The Britis

'The 2010 election was like no other. There is still much to learn about what happened during the campaign and Cowley and Kavanagh lay out all the facts in clear, comprehensible detail. Access to sources at the very top of the political parties ensures this book is essential reading if you want to know what really went on behind the scenes.'
Andrew Hawkins, Chief Executive, ComRes

'The 65-year-old series of books on British General Elections has become the Wisden of politics – essential reading for anyone wanting to know what happened during the campaigns and the significance of the outcome.'
Peter Riddell, Senior Fellow, The Institute for Government and former Chief Political Commentator of *The Times*

Praise for previous editions
'a unique cocktail of analysis, narrative and insider insight, are the authoritative guide to postwar electoral politics.'
Andrew Adonis, *Times Literary Supplement*

'A formidable achievement ... The studies have become by now almost part of our democratic fabric.'
Anthony Howard, *The Listener*

'The renowned ... election books demand shelf space and deserve frequent reference. Essential to the scholar of the British politics of our time.'
Robert Worcester, MORI, *Parliamentary History*

'Anyone familiar with previous volumes knows what a joy this book is, how it is packed with juicy morsels of political fact and incisive analysis.'
Jay Adams, *Times Higher Education Supplement*

'If generations to come want to know exactly what happened they have a reliable source to look it up in ... the solid, objective, verifiable story of what happened, when and why, set in impeccably numerate context.'
David McKie, *Guardian*

'The best series anywhere on national elections.'
Lancelot L. Farrar, *Annals of American Academy of Political and Social Science*

The British General Election of 2010

Dennis Kavanagh
Emeritus Professor of Politics, University of Liverpool, UK

Philip Cowley
Professor of Parliamentary Government, University of Nottingham, UK

with a Foreword by David Butler

First published 2010 by
PALGRAVE MACMILLAN

Palgrave Macmillan in the UK is an imprint of Macmillan Publishers Limited, registered in England, company number 785998, of Houndmills, Basingstoke, Hampshire RG21 6XS.

Palgrave Macmillan in the US is a division of St Martin's Press LLC, 175 Fifth Avenue, New York, NY 10010.

Palgrave Macmillan is the global academic imprint of the above companies and has companies and representatives throughout the world.

Palgrave® and Macmillan® are registered trademarks in the United States, the United Kingdom, Europe and other countries

ISBN   978–0–230–52189–6   hardback
ISBN   978–0–230–52190–2   paperback

This book is printed on paper suitable for recycling and made from fully managed and sustained forest sources. Logging, pulping and manufacturing processes are expected to conform to the environmental regulations of the country of origin.

A catalogue record for this book is available from the British Library.

A catalog record for this book is available from the Library of Congress.

10   9   8   7   6   5   4
19   18   17   16   15   14   13   12   11

Printed and bound in Great Britain by
CPI Antony Rowe, Chippenham and Eastbourne

Contents

List of Tables

List of Illustrations

Photographs

Party advertisements

Cartoons

Plates (bound between pages 126 and 127)

3. Nick Clegg, with his wife Miriam Gonzalez Durantez, addresses a campaign rally in Sheffield [Reuters/Phil Noble]
4. Peter Mandelson dances in the Tower Ballroom in Blackpool [Reuters/Stefan Wermuth]
5. Gordon Brown and Gillian Duffy in conversation in Rochdale [Reuters/Suzanne Plunkett]
6. A Conservative debate rehearsal, with Jeremy Hunt (as Clegg) and Damian Green (as Brown); Michael Gove asks the questions [Andrew Parsons]
7. A Labour debate rehearsal, with Alastair Campbell (as Cameron) and Theo Bertram (as Clegg) [Theo Bertram]
8. Not a rehearsal: the third and final televised debate in Birmingham on 29 April [Reuters/Gareth Fuller/Pool]
9. Gordon Brown's notes during the second televised debate [Reuters/Stefan Rousseau/Pool]
10. UKIP leader, Lord (Malcolm) Pearson [Reuters/Stefan Wermuth]
11. SNP leader, Alex Salmond [Reuters/David Moir]
12. Plaid leader, Ieuan Wyn Jones [Plaid]
13. Green leader, Caroline Lucas, after casting her vote in Brighton [Reuters/Luke MacGregor]
14. BNP leader, Nick Griffin, listening to Margaret Hodge after the declaration in Barking [Reuters/Kieran Doherty]
15. The wreckage of Nigel Farage's aircraft, 6 May [Reuters/Darren Staples]
16. The three party leaders at the VE day ceremony, 8 May [Reuters/Luke MacGregor]
17. The Conservative negotiating team: Letwin, Hague and Osborne (Ed Llewellyn not shown) [Reuters/Paul Hackett]
18. The Liberal Democrat negotiating team: Huhne, Stunell and Alexander (David Laws not shown) [Reuters/Paul Hackett]
19. The outgoing Prime Minister, with his wife Sarah and their two children, after he announced he was resigning, 11 May [Reuters/Toby Melville]
20. The incoming Prime Minister being greeted by Her Majesty the Queen, 11 May [Reuters/John Stillwell/Pool]
21. David Cameron and his wife Samantha meet Cabinet Secretary Gus O'Donnell after entering 10 Downing Street, 11 May 2010 [Reuters/Stefan Rousseau/Pool]

Foreword

David Butler

In 1945 Ronald McCallum made an original suggestion to the newly-founded Nuffield College. He wanted the country to be spared from the misinterpretations of the 1918 election that had so infuriated him in the inter-war years. He argued that when Britain went to the polls after the defeat of Hitler the campaign should be instantly recorded before partisan myths took popular root. Since then the authors of each Nuffield history have tried to stay true to this inspiration.

This is the eighteenth volume in a long-running series. Speaking personally, having been involved with each study from 1945 to 2005, I rejoice in the continuance of the tradition. In my retirement I have envied my successors as they strove to cope with the challenge of 2010, surely the most fascinating of recent contests.

Since the 1950s the table of contents of these books has stayed remarkably similar. But the substance has changed more than is generally realised. Between 1885 and 1955, elections changed surprisingly little. Party leaders toured the major cities, giving set speeches, carefully timed to catch the first editions of the national newspapers. The BBC, ludicrously conscientious about its neutrality, ignored the campaign. Candidates struggled individually in their own constituencies. There was little of the disciplined national campaign that has become so familiar nowadays.

The turning point came in 1959, with the arrival of television coverage, of party press conferences, of competitive opinion polls and of newspaper advertising. That paved the way to the centralised campaigns that we have now, with faxes and then emails coordinating party activities nationwide, and with an increasing focus on the relentless appetite of the 24/7 news coverage.

Every election study has to be similar as it records politicians going through similar routines. But every one also has to be different as the authors try to pinpoint new developments. In 2010 the challenge was exceptional as politicians, accustomed to the old world of uniform swing and a two-party duopoly, sought fresh ways (above all in televised debates) to catch the attention of a new and more sceptical electorate.

It should be appreciated that the following pages are based, not just on the media and the polls, but also on intensive and confidential interviews with most of the main players, interviews conducted before, during, and after the election. These contacts within the central arena of politics have been on a scale that Ronald McCallum could not have envisaged – yet the result is a proud monument to his inspiration, 65 years ago.

Preface

The opening book in the 'Nuffield' election series – *The British General Election of 1945* – lists a series of 'named' elections: 1874, when the Liberals went down in a flood of gin and beer; the Midlothian election of 1880; the Khaki election of 1900; the Chinese Slavery election of 1906; the People's Budget election of 1910; the 'Hang the Kaiser' election of 1918; and the 1924 'Zinovieff letter' election.

The study's authors, R.B. McCallum and Alison Readman, were sceptical that in reality these issues had ever been so dominant. They pointed out that in 1945, the key issue of the election had been housing – yet they rightly predicted that no-one in the future would ever talk about 1945 as the 'housing election'. And since then – and with the possible exception of February 1974, sometimes called the 'Who Governs Britain? election' – it is difficult to think of many modern equivalents.

This is largely, we suspect, because we now know so much more about elections. We know more about the manoeuvrings of the parties, their polling, their campaign strategies and personnel; but also more about how the public vote, what drives them (or not), and how their motivations are usually so mixed, and complex (if not downright contradictory), that it is ridiculous to think that any one thing is somehow responsible for deciding an election.

The 2005 election could no doubt have been labelled the 'Iraq election', given the extent to which national debate focused on the consequences and justifications of the 2003 war. Yet we know that for most voters Iraq came relatively low down the list of concerns. Even with the 1983 contest, which could easily be known as the 'Falklands election', there is plenty of evidence showing that the Falklands war was much less significant than people thought at the time.

Part of the reason we know so much more about modern elections is precisely because of the series of books which began with that volume in 1945. This volume is the eighteenth in that series. They have in the past always been sponsored by Nuffield College, Oxford. This year, for the first time, neither of the principal authors is based at Nuffield – although we are delighted to feature a foreword from David Butler, who had been involved in every one of the studies from 1945 until 2005. His foreword to this volume means that he can now claim to have been involved (so far) in 65 years' worth of election studies, a record we suspect will never be broken.

We would be dubious about attempts to name the 2010 election. In the run-up to the contest there were claims that it was going to be the 'internet election' – although that claim has now been made of every contest since 1997, and we remain as sceptical now as we were then. It was also going to be the 'expenses election', an issue which dominated the final year of the parliament, but which turned out to be much less significant during the election than many people had suspected.

It was, however, the first British election to feature televised debates between the three main party leaders, something that completely changed the rhythm and feel of the national campaign. Labour's campaign head, Douglas Alexander, compared the campaign to the green lines seen on ECG machines – three peaks, each marking a debate, with little taking place beyond the peaks. Yet, as will become clear, their impact on the result was less dramatic. We also note – much less remarked upon – the extent to which this was an election in which targeted literature sent from parties to voters played a crucial role. It was a direct mail election far more than it was an internet election, albeit only for voters in marginal seats.

What we are certain of is that the 2010 general election was one of the most fascinating contests of the last 100 or so years. It was the first contest since 1979 in which none of the three main party leaders had fought the previous election. It was the first since 1992 to be fought, from the beginning, with the realistic possibility of a hung parliament looming – and the first since February 1974 to produce one. It resulted in a coalition government; the first at Westminster since the Second World War, the first peace-time coalition since that formed in 1931, and the first formed by two parties afresh following a general election since modern British party politics began. The first substantive chapter of that very first election study in 1945 was entitled 'The break-up of the coalition'; this volume is the first to be able to include a chapter entitled 'The formation of the coalition'.

It is also the first to include a chapter about an election that did not take place. There was very nearly a book entitled *The British General Election of 2007*, with all of the parties primed and ready to fight a contest in October or November 2007. Gordon Brown's decision not to call that election – having allowed preparation for, and speculation about, it to build to unprecedented levels – is often seen as a fatal misjudgement. We regard this non-event as so significant in itself and bearing on much of what followed that we have devoted our opening chapter to it.

In the pages that follow we also deal with David Cameron's only partly successful efforts to change the image of the Conservative Party, Gordon

Brown's largely unsuccessful struggle to renew the Labour government after he took over as Prime Minister in June 2007, and Nick Clegg's equally unsuccessful attempt to achieve a Liberal Democrat electoral breakthrough. The election also marked yet another stage in the steady fragmentation of the British party system, as well as seeing a series of innovations in polling, broadcasting, the press, and campaigning techniques.

We conducted over 360 interviews for this book, with key players from all the main parties, and unattributed quotes in the volume are taken from those interviews. People gave generously and willingly of their time, and were very open and honest with us, and we are extremely grateful to them. We do not list them here, since many spoke to us on conditions of strict confidentiality. We hope they will recognise the picture we paint – even if not all of them will agree with every one of our conclusions. Many of them also agreed to look at draft chapters, helping to suggest a series of improvements, and again we are very grateful, as we are to the many friends and colleagues who also read early drafts of the book. Of course, all responsibility for any remaining errors rests with us alone.

We also have a debt to all our contributors whose names appear in the table of contents and who met demanding deadlines. In addition to writing Appendix 2, John Curtice, Stephen Fisher and Robert Ford also supplied the data which comprise Appendix 1. Mark Stuart was our Research Assistant, who dealt excellently with a series of challenging requests, and who was a delight to work with.

We also owe a debt of gratitude to all those who supplied, or allowed us to reproduce, material. The Conservatives, Labour, Liberal Democrats, Plaid, SNP, and UKIP all generously allowed us to reproduce campaign posters and images. Steve Bell, Dave Brown, Iain Martin, Martin Rowson, and Peter Schrank, as well as News International (for Peter Brookes) and the Telegraph Media Group (for Matt and Garland) granted us permission to print their excellent cartoons. The majority of photos in the plates come courtesy of Reuters. Other pictures, some thanks to the now-ubiquitous camera phone, come from Plaid, Theo Bertram, Rob Hutton, Sean Kemp, J. Lawrence and Andrew Parsons. We are grateful to all of them.

Alison Howson and Amber Stone-Galilee from Palgrave Macmillan have been supportive and encouraging. The research was generously funded by the Leverhulme Trust, who provided for teaching relief, research assistance, and travel. They have enabled us to tell what we think is a fascinating story.

Dennis Kavanagh
Philip Cowley
2010

1
The Election That Never Was: 2007

Harold Macmillan once said that he 'wanted to be an oak rather than a beech tree'. Other plants root and develop under oaks, nothing grows under a beech. It was not a sentiment Gordon Brown ever shared. When, in June 2007, he eventually became Labour leader and Prime Minister, it was the first time Labour had changed leaders without a contest since 1932, and the lack of a challenge was no accident. Brown had long wanted to ascend to the Premiership unopposed. Potential rivals who appeared to be gathering support had found their reputations subtly (and sometimes not so subtly) denigrated by the Chancellor's camp. Publicly, the Brown line was that he would 'welcome' a leadership contest; but behind the scenes, he was attempting to alter the rules to make it harder for rivals to stand.[1]

The Brown campaign team was formally headed by Jack Straw, chosen both for his experience but also for the symbolism, given that he had helped organise Tony Blair's campaign back in 1994. The campaign's fundamental goal was to win the leadership contest by preventing any rival emerging. 'Being campaign manager, in Jack's mind,' said one of those involved, 'meant that from day one there wasn't even going to be a contest.' It was not sufficient for Gordon Brown to be nominated; rather, the campaign team sought to ensure that Brown hoovered up so many nominations that no rival could gather the 45 nominations required to stand. The campaign team had twice weekly – and later, daily – meetings at which they collated intelligence about the intentions of every member of the Parliamentary Labour Party. Nominations went to Labour's HQ in Victoria Street, through the Office of the Parliamentary Labour Party, which was technically neutral but from where information leaked to the Brown camp on a daily basis, as to the state of play. MPs with doubts about the wisdom of the Chancellor's accession were made promises or

1

leant on. Brown, the argument went, was going to become Prime Minister, with or without their support, and whilst he would reward those who backed him, he would never forgive those who did not. With new MPs, in particular, his team found this argument proved especially persuasive.

There was a brief discussion within the campaign team – 'for about two minutes' – about allowing, or even engineering, a contest by 'lending' support to a leftish-rival. There were MPs who favoured Brown but who would have been willing to lend their support to Michael Meacher, a potential rival from the left of the party who was struggling to gain the number of nominations required, to facilitate a contest. Those in favour argued that Brown would still win, but that it would provide his leadership with more legitimacy. But as one of the team remarked: 'it was Gordon by acclaim, or Gordon by election. And Gordon wanted Gordon by acclaim.' When one MP had the temerity to come out in support of John McDonnell, another potential rival from the left of the party, the then Chancellor was soon on the phone to his fixer, and keeper of names, Nick Brown. 'How was this allowed to happen?' the Chancellor shouted down the phone, so loudly that he could be heard by all those sat with Nick Brown.

On 16 May Gordon Brown passed the 308 nomination mark, the point at which no other candidate could stand, and on 17 May he formally accepted the nomination for the leadership of the party. He became leader at Labour's Special Party Conference on 24 June in Manchester. Three days later, Tony Blair formally resigned, and Gordon Brown went to Buckingham Palace for an audience with the Queen, before making a statement outside Number 10, in which he used the words 'new' and 'change' on ten occasions, in an attempt to distinguish himself from his predecessor. He quoted his school motto ('I will try my utmost'), and ended with the words 'Let the work of change begin.' The work of change had both a short- and a medium-term plan. The former involved a grid for the first 56 days of his premiership, setting out what announcements were to be made, and when. This schedule was almost immediately thrown off course by two attempted terrorist attacks, one in London on 29 June, the other in Glasgow the following day. As one of the Brown team noted, this was the first time they realised that things were harder to schedule in Downing Street than in the Treasury. The medium-term plan was for an early election, something which had always been part of Team Brown's intentions. By 'early', however, they had originally pencilled in mid-2008. This date would have given the new Prime Minister around a year in office, enough time for him to establish himself with the electorate.

Opinion polls showed a noticeable early lift in his and the party's ratings. Before Brown became PM, the polls had consistently shown Labour trailing the Conservatives and him trailing the Conservative leader David Cameron. But on taking office, there was a visible 'Brown bounce' in the polls. The Prime Minister was lauded over the handling of three relatively low-level crises in quick succession: the acts of terrorism which had marked his first days in Downing Street (in which the only person to die had been one of the perpetrators); widespread flooding (which hit England and Wales in late July) and an outbreak of foot and mouth disease in August, the Prime Minister returning from holiday to chair COBRA. The Prime Minister and his team appeared to handle these various crises well, for which they received (exaggerated) praise from across the political spectrum. He was 'not an exhausted traveller ... but a man at the very start of a journey' (said Matthew d'Ancona, in the *Spectator*); 'masterly' (wrote Alice Thomson in the *Daily Telegraph*); 'Brown could be a great Prime Minister' (claimed Peter Oborne, in the *Daily Mail*).[2]

Meanwhile, Cameron's position – buoyant whilst Tony Blair had been in Number 10 – weakened. In July, at the Ealing Southall by-election, despite branding himself as representing 'Cameron's Conservatives' the Conservative candidate finished a poor third. During September, support for Labour in opinion polls averaged 40%, some five or six points ahead of the Conservatives. Conservative MPs sceptical about the Cameron project were said to be using the ironic acronym PODWAS: Poor Old Dave, What A Shame. Soon there was talk of an early general election. Much of this discussion was initially confined to commentators, short of a peg for a column. But some of Brown's aides encouraged the talk on the grounds that it could destabilise the Conservatives or would be an opportunity to close the Blair era, give Brown his own mandate and emphasise him as 'the change'.

In Number 10 Gordon Brown continued to rely on a group of young men, so-called 'Brownites', most of whom had worked for him since they were special advisers. Indeed, one Permanent Secretary, observing Brown at close quarters, thought that the Prime Minister continued to treat Ed Balls, Ed Miliband, and Douglas Alexander as special advisers, despite their new-found eminence as Cabinet ministers. At a political cabinet at Chequers in late July, ministers heard an up-beat polling presentation. Labour, they were told, had an 8% lead over the Conservatives, was ahead of the Conservatives on all issues except for immigration (although private Conservative research at the same time had Labour also trailing on crime and anti-social behaviour) and Brown outscored Cameron on most of the leadership attribute questions. A few ministers expressed support for an early election, Jacqui Smith, the new Home Secretary (who held a marginal seat and feared the impact of the money the Conservatives were putting into targeting seats like hers) prominently so. But nothing was decided and there was no concerted push by ministers for an early poll.

Spencer Livermore, the Prime Minister's strategy adviser, had been with Brown since 1999. He thought the idea of an early election had been ruled out too hurriedly at Chequers. On his return from holiday in late August he wrote a four-page memo to Brown, making the case for an early general election. Livermore pointed to the upturn in the polls, one that might not last, the prospects for a worsening economy and suggested that Autumn 2007 looked the best opportunity. Brown, who was still thinking of mid-2008, was taken aback by the memo which was then circulated to the three other key players along with Bob Shrum, who for three decades had been among the most prominent Democratic political consultants in America. Brown, however, did not engage fully with the memo, leaving it on his desk for three weeks while he dealt with other matters.

Peter Watt, the party's General Secretary, visited Brown at Number 10 in late August and spoke frankly about the party's weak financial position compared with the Conservatives, one that would worsen month by month if an autumn election was not held. An early election was a cheaper option because it would avoid tying up people and funds for several years and minimise the opportunity for the Conservatives to make use of the funding for key seats. Brown reacted grumpily, appearing to feel that his hand was being forced. Although there were early press reports that the party was being placed on an election alert and appeals were being made to donors, Brown had not been persuaded.[3]

Douglas Alexander, Labour's campaign coordinator as well as Minister for International Development, had already conducted an audit of the party machine at Victoria Street. He noted the poor state of the party's finances and the need for polling and an advertising agency but on the positive side the party's voter database was working well. He was convinced that the party's superiority over the Conservatives in this respect meant that they could use their contact data scheme to send direct mail to over 3 million target households at least four times in a short, Blitzkrieg-like, three-week election campaign. The Labour campaign would be funded almost entirely at a national level with centrally generated direct mail, with very little ground war, meaning that the lack of party activists and the poor state of organisation in many constituency parties would be less of a problem. Alexander went on holiday in August to New York where he arranged a shortlist of advertising agencies for the party to interview on his return.

Opinion was divided within the Labour Party about whether or not to go to the country in the autumn. Many Labour MPs in marginal seats were in favour of going early because of the anticipated effect of the Conservatives' targeting of their constituencies – and were saying so to the Chief Whip, Geoff Hoon. He however was doubtful about the wisdom of canvassing on cold dark nights in late October or November. Some of the more Blairite Cabinet ministers supported an early election precisely because they still had doubts about the new Prime Minister: 'we thought that Gordon had defied expectations by dealing with "events" better than was expected, but we feared that in the longer run some of his less endearing attributes would become more obvious to electors', as one put it.[4] There was some misleading discussion about a generational split with the so-called 'greybeards' urging caution and younger ministers and advisers calling for an election, but the reality was messier than that. Those with doubts, however, later regretted that they had not been more forceful. As one said: 'The danger is that you look split, but it would have been better than allowing the momentum to build up entirely on one side of the argument.'

But even if the chances of an early election were slight, preparations still needed to be made, just in case. The trouble, Labour's General Secretary later admitted, was that election preparations cannot be made in secret: too many people have to be informed for there to be such a thing as a 'snap', unexpected, election. Once mobilisation has begun, it is hard to conceal. Labour set up a media centre in Victoria Street, booked poster sites and prepared personalised letters to key voters in the marginals. The party also had reliable promises of funding if an election was held. Ed Miliband and members of the Policy Unit began to draft a manifesto, drawing largely on Brown's leadership acceptance speech, but it remained thin; brainstorming sessions to produce new policy ideas struggled to come up with much more than smaller class sizes and banning plastic bags. Preparations were made for a leader's tour and a 'war book' was drafted. Saatchi & Saatchi were commissioned, and produced a 'Not Flash, Just Gordon' poster. Despite the preparations, though, no decision had yet been taken, and the argument was still finely balanced. In his note to the Prime Minister in August, Livermore had explicitly noted that, whatever was decided, it was important that a decision was taken before Labour went to its party conference. But with no decision taken, the debate entered the pressure cooker of the party conference season.

Not flash, just Gordon.

www.labour.org.uk

Labour

The Liberal Democrats, whose party conference falls first, had begun making provisional plans for an early election since 2006 (they had even pencilled in the date: 25 October 2007). They still had around 200 candidates to select, but candidates were in place in most of their key seats and the party felt ready for what would have been an almost entirely defensive campaign, attempting to hold on to what they had gained in 2005, with the very occasional skirmish in enemy territory. Only a handful of Liberal Democrat MPs had announced their intentions to retire, and despite the party struggling in the polls, there was a feeling in their Cowley Street HQ that most were 'well dug in'.

Just before the Liberal Democrat conference, the party leader Sir Menzies Campbell announced that he wanted a draft manifesto ready by the end of the week. It was nowhere near ready, so Lib Dem policy staff worked long hours on the Sunday and Monday, drafting detailed sections. A series of meetings was held with various policy teams in a conference hotel suite, going over each section (at which point someone noticed that they had managed to leave out their policy on Trident entirely); and on the Thursday, Steve Webb, the chair of the manifesto writing group, worked until 4am polishing the draft. The following Saturday, the party held an Away Day in a hotel in London, at which the Shadow Cabinet discussed the draft in the morning, before the Federal Policy Committee meeting in the afternoon. The policy teams then went to work again on the Sunday, before the final version went off for copy-editing. Previous ambitious plans for a web-based manifesto, allowing comparison of each theme, by local, national and regional dimensions, were scrapped because of lack of time. Based on the *Free, Fair, Green* trinity the party had employed previously, the manifesto was entitled *Choose a Fairer and*

Greener Britain.[5] Menzies Campbell's tenure as Lib Dem leader was not a happy or successful one (see pp. 99–103), and was to end soon after, but many of those in the party hierarchy were impressed by the way he prepared the Party for the 2007 contest.

Labour Party delegates were in buoyant mood as they gathered in Bournemouth the following week for their annual party conference. Brown's speech on 25 September, largely written by Bob Shrum, received a broadly positive initial reaction, although *The Times* soon noticed that it contained many stock phrases from Shrum's repertoire, a discovery that caused a huge row between the pollster and the Prime Minister.[6] But the polls immediately after Brown's speech still appeared very positive: a YouGov poll, published for Channel 4 News on 26 September showed an 11% Labour lead, an Ipsos-MORI poll four days later revealed an even greater 13% Labour lead.

Opinion polls, both private and public, have become an important influence on decisions on election timing. For some years Brown had relied on Deborah Mattinson, of Opinion Leader Research, a focus group expert, for advice.[7] It was she who had given the presentation at Chequers on the positive national picture. But before any decision about calling an election was taken it was agreed the party would have to poll opinion in the marginal seats and that the party would look to the United States for a quantitative pollster. Mark Penn had been the party's pollster for the 2005 election but was now working for Hillary Clinton in her bid to win the Democratic nomination for the 2008 Presidential election. In late September Douglas Alexander therefore recruited Stan Greenberg, who had polled for the party in 2001 and 2005, this time to design a questionnaire and analyse the responses from a cluster of marginal seats with a sample size of around 1,800.

Greenberg's first presentation to Gordon Brown was made at the Bournemouth party conference the day after he had made his leader's speech. Contrary to the 100-plus seat majority some public opinion polls indicated, Greenberg cautiously indicated a majority of between 35 and 45. Brown was visibly disappointed. He was defending a 60+ majority and was looking to improve on it. He called on Greenberg to do further work, as if this extra effort would somehow produce a more favourable result. Amongst those present was Ed Miliband, who sat at the back of the room, muttering to himself, 'we don't have a story, we're not ready'. Despite the pro-election spin at the conference, behind the scenes there was still a vigorous debate amongst Brown's inner group. Some advisers were willing to contemplate a majority lower than the party won in

'Is Gordon Brown dithering?
a. Don't Know b. Undecided
c. Not Sure'

'Is Gordon Brown dithering?'

Matt, *Daily Telegraph*, 4 October 2007
(© Telegraph Media Group Ltd 2007)

2005. The question was: how much lower was acceptable? They were not helped by boundary changes which had worked to Labour's disadvantage; even if Labour performed as well as they had done in 2005, their majority would shrink to somewhere in the mid-40s. That would have been workable, although there were concerns that even that outcome could have been portrayed in the media as a setback for Brown. 'There's the real world,' said one of those closest to him, 'in which a majority of 40 is fine. There's the academic world, in which a majority of 40 is fine. And then there's the media world, in which they'll write stories about how his majority has fallen, where's his mandate?' But the difference in the calculations between a majority of 40 and one of, say, only 20, was what one aide called 'a whisker'. Moreover, when a handful of Brown's aides sat in the Cabinet room and worked through a seat-by-seat analysis of the seats that would make up their majority, those with intimate knowledge of particular constituencies queried some of the predictions. Would Labour really regain Birmingham Yardley? Or East Dunbartonshire? Yet whilst these discussions were going on in private, in public almost all the talk was of a forthcoming election, not least as a result of heavy briefing behind the scenes by some of Brown's closest aides and ministers throughout the conference. Many delegates and journalists left the Labour conference convinced the election was coming.

One of the aims of talking up an early election had been to destabilise the Conservatives. With the Tory poll lead gone, Brown's team hoped that the Conservative conference would be full of panicky Conservatives, scared that the party faced its fourth consecutive defeat. It had precisely the opposite reaction, rallying the party behind the leader, and producing a far more cohesive conference than would otherwise have occurred.

The Conservatives had initially been taken aback by the talk of an autumn election. Cameron's team had expected to spend the first two years of his leadership on their so-called 'decontamination' project before they turned their minds to a programme for an election. The party's policy review was still in its early stages and a frequent criticism of Cameron had been that the party was short of credible policies. There was, though, widespread scepticism amongst the Conservative high command about the likelihood of Brown calling an election, at least to begin with. The Conservatives' Shadow Chancellor and election coordinator, George Osborne, believed until almost the very end that Brown would not call an election, largely on the grounds that he thought the Prime Minister was an over-cautious politician. Steve Hilton, Cameron's strategy adviser, also claimed not to take the election talk seriously and even booked a holiday immediately following the party conference. But in July, as the rumours increased, Cameron and Osborne had moved their offices from the Commons to Conservative Campaign Headquarters at Millbank. Oliver Letwin oversaw the hasty development of a number of policies, adding to the early Cameron theme of personal responsibility and policies addressing traditional Tory themes of opportunity and security.

On 2 October, the first day of the Conservative conference in Blackpool, Gordon Brown paid his first visit as Prime Minister to Iraq, where he promised that British forces would be cut by 1,000 by the end of 2007. He had been warned by aides that the trip would look opportunistic – and his aides were right. Many commentators accused Brown of playing cynical pre-election politics, a charge reinforced when it emerged that the 1,000 figure included 500 troops whose withdrawal had already been announced in July. And with Brown stumbling in Basra, Cameron successfully called the Prime Minister's bluff in Blackpool by making it appear that the Conservatives were ready, willing and able to fight an early election. The conference mood was lifted by George Osborne's pledge that a Conservative government would increase to £1 million the threshold above which households would be liable to Inheritance Tax and the abolition of stamp duty for first-time buyers of homes up to £250,000, all to be financed by a levy on 'non-doms'. This proposal effectively ended inheritance tax for most middle class families. Although Labour criticised the concession as a tax break for the rich, it had been exhaustively tested in focus groups for the Conservatives and had proved very popular, even among the less well-off. It gained positive media coverage and set the agenda for the rest of the week. Mattinson's focus groups picked up the change of mood and she noted that the Conservative Party was now associated with hope, a new direction and new ideas, all symbolised by Osborne's announcement.

Livermore (who, like Mattinson, had for some months warned Brown of the case for doing something on inheritance tax) later reflected, 'From the moment George Osborne stood up at the Tory conference, the election was never going to happen ... the momentum had shifted.'

'World's Loneliest Decision'

Peter Brookes, *The Times*, 5 October 2007
(© Peter Brookes/*The Times*/N.I. Syndication 2007)

On Wednesday 3 October David Cameron gave a polished, notes-free speech, at the end of which he laid down the gauntlet to the Prime Minister, saying: 'So, Mr Brown, what's it going to be?' That evening many Conservative election staff left the conference early, to return to party headquarters, convinced that Brown had left it too late to call off an election. The Liberal Democrats too assumed the Prime Minister had gone too far to turn back, and Party Headquarters at Cowley Street moved into election mode. Some in Number 10 now voiced regret that the Prime Minister would be making a decision after a good Conservative conference rather than after a good Labour conference.

Special advisers and campaign strategists were called to what turned out to be the decisive meeting at Downing Street on the morning of Friday, 5 October. Before them were the results of Greenberg's second marginal seats poll. Some were irritated by Greenberg's qualifications to his data – for example 'voters as of today'. The meeting was already tense because of the positive reactions to Osborne's speech and rumours that early returns from public opinion polls were showing a Conservative recovery. Greenberg's latest poll showed a 1% Labour lead and a likely Labour majority of 20 seats. But it could be lower. Everybody was nervous as Brown entered the room. When the Prime Minister was given the numbers he 'dissolved into himself completely', as one of those present put it. He announced, 'We can't do it', turned and left the room. The atmosphere, according to another present, was 'like a wake'.

In the party headquarters in Victoria Street Peter Watt was still directing the campaign preparations and waiting for confirmation about the election date. He began to have doubts when his calls to Number 10 were ignored, and by late afternoon he guessed that there would not be an election; a phone call from Douglas Alexander then confirmed his suspicions. Telling only a handful of colleagues, he told staff to leave early, have a drink, and get a weekend's rest before the campaign began. It was his only way of stopping people working late into the night for an election he already knew had been called off.

Tory preparations had similarly gathered pace during and immediately following the party conference. Leaflets had been delivered to the printer, ready to be printed on the following Sunday and delivered on the Monday. An election war book included detailed plans for the first and final weeks, if more flexible for the intervening weeks. On the Friday most of the Cameron team were finally convinced the election was on, because Brown had left it too late to call it off, even if he had cold feet. Cameron departed to spend the weekend in his constituency. The next morning, the Conservatives heard that the broadcaster Andrew Marr was going in to see the Prime Minister, and they guessed what was happening. As news percolated through the Conservative staff that Brown had decided against an election many felt a sense of anti-climax, having psyched themselves up ready for the fight. Some remained unsure, and the Conservatives' head of research, James O'Shaughnessy, ignored teasing as he carried on polishing the party manifesto until he heard the news officially. Granted, they would only have been able to fight what one of them called 'a rough and ready campaign', but their tactical objectives had been to postpone an election and damage Gordon Brown, and they had succeeded.

Calling off the election incurred a cost of £1.2 million to Labour. Poster sites had been prepaid, letters to target voters had been printed and expensive polling had been commissioned. Wasting over a £1 million was serious for a party with a deficit of over £20 million. But the financial costs were nothing compared to the political fall-out. The press on 7 October was merciless. Andrew Rawnsley in the *Observer* wrote of 'Bottler Brown' (for a while afterwards, Tory supporters dressed as spoof Newcastle Brown bottles would follow the Prime Minister around), and the *Independent on Sunday* referred to 'a shambolic episode and a self-inflicted wound'. Brown was seen as somebody who funked contests – he had not stood in 1994 for the leadership and blocked potential leadership candidates in 2007. He wanted certainty and had scoffed at an adviser's forecast of a 40-seat majority. Philip Gould, a consistent advocate of an early election, argued that the act of calling an election would have transformed perceptions of Brown, making him look decisive. Instead, the episode reinforced his reputation as a ditherer.

Brown's problems were compounded by Labour's handling of the decision. Damian McBride, his press secretary, recommended that he pre-record on the Saturday afternoon an exclusive interview with Andrew Marr for his Sunday TV programme. The decision itself was a mistake, inevitably alienating other leading broadcasters. The Conservatives leaked the news that Marr had gone into Number 10 to journalists on other networks; Brown's decision, one of them said, 'pissed off every other journalist in the country'. Brown's claim to Marr that he decided against an election because he wanted more time to explain his 'vision for changing Britain', and not because of the polls, also failed to impress. As one of those closest to him put it, 'you needed an argument before you could have an interview'; and they had no plausible argument. At a press conference the next day, the Prime Minister's repeated claims that he had not been influenced by opinion polls prompted widespread ridicule. David Cameron mocked his decision not to call the election, as the only politician in history not to call an election because 'he thought he was going to win it'. Asked if there had been any prior thought about what Brown might say if he decided not to call an election, a member of his team replied 'That was the missing discussion'. Speaking at the end of Labour's conference, one MP close to Brown dismissed the idea that the Prime Minister had boxed himself in, and would suffer damage if he called the election off. 'Martin Kettle will wank off for a few weeks, but that'll be it,' he claimed. Yet it was not just Kettle – a *Guardian* columnist well-known for his scepticism about Brown – and it was not just a few weeks. The episode transformed the way Gordon Brown was discussed in the press. The hagiography of the early months of his premiership was gone, never to return.

The episode cast an unfavourable light on Brown's Number 10 and its working methods. There was an absence of any decision maker and no dominant person giving a lead. One Labour figure complained about the 'absence of any political strategy. It was basically reactive – "Let's see

TODAY HAS BEEN

CANCELLED

WE'RE SORRY TO INFORM YOU THAT

THE GENERAL ELECTION

PLANNED FOR TODAY HAS BEEN CANCELLED.

WE APOLOGISE FOR THE DELAY TO THE CHANGE BRITAIN NEEDS.

THE FOLLOWING SERVICES ARE AFFECTED:

Abolition of Stamp Duty for nine out of ten first-time buyers.

Abolition of Inheritance Tax for everyone except millionaires.

Stopping NHS cuts and the closure of District General Hospitals, A&E and maternity units.

Teaching by ability and more discipline in schools.

National Citizen Service for every school leaver.

Taxing pollution, not families.

Proper immigration controls and a new Border Police Force.

A vote on the European Constitution.

Ending the early release of prisoners.

THESE SERVICES ARE NOW DELAYED UNTIL

THE ELECTION OF A CONSERVATIVE GOVERNMENT.

Until then, please visit www.conservatives.com for further announcements.

Conservatives
It's time for change

where the polls go". Rather than polling, we should just have decided.'
The lack of direction and strategic discussion in Number 10 was to be a
recurring theme for much of the rest of the Parliament. The experience
had been so bruising for all that it would be a long time before Brown
allowed talk of an election in his presence. It was extraordinary that so few
senior Cabinet ministers were involved in the decision. The Cabinet was
effectively a bystander, not even informed of the final decision. Heath in

1974 held meetings of senior colleagues and Callaghan in 1979 informed the Cabinet of his decision not to hold an election.

It ruptured the previously loyal group around Brown. Although the Prime Minister said that he took full responsibility for the episode, both Livermore and Alexander suffered negative briefing from Number 10, as well as from some Cabinet ministers. Talk about the election had been encouraged by the favourable opinion polls but had got out of hand. Livermore had done no more than present the case for an election and Alexander had prepared a campaign so that Brown could, if he chose, call an election. Had he not taken these steps then he would have been failing the Prime Minister and the Party. Others around the Prime Minister were much more to blame in promoting the case so vigorously in public. Brown made no attempt to stop the briefing (or even to target it where it was deserved), and relationships with two of his previously most loyal lieutenants were irreparably damaged as a result. Livermore would leave Downing Street shortly after; Alexander remained in the Cabinet, but semi-detached from, and disillusioned about, Brown thereafter.

No matter how much collective discussion there is about calling an election, a Prime Minister cannot deflect his or her personal responsibility for the final decision. Deciding to go early is usually one of the Prime Minister's most difficult decisions. Even when opinion polls, local and by-elections are favourable a Prime Minister still agonises over the election date, as Mrs Thatcher did even when seemingly assured of landslide majorities in 1983 and 1987. To dissolve and lose is usually fatal, as Alec Douglas-Home in 1964, Ted Heath in 1974, James Callaghan in 1979 and John Major in 1997 all found. For Gordon Brown to call an election in September or October 2007 would have risked losing the three remaining Parliamentary sessions in office and terminating his premiership after a few short months. He risked being the shortest-lived Prime Minister in modern times.[8]

A Prime Minister who calls an 'early' election also has to think carefully about how they will explain it to the electorate. They can hardly state the most obvious reason, that it is their best chance to win. The trouble was that Brown never finally decided on the reason for calling an election and this may well have influenced (or perhaps reflected) his indecisiveness. When asked what Brown's message for the election would have been, an adviser said 'We could have said that he was asking for a personal mandate, but the policy agenda we had was insufficiently different or strong to support that argument.' Brown had a few months earlier promised to be 'the change'. But what was he changing, apart from Blair's style? He had been the co-architect of the New Labour programme over the previous ten years. It was redolent of Harold Wilson in 1970 suddenly calling an election on the back of a sudden up-turn in the opinion polls, with little to say about what he would do – and losing.

Brown's defenders argue that it is wrong to talk about a 'cancelled' election, because none was formally authorised. Even many of his critics accept that he was what one called 'the last person to be persuaded of the case for an early election'. Whilst true, it misses the point. There was, what a Cabinet minister, close to Brown, called 'a rolling conversation over weeks about yes and no', with 'constant prevarication' from Brown. Throughout, the Prime Minister had never said yes or no to an autumn election, but he had – as one aide put it – 'gone to the starting line'. Brown was subsequently to admit: 'I spent too much time thinking about having an election and not enough deciding to have one.'

Incoming Prime Ministers who succeed long-serving leaders are forced to consider almost every possible permutation for an election date that may or may not be to their electoral advantage. And all modern-day Prime Ministers face constant media speculation about the timing of a so-called 'snap' election. But Brown could have killed off, or at least dampened down, speculation about a possible election at any time. Instead, he acquiesced in the extended preparations and the intense scrutiny of public and private polls, printing of election material and preparation of a war book and a manifesto, all indicating that he was minded to go. Labour had even scheduled their Clause 5 meeting to sign off the manifesto (which was to have taken place at Church House) and a manifesto launch (at the Science Museum). His advisers, with his connivance, ramped up expectations of an election to such a degree that the decision to call it off was always going to be seen as a humiliating climbdown.

Contrasts were drawn with James Callaghan's decision not to call an election in 1978. Yet in two senses, Brown's decision is much the worse. First, because preparations in 2010 were significantly more advanced than they were in 1978; and, second, because although the latter had fluffed the timing of the election in 1978, Callaghan had at least fought and won a proper leadership contest. Brown appeared uniquely weak among modern Prime Ministers because he neither had a mandate from his party, following his coronation in June 2007, nor from the country. When he took over as PM in June relatively few had commented on the lack of a leadership contest, but after the non-election his unelected status became a running sore for him in focus groups. Asked why things had gone so wrong, one Brown aide later answered bluntly: 'Irresponsibility, inexperience, over-exuberance, immaturity.' He added: 'Not every person who is responsible is guilty of all four.'

Brown's standing was fatally damaged. An ICM poll for the *Sunday Telegraph* sampled on 10–11 October, shortly after the election call-off, showed a seven-point Tory lead over Labour, but with Brown still 20 points ahead of David Cameron on being the strongest leader; 11 points ahead on managing the economy properly.[9] It took a little more time for the Brown brand to collapse in the public's consciousness but Labour was never again able to sell Brown as a 'father of the nation' figure. Instead it faced growing accusations that he was a calculating, yet indecisive politician. As one of Brown's closest aides put it shortly afterwards: 'We've handed strength and competence away. We've not just lost it, we've given it away.' Few politicians have trashed their own brand in such a comprehensive way.

The negative fall-out from the non-election raises the intriguing question of whether or not Brown would have won any early election. Given what eventually happened in 2010, even a 20-seat Labour majority looks much more attractive than it did in 2007. Some of Brown's advisers, like Spencer Livermore, Douglas Alexander and Peter Watt thought, then and later, that whatever the problems 2007 offered Brown his best chance.

There are two caveats. The first is that no Labour victory, even with a small majority, can be assumed in 2007. For one thing, whilst Labour's own internal polling was pointing to a small Labour majority, the Conservative private polling was pointing to a hung parliament. Indeed, one private Conservative poll of 120 target seats, distributed only to a very small group at the highest levels of the party leadership just before the election was abandoned, was predicting the Conservatives to gain almost 90 seats (around 70 from Labour, 20 from the Liberal Democrats). This was not sufficient for a Conservative victory but it would have done more than just deny Labour a majority, it would have made the Conservatives the largest single party, and produced a result very similar to that which would eventually result in Labour losing office in 2010. If that poll was accurate, then Brown's decision not to call the election may not be as misguided as conventional wisdom holds.

Yet even if we assume that the Conservatives' polling was wrong, and that Labour's polls were the more accurate, given the speed at which the polls were changing, and the volatility in the electorate, who knew what change a three-week campaign could produce? A YouGov poll, conducted on 5–6 October for the *Sunday Times* showed a Tory lead of 3%; the same polling organisation had a week earlier revealed an 11% Labour lead at the end of the Labour Party conference. A swing of 7% in a week revealed an extremely volatile electorate. The truth is that no one knows what would have happened in an election that never took place.

There is one other counter-factual worth considering. What if Gordon Brown had not allowed expectation to run out of control, and stuck with the original 2008 plan? With none of the hype surrounding a forthcoming election, and behind in the polls, David Cameron may have had a very difficult 2007 Conservative conference. Labour could then have used the planned combined Comprehensive Spending Review and Pre-Budget Report to build on their lead in the polls. Perhaps Brown's poll lead would have remained high entering 2008, providing the launch pad for a Labour victory in early 2008. An election in an alternative 2008, in which Brown did not make such a hash of 2007, might well have proved better for the party than a rushed election in 2007. No one knows, but it is at least as plausible to argue that the key decision was not whether to have held the election or not, but whether to have allowed expectations to build up in such a way that not holding it was to prove so damaging.

Certain political events are sometimes seen as turning points, decisively shaping a party's prospects for the coming general election: such as the winter of discontent in 1978 and its impact on Labour's fortunes in the 1979 general election; or Britain's withdrawal from the Exchange Rate Mechanism (ERM) in September 1992 and its effect on Conservative standing for the rest of the Parliament. For most observers, Gordon Brown's 'cancelling' of the planned 2007 election comfortably falls into that category. No election in post-war history has come so close to being called, only then not to happen. It was a crucial moment in the Parliament, one which revealed much about the Prime Minister and his way of operating, and which was deeply damaging both to him and to his party. A key moment in the history of the British General Election of 2010 was the British General Election That Never Was of 2007. Having funked it in 2007, Gordon Brown then publicly ruled out 2008 as well. A Parliament he had planned would only last three years went on to run the full five, during which Labour would almost never again lead in an opinion poll.

Notes

1. Peter Watt, *Inside Out* (London: Biteback, 2010), p. 153.
2. These quotes are taken from Andy Beckett, 'So what happened?', *Guardian*, 3 June 2009.
3. Watt, *Inside Out*, pp. 169–70.
4. A view shared by some Brownites as well: see Watt, *Inside Out*, p. 170.

5. As in 2005, it would have been published in a tabloid format, on the insistence of Chris Rennard, the party's Chief Executive, on both cost and convenience grounds. A slightly worthy foreword on social justice by the party leader was followed by what one of its authors called The Chris Rennard page – a punchy list of five things that were fair, five that were free, five that were green – a page which was circulated to many Lib Dem candidates, to help them plan local literature.

6. See Andrew Rawnsley's *The End of the Party* (London: Penguin, 2010), p. 503. The speech also repeated the phrase 'British Jobs for British Workers', which Brown had earlier used at the GMB conference shortly before becoming Prime Minister. It was to cause him difficulties later, when people noted that it was a slogan the BNP had also employed, although this was not picked up much at the time. Moreover, it was probably illegal under EU law.

7. An experience described in her *Talking to a Brick Wall* (London: Biteback, 2010).

8. Had he lost, he would have been the second shortest-serving Prime Minister in history after George Canning in the nineteenth century.

9. David Cowling, BBC News, PollWatch, October 2007.

2
Recession, Scandal and War:
The Political Context

In Singapore, on 6 July 2005, Jacques Rogge, the President of the International Olympic Committee, opened an envelope which contained the result of the bidding process for the 2012 Olympic Games, and announced that the Games would be returning to London for the first time since 1948. After half a second's delay, the news was relayed to a packed Trafalgar Square, where celebrations commenced. Barely ten hours later London was hit by four terrorist explosions – three on the tube network, and one on a Number 30 bus in Tavistock Square. All were the result of suicide bombers, all British citizens, who killed another 52 people, and injured over 700. Tony Blair, who had been basking in the glory of London's triumph at the G8 leaders meeting at Gleneagles in Perthshire, left the summit to return to a sombre capital. The party, which had begun the night before, was over.

The 7/7 bombings, as they came to be known, marked, symbolically at least, an abrupt end to the optimism of much of the Blair era. For slightly less than a decade, Britain had enjoyed a period of uninterrupted economic growth. That economic success had formed the bedrock of Tony Blair's election victories in 2001 and 2005. As Chancellor since 1997, Gordon Brown would boast of having ended Britain's economic cycle of 'boom and bust'. But as Blair reluctantly handed over the premiership, the hubris of those boasts would become clear. Britain would face a series of crises over the next five years – economic and political – that would result in the 2010 election being fought against a very different backdrop.

The financial crisis was ostensibly caused by the collapse of trust in loans in the mortgage market in the United States. Financial institutions had bundled up bad ('toxic') loans and sold them on to investors as triple-A rated securities. When confidence in that market evaporated, banks stopped lending to one another on the money markets. Financial institutions like Northern Rock, based in the North East of England, which had relied almost entirely on the money markets to fund their mortgage business, were the first to suffer. In September 2007, shortly after Gordon Brown reached Number 10, Northern Rock's 140,000 customers triggered the first run on a bank in Britain for over 150 years, with queues of worried investors snaking round branches as they withdrew their money. The crisis continued for a fortnight, only ending when the Government stepped in to guarantee 100% of bank and building society savings up to £35,000. Northern Rock was eventually nationalised in February 2008.

At first, the only obvious signs of a more general economic slowdown were seen in falling house prices and a marked slowdown in the buy-to-let market. It was when the American investment bank, Lehman Brothers filed for bankruptcy in September 2008 that a chain of events occurred which ushered in the most turbulent month in the international money markets since the Wall Street Crash of 1929. Large American financial institutions such as investment bank Merrill Lynch, and insurance giant AIG, had to be rescued. In Britain, bank shares started to collapse as the FTSE 100, the index of leading shares, slid below 5,000 points for the first time since May 2005. In the financial equivalent of a shotgun wedding, Gordon Brown and his Chancellor, Alistair Darling, persuaded Lloyds TSB to take over Halifax Bank of Scotland (HBOS), Britain's largest home loan lender, who had lent recklessly. To stem the immediate panic on the markets, the Financial Services Authority announced a temporary ban on the short-selling of bank shares.

In the United States, Henry Paulson, the Treasury Secretary, announced a $700 billion bail-out plan to tax toxic mortgage assets in an effort to steady the markets, but Congress proved reluctant to agree to such a huge government bail-out. In Britain, the Government was forced to nationalise another troubled mortgage lender, Bradford & Bingley, at the end of September. Governments around the world – including Germany, Iceland and Ireland (the last two especially badly affected) – were also forced to bail out their ailing banks. After much delay, the US Senate belatedly voted for the Wall Street bail-out at the beginning of October. In a febrile atmosphere, Gordon Brown attended an emergency summit in Paris to discuss the financial crisis with his European counterparts. Share prices continued to fall – on 6 October, the FTSE 100 fell by a record 7.85% in one day. The following day, the Icelandic Bank, IceSave, blocked internet savers from withdrawing their money, leaving large numbers of charitable organisations and local councils in Britain unable to access their money.

On 8 October, after a weekend of frenetic activity in the Treasury, the Government announced the bare bones of a massive £500 billion bank rescue plan. As part of a coordinated move by central banks across the world, the Bank of England cut base rates from 5% to 4.5%. At first, financial markets reacted badly: the FTSE ended 10 October 8.85% lower, another record. Similar falls in share prices were seen throughout the world. Oil prices tumbled amid fears of a recession. The world financial system appeared on the brink of meltdown.

Against this backdrop, G7 finance ministers met in Washington on 11 October to discuss a coordinated response to the financial crisis, while Gordon Brown attended another EU summit in Paris the following day, where he persuaded most of his European partners to follow his bank bail-out plan. The contents of that plan became clear on 13 October when the Government announced an enormous emergency recapitalisation of three of Britain's biggest banks – Royal Bank of Scotland, HBOS and Lloyds TSB. In effect, the three were part-nationalised. At last, the financial markets responded positively to the news, the FTSE rising 8.3% in a single day.

In the next few months, the Bank of England and the Government used an aggressive combination of monetary and fiscal policy to try to kick-start the British economy. The Bank of England cut base rates from 4.5% to 3% in November, while the Chancellor of the Exchequer announced a fiscal package worth £20 billion, the centrepiece of which was a temporary reduction in the rate of VAT from 17.5% to 15% until 2010. The top rate of income tax would rise from 40% to 45% on those earning more than £150,000 from 2011. But despite further aggressive rate cuts from the Bank of England, which saw interest rates fall to 1.5% at the beginning of 2009, the banking crisis refused to abate, forcing the Government to announce a second major bail-out of British banks, this time increasing its stake in Royal Bank of Scotland to around 70%. By March 2009, the Government had assumed majority control of the newly-formed Lloyds Banking Group, with the taxpayer owning 65% of the shares. Meanwhile, the Bank of England, fearing more unemployment, had slashed base rates to an historic low of 0.5%, alongside an initial £75 billion programme known as 'quantitative easing', a new phrase for an old policy: printing money.

It took a further piece of international summitry – this time the G20 meeting in London hosted by Gordon Brown in April 2009 – to

'Dear Chancellor'

(Dave Brown, *Independent*, 18 June 2008)

convince the international money markets that the worst of the crisis was over. Fearing another financial collapse, this time in Eastern Europe, world leaders pledged an additional $1.1 trillion in financing to the International Monetary Fund, and declared a crackdown on tax havens and hedge funds. A new supervisory body would flag up problems in the global financial system, but there was no agreement on a fresh fiscal stimulus package, mainly due to opposition from the French and German governments.

Although world leaders and central bankers appeared to have prevented an economic meltdown, they had not stopped the financial crisis from spreading to the rest of the economy. Banks used the government cash to shore up their balance sheets, and to tighten their lending criteria to consumers and to businesses. By the end of 2008, economic output had fallen sharply as unemployment started to rise. The impact of the recession was felt especially acutely in the retail sector, with well-known high street firms Woolworths and MFI going out of business. Gross Domestic Product (GDP) decreased by 2.4% in the first quarter of 2009, while in the same period, unemployment rose past 2 million for the first time since 1997. Economic recovery proved sluggish, with GDP contracting by a further 0.8% in the second quarter of 2009.

The soaring debt burden and the economic recession transformed the political agenda. Politicians would have to offer a combination of tax rises and/or spending cuts, traditionally a formula for election defeat. Ministers were keen to argue that the crisis was global and had originated in the United States. Both were true but Britain was particularly exposed because of its heavy dependence on financial services for employment and tax revenues and because many households had become heavily indebted on the back of rising house prices. Criticism grew of Gordon Brown's economic legacy. From 2002 his budget and PBR predictions had always been over-optimistic with the result that public spending outstripped his revenues; and his removal of the regulatory oversight of the City from the Bank of England and sharing it between the bank and two other institutions had been found wanting.

Far from receiving political credit for having saved the world's financial system from collapse, governments on both sides of the Atlantic were increasingly blamed for bailing out the banks (and 'the bankers') while the rest of the economy suffered. In American parlance, there was a growing disconnect between the views of Wall Street and that of Main Street. Governments failed to communicate the message to the voters that they could not allow banks to fail because the fates of all financial institutions were intimately tied together. There developed a trade-off between recapitalising the banks and stimulating economic growth through increased bank lending to businesses. Public anger focused especially on the remuneration packages of high-ranking banking officials, first in February 2009 when Sir Fred 'the Shred' Goodwin, the former Chief Executive of the Royal Bank of Scotland, refused to give up his £693,000 per year pension package, despite pressure from government ministers, and then in June 2009 when the new Royal Bank of Scotland Chief Executive, Stephen Hester, received a £9.6 million pay package.

Beleaguered bankers, however, were about to be replaced as the focus of public anger, with public resentment instead shifting towards Britain's Members of Parliament and their expenses.

New Labour had suffered its fair share of sleaze stories in its first two terms, but the most serious and sustained episode that Tony Blair faced came in 2006 and 2007, during the 'cash-for-honours' investigations, also referred to as 'cash-for-peerages'. Blair had created more peerages – more than 380 by the time he stepped down – than any other previous Prime Minister. Most passed off without any comment, but in March 2006, several of the Prime Minister's nominations for life peerages were rejected by the House

Table 2.1   Economic and political indicators, 2005–10

		(1)	(2)	(3)	(4)	(5)	(6)	(7)
		Real Household Disposable Income (2005 =100)	Average earnings (2000 =100)	Retail sales index (2005 =100)	Year on Year inflation (CPI) (%)	Unemploy- ment (%)	Days lost in strikes (000s)	GDP (2005 =100)
2005	1	99.4	120.0	99.1	1.8	4.7	13	98.5
	2	99.4	121.0	99.9	2.1	4.8	43	100.0
	3	100.2	122.5	100.2	2.6	4.8	61	100.0
	4	101.0	124.0	100.8	2.3	5.2	41	101.6
2006	1	100.5	125.4	102.2	2.0	5.2	573	104.0
	2	101.4	127.1	103.8	2.3	5.5	92	104.6
	3	101.3	127.5	104.4	2.5	5.5	43	106.4
	4	99.6	128.9	105.1	2.9	5.5	47	107.9
2007	1	100.0	129.9	106.2	3.0	5.5	142	109.8
	2	100.6	131.3	107.7	2.7	5.4	204	111.0
	3	101.8	132.9	109.1	1.9	5.3	282	112.2
	4	102.3	133.5	108.6	2.0	5.2	412	113.2
2008	1	100.6	136.0	110.3	2.4	5.2	83	115.9
	2	103.5	135.8	110.6	3.4	5.3	156	116.1
	3	102.5	137.2	108.2	4.9	5.9	511	115.4
	4	104.6	137.9	108.3	4.5	6.4	9	114.6
2009	1	104.2	138.0	107.9	4.5	7.1	25	111.2
	2	106.7	138.5	109.3	3.5	7.8	54	110.2
	3	107.3	139.0	111.2	2.7	7.8	134	111.3
	4	106.3	139.8	111.7	2.8	7.8	243	112.6
2010	1	–	–	–	1.7	8.0	284	114.9

Sources: (1)–(8): Economic and Labour Market Review and Office for National Statistics; (9): Yahoo Finance; (10)–(12): Bank of England; (13): Department of Communities and Local Government; (14)–(15): Ipsos-MORI.

of Lords Appointments Commission. It later emerged that these men had loaned large sums of money to the Labour Party, at the suggestion of Blair's chief fundraiser, Lord Levy. Following a complaint from the SNP MP Angus MacNeil, the Metropolitan Police investigated the claim that the nominations had been granted in return for the loans. Levy was arrested and bailed, and Blair was interviewed on three separate occasions,

(8)	(9)	(10)	(11)	(12)	(13)	(14)	(15)		
Balance of Payments (as % of GDP)	*FTSE 100 share index (3 month average)*	*US $ to £*	*Sterling exchange rate index (Jan 2005 =100)*	*Interest (base) rates (%)*	*House prices (Feb 2002 =100)*	*Ipsos-MORI Economic Optimism Index*	*Ipsos-MORI polls (voting intention)*		
							C	L	LD
−2.3	4905	1.89	100.7	4.75	149.4	−15	30	41	20
−1.2	4960	1.85	101.6	4.75	160.0	−15	30	40	24
−3.7	5352	1.78	99.7	4.5	153.8	−26	29	40	25
−3.2	5453	1.75	99.6	4.5	153.1	−30	35	38	20
−2.9	5839	1.75	98.8	4.5	154.8	−26	37	39	18
−2.9	5860	1.83	100.2	4.5	159.0	−29	36	32	21
−3.6	5932	1.88	102.2	4.75	164.7	−32	36	34	22
−3.8	6133	1.92	103.6	5.0	167.0	−28	36	35	19
−3.4	6228	1.95	104.6	5.25	172.1	−39	40	34	18
−2.5	6560	1.99	104.1	5.5	177.0	−24	36	34	18
−3.4	6377	2.02	104.2	5.75	183.6	−26	34	41	15
−1.5	6537	2.04	101.4	5.5	183.8	−43	41	36	14
−0.4	5822	1.97	95.7	5.25	183.3	−53	40	35	16
−1.6	5922	1.97	92.8	5.0	181.7	−58	42	30	17
−2.2	5317	1.89	91.3	5.0	176.8	−60	49	25	14
−1.9	4367	1.57	83.4	2.0	167.4	−45	42	34	13
−1.2	3969	1.43	77.3	0.5	160.5	−36	45	30	16
−1.9	4304	1.55	80.8	0.5	159.4	2	40	23	20
−1.7	4884	1.64	82.5	0.5	166.0	7	39	25	20
0.1	5216	1.63	80.0	0.5	168.0	13	41	28	19
−2.7	5406	1.56	79.3	0.5	172.8	11	37	31	19

the first time that a serving Prime Minister had been interviewed by the police during a criminal investigation. After a prolonged investigation, overshadowing Blair's last year as Prime Minister, the Crown Prosecution Service announced in July 2007 that it would not be bringing any charges as there was no direct evidence that the nominations had been agreed in advance to be in return for the loans (which would have been required to proceed with a prosecution).

Gordon Brown's new administration fared even worse on the sleaze front. In March 2009, the husband of, and parliamentary aide to, the Home Secretary, Jacqui Smith, was forced to apologise after it emerged that he had claimed on her parliamentary expenses for the cost of two adult films. The affair, though embarrassing, might in normal circumstances have been relatively minor, but it came immediately after Ms Smith had been investigated by the Parliamentary Commissioner for Standards over her use of the Second Homes Allowance. She was widely criticised for designating her sister's home in London as her main residence, allowing her to claim for a second home in her Redditch constituency, where she lived with her family. The controversy over Smith's expenses, though, was merely the opening squall in what became a ferocious storm that engulfed the whole of Westminster in the spring and early summer of 2009.

The origins of the crisis over MPs' expenses dated back to the early 1980s. Fearing a public backlash, successive governments had refused to fund the recommendations of independent bodies which had sought to increase MPs' pay. MPs' allowances were discreetly and steadily increased instead to compensate. The distinction between pay and expenses became blurred. Some MPs would submit all manner of expense claims, leaving it up to the House of Commons Fees Office to decide whether or not they were valid.[1]

The Freedom of Information Act brought Parliament within the remit of freedom of information, but for several years the House of Commons authorities had fought its provisions, going to court to defend the right of MPs to keep the addresses of their properties secret. That legal battle was still ongoing when the *Daily Telegraph* acquired a CD containing the details of all MPs' expense claims.[2] The paper began publishing details in May 2009, and continued, with a drip-feed of damaging revelations, for weeks afterwards, dominating the media agenda throughout the summer of 2009. The paper dubbed the MPs' expenses scandal 'a systematic and deliberate misappropriation of public funds on an extravagant scale'.[3]

The paper uncovered several cases of 'flipping', where MPs had changed the designation of their second homes in order to maximise the benefits from their Additional Cost Allowance (ACA), the grant for MPs living outside London designed to reimburse MPs for having to stay close to Westminster. Several MPs claimed that their newly-sold second home was in fact their principal residence, thus avoiding paying capital gains tax. Others shifted the designation of their first and second homes to fund costly repairs. The most notorious example concerned Margaret Moran, the Labour MP for Luton South, who spent £22,500 treating dry rot at her Southampton house, located 100 miles from her constituency – only days after switching her 'second home' there.

The most serious cases concerned a handful of suspected fraudulent claims. Elliot Morley, the former Environment Minister, was alleged to have claimed £16,800 for a mortgage that had already been paid off. He blamed 'sloppy accounting', and revealed he had repaid the money, but that explanation was not enough to prevent him from being suspended from the Parliamentary Labour Party (PLP). The Bury North MP, David Chaytor, was similarly suspended from the PLP, after claiming almost £13,000 in interest payments for a mortgage that he had already paid. Along with Jim Devine, the MP for Livingston, all three would go on to face criminal charges under the Theft Act.

Alongside these significant abuses of the system were more petty – yet eye-catching – misdemeanours. Under the rules, MPs were supposed to claim for 'reasonable reimbursement' of expenses incurred in the course of their parliamentary duties up to the value of £24,222 a year. But the *Daily Telegraph* uncovered a bizarre list of items that had been claimed by MPs, including biscuits, dog food, horse manure, and two toilet seats. One of the most ridiculed was a claim for £1,600 for a floating duck island made by Sir Peter Viggers, the Tory MP for Gosport. The ducks became a charge of the public purse – as the Fees Office had rejected the claim – but it became emblematic of the scandal.

Whereas the details of some political 'scandals' pass the public by, the expenses scandal did not. It was easy to understand. Initially, MPs misjudged the extent of public anger by deploying two standard excuses: either 'I was acting in good faith', or 'I was acting within the rules'. When that failed, a string of MPs offered to pay money back. At one point, Hazel Blears, the Communities Secretary, who was found to have claimed for three different properties in one year, appeared on television, holding a cheque aloft for the sum of £13,332, a repayment for the capital gains tax she would have paid had she not declared the London flat she sold in 2004 to be her primary property.

The Commons authorities also badly misjudged the mood. The first thing that the Speaker, Michael Martin did was to call in the police to investigate – not the series of allegations against MPs, but how the information had been leaked to the *Daily Telegraph*. Martin was in a weak position. As Chairman of the House of Commons Commission, he had spent the previous four years trying to prevent the publication of MPs' expenses in the courts. He had attracted unfavourable publicity with his

'C'mon! There's still loads more meat left'

(Martin Rowson, *Guardian*, 23 May 2009)

own claims for expenses. In December 2008, Martin had attracted further controversy over his decision to allow a police raid on Conservative Immigration Spokesperson, Damian Green's Commons office, after Green was arrested in connection with leaking government documents. Martin had not insisted upon the police having a search warrant, and was later criticised for appearing to pin the blame on his colleague, the Serjeant-at-Arms. Then, at the height of the expenses crisis, more damaging revelations emerged in the *Daily Telegraph* of Martin's expense claims, including a bill for more than £1,400 for chauffeurs in his Glasgow constituency.

He sealed his own fate when, instead of issuing an apology for the expenses affair – as by that point, all three major party leaders had already done – he launched into tirades in the Commons directed against two MPs who questioned his stance – Kate Hoey and Norman Baker.[4] Whilst the leaders of the two main parties were bound by convention not to criticise the Speaker, Nick Clegg, the new Liberal Democrat leader, broke ranks by claiming that Martin had 'got it wrong, very wrong' and called on him to consider his position. Douglas Carswell, a junior Conservative backbencher, took the highly unusual step of putting down a motion of no confidence in the Speaker. On 18 May 2009, there followed extraordinary scenes in the Commons as Martin belatedly apologised for the expenses affair and instigated a meeting of all party leaders. However, several MPs from all sides of the House raised points of order, effectively calling on him to resign, and the following day – in a statement lasting just 33 seconds – he became the first Speaker to resign since 1695.

The election of a new Speaker, John Bercow, on 22 June 2009, did little to draw the sting from the crisis. When the Commons belatedly published the details of MPs' expense claims on 18 June 2009 (fully 40 days after the revelations had first appeared in the *Daily Telegraph*), large parts were left blacked out or 'redacted'. Crucially, the published data did not disclose the addresses of MPs' first and second homes, meaning that without the *Daily Telegraph*'s investigations in the uncensored material, one of the key aspects of the scandal – the alleged 'flipping' between first and second homes – would never have emerged.

The prolonged crisis over MPs' expenses not only contributed to the downfall of a Commons Speaker for the first time in over 300 years, it also led to much soul-searching amongst the political classes over the need for wholesale constitutional reform. Every constitutional reform activist and anorak jumped on the expenses bandwagon, as an excuse to push their particular reform. Some called for greater direct democracy, others favoured proportional representation. The *Guardian* called for 'a New Politics', even producing 'a blueprint for reforming government'. As well as specific measures to tighten up the expenses system, the Prime Minister hailed a new constitutional settlement, promising, amongst other things, reform of the House of Lords and the creation of a Bill of Rights.

It was never clear why any of this would solve the specific problem. New Labour had already engaged in substantial constitutional reform, and that had had little or no effect on the public's declining faith in its political institutions. Nevertheless, the public perception of Parliament as a tainted institution held sway and the scandal breathed extra life into the growing culture of anti-politics: the idea of a remote, Westminster-elite, greedily trousering taxpayers' cash.

One effect of the row was that serving MPs increasingly became disillusioned and demoralised. For any MP placed in the line of fire, it was a bruising experience. First came the fateful phone call from the *Daily Telegraph*, then an anxious wait for publication of the revelations and then a further wait for the local newspaper reactions. Within the confines of the Commons, there was a general view across the parties that many 'good' people had been effectively hanged for silly little mistakes.

There was particular concern on the Labour side about its 'star chamber', established by the party's ruling National Executive Committee (NEC) to 'try' MPs. A generation of MPs had been left bruised and shattered by the whole experience, and increasingly began asking themselves whether being an MP was worth the hassle. In August 2009, Alan Duncan, then Shadow Leader of the House, was caught on film lamenting the new culture of austerity: 'Basically, it's [the system of MPs' expenses] being nationalised, you have to live on rations and are treated like shit.' The scandal, Duncan claimed, would mean that no successful person outside politics would ever want to be an MP. Privately, plenty of other MPs agreed. Many simply gave up: the end of the 2005 Parliament saw the largest number of retirements among MPs in the post-war period – standing at 149, dwarfing the 128 MPs who retired in 1945. But to the general public, and a small number inside the Westminster village, it still seemed as if many MPs had failed to grasp what had happened. They didn't 'get it'. A senior Cabinet minister's adviser best summed up MPs' attitudes in the middle of 2009:

> Parliament is a load of people on a boat, which is swamped by a vicious storm. Some people go overboard (some are even pushed overboard by the captain), and then the storm subsides. Everyone's traumatised, but the waters are now calm, and the sky is clear, so they think that if they keep puffing on as they did before, they'll get to shore and be safe. What they haven't realised is that when they do, the harbour will be full of a mob with pitchforks.

In the middle of the expenses crisis, the broadcaster Stephen Fry had dubbed it 'a journalistic made up frenzy', warning: 'Let's not confuse what politicians really get wrong, things like wars, things where people die, with the rather tedious, bourgeois obsession with whether they've charged for their wisteria. It's not that important, it really isn't.'[5] And throughout the parliament, wars certainly cost – in both human and financial terms – far more than any duck islands.

Despite a rebellion involving over a hundred Labour MPs, in March 2007 Blair committed the Government to replacing Britain's ageing warheads on its fleet of Trident nuclear submarines. Two new aircraft carriers were also ordered. But declining economic fortunes meant that politicians and commentators alike increasingly questioned whether the Government could continue to devote the same high level of military commitments overseas as it had done in the past, particularly in Iraq and Afghanistan.

British soldiers remained in Iraq to train the indigenous army and police force, and to allow the fledgling Iraqi government time to assume administrative control of Basra. But that process took longer than expected. British combat operations in Iraq did not cease until 30 April 2009, and Britain's mandate did not formally expire until 31 July 2009. Britain lost 179 soldiers in the invasion and subsequent occupation, at an estimated cost of £6.5 billion. Opponents of the war called for a full public inquiry into the conflict, which was only ceded by the British Government once the bulk of troops had returned home. Even then, the Brown Government proved reluctant to concede the principle that most of the inquiry's hearings should be held in public. Overwhelming political pressure, including from Sir John Chilcot, the chairman of the inquiry panel, ensured that the vast majority of the hearings would be held in public, when consistent with national security considerations. The sheer scope of the inquiry would mean that it would not report until well after any general election, although it was to be a high-profile reminder of the Iraq invasion during the final months of the Parliament.

Political and public focus mostly shifted from Iraq to Afghanistan, where, by July 2009, British military deaths had surpassed those in Iraq. A large NATO-led offensive against the Taliban, entitled Operation Panther's Claw, left 22 British dead – the highest monthly tally since the conflict began in 2001. Public support for the war in Afghanistan at the beginning of the summer of 2009 was fairly evenly divided: an ICM poll in July 2009 found 47% support for the war, against 46% who opposed it. Mounting casualties meant that by the end of the summer, support for British troops staying in Afghanistan had slumped to 26%.

These statistics masked a growing public affection for the armed forces, a phenomenon not seen since the Falklands War. Large crowds greeted British troops' homecoming parades and British soldiers killed in action were flown into RAF Lyneham, and driven through the nearby market town of Wootton Bassett, where people lined the high street to pay their respects. So frequent were these sombre occasions that the Wiltshire town became synonymous with public grieving over Britain's war dead.

The debate began to shift from divisions over the rights and wrongs of military conflicts to growing unease about British troops being under-resourced, and concerns that the military covenant – the understanding that society owes troops a particular obligation – was being broken by the Government. Following an increase in the use of Improvised Explosive Devices (IEDs) by both insurgents in Iraq and the Taliban in Afghanistan, the Government was forced to strengthen armoured vehicles against such roadside bombs. During the summer of 2009, a similar political row broke out over whether the Government was failing to provide sufficient helicopters to give British troops air support in Afghanistan.

Against this backdrop of growing public empathy for the armed forces, the Home Office came under fire for its treatment of ex-soldiers. In April 2009, the Government was defeated in the House of Commons over its plans to allow only Ghurkhas who retired after 1997 to settle in Britain. The Commons defeat was preceded by a high-profile campaign led by the British actress Joanna Lumley, whose father had served with the Ghurkhas. The Government was forced into a major U-turn, relaxing the criteria for entry. The Ministry of Defence was also widely criticised for contesting in the courts increases in compensation payouts made to British soldiers injured while serving in Iraq.

Britain had experienced a surge in immigration after ten new countries acceded to the European Union in May 2004. Research published in 2006 appeared to suggest that these large inflows of migrant workers had provided a significant boost to UK economic growth in terms of increased tax receipts to the Treasury. However, it acknowledged that gains to the economy were not evenly distributed.[6] In the pockets of the highest immigration pressure was put on educational and social services, as well as housing, leading to widespread fears that the indigenous population was losing out. In 2009, detailed analysis of social housing allocation policies revealed no evidence that social housing allocation favoured foreign migrants over UK citizens.[7] But no amount of sober research findings assuaged growing public unease about the scale and impact of immigration. Politicians' encounters with voters confirmed the surveys showing that immigration was one of the top two or three concerns of voters.

In 2007 Gordon Brown pledged to secure 'British jobs for British workers'. It was a phrase that sounded good at the time, but which the Government came to regret in February 2009 when contract workers at the Lindsey refinery in north Lincolnshire and elsewhere took part in unofficial industrial action. They were protesting that a contract awarded to an Italian firm on the Lindsey site discriminated against British workers through the exclusive employment of Italian and Portuguese workers. As economic conditions worsened in Britain, so people's anxieties that their jobs were being somehow 'taken' by foreigners, increasingly held sway. In 2009, 41 years after Enoch Powell's controversial 'Rivers of Blood' speech, two British National Party MEPs were elected at the European elections.

The Government responded to public concern by moving to a points-based system for immigrants seeking to gain British citizenship.

Applicants could 'earn' points by engaging in voluntary work, speaking English, paying taxes or having useful skills. Equally, they could lose points for being convicted of a crime. Ironically, as the recession in Britain began to bite, so work applications from Eastern and Central European countries began to drop, leading to a dramatic slowdown in immigration.

By the end of 2008, the British Crime Survey reported the lowest level of crime since its first results were published in 1981. The murder rate fell by 17%, its lowest level for 20 years. The risk of being a victim of a crime of any kind had been 40% in 1995, and was 22% by the end of 2008.[8] Yet three-quarters of voters remained convinced that crime was rising, almost out of control. Nevertheless, by the middle of 2009, Britain's public sector braced itself for the full impact of the recession. In August 2009, an Audit Commission report warned local councils to prepare for the adverse social impact, including higher rates of debt, domestic violence, welfare and benefit queries, and even fly-tipping as the recession deepened.[9]

Yet at the very point at which the economic downturn kicked in, public satisfaction with the public services was at a record high. In January 2009, a British Social Attitudes Report found that voters were more satisfied with the service provided by the NHS than at any time since 1984. One in two people (51%) said they were satisfied with the NHS, compared with just a third of people (34%) in 1997 when New Labour came to power. The report concluded: 'It is hard to resist the conclusion that massively increased NHS spending over the last seven years, enabling [the service] to increase its staffing considerably ... and reduce waiting times to their lowest level since the inception of the NHS, must have played a significant part in boosting satisfaction.'[10]

But the UK was only beginning to face up to the twin impact of rising life expectancy and historically low rates of savings. In November 2005, the Turner Report recommended steadily increasing the state pension age for men and women from 66 by 2030 to 67 by 2040 and 68 by 2050, as well as the establishment of a new National Pension Savings Scheme.[11] The Report's chairman, Adair Turner, also came out in favour of restoring the link between the state pension and earnings, something which the Labour Government pledged to honour by 2012. However, the problems associated with the greying of Britain accelerated as the economic recession started to bite. Householders, who had increasingly seen bricks and mortar as their main source of income in retirement, saw house prices fall sharply, while most large British companies, facing very large deficits in their pension funds, closed their final salaries schemes to new entrants.

The nation also experienced a modest population boom. In August 2009, the Office for National Statistics published estimates that Britain's population in mid-2008 stood at 61.4 million, up 408,000 on the previous year, the biggest annual increase since 1973. Fertility rates from mothers born outside the UK rose from 14% in 1998 to 24% in 2008, as immigrants who had settled in Britain started having a family. Instead of viewing a baby boom as a positive development, providing young workers of the future to support an ageing population, sections of the British press saw it otherwise. Both the *Daily Mail* and the *Daily Express* voiced concern that one in four babies born were now born to a mother from overseas. It indicated, as *The Times* pointed out in a more measured way, that the ethnic balance of Britain was shifting.

By the end of 2009, the British people could look back on a decade of prosperity and investment in public services, in which public spending had risen from 40% to 48% of GDP. But the public mood had darkened over the five years of the Parliament. The expenses scandal had led to a further decline in trust in the political class and surveys found that many voters regarded Britain as a nation in decline. Families looked uneasily forward to an uncertain future, characterised by stagnant economic growth, growing unemployment, increases in tax, and large cuts in public expenditure, regardless of whichever political party won the 2010 election. It presented political parties with a difficult political battleground.

Chronology of events, from May 2005 to December 2009

2005

6 May	M. Howard announces intention to step down as Con leader, despite achieving a net gain of 31 seats.
30 May	French voters reject EU constitution.
2 Jun	Dutch voters reject EU constitution.
6–8 Jul	G8 annual summit at Gleneagles.
6 Jul	London wins 2012 Olympics.
7 Jul	London bombings.
22 Jul	Brazilian John Charles de Menezes, 27, is shot dead by police at Stockwell tube station.
29–31 Aug	Hurricane Katrina leaves most of New Orleans under water.
4 Oct	Tory leadership candidate, D. Cameron, delivers a speech without notes to the Con Party conference in Blackpool.

2 Nov	D. Blunkett, the Work and Pensions Secretary, resigns.
9 Nov	Government defeated twice in one night in the Commons over plans to detain terrorist suspects.
30 Nov	The second Turner Report concludes state pension age for men and women should rise to 66 by 2030, to 67 by 2040 and to 68 by 2050.
6 Dec	D. Cameron elected as Con Party leader.

2006

5 Jan	C. Kennedy admits to an alcohol problem, but says he wants to carry on as LD leader.
7 Jan	C. Kennedy resigns as LD leader.
19 Jan	M. Oaten pulls out of LD leadership race, claiming lack of support.
31 Jan	Government defeated twice in Commons over new offence of incitement to religious hatred in Racial and Religious Hatred Bill. T. Blair absent from the second vote, which the Government loses by one.
9 Feb	LD win the Dunfermline & West Fife by-election, from Labour.
14 Feb	On a free vote, MPs vote in favour of a total ban on smoking in public places.
2 Mar	Sir M. Campbell is elected LD Leader, defeating C. Huhne and S. Hughes.
21 Mar	Metropolitan Police are called in to investigate the 'cash-for-honours' allegations.
4 May	Lab lose 254 councillors and control of 18 town halls in the English local elections.
5 May	T. Blair's biggest ever government reshuffle.
30 Jun	Con narrowly hold Bromley & Chislehurst by-election.
12 Jul	Lord Levy, Blair's chief fundraiser, is arrested and bailed in connection with the 'cash-for-honours' inquiry.
12 Jul– 14 Aug	Israeli–Hezbollah war in Lebanon and Northern Israel.
4 Sep	15 Lab MPs write to PM calling on him to stand down.
6 Sep	T. Watson resigns as a junior defence minister, along with seven PPSs.
7 Sep	T. Blair confirms that the 2006 Labour Party conference will be his last as Lab leader.
26 Sep	Blair's final conference speech as Prime Minister.
20 Oct	C. Short resigns the Labour whip.

| 14 Dec | T. Blair interviewed by police investigating the 'cash-for-honours' allegations. |

2007

14 Mar	102 Lab MPs oppose decision to replace Trident.
15 Mar	Phillips' final report on party funding, recommends a cap on both donations and overall campaign spending, as well as a limited increase in state funding of parties.
21 Mar	In his final Budget as Chancellor, G. Brown pays for a 2p cut in the basic rate of income tax by abolishing the lower 10p starting rate.
1 May	T. Blair celebrates ten years as Prime Minister, endorsing G. Brown as his successor.
6 May	The SNP narrowly wins power over Lab in the Scottish parliamentary elections, Lab loses overall control in the Welsh Assembly elections. Con poll 40% in the English local elections.
8 May	Restoration of the devolved assembly in Northern Ireland.
10 May	T. Blair formally announces his decision to step down as Lab leader and PM. J. Prescott announces he is stepping down as Deputy Leader of the Labour Party.
17 May	Nominations close for Lab leadership. G. Brown secures the support of 313 MPs.
24 Jun	G. Brown is elected unopposed as Lab leader at a Special Conference in Manchester. H. Harman is elected Deputy Leader.
26 Jun	Q. Davies, the Con MP for Grantham and Stamford, defects to Lab.
27 Jun	T. Blair resigns as Prime Minister, and receives a standing ovation in the Commons. G. Brown enters Number 10, promising 'change'.
30 Jun	ICM poll gives Lab a four-point lead, for first time since Mar 2006.
19 Jul	Lab holds Sedgefield by-election and Ealing Southall by-election, where 'David Cameron's Conservatives' finish a poor third.
20 Jul	The Crown Prosecution Service decides not to bring any charges against anyone following the 'cash-for-honours' affair.
4 Jul	Government Green Paper on constitutional reform.
17 Jul	G. Galloway suspended from the Commons for 18 days.

27 Jul	B. Johnson selected, using a primary system, as Con mayoral candidate for London.
14 Sep	Customers begin a run on Northern Rock bank.
24 Sep	G. Brown delivers his first conference speech as Lab leader and PM.
1 Oct	Government announces it will guarantee 100% of bank and building society savings up to £35,000.
2 Oct	G. Brown makes his first visit to Iraq as PM, promising that 1,000 British troops will be home by Christmas. Shadow Chancellor, G. Osborne pledges next Conservative Government will raise the Inheritance Tax Threshold to £1 million.
6 Oct	G. Brown calls off a November election.
10 Oct	Government's joint Comprehensive Spending Review and Pre-Budget Report.
15 Oct	Sir M. Campbell resigns as LD leader. V. Cable becomes Acting Leader.
20 Nov	'Discgate': Government admits to losing two CDs containing bank details and addresses of 25 million people from HM Revenue and Customs.
26 Nov	P. Watt, General Secretary of the Labour Party, resigns after money donated to Labour through middlemen 'was not lawfully declared'.
28 Nov	V. Cable notes 'the Prime Minister's remarkable transformation in the past few weeks from Stalin to Mr Bean'.
8 Dec	N. Clegg narrowly defeats C. Huhne to win the LD leadership contest.
27 Dec	Former Pakistani Prime Minister, Benazir Bhutto assassinated.

2008

10 Jan	Work and Pensions Secretary and Welsh Secretary, P. Hain fails to declare £103,000 in donations relating to his failed deputy leadership bid.
24 Jan	P. Hain forced to resign as Electoral Commission refers his case to the Metropolitan Police. Cabinet reshuffle: J. Purnell promoted to Department of Work and Pensions.
30 Jan	D. Conway agrees to stand down at the next general election. The following day, the House of Commons suspends him for ten days.
7 Feb	Bank of England cuts base rates from 5.5% to 5.25%.

17 Feb	Northern Rock is placed into 'a temporary period of public ownership'.
4 Mar	The Rev I. Paisley announces his intention to retire as leader of the DUP.
5 Mar	House of Commons votes against a referendum on Treaty of Lisbon.
12 Mar	A. Darling's first Budget as Chancellor.
14 Apr	P. Robinson chosen to succeed the Rev I. Paisley as leader of the Democratic Unionist Party.
22 Apr	UKIP gains its first MP as former Con MP, Bob Spink announces his defection.
23 Apr	Facing defeat, Government makes concessions over the abolition of the 10p rate of income tax.
1–2 May	Lab routed in local elections in England and Wales, suffering a net loss of 334 council seats, their worst result for 40 years. Con net gain of 257 seats, LD gain 33 seats. Con Boris Johnson is declared Mayor of London.
22 May	Con win the Crewe & Nantwich by-election, on a 17.6% swing.
11 Jun	Government wins crucial Commons vote on 42 days pre-charge detention, by nine votes, largely thanks to the support of nine DUP MPs.
12 Jun	Shadow Home Secretary, D. Davis, announces his intention to resign his Haltemprice & Howden seat, forcing a by-election on the issue of 42 days.
13 Jun	The Irish people reject the Lisbon Treaty.
26 Jun	Con hold Henley by-election. Lab comes fifth behind the Greens and the BNP.
28 Jun	W. Alexander resigns as Scottish Labour leader after breaking rules on declaring donations.
24 Jul	The SNP gain Glasgow East from Labour on a by-election swing of 22.5%.
15 Sep	American investment bank, Lehman Brothers, files for bankruptcy.
16 Sep	US Federal Reserve Board rescues American insurance giant, AIG.
17 Sep	FTSE closes below 5,000 points for the first time since May 2005, amid widespread selling of bank shares.
18 Sep	Lloyds TSB agrees to buy troubled HBOS, Britain's biggest home loan lender. G. Brown vows to end 'irresponsible behaviour' in the City, as the Financial Services Authority

announces a temporary ban of the short-selling of bank shares.

19 Sep	US Treasury Secretary, Henry Paulson announces a $700 billion bail-out plan to of financial companies.
23 Sep	G. Brown tells Lab Conference that this is a time for experience, not a novice at Number 10.
26 Sep	Failure of Washington Mutual, a huge American bank.
29 Sep	Britain announces the nationalisation of mortgage lender, Bradford & Bingley.
30 Sep	The Irish Government guarantees all bank deposits.
3 Oct	Government bank deposit guarantees are increased from £35,000 to £50,000. Cabinet reshuffle sees P. Mandelson return as Secretary of State for Business, Enterprise and Regulatory Reform.
6 Oct	FTSE falls by a record 7.85% in one day.
7 Oct	Icelandic Bank, IceSave blocks internet savers from withdrawing their money.
8 Oct	The Treasury outlines a £500 billion bank rescue plan to try to prevent financial meltdown. The Bank of England cuts base rates from 5% to 4.5%.
10 Oct	The FTSE closes 8.85% lower in just one day. The Dow Jones falls 8%. The Nikkei index falls 10%. Oil prices tumble.
11 Oct	Emergency meeting of G7 finance ministers in Washington discusses a coordinated response to the financial crisis.
12 Oct	EU Summit in Paris.
13 Oct	Government announces a £37 billion emergency recapitalisation of RBS, HBOS and Lloyds TSB. Government drops its plans for 42-day detention of terrorist suspects after a defeat in the House of Lords.
4 Nov	Senator Barack Obama becomes the first black President of the United States.
6 Nov	Bank of England cuts base rates from 4.5% to 3%. Lab holds Glenrothes in by-election, despite a 5% swing to the SNP.
24 Nov	Chancellor of the Exchequer, A. Darling announces a fiscal stimulus package worth £20 billion, reduction in the rate of VAT from 17.5% to 15% until 2010. Top rate of income tax to 45% on those earning more than £150,000 from 2011.
26 Nov	Terrorists attack two Mumbai hotels, killing over 100 people. Retailer Woolworths goes into administration.
28 Nov	D. Green, Shadow Immigration Minister, is arrested at his home in Kent by counter-terrorism officers, following

	leaks from the Home Office to the Conservatives about immigration policy.
4 Dec	Bank of England cuts base rates from 3% to 2%.
10 Dec	In a slip of the tongue, Gordon Brown claims to have 'saved the world'.
27 Dec–	
20 Jan	Israeli offensive against Hamas in Gaza.

2009

8 Jan	Bank of England cuts base rates from 2% to 1.5%.
19 Jan	Government announces a second major bail-out of British banks, including increasing its stake in RBS to around 70%. Con reshuffle sees K. Clarke appointed Shadow Secretary of State for Business, Enterprise and Regulatory Reform. E. Pickles succeeds C. Spelman as Party Chairman.
29 Jan	Contract workers at the Lindsey Oil Refinery in north Lincolnshire take part in unofficial industrial action.
5 Feb	Bank of England cuts base rates from 1.5% to an all-time low of 1%.
26 Feb	Sir Fred Goodwin, the former Chief Executive of RBS refuses to give up his pension.
5 Mar	Bank of England cuts base rates from 1% to a new historic low of 0.5%, and announces a £75 billion asset purchase programme.
7 Mar	Government takes majority control of Lloyds Banking Group, with the taxpayer owning 65% of shares.
18 Mar	Unemployment passes 2 million for the first time since 1997.
2 Apr	G20 Summit in London pledges an additional $1.1 trillion in financing to the International Monetary Fund and declares a crackdown on tax havens and hedge funds. A new supervisory body would flag up problems in the global financial system, but G20 leaders failed to agree on a new fiscal stimulus package.
11 Apr	D. McBride, a close adviser to the Prime Minister, resigns after it emerged he had written 'juvenile and inappropriate' emails about the alleged private lives of leading Conservatives.
16 Apr	The Crown Prosecution Service announces that D. Green will not face charges.
22 Apr	A. Darling's second Budget. Growth forecasts downgraded for 2009; government borrowing forecasts upgraded to 12% of GDP. New top rate of income tax of 50% for those earning over £150,000 a year to be introduced in April 2010.

29 Apr	G. Brown suffers his first House of Commons defeat on the issue of Ghurkhas' rights of abode in Britain.
30 Apr	Government wins votes on MPs' expenses, after it agrees to delay a decision on the second homes allowance.
30 Apr	British combat operations end in Iraq.
7 May	Bank of England maintains base rates at 0.5%, but increases quantitative easing by £50 billion to £125 billion.
8 May	The *Daily Telegraph* publishes details of MPs' expenses, heralding a wave of damaging revelations that lasts over three weeks.
12 May	Unemployment rate rises to 7.1%, up 0.8% in the first quarter of 2009. D. Hogg, Con MP for Sleaford & North Hykeham, claims the cost of having his moat cleared at his country manor house. H. Blears responds to public anger by announcing that she will pay back over £13,000 to cover the capital gains tax on a London flat she sold.
14 May	Tory MP, A. Mackay resigns as PPS to the Con leader over 'unacceptable expense claims'. Scunthorpe MP, E. Morley suspended from the Parliamentary Labour Party after claiming £16,000 for interest payments on a mortgage that he had already paid off.
15 May	Dewsbury Labour MP, S. Malik steps downs as Justice Minister pending the outcome of an inquiry into his expense claims.
16 May	D. Chaytor, Labour MP for Bury North, is suspended from the Parliamentary Labour Party after claiming almost £13,000 in interest payments for a mortgage that he had already repaid.
18 May	Tory backbencher, D. Carswell tables a motion of no confidence in the Speaker. The Speaker faces calls from MPs of all three main parties to resign.
19 May	The Speaker resigns. Retail prices index falls to –1.2%.
20 May	Two Labour peers – Lord Truscott and Lord Taylor of Blackburn – are suspended from the House of Lords after they are found guilty of offering to change the law in return for money.
21 May	Revealed that Sir P. Viggers, Con MP for Gosport, claimed £1,600 for a floating duck island. Norwich North Labour MP, Dr I. Gibson agrees to stand down at the next election, after claiming almost £80,000 in four years for mortgage interest and bills on a London flat which was the main home of his daughter.

24 May	Con MP A. Mackay decides to stand down at the next general election, following a phone call from Con leader.
2 Jun	Home Secretary J. Smith announces her resignation from the Government ahead of an expected reshuffle. Lab 'star chamber' bars four Labour MPs implicated in the expenses row – B. Chapman, D. Chaytor, Dr I. Gibson and E. Morley – from standing as candidates at the next election.
3 Jun	H. Blears, the Communities Secretary, resigns from the Government. *Guardian* editorial calls on Lab 'to cut Gordon Brown loose'.
4 Jun	Just before polls close at the European and local elections, J. Purnell, the Work and Pensions Minister resigns, urging PM to go. Local election results: Con gain 265 seats; Lab lose 305, losing control of their last four county councils.
5 Jun	G. Brown vows 'I will not walk away.' Norwich North Labour MP, Dr I. Gibson resigns, prompting a by-election.
7 Jun	European elections results: Cons top the poll, UKIP push Labour into third.
8 Jun	Environment minister, J. Kennedy is sacked for refusing to give a pledge of support to the PM.
11 Jun	The World Health Organisation declares swine flu a global pandemic.
13 Jun	Iran's President Ahmadinejad is reelected following disputed elections.
16 Jun	Government announces an inquiry into the war in Iraq, but with evidence to be taken in private. J. Devine, Lab MP for Livingston, is deselected by 'star chamber' endorsements panel.
17 Jun	K. Ussher, junior Treasury minister, is sacked, following evidence that she 'flipped' her homes to avoid paying capital gains tax.
18 Jun	The House of Commons publishes MPs' expense claims, but with large sections redacted or 'blacked out'.
22 Jun	Con MP, J. Bercow, is elected Speaker of the House of Commons.
29 Jun	The PM attempts to relaunch his Government with *Building Britain's Future*.
30 Jun	Government announces that the ID cards scheme will remain voluntary, as plans for compulsory ID cards for pilots and other airport workers are shelved.

1 Jul	Government abandons plans to part-privatise the Royal Mail. Government defeated during the passage of the Parliamentary Standards Bill.
23 Jul	Con gain Norwich North from Labour, with a 16.5% swing.
30 Jul	MoD release figures for British soldiers wounded in Operation Panther's Claw in Helmand Province, Afghanistan.
31 Jul	Britain's mandate formally ends in Iraq.
3 Aug	Home Office unveils new points system for immigrants seeking British citizenship.
6 Aug	Bank of England maintains base rates at 0.5%, but increases quantitative easing by a further £50 billion to £175 billion.
12 Aug	Unemployment hits 2.43 million, its highest level in 14 years. A. Duncan, Shadow Leader of the House, is forced to apologise over comments on expenses.
20 Aug	Lockerbie bomber, Abdelbaset Al Mohmed al Megrahi, suffering from prostate cancer, is released from prison in Scotland on compassionate grounds, and is free to return to Libya.
7 Sep	A. Duncan is stripped of his role as Shadow Leader of the Commons, demoted to Shadow Justice Minister with responsibility for prisons.
29 Sep	G. Brown's last party conference speech as Prime Minister.
30 Sep	The *Sun* switches support from Labour to Conservative, claiming 'Labour's lost it'.
3 Oct	In a second referendum, 67.1% of Ireland's voters back the Lisbon Treaty. On the eve of the Tory Party conference, G. Brown declares his willingness to take part in television debates in the run-up to the election.
12 Oct	Sir Thomas Legg's inquiry into five years of MPs' expenses, seeks retrospective repayments for gardening and cleaning. G. Brown is asked to pay back £12,415 for overpayments.
14 Oct	Unemployment rises to 7.9% for the three months to August 2009, up 88,000, but the rate of increase slows.
23 Oct	A 0.4% drop in GDP in the third quarter of 2009, to the surprise of economists who had expected the recession to end.
3 Nov	Czech President, Vaclav Klaus signs the Lisbon Treaty, completing its ratification.
4 Nov	Publication of the Kelly Report into MPs' expenses. Following ratification in the rest of Europe, David Cameron reneges

	on his 'cast-iron guarantee' to hold a referendum on the Lisbon Treaty.
12 Nov	Lab hold Glasgow North East.
20 Nov	Belgian Prime Minister Herman von Rompuy is named as the new EU President of the Council of Ministers, and the UK's Baroness Ashton becomes the EU's foreign policy chief.
1 Dec	C. Jones is elected to succeed R. Morgan as leader of the Welsh Labour Party.
7–18 Dec	At Conference of the United Nations Convention for Climate Change, world leaders fail to reach an agreement to replace the Kyoto Protocol.
9 Dec	Pre-Budget Report introduces a 50% one-off levy on bankers' bonuses, plus 0.5% rise in national insurance in 2011–12; public sector pay to be capped at 1% for two years in a row.
22 Dec	The PM announces three live televised debates – on ITV, Sky and the BBC – between the three main party leaders for the 2010 general election campaign.

Notes

1. See A. Kelso, 'Parliament on its Knees: MPs' Expenses and the Crisis of Transparency at Westminster', *Political Quarterly*, 80:3 (2009), 329–38.
2. See R. Winnett and G. Rayner, *No Expenses Spared* (London: Bantam, 2009).
3. Leading Article, 'A flipping outrage', *Daily Telegraph*, 9 May 2009.
4. HC Debs, 11 May 2009, c. 548.
5. *Newsnight*, 11 May 2009.
6. M. Weale and R. Riley, 'Immigration and its Effects', *National Institute Economic Review*, 198 (2006), 4–9.
7. J. Rutter and M. Latorre, *Social Housing Allocation and Immigrant Communities*, IPPR Report for Equality and Human Rights Commission, 2009, p. ix.
8. Home Office, *Crime in England and Wales 2007/08* (April 2009), p. 2.
9. Audit Commission, *When it Comes to the Crunch. How Councils are Responding to the Recession* (August 2009).
10. J. Appleby and M. Phillips, 'The NHS: Satisfied Now?', *British Social Attitudes. The 25th Report*, 2009, Ch. 2.
11. Pensions Commission, *A New Pension Settlement for the Twenty-First Century. The Second Report of the Pensions Commission* (Turner Report, 2005).

3
From Blair to Brown: Labour

Tony Blair had fought the 2005 election making two promises to the electorate. He promised that it would be the last election he would fight as Labour leader; and that, if elected, he would serve a full term. Only one of those promises was kept. Blair would be forced from office in 2007, just two years into the Parliament – not a full term by anyone's definition – and he struggled even to make it that far. Despite winning that 'historic' third term for Labour, something the party had never before managed, he had been almost crestfallen as the results had come in on election night. He knew that the modest victory meant that remaining in office for the rest of the Parliament would be a struggle, and that his hopes of removing Gordon Brown from the Treasury would have to be abandoned.

Labour MPs attacked Blair at the first meeting of the Parliamentary Labour Party after the election, complaining that they would have had a larger majority had he stepped down earlier, and his continuing refusal to set a date for his departure led to endless speculation and intrigue, dominating political life for the next two years. Pressure began to build among those MPs who wanted a quick transition from Blair to Brown and was so strong that the hoped-for 'orderly transition' frequently looked like turning disorderly.

Blair's eventual removal, and replacement by Gordon Brown, may have brought to an end the factionalism and intense personal rivalry between the top two figures that at times had been crippling for the Government, but it did not see an end to complaints about the Labour leadership. For almost all of Brown's tenure in Number 10 – other than right at the beginning, when he was enjoying an initial honeymoon, and right at the end in 2010 – the threat of a coup was ever-present. Those around Brown, many of them no strangers to scheming against a prime minister, found themselves on the receiving end. 'Sometimes, on conference calls

I'd hear people saying "how can they behave like this?, don't they know the damage it's doing?",' said one of those working in Brown's Number 10, 'and I'd have to stop myself laughing.'

Leadership and the economy had been two of Labour's trump cards in previous elections. On both, the party struggled after 2007. The economic recession starting in 2008 (see Chapter 2) hung over the life of Brown's Government. Plans for spending cuts would have to replace those for further investment in public services and Brown's decade-long boasts of having ended a boom-and-bust economy were held up to ridicule. But Brown's leadership was also a factor. He struggled to adapt to the demands of life in Number 10. Being Prime Minister, he and his team soon found out, was harder than it looked. Compared with his time as Chancellor he proved to be a diminished political force as Prime Minister.

Tony Blair began his third term with an ambitious agenda of public service reform, hoping to expand city academies with the aid of business sponsorship, establish foundation schools and increase private sector involvement in the NHS. That reform agenda became sidetracked following the 7/7 bombings in London, after which the Home Office brought forward a Terrorism Bill, the centrepiece of which was plans to detain terrorist suspects without charge for up to 90 days. Getting it through the Commons looked difficult enough, but Blair set his face against compromise. It was a political style which he had deployed successfully before, but it no longer worked without the benefit of a three-figure parliamentary majority. The Government duly went down to a heavy defeat. Blair, however, saw political benefits to making the Conservatives appear 'weak' on Terrorism. As one of his whips admitted, 'If you are going to lose, then what better way to lose than on an issue where 70–80% of the public support you, including the tabloids, and where you've split the Tories and made them look weak on terror and anti-police.'

After disastrous English local elections results in May 2006, in which Labour lost control of 18 town halls, Blair was confronted with concerted and coordinated pressure from allies of Gordon Brown to set a date for his departure, or else face a formal leadership challenge. He attempted to reassert his authority, sacking Charles Clarke as Home Secretary following criticism over the release of hundreds of foreign prisoners who should have been considered for deportation at the end of their sentences. Clarke was replaced by John Reid, a close ally of Blair's. In the most radical reshuffle of his premiership, the Prime Minister also stripped John Prescott, his Deputy, of a government department weeks after revelations about Prescott's affair with his secretary. Jack Straw, the Foreign Secretary, was demoted to Leader of the House of Commons. Key Blair allies earned promotion: Alan Johnson took over Education; Jacqui Smith replaced Hilary Armstrong as Chief Whip; and Hazel Blears became Party Chair. The night before the reshuffle, Blair had decided to appoint David Miliband as Foreign Secretary, only to change his mind at the last minute. Instead, Margaret Beckett became the first ever female Foreign Secretary, whilst Miliband became Environment Secretary.

The pressure for a departure date, however, continued to increase. Labour MPs, particularly those from Scotland and Wales, felt that Blair's refusal to set a date would hurt the party in the devolved elections in May 2007, and that he needed to stand down well in advance. A few MPs were going public, but plenty of others expressed their views in private.

The eventual trigger for a coup against the Prime Minister turned out not to be a domestic political issue, but the Israeli invasion of Southern Lebanon. Blair refused to join in international calls for a ceasefire, seeing it as a tokenistic gesture. Many within the party saw his stance as provocative and antagonistic. Discontent over the Government's policy in the Middle East spilled over into the growing impatience with Blair's continued refusal to set a date for his departure. At Chequers in August, the Prime Minister gave an interview to *The Times*, telling an aide immediately afterwards, 'It'll calm things down.' Instead, it made things worse. *The Times* reported him repeatedly deflecting attempts to set a departure date, saying that he should be allowed to get on with the job, and would serve a full third term as Prime Minister.

On 4 September 15 Labour MPs, all drawn from the 2001 intake, wrote to the Prime Minister calling on him to step down. They included Tom Watson, a close ally of Gordon Brown, who resigned as a junior defence minister, along with seven parliamentary private secretaries. In his resignation letter, Watson wrote: 'I have to say that I no longer believe that your remaining in office is in the interest of either the party or the country.' Other letters were planned for delivery in a sequence of events that would have culminated in a ministerial delegation telling the Prime Minister to go. The aim was to force Blair out by the end of the week.

When they saw the identity of some of those who were prepared to go public, Blair's staff at Number 10 realised the threat was serious. They were not the usual malcontents (as one of the No 10 team put it: 'who'd be impressed if Jeremy Corbyn was a signatory?'), but a carefully chosen selection of previously loyal MPs. The No 10 counter-attack had two components. First, David Miliband was authorised to go onto Radio 4, to make clear that a new leader would be in place by the

Labour Party conference in 2007. Without naming an exact departure date, this concession removed the fears amongst some MPs – especially those around Gordon Brown – that Blair would simply hang on for as long as possible in Number 10. This announcement was backed up by a counter-letter, signed by 56 MPs, calling on the plotters to 'end damaging speculation about the leadership'. It was a sign of the trouble the Prime Minister was in that half the signatories to a letter purporting to represent the views of Labour backbenchers were in fact serving parliamentary private secretaries. Just 28 loyal backbenchers could be found.

Given his close links to the Chancellor Watson's involvement had already raised suspicions, which increased when it became known that he had visited Brown at home shortly beforehand. Few believed his claim that he had been delivering a present to Brown's children, and that they had merely spent their time watching Postman Pat videos. But as important as whether he knew in advance was what Brown did once the coup attempt began. 'We did notice', remarked one of Blair's aides, dryly, 'he didn't help much.'

On 6 September Blair and Brown held two separate meetings in Downing Street during which they tried to establish exactly what they both meant by 'a stable and orderly transition'. Brown thought that meant Blair announcing a timetable for his departure so that a new leader could be in place in good time before the local, Scottish and Welsh elections in May 2007. He demanded that Blair discourage other Cabinet ministers from standing against him in any future leadership contest and accept a system of 'co-decision', giving the Chancellor a veto over major policy decisions in the run-up to the handover. In sometimes heated exchanges, Blair refused to accept these conditions. The following day Blair used a visit to a school in north London to announce that the 2006 Labour Party conference would be his last as leader, but he stopped short of setting a firm date for his departure. He also apologised on behalf of the Labour Party, saying it had not been 'our finest hour'.

The attempted coup forced Blair to confirm an end-date for his premiership, but in the short term it did at least as much damage to Brown's reputation. Charles Clarke delivered an astonishing tirade against Brown, claiming he had 'psychological' issues, was a 'control freak' and 'totally uncollegiate'. If Brown could ignore the views of a known enemy, he could not so easily brush aside the bad press he received in the immediate wake of the coup attempt; and in the following weeks, the Blairites gained in confidence, believing there was still a possibility of an ABG – an 'Anyone but Gordon' – candidate. But a split had opened up between the older Blairites, such as Clarke, Reid, Alan Milburn and

Stephen Byers, who still cast around for someone to challenge Brown for the leadership (most often mentioning Alan Johnson, the Education Secretary), and a younger generation of Blairites, including David Miliband, James Purnell and Andy Burnham, who increasingly took the view that Brown's accession was inevitable, and who began making statements in support of the Chancellor. Some still hoped that Miliband would stand but he thought it not only unlikely he would win but also that the contest would be divisive and that some of Brown's aides would make life uncomfortable for his supporters.

Blair was determined to use his remaining months in power to tie his successor to his version of New Labour. The Government rushed through a series of measures in an effort to secure Blair's legacy, including a rapid expansion of business-sponsored city academies and the renewal of Trident in March 2007, both won only with Conservative support. After the bad feeling generated by the attempted coup the previous autumn the final phase in the transition from Blair to Brown was smooth and carefully choreographed by the Labour Party machine. On 1 May 2007, Tony Blair celebrated ten years as Prime Minister, and used the occasion to endorse his likely successor, although it proved too much to mention Brown by name: 'Within the next few weeks, I won't be prime minister of this country. In all probability, a Scot will be prime minister of the United Kingdom, someone who has built one of the strongest economies in the world and who, I've always said, will make a great prime minister for Britain.' Five days later, on 6 May, Labour narrowly lost power to the SNP in the Scottish parliamentary elections and in Wales lost overall control of the Welsh Assembly.[1]

Given the absence of a leadership contest, the Deputy Leadership contest became a low-grade substitute and the Manchester conference in June 2007 at which Brown became party leader saw Harriet Harman narrowly elected Deputy Leader, beating the favourite, Alan Johnson, by 50.4% to 49.6%. Harman had campaigned as if she wanted the job; Johnson had campaigned as if he wanted any other job. On being told who his deputy was to be, Brown's reaction was a long pause, followed by the words: 'It will be all right. We'll make it all right.'[2] Harman was given five different jobs, presumably in the hope that they would swamp her and stop her causing trouble.

There was much speculation about where Brown would lead Labour, now that he no longer had Blair at his side. Brown's first Cabinet saw significant changes of personnel from the Blair era, along with yet another rearrangement of Whitehall departments. Brown's long-time ally, Alistair Darling became Chancellor, and Ed Balls was sent to the new Department for Children, Schools and Families to gain some experience in a non-Treasury post. David Miliband earned a rapid promotion to Foreign Secretary, as did Jacqui Smith who became the first woman Home Secretary, albeit in a shake-up which saw the Home Office split in two, with Jack Straw heading up a new Department for Justice. Hilary Armstrong, Lord (Charlie) Falconer, Margaret Beckett, Patricia Hewitt, John Prescott and John Reid all left the Government.

Over the next few days as part of a move to demonstrate a belief in pluralism Brown assembled a 'government of all the talents' (GOATS) among the lower ranks of government ministers.[3] Three leading Liberal Democrats – Lord Lester, Baroness (Julia) Neuberger and Baroness (Shirley) Williams – agreed to undertake projects on behalf of the Government. In September he announced that another Lib Dem, Matthew Taylor, would be acting as a government adviser, as would two Conservative MPs – Patrick Mercer and John Bercow. He also invited Baroness Thatcher to a public visit to Number 10.

The first substantive policy move came with a Green Paper entitled, *The Governance of Britain*.[4] The document had been put together in draft form in the Treasury during the run-up to the leadership transition. Some of those involved had not been especially impressed by the process; one who took part in the Treasury pre-meetings recalls coming away thinking 'he hasn't got a clue ... he was just grateful for the ideas'. The Cabinet discussed constitutional reform in its first meeting after Brown became Prime Minister, and was said to have agreed the proposals. In reality, the document went through repeated redrafts over the following weekend, with Ministry of Justice officials attempting to iron out the many problems, before being agreed at the next Cabinet meeting. One Cabinet minister involved remarked that 'this was no way to run a chip shop'. The resulting document was a curious mixture of micro and macro ideas for constitutional reform, many of which went out to consultation and got no further. Little of substance occurred.[5]

The new Prime Minister also promised a change from showmanship to substance and a more collegiate style of leadership. There were a number of reviews and inquiries, including one into the Iraq War, and a reversal of the Blair Government's policy on gambling (so-called 'super casinos'). It did not amount to much. The Conservatives had carried out their own internal audit exercise to work out in advance what they could expect from a Brown government, and were surprised by the timidity of what was produced. Some Labour politicians – and not only predictable Blairites – began to have doubts about whether Brown had any agenda for radical change. They had thought that over the previous decade Brown had developed many radical plans, merely waiting for the opportunity to deliver them. They began to wonder if his 13-year campaign to become Prime Minister had more to do with just being Prime Minister rather than for what he would do once he had the office. A few observers doubted whether Brown had successfully made the crucial 'change' argument, setting out clearly how and why he would be different from Tony Blair.

In 2008 economic difficulties began to dominate British party politics for the first time since New Labour came to power in 1997. For fully a decade, the economy had been the Government's strongest card. The first crack in that reputation appeared with the collapse of Northern Rock in September 2007. Brown and Darling remained reluctant to nationalise the ailing bank, fearing negative associations with past Labour governments. But when no buyer could be found, they were forced to place Northern Rock into what was euphemistically termed 'a period of temporary public ownership'.

Darling's first Budget in March 2008 was overshadowed by the controversy caused by his predecessor's final Budget the previous year. To portray Labour as the tax-cutting party Brown had announced that he was cutting the basic rate of income tax by 2p to 22%, its lowest basic rate for 75 years. To pay for this reduction, he planned to abolish the 10p starting rate for income tax. Some of Brown's Treasury aides had opposed the measure but were overruled and Brown was fortified by the support of Ed Balls. A handful of Labour MPs had expressed concerns immediately after the 2007 Budget, but complaints from others increased in number and ferocity as the date for the change approached. It was estimated that over 5 million of the poorest people living in Britain – earning less than £18,500 a year – would find themselves worse off. Yet when Labour MPs raised the issue with the Prime Minister, they found him obdurate. When he appeared in front of a meeting of the PLP on 31 March 2008, his denial that there would be losers from the tax changes was met with audible gasps from the audience. It would take two more appearances in front of the PLP – and the whips office making clear that they were going to lose a vote on the budget if they did not change course – before the Government carried out a U-turn. Concessions were rushed out in an attempt to save Gordon Brown's blushes at Prime Minister's Question Time, although they did not stop David Cameron from giving his opposite number a torrid time: 'Does the Prime Minister have any idea what a pathetic figure he cuts today? He is making these changes because he would lose the vote. Or is it like the general election that he cancelled even though he thought he was going to win it? Is he not just taking people for fools again?'[6]

The Government's change of heart came too late to spare Labour the wrath of the voters at the local elections in May 2008 when it suffered its worst result for 40 years. Based on the results in England and Wales the BBC's projected share of the national vote put Labour trailing a poor third, on 24%.[7] The Conservative Boris Johnson won the mayoral race in London, ousting Labour's Ken Livingstone. Later that month the Conservatives also won the Crewe & Nantwich by-election, held following the death of Gwyneth Dunwoody, on a 17.6% swing.

To many people's surprise the Brown Government attempted to reintroduce extensions to pre-charge detention for terrorist offences, which the Blair Government had failed to implement. This time, they aimed for 42 days rather than 90, but the parliamentary arithmetic did not alter much. On the day of the crucial vote, one member of the whips office remarked that it was 'brown underpants day', but they managed, narrowly and after much effort, to secure a narrow victory for the Government; the votes of nine Democratic Unionist MPs were crucial and the newspapers the following day focused on the price extracted by the Ulstermen. After all the effort exerted by the whips to win the vote in the Commons, 42 days was effectively killed off after a heavy defeat in the House of Lords on 13 October. A measure that had caused so much difficulty for the Government was quietly dropped at the height of the banking crisis, almost without a murmur.

Brown had difficulties adjusting to life in Number 10 and struggled to grasp the job of being Prime Minister as he had been able to grasp being Chancellor of the Exchequer. In the Treasury, he had had time to formulate his plans; in Downing Street he had little or no time to deal with many competing demands. As one Brown aide who moved with him from the Treasury to Number 10 noted: 'In the Treasury, we could draw breath, allow Tony Blair in Number 10 to soak up the pressure.' In Number 10, however, the pressure was remorseless. As another Brown aide put it: 'Whereas Number 10 was always in the firing line, the Treasury only had two big media events a year – the Pre-Budget Report and the Budget itself – to deal with.' Brown had developed a style in the Treasury that one of his team described as 'government by speech'. That approach did not work in Number 10.

On 15 November 2006, during the debate on the Queen's Speech, Tony Blair had claimed:

The next election will be a flyweight versus a heavyweight. However much the right hon. Gentleman [David Cameron] may dance around the ring beforehand, at some point, he will come within reach of a big clunking fist, and you know what, he will be out on his feet, carried out of the ring – the fifth Tory leader to be carried out, and a fourth term Labour Government still standing.

The Labour benches cheered their approval, and Brown, sitting behind the Prime Minister, patted him on the back as he sat down, clearly liking the analogy. But the comparison could also have been interpreted in a more negative light: that Brown was slow-footed. The more Brown's premiership went on, the more the second interpretation seemed apt. His performances at PMQs rarely showed any lightness of touch or dexterity. He struggled in speeches to break out of his habit of piling fact upon fact, jargon upon jargon. At times, especially in his repetition of key phrases, he could sound like a political speak-your-weight machine, as in: 'We have got to get on with the job. People want us to get on with the job. Getting on with the job is the most important thing at the moment.'

He was hampered by a remarkable turnover of senior staff. Initially, Brown brought with him many long-serving staff from the Treasury. They included Sue Nye, his political secretary, Spencer Livermore, strategy adviser, Tom Scholar, chief of staff, Ian Austin, his PPS, Mike Ellam, his official spokesman, and Damian McBride his special adviser. Almost no one remained at senior level from the Blair era. As one of the incoming team noted: 'It was more like a change of Government than a change of Prime Minister. We were at a big disadvantage, we knew very little about how Number 10 operated.' After less than six months learning how to work Number 10, Brown's initial team split as a result of the events of October 2007. Within a few months, Livermore, the American consultant Bob Shrum, and Tom Scholar had all left, the last returning to the Treasury. Great hopes were invested in a new head of strategy, Stephen Carter, appointed in February 2008. A former chief executive of Ofcom, he came from City PR agency Brunswick. But vicious turf wars with other aides in Number 10, and his inability to carve out a credible role for himself, led to him leaving in late 2008. Nick Stace, the strategic communications chief recruited from the consumer magazine, *Which?*, and Jennifer Moses who came from Goldman Sachs, did not last long. No effective way had been reached of making Brown's Number 10 function. Brown failed to define clear roles for his staff and was reluctant to delegate. As one of those departing complained, shortly before leaving: 'Everything is so thoroughly disorganised. Politicians only turn to make the decision at the eleventh hour, and then only when they're forced to, when there's minutes to go … You start to feel deskilled working in here, you have to remind yourself that you've got good judgement, else it will soon suck all the confidence out of you.' Or, as another put it: 'It was distressing to work there. You'd look at it, and weep for the Labour Party.'

'That clunking fist again…'

(Peter Shrank, *Independent*, 25 April 2008)

Complaints continued from other departments and MPs that Number 10 was not working well – 'dysfunctional' was the word used most often – and lacked leadership. One member of Brown's team admitted, 'We have a grid but we have no plan.' 'On every single issue', complained one adviser, 'there is a horrendous period of void, when the thing tumbles into Number 10 … It's like dropping a stone into a well, and waiting to hear how deep it is, and then realising it's very deep – and anyway, your stone is now sitting on the bottom along with loads of other stones.' A senior official who had worked in Number 10 under Blair and now advised Brown was aghast at what he found. Complaints about Brown's personal style also began to circulate widely – about his short temper, thrown telephones, verbal abuse, a laser printer pushed off a table in a rage.[8] Much of this behaviour, those who knew him well claimed, was born out of frustration, with himself, and his failure to achieve what he wanted. 'There is', one of Brown's team claimed, 'no worse critic of Gordon Brown than Gordon Brown.' Or, as another of those working with the Prime Minister put it: 'I don't think he can quite come to terms with the fact that he's not good enough.'

The exception to the exodus of staff was David Muir, with expertise in advertising and market research, a recruit from WPP in March 2008 to replace Spencer Livermore. Eventually he took over much of Carter's remit as head of strategy. He was to remain a key figure in Downing Street until the 2010 election, and given credit for being a unifying force in Number 10 and for winning Brown's confidence. He was the only political adviser regularly to attend Cabinet strategy meetings. Brown came to rely on him heavily and few papers came to Brown that had not first been seen and commented on by him. He bore much of the brunt of the frustrations that colleagues felt with Brown. But by 2009, thanks to the efforts of Muir, Gavin Kelly, the deputy chief of staff, Justin Forsyth the director of communications and campaigning, and Jeremy Heywood the Permanent Secretary, Number 10 had begun to function better.

Brown's electoral honeymoon lasted under six months. As we show in Chapter 1 his caution and indecisiveness came to the fore in his mishandling of the question of calling a general election in October/November 2007, a watershed in the life of the Government. Thereafter focus groups and opinion polls were uniformly depressing. Labour's support had already weakened by 2005, notably among the young, the south and the middle class. It had now lost many of its longstanding electoral advantages on economic management, leadership, sleaze (it was to be hurt more than the other parties by the MPs' expenses scandal in 2009), standing up for hard-working families, and for being the party of change.

No Labour leader could have done much about the burdens of the party being in office for so long or the effect of the global economic recession. But Brown himself was another matter. Surveys showed that even when the Conservatives had a big polling lead Labour was almost level on the question of party identification. Changing the leader would not guarantee election victory – and one factor that worked in Brown's favour was that there was no evidence that his rivals were more electorally appealing – but it might, in the words of one party strategist, 'give us the opportunity to at least get on the playing field'. Voters still regarded Brown as a successful Chancellor and did not blame him for the credit crunch. But they did not rate him highly as a Prime Minister and polls reported that Cameron was more trusted to be a leader for political change and acting decisively.

There was intense disappointment among Brown's backers. Ed Balls told another Brownite MP, 'He can't connect. We always feared he couldn't.' Another minister said, 'We had our doubts, but he has performed at the lower end of our expectations.' Former cheerleaders in the press also changed their minds. Jonathan Freedland in the *Guardian* wrote, 'We got Brown wrong. He is simply not up to the job' (18 June 2008). Nearly 12 months later Polly Toynbee, who had enthusiastically welcomed Brown into Number 10, was calling for him to go: 'Plot it now. Do it fast. Brown must go' (12 May 2009).

Many of his fresh starts and relaunches, usually timed to coincide with party conferences, Cabinet reshuffles, and spending reviews, had little impact on the party's standing in the opinion polls. He conducted two major Cabinet reshuffles. The first followed his survival of a potential leadership threat from David Miliband, who wrote an article in the *Guardian* suggesting how Labour could renew itself – 'a radical new phase' – without mentioning Brown's name once, and the resignation of junior ministers and the call by a dozen MPs for a leadership election on the eve of the Manchester party conference in September 2008. Brown survived and when he reshuffled the Cabinet the following month he shocked most people, and dazzled others, with a recall from Brussels of Peter Mandelson to the new post of Secretary of State for Business, Enterprise and Regulatory Reform.[9]

The Prime Minister and some of his aides had held a series of discussions, some over dinner, with Mandelson since June about strategy and tactics, and Brown had increasingly come to appreciate his political advice. Although they had fallen out in 1994 when Mandelson backed Blair over Brown for the Labour leadership, they remained oddly dependent on one another: 'Peter was at his best in running a Prime Minister', and Gordon saw Peter, in the words of one Labour insider, as 'the guy who I need to run me'. Prior to his recall, however, a No 10 focus group examined how the public would view Mandelson's return to government. The public verdict was, according to a No 10 aide, 'mixed'.

The move divided the Blairites, some of whom claimed Mandelson had saved Brown and stymied the leadership prospects of David Miliband. The growing financial crisis and credit crunch also helped Brown; it hardly seemed an opportune moment to change from an experienced leader to, what he called in his conference speech, 'a novice', a remark that could have referred to David Cameron but was widely regarded as a rebuke to David Miliband. By the end of 2008 it seemed as if Brown had achieved a modest revival in his party's fortunes: whereas opinion polls during September had shown an average Tory lead over Labour of 19%; by December that average lead had been cut to just 5% and remained low at the time of the G20 conference the following April. Although the Prime Minister and the Chancellor of the Exchequer had successfully shored up the banking system, preventing meltdown, the economic fallout from the banking crisis rapidly spread to the rest of the economy as banks stopped lending to businesses and consumers. Economic activity was slowing, companies began going out of business at an alarming rate, and unemployment rose rapidly. By the early summer of 2009, the double-digit Tory lead over Labour had re-emerged.

A second reshuffle was held in June 2009 amid much speculation over the future of the Chancellor, Alistair Darling. Darling had been the target of much negative briefing from Number 10 and the Prime Minister began to refer to the Chancellor in the past tense. In summer 2008 Darling had given an interview to the *Guardian*, warning that the coming economic downturn would 'arguably' be the worst the country had had in sixty years. It angered Brown and his mood worsened at the time of the 2009 Budget when the Treasury announced that the borrowing requirement would rise to £175 billion. A split opened up, between Brown and some of his aides – who wanted the Treasury to be more political, launching attacks on the Conservatives over their plans to cut public expenditure – and Darling, who argued that such a stance was politically and economically unwise. The Chancellor told friends, 'I am not a prisoner of the Treasury and nor am I not thinking politically.' Given that Britain was so reliant on foreign investors buying government debt in the form of gilts, the Treasury could not afford to send out signals that Labour did not take spiralling government debt seriously. Darling frequently expressed private frustration to Treasury colleagues at Brown's failure to grasp economic reality.

The reshuffle took place against the background of imminent local and European election results – Labour came third in both, gaining just 16% of the vote in the latter – and a disintegrating Cabinet. On 2 June, Jacqui Smith announced her resignation as Home Secretary, pre-empting an almost certain dismissal following the furore over her husband's claim for adult films using the public purse (see p. 26). Hazel Blears' resignation as Communities Secretary on 3 June, just a day before the polls closed, infuriated Brown. Mischievously, she sported a brooch carrying the motto, 'Rocking the boat'. On the same day, the *Guardian*'s leader called on the Labour Party to cut Gordon Brown loose. Word began to spread of an email letter being circulated to Labour MPs, calling on Brown to quit. A few apparently unconnected ministerial resignations appeared to be shaping into a full-scale plot to unseat the Prime Minister.

Just as polls closed at the European and local elections, James Purnell, the Work and Pensions Minister, resigned, urging Brown to do the same and stating that Labour could not win under his leadership. He had grown increasingly disillusioned with Brown and the two had clashed over Purnell's call for a spending review in view of the economic downturn. By the end they had almost no working relationship. Fearing Purnell's move was part of a coordinated coup, Brown's aides and Mandelson gathered in the No 10 war room late at night, to begin phoning other Cabinet ministers, some of whom were asleep, seeking assurances that they were not planning to resign. One of those present said it reminded him of the scene in the Godfather, when the family all gather at the Corleone mall, and Clemenza remarks that 'it's like a fortress in here'. The crucial phone call was made by Peter Mandelson, to David Miliband. 'Had Miliband decided to resign, we were finished,' said a Brown aide.

Purnell's resignation had not been part of a plot but Brown's plans to promote Ed Balls to the Treasury in place of Darling, and Andrew Adonis and Purnell to Education and Health respectively were now aborted. Darling made clear he would rather return to the back benches than give up the Treasury and some Cabinet ministers had objected to Balls's promotion on the grounds that he was too divisive. Brown emerged a weaker figure from the reshuffle, no longer master of his Cabinet. He now had to work with a Chancellor who doubted his economic and political judgement. The person who gained most from the reshuffle was Mandelson, now effectively Deputy Prime Minister, armed with a raft of other titles, including Lord President of the Council, although not the DPM office that his grandfather Herbert Morrison held in the 1945–51 government, that he may have hoped for.[10]

Mandelson's support for Brown and the decision of Miliband not to resign split the Blairites; those who thought the resignations had been their best opportunity to change the leader were furious with Mandelson. The waverers had been brought back into line only by the threat that the replacement of Brown by a new leader for the second time in the Parliament would mean an immediate general election and a certain Labour defeat. There was also no obvious alternative to Brown. As Mandelson remarked, 'The idea that we'll do all of this, bring him down, for Alan Johnson is not serious.' Although a junior Environment Minister Jane Kennedy was sacked on 8 June for refusing to pledge loyalty to the Prime Minister, and a former Cabinet minister Charlie Falconer also called on Brown to go, the rebellion ran out of steam. At a packed meeting of the PLP a handful of MPs told Brown to his face that he should go but many more supported him. It did not prevent plots continuing. Disgruntled Labour MPs toyed with other schemes to bring down the Prime Minister: a candidate to stand on an anti-Brown platform against the chair of the PLP, or even a programme of resignations, triggering by-elections. They all came to naught, but the threat was ever-present. Only after the failure of the 'snow plot' in January 2010 – when, amidst freezing weather, Patricia Hewitt and Geoff Hoon called for a secret ballot on the leadership, only to find almost no one rallied to their cause, despite previous pledges from some senior figures to do so – was Brown's leadership secure.

Brown's response was yet another relaunch, including legally enforced entitlements about public services. However, *Building Britain's Future* appeared to be little more than a hasty rehash of old announcements, without the benefit of any new money. Moreover, the Government's two other announcements – that its much-vaunted ID cards scheme would remain voluntary and the abandonment of plans to part-privatise the Royal Mail – smacked of a government that had run out of steam. Despite a slight improvement in economic optimism over the late summer of 2009 voters did not reward the incumbent government.

In early April 2009 the Prime Minister used his hosting of an important meeting of the G20 Summit in London as the launch pad for another revival in his fortunes. Brown performed well, embarking on a tour of foreign countries, meeting the key players. The conference was hailed a success, especially by the international money markets, which reacted positively to an additional $1.1 trillion re-financing of the International Monetary Fund (IMF). The credit crunch and the economic slowdown provided an opportunity for Gordon Brown to deploy some of his experience and expertise. He was in his element. Where Cameron could only talk, Brown could act and where Cameron claimed the way ahead was to shrink the state, Brown could point to the constructive role of the active state. 'What rescued Gordon', one of his closest political allies noted, 'has been the global downturn.'

Any political advantage gained from the summit was lost as a result of the Damian McBride affair. On 11 April the Prime Minister's close adviser was forced to resign after it emerged he had written 'juvenile and inappropriate' emails to ex-Labour spin doctor, Derek Draper, about the alleged private lives of leading Conservatives. Few of Brown's colleagues – some of whom had suffered negative briefings – expressed much sympathy for McBride. After five days of media pressure Brown apologised for 'smeargate', but the political damage had been done.

Although the Prime Minister denied any knowledge of such activities, the impression gained was of a Richard Nixon-style leader, who kept unseemly company, and was willing to go to almost any lengths to stuff his political opponents. Gordon Brown's Number 10 was made in the image of the Prime Minister: an indecisive, often chaotic, combination of erudition and aggression. It could practise the dark arts of politics with ruthlessness, but it also contained several extremely thoughtful and intelligent individuals.

No sooner had Brown stumbled out of the McBride scandal than he faced a far larger one – the MPs' expenses scandal (see Chapter 2). Brown had known that details of MPs' expenses were scheduled to be published by the Commons authorities in July 2009, and he had moved early to try to prevent a public backlash. His plan had been to abolish the controversial MPs' second homes allowance (permitted for MPs living outside London), and replace it with a daily attendance allowance. The idea of appearing to 'pay' MPs twice – a salary and a separate sum of money to attend the Commons – was not an obvious winner. Worse still, however, was the manner of the Prime Minister's announcement. On 21 April, he made a disastrous – and much-mocked – video, uploaded to Youtube, in which he grinned at all the wrong moments.

Although some measures tightening aspects of MPs' expenses were passed, the Prime Minister was forced to delay a decision on reforming the second homes allowance. That meant that when the *Daily Telegraph* started publishing damaging details of MPs' expense claims on a daily basis from 8 May onwards, the Government appeared powerless to prevent it. After weeks of hesitating, the Prime Minister came up with a route map out of the crisis. He outlined plans to dismantle what he described as the 'gentleman's club' of Parliament by handing over the oversight of MPs' pay and allowances to a new statutory independent regulator. Legislation followed in the Parliamentary Standards Bill, which established the Independent Parliamentary Standards Authority (IPSA) to oversee MPs' expenses.

Brown faced a growing backlash from Labour backbenchers who felt he was leaning too heavily on them and they complained bitterly about the NEC's 'Star Chamber' which had meted out summary justice on their fellow MPs by banning four of them implicated in the expenses affair from standing as candidates at the next election. There was particular sympathy at Westminster for the fate of Dr Ian Gibson, who reacted to the decision by resigning his seat and provoking a by-election in Norwich North, which was easily gained by the Conservatives on a swing of 16.5%.

The opinion polls obstinately refused to turn. Labour's private polling in September 2009 reported that 74% of the public thought the country was heading in the wrong direction, and Brown lagged Cameron on 'strong personal values' by 24% and on 'strong leadership' by 34%. On party attributes the Conservatives led on every characteristic tested except for 'fairness for all' and 'tolerance'. Even slight improvements in Labour's standing could be seized on by critics to claim that with a change of leader Labour might be able to win or at least deny the Conservatives a clear election victory. But even if the Conservatives had not won over the public, Labour's problem was that it was no longer seen as the party for 'ordinary working people'. In June 2009 a YouGov poll asked which of the parties used to care for ordinary people and which did so now. 63% said Labour used to care but only 19% said it did now. The Conservative figures were 29% and 37% respectively. Labour was no longer perceived as the party for people like themselves but seemed to stand up for welfare shirkers and immigrants. YouGov's Peter Kellner recommended that Labour should start to address this negative image by reminding voters of its achievements: Sure Start, tax credits, winter fuel allowance, minimum wage. Even though many of them preceded 2007 they had been Brown's achievements. Here, however, was a central problem for Brown. He had wanted to come to Number 10, talking about change – which had meant distancing himself from events before 2007. A Cabinet colleague said: 'He'd spent so long opposing the record that he couldn't claim the credit for the good bits, and he was trapped by the bad bits.'

The party machine in Victoria Street suffered like most such organisations when a party is in government for a long time. It was run down as talented staff were drawn into government jobs and, even if resources had allowed, it was difficult to attract high calibre replacements for what seemed a doomed enterprise. While ministers were busy governing the country it was easy to forget that they had to prepare for an election campaign.

Matt Carter resigned as party general secretary soon after the 2005 general election. His replacement was Peter Watt, already an official at party headquarters. He had a poor legacy. Party membership was falling – heading towards 160,000 from the 405,000 in the heady days of 1998 – activism had declined, and funds were short. Most mass political parties are in decline everywhere and the declines often accompany a party's long spell in government. Watt had prepared the party machine for an autumn general election campaign and was disillusioned when it did not take place, noting in October 2007, 'It will be downhill all the way from here.' He was not far wrong. He was forced to resign his post when it was revealed that he had not lawfully declared an anonymous donation to the party received through a third party. A police investigation followed but there was no prosecution. The fund manager David Pitt-Watson was offered and accepted the post but subsequently changed his mind. Eventually, Ray Collins, an official in the Unite union, was appointed. He was one of the rare holders of the post not to have had experience in party organisation, campaigns or communications, but he had a reputation as a shrewd manager of finances. One result of his appointment was that the Task Force leaders exercised greater influence in Victoria Street. Hazel Blears and her successor Harriet Harman were both active party chairs, Harman successfully pushing for all-women shortlists in a number of competitive Labour seats where vacancies occurred.

Tackling the party's £18 million debt was a major challenge. Under Blair Labour had managed to reduce its heavy reliance on union funding and succeeded in attracting funds from businesses and wealthy individuals. But following the revelations in 2006 about the connection between political honours and party donations (and loans), and the involvement of the police (see Chapter 2), such funding soon tailed off. Collins made the most of his union contacts and managed to persuade a number of donors who had made loans to defer repayments, but the finances of the party were in a dire state. Although the Harry Potter author J.K. Rowling made a £1 million donation in 2008, the party was once again increasingly reliant on the unions for finance; the Unite, GMB and Unison unions contributed some 60% of the party's finances. For all the talk of the party's financial predicament it still raised over £70 million during the Parliament.

In response to urgings from senior colleagues Brown set up a Cabinet political strategy group of a dozen Cabinet ministers to develop themes for the election campaign. In Number 10 he relied on a group of trusted aides, particularly Muir, Kelly, Forsyth, Nick Pearce, head of his Policy Unit, and Stewart Wood, adviser on Europe. In addition, figures prominently associated with past Labour election victories returned to the fray. Mandelson, now in the Cabinet, was a major player in deciding the election strategy; Philip Gould would, health permitting, help once the uncertainty over the leadership was resolved; Alastair Campbell had rejected Brown's offers of a Cabinet post (with a peerage) and a role in Victoria Street but helped increasingly with advice and speeches.

During 2009 Brown made regular (often twice a week) home visits to mingle with small groups of between 15 and 20 people who came to 'meet and talk with Gordon Brown' in an informal setting; at times he would participate in phone-ins from the house with the local radio station. The hope was that those invited would talk favourably about Brown with other people. He also took part in several question and answer sessions with voluntary organisations, often sponsored by the local media. David Muir, inspired by the success which Barack Obama had with this 'person to person' approach, and Justin Forsyth were the moving spirits behind it. This activity was hardly reported by the national press. Brown, having grown frustrated at what he regarded as the national media's failure to concentrate on government measures to combat the economic challenges, was prepared to go direct to the voters. Muir also identified three groups of voters Labour needed to win back if it was to be competitive again. They included the liberal middle class, many of whom had been alienated by Iraq and Labour's record on civil liberties; young couples with children who were feeling the economic pinch, and C1 and C2 voters, in the lower middle and working class.

Brown and his aides struggled to come up with a compelling statement of why Labour should have a fourth term of office. A political message is more than a soundbite. It is a summation of the party's purpose, its identity, what it stands for. In 1997, Labour's appeal to voters had been the straightforward one of most political oppositions: Time for Change. In 2001, it could reasonably claim that it needed more time to deliver on its policies. In 2005 it had warned of the dangers of a Conservative victory. But support for Labour was on a downward trend; its vote share in 2005 was little higher than in the 1992 election which it had lost. The nature of its vote was changing; it was more middle class and more southern, and voters thought the party had moved steadily to the political right.

As Prime Minister, Brown had a continuing problem in striking a balance between continuity (from 1997) and change. 'Let the work of change begin,' he said on entering Number 10, promising 'a new politics', an end to confrontational politics, 'a new constitutional settlement', and continuing 'to listen and learn'. He had not called a general election in October 2007, he told interviewers, because he needed more time to spell out his vision. But not much progress was made in articulating a vision that was sufficiently his own (and distinct from Blair's). In September 2009 the Labour MP Jon Cruddas, addressing the centre-left Compass think tank in September 2009, warned that the party had made 'no compelling case for re-election'.

There were numerous suggestions for the message. There was Brown's much-loved dividing line of Labour investment versus Tory cuts, which had worked well in the 2001 and 2005 general elections. Before the credit crunch the Conservatives had sought to counter this assertion by promising they would match Labour's spending plans, but by 2009 Cameron and Osborne attached a higher priority to cutting the deficit and abandoned the matching pledge.

In late November 2009 Philip Gould, a key figure in Labour's election campaigns since 1983, made a presentation to the Cabinet's strategy group. Drawing on the findings of the party's private poll in August, of other polling data, and of focus groups, he did not pull any punches about the public's negativity about politics and Labour's (and Brown's) dire plight:

> The central driver of the electoral dynamic is hostility to Labour and its leadership. This hostility blocks any appreciation of Labour's record, and protects the Tories from proper scrutiny. Appreciation of Labour's achievements is negligible, and focuses on public services … The best way of summarising this is that we now own very little political ground – far less than in the last election. In 2005 we were ahead on leadership, the economy, public services and on crime. Now we really have only the NHS and fairness.

However, Gould identified five Conservative weaknesses, which showed much of their support was still an anti-Labour protest vote:

> The public do not believe the Tories have changed;
> They are not sure what the Tories stand for;
> They are not sure that Cameron has substance;
> They do not fully trust the Tories on their values;
> They still put the better off first.

Cameron was receiving remarkably similar warnings from his party's private polls. It was a prophetic list of the charges Brown was later to make against the Conservatives in the general election campaign.

The presentation, supported by Mandelson, was an attempt to steer Brown away from the investment versus cuts approach and offer an alternative strategy in which Labour focused on the future and aspiration, and would 'put Britain first'. Some ministers expressed approval for the approach but Brown's concluding remarks made clear that he still believed Labour investment versus Tory cuts was the way ahead.

There was general agreement that the economy was the crucial election ground. Darling, supported by Mandelson, wanted to maximise honesty about the deficit and the need for cuts. They, and some Cabinet colleagues, thought it essential for ministers to concede that cuts in spending after the election were inevitable if the voters and the markets were to be convinced that the deficit would be tackled effectively. Darling had already set in motion in his 2009 Budget a package of measures to halve the size of the deficit over four years (a new top rate of income tax on incomes of over £150,000, a rise in national insurance contributions from 2011, a levy on bankers' bonuses, and a cap of 1% on public sector pay for two years).

Brown was reluctant to hear any talk of spending cuts and had been angered by Treasury leaks about cuts of the order of 10% or more being planned. In a series of meetings Darling, Mandelson, Balls and Brown, with Muir and Kelly in attendance, met to agree an economic package for the December Pre-Budget Report and an economic message for the election. Darling shocked Brown with his proposal to raise VAT to 18 or 19%. Mandelson was cautiously supportive. But Brown, looking for a dividing line with the Conservatives, vetoed the idea and was supported by the other members of the group. 'It would split the party and be electorally disastrous,' said one. Brown, supported by Balls, suggested ruling out a VAT increase for the life of the next Parliament, Balls wanting to include the pledge in the manifesto. Darling refused, dismissing the suggestion as 'financially irresponsible' for any Chancellor to tie his hands in this way; his aides later expressed astonishment that Brown, as a former Chancellor, should even have proposed the idea. As a counter Brown proposed an increase in National Insurance Contributions and that carried the day, although Darling and Mandelson were both concerned that it might be portrayed as a 'jobs tax'. Darling welcomed the presence of Mandelson as a check on what he thought was Brown's irresponsibility, saying, 'I was an admirer of Peter's, long before it was fashionable.' Darling's only concession was to agree that VAT would not be extended to items like food, children's clothing and books and newspapers.

In an effort to find some common ground between Darling and Brown, Treasury and No 10 advisers had begun meeting while Cabinet was in session. Most felt the state of the economy meant that Brown's investment versus cuts message was no longer credible. Muir's focus groups found much voter hostility to Tory plans to cut child tax credits and defending the credits was something both sides agreed on. What emerged from the talks was a compromise. At Prime Minister's Questions Brown would attack the Conservatives for harming families (meaning cutting the tax credits) and Darling would attack Tory plans to give tax breaks to the well-off with their plans for easing inheritance tax. Brown claimed that the inheritance tax cut was 'one of the few in history where those proposing it probably knew personally each of the recipients'.

The new position was that Labour cuts would differ from the Conservatives' (nice versus nasty cuts), protecting front-line services and the poor and would be introduced only when the economic recovery was assured. Brown was still unconvinced, telling one aide he thought it was not possible to fight an election merely on the timing of cuts. Above all, there was a renewed emphasis on attacking the Conservatives and the dangers their economic policies would pose for the economic recovery and public services. Ministers claimed that the Government's fiscal stimulus and rescue of the banks had saved Britain from an economic depression and mass unemployment into which the 'do nothing' Conservatives would have taken Britain. In Number 10 David Muir observed, 'We must make it clear that people can't have Labour public services with Conservative taxes.'

By the end of 2009 the outlines of a Labour campaign were emerging. Douglas Alexander and Spencer Livermore had drafted a war book in April and had sent it to Brown but it had disappeared without trace. 'Because of the absence of structures, there was nowhere for it to go,' Alexander noted acidly. Brown complained he had not seen it, and was expressing concern at what he regarded as Alexander's defeatism and lack of activity. Another draft was produced by 18 December, the work of Alexander, Gould, and Patrick Loughran (Mandelson's special adviser), with late input from Muir, before it was delivered to Brown. Cabinet ministers decided to abandon the theme of change (which had been the centrepiece of Gordon Brown's acceptance speech of the party leadership in 2007) and emphasise instead a positive vision about the future.

There was still no formal announcement about who would be in charge of the election strategy. It was widely assumed that it would be (indeed could only be) Mandelson. He was frustrated and had appealed in vain in memos to Gordon Brown in February, June and October for the matter to be resolved. Other Cabinet ministers were aware of the complaints among MPs at the lack of direction. Brown's aides mentioned his fear of a negative reaction from Alexander if Mandelson had such a role (although the two had been cooperating for some months) or that Harriet Harman would feel resentful. Others said Brown simply thought it 'inappropriate' to be seen to be preparing for an election at a time when the public was angry over the expenses scandal and at a time of economic crisis. The truth was, in the words of an aide, 'Gordon did not focus on the election till late 2009. He was worried about the personalities and was never good at defining the roles of key people. That was always a problem with his Number 10.' It was a deeply frustrating period for those involved in preparing an election strategy.

Peter Mandelson and Ed Balls held regular meetings on Monday evenings and Thursday mornings with No 10 staff, Pearce, Muir, Kelly, Forsyth, and Patrick Diamond who had joined Number 10 to work on the manifesto. After the meetings, lasting up to an hour, the two Cabinet ministers and Muir would proceed to discuss their thoughts with Gordon Brown. Brown insisted on the two ministers, who represented different thinking about political strategy, being together. 'Gordon gets upset if we are known to be in disagreement,' one of them said. Ed Miliband, usually accompanied by Nick Pearce and Patrick Diamond, began to hold meetings with individual Cabinet ministers to discuss ideas for the manifesto. If a campaign was at last taking shape most of the participants still admitted they were well behind where they had been at a similar stage in the build up to previous general elections.

In 2005 the Labour Party's continued dominance of British politics had seemed assured. It had been returned for a third successive election, with what was a commanding, albeit reduced, majority. By the end of the Parliament it would have been in continuous power for 13 years. But much of those past five years had been a harrowing experience for Labour MPs and the Government. As it entered election year Labour had begun, slowly, to narrow the gap, but still trailed badly in the polls and Brown complained to aides that too many Cabinet ministers were pessimistic about the coming general election.

Notes

1. See D. Denver, '"A Historic Moment?" The Results of the Scottish Parliament Elections 2007', *Scottish Affairs*, 60 (2007), 6–23; L. McAllister and M. Cole, 'Pioneering New Politics or Re-Arranging the Deckchairs? The 2007 National Assembly for Wales Elections and Results', *The Political Quarterly*, 78:4 (2007), 536–46.
2. Peter Watt, *Inside Out* (London: Biteback, 2010), p. 158.
3. Sir Digby Jones, former Director General of the Confederation of British Industry (CBI), was appointed to the Department for Business, Enterprise and Regulatory Reform; Professor Sir Ara Darzi to the Department of Health; and Shriti Vadera, previously a special adviser to Brown at the Treasury, to the Department for International Development.
4. Cm. 7170, 3 July 2007.
5. *Failing Politics? A Response to the Governance of Britain Green Paper* (Political Studies Association, 2007).
6. HC Debs, 23 April 2008, c. 1303.

7. All local election figures for national shares are projections, and – like all projections – can be calculated in different ways. The separate Rallings and Thrasher estimates put Labour in second place, although only just.
8. The most detailed account of Brown's behaviour in Number 10 is contained in Rawnsley's *The End of the Party*. Although many of the details of Rawnsley's account have been disputed, the general thrust of the allegations is not, and in various forms allegations about Brown's temper and behaviour had circulated for most of the Brown premiership, especially in a piece published by Bloomberg in April 2009.
9. Peter Mandelson, *The Third Man* (London: HarperPress, 2010), pp. 431–41.
10. Ibid., pp. 471–2.

4
A Coup of Chums:
The Conservatives

Michael Howard announced his intention to resign as Conservative leader the day after the 2005 general election. The party had gained more than 30 seats, but had still managed to win just 198, lower even than Labour's tally in its disastrous 1983 performance. The Conservative share of the vote had barely shifted, up by less than one percentage point. Whoever replaced Howard would be the fifth Conservative leader Tony Blair had faced in 11 years. Each of the three Conservative Party leaders who followed John Major after his resignation in 1997 had started out taking steps described in some quarters as 'modernising', but when the opinion polls did not improve they had retreated to their comfort zones, the so-called core vote strategy. The very term core vote, however, was misleading because the party had lost so much support in its traditionally strong area of the South East and among women and urban professionals. If the twentieth century was sometimes called the Conservative Century the prospects did not seem bright for the twenty-first.[1]

There had long been a recognisable body of so-called modernisers in the Conservative Party, frustrated by its failure to reform. Conservative MPs such as David Willetts, Oliver Letwin, Theresa May, Andrew Lansley and Francis Maude had for some years favoured a change in the party's approach and appeal. But following the 2005 defeat, a younger generation came to the fore. Many had been associated with or were promoted by Michael Howard in his final shadow cabinet. Howard appointed David Cameron, elected in 2001, shadow minister for education and George Osborne, also elected in 2001, as shadow chancellor, and encouraged the latter to run for the party leadership. Osborne had no doubt about the scale of the challenge facing the party. Shortly after the 2005 election, he described it as 'a very bad result'. 'We did not do much better than in 2001, when circumstances were much more difficult for us. When you think about eight years of Labour government, the Iraq War and the failures on public services, we should have done so much better.'

The modernisers wanted a break with the party's emphasis in recent elections on tax cuts, immigration and Europe; they called for the party to regain the centre ground, by stressing the importance of the environment and placing economic stability and protecting core services ahead of tax cuts. But policies were only one element in the new approach. Conservatives, they felt, had to show they were at ease with modern Britain, with a multicultural society and with people who had different lifestyles and sexual preferences. 'Modernisation', said one of them, 'is something you are, as much as, if not more than, something you do.' The test should be that people felt comfortable about themselves when they voted Conservative. Modernisers were influenced by polls which showed that public support for particular policies noticeably dropped once respondents knew they were Conservative policies. Modernisers concluded that having fresh policies was not much use as long as people were not listening. The party's image had to change radically before voters would listen to it. The brand needed 'de-toxifying'.

Within a few weeks of the 2005 general election Lord Ashcroft published his *Smell the Coffee. A Wake-up Call for the Conservative Party*. The book drew on an extensive research programme he had commissioned from Populus and YouGov during that election. Prompted by Ashcroft's disagreement over electoral strategy with the party co-chairman Lord Saatchi, the book – a seminal text for the modernisers – showed how out of touch the party was, not least in its traditionally strong groups of middle class and women voters, and concluded: 'The problem was not that millions of people in Britain thought that the Conservative party didn't like them, and didn't understand them: the problem was that they were right.'[2]

The modernising group was sometimes known as the Notting Hill set, even though many of them did not live there. They were friends, usually from their time as students at Oxford and the Conservative Research Department (CRD); the 'Smith Square set' would be a more accurate description. Even if they disagreed about individual issues, they all agreed on the need for the party to change, and were impatient with how the older generation had messed up what they saw as their political inheritance. David Cameron himself was a late arrival to the group's political viewpoint. Just before the 2005 election campaign began, three of them – Cameron, George Osborne and Steve Hilton – had met to discuss what they might say on election night in the likely event of an election defeat. They accepted that no young moderniser was ready to challenge for the leadership but they did not want to waste another Parliament which they expected would be the case if one of what they regarded as the old guard – they assumed it would be David Davis – was elected.

Howard was not a party to their thinking and they were dismayed at his decision to resign, which they feared played into the hands of established and better-known figures. They failed to dissuade him, although he agreed to stay on until a new system for electing the Conservative leader had been agreed. This angered supporters of David Davis, who saw the delay as part of a plot to deny their man the leadership.

By electing Michael Howard unopposed in 2003 Conservative MPs had effectively disenfranchised the grassroots members. Even William Hague, architect of the scheme to elect the leader, now thought that his introduction of electing the leader by a second-stage ballot of party members had not worked well in 2001. But the modernisers wondered how they could reform the party's rules and culture when any changes had to be approved by a membership that was predominantly elderly, retired and based in the South East.

Proposed new rules, which would return the election of the leader to MPs, were drawn up by Francis Maude, the new party chairman, and Raymond Monbiot, a businessman and chair of the party's National Convention. The speed and minimal consultation with which the proposals were introduced caused widespread resentment, even among MPs, who were to be the gainers. After a series of false starts (in which the leadership rule changes were initially and ultimately unsuccessfully tagged on to other party rule changes) the proposals required a two-thirds majority among the different party constituencies.[3] Although some 61% voted for the reforms, they failed to gain the two-thirds support in each of the required categories and so the rules remained unchanged. The result was an unsatisfactory end to Michael Howard's leadership; several months appeared to have been wasted in fruitless internal debates, but in those months, David Cameron had been granted precious time to emerge from relative obscurity.

Liam Fox, David Davis and David Cameron soon declared their candidacy for the leadership and were followed by the perennial candidate Kenneth Clarke and Malcolm Rifkind, only recently returned to the House of Commons. Rifkind attracted little support and withdrew before the first ballot among MPs. Davis, the overwhelming favourite, and Fox were on the right of the party. Clarke and Cameron were on the social liberal side, although Clarke was distinctive because of his pro-European stance. Cameron made an impressive launch to his campaign, managed by Osborne, with Hilton as strategist and speechwriter. But he made little progress among MPs, and his poll ratings were poor right up to the party conference in early October.

The party conference at Blackpool in October 2005 proved crucial in shaping the fortunes of the leadership contenders.[4] Each of the candidates was given a slot to advance their vision for the party. Cameron's speech, 20 minutes long, delivered without notes, and with him walking round the platform, was a triumph. Davis's speech, the following day, was delivered poorly and was so underwhelming that he had to gesture to the audience to rouse them into the normally guaranteed standing ovation. Cameron had shown himself to be the best communicator among the four candidates, and was quickly seen as the more likely to win a general election. His campaign slogan 'Change to Win' made clear his determination to change the party and its previous election strategies. Most Conservatives were fed up of losing and wanted a winner, someone who could put the party back on the path to government.

David Davis finished top on the first ballot of MPs with 62 votes, but Cameron was a close second on 56, with Liam Fox on a better-than-expected 42. As so often in Tory leadership contests, the candidate that attracted the least opposition – in this case David Cameron – now emerged as the clear favourite, especially since Fox could be expected to draw off votes from Davis as the rival candidate on the right of the party. In the second ballot, Cameron added a further 34 votes, bringing his tally to 90, while Davis's vote actually fell by five votes to 57. Fox was then eliminated, leaving Cameron and Davis to compete in the final ballot among the party members. A six-week campaign followed, which everyone assumed that Cameron would win. On 6 December 2005, he defeated Davis by 134,446 votes to 64,398, a clear 2:1 margin. It had taken seven months to choose the new leader but, contrary to some doubters, the contest had not been divisive and the party had improved its standing in the polls. An average Labour lead of more than 5% in November 2005 was transformed into a small Conservative lead by December.

Cameron's was a remarkable rise. Aged 39, he had been an MP for just four years and a shadow minister for a few months. Much comment centred on his social background and independent wealth. He was the first Old Etonian leader of the party since Sir Alec Douglas-Home (1963–65).

He was distantly related to the Queen, on his mother's side numbered three Conservative MPs among his forebears, and liked country sports. But he was also a meritocrat, gaining an outstanding first class degree at Oxford. Voters did not seem bothered by his privileged background and he was always a more convincing spokesman for modernisation than his recent predecessors. He said privately that he wanted to be an heir to Blair. He may have had in mind Blair's political style, reforms of the Labour Party and successful use of the mantra of modernity. Some commentators spoke of him as a 'blue rinse Blair': self-assured, relaxed on the public stage, and with a young family he epitomised change as the young Blair had. But much of the hard work of modernising the Labour Party had been done before Blair became leader. Cameron's Conservatives were trying to do in two-to-three years what it had taken Labour 12–15 years. And Blair in 1994 had started off with a lead of 10% in the polls. Cameron, by contrast, had to make up a lot of ground.

Cameron's claim, in a speech to Policy Exchange on 29 June 2005, that 'We do think there's such a thing as society, we just don't think it's the same as the state', was less an outright rejection of Thatcherism than a belated recognition that she was now part of Conservative history.[5] Cameron believed Thatcher and Thatcherism had been appropriate for the economic problems of the 1980s – tackling inflation, the trade unions, and overmanned nationalised industries – but the nation now faced new challenges. She would not, however, have approved of Cameron's reconnection with some of the One Nation traditions in the party and his wish to reclaim the idea of the Conservatives as the progressive party.

Before Cameron could change the party he had first to establish his authority. Disloyalty to the party leader had become part of the DNA of Conservative MPs. The final ballot of MPs in 2005 showing that a majority voted for candidates on the centre-right – Fox and Davis – suggested he might face an uphill task. In the parliamentary party the 30 or so members of the Cornerstone Group – most of whom had voted for Fox – favoured the thrust of the 2005 election programme of tax cuts, firmer limits on immigration and hostility to the EU. But Cameron insisted he had a clear mandate to lead the Conservative Party, and unlike his three predecessors, there were no problems in getting his more senior rivals to serve in his Shadow Cabinet. David Davis remained as Shadow Home Secretary, Liam Fox shifted from the Foreign Office to Defence, while William Hague took Fox's place as Shadow Foreign Secretary. Cameron also showed a willingness to crack the whip over frontbenchers who went off message. In March 2007 Patrick Mercer, the frontbench spokesperson on homeland security, gave an interview in which he claimed that there were 'a lot of ethnic minority soldiers who were idle and useless, but who used racism as a cover for their misdemeanours'; he argued that racist taunts such as 'you black bastard' should be viewed in much the same way if recruits were fat or red-haired. Within hours of the story emerging, Cameron insisted that Mercer stand down from this frontbench post.

Not all Conservatives accepted Cameron's route map for the party. The former party chairman Lord Tebbit was a reliable spokesman for the Conservatism associated with the now silenced Mrs Thatcher and argued that the party had lost the last three general elections because of its pursuit of a middle ground largely defined by New Labour; he complained that Cameron was going down the same path and attacked his refusals, if he formed a government, to prioritise tax cuts and, later, to open new grammar schools. Cameron's statement that 'We believe in the role of government as a force for good' was too much for such an unreconstructed Thatcherite. Tebbit warned that if Cameron was insufficiently robust on Europe and immigration he risked losing support to UKIP and the BNP. Surveys of Tory candidates in 2009 also showed that a majority did not agree with Cameron's pledge to protect the NHS and international aid from spending cuts. More outspoken criticism of the Cameron project and the ideas of social liberalism and modernisation were voiced by Simon Heffer and Janet Daley in their political columns in the *Telegraph* and by Peter Hitchens in the *Mail on Sunday*, both Conservative-supporting papers. On the ConservativeHome website many activists expressed not dissimilar views. Tim Montgomerie, the editor of the site, called for Cameron to be an 'and' not an 'or' Conservative, one who addressed the activists' concerns about tax, immigration and Europe as well as the modernisers' agenda. YouGov surveys of party members showed an even split between those wanting the party to move to the right and those wanting it to move to the centre. But Montgomerie's high media profile and success in airing the (usually critical) views of the party activists were a persistent irritant to Cameron's team. Cameron made some concessions to the Eurosceptic section of his party with his leadership election pledge to take his party's MEPs out of the European People's Party in the European Parliament and, later, not to sign the Lisbon Treaty unless it had been approved in a British referendum.

If Blair and Brown had been scarred by Labour's election defeats in the 1980s, Cameron and Osborne had been similarly affected by Labour's successes in recent general elections, notably its ability to translate Conservative talk or hints of tax cuts into negative messages about Conservative cuts in spending on key services, such as health and education. Labour had learned from Conservative success in turning Labour spending pledges into threats of tax increases at the 1992 general election. The two men were determined not to provide up-front or unfunded tax cuts and therefore announced that they accepted Labour's spending plans up to 2010. This did not stop them, however, from offering in 2007 and 2008 reductions in inheritance tax and stamp duty on modestly priced house purchases, relief on council tax and help for employers taking on the long-term unemployed. Some of them quoted Philip Gould's book on the making of New Labour, *The Unfinished Revolution*, about the need for modernisation to involve changing the party from top to bottom, moving on from failed policies, holding the centre ground, and looking beyond the party's core vote at a time when party loyalties and tribal politics were declining.

Cameron's *Built to Last* (2006) was a statement of his aims and values and was written as a guide to the six policy commissions he set up when he became leader. With its emphasis on economic stability and fiscal responsibility over tax cuts, poverty and social justice, community, protecting the environment, and enhancing the role of voluntary organisations, it struck a note that had been absent in recent Conservative exercises. The six commissions deliberately covered cross-cutting themes including: economic competitiveness, public service reform, quality of life, social justice, national and international security, and overseas aid. Several former Tory leadership contenders (and potential irritants) were kept busy by chairing these groups. For instance, Iain Duncan Smith built on his Centre for Social Justice in chairing the social justice group. The group emphasised the importance of marriage and strong family values and the need to reverse the dependency culture of people spending long periods on benefit. John Redwood headed up the competitiveness group, while a former deputy leader, Peter Lilley chaired the overseas aid team. Cameron invited non-politicians to contribute, including Bob Geldof (overseas aid), while Zac Goldsmith, editor of the *Ecologist* magazine, and John Selwyn Gummer were co-chairs of the quality of life commission.

The policy review was part of a long tradition of far-reaching reviews the party had conducted before the 1950, 1970 and 1979 general elections, as it sought to refresh and renew its policies in the wake of electoral defeat. But unlike Heath's obsession with detail, Cameron's review was more broad-brush, reflecting his wariness of committing the party to policies that might become redundant by the time of the election, or be stolen by the other parties. Nor would Cameron allow himself to become bound by the various recommendations in the policy review reports. All Shadow minister speeches had to be cleared with Matthew

Hancock, George Osborne's chief of staff, so that, in the words of a Cameron aide, they were 'bomb-proof against spending commitments'. Cameron treated the policy review reports as an à la carte menu, from which he would select his favourite dishes, while rejecting less palatable ones. He quickly distanced the party from some of the policies of the 2005 election manifesto – which he had helped to write. Reversed were up-front tax cuts and incentives for patients and parents to opt out of the NHS or state schools, particularly the abandonment of the 'pupil's passport', a scheme involving state subsidies for those parents who sent their children to private schools.

The groups drew widely on a range of think tanks (including Policy Exchange, and, to a lesser extent, Civitas and the Centre for Policy Studies), experts, shadow ministers, former Cabinet ministers and former civil servants. They were expected to report in time for the 2007 party conference and, if time permitted, generate a series of green papers for wider discussion. For the first time since 1992, a manifesto could be prepared with a reasonable chance that it would inform the work of a new Conservative government. Some of the proposals were included in the draft manifesto for a November 2007 general election (see Chapter 1). Once that deadline had passed the party produced a series of green policy papers, many of which received favourable media comment. The first was on education in November 2007 and outlined Michael Gove's plans for setting up a British version of Sweden's 'Free Schools' in which groups could set up schools independent of the local authority but still financed by the state. Over the following two years nearly 20 papers were published. Cameron was still careful not to commit himself to most of the proposals but the exercise gained coverage and showed that the party was receptive to new thinking.

While the commissions deliberated, Cameron wrote and spoke frequently on themes promoting his ideas of modern Conservatism.[6] Several internal party studies had demonstrated that many voters still viewed even new Conservative policies and statements through the prism of the party's unattractive brand. To counter the charge that Thatcherism had concentrated too much on the economy and wealth creation, Cameron talked frequently of the need to foster general well-being and a softer, greener Conservatism. The Tory leader was seen to travel to the Commons on his bicycle (though any political gain was lost when the *Mirror* discovered that a Cameron aide drove a Lexus behind, carrying his shoes, papers and suit). In the middle of the 2006 local elections – built around the slogan, 'Vote Blue, Go Green' – Cameron visited the Arctic,

'Vote blue, go green'

(Dave Brown, *Independent*, 18 June 2008)

supposedly investigating first-hand the effects of global warming, but critics accused him of succumbing to photo opportunities.

Being filmed with huskies was, though, all part of a broader decontamination strategy that appeared to be working. The Conservatives polled 40% in the local elections, making over 300 gains in the process. The results only left room for cautious optimism; so-called 'traction' had not yet been achieved in the crucial election battlegrounds of the West Midlands, or in the North, where a Northern Board under William Hague had been established to try to reverse voters' long-standing resistance to the party.

Cameron's speeches in his first 18 months as leader were just as interesting not only for what he talked about, but also what he did not talk about. Europe, immigration and tax cuts – known as the 'Tebbit Trinity' – were temporarily put on the sidelines. On tax, George Osborne's mantra was that from 2010/11 a Conservative government would 'share the proceeds of economic growth' between spending, tax reduction and cutting borrowing.

During his first party conference speech as leader, Cameron made a concerted effort personally to identify himself with the NHS. It helped his cause enormously that he had sat for hours in NHS corridors, waiting to see how his disabled son Ivan's latest operation had fared; Ivan would later die in 2009. At the Tory Party conference in Bournemouth in October 2006, Cameron remarked: 'Tony Blair once explained his priority in three words: education, education, education. I can do it in three letters: NHS.'

The first phase of the policy review was predicated on prosperity, relying on economic growth to fund public service reform.[7] Cameron's team believed that in future the political debate would be conducted not so much on the economy (where there existed some agreement between the two major parties), but about 'quality of life' issues. In an article in the *Daily Mail* in May 2006, Cameron set out what would become a familiar theme of his first two years: 'It's time we admitted that there's more to life than money, and it's time we focused not just on GDP, but on GWB – general well-being.'[8] Yet events soon placed the economy back at the centre of political debate.

Cameron seized on Iain Duncan Smith's work on the broken society and emphasised the importance of the family. He was convinced by the evidence of the link between broken families and problems of poverty, drug addiction, unemployment and poor education. He therefore promised tax relief for married couples, a policy he had broached when launching his leadership campaign in 2007: 'A modern Conservative Party should support marriage', using the law and the tax and benefits system to do so. He showed his modernising credentials by extending beyond traditional marriage, 'whether you are a man and a woman, a woman and a woman, or a man and a man'.

A recurring theme in the early speeches was one of personal responsibility and community. 'Instead of asking the state to do things, we ask what individuals can do, what society can do.' An emphasis on the NHS ('We are the party of the NHS') and social justice was important for establishing in voters' minds that the Tories were the 'progressive' party in British politics. Just as Blair had not wanted to be outflanked on his right on immigration, Europe, crime and tax, Labour's old weaknesses, so Cameron's 'decontamination' strategy had the aim on camping his party on the traditional Labour turf of social justice and poverty. His alternative to Labour's top-down politics, was greater localism and scope for families and charities, what he called post-bureaucratic politics. He wanted to reduce the amount of bureaucracy and number of targets in public services and listen more to the professionals and users. On the NHS, the party would accept Labour's reforms but promised no future reorganisation.

The leader also addressed several recognisably Tory themes. Thus national sovereignty should be defended against incursions from the EU, the Union upheld, border controls strengthened, and radical constitutional change particularly a change to first past the post, resisted; civil society should be bolstered and scope should be provided for a more active localism and the third sector; threats to the citizen's freedom in the form of ID cards and 42 days detention should be resisted; and policies in the form of heavy regulation and controls should be reversed.

If in the 1990s Labour had played 'catch-up' to Thatcher's changes over the previous decade, so in a reverse flow of influence the Conservatives now accepted most of Labour's constitutional reforms, its spending plans on the NHS and international development, the national minimum wage, and target of reducing child poverty. But there was a good deal of policy convergence and cross-dressing. For all the talk of a great divide the differences between the parties were mainly of emphasis and timing on such issues as tackling the debt, Europe (once Cameron had ruled out a referendum on the Lisbon Treaty), inheritance tax, using the private sector and charities to get people off welfare and into work, limiting immigration from non-EU countries, and protecting NHS spending. Conservative plans for new independent schools and more patient choice built on Labour's reforms. The convergence did not please many Tory activists on the right who wanted a sharper choice between the parties and claimed that a more radical approach would be electorally appealing. But they acquiesced as long as Cameron looked like an election winner.

Cameron got off to a good political start in his first 18 months as leader. As a young aide, he had helped John Major, Iain Duncan Smith and Michael Howard prepare for their regular parliamentary jousts. Such a background did not, however, guarantee the quick-wittedness and calmness under fire that he showed in his weekly sessions with Tony Blair. His quip to Blair that he 'was the future once' stung a Labour leader whose best days were behind him.[9] Cameron's parliamentary strategy was to kill Blair with kindness. His support for the Prime Minister's introduction of trust schools exposed the extent of the splits within the Parliamentary Labour Party. As the handover between Blair and Brown approached, the Conservatives' aim was to trash Brown's reputation, particularly on the economy. Cameron seized his chance in a feisty reply to Brown's tenth Budget, in which he described the Chancellor as 'an analogue politician in a digital age'.[10]

By way of contrast, the Conservatives sought to 'love bomb' Liberal Democrat voters in the run-up to the May 2007 local elections. Thousands of personalised letters were sent out to Liberal Democrat voters in key marginals in time for the local council elections, pressing home the message that Cameron's moderate views on civil liberties and the environment were close to Lib Dem values. The tactic appeared to work. The Conservatives made over 900 gains in terms of council seats, though their lacklustre performance in both the Welsh and Scottish elections showed that the party was still not gaining significant traction outside its traditional heartlands.

Instead of gaining momentum from these election results, Cameron suffered his worst wobble as leader over the totemic Tory issue of grammar schools. The extent of the furore over a speech by David Willetts – in which he claimed that there was 'overwhelming evidence that such academic selection entrenches advantage, it does not spread it' – was odd in retrospect because Cameron had announced a full year before that he wasn't going to return to a policy of opening any new grammar schools. Willetts had spent weeks researching the issue, and had discovered that far from being a means of social mobility as they were a generation ago, grammar schools now reinforced social inequality. He therefore proposed to end selection for new schools. The day before, however, members of the Shadow Cabinet expressed concerns. However, David Cameron was away and William Hague was in the chair, one of a series of accidents that day, including the fact that everyone Willetts tried to brief in the media was unavailable. Having failed to get his pitch in beforehand, his speech struck a raw nerve with traditional Conservative supporters and the Tory press, which was uniformly negative. The frontbencher Graham Brady resigned in protest at the policy. A compromise was announced that more grammar schools could be built in the future in those parts of the country where the 11-plus exam existed, and where population growth demanded it.

In summer 2007, the Conservative Party lost ground when Gordon Brown took over from Tony Blair as Prime Minister. There were growing complaints from the Tory right that Cameron's themes of compassionate conservatism and personal responsibility lacked a cutting edge. Such sniping increased after the Tories finished a poor third in the Ealing Southall by-election on 19 July,[11] despite the Conservative candidate, Tony Lit (who had incredibly donated money to the Labour Party only eight days before being selected for the Tories), standing under the label, 'David Cameron's Conservatives'. Misfortune then struck Cameron on the eve of his long-planned visit to Rwanda. The aim had been to demonstrate the Cameron commitment to international development but Cameron was accused in the Tory tabloids of being more concerned about the plight of foreigners than his own constituents in Witney, who were flooded out. Both Cameron and Osborne knew that complaints about Rwanda – and about David Willetts' schools policy – were lightning conductors for the right's discontent with their kind of Conservatism.

Other critics held that waiting on the policy reviews was dilatory when an election might be held soon. Steve Hilton, seeking to counter an anticipated Brown media blitz over the summer, attempted but failed to cherry pick some of the groups' proposals.[12] As part of the fight back Cameron's team decided to reconnect with the values of opportunity and security, traditional Conservative themes, and he gave speeches on immigration and crime. Cameron acknowledged that the party's emphasis to date on personal responsibility had resulted in a lack of balance in public perceptions of what his modern Conservatism was about. Some commentators over-interpreted the change of gear as Cameron retreating from his social-liberal agenda, just as his three predecessors had done when the polls turned against them. The original Cameron plan had always been to return to more traditional issues once they had gained 'permission to be heard'. Cameron's team reckoned that the 'decontamination' process had succeeded enough to allow the party to broach these 'core' issues.

In anticipation of a 2007 election defeat, Cameron's critics and Tory journalists alike began sharpening their knives. Cameron's leadership came under intense pressure on the eve of the 2007 Conservative Party conference. A former deputy leader and party chairman Michael Ancram reflected some of the concern over Cameron's agenda when he produced a pamphlet attacking the leader for 'trashing our past or appearing ashamed of our history', and called for bolder policies on marriage, tax cuts and Europe. On 29 September Fraser Nelson in his *Spectator* column noted how the turnaround in just a few weeks in Cameron and Brown standings in the polls meant that '... the Tory leader's stardust has been replaced by the aura of a loser', and 'All this makes a murderous backdrop for what will be Mr Cameron's second, and possibly last, conference as Tory leader.'[13] Anthony King even went as far as to liken Cameron to 'a rich man's Iain Duncan Smith: well-meaning but ineffectual and politically inept'.[14]

But Cameron held his nerve, unlike Gordon Brown (see Chapter 1). Osborne's stock rose with his speech on 1 October to the party conference, when he promised that as Chancellor he would raise the inheritance tax threshold from £300,000 to £1 million and scrap stamp duty on house purchases up to £250,000, all to be financed by an annual £25,000 levy on non-domiciles. The speech – and the almost immediate pro-Tory shift in the polls – was important in frightening Brown from calling an election and changing Labour's economic policies.

The 'Cameroons' were overwhelmingly from elite public schools (with a strong Eton representation) and Oxbridge-educated, posh, and metropolitan. But Team Cameron was also highly talented and as much a social as an intellectual or ideological group. The political commentator Rachel Sylvester quoted a frontbencher, 'It's dinner party politics. There's been a coup of chums.'[15] One senior shadow minister, educated at independent school and Oxbridge, admitted that at times he could feel socially inferior when mixing with Cameroons.

They were a close-knit group. Steve Hilton had been a close friend since the two were students at Oxford and young colleagues in the Conservative Research Department, and was godfather to Cameron's first child. His firm, Good Business, advised firms on how to be socially responsible. Having in 2004 abandoned his ambitions to seek a seat he took leave from his firm to act as a Director of Strategy to Cameron when he became leader. He spent much time with Cameron, was energetic, creative and opinionated, but remained low profile. He encountered some jealousy, partly because of his salary, a reputed £250,000 a year, and his closeness to the leader. When Cameron seemed to make decisions without much reference to the shadow cabinet or other key groups or reversed a general shadow cabinet view, some were quick to attribute the outcome to Hilton. Highly individualistic he was difficult to place in an organisation chart of the Cameron team. He disliked big meetings and seemed to think the ideal meeting would be between himself and Cameron and, maybe occasionally, Osborne. He was mercurial – quick to flare up, if also quick to calm down afterwards – and did not dress like a traditional Conservative. The tie-less look became common amongst Cameron's team, but Hilton was often so casual that some critics said he could look like the man on a Spanish beach from whom you buy drinks. Some of the opposition was also political, from the right who disliked his social liberal agenda. Hilton's task was to refine the party's 'message', particularly emphasising social liberal values and shape party messages and Cameron's key speeches. He buzzed with ideas, was credited with the social responsibility theme in Cameron's speeches and such early initiatives as the leader's 'hug a hoodie' speech and trip to Norwegian glaciers. He was behind the 'social action' projects in the battleground seats where the candidates and volunteers worked on community projects. Expectations that his influence would wane when he departed for a year to California between July 2008 and July 2009, were confounded. He was as active as ever by email and video link and returned to the UK every three weeks or so. He 'very much carried the [Cameron] project round in his head', as one Tory insider put it. He could be forceful at meetings, arguing strongly against an initiative if he thought that it ran counter to the central decontaminating strategy and was given great leeway by Cameron. He was a key believer in the ideas that led to the Big Society theme, the essence of Cameron's modern Conservatism.

George Osborne did nothing to discourage the notion that he was something of a Gordon Brown to Cameron's Tony Blair, although there were warmer relations between them and he did not challenge Cameron's authority. Like Cameron he had been close to the centre of power in the party as a young man, having been political secretary to William Hague between 1997 and 2001. Hague and Howard had come to respect his advice about political tactics and positioning. He was a keen student of American politics and, like Hilton, was impressed by Blair's achievement in changing the Labour Party. He proved to be the only Conservative shadow chancellor to hold his own with Gordon Brown. Although privately he had regarded Brown as the dominant political figure of his times he dismissed claims that he had been a good Chancellor. As tax revenues failed to keep up with spending the public finances were already deteriorating before the credit crunch. 'He didn't fix the roof when the sun was shining,' he charged. Like Brown in 2001, Osborne also took on the role of election coordinator. Campaign headquarters were moved to Millbank, where he chaired the weekly General Election Planning Committee (GEPC) on Tuesday mornings. He wanted the party headquarters to play a more political role ('It costs us over £17 million a year and we want more politics for our money') and to integrate it more closely with Cameron's priorities.

In July 2007 Osborne recruited Andy Coulson, former editor of *News of the World*, as Director of Communications and Planning. Coulson had resigned his editorial post in January 2007 after it was revealed that one of his staff had hacked into the phone messages of aides to the royal family. He quickly won the respect of colleagues for organising an effective team and broadening the party's image, so that the party addressed voters' concerns about crime, immigration and welfare reform. More than any other previous Tory communications chief he played an important role in shaping strategy. His background differed from the 'Cameroons' and he was more sensitive to the concerns of the C1 voters. But he shared Osborne's view that a key to Conservative success was pinning blame for the economic recession on Brown. He played a crucial role in cultivating the support of the press which the party went on to enjoy at the election.

Cameron's chief of staff was Ed Llewellyn, another Old Etonian, and friend of Cameron since their time at the party's research department. Llewellyn had worked closely with Mrs Thatcher, Lord Patten in Hong Kong and Brussels, and Lord Ashdown in Kosovo, and had been planning to return to the UK to seek a seat when Cameron asked him to help in his leadership bid in October 2005. He ran Cameron's office and was the link between the leader and the shadow cabinet. The chief of staff in campaign headquarters was Andrew Feldman, another Cameron friend from university days, who had raised the funds for his leadership campaign.

In September 2007, James O'Shaughnessy was recruited from Policy Exchange, the right-leaning thinktank, to become Director of the party's research department. The department supplied a secretary for each of the policy review groups and a four-strong Political Unit covered briefings and rebuttals. Its operations were made easier by the greater availability of information through the Freedom of Information Act, campaign groups like Open Europe and the Taxpayers' Alliance and websites like TheyWorkForYou.com (along with a state-provided policy development grant of some £450,000). O'Shaughnessy later became a member of the election team, drafting the party's manifestos for the non-election in November 2007 and in 2010. He provided the core text for many statements and the manifesto, leaving Steve Hilton to fine-tune the messages and the headlines.

Another key member of the Cameron team was Oliver Letwin, Director of Policy and Chairman of the research department. Letwin had been a senior figure in the shadow cabinet since 2001 and an early moderniser. His role as Director of Policy was to oversee and coordinate the work of the policy groups. Letwin sat on the Policy Board, chaired by David Cameron.[16] Although the fortnightly meetings of this board inevitably led to accusations of sofa government it operated in an orderly way and was effectively a sub-committee of the Shadow Cabinet. By late 2009 O'Shaughnessy had completed a manifesto draft and sent sections to the relevant shadow ministers for discussion. These were then referred back to Steve Hilton and a revised draft reviewed by the Shadow Cabinet. The final word, however, rested with Cameron, Osborne and Letwin.

Michael Howard had made Lord (Michael Ashcroft) a deputy chairman of the party and a member of the party's board. The cash-strapped party accepted Ashcroft's offer to oversee the party's polling and manage the target seats campaign. Not until June 2007 was the Ashcroft operation moved to the party's campaign headquarters. Cameron and Osborne held inconclusive talks with Lynton Crosby, who had directed the party's election campaign in 2005, about returning to run CCHQ. One potential difficulty would have been the Ashcroft–Crosby relationship, given the former's forthright criticism of the 2005 campaign.

Ashcroft was a controversial figure, partly because of unanswered questions about his tax status – whether he was a UK taxpayer, a requirement if he was a party contributor, and because he channelled his contributions through Bearwood Corporate Services. Bearwood's aggregate contributions to the party, which exceeded £4 million between 2003 and 2009, concentrated on the target or battleground seats. Ashcroft provided about a quarter of the target seats fund and also raised earmarked contributions from other donors. Stephen Gilbert, a long-time official at Tory Central Office, and Gavin Barwell, also a former party official and latterly prospective Conservative candidate for Croydon Central, directed the key seats operation. To receive funding candidates and associations in battleground seats had to provide an approved business plan. In turn, each local association provided a six-monthly update on progress. Ashcroft and his 20-odd aides, drawn from existing party staff, ran the so-called ground war team, consisting of units on campaigning, opinion research and logistics, all of whom reported to Stephen Gilbert.

Labour MPs, especially those in marginal seats, complained bitterly about the advantages they claimed the Ashcroft operation – what they called 'Ashcroft money' – was giving to their Conservative opponents. They had hoped that Jack Straw's planned Political Parties and Elections bill would rule out such operations.

Francis Maude had been appointed by Michael Howard as Party Chairman after the election defeat in 2005. Howard had wanted to make the appointment when he first became leader in 2003, but had deferred to opposition from the ousted leader, Iain Duncan Smith. Maude had been a moderniser long before Cameron, and despite some opposition tackled his brief energetically. His main task was to implement Cameron's first pledge as leader to recruit more Conservative women MPs, regarded by both men as an important visible indicator of the party's determination to change. In the new 2005 House of Commons there were only 17 Tory women, compared with 97 Labour women. Fitful efforts by the Conservative leadership for over 40 years to persuade local constituency associations to select candidates more representative of the electorate had made little progress. Maude drew up an A-list of some 160 approved candidates which included several female and ethnic minority candidates, as well as some celebrities such as Adam Rickitt, a former *Coronation Street* actor. Maude insisted that target seats – the held and winnable ones – select candidates from the list. In July 2007 he was disappointed to be replaced as Chairman by Caroline Spelman, Cameron arguing that he needed a woman in a front-line position. Because of the presence of Osborne, Ashcroft and Andrew Feldman in CCHQ Ms Spelman found that her role was more limited in scope than her predecessors'.

Maude had also been consistently cautious (some said gloomy) about his party's election prospects; 'progress made, but still progress to make' was his watchword. He was right to remain cautious. The reform of the candidates' list faced stiff resistance both from aspiring candidates who failed to make it onto the A-list, many involved with Conservative-Home, and, just as importantly, from local Tory associations who defied the leadership by preferring local figures. Having made some progress, the party's Board agreed in January 2007 on a compromise that 50% of any final shortlist would be women. Some critics noted that many female and ethnic minority candidates simply replicated features of their white male counterparts, being middle class and well-connected with Cameroons. Ironically, the likes of Cameron, Osborne, Maude and Letwin were hardly A-list material themselves. Local associations were also permitted, having chosen a shortlist of three or four candidates, to hold primaries at which non-Conservatives could help select the prospective candidate. But by 2009 only about a third of the candidates in winnable seats were female. The episode showed that there were limits to how far Cameron was prepared to go to achieve greater representation for women.[17] In October 2009 the leadership took the initiative again and decided to impose all-women shortlists in some winnable seats from 1 January 2010.

Money was not the problem for the party it had been over the previous decade. In 2005 the party carried £23 million in outstanding loans; the figure had been reduced to £3 million by 2010. The new leader energetically and successfully tackled the party's funding problem. The donations averaged over £18 million for each year between 2006 and 2009. The various dining clubs and events with shadow ministers and advisers in attendance raised substantial sums, particularly if Cameron or Osborne were expected to be present. The Leader's Group, with 220 members contributing £50,000 a year by 2010, and the Treasurer's Group with members donating £25,000, were particularly lucrative operations. In addition, the party sold off its old party headquarters in Smith Square for £30 million.

Cameron was comfortable with his associates but also uneasily aware of the socially exclusive image they conveyed, particularly at a time of looming austerity, which was confirmed in the party's private polling.

Writing against the background of the economic recession in the *Observer* in January 2009, the political commentator Peter Oborne warned Cameron that if he wanted to deliver effectively an uncompromising message on the economic challenges ahead, the task 'cannot be only entrusted to wealthy young men who have at best a tenuous connection to the world as it is lived by the great majority of the British people ... [and] those with whom he would enjoy a country house weekend'.[18]

Somehow, Cameron needed to counter the image of the Conservatives as being too posh and immune to the hard times many voters were experiencing. On 20 January 2009, as part of a substantial reshuffle of the Conservative front bench, Cameron promoted some Tory politicians from a wider social background. Kenneth Clarke was brought back as Shadow Secretary of State for Business, Enterprise and Regulatory Reform, Mark Francois was appointed shadow minister for Europe, with the right to attend shadow cabinet; and Eric Pickles took over from Caroline Spelman as Party Chairman. 'It was', some of those at Conservative HQ said, 'nice to have a party chairman who actually liked the party.' And Cameron changed his tone to match the more sombre political mood. At a business conference in Davos ten days later he warned his affluent audience that markets should serve society not the other way round.

The Conservatives reaped the electoral reward of Labour's implosion – particularly from the Government's travails over Brown's abolition of the 10p rate of income tax which had just come into effect – at the local elections in May 2008. The Conservatives made a net gain of 257 seats, mostly at the expense of Labour. The projected Conservative share of the vote now stood at 44% as against 25% for the Liberal Democrats, with Labour trailing in third place on 24%. In the election for the London mayor Boris Johnson unseated Labour's Ken Livingstone. Later that same month, the Conservatives won the Crewe & Nantwich by-election on a swing of 17.6%, their first gain over Labour in a by-election since Ilford North in March 1978. A jubilant Cameron hailed the end of New Labour.

A setback in June was the announcement that the Shadow Home Secretary, David Davis, would resign his Haltemprice & Howden seat, forcing a by-election on the issue of 42 days pre-charge detention. Cameron's initial surprise gave way to anger at what he regarded as a self-indulgent act. Davis told friends he wanted to be free to speak out on issues. Cameron's view was that such a stance was incompatible with being a member of a team. Once the shock factor of Davis's resignation subsided, members of Cameron's team saw a bright side. One of them admitted privately, 'We have solved the DD problem.' Although Davis won the subsequent by-election easily, he was not invited back into the Shadow Cabinet. Cameron was not prepared to risk having such an unpredictable politician as a member of his inner team and a potentially disruptive member of a Cabinet.

Despite some improvement in voters' perceptions, voters were still unsure about the Conservative Party's central message. One who was involved in the polling exercise acknowledged Cameron's success in decontaminating the party's image but cautioned in February 2009: 'The Conservatives are no longer the nasty party. But people are not sure what they are. They will win the next election but they could have won it by a bigger margin and with a bolder mandate if they had been more radical.'

Surveys of public attitudes during the Parliament showed that voters warmed to Cameron – his youth, family image, freshness and optimism – but were less convinced by his party. One respondent in a focus group likened the Tories to 'a British telephone box, which looks appealing on the outside, but if you open the door, it smells of piss'.[19] From 2009 the party built a steady lead over Labour on most issues and party attributes, and no longer trailed on its traditionally weak but crucial issues of health, education and the economy. But voters had no detailed knowledge of what were the party's policies; the Conservatives, it seemed, were the voters' default rather than preferred choice.

Cameron continued to profit from the continued mishaps that befell the Government. He was widely held to have had a 'better' expenses scandal than Gordon Brown. After experiencing a week of unwelcome headlines, involving revelations that some of his wealthier MPs had used public money to pay for housekeepers, dredge their moats and maintain their swimming pools, Cameron appeared to set an example by repaying £680 for the removal of wisteria at his second home in Oxfordshire, though little was said about his mortgage interest claims. However, the Tory leader acted decisively by ordering his frontbench MPs to repay many of their more outlandish claims, instigating an immediate internal audit of the expense claims of all Tory MPs, and announcing that all new claims by his MPs would be placed online in full public view. The Conservatives had been regarded as bad as Labour on the issue but Cameron's press conference in which he apologised for what had happened, and his tough action against his shadow colleagues made a contrast to Brown's dithering. Andrew Mackay, Cameron's PPS, was forced to resign after it emerged that he had claimed a full second home allowance on his London address, while his wife and fellow Conservative MP, Julie Kirkbride, claimed the full allowance for another home. Both were later forced by local constituency pressure – and lack of support from

David Cameron – to retire as MPs in time for the 2010 general election. Other similarly offending Conservative MPs were also shown the door. Most observers were impressed with the decisiveness, even brutality.

Labour as the government party suffered most at the polls and local elections in the wake of the expenses scandal. But the Conservative share of the vote also fell, to 38%, down 6% from the previous year (and the Conservatives estimated that 3–4% of that was entirely due to the expenses issue). In the European elections the 28% share of the vote was also disappointing. Cameron's long-promised decision to withdraw from the European People's Party within the European Parliament had little impact apart from angering most liberal commentators.[20] Cameron's supposed image as a moderate Conservative did not sit well with a new grouping that included the hard-right Czech Civic Democrats and the Polish Law and Justice Party.

In the wake of the expenses scandal Cameron used his speech at the Open University in May 2009 to outline a programme of political and constitutional reform, including fixed term Parliaments. Later he broadened his attack on Brown's economic stewardship into a critique of the state, particularly in his October 2009 conference speech in Manchester when he attacked what he termed the big state, represented by Labour's targets, over-regulation, incursions on civil liberties and waste. In the Hugo Young Memorial Lecture the following month he developed his positive alternative, the idea of the Big Society with its call for greater citizen involvement and empowerment, and a bigger role for cooperatives, private service providers, and voluntary groups. Here was the amplification and development of earlier ideas of compassionate conservatism and post-bureaucratic politics. It was something to which the leader and Steve Hilton were strongly committed, and wanted to make it a centrepiece of the party's election campaign. Other senior colleagues were less enthusiastic.

In 2009, as part of its preparation for government, the party established an implementation unit, led by Francis Maude and Nick Boles, the party's prospective candidate for Grantham. It drew on the advice of former Cabinet ministers and senior civil servants and arranged meetings for shadow ministers and Whitehall officials. The leadership was determined not to repeat what it regarded as the errors of Blair's first two to three years in government, when it felt that he had wasted the opportunity for radical action. Shadow ministers prepared three-year rolling business plans for work in government. In late 2009 Maude, along with Steve Hilton and Treasury spokesman, Philip Hammond, interviewed shadow ministers about their business plans, covering priorities, milestones,

anticipated risks, likely interactions with other departments and who would be accountable for delivering which parts of the policy programme in government.

In another echo of New Labour, Cameron and Osborne ran a top-down party, and many key decisions were shaped in informal discussions between Cameron and his close colleagues. The Tory day usually began at 8.45 when Coulson's team met to consider a media summary and agree lines to take for the day. At 9.15 Cameron convened his meeting with senior politicians (Clarke, Hague, Osborne, Grayling and Pickles) and advisers. At 4pm many of the team would meet again to make decisions about the next day and the medium term. It was easy for many shadow ministers to feel bystanders to the Cameron project, a dissatisfaction that extended to senior figures. The potential resentment was increased when the Cameron and Osborne teams decided to share an open plan office in Norman Shaw South. 'We're all mates,' said one, adding that a shadow meeting of about 30 was hardly suitable for taking decisions. Cameron stuck to this routine until the election was called, although the meetings slowly got bigger and more unwieldy.

In a risky move, Cameron and George Osborne had gone on the attack over the collapse in Northern Rock in September 2007. While some more senior Tories quietly urged a bi-partisan approach to Britain's first run on a bank for over 150 years, Cameron pinned the blame firmly at the door of Gordon Brown and opposed the nationalisation of the bank, the temporary cut in VAT and the fiscal stimulus.[21] In the short term, the tactic appeared to backfire as Brown and Labour gained a temporary boost in their polling fortunes, although they still trailed Cameron and the Conservatives respectively.

During 2009 the growing financial crisis forced Cameron and Osborne into a more substantial change in economic policy. The policy of 'sharing the proceeds of growth' between spending and tax cuts and agreeing with Labour's public spending plans was abandoned. There would not be any proceeds to share. Tackling the debt became the priority. In January 2009 the party launched a poster campaign featuring a new baby born with 'Dad's Nose. Mum's Eyes. Gordon Brown's Debt', the debt amounting to £17,000 per person. Conservative leaders also claimed that an increasing number of voters felt they had not received good value from the extra public spending and the extra taxes they had paid. The party would no longer stick to Labour's spending plans after 2010–11, but would be making cuts early in the life of a Conservative government. It was a decision over which Cameron and Osborne agonised for weeks. If for Labour a more active state was the answer to the economic crisis, for Conservatives it was one that played a more modest role.

What had still not been resolved by late 2009 was the status of some of the party's policies formulated in anticipation of a growing economy. How much localism and mending of the 'broken society' would survive the need for cuts? How would the Big Society project fare in a recession when unemployment would increase and funding for voluntary groups would be cut? If NHS spending was to be protected then cuts of some 10% or more would have to be found across other programmes. Some policies, for example, the creation of new schools, would involve extra expenditure to expand capacity early on, as would attracting private companies to handle welfare.

Labour's Debt Crisis: Every child in Britain is born owing £17,000. They deserve better.

By autumn 2009 Cameron decided to use the annual Conservative Party conference in Manchester to spell out some of the policies he would adopt to tackle the debt burden. That way he could keep interest rates low, encourage business to invest and get the economy growing again. He wanted a mandate for the tough action that a Conservative government would have to take. George Osborne had been more cautious, preferring to restate the rider that he would need to see the books first. He also recalled the party's ambitious James spending review in the 2005 election which suggested a wide range of cuts for a Conservative government and succeeded only in presenting inviting targets for Labour's campaign on 'Tory cuts'. However, private polling showed that voters did not regard 'waiting to see the books' as a tenable position; if Osborne was to be taken seriously about cutting the deficit he would have to present some specific proposals. In his conference speech he announced a cuts package, which included a one year public sector pay freeze for those earning over £18,000, a one year increase in the pension age for males starting in 2016, and a review of public sector pensions, a curb on top public sector salaries, reforming welfare, scrapping some programmes and the usual attack on waste and inefficiency. But this amounted only to some £16 billion of the £175 billion total debt.

The Shadow Chancellor delivered perhaps the gloomiest speech ever delivered by a frontbench spokesperson at an annual party conference. He had overdone the fiscal conservatism, at least in tone, if not in substance. Surveys soon showed that his message of a coming age of austerity depressed Tory support. As one member of the Shadow Cabinet put it, 'The rhetoric became over-heated. It made it sound as if we were licking our lips at the thought of cutting spending. We need to make it a bit more in sorrow than in anger.' It was left to Cameron to lift the delegates from their gloom, with his promise to build a stronger society to replace Brown's big state and admission that 'it will be a steep climb. But the view from the summit will be worth it.' However, the call for quicker and bolder action to cut the deficit than Labour was planning was a political and economic risk. Many economists warned it might drive Britain back into a so-called 'double-dip' recession before recovery was assured. Whether to cut now as the Conservatives proposed or cut later, as Labour favoured would become one of the main battle lines of 2010.

One fear the Conservatives had was complacency. They knew the workings of the electoral system went against them. They needed a double-digit lead in vote share to win an overall majority. Allowing for boundary changes, they needed to win an additional 117 seats, with a 6.9% swing, the largest swing to the Conservatives seen since 1931. An internal presentation – entitled 'Uphill challenge' – hammered home just what the party faced. Its final slide included the sentence: 'We have never won a general election from a starting point as weak as this.' A document entitled 'Why We Might Lose' – containing many of the same facts – was circulated more widely, including to the media. Within CCHQ, there was almost no-one who really thought they might lose. But there were plenty who worried privately that they might not win.

Notes

1. For excellent accounts of the recent history of the party, see Tim Bale, *The Conservative Party from Thatcher to Cameron* (London: Polity Press, 2010) and Peter Snowdon, *Back from the Brink* (London: HarperPress, 2010).
2. Michael A. Ashcroft, *Smell the Coffee. A Wake-up Call for the Conservative Party*, 2005, p. 111.
3. Conservative Party, *A Twentieth Century Party* (Conservative Party, 2005).
4. Andrew Denham and Peter Dorey, 'A Tale of Two Speeches: The Conservative Party Leadership Election', *The Political Quarterly*, 77:1 (2006), 35–41.
5. Stephen Evans, 'Consigning its Past to History? David Cameron and the Conservative Party', *Parliamentary Affairs*, 61:2 (2008), 291–314.
6. See David Cameron, *Social Responsibility: The Big Idea for Britain's Future* (2007).
7. Peter Dorey, '"Sharing the Proceeds of Growth": Conservative Economic Policy under David Cameron', *The Political Quarterly*, 80:2 (2009), 259–69.
8. David Cameron, 'Money isn't all ... family life is', *Daily Mail*, 24 May 2006.
9. HC Debs, 7 December 2005, c. 861.
10. HC Debs, 22 March 2006, c. 305.
11. On the same day, the Conservatives also finished a poor third in Sedgefield – the seat vacated by Tony Blair.
12. For instance, Zac Goldsmith's more radical plans for retail parks to charge for parking were rejected, following the publication of the Quality of Life group's *Blueprint for A Green Economy*. See Neil Carter, 'Vote Blue, Go Green? Cameron's Conservatives and the Environment', *The Political Quarterly*, 80:2 (2009), 233–42.
13. Fraser Nelson, 'David Cameron's judgement day', *Spectator*, 29 September 2009. For further expressions of doubt about David Cameron, see Michael Portillo, 'Is this the start of the Tory collapse?' *Sunday Times*, 24 June 2007; Tim Hames, 'The road to Blackpool, via Punxsutawney', *The Times*, 1 October 2007.
14. Anthony King, 'Not a single ray of sunshine amid the Tories' gloom', *Daily Telegraph*, 29 September 2007.
15. *The Times*, 28 July 2009.
16. Other members of the Policy Board included George Osborne, David Davis (until his resignation), Francis Maude, Philip Hammond and James O'Shaughnessy.
17. Sarah Childs, Paul Webb and Sally Marthaler, 'The Feminisation of the Conservative Parliamentary Party: Party Members' Attitudes', *The Political Quarterly*, 80:2 (2009), 204–13.
18. Peter Oborne, 'Cameron plans to transform Britain and has what it takes', *Observer*, 4 January 2009.

19. This phrase was reported in the press as 'smells really bad' (Vincent Moss, 'Tories are like old red phone boxes', *Sunday Mirror*, 29 April 2007); the original focus group respondent was more precise.

20. See for example, Timothy Garton Ash, 'The farce of Cameron's Latvian legion is bad for Britain and bad for Europe', *Guardian*, 11 June 2009. Cameron had made the promise during the Conservative leadership campaign in an effort to court the support of the right of the party. Liam Fox's team had come up with the idea first.

21. David Cameron, 'These are fruits of a reckless "prudence"', *Sunday Telegraph*, 16 September 2007.

5
Three Leaders, Little Progress: The Liberal Democrats

On the surface, the Liberal Democrats had a good election in 2005. At 22.6% their share of the vote was the highest achieved by a third party since the SDP–Liberal Alliance in 1987. They emerged from the contest with 62 seats, the best performance since December 1923. Yet within the party there were many who felt that 2005 had been a missed opportunity. Despite playing a trump card in its opposition to the Iraq War, and facing an unpopular government and an underperforming opposition, the party had failed to break through. Some spectacular gains from Labour were balanced by the failure of their so-called decapitation strategy against the Conservatives. If they could not break through in 2005, then when? Charles Kennedy, leader since 1999, enjoyed public popularity, but there were plenty in the party who were worried about both his style of leadership and his personal life, especially stories about his drinking. Within the parliamentary party and at fringe events at the party conference in late 2005, there was widespread grumbling about the direction the party was going. The party's rules require the re-election of a leader within a year of a general election; Kennedy's aides were sufficiently worried about his position to hand out the ballot papers to the parliamentary party within days of the 2005 election, to leave no time for anyone to mount a challenge. He was re-elected unopposed.[1] What no-one then realised was that Kennedy would be gone within the year, and the party would be on its third leader within two years. Nor that these changes of leadership would in fact do almost nothing to help the party. For all the changes at the top, the Liberal Democrats would end the parliament in roughly the same electoral position that they began it.

Despite being a perennial of the Westminster rumour-mill, as a result of a number of high profile events from which he had been unexpectedly absent due to 'illness', stories about Charles Kennedy's drinking rarely surfaced publicly.[2] There had been a *Newsnight* interview in 2002, in which Jeremy Paxman had brought the subject up (only to apologise subsequently), and in 2005, Kennedy had given a distinctly below-par performance at the Liberal Democrat manifesto launch, which had been blamed officially on tiredness caused by his recent fatherhood.[3] But behind the scenes, those at the top of the party were much more aware of the problem, and its scale. In 2003, a press conference had been arranged at which Kennedy was to have announced he was seeking treatment for his drinking – only for him to cancel it at the last minute.

Fuelled by the growing sense of disappointment at the 2005 result, concerns continued, with increasingly open briefing against the leader. In mid-December, Kennedy raised the matter of his leadership at the party's weekly meeting of the Shadow Cabinet in an attempt to silence his critics, demanding that the briefing against him in the media must stop, and that anyone with concerns should see him personally. It took Sandra Gidley – the Lib Dem MP with the smallest majority – to challenge him, suggesting that MPs with concerns should be able to raise them with the Chief Whip. The following day, the subject of Kennedy's leadership was again raised at a meeting of the parliamentary party, after which Kennedy held a series of one-to-one meetings with Lib Dem MPs, which he described as 'a good end-of-year clearing of the air', but in private many of his MPs were giving him final warnings about his behaviour, and most were unimpressed by his response; at least half a dozen told him to his face that he should quit. Just before Christmas, Vince Cable drafted a letter telling Kennedy that he must step down, which was supported by ten of the party's frontbenchers. The letter was safely stored in Cable's safe, while he went off on holiday, hoping that the crisis would resolve itself.

On 5 January, the Lib Dem press office learnt that ITN News was about to run a story about Kennedy's drinking. Journalists knew not only that a meeting had taken place to discuss his problem, but also what had been said, and by whom. Someone within the party had leaked the details. In a desperate attempt to pre-empt the story, Kennedy called a press conference at which he confessed to 'coming to terms with' a serious drinking problem. Appealing over the heads of the parliamentary party to the party's membership, where he still enjoyed high levels of popularity, he offered himself for re-election as party leader against anyone who wanted to challenge him.

Yet whatever the formal rules of the party, it was inconceivable that any leader lacking the support of the party's MPs could continue in post. By mid-morning the following day, Nick Harvey let it be known that a motion of no confidence would be put to the parliamentary party, and by lunchtime, Vince Cable said on the BBC's *The World at One* that he had reached the 'sad conclusion' that Kennedy's position as leader was 'untenable'. Before the day was out, Ed Davey and Sarah Teather had emailed a joint statement which indicated that Kennedy had lost the confidence of some 25 MPs, including eight members of the Shadow Cabinet. Initially, Kennedy attempted to tough it out, claiming wide support from party members, but by the Saturday afternoon, he had resigned, citing lack of support in the parliamentary party.

There are essentially two views of the Kennedy leadership and its downfall. The first is summed up by the title of Greg Hurst's book, *A Tragic Flaw*. But for Kennedy's drinking, and his failure to come to terms with it, he would have been an excellent leader. It was his drinking that prevented him providing the dynamism the party needed, and his drinking which forced other people around him to lie, to become implicated in covering up his behaviour, and which resulted in the team around Kennedy, desperately loyal to him, developing a damaging bunker mentality, cutting him off from the rest of the party. Yet there is an alternative, and less flattering view, held by many of those at the top of the party: that the drinking was both a symptom and a symbol.[4] 'Had he been like Churchill,' said one of those based in Cowley Street, 'drinking a bottle of whisky a day, but able to take charge, we'd not have cared so much.' The problem was not just Kennedy's drinking, but his failure, even when sober, to offer much direction and discipline to the party. All acknowledged that he could be a brilliant communicator – when on form, one of the best there was – but he showed little or no interest in the development of policy, and could be half-hearted in the running of the party. 'They didn't see him at close quarters,' complained a member of the party's Federal Executive. 'They didn't realise how crap he was, the drift, the loss of direction.' When at the beginning of the 2005 conference, Richard Grayson, Kennedy's former speech writer and head of policy, wrote an article for the *Independent* in which he claimed that the Liberal Democrats needed leadership, and that Kennedy's style was 'more chairman than leader', the reaction from one member of the Federal Policy Committee was: 'if only! He would come in, crack a few jokes, and wander off.' Yet for all his flaws, in the month prior to Kennedy's resignation the Liberal Democrats averaged 19% in the opinion polls. With Kennedy gone, they would not manage that again until April 2010.

Kennedy's respected deputy, Sir Menzies 'Ming' Campbell, was installed as Acting Leader, and immediately announced his candidacy for the leadership. At his campaign launch on 19 January, Campbell said he wanted to be 'a bridge to the future', acting as a 'captain and coach', promoting and developing a younger generation of MPs. He attracted the support of more than half the party's MPs, including many of that same younger generation, such as Nick Clegg and David Laws, some of whom were doing so on the basis that young cardinals vote for old popes. But what many had thought would be something of a coronation ended up not being so straightforward. The early stages of the contest were overshadowed by revelations about two of Campbell's rivals for the leadership. Mark Oaten, the party's Home Affairs Spokesperson, pulled out of the race on 19 January, having failed to find sufficient MPs to nominate him. Two days later, he was forced to resign from the front bench when the *News of the World* uncovered his relationship with a male prostitute. Simon Hughes, the Party President, also stumbled over his sexuality, being forced to admit he was bisexual. Many within the party worried that these revelations, coming so soon after those about Kennedy's drinking, were beginning to turn the Liberal Democrats into a laughing stock.

Campbell also found himself under a more serious challenge than expected from Chris Huhne. An MP for less than a year, Huhne started the contest as a 300–1 outsider, and his decision to stand was not welcomed by many in the party's hierarchy, especially as he had previously pledged not to. But his pitch, including a proposal to exclude people on the minimum wage from paying income tax, to be paid for by environmental taxes, proved popular with activists. In the event, Campbell won fairly comfortably, although Huhne polled an impressive 42% of the final vote, once Simon Hughes' votes had been redistributed.[5]

Ming Campbell became party leader on 2 March 2006. The Ming dynasty – as it became known – would last just 18 months, the shortest reign of any leader of a major British political party since Robert Maclennan's brief spell as the leader of the pre-merger SDP in the 1980s, or before that, Arthur Henderson in the 1930s.

The Rt Hon Sir Menzies Campbell QC MP was supposed to be many of the things Charles 'Chatshow Charlie' Kennedy was not. He was reliable, serious, statesman-like, even prime ministerial. He did indeed prove to be a more effective internal leader of the party than Kennedy had been. He was tough, imposed discipline, and chaired meetings well. He took more of an interest in policy, driving through important policy changes. The Liberal Democrats produced *Trust in People: Make Britain Free, Fair and Green*,[6] which was debated at the 2006 Liberal Democrat conference. General in approach, *Trust in People* was endorsed with little fuss, largely due to a preceding comprehensive consultation process, but a separate policy paper on taxation saw a more intense debate, after which the leadership's proposals to abandon the 50p income tax rate for those earning over £100,000 was finally accepted.[7] In its place, the 40% income tax threshold was to be raised from £38,000 to £50,000, the 10p rate of income tax was to be abolished, while the basic rate would be cut from 22% to 20%. These tax-cutting measures were to be paid for by more environmental taxes, ending tax relief on pensions contributions for higher earners, and increases in capital gains tax.[8] The leadership claimed that the new policy was more redistributive. Critics argued that the party had merely abandoned a symbolically significant policy – the 50p rate for higher earners – in favour of a far less distinctive set of tax proposals, around a clumsy slogan of *Free, Fair and Green*. But the party's move away from its old tax and spend image had been set in motion. Campbell also personally took on those within his party who wanted the Lib Dems to sign up to the immediate scrapping of Trident, speaking from the floor in favour of the leadership's position, and narrowly winning a vote 454–414 at the party's spring conference in 2007. The vote was so close that some of those present believe the initial show of hands went against Campbell, only for some Lib Dems to change position when the formal vote was counted, in order not to embarrass the leadership. Either way, Campbell's intervention was crucial. Before he spoke, it looked as if the leadership position would be lost. Putting his authority on the line, his speech swung the debate.

Campbell was however also supposed to be a good communicator, and here the promise was not matched by the delivery. During the Ashdown years, Campbell had been one of the Leader's Office's go-to people when they needed someone for difficult media interviews; and as the party's Foreign Affairs Spokesperson during the Iraq War, he had earned a reputation as a polished television performer, providing cogent soundbites on *Newsnight* and other high-end outlets. But he struggled to recreate that success as leader, especially outside his comfort zone of defence and foreign policy. He had frequently been treated as a quasi-academic expert by the media, able to go into the television studios, give a short clip – part-analysis, part-criticism – and then leave, often without facing very much critical examination. As leader, however, he faced critical, sometimes hostile, questioning, with which he often struggled to cope. He also performed poorly in the Commons, stumbling badly at Prime Minister's Questions early in his leadership. Neither of his two predecessors had found it easy to make an impression in the Commons either, due to the constant heckling and rude, low-level chatter from the Government and Opposition benches, but Campbell seemed to find it especially difficult. An early question about pensions was floored by a heckle to 'declare your interest', an ill-judged question about temporary headmasters of failing schools prompted ridicule, and despite coaching on how to handle the Commons, he continued to struggle thereafter.

The media also began increasingly to focus on his age; he was just short of his 65th birthday when he was elected leader. In historic terms, there was nothing exceptional about his age at all (Gladstone was 82 when he became Prime Minister for the final time, Churchill was 76, Attlee a mere 62 when he became PM in 1945, as was Macmillan in 1957) and given the increasingly elderly population of the UK, it might have been thought an unusual criticism. But the cult of youth in modern British politics is strong, and the mockery was merciless. As Vince Cable remarked in his autobiography: 'To watch a decent man being kicked to death is not an edifying spectacle. To see cartoonists in otherwise liberal newspapers depict a sixty-five year old as a geriatric has been with a Zimmer frame went way beyond political wit.'[9] Campbell had also made a full recovery from cancer a couple of years before he became leader, and the radiotherapy had taken more out of him than many people realised at the time; what made things worse was that some of his mannerisms, his style, his language (he would refer to 'the motorcar' or the 'wireless'), even his clothes, appeared to hail from another, long-gone, political era. When he had first entered the House of Commons in 1987, several Tory MPs had mistakenly greeted him as one of their own and he could, at times, resemble a huntin'-shootin'-fishin' Edwardian laird more than a modern party leader.

Internally, there were also criticisms about his safety-first approach to the leadership, and his critics did not hesitate to brief against him. Destructive behaviour learnt during the Kennedy years continued, with some Lib Dem MPs having discovered the delights of anonymous briefing. Those around Campbell had no doubts where the briefings were coming from, identifying two close associates of Chris Huhne as the main culprits. There was, though, plenty to criticise. Campbell's leadership campaign had received an unexpected boost when – with him as Acting Leader – the party had won the Dunfermline & West Fife by-election in February 2006, overturning an 11,562 Labour majority. But nothing similar was achieved once he became leader proper. The Lib Dems won no Westminster by-elections. At the 2006 local elections they polled a national equivalent vote share of 25%, the party's lowest projected vote share from local elections since 1999, and a year later they suffered a net loss of 246 councillors in English local elections (a result Campbell described as 'a mixed bag').[10] In the Scottish elections in May 2007, they lost one seat and fell 1% in the polls compared with 2003. They fared no better in Wales, becalmed on six seats and 13% of the vote. Campbell's own ratings were also poor. Third party leaders traditionally poll relatively well (albeit with a higher than average number of don't knows); not so Ming Campbell. A June 2007 Ipsos-MORI poll found that just 5% of respondents chose him in response to the 'most capable Prime Minister' question; just before his downfall Charles Kennedy had been polling roughly three times that level. In September 2007, the same polling company found his satisfaction rating on a net score of –11 (24% approving of his leadership, 35% against). Even his party's supporters did not seem impressed: an ICM poll for *Newsnight*, four months into his leadership, found that not only did Lib Dem voters prefer Kennedy to Campbell, but they even thought that Brown and Cameron were more qualified to be Prime Minister.[11] And there were worrying signs that the party was suffering as a result. The month before Campbell stood down as party leader, the Liberal Democrats averaged 16%, but both a YouGov poll for the *Sunday Times* on 7 October 2007 and an Ipsos-MORI poll for the *Sun* on 12 October 2007 showed them on a mere 11%. Having a more coherent set of policies and some well-run meetings did not seem to be helping them very much.

Gordon Brown's arrival as Prime Minister and his offer to bring Lib Dems into his 'government of all the talents' – offering a Cabinet position to Paddy Ashdown, and advisory posts for others – further destabilised Ming Campbell's leadership. As Greg Hurst notes: 'The impact was deeply unsettling for the Lib Dems. It smacked of a crude attempt to divide the party's senior ranks ... it again called into question the judgement of Sir Menzies Campbell and his closest advisor Lord Kirkwood of Kirkhope, both of whom had presented his long-term friendship with Brown as an asset.'[12] But if Brown's arrival unsettled it, then his decision to call off the October 2007 election (see Chapter 1) killed off Campbell's leadership altogether. However disgruntled people had been, it had made no sense to change leaders with an election looming; but once that possibility was removed, and with Brown ruling out a contest in 2008 as well, a sizeable window of opportunity opened up, and pressure within the party increased. On GMTV on Sunday 14 October Simon Hughes claimed that 'the leader obviously has to do better'. The following day, Vince Cable admitted that the leadership was 'under discussion. But I don't think it's under threat.' Yet Campbell reasoned that he would be approaching 70 at the next election if Brown went on until 2010, and that questions over his advancing years would continue to dog him and his party. He asked himself, 'Can I trade my way out of this?'[13] The answer was no. Conscious of Charles Kennedy's brutal defenestration, and fearing that a similar fate would befall him if he stayed on, Sir Menzies Campbell stepped down from the leadership of his party at 6.30pm on 15 October. He gave no interviews, preferring to issue a written statement which Simon Hughes, Party President and Vince Cable, the new Acting Leader read out at a press conference.

Cable, ironically no spring chicken either at the age of 61, triumphed in his role as Acting Leader, excelling at Prime Minister's Questions, particularly with a well-received gag about Gordon Brown's 'remarkable transformation in the past few weeks from Stalin to Mr Bean'.[14] All those who dismiss the importance of Prime Minister's Questions should note that Cable's reputation was made there, just as Campbell's was damaged there. Cable pondered standing for the leadership, but decided against, annoyed by what he described as 'lazily ageist' assumptions that he was too old and that a new, younger, generation was needed. The ensuing leadership contest was that rare thing – a relatively exciting Liberal Democrat leadership election – and developed into a close two-horse race between virtual novices: Nick Clegg, the party's Home Affairs Spokesperson, and Chris Huhne, the party's Environment Spokesperson, both of whom had been elected to the Commons in 2005.[15]

Clegg was the candidate of the party establishment, gaining the backing of 38 MPs, the majority of whom had been supporters of Sir Menzies Campbell the previous year, in addition to the support of Paddy Ashdown. Huhne could claim support from just 11 MPs, but he had the advantage of having already stood against Campbell in 2006; not only did he enjoy name recognition among the party's membership, he also had a campaign infrastructure already in place, headed for the second time by Lynne Featherstone. The similarities between the candidates were striking: both were educated at Westminster School, both had served as MEPs, both even had foreign-born wives – and both made similar pitches. On 19 October, Clegg chose his constituency of Sheffield Hallam rather than Westminster from which to launch his campaign, claiming he wanted to lead an anti-establishment party, while at his manifesto launch on 31 October, Huhne said he wanted to 'revive our anti-establishment edge', adding 'we are the party that wants to change the system, not just change the people on the back of the ministerial limousine'.[16] Both candidates made bold policy announcements, Clegg promising to lead a grassroots campaign of civil disobedience against ID cards, while Huhne's manifesto, entitled *The Liberal Revolution*, pledged a 'revolution in democracy'. Unlike 2006, both campaign teams had access to telephone and membership party lists, which allowed them to use direct mailing and phone banks for the first time.

The effect of having two very similar candidates fighting it out for the leadership of a fairly small party tended to magnify the divisions between them, which were in reality relatively slight (as, in private, they would acknowledge). Writing for Lib Dem Voice, Stephen Tall characterised these differences as the 'purism' of Huhne and the 'pragmatism' of Clegg.[17] Such a tight-cornered, pedantic, and at times bad-tempered, contest suited Huhne, who was more of a natural street-fighter than Clegg, the former commenting early on in a GMTV Sunday interview on 4 November that he possessed 'sharp elbows' that would be able to gain greater coverage for his party. Clegg, on the other hand, wanted to broaden the party's appeal beyond the narrow confines of the party membership, but became frustrated when the contest became, as he put it, 'very introverted' with 'lots of point scoring and people dancing on the head of pins'.[18] Huhne positioned himself slightly to the left, most obviously over Trident, which he argued should be scrapped in favour of a smaller, minimal deterrent, while Clegg claimed that introducing such a new weapons system would undermine the UK's credibility in nuclear non-proliferation talks due to take place in 2010.

Despite Clegg being the early favourite, there were signs that Huhne was closing the gap, and the final result could not have been much closer. At the final count, on 18 December, both campaign teams were informed that there was a batch of unopened envelopes containing uncounted votes, delayed as a result of the Christmas post. Either of the two campaign teams could veto opening them. For Huhne, Lynne Featherstone wanted them opened. Richard Allan, the former Sheffield Hallam MP, who had organised Clegg's campaign, refused. With some 1,300 late votes sitting unopened in their envelopes, Clegg polled 20,988 votes (50.6%), just edging out Huhne on 20,477 votes (49.4%), a majority of just 511 votes. With a lower turnout, and with a yet smaller party membership, both candidates polled fewer votes than had voted for Huhne in the previous contest when he had finished second.

Under Charles Kennedy's leadership, the Liberal Democrats had positioned themselves clearly to the left of Labour, a stance that was popular with the party's generally left-leaning activists.[19] But the failure to break through in 2005, along with the election of David Cameron as Conservative leader, had already forced some into a rethink. Cameron portrayed himself as a Liberal Conservative, and was attempting to woo 'soft' Liberal Democrat voters.[20] As well as a pledge to 'at least' double the number of Liberal Democrat MPs within two general elections, Clegg soon made it clear to his MPs that he would restore the principle of equidistance in his party's dealings with Labour and the Conservatives, a policy that had been abandoned by Paddy Ashdown in 1995. In his first major policy speech in charge, on 12 January 2008, Clegg argued for the creation of 'free schools', liberated from local authorities, and guaranteed maximum waiting times for operations in the NHS, otherwise the NHS would have to pay for a patient to go private.

The global financial crisis, which hit early in Clegg's leadership, was a boon to the party. For one thing, it elevated Vince Cable from the humble status of Liberal Democrat spokesman to Global Financial Wizard. He became the far-sighted sage who had predicted what was to come, the man who saw what no Labour or Conservative politician had been able to see. Having previously found it difficult to get onto programmes such as *Question Time* (which had in the past been reluctant to book him – on the grounds that he was too gloomy and only wanted to talk about the forthcoming recession), suddenly Cable was everywhere, doing a good impression of a prophet returned from the wilderness, and being treated in much the same quasi-academic manner as Ming Campbell had been over foreign policy before he became leader. The truth was that his reputation for economic farsightedness was somewhat overplayed – Conservative MPs would joke that Cable had predicted nine out of the last one recessions – but perception is everything, and Cable and the Liberal Democrats made the most of the party's new reputation for economic competence. Until the election campaign began, Cable had at least as much prestige and kudos as the party's leader. When, in 2009, the *Telegraph* published its list of the 50 most influential Lib Dems it put Nick Clegg in second place; Vince Cable came first.

The recession also provided an opportunity for the leadership to begin to ditch or water down existing policies – on the grounds that they were now too expensive for the post-recession era. As a short-term economic fix, they successfully dusted off and re-branded Ming Campbell's policy of tax cuts for lower income workers paid for by a switch to green taxes, together with closing off tax loopholes – in order to show that the party had a plan to cope with the financial crisis. But the 'themes and values' document discussed at the 2008 conference – *Make it Happen* – contained an important shift in emphasis: savings from government spending programmes could now be channelled into extending tax cuts, in order to offer what Clegg termed 'the most radical and progressive package for ordinary people in living memory'.[21] That risked angering some activists, who suspected that policy had changed from cutting back on wasteful expenditure to fund investment to cutting public expenditure to finance tax cuts. At the 2008 conference, an amendment urging delegates not to vote for a cut in the overall tax level when there were so many pressing needs for investment in public services was defeated by about 2:1, but the debate aroused the same passions as the abandonment of the 50p tax rate for top-rate earners had done two years before.[22] In the aftermath of the debate, a slate of left-leaning Liberal Democrat members stood for, and were elected onto, the party's important Federal Policy Committee (FPC). The party leadership would always deny the existence of a left–right division within the party, but those on the left had no problem with the nomenclature; the leftish grouping was not especially well-organised, and punched below its weight, lacking a clear leader and failing to cohere, but it had some intellectual clout, and was large enough to serve as a significant restraint on further shifts in policy, and to cause several behind-the-scenes rows.[23]

The most noteworthy moment of the leadership campaign had come on the BBC's *The Politics Show* on 18 November, when Jon Sopel had challenged Huhne about a 'Calamity Clegg' briefing document which had been released by a member of Huhne's campaign team, and Clegg's leadership did indeed begin with a few stumbles. In an interview with Piers Morgan for *GQ* magazine, he got himself in trouble over questions about his sex life, appearing to have claimed to have slept with 'no more than' 30 women and earning the moniker 'Nick Cleggover'.[24] In another interview he erroneously thought that the state pension was about £30.[25] These early, relatively minor, stumbles caused concern amongst his team, who knew from their experience with Ming Campbell how early perceptions could prove difficult to dislodge, and who worried about Clegg's portrayal in the media as 'Cameron-lite'.

The Clegg strategy was to take risks with the media, deploying exactly those 'sharp elbows' Chris Huhne had claimed to possess, and eschewing Ming Campbell's more cautious strategy, in an attempt to force the Lib Dems into the public eye. One of Clegg's advisers would quote a maxim of Charles Kennedy's: 'The Prime Minister gets up every morning and thinks: what will I do today? The Leader of the Opposition gets up every morning and thinks: what will I say today? The Leader of the Liberal Democrats gets up every morning and thinks: what will I say or do today that will make anyone take any notice of me?' So the strategy was to be front-footed and aggressive in their political and media strategy, willing to take risks in order to force the party onto the media agenda. Parliamentary ratification of the Lisbon Treaty saw the party's MPs stage a walk-out from the Commons, when the Speaker did not select their amendment.[26] During the expenses scandal, Clegg was in the forefront of demands for the recall of miscreant MPs and for wide-ranging reform. He broke ranks with the other party leaders to call for the resignation of Michael Martin as Speaker. He began to question the role of British troops in Afghanistan. In April 2009, aided and abetted by the actress Joanna Lumley, the Lib Dems managed a rare parliamentary triumph, joining with the Conservatives to defeat the Government in the Commons on a Liberal Democrat Opposition Day motion over the settlement rights of the Ghurkhas.

For the most part, the benefits of this approach outweighed the greater risk of being ignored. But things did not always go to plan, resulting in Clegg's aides having to engage in what one of them described as 'a bit of sweeping up afterwards'. At the party's Bournemouth conference in 2009, Clegg used an interview with the *Guardian* to call for 'bold and even savage cuts' in public spending, a phrase that upset many members of the party. Even those who understood the need for them to be bold (and not all did) failed to see why they should be advocating 'savage' cuts.[27]

There was more than occasional frustration amongst the leadership with the policy apparatus of the party, and its ability to act as a break on speedy decision making. A senior member of the leadership described the party as 'a bit like an adolescent child ... its voice had broken and it had developed some muscles, but it still had child-like instincts'. Some party members, another member of the Shadow Cabinet complained, saw themselves as 'Keepers of the Holy Grail': 'Some of them, you feel, would rather consult for months on end, and go through 84 committees, rather than get any coverage. You can't lead a third party, get publicity, if everything has to be seen by 85 people. You need more freedom than that ... We ought to be very nimble, and able to innovate, but we can't.' The Leader's team saw it as their role to cut through the party 'technocratic' policy-making process to produce a much shorter, more distinctive manifesto. As one commented dryly: 'We've had ten policies for every issue, many expensive, some even costed.' That 'shopping list' approach had to go.

This was not a novel view. Shortly after Menzies Campbell stepped down as leader, he had argued that the Liberal Democrats suffered from 'too many alternative power sources' leaving its leaders with 'the responsibility but not the power'. Nick Clegg agreed, and shortly after becoming leader, asked Professor Christopher Bones, Dean of the Henley Business School, and a former Lib Dem constituency chair, to investigate ways in which the party might streamline its decision-making procedures. Part of the difficulty in decision-making arose because of the Lib Dems' federal policy-making structure. Having separate parties in Scotland, Wales and England meant, for instance, that setting the party's federal budget required nearly 20 meetings of five different committees.[28] As one of those close to Clegg put it: 'there is a multiplicity of committees in the name of transparency, but ultimately what happens is you don't get any decisions being made at all'. As part of his, albeit modest, streamlining agenda Bones recommended the creation of a Chief Officer's Group responsible for setting and delivering the party's overall strategy and budget. It also (less controversially) set out a strategy for broadening the political battlefield by strengthening regions and local parties in order to develop newly winnable seats.

In their defence, activists would point out that the party's worst problems frequently came from rushed, botched, ideas from the leadership that had not gone through the proper policy process. This was most obvious with the party's ill-thought-out proposals for a 'Mansion Tax', also announced at the Bournemouth conference. The initial proposal was for a 1% tax on homes worth £1 million or more, to pay for lifting 300,000 of the lowest-paid out of paying tax. It was a superb piece of political branding, but suffered from two drawbacks. For one thing, houses in South West London – where the Lib Dems held several constituencies – could reach a value of £1 million without being 'mansions', but more importantly the policy was launched half-cocked with none of the background detail worked out, and without consultation within the party. It later had to be relaunched, tweaked for the needs of their London electorate, as a 1% tax on all homes over £2 million. The leadership later admitted that this was 'slap-dash policy making', and there were mutterings amongst some MPs and activists about Vince Cable's willingness to make up policy on the hoof. At a subsequent FPC meeting, it was put to Cable that his behaviour emphasised the need for policy to go through the proper channels.

The issue that caused most trouble was the repeated attempts by the leadership to water down the party's policy of abolishing tuition fees. One of the party's high profile vote winners at the 2005 election – especially

'Mystery surrounds crash'

Garland, *Daily Telegraph*, 22 September 2009
(© Telegraph Media Group Ltd 2009)

in seats with large student populations – the policy became a target of those who felt that, however worthy, it was too expensive. In January 2009, the FPC voted by a wide margin of 18–5 against dropping the commitment to abolish tuition fees. Clegg, in the chair, was one of the minority. At the party's spring conference in Harrogate, delegates again voted overwhelmingly in favour of keeping the policy, but Clegg was determined to revisit the matter. When the matter came up at an FPC meeting in July to discuss the party's pre-manifesto document *A Fresh Start for Britain*, the discussions turned 'nasty and unpleasant' (according to one of those present). The document included a very small number of spending priorities, with everything else as an aspiration; and the abolition of tuition fees was not one of the priorities. There followed a series of long and heated disagreements, and the meeting, which should have finished shortly after 8pm, ran on until gone 11pm, by which time only a handful of items on the agenda had been dealt with. The leadership found the muleish stubbornness of the FPC frustrating beyond belief ('Lovely people, but every time they go into that room, they become policy Rottweilers'). For their part, members of the FPC found the leadership rude and patronising – with particular criticism of Clegg ('petulant') and Cable ('obnoxious', 'deeply arrogant'). When tempers had cooled, the FPC reconvened, this time with Danny Alexander, Head of the

Manifesto Group, taking Clegg's place as chair, after private complaints about Clegg's style of chairing. In a calmer atmosphere, the FPC agreed a compromise in which there would no longer be a division between top and lesser spending priorities. The eventual published paper then included 'sample priorities', of which tuition fees was still not one.

At the party's traditional Saturday Rally on the eve of its Bournemouth conference later in the year, Charles Kennedy issued a warning about abandoning policies that had 'served us well'. Then, on the opening day of the Bournemouth conference during a question-and-answer session, Clegg gave a carefully-worded reply: 'There is no question mark over the policy of the Liberal Democrats to scrap tuition fees. The only question mark is about when we can afford to scrap tuition fees.' In response, and in an unprecedented move, the FPC then moved an amendment to its own paper, making it clear that 'Nothing in this paper downgrades existing commitments', and on the suggestion of Evan Harris the majority of FPC members penned a letter to the *Guardian* on the day of Clegg's main party conference speech affirming that scrapping tuition fees remained the official policy of the party and predicting that that commitment would be included in the party's manifesto.[29] The leadership was not impressed, but the dispute became a symbol of everything those on the left of the party did not like about the party leadership's direction and style.

In 2009 the Liberal Democrats bade farewell to their Chief Executive, Lord (Chris) Rennard. The mastermind behind their recent election performances, Rennard had been a key figure at Cowley Street since at least 1989 when he had become Director of Campaigns; and had been Chief Executive since 2003. He was one of the – if not *the* – most experienced electioneers in modern British politics, and almost all Liberal Democrats were aware of the debt the party owed him. There had, however, been grumblings about his role, power and approach for a while. His position as something close to an all-powerful unelected Chief Executive was always a paradox in such a bottom-up participatory party; neither of the two larger parties – much more top-down in most other ways – had so much power concentrated in just one person. There were also complaints about Rennard's electoral approach – 'Rennardism', as it was known within the party – complaints that years of very localised, and largely non-ideological, campaigning had blunted the party's ability to outline a clear vision of what it stood for. One of the senior members of the party summed it up like so: 'You do a survey of the voters, get feedback from people telling you what they want, and then you put out endless literature in which you tell them they'll get it tomorrow ... At some stage this party is going to have to wake up and realise that it can't make advances using the same tactics as before.' Or, as one member of the Federal Executive complained: 'We've become a cult for people who like delivering leaflets ... If you're really lucky, work very hard, and deliver lots of leaflets, you'll get onto our fund-raising email list and be bombarded with emails asking for money.' Rennard himself preferred the phrase 'incremental targetting', and compared it to a man spinning plates on poles: 'It's possible to add more poles and more plates, but there comes a point at which you can't make any more progress than that – and if you try, the consequences could be disastrous.' Rennard's critics hoped that the immediate post-2005 campaign review would clip his wings a little (they were disappointed); they also saw the Bones Commission as having the same possibility. To accolades from Nick Clegg, in May 2009 Rennard announced that he would stand down from October 2009, citing family and health reasons. The announcement of his resignation was timed to ensure that the new Chief Executive would have sufficient time to prepare the party for a 2010 campaign. The timing also probably avoided any controversy arising from a claim in the *News of the World* that he had misused his House of Lords allowances, a claim which was rejected by the Lords authorities.[30]

Rennard's successor, Chris Fox, had originally been appointed as the Lib Dems' new Director of Policy and Communications in January 2009, in an attempt to strengthen the party's 'air war' operation. He could claim a long history with the party, including as a parliamentary candidate, but he also brought a more corporate feel to the post of Chief Executive – a bit more flipchart than barchart – and his arrival broke up the concentration of power within Cowley Street, creating a more normal management structure and ensuring that a wider number of voices were heard in terms of the decision-making processes of the party. Before his departure Rennard had begun work on a more ambitious electoral strategy, moving away from incremental targeting, and this work picked up under Fox.

There was, however, no evidence of an electoral breakthrough. The 2008 London Assembly elections saw the Lib Dems lose two seats out of five, with a share of the vote in the constituency elections of just 14%, 5% down on 2004. At the June 2009 European elections, the Lib Dems came fourth with just 14% of the vote, losing out to a plethora of minor parties. And although they finished second ahead of Labour on 25% in the local elections held on the same day, they lost three key counties to the Conservatives in their crucial election battleground of the South West, and failed to win the new Cornish local authority. By the end of 2009, the Liberal Democrats had not won a Westminster by-election since 2006, and in November 2009 the party reached a new low point, polling only 474 votes in the Glasgow North East by-election, finishing in an ignominious sixth place behind the British National Party (fourth) and Tommy Sheridan's Solidarity (fifth). More generally, there were no signs of the party picking up in the polls. Clegg's personal ratings were up on Ming Campbell's (in December 2009, he was polling +13 according to Ipsos-MORI's satisfaction rating) but there was less sign of the party picking up in the polls. The Liberal Democrats ended 2009 polling an average of 18% in December 2009, lower than they had been achieving under Charles Kennedy. Indeed, not only were they polling worse than they had under Kennedy, there was not even much evidence they were performing any better than they did under Ming Campbell; the party's position in the polls during both the Clegg and Campbell leaderships averaged at almost exactly the same. There was at least some evidence of polls beginning to pick up towards the end of the Parliament, although still not to a better position than they had been in 2005. Until the 2010 election campaign began, the brutal truth was that the Liberal Democrats had polled best when led by a drunk.

Notes

1. Just one MP, John Hemming, refused to sign Kennedy's papers.
2. For a full account of Kennedy's travails, see Greg Hurst, *Charles Kennedy. A Tragic Flaw* (London: Politico's, 2006).
3. Many observers present at the launch were sceptical of the official explanations at the time.
4. This view is set out clearly in Duncan Brack, 'Liberal Democrat Leadership: The Cases of Ashdown and Kennedy', *The Political Quarterly*, 78:1 (2007), 78–88.
5. In the first round of voting, Campbell polled 23,264 votes, Huhne 16,691 and Hughes 12,081. After Hughes' second preference votes were re-distributed, Campbell defeated Huhne by 29,697 votes to 21,628. See Andrew Denham and Peter Dorey, 'The Caretaker Leader Cleans Up: The Liberal Democrat Leadership Contest of 2006', *Parliamentary Affairs*, 60:1 (2007), 26–45.
6. Liberal Democrats, *Trust in People: Make Britain Free, Fair and Green*, Policy Paper 76 (Liberal Democrats, July 2006).
7. Liberal Democrats, *Fairer, Simpler, Greener*, Policy Paper 75 (Liberal Democrats, 2006).
8. Peter Dorey and Andrew Denham, '"Meeting the Challenge"? The Liberal Democrats' Policy Review of 2005–2006', *The Political Quarterly*, 78:1 (2007), 68–77.
9. Vince Cable, *Free Radical* (London: Atlantic Books, 2009), p. 287. Yet Cable still dismisses the 18-month Campbell leadership in just four pages.
10. The data reported here are those from Colin Rallings and Michael Thrasher's estimates, which differ somewhat from those reported by the BBC on election night (and which were slightly more flattering to the Lib Dems). Either way, the trends across the Parliament are similar, whichever data are utilised, with

the Lib Dem projected share of the vote dropping year-on-year from 2006 until 2008, before rising again in 2009 back to the 2006 level or similar.

11. When 65% of your *own party's* supporters don't think you cut the mustard you have a serious problem.

12. Greg Hurst, 'Path to Power: How the Lib Dems Made History', in *The Times Guide to the House of Commons 2010* (London: Times Books, 2010), p. 45.

13. Menzies Campbell, *My Autobiography* (Hodder & Stoughton, 2008), ch. 17.

14. HC Debs, 28 November 2007, c. 275.

15. See Matthew Francis, 'The Bland Leading the Bland: Electing the Liberal Democrat Leader 1988–2007', *Representation*, 46:1 (2010), 91–100.

16. See also Nick Clegg, 'Time for a power shift', *Guardian*, 22 November 2007, or Chris Huhne, 'Radicalism will serve us', *Guardian*, 23 November 2007.

17. Stephen Tall, 'The leadership contest – how's it looking so far?', Lib Dem Voice, 7 November 2007.

18. Alice Miles and Helen Rumbelow, 'A reformer troubled by Calamity Clegg tag', *The Times*, 24 November 2007.

19. The ideological tensions within Liberal Democrat members have been explored by Paul Whiteley, Patrick Seyd and Antony Billinghurst, *Third Force Politics: Liberal Democrats at the Grassroots* (Oxford: Oxford University Press, 2006).

20. See for example, David Cameron, 'A Lib Dem–Tory movement will vanquish Labour', *Observer*, 20 September 2009.

21. See Nick Clegg, 'We need big – and fair – tax cuts', *Independent*, 13 September 2008; or Nick Clegg, 'My Liberal Vision', *New Statesman*, 12 September 2008.

22. Paul Holmes MP, '"No" to Make it Happen's public spending cuts', Lib Dem Voice, 11 September 2008.

23. See for example the arguments contained in Duncan Brack, Richard Grayson and David Howarth (eds), *Reinventing the State: Social Liberalism for the 21st Century* (London: Politico's, 2007).

24. This claim deserves to join the list of things-politicians-never-said. In reality, faced with a series of questions about his sex life, Clegg had refused to answer, until, panicking slightly at the line of the questioning, he eventually responded to a question 'Thirty?' with 'No more than thirty', adding 'It's a lot less than that' – answers that, of course, could mean anything from zero upwards. It was, one of his media term admitted, the result of some naivety on their part, along with a tendency – widely deprecated by his aides – to engage with whatever question he has been asked, what one called his 'slightly nauseating desire to answer the question'.

25. At the time of the interview, the single person's pension was £90.70 a week, £145.45 for a couple.

26. The ratification of the Lisbon Treaty also triggered a damaging split in the party over the issue of a referendum – both within the Commons, triggering two large rebellions and the resignation of three frontbench spokespeople, and in the Lords, where Lib Dem peers adopted a different position from those in the Commons. The Liberal Democrat position on the Bill thus depended what chamber of Parliament the Bill happened to be in.

27. Allegra Stratton and Patrick Wintour, 'LibDem leader Nick Clegg fights to extend party appeal beyond the faithful', *Guardian*, 18 September 2009. In that interview, Clegg also suggested means-testing child benefit, something

that his Work and Pensions Spokesperson, Steve Webb, rejected outright on 21 September.
28. Chris Bones, 'The Party Reform Commission – taking the Lib Dems forward', Lib Dem Voice, 3 September 2008.
29. Letters to the Editor, 'Tuition fee lesson for Liberal Democrats', *Guardian*, 23 September 2009.
30. http://www.parliament.uk/documents/upload/lordrennard%20complaint. pdf

6
Fragmentation and Diversity: The Others

In his classic work *British Political Parties*, published in 1955, R.T. McKenzie allocated the Liberal Party just three pages, tucked away in what he described as a 'ghetto' of an appendix. Despite its distinguished history, the party had, he claimed, no chance of governing, and so it was not worth worrying about. To parties outside of the top three, he did not even allocate an appendix – and for the very good reason that they mattered even less. The fragmentation of the party system since then – beginning in the 1960s and 1970s, accelerating in the 1990s – has altered the political landscape almost beyond recognition. During the height of the expenses scandal in May 2009, a ComRes poll found 30% of respondents saying that they would vote for one of the minor parties, and that 80% thought that the main political parties had 'let the country down'. In the European elections just a month later a full 40% of the votes went to parties other than the Conservatives, Labour and the Lib Dems. Even at the Norwich North by-election in July 2009, some 28% of the vote went to parties other than the main three. The vote share being claimed for the 'others' in opinion polls diminished somewhat as the general election approached, and was down to between 10–12% by early 2010. This, though, was still noticeably up on the 6–10% seen prior to the 2005 election, and represented yet another ratcheting up in their presence on the political stage.

Put bluntly, the various 'others' now matter in a way that they did not, even a decade ago. They have become, in different ways, a constant presence throughout the Parliament. They represent a different political space, a diversification of voices and choices, and one which for the foreseeable future is here to stay. These parties are now often serious contenders for election and office, rather than merely a depository for the disgruntled and disaffected. Following the Scottish and Welsh elections in 2007, both Plaid Cymru and the Scottish National Party have become parties of government. In Northern Ireland, five separate parties constitute the Executive. The BNP, Greens, and UKIP are also all realistic contenders for seats in at least one parliament or assembly, as well as in local government. The parties also all matter as a constraint on the activities of the major parties, who are constantly aware of the manoeuvrings on their flanks. Even when the minor parties are unlikely to take seats, the major parties are always aware that the attractions of the minor parties can cost them votes. And finally, they matter because in a close contest like the one everyone expected in 2010, where the House of Commons could be very finely balanced, and where every seat could matter, there was the potential for minor parties to be the deciding ones in a coalition or agreement – something they were all aware of as they began the election campaign. Given the impact of the expenses scandal – and the disdain for politics that it fed – this should have been a good election for parties, and a plethora of independent candidates, that could claim to be different from the establishment.

United Kingdom Independence Party. In early 2006, the new Conservative leader, David Cameron, described the United Kingdom Independence Party (UKIP) as 'a bunch of fruitcakes and loonies and closet racists'. It was an image they would try to shake off for much of the Parliament, as they struggled to recover from a series of splits and scandals. In 2007, Ashley Mote, a UKIP MEP turned independent, was convicted and imprisoned for benefit fraud; in November 2009, Tom Wise, another MEP, was jailed for two years for false accounting and money laundering. And yet in the European elections in 2009 the 'fruitcakes and loonies' pushed the governing party into third place in a national election.

The politician charged with turning UKIP around was Nigel Farage, elected to replace Roger Knapman as party leader in September 2006. Farage claimed that there was 'an enormous vacuum in British politics'. He believed that David Cameron had abandoned Conservatism, and that 'on the big issues of the day you cannot put a cigarette paper between the three major parties'. Farage wanted to ditch UKIP's reputation for being a single issue pressure group, and instead be 'a party fighting on a broad range of domestic policies'. His pitch was right-of-centre, promising 'lower, simpler, flatter taxes', as well as supporting selective education, giving Britain its own independent trade policy, and instituting a five year freeze on immigration.

UKIP gained its first representation at Westminster in January 2007, when two peers – Lord Pearson of Rannoch and Lord Willoughby de Broke – defected from the Conservatives. In March 2008, Bob Spink, the Conservative MP for Castle Point resigned the Tory whip, prior to facing a re-selection meeting in his constituency, and a month later, he said he would join UKIP, although his association with the party was somewhat vague and short-lived.[1] In March 2009, UKIP's funds received a major boost when spread betting tycoon, Stuart Wheeler, donated £100,000 to UKIP, and was expelled from the Conservative Party a few days later.

In the June 2009 European elections, UKIP came second, winning 13 seats, one up from the 12 seats won when the party finished third in 2004. UKIP's vote share was up 0.3% to 16.5%. Farage had promised to resign if he did not better the result achieved in 2004 and he was able to argue that the result was 'no fluke'. But the party continued to struggle to perform well outside of European elections. In the 2008 London Assembly elections, they lost both of the seats they had won in 2004 (when they had benefitted from the European elections being held on the same day), while their candidate for the mayoral race polled only 0.9% of first preference votes, and finished in a distant seventh place. The party fared little better in the local elections held in 2009, winning a total of just seven seats.

In September 2009, Farage stepped down as UKIP leader to allow him to focus most of his energies on challenging the Speaker, John Bercow, in Buckingham. Explaining his decision to step down, Farage said, 'I may just have bitten off more than I can chew. I think I am better to the party doing fewer jobs better.' The identity of Farage's successor as UKIP leader was in little doubt, especially after the departing leader backed Lord Pearson of Rannoch as the only 'serious, credible candidate', and in November 2009, Pearson was elected leader. Despite ceasing to be leader, Farage remained high profile. In January 2010, he told the BBC's *Politics Show* that his party wanted to ban the burka in public. In March he was fined almost €4,000 for giving a speech in the European Parliament – where he remained the UKIP group leader – in which he described Belgium as 'pretty much a non-country', while attacking the new European Council President, Herman Van Rompuy as having 'the charisma of a damp rag, and the appearance of a low-grade bank clerk'.

UKIP continued to be dogged by internal disputes. In March 2010, Nikki Sinclaire, a newly elected UKIP MEP had the whip removed for refusing to sit with the Europe of Freedom and Democracy (EFD) grouping in the European Parliament. Lord Pearson also attracted criticism for inviting Geert Wilders, the leader of the Dutch anti-immigration Freedom

Party to the House of Lords to show his controversial film, *Fitna*, an attack on militant Islam, to an invited group of peers and MPs.

The party would go into the 2010 campaign fielding a record 558 candidates, although it declined to stand candidates in a handful of seats where there were hard Eurosceptic candidates standing, and in some cases Pearson would even go on to campaign for candidates from other parties himself. Farage was their most likely victor, but even he was starting with a notional 3.6% vote share whilst attempting to overturn a notional majority of 37.8%.

British National Party. The 'modernisation' strategy of the British National Party (BNP), under Nick Griffin, its Chairman since 1999, has been much commented upon, as the party bid to attract wider support. But there has been another shift in its approach, less remarked on but just as important, which was its embrace of anti-Muslim rhetoric. This shift in its rhetoric took it away from its previously crude and increasingly unfashionable anti-immigrant stance, and into a discourse which was more popularly acceptable.[2] It proved electorally successful: analysis of BNP support showed that the party did well in areas with low education levels but also large Muslim minority populations of Pakistani or African origin.[3]

For much of the Parliament the BNP continued to make slow progress in local elections, albeit in fits and starts. In 2006 they won 32 council seats, an increase of 27. This haul included 12 seats in Barking & Dagenham, where the BNP became the second largest party on the council. A year later, they stalled, with a net gain of just one council seat – although they came very close to winning a seat in the Welsh Assembly. In 2008 the BNP fared better, winning 37 council seats, a net gain of ten seats, and performed well enough in the elections for the London Assembly, polling 5.4%, to secure their first ever Assembly member. And in the 2009 local elections, they made a further net gain of three council seats.

An Excrescence:– a Fungus;—alias — a Toadstool upon a Dung-hill AFTER GILLRAY

'An excrescence: a fungus; alias a toadstool upon a dung-hill'

(Steve Bell, *Guardian*, 9 June 2009)

The high point of BNP success, though, occurred in the European elections in June 2009, when they polled 6.2% of the vote, and two BNP candidates – Nick Griffin, standing in the North West and Andrew Brons, standing in Yorkshire and the Humber – were elected as MEPs. This was the first time in the BNP's history (indeed, in the history of any British far-right party) that they had won seats in a national election. Success at the ballot box gave the BNP new and greater opportunities to be heard on the mainstream media and in October 2009 Griffin appeared on the BBC's *Question Time* show, in front of an audience of 8 million. Although Griffin was widely felt to have performed poorly (a subsequent YouGov poll found only 4% of voters would 'definitely consider' voting for the BNP), the publicity proved useful. Griffin could claim that he had been subject to unfair treatment by the BBC, and even if he had under-performed on this occasion, his party's new-found status as a mainstream party would guarantee him a right of reply to the Prime Ministerial debates during the 2010 general election campaign.

Despite cultivating the veneer of moderation, the BNP's constitution continued to forbid membership to non-whites (restricting membership to what it called 'indigenous caucasians'). In June 2009, the Equality and Human Rights Commission wrote to Griffin, requesting that the party change its constitution or face prosecution under the Race Relations Act. In January 2010, after a court hearing, the BNP agreed to change the constitution permitting non-whites to join, but the party stipulated that members would have to sign up to certain principles – such as opposing mixed race relationships – which the Commission felt still amounted to indirect discrimination. At a further court hearing in March 2010, the revised BNP Constitution was again declared illegal.

The BNP would stand some 338 candidates in the 2010 election, massively up on the 119 it had fielded in 2005, and more than the party or its predecessor had ever managed before. The party would target two seats – Stoke Central, and Barking, where the party had achieved its best result in 2005 and where Griffin himself would stand.

Greens. In September 2008 Caroline Lucas, the Green MEP for the South East Region since 1999, was elected as the first sole Green Party leader in England and Wales (winning 92% of the party vote), the party having dispensed with its joint leadership structure. The party's membership had liked the joint system – not least because it ensured that the party was represented publicly by both a man and a woman – but the media found it awkward, and political realities led to its abandonment.

With one notable exception, the period from 2005 until 2010 was one of steady progress for the Greens. In the 2006 local elections, they won 30 seats, an increase of 21. These included five seats in Lewisham and four in Norwich. A year later, they won 70 seats, making a net gain of 17 in England and eight in Scotland. The party could now boast 12 seats in both Brighton and Lancaster, as well as ten seats in Norwich and five in Glasgow. At the 2008 local elections, they won 47 seats, a net gain of five. The party increased its representation in Norwich to 13 seats, while it could boast seven councillors in Oxford and six in Stroud. Meanwhile, they maintained their position in the London Assembly elections, holding on to their two seats, and Siân Berry, the party's candidate in the Mayoral race polled 3.2% of first preference votes with 16.6% of second preferences, the latter a reasonable 3.4% improvement on 2004. The one notable exception was the Scottish parliamentary elections, where the separately-organised Scottish Green Party lost ground to the SNP surge (see below), losing five seats, and leaving it with just two MSPs, both in top-up seats, one in Glasgow, one in Edinburgh.

At the 2009 European elections, the Greens made modest progress, increasing their share of the vote by 2.4% on five years before, and retaining both their MEPs: Lucas and Jean Lambert (representing the London region). In the local elections held on the same day, the party won 18 seats, a further net gain of eight.

They would go into the 2010 election fielding 335 candidates, another record, and with three target seats. Significant efforts would go into Norwich South, where there was the chance to unseat Charles Clarke, but by far the most effort went into Brighton Pavilion, where Lucas was standing, and where they had polled over 20% in 2005.

Respect. Respect had been responsible for one of the most memorable results of the 2005 election, when George Galloway had taken the previously rock solid Labour seat of Bethnal Green & Bow. In the 2006 local elections, Respect won 16 seats, an increase of 13. Twelve of these gains were made in Tower Hamlets. In addition, the party's leader, Salma Yaqoob, who had stood unsuccessfully in the Birmingham Sparkbrook & Small Heath constituency at the 2005 election, was also elected with 50% of the vote in the Sparkbrook ward of Birmingham City Council.

But in 2007 Respect suffered from a serious internal rift when George Galloway, its only MP, split with members of the Socialist Workers' Party (SWP). Ostensibly, the split was caused by rows over candidate selection and internal democracy, although Galloway's decision to appear and behaviour whilst on the reality TV show *Celebrity Big Brother* did not help matters. The two factions argued over who would get to keep the party's name. Galloway eventually won that particular battle, while the breakaway SWP became known as Left List (and later Left Alternative). In the 2008 London elections, Respect chose not to field a candidate for the mayoralty race, but polled 2.5% of the vote in the London-wide (top-up) ballot.[4]

Respect was to stand just 11 candidates in 2010, down from 30 in 2005. Their best hope rested with Yaqoob, standing in Birmingham Hall Green. She was helped by the decision of the Greens not to field a candidate, and by comments from Dr Lynne Jones, the retiring Labour MP for nearby Birmingham Selly Oak who described her as 'an excellent candidate of great ability' and who refused to endorse the Labour candidate. Galloway did not stand again for the redrawn seat of Bethnal Green & Bow, preferring instead to stand in the neighbouring, newly-created, seat of Poplar & Limehouse.

Scottish National Party. The Scottish National Party (SNP) would fight the 2010 general election as a party of government. Under the skilful leadership of Alex Salmond they pushed Labour into second place in the 2007 Scottish elections, winning 47 seats to Labour's 46. The SNP made a remarkable 12 gains in the constituency seats (from nine in 2003 to 21 in 2007), along with eight further gains from the top-up seats (from 18 in 2003 to 26 in 2007). The latter came mostly at the expense of the smaller Scottish parties who suffered because of the media focus on the two 'big beasts' – the SNP and Labour. They were also helped by the splits inside the Scottish Socialist Party, when its former leader, Tommy Sheridan, broke away to form a rival party, Solidarity.

Salmond appealed not to a growing sense of nationalism, but to a general discontent among Scottish voters towards Labour, particularly Tony Blair's 'long goodbye' as Prime Minister. In an era of valence politics (where the two main parties in Scotland moved closer together ideologically), Scottish voters were more concerned with which party would best stand up for Scottish interests on the 'bread and butter' issues such as health and education. In line with Salmond's incremental route to independence, the SNP's 2007 campaign was 'independence-lite', assuaging residual fears among Scottish business figures, particularly the owner of Stagecoach, Brian Souter, whose donation of £500,000 represented a hefty sum for a small party not used to large individual gifts. The party's slogan, 'It's time... ', suggested a sense of anticipation among voters, in contrast to Scottish Labour under the leadership of Jack McConnell, who fought a negative campaign centred on the dangers of the break-up of the Union. Although Gordon Brown's intervention in the 2007 campaign narrowed the gap in the polls between Labour and the SNP in the final weeks, Salmond achieved a narrow victory on polling day, and formed a minority SNP administration at Holyrood. In the first ever set of Scottish local elections fought under the single transferable vote (held on the same day as the Scottish parliamentary elections), the SNP also did well, winning a total of 363 seats in Scotland, a net gain of 181 seats, to become the largest party in Scottish local government.

Salmond's long-term vision, outlined in February 2008, was of a modern, independent Scotland, part of an 'arc of prosperity' made up of small prosperous Northern European states such as Ireland, Iceland and Norway. His party's appeal reached its peak in the Glasgow East by-election in July 2008, when it defeated Labour on a by-election swing of 22.5%. But the banking crisis in the autumn of 2008, which adversely affected both Ireland and Iceland, as well as financial institutions with a Scotland heritage (most obviously RBS, where Salmond had been an economist before becoming an MP) cast doubts over Scotland's ability to survive economically as an independent nation. However, in June 2009, Salmond was still able to hail an 'historic' win in the European elections, winning the largest share of the vote in a European election in Scotland for the first time, polling 29.1% of the vote – a 10% increase on five years before – well ahead of Labour's 20.8%.

As the general election approached, commentators in Scotland questioned the SNP's ability to convince its supporters to turn out in a 'London' election where their leader wasn't even standing – Salmond having signalled his intention to stand down as a Westminster MP after 23 years. As Scottish voters contemplated the prospect of a Conservative government at Westminster, they started to drift back to Labour. In November 2008 Labour easily held off the SNP challenge in the Glenrothes by-election, as they did a year later in Glasgow North East, following the resignation of the former Speaker, Michael Martin. The First Minister set an ambitious target for the SNP of winning a total of 20 Westminster seats, meaning the SNP needed to take some unlikely targets, almost exclusively from Labour. It did not look likely. Going into the 2010 campaign, to be fought on the same boundaries as 2005, Scottish Labour would enjoy a poll lead of at least 10% (and in some cases more than 15%) over the SNP. A Nationalist electoral breakthrough looked distinctly unlikely, but a hung parliament could offer the party the potential for leverage.

Plaid. In 2006 Plaid Cymru engaged in an overhaul of its party structure, in which the Leader of the Party in the Assembly – Ieuan Wyn Jones – became its overall leader. The party also shortened its name to 'Plaid', although 'Plaid Cymru – The Party of Wales' remained its official title, and its party logo changed from the traditional green and red (depicting the red dragon and the triban, the three peaks of Wales) to a yellow Welsh

poppy. Plaid also professionalised its campaigning, smartening up the look of their posters and billboards.

In its new incarnation Plaid would also enter the 2010 general election as a party of government. In the 2007 Welsh Assembly elections, they won 15 seats, a modest gain of three seats on what they acknowledged was a poor performance in 2003. Initial expectations of an 'All-Wales' accord or rainbow coalition encompassing Plaid, the Liberal Democrats and the Conservatives faded, after the Welsh Liberal Democrats pulled out of the talks, and instead Ieuan Wyn Jones formed an unexpected 'One Wales' coalition with the Welsh Labour Party, which as the largest party, had won 26 seats. Jones was made Deputy First Minister and Minister for Economic Development and Transport in the new coalition government, working alongside the Labour Welsh First Minister. In February 2010, the National Assembly for Wales voted in favour of a referendum on whether the Assembly should be given law-making powers without the need to ask the Westminster Parliament for permission.

Plaid's electoral performance outside of the Assembly was more patchy. In the 2008 local elections in Wales, involving all 22 unitary authorities, Plaid won 205 seats, a modest gain of 31 on four years before. Their greatest gains were in Carmarthenshire (+14 seats) and Rhondda Cynon Taff (+7 seats) and their six gains in Caerphilly contributed to Labour losing overall control of the council. A year later, Plaid retained its one MEP in the European parliamentary elections, though its share of the vote was down slightly on 2004, finishing third behind Labour and the Conservatives.

Plaid Cymru (as was) won just three seats in the 2005 general election; Plaid were to target a further three in 2010. The aim was to forge a strong 'Celtic Alliance' with the SNP to ensure greater influence in any hung parliament – or what they preferred to call a 'balanced parliament'. The cooperation was symbolised during the election in a rare joint poster, '4 Wales, 4 Scotland', depicting two voters, one whose face has been painted with the Scottish Saltire, the other with the Welsh Red Dragon.

Northern Ireland. In March 2007, after an extended period in which the Northern Ireland Assembly had been suspended, two previously sworn enemies, Sinn Fein and the Democratic Unionist Party (DUP) agreed to enter government together. The result was a power-sharing government in which the DUP leader, Rev. Ian Paisley, became Northern Ireland's First Minister, while Sinn Fein's Martin McGuinness was appointed as his Deputy. It was, one commentator wrote, akin to the Molotov–Ribbentrop pact. The breakthrough was facilitated by a generous Treasury-funded settlement, and vital concessions from Sinn Fein which would eventually lead to the devolution of policing and justice to the Assembly.

At the 2007 Northern Ireland Assembly elections, the Province's two more 'extreme' parties, Sinn Fein and the DUP, continued to pick up votes at the expense of their more moderate rivals, the Social Democratic and Labour Party (SDLP) and the Ulster Unionist Party (UUP). Sinn Fein's share of the vote rose by 3%, and they gained four seats, whilst the SDLP lost 2% and two seats compared with 2003. On the other side of the sectarian divide, the DUP gained 4% and four seats at the expense of the UUP, whose vote share fell 8% on 2003, resulting in a loss of nine seats. Following its disastrous performance at the 2005 general election in which it had lost five out of its six Westminster seats, David Trimble had stood down as the UUP leader after ten years in charge, to be replaced by Sir Reg Empey. The change of leader, however, did not herald a change in fortunes for the Ulster Unionists: the (bad) joke doing the rounds was that the party was 'stuck on Empey'. In July 2008, in an effort to revive his party's fortunes, Empey established a joint working group with the Conservative Party to examine closer ties, and in February 2009, the Ulster Unionists agreed to field joint candidates in future elections to the House of Commons and the European Parliament under the name 'Ulster Conservative and Unionists – New Force'. The only remaining UUP MP at Westminster – Lady Sylvia Hermon – refused to join, immediately blunting the party's chances.

In June 2009, Sinn Fein topped the poll in the Northern Ireland European elections, when the party's MEP, Bairbre de Brun, was the only candidate to reach the required quota of 25% on her first preference votes. The Ulster Unionist/Conservative candidate, Jim Nicholson finished in second place, ahead of the DUP's Diane Dodds in third place. The DUP had suffered from a splintering of its vote, following the formation of a more hardline party calling itself Traditional Unionist Voice (TUV), which rejected the idea of the DUP entering into coalition with Sinn Fein. TUV's party leader, Jim Allister, finished fourth in European elections, but polled a respectable 66,197 first preference votes.

The DUP's long-serving leader, Rev. Ian Paisley, had stood down in April 2008. Peter Robinson, his successor as DUP leader, soon became mired in scandal. In January 2010, Robinson was forced to reveal that his wife, Iris Robinson, had had an extra-marital affair with a 19-year-old man. When it was revealed that the aptly-named Mrs Robinson had also failed to declare £50,000 in loans to her teenage lover, her husband temporarily stood down as Northern Ireland First Minister. Arlene Foster was appointed as Acting First Minister, but Peter Robinson carried on as Party Leader, heading crucial talks with Sinn Fein over the devolution of policing and justice powers to the Northern Ireland Assembly. Within weeks, Robinson resumed his post as First Minister. Meanwhile, two remaining paramilitary groups – the Ulster Defence Association (UDA) and the Irish National Liberation Army (INLA) – announced that they had decommissioned their weapons in time for the St Valentine's Day deadline. These carefully choreographed moves helped to facilitate the historic transfer of policing and justice powers to the Northern Ireland Assembly in February 2010. In the same month, the SDLP elected Margaret Ritchie to replace its leader Mark Durkan. As a result, by the time of the 2010 general election, Sinn Fein President Gerry Adams was the only main party leader in Northern Ireland to survive from the 2005 general election.

Notes

1. In April 2008, Spink had announced he was joining, and was labelled as 'UKIP' by the House authorities; by March 2009, he was describing himself as an independent, saying that he had never formally joined the party.
2. See Matthew Goodwin, 'In Search of the Winning Formula: Nick Griffin and the "Modernization" of the British National Party', in R. Eatwell and M.J. Goodwin (eds), *The New Extremism in 21st Century Britain* (London: Routledge, 2010), pp. 169–90.
3. See Robert Ford and Matthew Goodwin, 'Angry White Men: Individual and Contextual Predictors of Support for the British National Party', *Political Studies*, 58:1 (2010), 1–25.
4. In addition, Left List polled 0.9% in the London-wide (top-up) Assembly elections.

1. Surrounded by the Cabinet, Gordon Brown announces a general election to be held on 6 May.

2. David Cameron addresses a party rally in Bristol.

3. Nick Clegg, with his wife Miriam Gonzalez Durantez, addresses a campaign rally in Sheffield.

4. Peter Mandelson dances in the Tower Ballroom in Blackpool.

5. Gordon Brown and Gillian Duffy in conversation in Rochdale.

6. A Conservative debate rehearsal, with Jeremy Hunt (as Clegg, *left*) and Damian Green (as Brown, *right*); Michael Gove asks the questions.

7. A Labour debate rehearsal, with Alastair Campbell (as Cameron, *left*) and Theo Bertram (as Clegg, *centre*).

8. Not a rehearsal: Cameron, Clegg and Brown in the third and final televised debate in Birmingham on 29 April.

9. Gordon Brown's notes during the second televised debate.

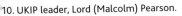
10. UKIP leader, Lord (Malcolm) Pearson.

11. SNP leader, Alex Salmond.

12. Plaid leader, Ieuan Wyn Jones.

13. Green leader, Caroline Lucas, after casting her vote in Brighton.

14. BNP leader, Nick Griffin, listening to Margaret Hodge after the declaration in Barking.

15. The wreckage of Nigel Farage's aircraft, 6 May.

16. The three party leaders at the VE day ceremony, 8 May.

17. The Conservative negotiating team: Oliver Letwin, William Hague and George Osborne (Ed Llewellyn not shown).

18. The Liberal Democrat negotiating team: Chris Huhne, Andrew Stunell and Danny Alexander (David Laws not shown).

19. The outgoing Prime Minister, with his wife Sarah and their two children, after he announced he was resigning, 11 May.

20. The incoming Prime Minister being greeted by Her Majesty the Queen, 11 May.

21. David Cameron and his wife Samantha meet Cabinet Secretary Gus O'Donnell after entering 10 Downing Street, 11 May 2010.

7
Losing It in January:
The Coming of the Election

In the last months of 2009 the Conservatives put the finishing touches to material for six weeks of campaigning, to begin at the start of January and to last until the party's Spring Forum. 'On 4 January,' said one member of the Cameron team, 'the election campaign begins.' In reality, though, what began in January was what US politicians would call the 'near-term campaign'. All parties have launched such campaigns in recent elections, some months before the general election proper begins. They do this in part to try to set the agenda, but also to test policies, themes and the effectiveness of their organisation. In 2010, neither of the main parties would go on to have a smooth near-term campaign, but it was especially difficult for the Conservatives. Looking back after the election, one of Cameron's most senior advisers would claim that 'we lost it in January'.

The Conservatives' preparations were lent some urgency as a result of the party's poll lead narrowing in December, and the chance of the Prime Minister calling an election in March 2010, a possibility some Conservatives took seriously. The plan was to 'hit January very very hard' (as one of those close to Cameron put it), releasing policies from the draft manifesto, backed up with statements, posters, and speeches. The draft manifesto's overall theme was both personal and governmental responsibility. Each policy chapter began with a statement of the party's values, what had gone wrong under Labour and how a Conservative government would bring improvement. The campaign began with the NHS chapter, and was to be followed by what Conservatives called the 'three brokens' – society, economy and politics – before moving on to other policies. It was later claimed that the party had promised (and then failed) to release a new policy a day, but this was never the intention.

Most of the policies were not new – the novelty was that they had been collected together, as preparation for the manifesto – and the aim had never been to make one announcement every day, a claim that frustrated Conservative campaigners who knew that they would never be able to live up to it.

The Conservative campaign slogan, 'Year for Change', was a deliberate echo of Barack Obama's 'Time for Change' in the 2008 US Presidential campaign. David Cameron and shadow ministers reinforced the message by declaring, 'We can't go on like this', a phrase Shadow Cabinet members were told to use repeatedly and which was to become a tag on the party's posters. 'We want', said Andy Coulson, 'people to become sick of that phrase by the time of the election', although the slogan soon disappeared. The emphasis on David Cameron recognised his popularity and the voters' ignorance of most other shadow ministers. The party launched a massive poster campaign, with posters on 1,000 sites, with a picture of a (tie-less) David Cameron, alongside the slogan: 'We can't go on like this. I'll cut the deficit, not the NHS.' The curious juxtaposition of the two phrases reflected the poster's genesis. Originating from a committee in which there was no agreement over the key message, it was an uneasy compromise between differing viewpoints. The slogan was what car mechanics call a cut-and-shut job, bolting together two phrases, each favoured by a different member of the committee.

Labour had been aware before Christmas that the Conservatives were planning their January offensive. Downing Street staff had seen the Conservative posters and had detailed knowledge of the poster sites. With no similar resources to buy up poster sites, Labour began its near-term campaign with a press conference and a bulky policy document – *Conservative Tax and Spending Promises* – highlighting an alleged £34 billion 'black hole' in Conservative spending plans. Work on the dossier had been ongoing since July 2009, growing out of the links between Treasury and No 10 aides (see p. 65) and there had been earlier discussions about when to deploy it, before deciding to use it to disrupt the Conservative campaign launch. Labour was sanguine about the effect it would have, assuming that the Conservatives would be prepared for the charges that would be thrown at them; some of the data from the dossier had been drip-fed to the media in late 2009 to little impact and the Chancellor's private view was that the dossier would throw some grit in the wheels of the Conservative campaign, but not much more. They were to be pleasantly surprised.

'We can't go on like this'

Peter Brookes, *The Times*, 5 January 2010
(© Peter Brookes/*The Times*/N.I. Syndication 2010)

Labour ministers had long complained that the Conservatives received an easy ride in the media. As part of a rethinking of policies drawn up before the economic downturn, the Conservatives had already back-tracked on some of their spending promises, abandoning plans to build an extra 5,000 prison places, to grant tax relief on the savings of standard rate taxpayers and introduce single rooms in hospitals. But the confusion over policy, created in part because of the Labour dossier, was more damaging. Under pressure over spending commitments, in a BBC interview on 4 January, Cameron suggested the proposed tax support for marriage – a distinctive and early Cameron pledge and a signifier of his support for the family – might not be delivered over the course of a parliament because of the state of the public finances. He quickly corrected himself and confessed to 'messing up' over whether it was a promise or an aspiration. Conservative claims that ending Child Tax Credits for families with an income of over £50,000 would produce savings of £400 million, were also challenged by both the Treasury and the independent Institute for Fiscal Studies. To raise that amount, the Treasury argued, the cuts would need to be applied to households with incomes of £30,000 and above. And Conservative charges that Labour had presided over a large rise in violent crime were rebuffed as 'misleading' by the UK Statistics Authority.

The Conservative poster itself caused controversy, with claims that the photo of David Cameron had been airbrushed; Conservatives' denials met widespread scepticism. It proved easy to spoof, and spoof versions circulated on the internet, helped by a website mydavidcameron.com, which allowed users to design their own versions.[1] There were some unforced errors, such as the typo in one briefing document, *Labour's Two Nations*, in which a misplaced decimal point inflated the teenage pregnancy rate in the most deprived parts of the UK from 5.4% to 54%. Relatively trivial in themselves these slips exposed a fragility in the Conservative operation, and boosted morale amongst Labour staff, who suddenly found that they could land blows. Labour's campaign manager, Douglas Alexander, privately expressed surprise and delight over the Conservatives' 'glass jaw'. Combined with a media focus on the impact of the wintry weather in Britain and extensive coverage of the earthquake in Haiti on 12 January, the Labour counter-attack had the effect of seriously blunting the Conservatives' planned policy launches, preventing the party building the momentum they had hoped for.

On 25 January Cameron, speaking at the World Economic Forum in Davos, stated that spending cuts under a Conservative government in 2010 would not be 'swingeing' and tackling the deficit in earnest would start in 2011. The speech was a shift in mood from the rhetoric of the previous autumn about the coming age of austerity and the need for deep and rapid cuts in spending to reassure the markets and protect Britain's triple-A credit rating. In part, the change could be explained by the reported 0.1% growth in the final quarter of 2009 which showed how fragile the economic recovery was (although growth was subsequently revised upwards to 0.4%) but the parties' private research revealed voter unease about anticipated cuts in front-line services. Not all Conservative campaigners appreciated that change was a double-edged message and might alarm voters seeking reassurance in difficult times. Voters acknowledged the need to tackle the deficit and cut spending but not at the cost of cutting specific services. Labour focus groups found that voters wanted change and associated the Conservatives with it. Yet when asked what they expected a Conservative Britain would be like the voters' response was often unsure. Peter Mandelson seized on apparent Conservative uncertainties over their policies in January to argue that the Conservatives could not be trusted and that they were therefore a risk; Labour, he argued, should emulate what the Conservatives had done to Labour in the run-up to the 1992 election, when they had attacked their credibility. 'You get them on credibility,' said one No 10 staffer, 'which leads on to trustworthiness. And then change becomes a risk.'

An ICM/*Guardian* poll in late January reported that two-thirds of voters agreed it was 'time for a change' (including 38% of 2005 Labour voters), compared with a quarter who favoured continuity. But a measure of the Conservatives' failure to build on the public mood was that less than 40% of the same poll indicated they would vote for the party. A private survey conducted for the Conservatives found voters' four main concerns about the party were: it would in a crisis take care of the rich; it would not make changes; the problems were so severe that no party could tackle them; and it would weaken the NHS. A common theme for all parties' focus groups was that the voters were fed up with Labour but were still unsure about the Conservatives. 'Voters like Cameron and many are seriously thinking of voting Tory, yet they struggle for a sense of what they will do that is different,' said the organiser of a Labour focus group.

Conservative commentators were growing impatient with Cameron's repeated emphasis on change and called for more policy substance and 'clear blue water' between Labour and Conservative. Tax cuts, quick spending reductions to tackle the deficit, and control of immigration were favoured policy prescriptions. Fraser Nelson, in his Sir Keith Joseph Memorial Lecture in February, complained that Cameron was in danger of becoming like the pre-Thatcher Conservative leaders who pursued the wisp of 'the middle ground' and argued 'It's hard to see what's Tory about the Tories.'

Within the Cameron camp, there was a long-running tension between those who wanted to remain positive about the Conservative 'brand' and those who felt that they should be attacking the Government more. The former group believed that Labour and Gordon Brown were finished – 'toast', as one described them – and the public needed no further reasons not to vote Labour. What they did need, however, were reasons to vote *for* the Conservatives, particularly in those parts of the country where reassurance was necessary. So focusing on Labour's failings was a waste of time. What the Conservatives needed to be doing instead was to strengthen their own brand. The latter group rejected this analysis, and wanted to keep their 'foot on Gordon Brown's neck' (a phrase George Osborne would use to his team) until the very end. Positive messages were all very well, but the biggest asset the Conservatives had was the record of the government and the prime minister and it was foolish to ignore it. Although the differences between the two of them could be exaggerated, key figures around Cameron reflected this different view. Andy Coulson, as befitted his media brief, wanted daily initiatives to keep the focus on Brown and the poor state of the economy, an approach consistent with the adage that oppositions don't win elections but governments lose them; Steve Hilton was more concerned about the long-term value of the Cameron brand and still pressed for a message of political change and positive Conservative values. The result was frequent confusion about the messages. A thoughtful speech in early February by Cameron on reforming 'broken politics', by cutting the number of MPs, ensuring greater transparency and reducing the cost of politics, was instead heavily pre-briefed as a personal attack on Gordon Brown, and reported as such.

A feature of the Conservative campaign team was that Osborne, Hilton and Coulson, all strong-minded individuals, had their own, not necessarily rival, views of the way ahead. Osborne regarded himself as a chairman rather than the director of the group. Until January 2010 they had looked to Cameron to adjudicate when there were differences of view between the main figures. But the decision was then taken that Cameron should stand back from day-to-day involvement. A result was a lack of direction – and confusion over the poster was an outcome of this failure. 'Instead of leading, George became part of the argument, as Coulson and Hilton did not recognise his authority', said a member of the leadership team. Tensions between Coulson and Hilton ('unless the two sort things out, nothing happens', said a Cameroon) were defused somewhat when they agreed to share an office together – a room known by those in Millbank as the 'love pod'. A colleague, relieved to see the men sharing an office, sent a bouquet of flowers to the pair. But the fundamental strategic issue of how to approach the election campaign was never resolved.

By mid-February the Conservatives had lost momentum. The Tory lead in the polls had been halved in recent weeks. In the *Spectator*, the well-informed James Forsyth commented that 'the Tory situation is now verging on the critical'.[2] Cameron's colleagues and advisers debated the steps needed for the party to consolidate its lead in the polls and ensure a clear working majority in the new House of Commons. Despite Cameron's small team meeting daily, often twice a day and sometimes more, and working in close proximity to one another on their corridor in the Norman Shaw South building, there still seemed to be a lack of an overarching theme. Insiders complained that the war book was behind schedule, the various policy announcements lacked coherence, meetings were long and rambling, and there was no clear sense of direction. George Osborne, combining the duties of campaign coordinator and shadow chancellor, appeared overstretched. To reduce the load on Osborne the party's former Research Director, George Bridges – an advocate of a more forceful approach to the fight with Labour – had been employed from January.

As an acknowledgement of the need for fresh thinking other additions were made to the campaign team. Michael Gove, the highly regarded education spokesman and a former journalist, joined in early February, ostensibly to help sharpen the attack on Labour. Gove operated largely, as did Hilton, by approaching Cameron privately. Such back channels to the leader were used at times to overturn decisions of formal meetings. Andrew Cooper, who had conducted much of the party's private polling over the Parliament, was invited to join the team at Millbank and given access to all the party's research as were the American political consultants who were helping with preparations for the television debates. Meetings became longer and less decisive. 'More people, more voices, the last thing we need at this stage,' said one disaffected member.

When the Conservatives gathered for their annual spring conference at Brighton on 27–28 February the mood was not upbeat. The eight weeks of the campaign had won few plaudits. The party had lost ground in the polls and appeared to lack a clear message. A YouGov poll for the *Sunday Times* that weekend had the Conservative lead down to 2%, a result which would have given Labour the most seats, and that despite a week of negative media stories concerning allegations about the Prime Minister's irascible behaviour. Before the conference Cameron invited colleagues and advisers to his home to discuss how the party could regain the initiative. One who attended the meeting said, 'We've allowed it to be a referendum on us rather than them. We've learnt that lesson and in future it will be more about the government.' Cameron's conclusion, texted to the team the following day, was that he had not found what he called 'the navel-gazing' useful and in future they should stick relentlessly to the message of change and highlight Brown's record as Prime Minister. His spring conference speech on 28 February laid out the party's six key pledges for the election campaign: boosting enterprise, shoring up families, dealing with the deficit, backing the NHS, raising standards in schools, and cleaning up politics.

Cameron's plans over the next ten days were lost in the media frenzy following Lord Ashcroft's admission on 1 March that as a non-domicile he did not pay UK tax on his considerable overseas earnings. It had been understood that the award of the peerage in 2000 had been conditional on his being a full UK taxpayer, but sections of the media had raised doubts about his status for several months. It was now revealed that he had renegotiated with officials his undertaking to become a permanent British resident to being a 'long term' one, enabling him to retain his non-dom status and gain the tax advantages. He had done nothing illegal but had not kept William Hague, who as party leader had nominated him for the peerage, fully informed about his status until six months earlier and Hague in turn had not informed Cameron until a month earlier.

For all the panic on the Labour side about the impact of 'Ashcroft money', Conservatives pointed out that Ashcroft's funding amounted to only 1% of party expenditure during 2009 and his contribution was more concerned with the ground war strategy, particularly the insistence on candidates having an approved business plan and taking a more hard-headed approach to the targeting of seats. After an 18-month-long investigation the Electoral Commission ruled that the £5.1 million funding to the party from Ashcroft's company Bearwood Services was legal. Ashcroft was not a hands-on executive and left the key decisions about target seats to his key staff, Gavin Barwell and Stephen Gilbert, and the private polling to the latter. He did not support Cameron's decision to take part in the TV debates, partly because it might offset the benefits from his ground war campaign and partly because he was confident he could measure the impact of the latter but not the former.

Apologists over his tax status pointed to Lord Paul, a Labour donor and a non-dom. But the media focus on Ashcroft damaged the Conservatives; a Cameroon admitted, 'It stopped us getting our messages across.' Cameron was said to have acknowledged in mid-2009 that he knew something needed to be done about Ashcroft, even before the details of his tax status became known, yet nothing was done. It was a self-inflicted blow, and the unflattering coverage fed charges that he led a party for the rich who played to a different set of rules from the general public and that the leadership was weak.

On 31 March, at the Coin Street neighbourhood centre on London's South Bank, Cameron and 11 members of his Shadow Cabinet launched their 'Big Society' proposals, trailed in the Hugo Young lecture of the year before (see p. 89). Cameron described the concept as 'both incredibly ambitious, but also refreshingly modest'. Ambitious because 'its aims are sweeping – building a fairer, richer, safer Britain, where opportunity is more equal and poverty is abolished'. But also modest, 'because it's not about some magic new plan dreamed up in Whitehall and imposed from on high. It's about enabling and encouraging people to come together to solve their problems and make life better.' The Big Society, he claimed, would replace the Big State – which he had attacked in his conference speech the year before. The policies themselves – such as allowing local groups to set up schools, or elected police commissioners – were not new, but the Coin Street event was the most ambitious attempt to stitch them together to create an overarching narrative about what the Conservatives stood for. Those around Cameron were pleased with the event and its coverage. For more than four years, they felt, they had been trying to explain the purpose of a Cameron administration. The Big Society, they believed, was it.

The failure of Labour's 'snow plot' of January 2010 (see p. 59) had the effect of confirming that Gordon Brown would be leading the Labour Party into the election. It also had what one Cabinet minister called 'a benign consequence' of forcing the Prime Minister to confirm to the PLP on 11 January that Peter Mandelson would be in charge of the election campaign strategy, while Harriet Harman would also have an enhanced role. Harman had told Brown the previous November that she had no objection to Mandelson directing the campaign; what she wanted was Brown to make a decision and to be more collegial. Mandelson and Harman, along with Douglas Alexander, chaired a meeting of Labour Party staff in Victoria Street that morning to emphasise their roles. Pressed by senior colleagues to be more collegial, Brown also announced that Cabinet ministers would be fully involved in preparing campaign strategy. Brown's empowering of senior figures broke what many had come to regard as the No 10 logjam. 'He wanted to run it himself,' said one of those close to him, 'and he's been made to realise that he can't; he is now the candidate.'

Mandelson's involvement in Labour's national campaigns went back as far as 1987. In November 2009, when he had hoped to be appointed the EU foreign policy chief (a post eventually given to Baroness Ashton), he had not been optimistic about the party's election prospects. But in the New Year he began to believe there were 'grounds for reassessing' the political situation, a phrase soon repeated by others in the campaign team. He reasoned that the recession and increase in unemployment had not been as bad as had been expected, that Brown could gain credit for his actions in tackling the economic crisis, and that David Cameron was showing brittleness under pressure. He believed that although the Conservatives were 'the public's default position' many voters had not yet been convinced by Cameron. Despite having his own department to run Mandelson spent a lot of time with Brown; the two were often on the phone and Mandelson frequently visited Number 10, often twice a day. When ministers and Brown's aides told him he was the only person who could stand up to the Prime Minister, he would reply, 'He did listen to me but he wouldn't heed the advice.' His continuing worry was that the party could not sound credible about the economy as long as Brown appeared to be in denial, and in disagreement with his Chancellor, about the need for cuts as part of the programme for tackling the deficit.

Douglas Alexander had been a key player in Labour's election campaigns since 1997 and was a close student of US politics and, in particular, the Obama campaign. He knew that 2010 would be held in a different context from the previous three general elections; Labour was the underdog, its leader was unpopular and economic growth could not be assumed, indeed the opposite. Whichever party won would have to introduce measures that would depress the living standards of most of the electorate. How could this package be presented persuasively? Alexander acknowledged Labour could not fight its traditional top-down campaign, directed from the centre. Influenced both by a shortage of funds and by the Obama campaign he wanted Labour to fight what he called a word of mouth election: backed by as much direct mail as they could afford, Labour activists should use phones, the internet and face-to-face meetings to address the concerns of target voters in the key seats. Believing that 'elections are a competition of questions' about the campaign agenda he was determined that the election should not be a referendum on Labour or about change – he saw both as certain losers. Instead, they had to make it a choice about the future.

Labour's war book stated presciently that the 2010 election would be the 'most presidential election to date', noting 'Labour lags on leadership'. Indeed, the war book listed so many potential negatives that when it came to analysis of the party's strengths and weaknesses the authors had to use a smaller font size to detail the weaknesses.[3] The strategy group of Cabinet ministers considered the war book on 9 February and the Cabinet on 23 February. There were two versions, the full one and a leakable one with key material removed, although neither leaked. Unlike the Conservative war book, which was a functional document, of around 100 pages (or the Lib Dem one which was a detailed policy discussion of almost 500 pages), Labour's campaign master plan was more strategic, a PowerPoint presentation of fewer than 30 slides, identifying the main battle lines around which the election was to be fought. The Conservative narrative, it predicted, would be: 'Britain is broken. Gordon Brown and Labour taxed, borrowed and spent in the good times and then, like every Labour Government before, ran out of money. Now we are all paying the price in higher borrowing, higher taxes and higher unemployment.' Labour's strategy was simple: 'Change is the default option for the public. Optimism and a better future is what they really want. This is the battle ground.'

Ed Miliband, with Nick Pearce and Patrick Diamond from Number 10, continued to hold meetings with Cabinet ministers about items for the manifesto; discussions followed a template of legislation, if necessary, and efficiency savings. Brown urged ministers at a political Cabinet in late November 2009 to come up with bold ideas. Ministers made presentations to a series of political Cabinets around such themes as living standards, crime and policing, economic growth and immigration. Some ministers were defensive, some appeared exhausted and some appeared to be held back by officials who were cautious about radical initiatives so late in the day. Brown and his staff found the collective discussion a useful lever to force ministers to be more active and imaginative. In contrast to previous Labour manifesto discussions ministers were discouraged from suggesting schemes which involved even modest expenditure. Ed Balls's proposal for free school meals for all primary school children was judged too costly. There was support for Andy Burnham's new policy on social care for the elderly, Andrew Adonis's plans for improved high speed rail links, and Jack Straw's political reforms. Despite operating within such clear guidelines, some insiders felt ministers never satisfactorily struck a balance between building on what Labour had done (from either 1997 or 2007) and starting anew.

Lack of money was a major and depressing constraint on Labour's election planning. In the 2005 general election the party had spent near to the permitted maximum of £18 million. A campaign in 2007 would have seen around £11 million spent but in 2010 the party was initially looking at a budget closer to £4 million. It had very limited resources for posters or press advertising whereas the Conservatives could put up 1,000 posters at the drop of a hat. Labour tried to make a virtue of its poverty; spending money on posters, literature, and election broadcasts was decried as 'old politics' and they stressed instead the extent to which they would be innovative with free media, including the internet. But complaining about 'old politics' is what you do when you do not have any money to spend on established techniques. Labour strategists acknowledged the limitations imposed by their financial position – they would have liked to have afforded proper poster campaigns, instead of occasionally using the 'launches' of virtual posters to generate publicity. Other key parts of their campaigning (including polling, direct mail and the leader's tour) had to be scaled back for lack of finance. The party was staffed at approximately one-third of the level it had been at the equivalent periods in 2004 and 2000. An early promise to provide direct mail support to seats that increased their voter contacts had to be temporarily withdrawn, simply because of insufficient funds.

Most of the focus groups were conducted by the veteran party official Greg Cook and the party's pollsters, the Benenson polling team, did some pre-campaign testing of messages. The agency suggested that the party's most effective message was that the Conservatives' inheritance tax proposals would deliver a large tax cut to 3,000 of the country's richest households.[4] The US advisers argued that Obama had never had any attack line as powerful. Other themes were Labour's 'fair' versus the Conservatives' 'unfair' spending cuts and the former's message of optimism versus the latter's of austerity. Mandelson, Alexander and Justin Forsyth from Number 10 prepared the initial campaign grid and Alexander held meetings with party officials at party headquarters to review the election nuts and bolts. The main players also gathered weekly in the Cabinet Office for brainstorming sessions.

A narrowing of the Conservative lead in the polls in the first weeks of 2010, Conservative mistakes, and reports that party support among the working class and in the north was consolidating, raised Labour spirits. Most, but not all, of the key campaigners felt that at last they were all working for a common purpose. However, the earlier prevarication over structures and responsibilities meant Labour was seriously behind in its election planning; one official estimated in March that they were still about six months behind schedule. As late as February there was still uncertainty about who would be doing what in Victoria Street in the campaign – and there remained disagreements between key figures about what Labour should say about the economy. Alistair Darling still argued privately with Gordon Brown over whether or not Labour should own up to future cuts in public expenditure. The Prime Minister (supported by Ed Balls) wanted to forbid any mention of cuts, and pressed for a manifesto pledge to rule out any increase in VAT in the next Parliament, so creating dividing lines with the Conservatives. The Chancellor, committed to halving the deficit over the next four years, and worried about adverse reactions from the financial markets, argued that was simply unsustainable given Brown's resistance to major spending cuts. He was supported by Mandelson and another Cabinet minister mocked the Brown view as 'simplistic'. Brown's mocking of David Cameron's inheritance tax policy as being dreamt up 'on the playing fields of Eton' at Prime Minister's Questions (a line suggested by Alastair Campbell) raised fears amongst some New Labour figures that the Prime Minister might be thinking of a 'core vote strategy'. 'He's not that stupid,' said Peter Mandelson, probably as much in hope as in expectation, 'and he never uses the phrase.'

No 10 staff and ministers took note of a report from Peter Kellner of YouGov of a trend for Lib Dem voters in Con–Lab marginals to support

Labour as a second choice (as had happened in 1997 and 2001). This encouraged Brown in February to press for a Commons vote promising a referendum on the Alternative Vote, a scheme which allowed voters to rank their preferences. The policy had been agreed by a Cabinet committee the previous November, but had been on hold, stymied by opposition from the Government whips, both individually (most of the senior whips opposed the plan) but also because they thought it would split the parliamentary party. When Jack Straw had addressed the PLP on the subject it was clear that Labour MPs were evenly divided over the proposal. The policy was almost dropped, but the polling evidence persuaded Brown to push on with it. Sceptical MPs had the politics of the issue explained to them. It would appeal to liberal-minded voters in the marginals, it might help appeal to the Lib Dems in the event of a hung parliament, and the predictable opposition of the Conservatives would show they were 'anti-reform', so creating another of the Prime Minister's much-loved dividing lines. But it would – as the whips reassured the most recalcitrant MPs – stand no chance of reaching the statute book before the election.

All surveys reported that Gordon Brown remained a drag on Labour's support. 'Toxic on the doorstep', more than one MP said. In an effort to show the leader's 'human side', an hour-long ITV interview with Piers Morgan in front of a live audience was arranged and Brown gave an interview with *Tesco* magazine ('At Home With the Browns') in which he talked about the death of his mother. Number 10 held several rehearsals for the Morgan interview, with Peter Mandelson, Alastair Campbell and others coaching the Prime Minister and being brutal with him when his performance was not adequate. The judgement of one of those present was, 'Better, but needs to be even better', reminiscent of a teacher grading an under-performing pupil. Some scoffed at the sight of Brown's (and his wife, Sarah's) emotional response to questioning about the loss of his first baby, but the programme had an audience of 4.2 million (peaking at 5.2 million), and Labour's polling found that it had 'an amazing cut through', reaching out especially to women, some of whom took a 'motherly attitude' to Brown. 'It was', one Labour staffer reported, 'the single most positive thing that Number 10 has done.'

Despite claims that No 10 staff would try to shield the Prime Minister from the extent of his unpopularity, he was well aware of the problem. Those around him sometimes joked with him that five more years of Gordon Brown did not seem like a particularly appealing sell to the electorate. Brown himself came up with the idea that he might announce that he would stand down a year into a new Parliament. After some discussion, the idea was dropped for the time, but not by Brown. On the eve of the campaign, on Good Friday 2 April, he astonished his aides and Mandelson by proposing that when the election was called he would ask for a year-long mandate to tackle the economic crisis and reform the political system. He would put a range of constitutional reforms to a referendum a year hence and if he lost he would resign. The logic was that whilst five more years with him might be excessive, pledging to stay on for a year, in which he resolved the economic crisis and brought in far-reaching constitutional reforms, might be more appealing, especially given voters' doubts about David Cameron. David Muir supported the idea, but others were more sceptical, not least because it might repeat what they saw as the mistake made by Tony Blair before the 2005 election, and after.

Allegations about Brown's bullying of staff and leadership style contained in Andrew Rawnsley's book, *The End of the Party*, created unflattering headlines but did not seem to damage Brown or Labour in the polls. During the height of the furore – when it was alleged that the Cabinet Secretary, Gus O'Donnell had confronted Brown about his bullying behaviour – Downing Street was forced to issue three separate denials. The story was soon bogged down in claim and counter-claim, and was seen as a Westminster-village story. Labour's focus groups showed that some people felt more favourably towards the Prime Minister, the allegations of bullying being seen as a proxy for strength (although usually 'by those who didn't understand the details').

Addressing delegates at the spring party conference in Warwick on 20 February Brown unveiled the party's election slogan, 'A Future Fair For All'. He pledged to support jobs, protect front-line services, and work for economic recovery and appealed to voters, particularly former supporters who had turned away from the party, to 'take a second look at us and take a long hard look at them'. He also unveiled the party's five election pledges:

- secure the economic recovery – including halving the deficit;
- raise family living standards;
- protect front-line services;
- build a high-tech economy;
- strengthen fairness in communities – including the introduction of a points system for immigration.

The pledge card had been a standard Labour gambit in the previous three general elections, but the pledges were less specific than in the past. In his speech, the Prime Minister reiterated the strategy of acknowledging Labour's position in the opinion polls and painting Labour as the underdogs. He also made a dig about Labour launching policy pledges whilst all the Conservatives could do was to announce a change of advertising team.

Labour, however, suffered three setbacks during March which eroded some of their momentum. On 5 March the Prime Minister gave his public evidence before the Chilcot Inquiry into Iraq. Chilcot's original intention had been to interview serving ministers, including the Prime Minister, after the election, but – in the face of opposition pressure – this delay proved unsustainable. Requiring days of preparation, the inquiry was a massive distraction in the run-up to the election, but Brown initially appeared to have come out of the session well; yet 12 days later he had to write to Chilcot to correct his evidence, in which he had erroneously claimed that the defence budget had risen in real terms in every year under Labour. Second, a strike amongst British Airways cabin crew gave the Conservatives the opportunity to remind voters of the links between Labour and the unions. And, in an unwelcome echo of the expenses scandal, three former Labour Cabinet ministers were filmed undercover by Channel 4's *Dispatches* discussing the fees they would charge a lobbying firm to use their contacts to influence public policy. Stephen Byers, Patricia Hewitt, and Geoff Hoon, along with a backbencher Margaret Moran, were quickly suspended from the PLP. Byers' comment that he was 'like a cab for hire' was particularly damaging.

The 'good news' in Alistair Darling's Budget on 24 March was that the deficit for the year was a slightly less staggering £167 billion compared with initial Treasury forecasts of £178 billion. Having reaffirmed the commitment to halve the deficit over four years, in a broadly revenue neutral Budget the Chancellor launched a 'smash-and-grab' raid on Conservative policy, by announcing a two-year stamp duty holiday on property purchases under £250,000 for first-time buyers and financed it with a permanent increase in the duty from 4 to 5% for the sale of properties above £1 million. Commentators noted the lack of detail on how and where the cuts would be made – with a Comprehensive Spending Review (CSR) scheduled for the autumn – and that much depended on growth forecasts that most independent forecasters considered optimistic. The other main theme of Darling's Budget was increasing the role that Government could play as a 'force for good' in unlocking private sector investment. 'Partnership not indifference', Darling argued, would help to secure economic recovery. This approach represented a philosophical change; New Labour had previously rejected the idea of 'picking winners' in British industry. Short term, however, it made good sense politically, not only challenging the Conservatives over their *laissez-faire* attitude towards British industry, but also turning the debate at the election into one about the future.

The Conservatives decided to commission advertising from M & C Saatchi. Earlier work had been by Euro RSCG, including a series of posters launched in mid-February featuring three people who were deciding to vote Conservative for the first time, which appeared at over 1,500 sites. The Conservatives denied the move had anything to do with their poll lead narrowing, and was merely an attempt to expand their campaign, although the February posters were the last work Euro RSCG undertook for the party before the election. The Saatchi posters – at another 850 poster sites – were much more negative.[5] Each depicted a smiling Prime Minister (rarely a happy sight) along with one of seven negative slogans:

- I let 80,000 criminals out early
- I doubled the tax rate for the poor
- I took billions from pensions
- I doubled the national debt
- I lost £6 billion selling off Britain's gold
- I caused record youth unemployment
- I increased the gap between rich and poor.

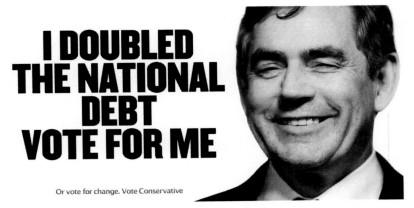

The various iterations of Conservative posters – and further posters would be both positive and negative in turn – were a microcosm of the broader debate within the Conservative campaign: should they go negative or positive? When negotiations between the parties to reach a measure of agreement on plans for tackling the social care of the elderly broke down, the Conservatives had quickly prepared a hard-hitting 'death tax' poster announcing 'Gordon Brown wants £20,000 when you die'. The debate was to remain essentially unresolved, and every time the party launched a set of posters, the Conservatives would have the same internal debate, between those who favoured attacks on Labour and those who favoured a positive message to bolstering the Conservatives' image.

Shortly after these posters appeared the *Guardian* claimed to have advance sight of Labour's response. Drawing on Brown's reputation for aggression, they claimed Labour intended to present 'the prime minister as a hard man, unafraid of confrontation, who is willing to take on David Cameron in "a bare-knuckle fistfight for the future of Britain"'. One poster featured the phrase 'Step Outside Posh Boy', along with the words 'Vote Labour. Or else.'[6] The *Guardian's* April Fool stunt was in fact relatively close to a poster design ('He's the toughest boss in Britain') that had been drawn up but not used; another, also eventually unused, aimed to target 'Conservative Family Butchers', with a liveried butchers van offering 'prime cuts', such as child tax credits. The advertising agency mocked up an uncooked steak in the shape of the UK.[7]

Labour's eventual response was a poster designed by one of its supporters. An example of how Labour tried to respond to its lack of finance imaginatively, it had launched a competition for poster ideas, attracting more than 1,000 suggestions.[8] The winner came from a 24-year-old Labour supporter, Jacob Quagliozzi, from St Albans. Quagliozzi's design was a mock-up of David Cameron as the character Gene Hunt, from the TV show *Ashes to Ashes*, along with the slogan: 'Don't let him take Britain back to the 1980s.' It was not an obvious success. The character of Gene Hunt was widely seen as an anti-hero, and as with earlier Conservative posters, ubiquitous photo-editing software merely meant that spoof versions of the poster were soon circulating on the internet. Within hours, the Conservatives had adopted the image, replacing the slogan with 'Fire up the Quattro. It's time for change.'

The Liberal Democrats' game plan as the election approached was simple: to fight off the Conservative challenge in those seats which the Lib Dems held, whilst making gains against Labour in seats where the Lib Dems were second. For much of 2009 party strategists worried about the former and feared that losses to the Conservatives could be in double figures. By early 2010, Cowley Street felt that they had reinvigorated the campaign in some of their vulnerable seats, and potential losses to the Conservatives were numbered at 'five or fewer'. With the party's poll ratings beginning to climb back to the levels they had enjoyed in 2005, they even held out the hope of taking a seat or two from the Conservatives.

They were far more confident of taking seats from Labour. In mid-2009, with Labour's fortunes floundering, Clegg had asked his General Election Campaign Committee to be more ambitious in how it targeted Labour. Some of the Lib Dems' Labour targets were obvious, seats in which the party had done well in local elections, in metropolitan areas such as Hull, Newcastle, or Burnley. But their target list extended beyond these. It was, however, important that this was kept quiet. Some of the party hierarchy had learnt two campaigning lessons from 2005: 'Don't go round talking about it. And be more ambitious in where you are targeting.'

John Sharkey chaired the party's General Election Campaign Committee, which met regularly – fortnightly before Christmas 2009 and weekly thereafter – in Cowley Street. A member of the Labour Party when at university, then an employee at Saatchi & Saatchi who worked on the Conservatives' 1987 campaign, Sharkey brought years of experience to a team that was otherwise relatively inexperienced, at least at the national level. His role was oversight, ensuring delivery, and answering directly to Nick Clegg. Hilary Stephenson, Director of Campaigns, headed the party's 'ground war', alongside two Lib Dem MPs, Andrew Stunell (who was Local Election Coordinator) and Willie Rennie (Chair of the Campaigns and Communications Committee). Jonny Oates was brought back from Bell Pottinger to fight the 'air war', alongside Chris Fox. There was a widespread acknowledgement amongst the team that the party's national campaign had mostly been disappointing in the past ('a liability at best', one called it), but there was an understanding that for the Liberal Democrats even the most effective air war ever would not succeed in winning seats. As one of them put it, 'Seats won't shower on us because of a brilliantly orchestrated air war.'

The manifesto writing committee was chaired by Danny Alexander, Clegg's Chief of Staff, although he had carried out much of the intellectual work in the Federal Policy Committee throughout 2009, persuading the party to agree to a less inclusive manifesto. 'The shorter the manifesto,' one of its members said, 'the more effort we've put into it.' As with the other two main parties, the deteriorating economy posed dilemmas as to how the party should pitch its message. Failure to acknowledge the scale of the economic mess would not be believed by the voters, and yet there were risks to offering too gloomy a message, as had been shown by Clegg's negative talk of 'savage cuts' the previous year. Just as David Cameron had tried to tell voters that there was a summit ahead after years of austerity, the Liberal Democrats also needed, in their use of political language and narrative to 'show the way out', as a leading party strategist put it. A full draft of the manifesto was ready by early March, but the headline messages were clear months before. The party would be campaigning on four key messages, linked by 'fairness':

- fair taxes (especially lifting the low paid out of paying tax);
- fair chances (the 'pupil premium' for poorer pupils);
- fair future (economy and environment);
- fair deal ('cleaning up politics').

This shorter and punchier manifesto was an attempt to impose better message discipline – something the party had been poor at in the past – and to link the party's efforts in the national campaign with its work in constituencies. The early identification of key messages meant that the ground war operation was able to prepare literature five months in advance, safe in the knowledge that the party's national campaign would be talking the same language.

They also took the decision to engage publicly with the issue of a hung parliament. In previous campaigns, the party had tried to avoid the subject – scarred by the experience in 1992, when the final weeks of the campaign became dominated by the question of whether a vote for the Liberal Democrats would enable Neil Kinnock to become Prime Minister. Yet it was impossible to avoid the question completely and, as one of the campaign team observed, trying to do so could come across as defensiveness; it 'said to people, "we've got something to hide", when we've got nothing to hide'. Aware that one of the few times the party became of interest to the media was when it looked like it might hold the balance of power, they hoped to be able to use the media interest to generate positive coverage for their policy programme, to 'leverage the issues that are of concern to us'.

The plan was to speak about how they would work with whichever party had a 'mandate' from the British public – thus hoping to kill off the procedural questions – and to stress instead the extent to which they would work with that party to advance their policy programme. The problem – as they all knew – turned on the word 'mandate'. Did that mean votes or seats? The workings of the electoral system meant it was perfectly possible for Labour to emerge with more seats than the Conservatives, but with fewer votes. In interviews, Clegg refused to be drawn on that question, arguing that it was merely a theoretical issue. The party knew that to answer would instantly be interpreted as indicating a preference. To say seats would mean Labour. To say votes would mean the Conservatives.

Behind-the-scenes the parties were preparing for the most high-profile innovation of the election: the Prime Ministerial debates. As soon as it became clear they were going to happen, everyone involved realised they would have a major impact on the forthcoming campaign. They would completely change its structure and become what one called the 'spine' of the campaign. They will 'totally change the rhythm of the campaign', predicted another.

The expectation of almost all of those involved in planning for the debates was that the first and the last debates would be the most important. The first, on domestic policy, would attract attention for its novelty value (more than one person involved suspected that the real importance will be the 'first half hour of the first one'). The final debate, on the economy, would be watched because it was the last before polling day. The middle debate would be on foreign affairs, and it would be on Sky, so almost all expected viewing figures to be much lower. 'Whoever drew Sky's lot,' said one of the Lib Dems involved, 'I'd never allow them to draw my lottery numbers.'

Gordon Brown had been initially reluctant to agree to participate. His reluctance was understandable. Not only was he being repeatedly told that he was a poor media performer, faced by two good media performers, but also he had to learn a completely new way of performing. 'He had to learn an entirely new format and genre,' said Peter Mandelson. 'It was completely virgin territory, which was easier for two virgins to adapt to.' He had been worked on, repeatedly, by Mandelson and Douglas Alexander, who saw the debates as a potential game-changing moment, as did David Muir.[9] Acknowledging Labour's disadvantages in finance, personnel and polling, 'to play by the usual rules is to programme in defeat', said Muir. For all the risks, the debates would give Labour hours of high profile airtime, for free, helping to counteract the Conservatives' massive advantage in campaign finance. One of those negotiating for Labour said that the Conservatives 'will rue the day they agreed to them'. Labour had pushed for the debates to be themed, to focus on specific areas of policy. They noted how well Cameron performed in his Cameron Direct sessions with the public but they believed that whilst he was good at generalities and the broad picture, he struggled to handle detail – one Downing Street insider described him as 'travelling policy-lite'. Labour also wanted to avoid any hint of the leaders being able to engage with the audience, anything at all 'touchy-feely', but to concentrate on policy issues, to try to make the debates as dry and prosaic as possible.

David Cameron had first called for a leaders' debate in 2005, when running for the party leadership. He had long believed they could help reconnect voters with politics. There was also a political calculation involved; almost all of his team believed that the party would do well out of the debates. They recognised the risk involved, but saw it as a calculated one, based on a belief that Cameron would outperform Gordon Brown. As one of those close to Cameron put it, 'We, as political aficionados, get used to Gordon Brown being hopeless. But very few people out there ever see that.' This, they argued, was a chance to show the public. They wanted the debates to be more free-flowing and general, rather than themed, and the eventual debate structure – half focusing on a theme, half on general topics – was a compromise between them and Labour.

For the Liberal Democrats, the potential benefits of the debates were obvious. Exposure, as one of their debate negotiators argued, is 'disproportionately important to us'. Their key negotiating stance was that the leaders had to be treated equally, their fear was that the other parties would push for unequal treatment, perhaps similar to the split between the party election broadcasts (which are on the ratio of 5:5:4). Their strategy therefore was to ensure that they nailed down the broad principles of the debates as early as possible, and signed off on those before discussing the details – a lesson they had learnt from reading about the Ford–Carter debates, the first to feature an incumbent US President, and where the Carter team had similarly insisted on agreeing key principles early, to stop Ford's Presidential status denying them equality.[10] They also studied the Clinton–Bush–Perot debates, and noted the way Perot's behaviour and stance became a story in and of itself.

All the parties began to prepare for the debates in earnest in the New Year. Despite some differences the core of their preparations was similar. They held different types of practice sessions – some full, 90-minute dress rehearsals (which were draining on those involved), other more focused sessions, working on quick-fire Q&A, phrasing and tone. Many sessions – and all of the full rehearsals – were filmed, because 'how you feel when you're in the room can seem completely different on screen', as one of those involved put it. They all accepted that what would matter was how things felt on screen. The key audience was the viewing public; the audience in the room were marginal. Even the journalists present would be watching in a different room, rather than in the venue itself. All the parties decided early on – as a result of watching play-backs – that it would be better to speak directly to the camera rather than to the audience. Why this did not happen, in practice, is discussed below (pp. 164–5).

Those involved in Labour's preparation complained that Brown struggled to find the time to prepare properly ('not taking as much time as anyone would want or like', complained one). The reason was partly because of the inevitable time pressures that arose from being Prime Minister and partly Brown's reluctance. The team tried to find two-hour slots on a Friday, either in Number 10 or in hotels, to go over particular areas. Key to Labour's preparation was Michael Sheehan, a US voice coach, whom Labour's pollster Joel Benneson recommended. Because the party paid Sheehan highly, Brown – who did not handle criticism well – had to behave, control his temper and not sulk, when Sheehan was present. The American could be direct with him in a way the rest of the team could not, and forced him to watch play-backs of interviews and debates. Sheehan told him what to do with his hands, to avoid deploying his unfortunate smile and to try to lift his jowls. And it was Sheehan who told him that he needed to be combative, there was no point trying to win a likeability contest: 'you'll lose'.

The Prime Minister was advised to keep the detail light and there were concerns about whether he would struggle with the concise time slots allocated by the debate rules. His habit of piling detail upon detail was not helped by his poor eyesight, which meant he struggled to see the clock properly, and in rehearsal, he kept running over the allotted time. This laid him open to a charge – used against him during Labour's rehearsals – that 'here was a Prime Minister who didn't know when his time was up'.

Sheehan's involvement had the added benefit that Brown's other media appearances noticeably improved during the run-up to the election, and the team around the Prime Minister took some satisfaction from improvements in his performance. They still knew the performances were not great and that the chance of Cameron slipping up was slim, but they hoped that they might be able to emerge from the first debate with a small bounce in the polls.

Like Labour, the Conservatives took advice from US consultants. Osborne recruited Anita Dunn, a former Communications Director at the White House, and Bill Knapp of Squier Knapp Dunn Communications, on the recommendation of Mayor Bloomberg of New York. The party set up its press conference room to use for rehearsals. The US advisers helped with work on condensing the message, especially on NICs, and focusing on anecdotes. Don't be too aggressive. Be reasonable. Damian Green played Gordon Brown ('he couldn't do the accent', said one of the Conservative team, 'but he got the relentlessly political thud, thud, thud of his delivery'), Jeremy Hunt played Clegg. Of all the three parties, they began full dress rehearsals the latest, less than a month before the election campaign began.

'Let me tell you an anecdote'

Conservative debate rehearsal, in the party's London HQ. Jeremy Hunt (playing Nick Clegg) and Damian Green (Gordon Brown) flank David Cameron.

(© Andrew Parsons)

The Lib Dems would later credit their success in the debates to not having hired any US consultants – arguing that their home-spun advice was more suitable for a UK audience – although they did talk to the US consultant Rick Ridder for advice on how to handle the post-debate spin, and Clegg continued to work with Scott Chisholm, who had been media training Clegg since he became party leader. The party scheduled full rehearsals, which they did almost weekly and earlier than the other two parties. They were also more systematic in their analysis of the performances.[11] Much of their early focus was not on the precise wording of answers, but on tone and body language. They worked on the basis that there might possibly be some gaffe, or mistake (by Nick Clegg or anyone else) during one of the debates, but it was more likely that 'a lot of it is – do people like this person? Is he a human being? And particularly for us, it's that parity thing, parity of esteem.'

Many of the techniques used by Nick Clegg in the debates emerged from these practice sessions. Try to mention the questioner in his answer, since that produced a cutaway shot of the audience nodding and looking engaged. Answer any question directly and briefly, which changed the tone of his voice, and enabled him to range more widely in his remaining time. Like all the parties they began using anecdotes but soon realised that an excessive number jarred, and so they cut down the number. Clegg had one annoying habit which frustrated several of his advisers: he kept putting his hand in his pocket when answering questions. Oates tried to dissuade him; Clegg insisted it made him feel comfortable.

Both Labour and the Conservatives soon realised that they had a serious problem on their hands – what one of them called 'a Nick Clegg problem'. Both had accepted that the Lib Dems would raise their profile because of participating in the debates; that Clegg would receive a boost by appearing on an equal footing with Cameron and Brown was taken as given. Some Conservatives were concerned but most expected that any disadvantage would be outweighed by Cameron's anticipated superiority over Brown. But as soon as they began rehearsals they realised the problem was more serious than they had anticipated. During Labour's rehearsals, Theo Bertram, a No 10 staffer who was acting as Nick Clegg, would play the anti-establishment card hard, blaming the 'two old parties' for their failings and presenting himself as a real alternative. Bertram's anticipation of Clegg's arguments was so good that at one point in the debates, when the real Clegg employed exactly the same phrases, Brown found himself smiling in recognition. When Brown and Alastair Campbell (who played Cameron) would argue, Bertram would stand back, gesturing with his arms, and say, in a resigned tone of voice, 'there they go again, the two old parties'. A watching Peter Mandelson could contain himself no more: 'Sanctimonious wanker' he remarked from the back of the room. Labour's plan to combat Clegg was to try to 'hug him close', compiling a list of areas on which Labour and the Liberal Democrats were in agreement. The very same realisation dawned on the Conservatives early in their preparations. As soon as their first dress rehearsal – in which Jeremy Hunt deployed arguments almost identical to those Clegg would go on to use – had finished, Anita Dunn simply said, 'Well, I'm voting for Nick Clegg.' But the team 'under-thought' what to do about the Lib Dem threat: 'We weren't disciplined enough to work out what to do about it,' one of those involved admitted. As a result, David Cameron would go into the first debate with no strategy for dealing with the Liberal Democrat leader.

Given the inviting targets the Conservatives and Labour presented to their opponents, a negative campaign seemed inevitable. In the *Financial Times* (11 March 2010) Martin Wolf complained of 'the British election that both sides deserve to lose'. One of the parties' researchers compared the mood of his focus groups in 2010 with that in 2005: 'The wish to oust Labour now is stronger than the wish to elect the Conservatives, whereas in 2005 the wish to elect Labour was stronger than the hostility to the Conservatives.'

The stakes for the parties were high. Liberal Democrats knew it was both their best chance to achieve a hung parliament and to become kingmakers, for decades. Labour was attempting to gain a fourth consecutive victory – achieved only once before since Britain had become a democracy – and to do so despite adverse political and economic circumstances. Conversely, the Conservatives had never before suffered four successive defeats. And if the party failed to achieve what for most of the Parliament had seemed an inevitable victory what would that mean for Cameron's modernising project?

Chronology of events, from 1 January 2010 to 5 April 2010

2 Jan	D. Cameron claims 2010 is the 'Year for Change'.
4 Jan	Con launch Ch.1 of their draft manifesto, plus 1,000 posters. Lab publish a 148-page dossier, *Conservative Tax and Spending Promises*. Cameron claims that tax benefits for married couples cannot be guaranteed because of the fiscal deficit; then he says that he will introduce some form of tax breaks within the lifetime of the next Parliament.
6 Jan	Former ministers G. Hoon and P. Hewitt call for a secret ballot to resolve the issue of Lab leadership. Northern Ireland First Minister, P. Robinson, admits his wife, Iris, has had an extra-marital affair. The Ulster Defence Association claims to have decommissioned its weapons.
8 Jan	It emerges that I. Robinson has had an affair with a 19-year-old man, and gave loans to him for £50,000, which she failed to declare.
9 Jan	A. Darling warns of the toughest spending round in 20 years if Labour is re-elected.

11 Jan	P. Robinson temporarily steps down as Northern Ireland's First Minister. A. Foster is appointed as his Acting First Minister.
12 Jan	Massive earthquake hits Haiti.
20 Jan	Unemployment falls by 7,000 to 2.46 million, the first fall since May 2008.
26 Jan	Britain limps out of recession – GDP increases by only 0.1% in the fourth quarter of 2009.
27 Jan	Launch of P. Watt's book, *Inside Out* paints a picture of a dysfunctional Downing Street under Gordon Brown.
29 Jan	T. Blair gives evidence before the Iraq Inquiry.
2 Feb	G. Brown comes out in favour of the alternative vote for Westminster elections. G. Osborne publishes *A New Economic Model. Eight Benchmarks for Britain.*
4 Feb	DUP and Sinn Fein agree a deal to devolve policing and justice powers to the Northern Ireland Assembly.
5 Feb	Three Labour MPs – D. Chaytor, J. Devine and E. Morley – and one Conservative peer – Lord Hanningfield – to face prosecution on charges of false accounting.
6 Feb	The Irish National Liberation Army (INLA) says it has decommissioned its weapons.
7 Feb	M. Ritchie is elected leader of the Social Democratic and Labour Party.
9 Feb	National Assembly for Wales votes in favour of a referendum asking if the Assembly can make laws without asking the Westminster Parliament for permission. House of Commons votes in favour of introducing the alternative vote for Westminster general elections by a majority of 178; the Bill will fail to become law because of the calling of the election.
16 Feb	Consumer price inflation rises sharply to 3.5%.
17 Feb	Unemployment falls by 3,000 to 2.46 million, although numbers claiming job seeker's allowance is at its highest level since 1997. Conservatives re-launch their worker cooperative plan for public sector workers.
20 Feb	At Labour spring conference, G. Brown says Labour will campaign under the slogan 'A Future Fair For All'.
21 Feb	A. Rawnsley's book, *The End of the Party* claims that Gordon Brown was confronted about his bullying behaviour by Cabinet Secretary, G. O'Donnell. Downing Street issue three separate denials.

24 Feb	Electoral Commission report shows that Con donations totalled £10.48 million, as compared to less than £5 million for Lab and £1 million for the LD in the last quarter of 2009.
27 Feb	Earthquake in Chile measures 8.8 on the Richter Scale. The Conservatives launch their six key pledges at their spring conference in Brighton.
27–28 Feb	Con spring conference.
1 Mar	Lord Ashcroft admits to 'non-dom' status.
2 Mar	Final agreement reached on televised Leaders' Debates – renamed 'Prime Ministerial Debates'.
3 Mar	M. Foot, Labour Party leader (1980–83) dies, aged 96.
5 Mar	G. Brown gives evidence to the Iraq Inquiry.
12 Mar	E. Macmillan-Scott MEP defects from Con to the LD. Judge declares BNP Constitution illegal because of its refusal to accept non-whites as members.
15 Mar	A. Kumar, Labour MP for Middlesbrough South & East Cleveland dies, aged 53.
17 Mar	G. Brown writes to Sir John Chilcot to correct evidence he gave to the Iraq Inquiry, claiming the defence budget had risen in real terms in every year under Lab. Unemployment falls by 33,000 in February to 2.45 million.
20 Mar	D. Cameron claims a future Con Government will introduce a banking levy, even if other countries did not do so. BA cabin crew begin three days of industrial action. SNP hold pre-election conference in Aviemore.
21 Mar	*The Sunday Times* uncovers three former Cabinet ministers – S. Byers, P. Hewitt and G. Hoon – in a 'cash for influence' scandal. Byers is recorded as offering to work for lobbyists – 'like a sort of cab for hire' – for up to £5,000 a day.
22 Mar	Byers, Hewitt and Hoon are suspended from the PLP. It is announced that Samantha Cameron is expecting a baby. LD plan to cut the winter fuel allowance for the under-65s earlier than Labour to save £400 million.
24 Mar	In the Budget, A. Darling announces a £2.5 billion package of support for business financed by better-than-expected revenues from the tax on bank bonuses. In a 'smash-and-grab' raid on Con policy, he introduces a two year stamp duty holiday for first-time buyers on houses up to £250,000, paid for by a permanent increase in stamp duty from 4% to 5% for houses over £1 million. Inheritance tax thresholds frozen for four years to help fund social care; winter fuel

allowance increases preserved for a further year, paid for
by introducing tax avoidance agreements with Dominica,
Grenada and Belize. Other measures: income tax thresholds
frozen; fuel duty rises are staged; cider duty increased by 10%
above inflation. The inflation rate falls from 3.5% to 3% in
February.

25 Mar   The Conservatives hire M & C Saatchi, the advertising agency,
to spice up their election advertising.

26 Mar   US and Russian presidents agree a new nuclear arms reduction
treaty, cutting warheads by about 30%.

27 Mar   At the Scottish Labour Party conference in Glasgow, Gordon
Brown unveils his five key election pledges. British Airways
cabin crew begin their second three-day strike.

28 Mar   Conservatives unveil their anti-Brown posters.

29 Mar   George Osborne announces plan to reverse around half of
Labour's planned rise in National Insurance Contributions
paid for by £6 billion in efficiency savings. Full 1% rise to
go ahead for those earning £45,000+. 'Ask the Chancellors'
Debate on Channel 4. IPSA Report bans claims for: 1st class
rail travel and mortgages on second homes. Basic bills covered
only, including rent (up to £1,400), council tax and utilities.
All claims to require receipts and to be published online. In a
change from the Kelly Report, one family member permitted
to be employed by each MP.

30 Mar   Tony Blair returns to the political fray. Government launches
a National Care Service, but questions of funding are left
to an independent commission. Growth figures for the last
quarter of 2009 are revised upwards from 0.1% to 0.4%.

31 Mar   SNP and Plaid Cymru publish a joint programme in the event
of a hung parliament.

1 Apr   In a letter to the *Daily Telegraph*, 23 senior businessmen
endorse Con plan to partly halt Labour's National Insurance
Contribution increase.

4 Apr   C. Grayling, the Shadow Home Secretary is secretly taped
saying that people who run B&Bs should have the right to
decide whether homosexuals stay in their homes.

5 Apr   Labour poster depicts Cameron as Gene Hunt from the BBC
series, *Ashes to Ashes*: 'Don't let him take Britain back to the
1980s.' Four hours later, the Conservatives respond with:
'Fire up the Quattro. It's time for change.'

Notes

1. In its first six weeks, more than 250,000 people visited the site.
2. James Forsyth, 'The Tory situation is now verging on critical', *Spectator*, 24 February 2010.
3. Labour's war book's SWOT analysis contained five Strengths, five Opportunities, and five Threats – but ten Weaknesses.
4. This contradicted the earlier findings, in both Labour and Conservative focus groups (see Chapter 1) that found the IHT cuts were very popular.
5. Ironically, whilst Labour's focus groups reported the posters making an impact, Conservative focus groups found that voters did not especially like the posters, thinking them cruel and personal.
6. *Guardian*, 1 April 2010.
7. 'Made in Scotland from Girders' was also not used.
8. It was hardly an innovation, however: Labour had first asked supporters to send in poster ideas as far back as 1908.
9. Muir had been influenced by an article he had read in the *New Yorker*, arguing that the best way for David to beat Goliath was not to play by Goliath's rules ('How David beats Goliath. When underdogs break the rules', *New Yorker*, 11 May 2009).
10. John W. Self, 'Debating the 1976 Debates: Establishing a Tradition of Negotiations', *Presidential Studies Quarterly*, 37:2 (2007), 331–48.
11. Three password-protected DVD copies were made of each session. Nick Clegg had one, and the others circulated around four other people: Jonny Oates, John Sharkey, Lena Pietsch, and Sean Kemp, the Head of Media. There was an immediate viewing after each mock debate, with Clegg, Oates, and Pietsch followed by a later meeting of all five to discuss the performance.

8
Cleggmania and Bigotgate: The National Campaign

After all the plots and attempted coups, and multiple rumours of snap elections, it was Gordon Brown who called the election and for what had long been the most predictable day: 6 May 2010. The announcement was confirmed to the media on Easter Monday, and on Tuesday 6 April the Prime Minister went to Buckingham Palace just after 10am. A 20-minute audience with the Queen was followed by a photocall outside Number 10, along with the entire Cabinet, in which Brown stressed he was 'not a team of one', but 'one of a team'. The Prime Minister described himself as coming from 'an ordinary middle-class family in an ordinary town' (a less than subtle way of reminding the electorate that David Cameron did not), ending with a slightly awkward, and passionless, exhortation: 'Let's go to it!' And so began the 2010 election campaign.

It was the first election since 1987 in which the Conservatives had gone into the campaign with a clear lead in the opinion polls; a YouGov poll in the *Sun* on the day the election was called put them 8% ahead. Yet on a uniform national swing this would not have been enough to produce a majority Conservative government, and so it was also the first campaign since 1992 to be fought, from the beginning, with the realistic possibility of a hung parliament looming.

It was the first ever campaign to feature televised debates between the three main party leaders, something which all involved in the campaigns – participants and observers – accepted would alter the shape and feel of the campaign, although there was less confidence that they would have much effect on the outcome. In the event, the debates had a much greater impact on the rhythm and feel of the campaign than almost anyone had predicted. They effectively became the national campaign, sucking the life out of many of the more traditional aspects of campaigning.

Between Brown's return from the Palace and the appearance in front of Number 10, the Conservatives conducted their own launch event on the south bank of the Thames, with David Cameron speaking to a small group of party candidates and activists. Cameron appeared as the outsider for the day, standing across the river from Westminster. His speech was more presidential than Brown's: he spoke of fighting the election for what he called 'the great ignored' – whether they were black or white, rich or poor, from the town or the country, people who 'work hard, pay taxes' – and claimed that the Conservatives promised 'real changes', which he contrasted with 'five more years of Gordon Brown'. The 'great ignored' was supposed to speak to a sense that the state would support you if you worked hard and played by the rules but, as one Cameroon noted, it was defined too broadly ('we didn't actually leave anyone out').[1] The 'great ignored' joined a long list of used and discarded Conservative slogans, not to be heard of again during the campaign, although 'five more years of Gordon Brown' survived.

The Liberal Democrats attempted several launch speeches of which the first, before the Prime Minister's announcement, was a low-key event held in Cowley Street. 'So far as I could see,' joked the Conservative chairman Eric Pickles, 'the Liberal Democrats' launch took place in the photocopying room.' With Vince Cable at his side, Nick Clegg called for voters to 'do something different' by choosing 'change that works for you'.

Leaders' tours then began in the marginal seats. Gordon Brown toured three Labour marginals in Kent, while David Cameron visited a hospital in Birmingham Edgbaston, before travelling to Leeds. Nick Clegg, meanwhile, began his campaign in the three-way marginal of Watford. They could just as well have stayed at home: not one of the seats visited by the party leaders on the first day of the campaign went on to be won by their party.

The final few days of the 2005 Parliament were spent with the frontbenches engaged in talks about which pieces of legislation would make it to the Statute Book. As expected, two major planks of the Government's Constitutional Reform and Governance Bill – a referendum on the Alternative Vote and ending the by-election system for the remaining hereditary peers – were shelved.[2] Haggled over to the bitter end was the Digital Economy Bill which proposed giving the Business Secretary power to block pirate websites infringing copyright.

Twenty-three Labour MPs voted against the bill's Third Reading, the last major Labour rebellion of a very rebellious Parliament. Parliament was prorogued on Thursday 8 April, and formally dissolved by the Queen at 11.41am on Tuesday 13 April. The so-called 'Rotten' or 'Manure' Parliament had ended.

One policy issue dominated the first week's campaigning: National Insurance. At the beginning of April, George Osborne had announced that he would partially reverse the Government's planned 1% increase in national insurance contributions, claiming that it amounted to 'Labour's Tax on Jobs'. The Conservatives enlisted the help of 23 senior businessmen, who wrote a letter to the *Daily Telegraph* on 1 April opposing the rise, and over the following days, more businessmen came out against the Government; by Wednesday 7 April, when Cameron deployed the issue at the last Prime Minister's Questions of the Parliament, the number had reached 68.

Labour's initial response was to suggest that the businessmen were being somehow 'deceived', a phrase both Peter Mandelson and Gordon Brown used. To Tory delight, this merely provoked counter-attacks from outraged businessmen, and so instead Labour regrouped and launched a counter-attack, at a press conference on 8 April. As the number of business leaders supporting Cameron reached 81, Labour attempted to turn the debate into one of credibility, claiming that Conservative proposals to cut £6 billion in waste in 2010–11 to pay for the national insurance reversal did not add up. At the press conference, Brown held aloft a four-page Tory document compiled by Dr Martin Read and Sir Peter Gershon (damagingly for the Government, two of its former advisers), which he dismissed as 'flimsy'. Deliberately vague, to prevent journalists poring over the detail, the document was certainly in sharp contrast to the 128-page James Report which the Conservatives had produced during the 2005 campaign.[3] Alistair Darling and George Osborne then engaged in a lively head-to-head debate on College Green, broadcast live on the BBC's One O'clock News, during which the Chancellor claimed that the Conservative plans were 'reckless'. Labour's counter-attack forced the Conservatives to put more flesh on the bones of their efficiency savings, and while the Government clearly lost the debate in terms of business support (eventually the number of businessmen opposing the NI rise swelled to over 1,100), they did eventually publish a rejoinder letter, from 58 leading economists in the *Daily Telegraph* on 15 April warning that 'only when the recovery is well under way will it be safe to have extra cuts in expenditure'.[4] The Liberal Democrat response was to recycle an old Conservative poster from 1992, claiming that the Conservatives planned to deliver a £389-a-year 'VAT Bombshell' to pay for their tax cuts. It was a poster that would come back to haunt them after the election.

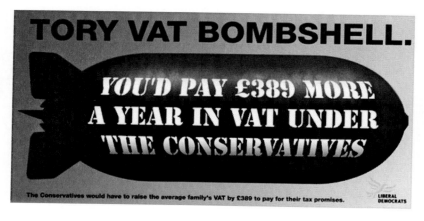

The national insurance debate dwarfed the parties' efforts in other policy areas. Labour strategists had grudging admiration for George Osborne's political nous in the way he played the National Insurance card. Osborne was aware of how his party had been derailed by Brown over the economy in 2001 and 2005. He took pride in putting Labour on the back foot. Labour's aim for the first week of the campaign had been to focus on economic recovery – or, in the language of its war book:

'Week one: Building an economic future for all Britain's people, not change you can't afford' – and instead it was forced onto the defensive. On 7 April Gordon Brown unveiled a package of constitutional reforms, designed to attract supposedly 'soft' Liberal Democrat voters, especially in Conservative–Labour marginals. This was the occasion upon which Brown was to have trailed his resignation (see p. 141), but without it the speech attracted relatively little publicity. The following day the Conservatives launched their plans for a National Citizen's Service, in which young people would undertake two months' voluntary community service during the summer. The event saw a walk-on part by Sir Michael Caine – the actor fluffing his lines by praising the Government rather than the Conservatives.

The Conservatives also announced their long-delayed plans for a married couples tax break worth £150 a year for 4 million families, including civil partnerships. Couples earning less than £44,000 a year would be able to transfer their allowance to their partners. The scope of the plans was wider than anticipated (for instance, childless married couples would benefit) but the overall cost of the measure was a modest £550 million a year and the amount on offer, just £3 a week, seemed minimal. The Conservatives claimed that the new allowance was intended as a symbol of its support for the institution of marriage. The Conservatives fared little better when they announced a crackdown on benefit cheats with their 'three strikes and you are out' policy. The BBC discovered that the number of people currently on three strikes was zero, those on two strikes was 69, amounting to an annual saving of only £100,000.

More significant was Labour's conversion to a hands-on industrial policy. Following the controversy over the takeover of Cadbury's by Kraft in 2009 (an especially sensitive issue in marginal seats in the West Midlands), they proposed the introduction of a national interest test for foreign takeovers, a so-called 'Cadbury's Law'. The Government claimed that in the wake of the banking crisis, most other major industrial countries were protecting their key industries from foreign takeovers, so Britain should do the same. It would also serve to create another dividing line between itself and the Conservatives' preference for *laissez-faire* economics and deregulation.

By the end of the week most commentators argued that the Conservatives were having the better of the campaign (although a YouGov poll of the public's own impressions put the Lib Dems narrowly on top). Two polls of voting intention on 11 April – an ICM poll for the *Sunday Telegraph* and a YouGov poll for the *Sunday Times* – both showed a Tory lead of eight points. But many of those involved in the campaigns in party HQs saw the first week as a phoney war, the calm before the storm of the TV debates, and the overall reaction of the public was muted at best. A Populus poll for *The Times* revealed that more than two-fifths (43%) of voters including 50% of women, said 'none of the parties' or 'don't know' when asked which party was putting across a convincing case. Just 25% named the Conservatives, 18% named Labour.

The second week began with the major parties launching their manifestos. Labour launched *A Future Fair For All* on 12 April in a newly-built hospital in Birmingham, in the marginal Edgbaston constituency where nine years before Tony Blair had been harangued by the partner of a cancer patient.[5] The manifesto cover – a retro 1930s-style image of a family staring into a bright sunshine – was eerily like the Conservatives' 1929 'Sun Ray Treatment' poster. Labour aides had been emphasising to the creative staff at Saatchi & Saatchi that they wanted something that reminded people of 1945 ('a reference that was rather lost on some of them'), although the main inspiration was a 2002 album cover by the band Lemon Jelly, one of several images initially shown to Peter Mandelson by Saatchi & Saatchi. Mandelson liked the image eventually developed, because it emphasised the future: 'We could not argue on change. We were patently not the change.' But unknown to Mandelson, the album on which the image was based was prophetically entitled 'Lost Horizon'.

Labour's manifesto launch audience comprised both press and Labour Party supporters, with the latter booing the former whenever a difficult question was asked; Paul Waugh of the *Evening Standard* described it as having a 'North Korean rally atmosphere'. The manifesto was published in hard copy, but as with all the parties it was also available online. For the photocall, Gordon Brown, Alistair Darling and Harriet Harman were allowed to hold printed versions of the manifesto; the rest of the Cabinet had to make do with Labour-branded data sticks.

Brown stressed that his party were the custodians of economic recovery, and that they had got the 'big decisions' right. Labour's manifesto was deliberately long and detailed (it ran to 115 pages), reflecting a determination to show that it had not run out of ideas, a point emphasised by the Prime Minister when he said that Labour was comprised of 'restless and relentless reformers', and in a clunking phrase of his own to match David Cameron's 'great ignored', he announced 'we are in the future business'.

Labour pledged not to increase income tax rates and not to increase the scope of VAT. It planned a programme of constitutional reform, including a referendum on AV and an elected House of Lords. The manifesto was crammed full of micro-measures – such as DIY ASBOs, a 'cancer guarantee', an English language test for migrants, and doubling paternity leave for fathers – but it was less clear what the grand vision was. One of its authors explicitly saw it as a mongrel: New Labour in its public sector reform, high Liberal in its political reform, and social democratic in its economic interventionism. The emphasis on Blairite themes such as public service reform led Peter Mandelson to describe the manifesto as 'Blair Plus', much to Ed Balls' subsequent irritation. The impact of the launch was dented somewhat by the news the same day that the three Labour MPs charged with fraud over their expense claims were to receive legal aid.

The Conservatives launched their manifesto the following day, at Battersea Power Station. As with Labour, the chosen site was supposed to be symbolic of something wider (although what that was, was more open to debate).[6] The night before the launch, the Conservatives attempted to create a sense of anticipation by projecting the words 'Who is the New Member of Cameron's Team?' onto the building. The answer – the public – was to be found the following morning in *An Invitation to Join the Government of Britain*, a lavish production hardback in what the *Guardian* described as 'hymn book blue'. Referring to 'the biggest call to arms in a generation', David Cameron invited people to take control over their own lives, to become part of the Big Society. Parents would be given the power to set up their own schools; residents could veto disproportionate council tax increases in referendums; people could take over the running of their local pub or Post Office; constituents would have the power to oust errant MPs; and people could elect police commissioners to replace local police authorities. In an effort to clean up politics, the number of MPs would be cut by 10%, while ministerial pay would be cut by 5%, and then subject to a five-year pay freeze. Cameron maintained his party's policy of ring-fencing NHS spending, while offering access to GPs' surgeries seven days a week. More traditional Tory policies included placing an annual cap on immigration (as well as placing limits on work permits for non-EU workers) and a referendum if further powers were being given to the EU. Unlike Labour, the Conservatives were silent on income tax and VAT rates.

The idea behind the Big Society was soon widely mocked, and rarely featured again in the campaign, although Cameron would mention it in his stump speeches. The Conservatives were criticised both for the idea itself (how many parents, for example, really wanted to take over the running of their schools?), and for springing it on the public. In their defence the Conservatives did at least have a clear underpinning idea – the Big Society was a Big Idea, of the sort which pundits always call for – and one which Cameron and his team had been going on about in different guises for years. And yet despite the extensive work that the Conservatives put in to market-testing most of their policies, and the language used to sell those policies, at the point at which it was launched neither the general theme of the Big Society nor the individual policy items contained within it had been market-tested – either in polls or focus groups – and it soon became obvious that the central concept of the manifesto, however worthy, did not resonate on the doorstep.

The Liberal Democrats launched their manifesto, *Change That Works For You: Building a Fairer Britain* at the London offices of Bloomberg. Nick Clegg lauded his party's 'four-step manifesto' which would 'hardwire fairness into British society'. The four key pledges, much trailed in advance, were fair taxes; the pupil premium; a fair economy; and cleaning up politics (by proportional representation; giving people the power to sack MPs between elections; and introducing a £10,000 cap on donations to parties).

Britain's first television debate between the candidates seeking to be Prime Minister took place on Thursday 15 April at Granada Studios in Manchester – normally the venue for the filming of *Coronation Street*. An audience of marginally under 10 million watched 90 minutes of live, uninterrupted politics on television. Gordon Brown occupied the right hand podium (from the viewer's point of view), as he did in all three debates, because of his poor eyesight. Cameron occupied the centre podium, with Nick Clegg on the left. The debate, moderated by Alastair Stewart, covered domestic affairs. The honour of asking the very first question fell to Gerard Oliver, a retired toxicologist, who asked about immigration policy, a subject which would feature in each of the three debates. All three speakers had any over-running contributions cut short in mid-sentence by Alastair Stewart, who interpreted the rules rigidly and vigorously.

From an early stage, it was apparent that Nick Clegg was performing well, and that all the Liberal Democrats' pre-debate rehearsals had paid off. Clegg talked directly into camera, made a special point of mentioning the audience members' names, and seemed comfortable in the format. As planned, he portrayed himself as the fresh alternative to the 'two old parties who have been playing pass the parcel with your government for 65 years'.

By contrast, Gordon Brown used too many statistics, his scripted jokes didn't quite work, and he struggled to connect. Once on stage, he found that his eyesight meant that he could not see the camera properly and he was unable to talk down the camera lens, as rehearsed.[7] As part of their preparations, the Labour debate team had compiled a long list of areas in which they agreed with the Liberal Democrats, and Brown had always intended to 'hug Clegg close'. He had, however, been supposed to show a little variety in the way he did it, instead of which he constantly repeated the phrase (or mild variations): 'I agree with Nick.'[8]

David Cameron was clearly nervous, and underperformed from the beginning. He was thrown by the vigorous interruptions of the moderator (more vigorous than anything that the Conservatives had rehearsed), and he too struggled to look down the lens. His problem was not an inability to see the camera, but merely a natural desire to work the room ('all the instincts of a British politician is to work the audience', said one of those who had worked with him); the Conservatives had not done enough rehearsals to repress that instinct. He also seemed flummoxed by Clegg's success in connecting with the audience, and used too many of the folksy anecdotes his American advisers had encouraged him to practise. Within hours, one website had created an online 'David Cameron Anecdote Generator', which could come up with any number of anecdotes from the Tory leader.

What was obvious to most people watching offstage was less obvious onstage, and coming off stage, Brown was surprised to be told by his team that Clegg had 'won'. The instant polls, though, were unequivocal: all except the 'voodoo' polls – self-selecting phone-ins and so on – showed Clegg the clear winner. Despite coming a clear third, Labour saw it as an opportunity: by praising Clegg's performance, which they did shamelessly, they hoped to take the shine off David Cameron. The Liberal Democrat debate team went back to their hotel and celebrated with a glass of wine, reflecting on a job well done, and hoping for a bounce in the polls as a result. That night, David Laws quipped on *Question Time* that he had played David Cameron rather better in rehearsals than the real Cameron.

The Liberal Democrats surged in the polls and some surveys showed the party in the lead. They appeared to have increased their support by 50% in the space of just four days. One 90-minute TV appearance appeared to have done more to transform the standing of the political parties in an election campaign than anything else since polling began. As the Liberal Democrats started to get news of their poll surge over the weekend, Nick Clegg spoke to his senior colleagues on the phone. None could quite believe what was happening, but they agreed on one thing: 'They're going to come for us.'

On the same day as the first debate, the Eyjafjallajokull volcano in Iceland erupted, releasing a massive ash cloud into the sky. All UK flights were grounded as a result, and were to remain so for days. 'It feels like 1906,' said one Conservative campaigner, 'the Liberals ahead in the polls and not a plane in the sky.' It provided a curious backdrop to the campaign, as well as causing some logistical difficulties for the party leaders, who were unable to use aircraft. Meanwhile, the political eruption continued. The newspaper headlines over the weekend of 17–18 April were extraordinary. The *Sunday Times* ran with a poll finding which they claimed showed that Clegg was nearly as popular as Winston Churchill; he enjoyed an approval rating of 72%, only 9 points less than Churchill had enjoyed at the end of World War II. There were also comparisons with Barack Obama. Within 24 hours, the Lib Dems claimed to have received £120,000 in small donations; by Monday, 19 April, over 100,000 Facebook users – more than the party's entire membership – had joined a group dedicated to supporting a Liberal Democrat victory.

'I don't want to ask him about the NHS – I want him to heal me'

'Here Nick Clegg'

Matt, *Daily Telegraph*, 21 April 2010
(© Telegraph Media Group Ltd 2010)

The *Guardian*'s headline of 16 April – 'Knives Out for Nick Clegg' – foreshadowed what was to come. The *Mail on Sunday*'s contribution began, 'His wife is Spanish, his mother Dutch, his father half-Russian and his spin-doctor German. Is there anything British about the Lib Dem leader?' On the Monday (19 April), the *Sun* ran with 'Don't Trust Dem', showing a YouGov poll in which six out of ten Lib Dem policies were given 'a resounding thumbs down', while its former political editor, Trevor Kavanagh, warned, 'Vote Lib, Get Lab.' The onslaught reached a peak on 22 April, the morning of the second leaders' debate: 'Nick Clegg, the Lib Dem donors and payments into his private account' (*Daily Telegraph*); 'Clegg's crazy immigration policies' (*Daily Express*); 'Wobble Democrat' (*Sun*); and 'Clegg in Nazi Slur on Britain' (*Daily Mail*). The last of these unearthed an eight-year-old article written by Clegg for the *Guardian* in which he had criticised British attitudes towards Germany.

Many of these stories were fed to the press by Conservative HQ, as the love bombing of the previous few years was replaced by old fashioned political carpet bombing. 'We did a pretty comprehensive job on them,' admitted one of the Cameron team, 'however dirty it was.' 'That was the machine swinging into action.' All but one of the stories to feature on newspaper front pages that day came from Conservative sources. It provoked the rare sight of a politician coming to an opponent's defence, when Peter Mandelson accused Andy Coulson of orchestrating the headlines. The Lib Dem press office (which also had no doubts about where these stories were coming from) began to appreciate that there was a downside to being taken seriously. The stories that made it into the press were a tiny proportion of those that were thrown at the party, and whilst they felt able to rebut most of the attacks, they ate up staff time, time that a small party did not have. The *Telegraph* story about Clegg's donations, for example, required three staff for the best part of an entire day (including their Head of Communications Jonny Oates, who had to withdraw from Clegg's debate prep) to study Nick Clegg's personal bank statements until they could disprove the story.

Some of the younger members of the Lib Dem team – unused to such treatment – were shocked at the attacks. On the Monday morning after the debate, some Lib Dem MPs took to the airwaves to complain about the coverage, but Cowley Street rowed them back, discouraging complaints, arguing that they could be counter-productive, and you had to 'take the heat' that came with being taken seriously. There was however, a public backlash, picked up on Twitter, where thousands of people began using the hashtag #nickcleggsfault as an explanation for anything that went wrong.[9] By midday on 22 April, it had become the UK's top hashtag, and the Lib Dem debate team read out some of the sillier ones as a distraction from their preparation for the second debate.

The Tory press engineered a tactical retreat. As Andrew Marr pointed out the following weekend, it was the moment when 'Fleet Street lost touch with the High Street'. But if the bludgeoning tone dropped off, for the rest of the campaign the Liberal Democrats were still subject to a more serious examination of their policies than ever before. Conservative private focus groups found that whilst awareness of the Lib Dems was noticeably up (as was approval of Nick Clegg personally) there was also growing disapproval of their individual policies, especially on immigration and Trident ('not that important overall', said one Conservative strategist, 'but important to our people'). Labour focus groups found something similar: awareness of, and hostility to, the Lib Dem policy on immigration grew, along with the 'discovery that these nice Liberal Democrats were going to take away their tax credits'.

Once it became clear that the Lib Dem surge was not just some temporary blip, the other parties had to decide how to respond. On Monday 19 April the Conservative team met for a prolonged discussion. One idea aired was to tear up the rules of the remaining debates, replacing the staged encounters with a more open debate, in which the inconsistencies of Liberal Democrat policy could be revealed. The practical problems inherent in the suggestion (why would the other parties agree?), along with the fact that many of the more pedantic rules had initially been requested by the Conservative negotiating team, soon led to that suggestion being dropped. Some advocated what they called a 'we got it too' moment, in which the party would show that it understood voters' anger. Another meeting descended into an obtuse discussion between George Bridges and Steve Hilton, in which they began to argue about exactly when during the 1997 campaign Labour had launched its attack on Conservative pensions policy. Even Cameron, normally very calm in meetings, began to show his annoyance at this.

The Conservatives reacted by pulling a planned Party Election Broadcast on the failures of the Brown Government, replacing it with one produced, at very short notice, focusing on Cameron's belief in 'change', filmed in the leader's back garden, with him talking directly to camera. Less publicly, on 20 April they also changed their list of target seats, removing most of their Liberal Democrat seats and adding 14 new Labour ones in an attempt to compensate for the expected Lib Dem surge.

At first, Labour's reaction to Cleggmania had been broadly positive, believing that more of the new Lib Dem votes had come from the Conservatives than from Labour. A hung parliament in which Labour were the largest single party was again a realistic possibility, even if it finished third in votes. Labour's strategists had been struggling for months to think of ways to break out of the 40/30/20 pattern into which the polls seemed to have stuck – and the debate had provided the necessary stick of dynamite. Ironically, Labour was more relevant in third place but with a resurgent Lib Dems than they had been as a distant second. It meant that journalists kept discussing the party seriously, rather than writing it off, and Labour found that it encouraged grassroots activists who felt that they were still in the game. But, privately, within Labour HQ there were also real concerns about what would happen if Labour continued in third place, and the Lib Dems started to erode Labour's heartlands, especially in the North of England. Douglas Alexander told Labour staff that they were 'playing Russian roulette with the future of the Labour Party'. And just like the Conservatives, Labour also shifted its battleground seats slightly in response to the Lib Dem advance; using its National Call Centre to do spot polling in potential Lib Dem targets, they added another 20 seats, all seats the party could lose to the Lib Dems, to the list of those they were helping from the centre.

The second televised debate was held in Bristol, on 22 April, and broadcast on Sky. Chaired by Adam Boulton, it covered foreign and defence matters for the first 45 minutes, before switching to a more general series of topics (several of which reprised those of the week before) for the second 45. The viewing audience was far smaller – estimated at around 4 million – although the debate was also carried on Radio 4 and then shown later, 'as live', on other channels, especially BBC Two.

There were more offbeat questions during the foreign policy section of the programme, including a question on the candidates' views on the Pope's forthcoming visit to the UK which was not in the script for any parties' preparations (and it showed), and the Lib Dems were privately annoyed about some of the areas which were not asked about (there was no question about Iraq, for example, and a question about the environment was about each leader's individual behaviour rather than their party's policies). The debate was widely considered to be slightly livelier – the candidates all looking more relaxed, and prepared to be a bit more confrontational – and the anecdote count was noticeably lower, all the parties having realised that there were too many the week before. When the subject of expenses came up, Boulton appeared to break the spirit, if not the letter, of the debate rules by mentioning the press coverage that morning about Clegg's bank accounts.[10]

Brown's advisers had privately been most worried about this debate, partly because of the outlet (both Labour and the Liberal Democrats were concerned about the possibility that Sky might try something to generate publicity), but also because of the subject material. Their nightmare scenario was a question asked by a member of the armed forces. The debate rules specified that every candidate must be asked the same questions, but in reality such a question would be aimed at the only man who had been responsible for putting troops in harm's way in either Iraq or Afghanistan. But both Brown and Cameron performed better than they had in the first debate, and they managed to land blows on Clegg, especially over immigration, Trident, and MPs' expenses. The 'I agree with Nick' phrase had gone; instead, at one point, discussing Trident, the Lib Dem leader was told to 'get real' by the Prime Minister, in one of his more effective passages. And a large piece of orange cardboard placed around the television camera meant that he was able to identify the camera. Less effective was the Prime Minister's attempt at engaging with a questioner – 'women, and you are one...', he told her helpfully.

Polls showed that the outcome of the debate was closer than the previous week (see p. 247). Although spinners for each of the parties tried to present the results as showing how well their man had done (and the Conservative spin operation in particular was better than it had been the week before), most of the poll results were merely within the margin of error of each other, and showed a broadly tied result. An early edition of *The Times* was headlined 'Neck and Neck', which was more accurate than its later edition proclaiming David Cameron the winner.

David Cameron had ignored those who had advised him to be more aggressive and confrontational in the debate – instead stressing repeatedly the things he would do 'if I were to become Prime Minister'. The exception was an exchange with Gordon Brown over state support for the elderly. Cameron listed a series of things that he said the Conservative Party was pledged to keep – the free television licence, pension credit, winter fuel allowance and free bus pass – and complained of Labour leaflets suggesting otherwise, which he said were 'pure and simple lies'. He challenged Brown to withdraw the leaflets; the Prime Minister's somewhat awkward response was to claim that he had not authorised any such leaflets. Even before the debate had finished, however, the Conservative press team were able to produce copies of multiple Labour leaflets making similar claims, and scheduled a press conference for the following morning to discuss them. Privately, Labour admitted the leaflets were going out. 'To be honest, they work,' admitted one of the Victoria Street team. 'They're about the only thing we're doing that does work.'

Scaremongering was universal. Nick Clegg had begun the campaign warning of 'Greek-style unrest' if a government elected with no mandate began carrying out savage spending cuts, reducing public services and putting up VAT. 'And so my warning to people who think the old politics still works, is be careful for what you wish for.' When pressed, the Lib Dem leader claimed his comments were merely 'stating the obvious'.

For their part, the Conservatives repeatedly raised the prospect of a hung parliament and the chaos that they claimed would ensue. Shadow Business Secretary, Kenneth Clarke, had been warning of the problems for business and the markets even before the campaign began, and during the campaign he went so far as to argue that the IMF might be called in if there was a hung parliament. The Conservatives devoted two press conferences to the dangers of a hung parliament, including one on 26 April, at which George Osborne and Jeremy Hunt launched their latest party election broadcast, a *faux* broadcast from the Hung Parliament Party and its vision for Britain – 'behind-closed doors politics, indecision, weak government, a paralysed economy and yet another election within the calendar year'. Every poll during the campaign – from the first to the last – would, on a uniform national swing, have produced a hung parliament. The problem for the Conservatives was that there was no evidence that the prospect of a hung parliament particularly turned voters off.

As the polls continued, relentlessly, to predict no party winning an overall majority, so inevitably the pressure increased on Nick Clegg to say more about what he would do in the event of a hung parliament – pressure made worse by Labour running fairly consistently in third place in the polls. In an interview Clegg gave to Jeremy Paxman on the BBC on 12 April, he had made it clear that any party that came ahead in both votes and seats would be considered to have a mandate, although he had still swerved the question about what would happen if one party came ahead in votes but behind in seats. Clegg's tactic was to look puzzled at the very question, implying it was some extremely unlikely hypothetical scenario ('a dead heat?'), rather than – as he well knew – a distinctly possible outcome. Labour's poor performance made this question harder to dodge; it could be third in votes, but still come first in seats. 'We've got to hold that line,' insisted one Cowley Street insider on 20 April, 'the electoral logic of saying one or the other is too obvious, and whatever we say, we lose votes either way.'

But on Sunday 25 April the line broke. In an interview for the *Sunday Times*, and then with Andrew Marr on BBC One, Clegg went further than he had before, and made it clear that if Labour finished with the largest number of MPs, but came third in the share of the popular vote, then he would not support Gordon Brown remaining in Downing Street. 'I think it's a complete nonsense,' he said. 'I mean, how on earth? You can't have Gordon Brown squatting in Number 10 just because of the irrational idiosyncrasies of our electoral system.'

Was this change in stance a deliberate strategy? 'To call it strategic would be overgenerous,' one of the Clegg's team remarked, 'but it was a decision.' It was, though, not one that all of his team favoured, and a discussion the day before had concluded that they should hold firm to the existing position. As one of those involved in the discussion argued: 'You're never going to give them [the media] what they want, so don't bother trying. Just fob them off, and they'll eventually get bored and give up trying in the end.'

But Clegg was hearing that his party was being hurt by the warnings from the Conservatives and their press allies that a Lib Dem vote would keep Brown in Downing Street. Supporters of a shift in position argued that it would 'reduce the pressure' which the party was facing on the issue, but – as those against predicted – all it did was pose further questions. Would he work with a different Labour leader? Would he work with the Prime Minister if Brown came second in votes but ahead in seats? One of his team described the pressure over post-election arrangements as like a fairground splat-a-rat machine; no sooner would they knock the argument down in one place, it would pop up somewhere else. It was not only a distraction into discussion of process at the expense of policy, but it also meant that the 'vote Clegg, get Cameron' message would now hit home in Labour seats. The following day, Clegg appeared to soften his stance by indicating that he might be prepared to work with Brown, as long as Labour had not come third in the vote.

The only good news for the Liberal Democrats was that the media also started quizzing politicians from the other parties about what they would do in the event of a hung parliament, but in general these were exactly the sort of process issues which the Lib Dems had begun the campaign desperate to avoid. Instead of talking about their key policies, they were dragged into days of discussion over the intricacies of hypothetical questions about who would work with whom, and under what circumstances. 'We struggled to get it under control,' complained a key member of the team, 'and lost a week of the campaign.'

Almost since the first day of the campaign there had been criticism that Gordon Brown's tours consisted solely of him visiting small groups of Labour supporters, in extremely tightly organised events – 'from safe house to safe house', as one Conservative MP put it. His advance team was accused of keeping events as tame as possible. But Brown was continuing the home visits with which he had some success during 2009. The problem was that these 'under the radar' events were not working in a general election campaign; the national media showed no interest in them. After a week following the Prime Minister a journalist on the Brown bus remarked that he knew he had not been where the war was. These criticisms were shared by some within the party machine, who argued that they needed to get the PM into more contact with voters, although others, bluntly, saw him as a liability, and wanted to keep him out of the way. Brown and aides with him were also dissatisfied, frustrated that his policies, particularly on crime, were not being reported. After much internal wrangling, those favouring more spontaneous visits and walkabouts won the day.

'From safe house to safe house'
The Prime Minister and Chancellor meet the voters at home.

On 24 April, an Elvis impersonator sang to the Prime Minister and a small audience of Labour supporters. One of those responsible for the tours blamed the obsession many Labour politicos have with US politics. 'But 150 people in a hall in Corby listening to an Elvis impersonator is not quite the same as Beyoncé at the Hollywood Bowl, is it?' Many thought that would prove to be the most embarrassing event of the campaign. They were wrong.

On Wednesday 28 April, the Prime Minister was about to finish a visit, to Rochdale, when he began to be heckled by a 66-year-old pensioner, Gillian Duffy, who had popped out of her house to buy a loaf of bread, and on encountering the Prime Minister decided to give him a piece of her mind. She was brought across to meet Brown, and they engaged in a discussion about a range of issues, including the national debt, education, and immigration. Although Mrs Duffy began by admitting she was 'ashamed of saying I'm Labour', the Prime Minister responded to her points well, and the two appeared to part on good terms. She even told reporters she would be voting Labour.

However, after Brown got into his car to leave, he forgot that his radio microphone – worn to enable the media to hear his encounters with voters – was still switched on, and his subsequent conversation with his aide Justin Forsyth was recorded:

Brown:	That was a disaster. Should never have put me with that woman. Whose idea was that?
Forsyth:	I don't know, I didn't see.
Brown:	Sue's, I think. Just ridiculous.
Forsyth:	Not sure if they'll go with that one.
Brown:	Oh they will.
Forsyth:	What did she say?
Brown:	Everything. She's just this sort of bigoted woman who said she used to be a Labour voter. Ridiculous.

As the words began to be broadcast on every TV channel, those watching at Victoria Street – who had thought the initial encounter had gone well – went silent. Labour staff stopped and stared at the screen. It was not just that the Prime Minister appeared tetchy, it was also that Mrs Duffy was white, female, northern, working class – 'the physical embodiment of our core vote' – and that the issue on which the Prime Minister appeared to be especially critical of her was immigration, an issue which almost all Labour candidates reported as huge on the doorstep. But also, as another key member of the campaign noted, 'we knew how, given half the chance, the press focused on process, and we'd just given them a whopping big process story'.

The media immediately tracked down Mrs Duffy, who expressed shock when she was told what Brown had said about her ('You're joking! I can't believe it. All me life damn well Labour'). Shortly afterwards, during his appearance live on the Jeremy Vine Show on BBC Radio 2, the Prime Minister was played a recording of his remarks for the first time. Despite knowing that he was being filmed whilst on air – he had been told three times by his staff that the interview was to be filmed as well as broadcast – the Prime Minister slumped down on hearing the recording, with his head in his hands, an image that was used repeatedly during the rest of the campaign. Those who knew Brown well knew that that action was not especially significant, something Brown often

'How to win friends and influence people'

(Iain Green, *Scotsman*, 29 April 2010)

did to rest his eyes. The telling reaction was when he raised and tilted back his head.

He had phoned Mrs Duffy to apologise to her before his appearance on the radio, but believing that such an apology was insufficient to close the story down, he and his entourage then ripped up their schedule for the day and returned from Manchester to Rochdale, to pay a visit to Mrs Duffy's house. Following a 40-minute conversation behind closed curtains – more than some foreign leaders get – the Prime Minister emerged in front of a sea of reporters and cameramen, wearing his awkward smile. He said he was 'mortified' about what had happened, claimed that the comments were as the result of a misunderstanding, and asked for forgiveness, describing himself as a 'penitent sinner'. Later that day, he also sent an email to Labour supporters apologising for what had happened. The incident – which he later described as his 'worst day in politics' – was the product of many accidents. Only a few days earlier, Brown had agreed to the media request to wear the microphone because multiple boom mikes were proving too obtrusive. And because the media had arrived late for the Duffy exchange there was such a scrum around Brown that his press aide was unable to remove the microphone before he got into his car.

There was some relief among Labour aides that what had been recorded was not worse. But the media that day, and press reaction the following day (see pp. 271–2, 299) were negative enough. It was possible to take the Prime Minister's words – all 42 of them – and to construct a detailed psychoanalytical critique of his behaviour and personality, and plenty of journalists did. For those in the trade, it was an astonishing moment; one political party's media chief described it as 'one of the most compelling bits of 24-hour TV ever … It's what 24-hour TV was invented for.' Yet, for all the fuss, there was relatively little evidence that the public cared very much. The incident with Mrs Duffy was so close to the third leaders' debate the following day that disentangling one set of polls from the other is almost impossible, but the only poll that was conducted between 'bigotgate' (as it became known) and the leaders' debate showed almost no changes in the parties' standing.

In their private focus groups, and on the doorstep Labour found that the incident was mentioned, but largely as something which confirmed people's pre-existing views, something that made people who already disliked Gordon Brown feel more open about saying so.[11] Bigotgate was unedifying, distracting, painful, and humiliating, but it was not all that significant. It was the most memorable moment of the 2010 campaign, for sure, but it was not the most important.

The Prime Ministerial debates ate massively into the schedule of the campaign. Gordon Brown usually did preparation on the Saturday and Sunday before each debate, leaving time for one or two short 'pop-out' visits to nearby locations. On the Tuesday morning, his debate team would go to a hotel, near the debate venue and set up what they called 'Debate Camp'. He would then do similar local visits on the Tuesday and Wednesdays, although again, these were limited by the need to do preparation (including, a full 90-minute rehearsal on the Tuesday evening before the debate), and Thursday was given over almost entirely to debate preparation. In other words, there was some debate prep on the majority of days during an average week's campaigning. David Cameron and Nick Clegg's schedules differed slightly in the detail – the Lib Dems, for example, did not do full 90-minute rehearsals once the campaign was underway – but were similarly intensive.

Moreover, what one campaign head called the media 'frenzy' around the debates – which would begin on the Tuesday of each week, and continue through until the Saturday morning – meant that it was much harder for any of the parties to get traction on any campaigns or issues for at least half of each week. 'It wasn't even a good idea to try,' one said.

'The day before Duffy'

Labour debate rehearsal, in a Manchester hotel room.
Alastair Campbell and Theo Bertram behind podiums;
Gordon Brown on monitor screen; Douglas Alexander
with hands on head.

Other traditional features of the national campaign declined as a result. The most obvious casualty was the national press conference, a staple of UK elections for decades, which vanished almost completely.[12] There was no single day during the campaign when all three parties held London-based press conferences, and when they did occur they were ad hoc events, often decided the night before, responding to issues or events, rather than being scheduled in advance. All parties had originally intended to hold more press conferences, but soon discovered that there was little point.

This became mutually reinforcing; once one party stopped having them, there was less benefit to others holding them. It is, as one of Labour's team put it, 'difficult to have an argument if the other side don't turn up'. When Labour hastily organised a Saturday press conference fronted by Ed Balls and Yvette Cooper, together with Liam Byrne, Chief Secretary to the Treasury, to rebut Conservative plans on the marriage tax allowance, a photographer snapped a private note between Cooper and Byrne in which she described the event as 'second division'. (Byrne's scribbled reply: 'Sort of like being allowed to play in the sand pit'.) But the truth was that all press conferences were now second division. A side effect was that fewer members of the Shadow Cabinet received much media coverage – and in turn, given that the three main party leaders were men, this meant that there were complaints about reduced coverage of women politicians.[13] But it also meant that the old structure of a campaign day – with questions posed at one press conference, then taken to another, to be answered or rebutted – disappeared entirely from the campaign.

A familiar complaint from both the major parties was that too much of the media's coverage of the election was on process, particularly around the debates, and 'horse-race' issues, rather than policy. One key Conservative strategist complained of the media's 'obsession with strategy, why we were doing things, where we were going, and very little on policy differences between us'. Labour even complained officially to the media, although it was unfortunate that the letter came immediately after the Elvis stunt in Corby. They had approached the other two parties without success to make it a collective complaint. The Liberal Democrats were more relaxed about the horse-race discussion, if only because doing well in the horse race was so novel to them.

Those who could recall earlier campaigns, though, noted the absence of the to and fro of policy arguments. 'In 2005,' said one Conservative, 'I remember mortars dropping in the middle of the Research Department.' Another Labour strategist recalled that Evan Davis of the BBC, was always on the phone in 2005, challenging facts and figures. This time, he said, there was much less of that. However, those journalists who did attempt to raise policy issues hardly found politicians eager to engage; complaining about process, pointed out one journalist, 'is what parties say about stories they don't like'.

The Party Election Broadcasts (PEBs), which once provided a structure of the campaign, have also become relatively minor matters, often produced on the cheap, and sometimes at very short notice (see pp. 273–7). They were still illustrative of the themes of the campaign – it was striking that Gordon Brown hardly featured in Labour's, whereas three of the Conservative PEBs made extensive use of David Cameron – but they are no longer as significant as they were even 13 years before.

One aspect of the more traditional, pre-debate, campaigning that did survive, however, was the leaders' tours – albeit scaled back for reasons of time. Post-election estimates were that Brown travelled around 7,000 miles, Clegg around 7,500, and Cameron – aided by more use of planes than the other party leaders – just over 10,000 miles. The parties employed different organisational strategies for their tours, which revealed the relative wealth of the campaigns. The Conservatives deployed three state-of-the-art tour buses, nick-named Tom, Dick and Harry. All were in campaign livery, which changed mid-way through the campaign, in line with the campaign slogan. The buses were despatched around the country, to meet Cameron as he came off trains or (ash cloud notwithstanding) planes. For all the criticism of the Brown campaign for being tightly controlled, the Conservatives took relatively few core media with them on the bus, allowing just one place per day for a visiting reporter from another outlet. The rest of the media pack were issued with Operational Notes the day before, and told to make their own way there. Many gave up trying; 'There wasn't any point,' said one journalist. When they occurred, Conservative events were more free-flowing than the Labour ones – Cameron did not just meet Conservative activists – but the campaign itself was as tightly controlled as any of the parties', with far fewer media in attendance.

The Liberal Democrats could afford two tour buses, each decorated with a large photo of both Vince Cable and Nick Clegg, and supplying plenty of drinks and food for the travelling journalists. Clegg would often travel on the bus with the journalists, and there were few complaints about a lack of access. To begin with some of the journalists did not take the Lib Dem campaign very seriously, asking Clegg silly questions to fill the time.[14] But after the first debate the Liberal Democrat bus suddenly became the place to be, and the party was forced to hire an additional coach, to accommodate all the foreign press who suddenly wanted to know about the new political phenomenon.

Whilst the extra media attention (and accompanying money) was welcome, foreign correspondents demanded things in return. At one point, a Russian TV station contacted Clegg's press secretary asking if they could be filmed taking a sample of his blood so that they could use the DNA to trace his Russian ancestry. There being relatively few Liberal Democrat voters in Russia, they were politely declined. Cowley Street also organised tours for Vince Cable and Paddy Ashdown, the latter focusing primarily on seats in the South West. Cable's tours had originally been intended to be more high profile, but with the post-debate attention now focusing almost exclusively on the leader, Cable would occasionally wonder out loud why there were so few journalists present.

Despite charging media outlets £13,000 for a space on the Brown media bus, Labour's operation was more basic, a standard coach with the bare minimum of facilities. The party tried to make an environmental virtue out of its more extensive use of public transport, but the truth was they had no money for anything more glamorous. Gone were the helicopters which used to ferry the press pack around in the Blair days. The media bus trailed behind the Prime Minister's entourage, often getting lost and arriving late, and missing some events altogether. Journalists would complain about the lack of access – the Prime Minister was not allowed on the bus for security reasons – as well as the lack of food. The latter received short shrift from the Labour organisers ('they had better food than we did'), even if it did obsess some journalists: the Labour press office faced continual requests from one news outlet for the name of the onboard chef, even though there was no chef onboard. Occasionally, Labour would arrange for Cabinet ministers to travel with the bus, and to provide briefings. Peter Mandelson's excursion with the press pack, in which they went to Blackpool, where he danced in the Ballroom and went up the Tower, was one of few highlights.

'The walk of faith'

Peter Mandelson gives journalists a gift of a photo opportunity.

Labour's campaign suffered from a lack of organisation and direction, as well as of money. The 'grid', which once ruled campaigns, was close to non-existent, with events decided on almost a day-to-day basis. Scheduled visits were routinely dropped or rearranged, often at a day's notice. All of this made it impossible to prepare sufficiently or for the party's advance team to do proper work.[15] 'They can't make decisions,' one of those involved in the tours complained. There was admiration amongst some at Victoria Street for how well those involved in the leaders' tours did, given the circumstances.

Another effect of the leaders' debates was to crowd out the minor parties. The SNP leader, Alex Salmond, had launched a high profile legal challenge to be included in the debates, but was eventually rebuffed at the Court of Session in Edinburgh (see p. 267). Excluded from the UK TV debates, there were instead separate debates held outside of England – three in Scotland and Wales, and two in Northern Ireland. Yet these were much less high profile, not helped by being shown at what were hardly prime-time slots. The first Welsh debate, for example, was shown on Sky at 10.30am on a Sunday. Even those shown at more sensible times were overshadowed by the UK-wide debates, and prevented distinctly Scottish or Welsh elections emerging.

The same applied to the minor UK-wide parties, who were also excluded from the debates. UKIP attracted relatively little publicity for its manifesto launch, apart from the unveiling of the party's irreverent 'Sod the Lot' poster, depicting Gordon Brown, David Cameron and Nick Clegg. Probably the most high profile UKIP event of the entire campaign came on polling day itself, when the party's former leader, Nigel Farage survived a plane crash – a light aircraft, containing Farage and a pilot had been towing a UKIP banner when it had crashed in Northamptonshire.

The BNP attracted probably as much publicity for the protests or scuffles that broke out around their events – including a fight between their candidate for Romford and a group of Asian men – as for anything else that happened during the campaign. And outside of one or two seats, the Greens were virtually invisible during the election campaign. During the campaign, the party's leader Caroline Lucas said she believed that the Greens had reached a 'tipping point', commenting: 'It's massively important for people to know that we can win.' She also made clear that no Green MPs would 'prop up' a Conservative government in the event of a hung parliament.

In Scotland, Wales, and Northern Ireland, there were separate election campaigns, fought with separate manifestos (albeit often similar in content, save for a change of name), with separate manifesto launches, different publicity material, and with different party leaders. They were also fought in different contexts. Scottish Labour had the advantage, denied elsewhere, of being able to fight against the incumbent, SNP, government; Jim Murphy, the Secretary of State for Scotland, was extremely confident about his party's fortunes in Scotland and had been given a free hand from London. Labour trumpeted the benefits that Scotland got from having a Labour government in Westminster and that a vote for Labour was the only way of avoiding a 'harsh' Tory government. Nationalist parties and those in Northern Ireland made much of the influence that they could have in a hung parliament – what the SNP called 'local champions' – although the very tactic summed up the somewhat peripheral role the parties play in Westminster elections.

The third Prime Ministerial debate was held on Thursday 29 April in the Great Hall at the University of Birmingham. The debate was aired on BBC One, and moderated by David Dimbleby, who took a more activist role throughout, constantly repeating the questions that had been posed by the audience. (This prompted complaints from Labour, annoyed that he was eating up too much time – 'these people and their fucking egos' moaned one of Brown's team.) The first half of the debate was on economic issues, the second half covered a miscellaneous selection (including, for the third debate running, immigration). In his opening statement, the Prime Minister attempted to put the events of the previous day behind him ('there's a lot to this job, and as you saw yesterday, I don't get all of it right'); had he not done so, the other parties were not intending to bring it up.

The previous day's encounter in Rochdale and its aftermath had wiped out Labour's intended preparation and afterwards Brown was in no condition to focus properly on detailed Q and A. One of those with him admitted that he was in a 'terrible state', unable to concentrate properly on the work in hand. But Labour's tactic for the debate was, anyway, pretty straightforward: to 'set up the contrast'. 'Fuck Clegg, and shape the contrast with Cameron.' Insofar as Clegg mattered, the aim was to rope him in as 'part of a coalition of cuts'. Brown was relentlessly negative, attacking Cameron's plans for inheritance tax cuts, and warning that both Opposition parties intended to cut child tax credits for middle income families. Labour played this card hard in the final week and Conservatives found it was a concern in their private focus groups and on the doorstep. Cameron more or less ignored Brown's questioning throughout, portraying him as a desperate man who had run out of things to say. He turned his fire instead on Clegg, particularly the Liberal Democrats' support for the euro as well as their amnesty for illegal immigrants. The Tory leader directed his remarks at those people 'who do the right thing', and 'play by the rules', arguments which worked well when the debate turned to immigration and benefits. The Lib Dems had prepared more for this debate than for the previous one, and had worked on the assumption that Cameron would indeed attempt to attack them, that the Tories 'would come for us hard'. They tried to tone down slightly what one of them called 'Nick's schtick' about the 'two old parties', aware it was wearing thin, but they also worked on the assumption that most voters had not watched all three programmes, and so some repetition was necessary. For those who had watched all three debates, however, the risk was that Clegg's lines became stale, and afterwards some Lib Dems would admit that they should have thought of a way of carrying the debates forward.[16]

'The Final Debate'

(Steve Bell, *Guardian*, 30 April 2010)

Labour strategists were unhappy with the way the debate went, making multiple complaints to the BBC: in addition to Dimbleby's repetition of the questions, they also complained about the over-running of the section on immigration, given the fact that it had previously been debated twice.

There was also a widespread impression that none of the three politicians had anything new to say; many of the arguments used in the previous debates were repeated.

This time Cameron was the clear winner: all the polls put him top (albeit in one case, jointly), whilst all but one had Brown in third (see p. 247). Cameron had moved from second in the first debate, to neck-and-neck in the second, to first place in the third, although the overall outcome was still far less favourable then that predicted by Cameroons when they had been advocating the debates.

In the pre-election discussion of the role of the internet, one common theme was that it would be someone's undoing. As Alex Smith who ran the LabourList website said in early 2010: 'The web really concentrates and intensifies news – and disseminates information quickly. If some young candidate quietly says something stupid in a marginal somewhere, the internet has the potential to make that into a very big story very quickly.' That young candidate turned out to be Stuart Maclennan, who had been chosen as the Labour candidate (albeit not in a marginal seat) for Moray, and who right at the beginning of the campaign was found to have posted a series of offensive comments on Twitter. The story had been broken by the *Scottish Sun*, and after a fairly half-hearted attempt by Labour to make light of the incident, by noon the same day Maclennan's candidature was over. He was Britain's first political suicide by Twitter.

Yet the defenestration of candidates for saying daft things is hardly an innovation; all that differed here was the method of delivery. As one of Cameron's team had noted some six months before the campaign, whilst anticipating what he called 'a YouTube moment', dealing with it 'will be the same as dealing with any old screw up'.

For anyone who was already politically interested, of course, the internet provided a mass of information and data about the campaign, more than anyone could possibly want or need. But for the rest of the population its impact was less dramatic. Evidence of parties' contacts with voters showed that the old fashioned techniques outstripped the new – those contacted by mail and leaflets outnumbered all of those contacted by other campaigning techniques combined. Just 9% of voters questioned in a poll by Opinion Matters for the National Endowment for Science, Technology and the Arts (Nesta) said they expected to get information from political websites and 5% from emails sent by politicians. Compare that to 63% who said they would find out about the election from the TV, 47% from newspapers and 27% from radio. The key moments of the campaign all took place on TV, a medium invented in 1925; 'bigotgate' came about because of a radio microphone, a technology that has existed since 1949. Those who were seeking evidence to prove that 2010 was Britain's first 'internet election' – a claim that has now rather tediously been made of every contest since 1997 – tended to be frustrated.

One senior party official was especially sceptical. 'No British political party has demonstrated a significant change in its fortunes as a result of e-campaigning ... Will we build it? Yes. But are the benefits over-stated? Yes.' This was, however, as much about ensuring respectability with the commentariat as anything else: 'as much about credibility as it is about real votes'. On this reading, old media clearly trumped new.

Yet at the same time as its importance has grown, so all the parties take the web and new social media far more seriously than they did, and whilst the medium may not have dominated anywhere, its influence was almost everywhere. Manifestos could be, and were, downloaded at a rate far outstripping printed copies. (Sinn Fein's manifesto was only available online.) Online material frequently augmented the offline – such as the online video that accompanied Labour's manifesto, the Conservative posters with accompanying videos in which people explained why they were voting Conservative, or the Liberal Democrats' Labservative spoof ('We've had 65 years to get it right. So what's another 5?'). Labour sold 9,000 copies of their manifesto in 2005; in 2010 their online mini-manifesto cartoon managed 100,000 views, with similar figures for downloads of the manifesto itself. PEBs were now released online before being broadcast, on YouTube or similar, in an attempt to generate more than one day's interest out of them; they had to 'live online', as one Labour strategist put it. All the parties' press teams used tweets and blogs, to disseminate stories, to enable them to reach the mainstream media. David Cameron himself – the first 'blackberry prime minister' one of his team called him – was an avid reader of political blogs; he was said to be a particular fan of the *Spectator*'s Coffee House, ConservativeHome, Guido Fawkes, and Iain Dale. He could also be found reading the politicalbetting.com site. Almost all candidates fighting marginal seats had an online presence of some sort. In the past, one Conservative staffer said, the person in charge of the website was also the person you went to 'if your Outlook broke'.[17] That is no longer the case.

There is what one Conservative involved in their online operation described as a 'giant straw man' involved in any discussion of the internet election, a world in which hierarchies are somehow cast aside, and everyone is suddenly plugged in to political data. The reality is not like that. Instead, new technology has been put to work serving fairly well-established political techniques. There is an inverse relationship between the media attention given to aspects of technology and their real importance. Many of those involved argue that email is still the most important of the 'new' campaigning techniques (the Conservatives had some 500,000 email addresses that they would contact on a regular basis) rather than the various Web 2.0 platforms. Also, and a development largely missed outside of the specialist press, the Conservatives invested considerable time and money buying up google adwords, allowing them to target their message online – 'Effectively,' one said, 'we bought google.' This was old fashioned advertising, albeit with an ability to segment and target audiences previously unavailable.

There is an obsession in elements of the media about the role of internet in politics, but dismissing the hype is not to dismiss the medium, which is now a mainstream tool of political campaigning in the UK, where the new media has meshed with the old.

Even before the rise in the Liberal Democrat share of the vote, Labour had been attempting to appeal to Lib Dem voters to vote tactically. Early on in the campaign, the Transport Secretary, Andrew Adonis penned an article in the *Independent* (9 April) in which he called on voters to 'grasp the fundamental Labour–Lib Dem identity of interest'. Once Labour went into third place in the polls, there was talk of Alan Johnson entering the ring as someone who might be prepared to work with the Liberal Democrats. In an interview with *The Times* (17 April), the Home Secretary commented: 'I am a supporter of PR and so I believe that we have to kill this argument that coalition government is dangerous. Leaving this election aside, I don't have a horror of coalitions. You see what happens in many other progressive countries.'

As the election approached, Labour's attempts to appeal to Lib Dem voters became more overt. They also became less one-sided, coming very close to recommending not just that Lib Dem voters vote Labour, but also that Labour voters vote Lib Dem. On 4 May, two days before polling, the Schools Secretary Ed Balls told the *New Statesman* that whilst he always wanted Labour to win, he recognised the need for tactical voting because 'I want to keep the Tories out'. The same day saw the Welsh Secretary Peter Hain say that it was important 'for people to act intelligently in this election' and 'draw their own conclusions'. The Prime Minister – making an appearance on the GMTV sofa – was forced to reject tactical voting, but others had done his work for him. These appeals to tactical voting came very close to breaking Labour Party rules, which prohibit support for any candidate other than the Labour candidate.

The Lib Dems rejected these comments as 'desperate'. They had known that they would get appeals for tactical voting from Labour. 'The surprise', as one of their campaign team observed, 'was how early, how intense and how desperate it was.' But before the campaign began they had ruled out any reciprocity. The problem was not just that they feared it would squeeze their vote – putting off Conservative-leaning Liberal Democrats – it would also undermine their brand. You could not, they argued, claim to be for honest, different, politics, and yet advocate tactical voting.

Debates over, the final week of the election more closely resembled a traditional election campaign. Without the need for debate prep, the bank holiday weekend before polling was a frenetic sequence of leaders' visits. 'Once you're into an election campaign,' admitted one Conservative strategist, 'there's not an awful lot you can change. After the first week, all your posters are done. About 15 days out, all your direct mail is written … You can divert the bus, but you can't reprint the posters.' And so the buses zipped back and forth across the country, as the campaigning became ever more frantic. Both Cameron and Brown enjoyed the final week of the campaign, and its more traditional campaigning, much more than what had gone before. On the Sunday before polling Gordon Brown managed to visit ten South London constituencies in one day, from which, according to one of those involved, he came back 'visibly fizzing'.

Bank Holiday Monday saw all three prime ministerial candidates address a meeting of CitizensUK at a packed Westminster Central Hall. All received good responses, but Brown in particular was in his element, enthused by the quasi-religious atmosphere. He began to give the sort of performances that some of his campaign team had been encouraging from the beginning. 'Wow,' thought one of Cameron's speechwriters, 'why has he not been doing this for the whole campaign?', a sentiment echoed by many in Labour Head Office.

David Cameron then undertook a 24-hour non-stop tour from the Tuesday night through to the Wednesday night, beginning in East Renfrewshire and going through the night including a 3.15am visit to a Morrisons supermarket distribution centre in Wakefield and a 5.30am visit to Grimsby Fish Market. The idea was a direct US import, and like many US imports it did not translate seamlessly. 'They can do planes to Chicago,' said one of the Conservative team, 'we do coaches to Grimsby.' But the Conservatives claimed that the idea did at least reinterest the media in the campaign, 'who by then had lost any interest in policy, if they ever had any'.

There were nine opinion polls on the eve of the election, almost double the number in 2005. Just as at the start of the campaign, none of the polls – assuming a uniform national swing – would have given the Conservatives a majority of seats, although they would have been pretty close on some. All predicted a hung parliament, but with both the Conservatives and the Lib Dems making large gains. And there was still the possibility of Labour, the party of government, ending up third in the share of the popular vote.

On the morning of polling day Cameron's team sat round Steve Hilton's kitchen table in Oxfordshire and made their predictions; most were for the Conservatives being the largest party but without a majority. Until a couple of days out Brown had still believed Labour would be the largest party and that he would be well placed to form a coalition with the Lib Dems; as he drove around the country, his team would play 'Don't Stop Believing' in the car. But by the end of the campaign, reality had dawned. On his way back to his constituency, on the eve of poll, he rang Douglas Alexander and apologised. 'I'm so sorry,' he said, 'I thought I could turn it around.'

Campaign Chronology

6 Apr   Election called.

7 Apr   Senior businessmen support Con National Insurance plans; G. Brown claims on GMTV that they have been 'deceived'. Brown unveils comprehensive package of constitutional reform.

8 Apr   Brown claims that Con plans were drawn up on 'the back of an envelope'; LD claim Con planning a VAT bombshell. Con launch National Citizens Scheme. Plaid launch campaign with slogan 'Think Different, Think Plaid'.

9 Apr   Con announce married couples tax break. S. Maclennan, Lab candidate for Moray, resigns for a string of offensive comments posted on Twitter.

10 Apr   Polish President, Lech Kaczynski and entourage are killed as an aeroplane crashes in Russia.

12 Apr   Queen dissolves Parliament. Lab launch manifesto, *A Future Fair For All*. SNP campaign launch.

13 Apr   Con launch manifesto, *Invitation to Join the Government of Britain*. Plaid launch manifesto, *Think Different, Think Plaid*. UKIP launch manifesto, *Empowering the People*.

14 Apr   LD launch manifesto, *Change that Works For You: Building a Fairer Britain*.

15 Apr	First Prime Ministerial TV debate, held in Manchester, and broadcast on ITV1. N. Clegg emerges as the clear winner. All UK flights grounded following a volcanic eruption in Iceland. Green Party launch manifesto, *Fair is Worth Fighting For*.
17 Apr	English Democrats launch manifesto.
19 Apr	Government sends three Royal Navy warships to the continent to help British citizens stranded by the ban on flights caused by the volcanic ash crisis. Con Party Election Broadcast calls for 'a clear, decisive result'. DUP launch manifesto, *Let's Keep Northern Ireland Moving Forward*.
20 Apr	SNP manifesto launch, *Elect a Local Champion*. UK airspace is reopened.
21 Apr	Unemployment rises 43,000 to 2.5 million. SDLP launch manifesto, *A Better Way to a Better Ireland*.
22 Apr	Tory-leaning press round on N. Clegg. Second Prime Ministerial debate, in Bristol, broadcast on Sky. The leaders debate international affairs and general matters. British Crime Survey shows levels of crime down 7%, and at its lowest level since 1981. Government borrowing is £163.4 billion, £3 billion below the Budget forecast, but still the highest in peacetime history.
23 Apr	Growth figures published for the first quarter of 2010 show a rise of only 0.2%. Greeks forced to implement rescue deal from IMF and the European Union. D. Cameron is interviewed by J. Paxman, and says the relative size of the public sector is too high in Northern Ireland (69%) and the North East of England (63%). BNP launch manifesto, *Democracy, Freedom, Culture and Identity*.
24 Apr	D. Cameron calls for a decisive victory, claiming a hung parliament would be a threat to the economy.
25 Apr	N. Clegg claims he won't have Brown 'squatting in Downing Street' if Lab finishes with the most seats, but third in the popular vote. Lab complains to the BBC about reporting of polls at expense of policies.
26 Apr	UUP launch the same manifesto as the Conservatives. Respect launch manifesto, *Peace, Justice and Equality*.
27 Apr	IFS Report claims the three main parties are being 'strikingly reticent' about the scale of public spending cuts required to cut the deficit. Con air 'Hung Parliament Party' spoof election broadcast. Greek bonds reduced to junk status by a leading credit agency; FTSE 100 falls 150 points on the news.

28 Apr   The Prime Minister, not realising that he has a microphone attached to him, describes a 66-year-old pensioner as a 'bigoted woman', and is later forced to apologise. Sinn Fein launch their manifesto exclusively online, *2010 Westminster Election Manifesto*.

29 Apr   Negative press headlines on 'bigotgate'. At the third and final Prime Ministerial debate on BBC One held in Birmingham, the three leaders mainly debate the economy.

30 Apr   T. Blair re-enters the election fray briefly having his blood pressure tested at a health centre in Harlow. He makes a joke about turning his microphone off. Car crashes into a bus stop near the launch of Labour's new poster campaign in Birmingham. SNP and Plaid Cymru hold a joint conference after TV debates, aiming to build a 'strong block of Plaid and SNP MPs'.

2 May   Mrs Duffy explains in the *Mail on Sunday* why 'Gordon won't be getting my vote'.

3 May   Ipsos-MORI poll in the marginals gives Con the 7% swing they need to gain a small majority. All three main party leaders address a CitizensUK event in London.

4 May   G. and S. Brown appear on GMTV with Lorraine Kelly. Three Labour cabinet ministers – E. Balls, P. Hain and T. Jowell – appear to endorse tactical voting. M. Sood, Lab candidate for Norfolk North West, claims G. Brown is 'the worst Prime Minister' Britain has ever had.

Notes

1. It was, however, noted that the pairing 'gay or straight' was not included, something which the Conservatives claimed was merely an oversight. But it came just days after Chris Grayling, the Conservative Shadow Home Secretary, had been recorded expressing personal doubts about the law which prevented B&B owners from turning away gay couples. The Conservatives had promptly issued a statement explaining that he had no desire to change the law, and the Shadow Home Secretary was then hardly seen until the party's manifesto launch more than a week later.

2. Other abandoned pieces of legislation included changes to the libel laws, one-to-one schooling and the Government's plans for compulsory sex education in schools, along with the backbench Business Committee (a key recommendation of the Wright Report into reform of the House of Commons) and three tax measures in the Budget, including the 10% increase in the duty on cider.

3. See D. Kavanagh and D. Butler, *The British General Election of 2005* (Basingstoke: Palgrave Macmillan), p. 59.

4. The party had had the letter for several days before, but there was an internal debate about how many signatories they needed before it was released, with some arguing that they should hold it back until it had at least 100 names.

5. Cabinet Office guidelines rule out election events on NHS property, but the hospital – built via PFI – had not yet become NHS property, thus providing a convenient loophole.

6. The building, unused since 1983, was meant to symbolise the need for change and renewal; but the alternate symbolism was pretty obvious: Battersea Power Station may look impressive on the outside, but inside is a void.

7. This explanation is dismissed by some Conservatives and Lib Dems ('sounds like a retrospective excuse to me'), but is confirmed by multiple members of Labour's debate team.

8. The phrase subsequently appeared on placards held aloft by Lib Dem activists as they accompanied Clegg on his tour across the country.

9. As in: 'The BP Garage near my house running out of Double Decker bars. #nickcleggsfault'.

10. This provoked over 600 complaints to Ofcom, arguing that Boulton had broken rule 63 of the debate rules. Ofcom did not have responsibility for the rules, and rejected the complaints. But even if it had had responsibility, it was not clear that Boulton had broken any rules. Sections 58–64 of the rules dealt with the role of the moderator. The role of the moderator is to 'moderate the debate' (rule 58), and it is 'not the moderator's role to criticise or comment on the leaders' answers' (rule 63). Yet Boulton neither criticised nor commented on an *answer*. Rule 37 sets out that all 'questions will be addressed to and answered by all three leaders', and whilst the question was addressed to all three, by inserting an extra comment before he asked for Clegg's response, his behaviour could perhaps be argued to break the spirit of that rule, but not the letter.

11. Similarly, a YouGov poll found just 9% of voters who said that they were less likely to vote Labour as a result of the Prime Minister's comments – almost all of whom anyway were already Conservative or Lib Dem supporters.

12. Both Labour and the Conservatives had attempted to do away with national press conferences in 2005, but had soon recanted.

13. There was, however, a lot of coverage of the leaders' *wives*, with close attention to what they were doing.

14. Including: 'How many members are there in a rugby league team?'

15. On 27 April, for example, the Prime Minister made a visit to Scotland. The decision to visit Scotland was only made at noon the day before (until then, the team had prepared both a Scotland and an England plan); exactly where in Scotland was then only decided in the late-afternoon, leaving very little time for preparation. 'Ridiculous', said one of those involved.

16. One reflected that in their preparation they had treated each debate as if it was self-contained, instead of seeing them as a linked series. 'We needed to think, how do we develop the argument.'

17. James Crabtree, 'David Cameron's battle to connect', *Wired*, 24 March 2010.

9
A Long Night, With No Winner: Election Night

As soon as polls closed on 6 May, two stories dominated the media. The first, coming sharp at 10pm, was the exit poll. Broadcast on BBC, ITN and Sky simultaneously, it predicted a hung parliament, with seat shares of: Conservative 307, Labour 255, Liberal Democrats 59 and others 29. That it predicted a hung parliament was no great surprise; that it predicted the Lib Dems to lose seats, after the campaign they had experienced, was much more of a shock, and the poll was met with disbelief by most commentators and those in the parties' HQs. Even the very accurate exit poll of 2005 had erred when it came to the Lib Dems, and there was a widespread belief that the same might well be true five years on.

The second story, filtering through in the hour or so after the polls closed, was of problems at polling stations, of long queues resulting in people being turned away, unable to vote. These included voters in Nick Clegg's constituency of Sheffield Hallam, where some students, angry that they had been denied the right to vote, tried to stop the transfer of ballot boxes, as well as in Leeds, Manchester, Birmingham, Newcastle, London, and Chester.[1] In Hackney, the police were called in to deal with protestors holding sit-ins.[2]

Initial explanations blamed the queues on a 'surge' in voting – with talk of high turnout reported across the UK. The Chair of the Electoral Commission, Jenny Watson, was hauled around various media outlets to be questioned on what had gone wrong, and there were a number of calls for her to resign or to be sacked. Yet it soon became clear, as results from the first few seats came through, there was in fact no large increase in turnout. It was to end up at 65%, up on its levels in 2001 and 2005, but still lower than at any election from 1922 until 1997.[3]

192

The cause of the problems was incompetence and penny-pinching by various local councils. Some (Acting) Returning Officers ignored guidelines about the correct ratio of population to polling stations.[4] Others did not allow enough staff, allocating just one Presiding Officer and Poll Clerk to each polling station regardless of the size of the population being serviced. And, worst of all, some councils based their assumptions of turnout on the levels in 'local government elections since 2006'. As the Electoral Commission's post-election *Interim Report* dryly noted, 'plans were not always based on robust, reasonable assumptions about the possible levels of turnout'.[5]

The first result came at 10.52pm in Houghton & Sunderland South, maintaining Sunderland South's record of declaring first in every contest since 1992. It produced the predicted Labour hold, but the 8.4% swing to the Conservatives would, if replicated elsewhere, have produced an outright Tory victory in the country as a whole. Washington & Sunderland West, the next to declare, had an even larger swing to the Conservatives. But Sunderland Central, which declared at 11.43pm, and which had been a long-shot Conservative target, produced a comfortable Labour hold on a swing to the Conservatives of just 4.8%, suggesting that Labour may be able to hold off the Conservatives where it mattered. Between them, the three Sunderland seats also revealed the first signs that there had in fact been no noticeable increase in turnout, and absolutely no evidence of any significant Lib Dem advance, up by a maximum of just 0.9%. The three seats also shared one other distinction: all returned MPs elected for the first time, all of whom were women. As of midnight on Thursday 6 May the UK had a 100% female House of Commons.

The first shock of the night came at 12.49am. Northern Ireland's embattled First Minister and DUP leader, Peter Robinson lost his seat in Belfast East to the Alliance Party, who were winning their first ever seat in the Westminster Parliament. The swing was an astonishing 22.9%. Robinson gave a dignified speech in which he noted that he had always preferred not to stand in the election. 'You should', he said 'always be careful what you wish for in politics.'

Other results from Northern Ireland – which was counting on election night for the first time – were less dramatic. David Cameron's attempt to break into Northern Irish politics came to naught, when Sylvia Hermon, the former Ulster Unionist MP, defeated the Ulster Conservatives and Unionists – New Force candidate to hold Down North. In neighbouring Down South, UCU leader Sir Reg Empey failed in his attempt to unseat the sitting DUP MP, William McCrea, leaving the UCU with no representation at all at Westminster. Empey resigned soon after the election, yet another unionist leader to bite the dust.[6]

In Fermanagh & South Tyrone, Michelle Gildernew hung on for Sinn Fein, fighting off a challenge from an independent Unionist backed by both the DUP and the UCU, winning by a mere four votes, the closest result of the election. Meanwhile, the SDLP doggedly held on to their existing three seats. More generally, however, the results confirmed the recent pattern of Northern Irish elections, in which the former 'extremist' parties outpolled what had previously been their more respectable rivals. Sinn Fein gained a larger share of the vote than they had in any Westminster election since they began contesting general elections in 1983, outpolling all the other parties for the first time in a Westminster election, albeit still coming second to the DUP in terms of seats.

Just after 1am, the Conservatives made their first gain of the night, taking Kingswood, 135th on their target list, on a massive swing of 9.4%, enough to get David Cameron into Downing Street with a majority. But the swing seen in Kingswood would be the exception rather than the rule, and as the night wore on it soon became clear that the exit poll had not been wrong. At 1.10am, the Conservatives failed to take Torbay (the seat even showing a swing away from the Conservatives to the Lib Dems), the first Con–Lib Dem seat that the Conservatives needed but had failed to gain. Of the 19 most marginal Con–Lib Dem seats, a mere five would fall to the Conservatives, and there were no signs of the extra gains from Labour needed to compensate. Of the 14 Con–Lab seats that the Conservatives had added to their battleground in April, to compensate for the rise in the popularity of the Lib Dems, they took just five.

There were other early signs that the expected Liberal Democrat surge had not materialised. Just after 1.30am, the Lib Dems failed to take City of Durham from Labour, and at 1.47am the top Liberal Democrat target seat of Guildford stayed resolutely Conservative.

At 1.43am, with just 40 seats declared, Gordon Brown held his own seat of Kirkcaldy & Cowdenbeath with a majority up 6.4% on 2005. In his acceptance speech he said that whilst the outcome of the country's vote was 'not yet known', his duty was to play his part 'in Britain having a strong, stable and principled government; able to lead Britain into sustained economic recovery; and able to implement our commitments to far-reaching reform to our political system, upon which there is a growing consensus in our country'. The Prime Minister then joined

Labour activists at a Kirkcaldy hotel in time to see Labour regain Glasgow East, lost to the SNP in a by-election in July 2008. Brown was said to have punched the air in delight at the news. At around 3am, the Prime Minister boarded a chartered jet at Edinburgh, bound for London. The travelling journalist pack – previously so frustrated by their lack of access – now found him in an expansive mood, talking about how he intended to remain Prime Minister. He had been worried about missing any key results whilst airborne, but as his plane landed cheers greeted the news that Labour had won Rochdale – the scene of bigotgate.[7] Mrs Duffy may not have voted for him, but Rochdale now had a Labour MP.[8]

Brown went straight to Labour HQ in Victoria Street, where he gave a brief speech to party workers ('the most human I've ever seen him', one of those present claimed). He told his staff he was proud of them, and that he knew the campaign had been a success, because the Labour Party had, at last, come to love Peter Mandelson. He was then taken off into a conference room by Mandelson and Alastair Campbell, to be briefed

In a Victoria Street meeting room, in the early hours of 7 May, Gordon Brown studies the numbers, flanked by Peter Mandelson (sending text messages) and Alastair Campbell (looking pensive). Sue Nye has her back to the camera.

(© J. Lawrence, Labour Party Archive)

by David Muir and Greg Cook, who told him that the Conservatives were poised to win over 300 seats, but that a hung parliament, in which Labour and the Liberal Democrats might be able to combine forces, was still a possibility.

The mood in Victoria Street was relatively upbeat; despite losing so many seats, staff felt they had avoided what could have been a much worse result, and achieved what they had been aiming for since the beginning of the year: to prevent a Conservative majority. Many still thought the Conservatives would govern as a minority administration, but Brown was not ready to concede, focusing relentlessly on the various permutations that would enable him to remain in Downing Street. During television interviews on election night, both Peter Mandelson and Alan Johnson talked up the idea of a 'progressive alliance' with the Liberal Democrats. Filled with the hope that some sort of accommodation with the Lib Dems might be feasible, Brown returned to Downing Street to catch up on a few hours' sleep.

At 2.02am Labour held Gedling in Nottinghamshire, 92nd on the Tories' target list. It was the first obvious manifestation of something identified in the exit poll (and discussed in more detail in Appendix 2), where a hard-working Labour incumbent – in this case the Schools Minister, Vernon Coaker – could manage to survive against the swing. The Conservatives would end the night having taken almost a clean sweep of seats from Labour in their top 100 targets. But of the nine they failed to take, eight were held by an incumbent Labour MP. A growing incumbency factor had been building up in recent Westminster elections.[9] But most observers (and many politicians) suspected that the expenses scandal would negate it this time, that 2010 would be the very worst election to be an incumbent, the best to be a challenger. But with most of the 'worst' expenses offenders gone, many of the remaining MPs were still able to reap the benefits of incumbency. The same also applied to the Liberal Democrats, who lost a majority of seats where their incumbent MP stood down, whilst managing to hold comfortably several seats which they had first won in 2005.

At 3.10am David Cameron was re-elected in Witney. Like the Prime Minister, he too had an increased majority. In his victory speech, he said that Labour had 'lost its mandate to govern', but he did not demand Gordon Brown's immediate resignation. He travelled down to Conservative HQ, where the mood was tense.

Initial scepticism at the exit poll had faded relatively early on, when seats such as Tooting (where there was just a 3.6% swing to the Conservatives) came through, and the party hierarchy soon realised that an overall majority was unlikely. A handful of larger swings in long-shot seats (such as Cannock Chase) later in the night gave some hope that they might just manage to win enough seats to be able to form a majority with the support of the DUP, but most of the night was spent with a grudging acceptance that an overall majority was out of reach.

There were two big display boards standing outside the Party Chairman's office at Millbank. One listed the 326 seats the party needed to form a majority, the second the remainder. As results came in, party workers stuck a coloured dot on each seat. Each red or yellow dot on the first board required a blue dot on the second board. Cameron arrived at Campaign Headquarters at about 4am, and stood in front of the board, looking at the dots, and asking questions about what was expected in individual seats. 'He knew exactly what it meant,' said one of his team. By that point, the internal calculation was that the maximum number of seats the party could win was 309, nowhere near enough for a majority, even with the support of the DUP.

Lord Ashcroft, the party's Deputy Chairman and architect of its key seats strategy, sat in Millbank for most of the evening, working his phone, sending texts and making calls to candidates his operation had helped. He was, and would remain, utterly unrepentant about his work for the party. Later that night, he slipped out of the building, to give an interview to Andrew Neil on BBC One's election night programme. Neil's first question ('What's gone wrong?') produced not a denial, but the observation that the debates had turned 'everything topsy turvey', and had reduced the Conservative lead. So were they a mistake, Neil asked? It was, Ashcroft claimed, 'a balanced argument in a way', although it was notable that the 'balance' consisted only of altruistic arguments in favour – the debates had raised awareness, turnout, discussion. It was clear that from what he called a 'pure strategic hindsight view' Ashcroft thought they had been a disaster, a view he was to expand upon privately and publicly over the coming months. He had told almost no one in Conservative HQ what he was going to do, and when he suddenly appeared on TV, it was the only time that night that Conservative headquarters went quiet.

At 3.54am, Labour gained Blaenau Gwent from the Independent MP, Dai Davies. Labour had lost the formerly rock-solid Labour seat in 2005, after the botched imposition of an all-women shortlist. About half an hour later, at 4.23am, Dr Richard Taylor, the independent MP for Wyre

Forest since 2001 lost his seat to the Conservatives. In the space of 30 minutes, the two 'independent' MPs in the Commons had gone.[10] With the exception of the party retread Sylvia Hermon in Down North, many other independents polled equally poorly. Ten minutes after Taylor's result, the former BBC presenter, Esther Rantzen polled a mere 1,872 votes, and lost her deposit, as Labour held on in Luton South. The newspaper columnist Suzanne Moore, who stood in Hackney North & Stoke Newington received a derisory 285 votes (0.6%). The better independent performances are listed in Appendix 1, but overall it is not a record of glory. Given the public anger of the preceding year following the expenses scandal, this was a poor return on so much anti-politics sentiment. The share of the vote going to the main parties was in decline (as John Curtice and colleagues discuss in Appendix 2) – but votes were seeping away to other political parties, not to independent candidates.

Many councils had initially planned to abandon counting throughout the night and move to Friday counts. A campaign to 'save' the 'traditional' election night had mobilised (although, like several British traditions, overnight counting was a reasonably modern invention, dating back to 1950), even roping in support from the Speaker.[11] Resulting measures in the government's Constitutional Reform and Governance Bill (which received support from all the main parties) compelled returning officers to hold counts within four hours of the close of poll except in exceptional circumstances, and the predicted number of Friday counts diminished dramatically, to just 22.

However, a combination of widespread local elections along with an increased requirement to verify last-minute postal votes, meant that the declarations had always been expected later than in previous elections.[12] The local elections required ballot papers to be separated before being counted.[13] The verification process, introduced by the Electoral Administration Act of 2006, introduced a tougher regime for postal votes to prevent fraud: Returning Officers had to check at least 20% of all postal votes against personal identifiers; many were aiming to check 100%.

Estimates for the number of seats expected to declare by 2am in 2010 were a mere 57.[14] In the event, counting in many seats overran considerably, stretching election night out over a much longer period than anticipated. By 4am there had been 313 declarations, fewer than half the Commons. Some 265 constituencies declared between 4am and 7am, and six declared so late on the Friday that they were overtaken by those which had not even begun counting until that morning.[15] For all involved, it was a long night.

At 4.27am Vera Baird, the Solicitor-General, lost her seat in Redcar to the Liberal Democrats, on a massive swing of 21.8%. Redcar – where the Corus steel plant had closed with widespread job losses – had been one of the long-shot Lib Dem gains, planned in secret by the party in 2009, but it was the only one the party went on to win. They would come close in Ashfield, where Geoff Hoon was standing down, but Labour held on by under 200 votes. What one of the Lib Dem campaign committee called their 'Northern Strategy' failed almost completely.

Five minutes later, the Schools Secretary Ed Balls clung on by 1,100 votes in Morley & Outwood. The seat had been a long-shot target for the Conservatives and, helped by an energetic local campaign, one of their few hopes of claiming a Cabinet scalp. There was no 'Portillo moment' in 2010, although two former Home Secretaries fell to defeat: at 4.36am Jacqui Smith lost Redditch to the Conservatives and at 4.55am Charles Clarke lost Norwich North to the Liberal Democrats.

Further down the ministerial hierarchy, however, there were more defeats. In addition to Baird, some 18 serving ministers and whips lost their seats. The landslide of 1997 aside, this was more than at any election since 1945.

At 4.53am, and after a recount, Edinburgh South was held by Labour by just 316 votes. What had been the top Lib Dem target in Scotland saw the party achieve a miserable 0.1% swing. Yet another Lib Dem failure (one of a dozen seats the party lost by fewer than 1,000 votes), it was also the closest Scotland saw to a seat changing hands. For the results in Scotland were remarkable for both their continuity and also their contrast with the rest of the UK.

The continuity was that, by-election results notwithstanding, not a seat changed hands. Labour regained two seats lost in by-elections (one of which had formerly been held by the Speaker Michael Martin), but no other constituency changed colour. With constituencies in flux everywhere else, the Scottish political map was constant.

The contrast was with the result in the rest of Great Britain. Labour's vote fell almost everywhere else, but in Scotland it went up – and by an impressive 2.5%. Yet again, the exit poll – which had detected a much better performance by Labour in Scotland – had got it right. The result was also a relief for the Lib Dems (whose vote fell badly in Scotland, whilst increasing across most of the rest of Great Britain) but who still managed to hold on to their 11 seats, as well as a bitter disappointment to the Conservatives. Thirteen years after the wipeout of 1997, the Conservative vote went up by a mere 0.9%, they came fourth in share of the vote, and ended the night still with just one seat in the whole of Scotland. The SNP gained votes but no extra seats.

The situation in Wales was different. Labour's vote there fell to the lowest level in any general election since 1918, losing four seats in the process. The Conservatives made reasonable advances, picking up five seats, and increasing their vote to 26.1%, although this was still lower than they gained between 1979 and 1992. Plaid saw their vote fall, and the Lib Dems made small advances in votes, whilst losing one seat – Lembit Öpik managing to lose Montgomeryshire, held by the Liberals more or less continuously since 1880, to the Conservatives.

At 5.22am Joanne Cash, the controversial Tory A-lister failed to take Westminster North from Labour, complaining about media 'lies'. About ten minutes later, Labour also held Hammersmith, where another leading Tory moderniser, Shaun Bailey, failed to take the Conservatives' 78th target seat. After the election there were criticisms from within Conservative ranks about the performance of the A-list candidates. But both Hammersmith and Westminster were also evidence of another trend of the night, again picked up in the exit poll: of seats with above average numbers of ethnic minority voters performing better for Labour, and as Appendix 2 demonstrates, the ethnicity of seats was much more significant than the failings of individual candidates.

Just before 6am, Caroline Lucas became the UK's first Green MP by taking Brighton Pavilion from Labour, and ten minutes later, the BNP leader, Nick Griffin, was heavily defeated in Barking by Labour's Margaret Hodge, with the Conservatives even managing to keep the BNP in third place. Overall, however, the total number of votes received by the BNP was the largest for any far-right party in British political history, albeit largely as a result of standing so many candidates. Its share of the vote in seats where it stood was lower than in 2005, and the failure to break through – allied with disappointing council election results – was to trigger a post-election split within the party. The Greens had stood roughly the same number of candidates yet saved a mere seven deposits, and averaged only 1.8% of the vote where they stood (also down on their performance in 2005). By most criteria it had been a much more successful night for the BNP than for the Greens, but the Greens had won a Westminster seat, and that achievement was enough to more than compensate for failures elsewhere.

In Sheffield, Liberal Democrat leader Nick Clegg had endured a miserable night. He had watched the exit poll in disbelief on TV at his home, and then gone to the count at a nearby leisure centre. But the result had been repeatedly delayed, and he was stuck there for hours, receiving news of friends and colleagues who had failed to win their seats, and with a growing sense of frustration. As one of those with him said, 'if we can't do it now, then when can we?' When his result was eventually announced just after 6.30am, he too had increased his majority – the third major party leader to do so – but he admitted that overall it had been a 'disappointing night'. 'We simply haven't achieved what we hoped.' There had been a brief discussion about whether to use the word 'disappointing', but Clegg's view was that the result was so clearly a disappointment that he may as well say so. The party had increased its share of the vote but would end the election with five fewer MPs. It was now too late to drive to London as originally planned without getting stuck in rush hour traffic, so he and the team returned to London by train, contemplating that although his party had lost seats, it held the balance of power. En route, he spoke to Paddy Ashdown and Danny Alexander, and discussed what to do next.

At Cowley Street the mood was flat. The Lib Dems had not organised an election night party for staff – they hoped to be working the next morning, and wanted people as fresh as possible – but many staffers had drifted off to an ad hoc party at the National Liberal Club, where there had not been much to cheer. On his arrival at Cowley Street, Clegg spoke to the press, and then gave a short speech to staff – many of whom were in tears.

Results continued to trickle in on the Friday. The Respect candidate, George Galloway lost decisively to Labour's Jim Fitzpatrick in Poplar & Limehouse; Labour regained Galloway's former seat of Bethnal Green & Bow. At just gone 2pm, the Speaker, John Bercow, easily held his Buckingham seat. The hospitalised Nigel Farage came third. UKIP saved just under 100 deposits, averaged 3.5% of the vote where they stood, and polled the best result of any 'minor' party, yet ended up without a seat.

By then, however, attention had shifted away from the remaining results, and onto the possible post-election scenarios. In private, contacts had already begun between the political parties. The parliamentary arithmetic was clear, and – despite the occasional blip – had been since relatively early on in the night. The short-hand figure used throughout the campaign as the target for a Commons majority was 326 (that is, half of the Commons, plus one). In fact, given that the five Sinn Fein MPs did not take their seats, the real target figure was 323, and – given predictably low rates of turnout from minor parties – a bearable *de facto* majority could be achievable with even fewer MPs. There were four key facts about the result:

1. No party could reach 323 alone.
2. The Conservatives and the DUP combined (314 seats) was not enough for a majority.
3. Labour and the Liberal Democrats combined (315) had more seats than the Conservatives but together could also not command a majority.
4. The Conservatives and the Liberal Democrats together (353) could command a comfortable majority.[16]

Based purely on the numbers, the most logical outcome was for a Conservative–Lib Dem deal. Yet there were obvious political problems with that would-be arrangement, and the results were close enough that other potential deals looked at least plausible. A Labour–Lib Dem deal might not deliver enough for a majority on its own, but it was close enough that if arrangements could be made with the minor parties at least not to vote against them in a vote of confidence, they could form an administration.

Britain had had an election, and no party had won. The hung parliament, which had long been predicted, was a reality. The post-election negotiations were about to begin.

Notes

1. In Hallam, there were also complaints that students were made to queue in one line, while long-term residents were fast-tracked.
2. In total, the Electoral Commission's report noted that problems occurred at 27 polling stations, across 16 constituencies, and involved at least 1,200 would-be voters. But these were minima, based on those still bothering to queue at 10pm. As a proportion of the 40,000 polling stations in action during the day (or the almost 30 million people who voted), it was a tiny proportion, but still concerning.
3. The size of the British population had, of course, grown in the meantime, and in total more people voted in 2010 than in every election up to and including 1970. But postal voting is now much more commonly available, and so the footfall in polling stations on the day of the election was noticeably down on

almost all post-war elections. Plus, polling stations now stay open for longer (until 10pm, as opposed to 9pm).

4. In one of the worst cases, in Sheffield Hallam, one polling station had some 4,469 electors (excluding postal voters), compared to the recommended limit of 2,500.

5. Electoral Commission, *Interim Report: Review of Problems at Polling Stations at Close of Poll on 6 May 2010*, 2010, p. 27.

6. See J. Tonge and J. Evans, 'Northern Ireland: Unionism Loses More Leaders', *Parliamentary Affairs*, 63:4 (2010), 158–75.

7. Isabel Oakeshott, Marie Woolf and Jonathan Oliver, 'Against the wall', *The Sunday Times*, 16 May 2010.

8. As a result of boundary changes, Rochdale was nominally a Labour seat, albeit one with an incumbent Liberal Democrat MP, and it is therefore technically not counted as a Labour 'gain'. But most within Labour had written it off following the previous week's events.

9. See J. Curtice et al., 'Appendix 2: The Results Analysed', in D. Kavanagh and D. Butler, *The British General Election of 2005* (Basingstoke: Palgrave Macmillan, 2005), pp. 247–9.

10. Both were self-identifying 'independents', although both were in fact members of political parties, albeit parochial parties – Kidderminster Hospital and Health Concern and Blaenau Gwent People's Voice. See P. Cowley and M. Stuart, 'There Was a Doctor, a Journalist and Two Welshmen: The Voting Behaviour of Independent MPs in the United Kingdom House of Commons, 1997–2007', *Parliamentary Affairs*, 62:1 (2009), 19–31.

11. HC Debs, 18 January 2010, c.23.

12. Local elections were taking place in the London Boroughs, Metropolitan Districts as well as in a number of other councils in England.

13. Even in areas where councils use separate ballot boxes for local and general elections, verification of both sets of ballots is required before counting can begin.

14. By 2am in the 1992 election (when there had been no local elections), some 464 seats had been declared. By 2am in 2005 (with local elections), there had been 166.

15. Hackney North & Stoke Newington (which had been expected to declare at 4am on the Friday morning), ended up doing so at 3.31pm on the Friday, along with Dudley North (which had been expected to declare as early as 2am on the Friday morning).

16. These calculations exclude the Speaker, and assume – as everyone rightly did – that the Conservative would hold the seat of Thirsk & Malton, where the contest had been postponed due to the death of the UKIP candidate.

10
Five Days in May:
The Formation of the Coalition

Midway through the election campaign, and with a hung parliament looking likely, one Labour Cabinet Minister had a long discussion with his former Special Adviser about the different post-election scenarios. His SpAd explained the various permutations in loving detail: how Labour could trail in votes but be ahead in seats; the difference between a full coalition and a 'confidence and supply' agreement, which would allow a minority government supported by another party; the possibility that the Liberal Democrats might refuse to deal with Labour unless they were led by a different leader than Gordon Brown; and the chronology of coalition, the timing of the various decisions that would need to be made. The Minister listened intently, and then remarked that it all sounded very complicated and he really hoped someone was thinking about it.

Thankfully, both the political system and the parties had prepared for the result, albeit to differing degrees. The likelihood of a hung parliament had generated several reports and much discussion over the preceding five years.[1] In 2009, a high-level conference at Ditchley Park, attended by a mixture of the constitutional great and the good, had discussed the process of managing changes of government.[2] Participants broadly agreed on the conventions themselves, but felt that the previous position of the rules being understood at elite level but not published was unsatisfactory in the age of 24-hour news, and febrile financial markets.

Separately, the Cabinet Secretary had reached the conclusion – based both on reading the various published reports, and on contacts with his opposite number in New Zealand – that it would be useful to pull together the conventions in a Cabinet manual and publish them in advance of the election. The problem was how to make them public. Both the Palace and the Cabinet Office could not do so, wary of appearing to prejudge the outcome of the election. After some private discussions amongst some of the conference participants, it was agreed that a suitable mechanism would be a select committee inquiry, which Alan Beith, the chair of the Justice Select Committee, agreed to hold.[3] The inquiry provided a vehicle for the Cabinet Office to publish the relevant chapter of its Cabinet Manual, on Elections and Government Formation, prior to the election.

The aim was to demystify the process, but also to avoid involving the Queen in the process, with the chapter stressing that it was for the political parties and not the Monarch to work out who could command confidence in the Commons: 'Where a range of different administrations could potentially be formed, the expectation is that discussions will take place between political parties on who should form the next Government. The Monarch would not expect to become involved in such discussions, although the political parties and the Cabinet Secretary would have a role in ensuring that the Palace is informed of progress.'[4] The Palace was to be an observer, not a participant. The guidance also made it clear that the incumbent Prime Minister would remain in office until it was apparent who could form a new government, while Gordon Brown agreed that the civil service could facilitate any negotiations and offer factual advice to the participants in any talks.[5]

The Cabinet Office also organised role play exercises to cover different electoral outcomes, with civil servants playing the roles of the different party leaders. As the Cabinet Secretary later revealed, they managed to reach a successful conclusion under almost all the scenarios they could envisage. The exception was 'Scenario Four' – the closest of all the scenarios to the results on 6 May.[6]

Preparations by the political parties were more varied and ad hoc. Not surprisingly, the best prepared were the Liberal Democrats. In December 2009, Clegg appointed the four individuals who would serve as their negotiating team in the event of a hung parliament: Danny Alexander, Chris Huhne, David Laws, and Andrew Stunell. After an initial meeting with Clegg, Vince Cable, and the Party President Ros Scott, to agree on ground rules, the team then met once or twice a month until the election, working on both the policy outcomes that they wanted from, but also the approach they would take in, any negotiations. They spoke to Jim Wallace, to draw on the experience in Scotland.[7] This resulted in two substantive policy documents drawn up by Alexander – one on policy demands for a coalition (about 15 pages long) and another on demands for a confidence and supply agreement (ten pages). There was also a document on tactics, drawn up by Andrew Stunell. (One senior Lib Dem was later to describe Stunell as the party's secret weapon.) Circulation of the documents was confined to a very small group at the top of the party.

Both Labour and the Conservatives were noticeably less well-prepared. Despite the likelihood that a hung parliament would be the outcome of the election, the majority of Labour and Conservative preparations were undertaken only during the election campaign itself. Various Labour figures had for some months made tentative and private enquiries towards the Lib Dems but had always been rebuffed. Brown's Head of Policy, Nick Pearce and Gavin Kelly, his Deputy Chief of Staff, had done some preparatory work in the new year on possible post-election outcomes. And on the Monday of election week, the Prime Minister asked Pearce to prepare a document on Liberal Democrat policy, identifying the areas where Labour felt they could do business. It ran to ten pages, under seven different headings: electoral reform, nuclear energy, Trident, tax credits, ID cards, National Insurance, and the pupil premium. The document was passed to Brown on the day before polling, and then circulated to Peter Mandelson and Andrew Adonis.

Around 9.30pm on polling day, before the polls closed, David Muir contacted the former Lib Dem leader, Paddy Ashdown, via an intermediary, to ask that the Lib Dems keep their options open during election night, and not rush into any arrangement with the Conservatives in the event of a hung parliament. The request was largely redundant – the Liberal Democrats were already intending to say that there was no need to rush to a decision – but it was to establish a useful back channel open throughout the negotiations, as a way of keeping Downing Street in touch with Labour-minded Liberal Democrats.

In the event that they failed to achieve a majority, most Conservatives had hoped to be able to do a deal with the DUP to generate a narrow majority or at worst to govern as a minority administration, bringing forward a budget and daring the others to defeat it ('Nick Clegg won't vote against our first budget', one of them had predicted). This was also the dominant view in the senior civil service. None of the work of Francis Maude's Implementation Unit (see p. 89) had even contemplated a post-election coalition. But amongst a small group at the top of the party, there had been pre-election discussions about various other possibilities, including coalition. Privately, they would distinguish between what they called Route A (a full coalition) and Route B (a confidence and supply agreement). Despite attacking the idea of a post-election deal publicly, Cameron mentioned to both William Hague and George Osborne during the campaign that coalition might be an option.[8] Preparations stepped up a gear after the first leaders' debate, and Oliver Letwin was charged with drawing up a paper on the Lib Dems and their possible policy demands. The four Conservative negotiators – Letwin, Osborne, Hague and Ed Llewellyn – were appointed during the election campaign, and held two meetings at Osborne's house to discuss the work. The resulting paper noted overlap but also tensions, going into Lib Dem policy platforms in detail. Some Labour figures occasionally mocked Letwin for his slightly wonkish other-worldly nature, but in a task like this, involving close reading of policy detail, he was in his element, and Liberal Democrats during the negotiations would praise his understanding of their policy.[9]

Ed Llewellyn also supplied some personal contact, being an old friend of both Nick Clegg and his wife, Miriam, who used to work with Llewellyn in European Commissioner Chris Patten's Brussels office – as well as having worked for Paddy Ashdown in Bosnia. Around 4am on the morning after the election, once it was obvious that the Conservatives would not achieve an overall majority, the Conservative leader authorised his team to make contact with the Liberal Democrats. Llewellyn, who had returned to London from Witney ahead of Cameron, texted Danny Alexander, followed by a quick conversation, and they agreed to speak again later in the day. After a few hours' sleep, the Conservative team gathered on the Friday morning in David Cameron's hotel suite, across the river from Westminster. By then, it was clear that Route A was his favoured option. Given the economic crisis, and the need to make unpopular decisions, he felt any government would need to serve for the full parliament. 'It wasn't just about getting into No 10,' one of those close to him noted, 'it was about getting things done.' This, however, was not the unanimous view of the room, several present preferring to go for a minority administration, but the majority view – and Cameron's himself – was strongly in favour of a coalition.

Having won more votes and most seats, Cameron had the 'mandate' Nick Clegg had talked about during the election, and assumed that they would begin negotiations with the Liberal Democrats shortly. But until they heard the Liberal Democrat leader say so explicitly – which he did outside Cowley Street that morning in front of a media scrum – there were concerns amongst the Conservative team that Clegg would find some way to wriggle out of his earlier position, and open negotiations with Gordon Brown instead. Cameron's counter-statement just after 2.30pm on the Friday, delivered at St Stephen's Club, included what he called a 'big, open and comprehensive offer' towards the Liberal Democrats, a phrase that had been agreed on during that morning's discussions. Cameron's speech did not include the word 'coalition', but it explicitly said that he was willing to go further than merely a confidence and supply agreement. The Liberal Democrat negotiating team realised the significance of what was being offered.

The view from a Cowley Street window, as Nick Clegg says he will open talks with the Conservatives

Direct talks between the Conservatives and the Liberal Democrats began that evening in the Cabinet Office in 70 Whitehall. Various alternate venues had been prepared, but the parties chose the Cabinet Office, to symbolise getting their feet in the door of government. George Osborne also favoured the venue as a way of putting pressure on Gordon Brown ('being physically in the building, I knew would drive him wild'). In addition to the four lead negotiators, and out of the sight of the media, there was also a rotating cast list of other party staff present, to contribute on aspects of policy. Initial discussions focused on matters of process – when they would meet, how they would conduct the meetings – and their first decision was to dispense with the offer of civil service note-takers. 'We all looked at each other,' one of them said, 'and thought "no thank you very much".'[10] The wisdom of that decision became clear two days later when it was revealed that the Cabinet Office had already had Freedom of Information requests for the meeting's paperwork. Despite the room being stiflingly hot due to a faulty central heating system, the discussions were friendly and professional. 'It was clear from the off', said one of the Conservatives, 'that it was very comfortable. They were just reasonable people to deal with. There was a fair bit of humour, joshing and laughter.'

During that first meeting, the participants also outlined their own internal party procedures. For the Conservatives, things were straightforward: William Hague said that they would occasionally need to consult with David Cameron, and at some point they would have to consult with the parliamentary party. The Liberal Democrats then explained the party's complicated 'triple lock' rules.[11] 'They all looked at us as if we were mad,' said one Lib Dem.

In addition to the meetings of the negotiating teams – each of which would attract a massive media scrum, largely in order to film groups of middle-aged men going into and then later out of a building – there was a second strand to the negotiations, involving direct contact between the party leaders, either by phone or face-to-face. The full extent and importance of these contacts only became clear after the negotiations had been concluded. Clegg and Cameron had spoken by phone at 4pm, prior to the formal negotiations beginning. Later that night, Gordon Brown also telephoned Clegg, at the request of both Danny Alexander and some senior Liberal Democrats who preferred cooperation with Labour. The conversation was tense, with Clegg feeling that he had been talked at by Brown, rather than engaging in two-way discussion, but it was not the angry exchange reported at the time in the media. Clegg summed it up later: 'He spoke more than I did.'[12]

In addition, there were countless text messages and phone calls between various members of the negotiating teams. As one of the Lib Dems involved put it, 'the role of texts in modern politics is one of the unwritten stories'. Peter Mandelson had first texted Danny Alexander after noon on the Friday: 'Between us (pl protect) ask Nick how big an obstacle is GB for LDs'.[13] Much was later made of the difficulties Brown and Clegg had in clicking during the negotiations. Clegg had previously found Brown difficult to deal with, whereas he struck up an easy relationship with David Cameron.[14] This was often put down to their backgrounds – both were young, English, public-school educated – but it was also about the positions they found themselves in. Both Cameron and Clegg had been MPs for less than a decade, in which they had only known opposition (and opposition to a government in which Gordon

Brown was a key, or the key, figure). Moreover, any putative Clegg–Brown relationship was inhibited somewhat by what Danny Alexander termed the 'personnel' question – the issue of 'GB' and the extent to which his remaining in office was a barrier for the Lib Dems. It was a constant theme in the negotiations and was unlikely to facilitate a firm bond developing between the two men.

One of Brown's closest aides observed that the Prime Minister's view was that the shared values and policies of the two parties made a Labour–Lib Dem deal easy to achieve; it was, he said, typical of Brown that he did not think personal chemistry mattered. Many of the approaches Labour politicians made to Liberal Democrats made the same assumption as Brown: that Labour and the Liberal Democrats were natural partners in some 'progressive alliance'. Such a stance irked many Lib Dems – as did the continual use by some Labour figures, including Brown, of 'Liberal' for their party's name. It overlooked both the number of Lib Dem–Conservative councils that were functioning well around the country and the extent to which there had been a generational shift at the top of the Liberal Democrats. The new generation had not cut their political teeth fighting against Margaret Thatcher or John Major; every member of the Lib Dem negotiating team – and their Leader – had entered the Commons after 1997. Labour politicians saw their party as a progressive party; that was not how it looked to many of the key Liberal Democrats, who had been voting against Labour policy, day-in, day-out, in the House of Commons for years. This did not mean they necessarily favoured a deal with the Conservatives – most would still have instinctively preferred a deal with Labour – but it meant that they did not see an arrangement with the Conservatives as impossible. Many of Labour's high command enjoyed excellent links with previous Lib Dem leaders. During the negotiations, they had no problem persuading Ming Campbell or Charles Kennedy that a deal with Labour was the right way to proceed. Where they struggled was with the Lib Dems who actually mattered.

Saturday saw Nick Clegg consult with his party's MPs and peers, at a three-hour meeting at Local Government House in Smith Square, ironically the former headquarters of the Labour Party. For all the criticisms there had been about Clegg's style of leadership in the preceding years (see p. 109), there were few Lib Dem complaints about a lack of consultation during the negotiations and it was to be the first of many meetings the leadership would have with the party before any agreement was reached. Outside the meeting, a group of several hundred pro-PR supporters urged no sell-out on electoral reform. The general mood among the Lib Dem parliamentarians inside was that they did indeed need a more concrete deal on voting reform from the Conservatives, rather than merely a committee of inquiry which they had been promised. The meeting ended with Clegg's MPs endorsing his strategy of pursuing a deal in 'the national interest', as did the party's Federal Executive later. That evening, Nick Clegg met with David Cameron at Admiralty House for 70 minutes of secret talks, one-on-one, but, unknown to the Conservatives, he also spoke again on the telephone with Gordon Brown, and a Labour negotiating team met with Liberal Democrats in secret for exploratory talks. The Liberal Democrat leader was keeping both potential negotiating partners in play, a strategy he was to follow for most of the negotiations.

The first Labour–Liberal Democrat meeting took place in secret in Portcullis House, rather than the Cabinet Office. The Lib Dems were aware what it would look like to be negotiating with two different parties, and they did not want pictures of them going into the same venue, but with different partners. Five Labour negotiators met them, including Labour's Deputy Leader Harriet Harman. After introductions, much of the meeting was spent discussing the possibilities for electoral reform in the event of any deal. Despite later claims that Labour had not prepared for the meeting properly – no negotiating lines, no agreement on who was to do what – a memo on electoral reform had been prepared for Peter Mandelson's use before the meeting, and he stuck carefully to it during the meeting. Lib Dem negotiators picked up a sense of division within the Labour team – which reflected the fact that they were divided between those who were enthusiastic for a deal, like Mandelson and Andrew Adonis, and those who were sceptical, like Ed Balls and Ed Miliband. For their part, Labour negotiators ended the meeting not entirely clear what the Lib Dems were after in terms of electoral reform.

The Prime Minister had flown to Scotland on Saturday, not wanting to appear to be 'squatting' in Downing Street, but continuing to cling to the idea that perhaps he could stay on for a number of months. But other figures in Downing Street, particularly Peter Mandelson, were increasingly impressing upon him that he needed to step down soon in order to facilitate a deal with the Liberal Democrats. Brown initially appeared to accept this idea, promising to go by October, as part of a comprehensive reform package, including a full coalition with the Liberal Democrats. He was given the same message very early on the Sunday morning by Vince Cable, who told him that a vague promise by him to step down would not be enough to initiate formal talks with the Liberal Democrats. He would have to be much more specific. On his return from Scotland, Brown met with Clegg for 75 minutes of talks in the office of Sir Peter Ricketts, the

Permanent Under-Secretary at the Foreign Office. He offered to resign in the autumn, once he had secured measures on electoral reform.[15]

Meanwhile, formal talks between the Conservatives and the Liberal Democrats had resumed, and lasted some six-and-a-half hours. The teams negotiated in blocks of 90 minutes or so, breaking occasionally for coffee, or to 'seek higher authority', going off to adjacent suites of offices to speak to the party leaders over the phone. They focused almost exclusively on policy, leaving issues of personnel to the leaders themselves. Much of the initial discussion dealt with areas where the parties agreed, in an attempt to build up confidence by dealing with the easier issues first – a process one negotiator described as 'clearing the undergrowth' – and largely deferred consideration of the trickier issues, including electoral reform. Yet they all knew it was a crucial issue and could yet prove to be the stumbling block.

The Conservatives showed no signs of giving ground on electoral reform, and Cameron correctly suspected Clegg was now engaged in parallel talks with Labour. At around midnight, Brown and Nick Clegg met again, this time with Peter Mandelson and Danny Alexander also in attendance. On this occasion, the Prime Minister reneged from his pledge to have gone by October, promising only to step down 'sometime during the parliament'. Brown claims not to have been prevaricating, but feared others in the room might leak the information if he was specific.[16] The problem with this defence of his behaviour is that it poses at least as many questions as it answers, of which the most important is: how, given his reputation as someone who dithered when making important decisions, Brown could have failed to understand the impact that any apparent prevarication would have on Clegg and the Liberal Democrats? It may well be that this is the correct defence of Brown's behaviour that Sunday night, but if so it is one which reflects poorly on his judgement. Those Lib Dems who favoured a deal with Labour were appalled, and in an effort to get the process back on board, Paddy Ashdown even telephoned Tony Blair in the Middle East to try to persuade him to talk Brown into standing down by the autumn.[17]

At a Downing Street meeting early on Monday morning, Alastair Campbell, Andrew Adonis and Peter Mandelson all strongly advised the Prime Minister to revert to his October departure date. Shortly after 10.30am, Brown and Mandelson left Downing Street for talks with Clegg, whilst the Lib Dem negotiating team met for a further round of talks with the Conservatives. This time, Brown agreed to go by the autumn. Clegg then held an extended meeting with his MPs at 1.30pm. Afterwards, David Laws made a statement in which he indicated that progress had been made with the Conservatives, but that Lib Dem MPs were asking for 'clarification' in terms of education funding, fair taxes and voting reform.

Around 4pm, Nick Clegg telephoned David Cameron, and during a 15-minute conversation, asked him to match or at least nearly match Labour's offer, including Conservative backing for the Alternative Vote (AV), not simply holding a referendum where the Conservative Party could campaign for a 'no' vote. Clegg then told Cameron that he would open talks formally with Labour, causing Cameron to end the conversation abruptly.

At 5pm, on the Monday, in a dramatic statement outside Number 10, Gordon Brown announced his party's intention to take forward formal discussions with the Liberal Democrats in order to create 'a progressive coalition government'. Brown expressed a desire not to stay on in his position as leader of the Labour Party any longer than necessary, saying a timetable would be put in place for a Labour leadership contest, with a view to a new leader being in place by the time of the Labour Party conference in September. He walked back into the war room in Number 12, where the staff all stood up and applauded. An emotional Peter Mandelson went into a side room, and shed a tear. Alastair Campbell and Andrew Adonis, both enthusiasts for a deal with the Lib Dems, toured the television studios praising Brown's ultimate sacrifice, while claiming that there existed a greater commonality of purpose between the Liberal Democrats and Labour than with the Lib Dems and the Conservatives. The Cabinet met at 6pm to endorse the Prime Minister's strategy. There were three dissenters – Andy Burnham, Jack Straw and Liam Byrne were all sceptical about a deal with the Liberal Democrats. But the majority was in favour, and potential Labour leadership contenders agreed to hold their fire, and not to announce their candidatures for the time being.

Earlier in the day there had been rumours a deal with the Conservatives was imminent. Instead, suddenly, the momentum now appeared to be with a Lib–Lab deal, and things looked bleak for the Conservatives. Calling a second meeting of his Shadow Cabinet the same day, Cameron sought agreement to concede to the Lib Dem demand for a referendum on AV. Chris Grayling dissented, but otherwise Cameron succeeded in winning over the Shadow Cabinet.

At a later meeting with his parliamentary party, in Committee Room 14 in the Commons, Cameron stressed that failure to agree to a referendum would only result in the Liberal Democrats doing a deal with Labour. He told his MPs – as he had told the Shadow Cabinet – that Labour was offering the Liberal Democrats AV without a referendum. Object to a

Con–Lib coalition government *with* a referendum on AV, he said, and Conservative MPs would be faced with a Lab–Lib coalition and AV *without* a referendum. Reluctant Conservative MPs appeared to have nowhere to go, and with a handful of right-wing Conservative MPs dissenting, Cameron's view won the day by acclaim.

The Shadow Cabinet watch Gordon Brown announce his decision to resign
(© Andrew Parsons)

Yet at no point, in any of the formal meetings they held did Labour ever offer the Liberal Democrats electoral reform without a referendum. They had discussed different options for electoral reform, including a referendum on proportional representation (either alone, or as part of a multi-question referendum, or to follow the introduction of AV), but insisted at the very first meeting that a referendum must be part of the deal. On the authority of Nick Brown, the Chief Whip, they made it clear that they could not carry an AV bill without a referendum through the Parliamentary Labour Party. It is possible that legislating for AV without a referendum was offered in one of the private meetings between Brown and Clegg, but both Clegg and Brown deny this. After one meeting with Clegg, Brown said that he didn't think it was an option, telling an aide 'we'd get killed and the party would not have it'. Clegg has confirmed that he was not offered it either in the formal meetings or by Brown personally.[18]

Cameron's defence is that he did not deceive his backbenchers, because he believed it at the time. Several of those involved in the negotiations still remain convinced that the offer was made at some point – there were, one said, 'lots of channels', and Brown was 'offering anything'. Certainly several senior Lib Dems genuinely believed at the time the offer had been made. Rumours even circulated of a draft Queen's speech, shown to the Lib Dem negotiators, containing the pledge.[19] Clegg's post-coalition explanation was that there were 'discussions around [the subject], and it might have been an offer that might have been made and might have been considered', which does not help much, but at one of the Clegg–Brown meetings, Brown is said to have remarked 'we can do it any way that you want'.

Both Lib Dems and Conservatives deny they were the source of the story, although it suited both. For the Lib Dems it helped put the pressure on the Conservatives to raise their offer on electoral reform. For the Conservative leadership it helped because it increased the pressure on their MPs, and allowed them to paint Gordon Brown and Labour as unscrupulous, willing to do anything to stay in power.

When it later became clear that no such formal offer had been made there was understandable unhappiness on the Conservative benches, prompting the charge that the coalition had been formed on a lie.[20] Whether it was a lie or just a misunderstanding is still not clear, but it may not have been as crucial as this claim implies either. Without the disputed claims about AV without a referendum, the situation was as follows: Labour was offering a referendum on AV and/or other electoral systems, and the Conservatives were merely offering a commission of inquiry. Given the importance of electoral reform to the Liberal Democrats, it was close to impossible for them to have made a deal with the Conservatives without gaining an improvement on that offer – as several of the Conservative negotiating team admit. In other words, the Conservatives needed to up their offer, whether or not Labour had offered AV without a referendum. The stories may have helped put pressure on Conservative backbenchers, but they did not change a fundamental reality under-pinning the negotiations.

Just after 7pm, William Hague made a statement in which he said that the Conservatives were willing to make 'a final offer' of a post-legislative referendum on AV, meaning that a referendum bill would be whipped through the Commons, but with the Conservatives free to campaign against it during the referendum campaign. It was not quite what Clegg had asked for, nor was it as much as Labour had offered, but it represented a huge shift in the Conservative position.

Formal public talks between the Liberal Democrats and Labour began later that evening. What occurred in this meeting is just as contested.

Labour's negotiating team had now shrunk to four – Harman was not present, leaving Adonis, Balls, Mandelson, and Ed Miliband. The Liberal Democrats claimed Labour's tone was all wrong, too arrogant, as though they were not interested in a proper partnership of equals, and contrasted sharply with what had been the more respectful tone of the Conservative negotiating team. Labour tended to see the 'new government as a continuation of the old government, just with a few irritants added in', as one of the Lib Dem negotiators put it. They singled out the two Eds as being especially problematic. And besides, the Liberal Democrat negotiators were coming increasingly to the view that the Conservatives, as one put it, had 'given us virtually the whole Lib Dem manifesto'. Several of the Lib Dem negotiating team had, by this stage, real doubts about the possibility of any deal with Labour, but continued to negotiate, urged on by their MPs who still preferred a pro-Labour arrangement, and in order to lever further concessions out of the Conservatives. That night, Clegg reported back to his parliamentary party, telling Lib Dem MPs: 'I'm afraid the meeting with Labour was terrible … They don't seem to be serious about dealing with us.'

This view is challenged strongly by Labour figures present, many of whom claim the Lib Dem negotiators were looking for a way out, a way to justify doing a deal with the Conservatives.[21] But true or not it was an influential argument with the Lib Dem parliamentarians. Norman Baker and Don Foster spoke up, suggesting that the party had little option but to make a deal with the Conservatives. Even Vince Cable, one of the more Labour-inclined Liberal Democrats, got up and said, 'I hate the Tories. I have spent my whole life fighting them. But I think we could be quite influential if we go with the Tories.'[22]

David Cameron and his team were waiting for news of the talks in Cameron's office in Norman Shaw South, with Cameron joking that they should perhaps begin to put the pictures back on the wall – and were sent word that a deal was still a possibility. In retrospect, the various meetings late on the Monday were to prove the turning point. It was the moment Cameron persuaded his party to move ground sufficiently to facilitate an agreement, and at which the mass of Liberal Democrat MPs finally accepted that they would be able to do a deal with the Conservatives. Cameron claims to have gone home that night and told his wife that he thought it was all falling apart. It was not a view shared by his negotiating team. When one of them reached home, to be greeted by his wife who had been watching TV reports of a probable Lib–Lab deal, he told her not to worry: 'it's going to be fine'. One of the few things that all the negotiating teams agree on is that the news media – not used to reporting coalition-formation, and denied access to the negotiations – was consistently about six hours behind the story.

The Tory-leaning press vented their spleen against both Labour and Nick Clegg the following morning. The *Daily Mail* described the previous day's events as 'a squalid day for democracy', while the *Daily Express* dubbed the Lib–Lab plan as a 'shabby stitch-up'. Nor were many Conservatives happy with the way that Nick Clegg had behaved. The right-wing Conservative Way Forward group announced it was opposed to a Liberal Democrat–Conservative coalition, and in an unusual display of undiplomatic language, the former Foreign Secretary, Sir Malcolm Rifkind accused the Lib Dems of 'two-timing'.

Meanwhile, beyond those leading Labour figures such as Peter Mandelson, Andrew Adonis and Alan Johnson who had always been keen on some sort of progressive alliance, few Labour backbenchers could be found who agreed that the idea of a Lib–Lab coalition was a runner. Over the weekend of 8–9 May, most Labour MPs had held their tongues.[23] But on the Monday and Tuesday, a widespread view emerged inside the PLP that Labour had been defeated, and that the party needed to reconcile itself to a period in Opposition. Despite having stepped down as an MP, John Reid, the former Home Secretary, waded into the controversy on Monday night, claiming that a Lib–Lab pact would not be welcomed by the country. It would, he claimed, be 'pretty disastrous' to include the SNP in any coalition. The following morning (Tuesday 11 May), David Blunkett, another former Labour Home Secretary, told the *Today* programme that he did not like the attempts being made to form a Lib–Lab coalition. The Lib Dems, he said, were 'behaving like every harlot in history', echoing the view of the *Daily Telegraph* that morning. Tom Harris, the Labour MP for Glasgow South, who had already aired his doubts on *Newsnight* the previous evening, also expressed concern to the BBC that his party might be seen to be 'scrabbling around in a very ungracious way' to hold on to power. Liberal Democrats who favoured a deal with Labour looked on in horror.

Talks between Labour and the Liberal Democrats resumed on Tuesday morning, but they fared no better than the night before, and broke up just before 1pm. Number 10 was picking up increasingly unfavourable vibes from the Liberal Democrats; a 2pm email from Downing Street read, 'We are increasingly worried they [Lib Dems] are playing games.' A senior Liberal Democrat made it known that his party now wanted the main Labour leadership contenders to offer public statements of support (as opposed to mere private assurances) for any Lib–Lab deal. Events were clearly moving away from Labour, and Brown's advisers were coming to the view that the Liberal Democrats were looking for an excuse to justify an impending deal with the Conservatives. In an email to Downing Street, a Labour go-between with the Liberal Democrats wrote: 'Game over? I think there is now deadlock. Too many of them don't trust us, and too many of us don't trust them. What a shame: I believe it could have been different.'

By contrast, Liberal Democrat and Conservative negotiations, which resumed at 2pm, and would go on for more than five hours, were reaching the end-game, and a draft coalition document was taking shape. The document focused on issues where the parties overlapped (to identify strengths, to help bind them together) and those where there were obvious differences (to set out how those tensions were to be resolved). Issues that fell in the middle were to be deferred, left to a fuller agreement that would come out later. Throughout the afternoon, a succession of Labour figures continued to speak out against a Lib–Lab deal. The *Evening Standard* reported Andy Burnham's Cabinet opposition; Lord Falconer claimed, during an interview on the BBC, that Labour were 'doing ourselves damage now in trying to do a deal. The sense that people will bargain on any basis in order to stay in power is unacceptable.' He called on Labour to 'call it quits'; and David Lammy, the Business and Skills Minister, said that it was 'deeply unfortunate' that the PLP had not been consulted.

The Prime Minister and his staff had gathered in the horseshoe war room in No 12 Downing Street. As the afternoon wore on, it was obvious that the game was up. Clegg made a series of phone calls which ended when Brown refused to delay a visit to the Palace any longer. His staff could hear the Prime Minister's end of the conversation: 'Nick, Nick. I can't hold on any longer. Nick. I've got to go to the Palace. The country expects me to. I can't go on any longer.'[24] The Prime Minister said goodbye to his closest aides. His two sons, John and Fraser, came in and stood on one of the desks, posing for photographs, taken by *Guardian* photographer, Martin Argles, who had been given exclusive access during these final hours of the Brown premiership. Brown walked through to the foyer of Number 10, thanking staff as he went.

At 7.17pm, the Prime Minister, standing outside Number 10, announced that he was resigning with immediate effect. He said that it had been a privilege to serve as Prime Minister; he had enjoyed doing the second best job in the land, second only to being a husband to his wife, Sarah, and a father to his two sons. Sarah and Gordon each held a hand of one of their sons as they left Downing Street. At 7.43pm, Brown left Buckingham Palace, after a 15-minute audience with the Queen. From there, he was taken to Labour Party HQ in Victoria Street, where he made an emotional speech, thanking party workers for all the work they had done, claiming that Labour had not been routed.

Amongst those watching Brown's resignation on television were most – though not all – of the Lib Dem and Conservative negotiators, still locked in the Cabinet Office. Alerted by increasingly frequent text messages that something was up, Ed Llewellyn had slipped out of the building and returned to David Cameron's office to arrange the next stage of the process, where he was joined by Nick Clegg.

At 8pm, David Cameron and his wife – who had rushed over from their house in West London – were driven to the Palace in a silver Jaguar for a short audience with the Queen, accepting her invitation to form a Government, becoming the twelfth politician of her reign to do so. Aged a mere 43, he was the youngest Prime Minister since Lord Liverpool in 1812 – and the nineteenth Old Etonian to become Prime Minister. Dispensing with police motorcycle outriders, Cameron's car made its way back to Downing Street, where at 8.43pm, the new Prime Minister gave a short speech, saying he wanted to form 'a proper and full coalition' with the Liberal Democrats in order to ensure strong and stable government. His administration would be based on freedom, fairness and responsibility. It was necessary to rebuild trust with the electorate, but also to be honest about what governments could achieve. As Prime Minister, he hoped to create a more responsible society, where people asked, not 'what are my entitlements?', but 'what can I do?'

Yet at this point, and with the new Prime Minister ensconced in Downing Street, there was still no formal coalition agreement. By departing when he did, Brown had forced Cameron's hand, and neither David Cameron nor Nick Clegg's respective parties had yet to accept the draft coalition agreement. Brown's decision to go annoyed Clegg, who felt he should have stayed until the new government was ready (as did some at the Palace), and several of the Conservatives believed it was a final attempt to destabilise a potential Con–Lib deal. For their part, those around Brown felt he could not simply be left hanging on, and wanted to avoid pictures of him leaving in the dark.[25] He was also acting according to convention: it was now clear that he could not form a government, and that only David Cameron was in a position to do so, even if the nature of that government was (as David Cameron told the Queen at their meeting) still unclear. Cameron said he hoped it would be a coalition but he could not be certain. The draft coalition agreement was at that stage around

95% completed, and all of his negotiating team knew that they had got a deal. What remained was to sell it to their parties.

At 10pm on the Tuesday evening, the Liberal Democrats held a joint meeting of their MPs, peers and the party's Federal Executive Committee – the first lock of their triple-lock process – in Local Government House. Both the Federal Executive and the MPs had had two previous meetings since the election, but this was their first joint session. The meeting had originally been scheduled for 5pm, then repeatedly put back as the negotiations dragged on, to 7pm, then 8.30pm, then eventually 9.30pm, and it would finish at 12.15am. It began with the four-page draft coalition agreement being handed out to those present. There was then a question-and-answer session with the members of the negotiating team, followed by a formal debate and a vote. Contributions were marked by support, concern, occasional angst, and more than a little hyperbole about the historic nature of the event, but there was almost no outright opposition. Charles Kennedy (speaking, he claimed, also for David Steel) said that he could not support what was on offer, although he offered no alternative strategy.[26] Paddy Ashdown, one of the strongest supporters of a deal with Labour, said he feared that his party had abandoned the left, and that he had initially thought he would leave politics, and 'return to my garden and books'. But when he read through the agreement, he said he was amazed at the extent to which chunks of the Liberal Democrat manifesto had been accepted by the Conservatives. 'Fuck it!', he said, 'I can't resist a fight. If this is what you're going to fight for, even with the bloody Tories, you better count me in!' He promptly apologised for what he described as barrack room language.[27] Gone midnight, Ros Scott wound the meeting up, noting that 47 people had made some contribution to the debate whereas Conservative MPs had not even seen the document at that point. She was followed by Nick Clegg, who said that he was humbled, and that the unity displayed throughout the last few days had helped him face down both Gordon Brown and David Cameron. There had been, he noted, 'no Lib Dem noises off'. He said that he knew that there would be difficulties ahead – that that unity would be 'tested to destruction', and he warned explicitly that there would be moments when they would think they had made a mistake. But they needed to be confident about what they had done. When it came to a vote, the MPs voted 50–0 to support the coalition, the peers voted 31–0, and the Federal Executive voted 27–1.[28] Kennedy abstained, as did a handful of others, quietly. The first lock had been cleared so decisively that there was no requirement for either of the remaining stages.[29]

Cumbersome it may have been, but the Lib Dem process of consultation had been useful. It had acted as a safety valve for the party, as a useful negotiating tool during meetings, and it gave the decision legitimacy. Despite the fact that the majority of members of the Federal Executive would have instinctively preferred a deal with Labour – that much had been obvious from the first post-election meeting – they felt included and consulted. Whether the coalition was a success or not over the coming months or years, it would be difficult for Liberal Democrat members seriously to claim that they had been bounced into it. For good or ill, going into coalition with the Conservatives was not a decision of the 'leadership', but of the party.

The difference with the Conservatives (or, for that matter, Labour) was striking. For Labour, the Cabinet had been involved in one meeting, but the Parliamentary Labour Party had not met at any point.[30] For the Conservatives the coalition process had similarly essentially been a top-down one, driven by a handful of Cameron's close confidants, and involving the Shadow Cabinet and Parliamentary Party only sporadically, and only when the leadership needed it. On the Tuesday night when Prime Minister Cameron went before Conservative MPs, it was essentially as a *fait accompli*. It was difficult for Conservative MPs who harboured doubts about the coalition deal to air them openly in an atmosphere where the new Prime Minister and his wife were being paraded triumphantly in front of them. Nor were they shown a copy of the coalition agreement which had been drawn up between the two parties.

Despite the chaos that had been predicted – not least by the Conservatives – the process of navigating a hung parliament had been relatively smooth and speedy. The coalition had taken a mere five days to create, resulting in a formal coalition agreement of just under 3,000 words, relatively short by international standards.[31] It was, though, merely an interim agreement, to be followed on 20 May by a fuller, and noticeably longer, document of around 16,000 words. The process had involved compromise on both sides, and the press pored over the agreement for examples of which party had won or lost. The Lib Dems had gleefully reported the willingness of the Conservative negotiators to offer up tricky policies for dumping – most obviously inheritance tax cuts. 'But then', said one Lib Dem negotiator, 'so were we.' The biggest Lib Dem compromises came on immigration (a policy which had caused them difficulties throughout the campaign), tuition fees (the subject of so much debate during the parliament – but where they still reserved the right to abstain on any rise in fees), and most controversially on public expenditure, where they agreed to £6 billion in spending cuts in 2010/11 (something which they had argued ferociously against during the campaign). Nick Clegg later claimed to have been converted to the need to tackle the deficit urgently as he became aware of the scale of the crisis in Greece and the warnings it held for the British economy – although if he had been, he kept it rather quiet.[32]

'Gee, Jiminy Liberal!'

(Martin Rowson, *Guardian*, 10 May 2010)

Once the coalition had been formed, a series of claims soon began to circulate about its formation, almost all of them *parti pris*. It suited Labour to try to claim that the Liberal Democrats never really wanted the deal, that they were merely playing games, and that they had wanted a deal with the Conservatives all along. It similarly suited the Liberal Democrats to claim that it was Labour's behaviour – both in and out of the negotiating room – that scuppered any hope of a deal. And it suited the Conservatives, at least the leadership, to claim that they were working in the national interest, that a deal with the Liberal Democrats was the best for Britain. These claims should be treated with scepticism, if only because for all that we know about the choreography of the negotiations, we still know relatively little about some of the detailed policy negotiations that went on – matters which will only become clear over the following years. But what we do already know suggests that the truth was more complicated than any of these simple claims.

Post-formation, there was also a claim that the outcome was somehow inevitable, that there was – to use a phrase beloved of Mrs Thatcher – no alternative. Yet there were several alternatives. Several figures around Cameron – though excluded from the negotiating team and his thinking – certainly favoured another approach. One option was to negotiate only on the basis of a confidence and supply arrangement and to refuse any requests for coalition. Others favoured an even riskier strategy – which was to imitate Harold Wilson's behaviour in 1974 and let the other parties take the lead. The sitting Prime Minister had the constitutional right to make the first move and they argued that Cameron should have let Brown do exactly that. Then, when negotiations between Labour and the Liberal Democrats failed, as they were sure they would, Cameron's authority would have been enhanced. He could then either govern as a minority PM, calling, and winning, another election within a year or two or negotiate an arrangement with the Liberal Democrats from a position of strength, knowing that Nick Clegg no longer had any alternative home. Ceding the initiative to Labour in this way would have been a high risk strategy, especially for Cameron personally (if Brown and Clegg did manage to patch together a deal, even one that only lasted for six months or so, that could have been the end of the Cameron leadership) and anyway there was no guarantee of winning another quickly-held election. In both 1910 and 1974, the last occasions to see two elections in one year, the results barely shifted at the second contest. Moreover, as John Curtice et al. show in Appendix 2, the political geography of the UK has changed in recent years, producing fewer marginal seats so making a victorious second election even less likely.

The Lib Dems also had choices, but they were not easy ones. Senior members of the party decided early on that a coalition was a better outcome than a confidence and supply arrangement, believing that the latter was one in which they would get the blame but none of the influence or credit, a lesson they learnt from the experience of the Lib–Lab pact in the late 1970s. They also wanted to try to kill the idea that a hung parliament always led to instability, and feared what might happen in any early second election (believing that if there was an early election, it would be one in which only the Conservatives would have any significant resources). The key question was with which party to do a deal. Focusing – as much of the post-formation discussion did – on the attitude of Labour negotiators is to ignore some of the larger, more substantive, hurdles that a Labour–Lib Dem deal faced.

The first was the electoral arithmetic. At around 10am, the morning after the election, and with Nick Clegg still en route down from Sheffield, when the Lib Dem campaign team gathered at Cowley Street, the very first thing they did was write the electoral arithmetic on a large whiteboard and go through the combinations. At the first Federal Executive meeting, the numbers of seats were also prominently displayed and Clegg made clear that he could see the problems they presented. Even Paddy Ashdown, an enthusiastic advocate of a deal with Labour, initially struggled to see how it was possible given what the electorate had served up.

The Liberal Democrats were faced with two possible arrangements. One delivered a *de facto* majority of 80, and possible government for four or more years. The other delivered a minority administration, still requiring the support or acquiescence of an assortment of parties from the political or geographic periphery. Labour tried hard to persuade Liberal Democrats that the numbers stacked up. If you added in the SDLP (a sister party of Labour), and the one Alliance MP (a sister party of the Liberal Democrats), you got to 319, very close to the 323 needed for a majority.[33] Assume the acquiescence of the one Green – who had said that she would not vote for a Conservative government – plus that of the four Plaid MPs (with whom Labour felt a deal could be reached), and a majority was just about plausible, even before allowing for deals to be reached with the DUP. There was, Labour claimed, an anti-Conservative majority in the House, and since Labour and the Lib Dems combined had more seats than the Conservatives they could outvote them as long as the other parties at least abstained.

The discussion about the majority, however, confused two things. The first was the ability of the government to *survive*. The second was the ability of the government to *function*. It was certainly true that a Lib–Lab arrangement could survive. It was very unlikely that enough of the minor parties would vote to bring down a Lib–Lab government and trigger an early election. But in terms of its day-to-day functioning – a Lib–Lab coalition's ability to win votes on run-of-the-mill legislation, as opposed to high politics votes of confidence – it was not an appetising prospect. On vote after vote, the government could be held hostage by one or more of the minor parties or by its own malcontents. As Peter Hennessy remarked at the time, such an arrangement would have 'too many moving parts'. There was, in political science terminology, a clear 'minimal winning coalition' – and that was the Conservatives and Liberal Democrats.

A slightly different result – with, say, another ten Labour and Lib Dem MPs – and things would have been different, but that was not what the electorate had delivered. The parliamentary arithmetic does not, in itself, explain the outcome of the negotiations, but that was the context in which all the discussions took place.

The second issue was doubts about the Labour leadership. Gordon Brown was a problem whilst he remained leader, but his going merely created another problem. On the Conservative side, the Liberal Democrats knew exactly with whom they would be dealing – and were, in fact, dealing with already. But on the Labour side, they had no idea who would be elected to lead Labour post-Brown, and what his or her attitude would be towards them. The Liberal Democrats had no guarantee that a fragile Lib–Lab deal brokered by a caretaker Prime Minister would not be upset by his successor once the winner of a future Labour leadership contest had been decided. Privately, as part of the negotiations, both Ed Balls and Ed Miliband were willing to give promises to the Lib Dems, but they were not willing to do so publicly, and that was before the attitude of other alternative candidates was considered.

And then, third, there was the ability to deliver. The promises being made by Gordon Brown were in some cases more impressive than those being made by the Conservatives but the Lib Dems doubted Labour's ability to deliver them, especially when it came to their key issue of electoral reform. The Lib Dems were careful to stress in their public pronouncements that they were interested in a range of issues, and not just voting reform, aware that it would be damaging to be seen as engaging in a Dutch auction on voting systems for the sake of narrow party interest. Senior Liberal Democrat figures who favoured a deal with Labour aired the idea of a wider policy deal on issues such as Trident, Europe and immigration – issues where the Conservatives and the Liberal Democrats would not be able to reach a compromise. Such a 'partnership of principle', as Labour's go-between put it in a text to Number 10, could then have been defended in the broader national interest. But the reality was that electoral reform, of some sort, *was* a deal breaker.[34] The initial Conservative offer of a committee of inquiry was not sufficient – something the Conservatives knew, although they felt it was a reasonable initial negotiating position – but the eventual offer of a referendum on AV was more significant.

Labour's offer of a referendum on STV was a more substantial offer, but what was the likelihood that it would be delivered? With every Conservative MP voting against, could Labour really deliver that policy – which went further than their manifesto – through the Parliamentary

Labour Party, given the number of Labour MPs and peers who were opposed? The same would have applied to AV without a referendum – which is why one Lib Dem answered a question on the subject by saying 'even if it was offered, it wasn't deliverable'. And anyway, what was the likelihood that a coalition with Labour would last long enough to bring either of these policies to fruition? These concerns were intensified by the reaction of Labour's voices off, but the doubts were present already – and for the very good reason that it was not obvious Labour could deliver such promises.

Given that the Alternative Vote is not a proportional electoral system, and falls well short of the Lib Dem aim of the Single Transferable Vote, there was some puzzlement about why the party would accept it, especially as Nick Clegg had been critical of it in the past. The answer is summed up in a phrase used by a member of the party's Federal Executive, at their first meeting after the election: 'this is as good as it's going to get, we can't get any better', a sentiment greeted with lots of nodding by other Federal Executive members. In both 2005 and 2010 the Liberal Democrats had thought that they had the chance to make serious gains, but in both cases they had fallen short. AV may not be proportional, and it may not generate a huge increase in the number of Lib Dem seats, but it does almost certainly still increase the number of Lib Dem MPs (by around 20, based on their performance in 2010), thus making future hung parliaments – in which the party could again hold the balance of power – more likely.[35] The Liberal Democrats accepted a referendum on AV on the basis that it was the best they could get; that something was better than nothing; and that it could be a stepping stone to future reform.

At 9.42am on Wednesday, 12 May, Nick Clegg and David Cameron shook hands outside Downing Street as they began a day of dealing over which jobs would go to Conservatives and which to Liberal Democrats. In all, five Lib Dems, including Clegg as Deputy Prime Minister, were given seats in Cabinet, and that afternoon, at just after 2pm, David Cameron and Nick Clegg held a joint press conference in the garden of Number 10. The rapport between the two leaders was obvious to all the journalists present. Each finished the other's sentences. The reporters had a field day. The BBC's Nick Robinson described it as 'Not so much a political marriage as a political civil partnership ceremony.' One of the earliest announcements, as part of the coalition agreement, was made by William Hague, discussing their plans for fixed-term parliaments. 'The next general election', he said, 'will be held on the first Thursday of May, 2015.' In other words, 7 May 2015. Despite the immediate post-election love-in, there were plenty of observers – as well as a good few of the participants – who wondered if the coalition could really last that long.

Notes

1. For example, Alex Brazier and Susanna Kalitowski (eds), *No Overall Control? The Impact of a 'Hung Parliament' on British Politics* (London: Hansard Society, 2008); Peter Riddell and Catherine Haddon, *Transitions: Preparing for Changes of Government* (London: Institute for Government, 2009); Robert Hazell and Akash Paun (eds), *Making Minority Government Work: Hung Parliaments and the Challenges for Westminster and Whitehall* (London: Constitution Unit and Institute for Government, 2009).
2. 'Managing the Machinery of Government in Periods of Change', 5–7 November 2009.
3. See Justice Select Committee, *Constitutional Processes Following a General Election*, HC 396 (2010).
4. 'Chapter 6: Elections and Government Formation', para. 17.
5. The convention on Whitehall purdah – limiting ministers from taking avoidable actions that might bind their successors – also changed. Previously, purdah had ceased on election day. In his evidence, Gus O'Donnell said it would now be extended until a stable government was formed.
6. *Five Days That Changed Britain*, BBC One, 29 July 2010.
7. David Laws also had experience of the Scottish negotiations, having been the party's Policy Director at the time, and responsible (with Malcolm Bruce) for drawing up a draft coalition agreement (which in turn had been based on a coalition document from New Zealand).
8. *Five Days That Changed Britain*.
9. As one of the Lib Dem negotiating team said: 'They had Oliver Letwin, which is a huge advantage. He had really thought about it, and knew our policy, and the potential synergies.'
10. There was some slight controversy caused when it later became known that the Cabinet Secretary had advised them at the first meeting that the 'more comprehensive the agreement, the better', in order to placate the markets (*Five Days That Changed Britain*), which some interpreted as support for a coalition.
11. Sometimes known as the 'Southport resolution', after the Spring Convention when they were introduced, the triple-lock was established in 1998 after the extent of Paddy Ashdown's negotiations with Labour in the run-up to the 1997 election had become clear; they were designed to ensure that the Lib Dems could never be joined in an arrangement with another party without being properly consulted. The first lock required support for any coalition or similar agreement from 75% of the parliamentary party and 75% of the Federal Party Executive. If both were not achieved, the second lock triggered a special conference, where two-thirds support was required. And if that was not achieved, then a full ballot of the party membership was required, at which point a majority sufficed.

12. Or as Peter Mandelson put it: 'I just think he might have given Nick more space, more opportunity to speak, rather than to be spoken to. There should have been a little bit more of "come to me", rather than "I'm telling you where to go"' (*Five Days That Changed Britain*).

13. Peter Mandelson, *The Third Man* (London: HarperPress, 2010), p. 543.

14. As one Lib Dem put it: 'He finds him arrogant, dismissive ... He doesn't listen.' Mandelson would later describe Brown's behaviour in the call as 'Gordonish' (*Five Days That Changed Britain*).

15. Other accounts have the resignation offer being made in a follow-up phone conversation, reported by the *Sunday Times* (16 May 2010) as:

    Brown: I don't want to get in the way of things.
    Clegg: That's very good of you.
    Brown: I'll stay as interim prime minister until then [October], but you can be the public face of the coalition.

    Either way, the offer was made by Brown on the Sunday, only then apparently to be retracted later that same day.

16. See Anthony Seldon's 'How Brown and Clegg let it slip', *Independent*, 29 July 2010, well informed, and based heavily on Brownite sources.

17. Isabel Oakeshott, Marie Woolf and Jonathan Oliver, 'Against the wall', *Sunday Times*, 16 May 2010.

18. See HC Debs, 7 June 2010, c. 44.

19. Of all the rumours, this one was the daftest. The idea that any of Labour's negotiators carried around draft Queen's speeches was especially silly.

20. See Michael Crick's 'Was the coalition built on a lie?', BBC Newsnight blog, 26 July 2010.

21. Views outlined in James Macintyre, 'The path to Con-Dem nation', *New Statesman*, 21 May 2010.

22. Oakeshott et al., 'Against the wall'.

23. Only John Mann, Malcolm Wicks and Kate Hoey had broken cover, publicly urging Brown to step down.

24. Martin Argles, 'The last hours', *Guardian*, 13 May 2010. Alastair Campbell's version of the same conversation was 'Time for what? Unless you can tell me you've broken off talks with the Tories in favour of discussion with us I'll assume you're going with the Tories. I'm now in an impossible position. I have to go to the Palace. Nick, Nick, Nick, I have to do this now. I can't stay on. It's a choice one way or the other. You've made the choice...' (*Five Days That Changed Britain*). Peter Mandelson's memoirs contain yet another version of it (p. 554).

25. Mandelson, *The Third Man*, p. 553.

26. He later outlined his objections in the *Observer*: Charles Kennedy, 'Why I couldn't support Clegg's deal with the Conservatives', *Observer*, 16 May 2010.

27. Ashdown's contribution has also been reported differently, although this account is from a near verbatim record taken at the time.

28. The lone opponent was the former Lib Dem MP, David Rendel.

29. There was, however, a special conference of the party on Sunday, 16 May, held in private, which also voted overwhelmingly to support the agreement. Because the parliamentary and Federal Executive votes had been so decisive, the conference was not formally required, but the decision to hold it regardless

had been taken at the very first post-election meeting of the Federal Executive, as a way of binding the party together with any decision.

30. It finally did so on late Wednesday afternoon, 12 May.
31. Tim Bale, 'Coalition deal is worth the paper it is written on', *Financial Times*, 14 May 2010.
32. Seldon ('How Brown and Clegg let it slip') reports claims that the Governor of the Bank of England, Mervyn King, had personally lobbied the Liberal Democrats to take a tougher line on spending cuts.
33. In the event, the one Alliance MP did not take the Lib Dem whip.
34. One (unscientific) poll of the Lib Dem membership for Lib Dem Voice, during the negotiations, found that although 90% supported discussions with the Conservatives, 80% of Lib Dems thought electoral reform was a deal breaker.
35. Such calculations are estimates based on data on the second preferences of voters. They can be no more than estimates, not least because any election fought under different electoral systems would be fought in an entirely different context.

11
Where We Work, We Win: The Constituency Battle

For all the attention that was focused on the high politics of the 'air war' – the campaign as seen through the eyes of the broadcasters and national press – there was also a 'ground war' fought by candidates, local party activists and volunteers in the 650 separate constituencies. Given that the majority of seats are considered 'safe' for one or other of the parties the party strategists have increasingly concentrated their resources on what are called, variously, marginal, key, or battleground seats. Within these seats the party strategists concentrate their political messages, via polling, direct mail, phone calls and visits, on the voters who say they are undecided.

Although there has been growing evidence in recent elections that local candidates and local campaigning are more important than was traditionally assumed, paradoxically the local campaign is becoming more centralised than ever. Because the stakes are so high party headquarters intervenes much more than in the past, leaving local candidates with less autonomy. In the 2010 election, as in previous elections, party headquarters determined the location of posters (although, in practice, this was a medium almost exclusively used by the Conservatives) and where it sent the leaders on their tours. But increasingly it was the national HQ that also determined the content of direct mail, as well as its printing and despatch, so much so that the local party was often left uninformed about what the centre had sent to voters.

New technology, including the use of centralised phone banks, enabled greater direct contact between party headquarters and the constituencies. It allowed much greater targeting of voters, helping the parties to deliver messages to particular types of voters more precisely than they had previously been able to do. Party headquarters also intervened increasingly in the selection of candidates (see Chapter 15), and from January 2010 Labour and Conservative headquarters assumed the power to impose shortlists in seats which had not by then selected a candidate.

Much of the discussion about the targeting of constituencies assumes a simple dichotomy: seats are either 'targets' (and get inundated with resources) or they are not (and get forgotten). The reality is more nuanced than this. The 'battleground' is a moveable feast, and seats fall off or come onto it. Parties change the allocation of resources to constituencies according to their political fortunes and performance within those seats. Even within any overall list of target seats, some seats get more resources than others, depending on where the parties feel they can best utilise them. In 2010 all of the parties changed their battleground seats as the election approached, and then again during the campaign itself.

Labour's ground war campaign was a defensive one – and it became more defensive and last ditch as the campaign progressed. Labour changed its battleground seats twice in the run-up to the campaign, once in June 2009 and then again in January 2010, and on both occasions they moved the list downwards, taking resources away from their most marginal seats and moving them into seats that on paper they held relatively comfortably. Theoretically, Labour's ground war strategy had three stages: first, prevent a Conservative victory; second, attempt to become the largest party; third, produce a Labour majority. But from January 2010 onwards, the reality was that the second and third stages existed largely for show, and the party's central resources were concentrated on holding those seats that would deny the Conservatives a majority. Douglas Alexander, the party's campaign coordinator, had been scarred by his experience in the Scottish Parliament elections in 2007 when seats had fallen to the SNP that he felt could have been held by Labour, had they marshalled their resources better. Labour began the campaign with a list of 146 target constituencies, but by the end of the campaign they were putting relatively little national resources into the most marginal of those seats. Mid-way through the campaign, and in response to the perceived Lib Dem threat, the party added another 20 seats to the list.

Given that Labour fears of being outgunned in national press came to be realised (see Chapter 14), it instead concentrated on local and regional media, particularly local radio and press, and 'free' papers like *Metro*. It also placed more reliance on direct communication with voters, making use of its central print creator and a contact creator system. Providing these services centrally would release local parties from the task of producing their own freepost communications. Three-quarters of

Constituency Labour Parties accepted the offer. The print creator could provide free localised and personalised mail to parties which achieved agreed targets of voter contact in their seats. Alexander regarded this as an incentivising scheme. To his disappointment, and that of a number of Labour MPs in marginals, Labour's National Executive Committee (NEC) curtailed the scheme in summer 2009 and again in January 2010 because of financial pressures, although the party's General Secretary, Ray Collins subsequently secured more funding, enabling it to resume.

Early on in the campaign, Labour was briefly embarrassed by a row concerning cancer patients, some of whom had received a personalised postcard from the party, sent with a message, 'Are the Tories a change you can afford?' The 250,000 postcards featured a breast cancer survivor praising her treatment on the NHS under Labour. Questions were raised by some cancer survivors and the Conservatives about the Government's use of personal data. It was the only time the parties' massive use of direct mail was noticed by the media at any point during the campaign. Labour was not targeting cancer sufferers – they did not have the data to do so – but the mailing was aimed at female swing voters, a large number of whom were bound to have either had, or known someone close who had had, cancer.[1] And for all the controversy, those in Labour HQ were convinced it worked: 'Cancer hit home,' one said.

The cancer mailing was merely one of around a dozen direct mailings sent out by Victoria Street during the election. For all three main parties, the campaign was what one senior Lib Dem campaigner called 'the direct mail election' – 'more paper delivered to more houses than any campaign in British history', and with much greater accuracy. Labour made no fewer than 8.3 million mail deliveries, spread across 138 seats between 2008 and early 2010. Three-quarters of its national election expenditure went on direct mail. A further 7.4 million letters were delivered during the campaign, some 4.8 million to swing voters and 2.6 million to core voters. So-called 'squeeze' mail was addressed to Liberal Democrat voters in the marginals. One letter warned that a Lib Dem vote could let in the Conservatives and another, written by the Cabinet minister Andrew Adonis (mirroring his pieces in national newspapers), pointed to the convergence around progressive values of the Labour and Liberal Democrat parties. Liberal Democrats admitted they had been squeezed by these appeals and Conservatives acknowledged the effectiveness of the 'scare' leaflets about the threat that a future Conservative government allegedly posed to tax credits and winter fuel payments and free bus passes for the elderly. 'The most powerful thing they did,' said a Conservative of Labour's tax credit leaflets.

All the parties made greater use of phone banks to telephone canvass potential supporters, to try to build up voter ID data. Labour's National Call Centre, staffed by activists and volunteers, was making between 4,000 and 7,000 calls a day, rising to 10,000 in the final week of the campaign. The party achieved a total of some 500,000 voter contacts between 1 January and polling day.[2] In addition, Labour was helped by phone banks provided by the Unite union, staffed by union members. The party also used its Call Centre for spot polling to check if there was a rise in Liberal Democrat support after the first debate. The lack of solid evidence of any surge was used to reassure some Labour MPs worried about a Liberal Democrat threat in their seats.[3] Another innovation in 2010 was that the national HQs had direct access to the local canvass returns in individual seats as they were uploaded (Labour activists were uploading 100,000 contacts in the final week of the campaign), enabling them to monitor the national picture more effectively.[4]

The parties were able to deploy direct mail with more accuracy, targeting particular leaflets at individuals, as a result of a combination of commercially produced data (all the major parties, and some of the minor ones, used Experian's MOSAIC data) and information gathered by themselves. Whereas many people talking about politics will do so in terms of broad social class categories – AB, C1, C2, or so on – those who organised the parties' direct mail operations would talk in terms of much more finely-nuanced MOSAIC codes, providing information about the social, demographic and consumer features of voters which divided the electorate into clusters or categories of individuals, groups and households which (somewhat disconcertingly) they could reel off without thinking. Labour's swing voter targets, for example, were groups B ('Bourgeois Prosperity'), C ('Career and Family'), D ('Comfortable Retirement') and H45 ('Older Right to Buy'). Around 15 years ago MOSAIC had allowed parties to target at postcode level only; at the last election it enabled them to target by households; in 2010 it allowed them to target individual voters based on their MOSAIC code. The parties overlaid the MOSAIC data with more overtly political voter ID data they gathered themselves, through door-to-door or telephone canvassing.[5] Of the three main parties, the Liberal Democrats found MOSAIC least useful – as a result of the nature of their support, and said they used it only when other data were not available to them – but they did still use it.

One problem the parties face is that – unlike commercial users of the data – they cannot trace the eventual 'transaction' (in their case, the vote) with any certainty. This prevents them from deploying more sophisticated models to target voters. But those with knowledge of the systems thought the parties' use of the data, whilst less sophisticated than many commercial clients, was often more opportunistic and agile ('There's a lot the commercial sector could learn from the way that the parties work'), and at times it was deployed at short notice. On the Friday before polling, Labour secured a one-off donation of £200,000, which they decided to use for a 'squeeze' mailing to Lib Dem voters. A series of conference calls took place on the Friday and Saturday to discuss the mailing and sign off the design; the literature was delivered to the post office by the Sunday; and 400,000 pieces of literature arrived on doorsteps on the Wednesday, the day before polling.

The fact that the Conservatives needed more than a hundred net gains to form a majority in Parliament made the ground war crucial to the success of their campaign. Tory headquarters therefore conducted probably the most ambitious and certainly the most expensive ground war in modern British election campaigning. The bulk of their £17 million war chest enabled them to dominate poster sites in the key seats; the sites had been booked the previous October and November at a generous discount. Such was the scale of resources the Tories were pumping into the marginal seats that polling companies issued health warnings during the election campaign that the Conservatives might be doing better than the national polling numbers suggested.

After 2005, as party deputy chairman, Lord Ashcroft oversaw a similar exercise in the seats the party needed to win if it was to gain a majority at the next general election, as he had run privately before 2005. Expectations were high because the party were investing in these seats for the best part of the Parliament; indeed some had been identified and supported before the 2005 general election. To receive support each candidate or local party had to submit a business plan to Ashcroft's team in CCHQ. The key figures in the team were Stephen Gilbert and Gavin Barwell, both former Directors of Organisation with the latter going on to be the prospective Parliamentary candidate (and then MP) for Croydon Central. The business plan was expected to cover local activities, targets, and benchmarks of progress. If successful the local party received substantial funding (certainly exceeding the £10,000 communications allowance paid to MPs each year) and direct support.

Where possible, candidates were selected early in the Parliament and expected to 'embed' themselves in the community through repeated canvassing, social action projects and campaigning on local issues, to appear to be 'local'. The party also tried to run the same candidates as in the previous election, to promote local name recognition. The lesson learned from previous campaigns was that money spent early was money well spent. Some candidates even changed jobs to base themselves in or near the seats they contested. They were backed by systematic targeted phoning, direct mail, and advertising. Gilbert monitored the progress in the battleground seats by regular private polling and feedback from his regional field staff. Most of the party's polling was done in the key seats, and as we report on page 259 the private polls identified problems that the party faced, even before the campaign. The 2 million-plus swing voters on the party's database were heavily direct-mailed on the issues that concerned them most. The team had a significant field force – of around 20 staff in key seats, plus ten regional directors, plus about ten staff in CCHQ. Many features of the battleground campaign were tested in by-elections and the capture from Labour of Crewe & Nantwich and Norwich North boosted the confidence of Conservative HQ.

The composition of the list of 'Ashcroft' seats was a closely guarded secret. The party did not put significant resources into its most marginal targets, believing that those would fall without too much extra resource. Instead, as the campaign approached the majority of the Ashcroft operation went into 69 seats, of which 45 were contests with Labour, 24 with the Lib Dems. During the campaign, in reaction to Cleggmania, they withdrew resources from some of the Lib Dem battlegrounds, and added two new Labour clusters, comprising 14 new seats, in two clusters called simply 'North' and 'Midlands & South'. The targeted seats could not be read off a list of what were on paper the party's most marginal seats – they ranged from Colne Valley (the 21st most marginal Conservative target) up to Bury South (211th). The 14 late additions were even longer-shots, ranging from Amber Valley (120th) up to Sunderland Central (234th). The party did especially well in the clusters of seats known as 'seaside towns', where they took all five targeted, and 'new towns', where they gained seven of the eight targeted. They did less well in the two Pennines clusters – winning eight of 19 targeted – and in the Northern additional seats (a mere one, out of seven). In the Labour-held target seats, the party's operation recorded an additional 1.6% in the rise of the Conservative vote over the national performance, a small but significant amount. Of the 21 seats the party gained but would not have done with a uniform swing, 20 were battleground seats.

Some Labour MPs were obsessive ('neurotic', said staff in Victoria Street) about the effect of the so-called 'Ashcroft money', although it showed up in association accounts as grants from Conservative headquarters. Martin Linton, defending highly marginal Battersea, for example, was a high-profile complainant about the unfairness of being targeted like that. His own party's organisers thought he protested too much and the Conservative Party claimed it had not provided any extra resources to their successful Battersea candidate, who won with some ease.

The Conservatives had, however, hoped for more from their investment in the battleground seats. They failed to capture some constituencies that even Labour had written off – most obviously Birmingham Edgbaston. In the most marginal 50 seats their vote share increased by 3.7%, similar to the national average, and by 4.3% in the next 50. Their main shortfall was the underperformance against the Liberal Democrats, gaining only six of the 24 they theoretically needed (but a further six beyond that). 'A mixture of achievement and disappointment' was the verdict of a strategist in Millbank.

Like Labour, the party invested heavily in direct mail, delivering nearly 16 million items of mail from 1 January, 8 million in the near term, 8 million during the campaign and another 4 million localised letters in the near term. And just like their Labour counterparts, Tory agents and candidates often had no idea what literature was being delivered in their constituencies. David Cameron's 'Contract' with the voter letter was prepared in the penultimate week and sent to some 2 million target voters. It was, said one insider, designed to 'help David break through the cynicism and distrust we found among some voters'. They had four direct rebuttal leaflets, covering the elderly, family tax credits, social housing and the NHS, all prepared in advance as a response to 'Labour's scares'. A magazine, addressed to older voters, included a direct rebuttal of Labour claims. A newsletter in the final days restated the Conservative policies on the three key issues of the economy, NHS and immigration. Most party organisers now believe that direct personalised mail scores over leaflets (put straight in the bin, according to research), posters and election broadcasts, in large part because of an anti-political mood.

Conservative candidates, deprived of the party's traditional weapon of tax cuts, exploited Osborne's pledge that a Conservative Chancellor would not go ahead with Labour's NIC rise, the 'tax on jobs'. The manifesto's Big Society theme seems to have been a particular bugbear for some activists and candidates who found the idea difficult to communicate on the doorstep. 'A good concept for some of the commentators,' said one, 'but we needed to present it in more retail politics terms.' As one strategist said: 'We tried to take an intellectual argument that there was a big Conservative idea (which was great for Matthew d'Ancona) and then tried to sell it to voters in Bury, rather than deconstructing the package, and selling the individual bits in Bury.' Promoting the idea of 'free schools' was also mentioned as a particular difficulty.

During the summer of 2009, with Labour performing particularly poorly in the polls, the Liberal Democrats had taken the decision to expand their number of target seats. The hope was that Labour would put resources into combating the Lib Dem threat in more obvious Lib Dem targets, but fail to spot these new, less obvious targets – with the expectation that the Lib Dems would then win at least as many 'unexpected' gains as expected ones ('Labour is effective at getting their ducks in a row in places where they know they're in a fight'). The trouble was that some of these new target seats lacked Lib Dem infrastructure, and so the party had to change its traditional model of campaigning. As one key Lib Dem campaigner put it, the old model went like this: 'You start with one activist, and their friends. They campaign in one ward, and then capture the ward next door, then the one next to that. Then the council, and then one of them stands for Westminster ... Well, we're hoping to short circuit that process.' This was still targeted campaigning ('we're not just dropping food parcels, hoping that stray voters will pick them up') but it was increasingly centrally-driven. The party added up to 20 Labour seats to its target list at this point, although many of these dropped off the list by the time the election approached.

Helped by a more professionalised fund-raising operation, the party aimed to use direct mail, supported by volunteer phone banks, to compensate for its lack of an activist base on the ground in these long-shot target seats. During the campaign, the party sent out about 9 million direct mails (four mailings of 1.6 million each, plus assorted extras), in addition to slightly more during the long campaign, a total of around 20 million letters from January until the end of the campaign. This was a step-change for the party (roughly a ten-fold increase in its use of direct mail from 2005) and placed them on a par with the two larger parties. In one sense the extra use of direct mail was a continuation of the party's normal strategy – outnumbered in the press, they have to get their message out to the doorstep – but using a very different delivery mechanism. Where they struggled to compete was with the use of phone banks, which the party only had running on a full-time basis by late 2009, and which never worked at capacity. It was supported by a series of regional phone banks, staffed by volunteers and paid staff, but the party accepted it was noticeably under-powered compared to the other two parties.

As the Lib Dems surged in the polls, so they too changed their target seats, expanding the target list yet further. The Joseph Rowntree Reform Trust Ltd, the party's longstanding generous donor, provided extra money during the campaign for direct mail in a number of 'new' seats; at the time the hope was that the party's rise in the opinion polls might enable it to gain seats which it had not targeted. Whilst the money was welcome, the nature of the donation showed a failure to understand how campaigning worked, that money cannot be dropped at short notice into seats where no preparatory work has been carried out. The party sensibly interpreted the requirement for the seats to be 'new' broadly, although it still failed to capture any of the extra seats.

The rise in Lib Dem support was not an unalloyed blessing for staff at Cowley Street. Their canvass returns – like those of the other parties – were not detecting the same surge in support for the party as that picked up by the polls ('it wasn't anything like what people would have imagined it was') and when it did occur it was not in the right place ('it was huge in places that weren't our target areas'). This rise in the prominence of the party upset their direct mail work: most of their pre-campaign planning had been predicated on mailings designed to raise the party's profile. They were now fighting a different campaign, and they struggled to respond quickly enough to the new opportunities. Cleggmania also caused a problem on the ground, as party activists – previously very willing to travel, often quite long distances, to help out in winnable seats – began to insist they could win their local constituency. Head Office started to receive requests for visits from the Leader, sometimes to utterly unwinnable constituencies but where party workers were convinced they could now win, and showing a reluctance to move to other seats to help out. 'Hubris', one of the key Lib Dems described it as. Needless to say, the party captured none of these seats, but the opinion-poll-driven optimism diverted activists away from seats where the chances of victory were greater.

The Liberal Democrats had been torn between operating in their traditional mode as a small party seeking incremental gains, and a small party intent on turning itself into a big party over a couple of elections. Lacking both the necessary infrastructure and the resources on the ground to implement the latter strategy, they had however still tried to behave as a larger party, and stretched to the limits of what they could logistically manage they had struggled to deliver the goods. They put resources into over 100 constituencies – around 30 of those that they already held, plus some 80 targets – and yet ended the election having lost seats. The move away from the incremental progress of 'Rennardism' (see p. 110) was not entirely successful.

Largely because of the MPs' expenses scandal, some party campaigners expected that voters' general revulsion with the behaviour of politicians would help the minor parties and damage incumbents. The first was only modestly confirmed and there was little evidence of the second, rather the opposite. MPs have become increasingly constituency-focused in recent years, and a study of the 2005 intake found that they were spending more than half of their time working in, or on, the constituency.[6] They were helped by a £10,000 annual communications allowance, introduced during the parliament to allow them to promote their parliamentary work (but which many used to promote themselves). Incumbency helped them to gain name recognition through their coverage in the local media.

As Appendix 2 shows, despite predictions that incumbency would be less of an advantage than in previous elections, it still proved to be a surprisingly useful weapon. Labour's analysis claimed that seven seats were held by margins in which incumbency may have been decisive. Conversely, eleven seats were lost by margins in which the retirement of the MP and loss of incumbency may have made the difference.[7] The party had reason to regret that so many Labour MPs decided to retire. A problem for the party is that whilst incumbency may have helped them this time, it will find it harder to unseat the many locally-based Conservative MPs who won for the first time in 2010. The evidence of an incumbency effect and the variance in results made some people at the centre acknowledge the importance of what one called 'relational politics', the rewards that could come from the candidate having regular contact and gaining a reputation as a local champion. One Labour strategist claimed that with the decline of party loyalty and growing disillusion with politics local political entrepreneurs stood to benefit the most.

But incumbency alone was not enough. It had to be coupled with an active local party or volunteers working long before the four-week campaign began. An MP's reputation as an effective constituency spokesman is built over years. Some had neglected their constituencies and suffered accordingly (or, in cases where they stood down, their successors suffered). The mantra of Alicia Kennedy, Labour's Director of Field Operations, was 'Where we work, we win', as the only way the party could counter the greater resources the Conservatives were deploying. Labour's organisers claimed a remarkable correlation between the election outcomes in the marginal seats which generated the greatest amount of voter ID work and Labour's electoral performance. In the ten seats with the highest Voter ID contact rates there was an average swing *to Labour* of 0.6%; in the 20 with the highest rates the swing away from Labour was only 0.97%. The exemplar was Andrew Smith's local party, in Oxford East, which had managed to contact some 40,000 voters between the start of the year and the election. As voter contact rates fell, so did Labour's performance.

The local candidate could also matter. As Appendix 2 shows, whilst there was no evidence of female candidates performing any differently to male candidates, there was a noticeable tendency for ethnic minority candidates to suffer adverse electoral swings. This was true for all three main parties, although in the case of the Lib Dems it was largely as a result of the type of seats for which they were selected. That this was more a comment on the prejudices of the electorate rather than the candidates is confirmed by the finding that, in the case of both Labour and the Conservatives, this was especially noticeable in seats with small ethnic minority populations.

In tandem with the nationally directed attempts to contact voters in constituencies – what we might call the national-local campaign – there was also the work of the party activists, the poor bloody infantry who would deliver leaflets, knock on doors, and act as tellers on polling day – what we might call the local-local campaign. The decline in party membership, which has affected all the major political parties, is one reason for the increase in use of nationally directed mechanisms for contacting voters; there are simply no longer the number of party activists on the ground that parties once deployed. It has also led to parties attempting to make greater use of registered volunteers and supporters, those who are sympathetic to the party's aims but who for whatever reason do not want to sign up for membership – what one key campaigner called 'the fuzzy bit between I-vote-for-you and I-am-a-member-of-your-organisation, the beyond membership bit'. One study of party agents found that volunteers were helping out in three-quarters of constituency campaigns, often in considerable numbers, albeit predominantly doing the grunt work of delivering leaflets and 'knocking up' on polling day, leaving party members to do the more complicated tasks of telephoning and canvassing.[8]

The same study also found that the parties were deploying their grassroots resources more effectively – that is, with relatively more in the target seats than in the seats they already held or knew they could not win. This indicated something of a shift in behaviour by Conservative activists, who had previously been especially resistant to moving outside of their 'home' constituency. 'Driving through the night to sleep on someone's sofa is not a traditional Tory value,' as a recent Conservative Party Chairman put it. The party was well aware that its curse had always been to build up majorities where they did not need them, and had tried to establish links between safe seats and target constituencies, in order to encourage activists to work where they were most needed. In the 2009 local elections, they had targeted very closely at ward level to encourage focused campaigning, and reported that party members were becoming more willing to move to where they were needed rather than where they happened to live. They were, one key Conservative campaigner noted in 2009, 'more flexible than they have ever been'.

The Lib Dems reported what one called 'a huge surge of Labour activists' in the final week, as the prospect of coming third galvanised their grassroots activists. One key Labour strategist agreed, claiming that the party had broadly the same number of bodies out on the ground in 2010 as they had had in 2005, especially towards the end of the campaign, when 'they came out of the woodwork to volunteer'. The Cowley Street staff blamed the resurgence of Labour activists for its failure to break through in the final week.[9]

Table 11.1 Voters contact, by parties

| | | Of those contacted, by which parties? | | |
| | | Con | Lab | LD |
	%	%	%	%
During the past few weeks, have you...				
had any political leaflets put through your letterbox?	93	79	76	76
been called on by a representative of any political party?	21	47	37	28
been telephoned by a representative of any political party?	5	39	39	21

Source: Ipsos-MORI

Voters, on the receiving end of all this activity, reported the activity seen in Table 11.1. Almost all said they had received some political leaflets (although this did not distinguish between leaflets delivered by hand and direct mail), around a fifth been called on, and one in 20 been telephoned. The key activity of local activists of all three parties in the run-up to the election was delivering leaflets.[10] The British Election Study's regular pre-election surveys noted a steady rise in the proportion of people contacted by the parties as the election approached, and with mail and leaflets by far the most common method used; in both their October 2009 and February 2010 surveys they found that the number of voters who said that they had received an item of literature through the post was greater than all other methods of contact combined, a finding that was true for all three of the major parties.[11]

On the figures in Table 11.1, the Conservatives' ground war advantage was clear, although relatively slight. Surveys from the British Election Study confirmed this, throughout the longer campaign.[12] Conservative polling, focusing solely on the battleground seats, found that in terms of mail, 10% more voters claimed to have received literature from the Conservatives than Labour or the Lib Dems; nearly 20% claimed to have been phoned by the Conservatives compared to 10% for Labour and the Lib Dems; and three-fifths reported receiving personally-addressed direct mail from the Conservatives compared with less than two-fifths for the other two parties. However, the trouble with measures such as these is that they do not take into account the *volume* of literature. Whilst 93% of voters may claim to have had some literature, in many seats that will be merely one leaflet from the candidates, as part of the election addresses distributed by Royal Mail. In battleground seats there will have been several leaflets, either from national or local directed campaigning. Some households in battleground seats were the lucky recipients of dozens of pieces of literature.

Following the Representation of the People Act 2000, which allowed for postal voting on demand, there had been a steady increase in the amount of postal voting election-on-election; by 2005, around 15% of the votes cast were postal voters. Ipsos-MORI's final election survey found the same figure was given by respondents this time – with 15% of respondents saying that they had voted by post.[13] Research by Rallings et al. argued that in 2005 postal voting had very little impact on either turnout or party support at that election.[14] But it does alter the focus and the structure of campaigns if not necessarily their outcome. Prior to the 2000 Act, everything the parties did built towards polling day. Whilst most campaign activity still builds towards polling day, local parties now also need to be aware of the significant block of voters who will be casting their votes before then. Widespread postal voting effectively creates multiple polling dates, and local parties make considerable efforts to sign up would-be supporters for postal votes. In 2010, postal votes landed on voters' doormats just after the polls showed Lib Dems rising and Labour in third place.

In terms of output, at least, the Conservatives won the ground war operation in 2010. They had learned from previous elections that they needed more local candidates in situ, and that resources needed to be put into constituencies much earlier than in the past if the party was to yield benefits at election time. But, as we have seen, the election still ended in relative disappointment for the Conservatives.

Nevertheless, the variability in the outcomes in constituencies gave all the three main parties food for thought about the supposedly positive impact of centrally-driven local campaigning. The Liberal Democrats found out the hard way that merely pumping funds into new target seats without the infrastructure and members on the ground to support it did not work. Labour, meanwhile, could console itself that it had held on remarkably well in some unexpected places, especially where they had a strong local candidate in place, perhaps suggesting that the party headquarters were wrong to place so much focus on direction and control from the centre. Conversely, where a Labour incumbent stood down, the Conservatives were able to make a handful of impressive gains in seats where in terms of the swing required they appeared to have little chance.

Notes

1. There were two versions of the mailing, one featuring a picture of an older woman, another a younger woman. Labour's assumption was that women were more likely both to open and then respond to direct mail, and so they were a disproportionately large part of its target group.
2. It would take an average of three calls to achieve every contact, more if the voter was in London.
3. They polled in, amongst others, Nottingham East, Holborn & St Pancras, and Dulwich & East Norwood. All stayed safely Labour.
4. In 2005, parties had asked agents to fax in canvass returns, but this system allowed for all manner of errors – and deceptions – to creep into the data.
5. Labour also used data on ethnicity, employing name-related software (useful at identifying voters of African and Asian background, but less so with Afro-Caribbean voters).
6. See G. Rosenblatt, *A Year in the Life* (London: Hansard Society, 2006).
7. The seven were Dudley North, Kingston upon Hull North, Newport East, Plymouth, Moor View, Tooting, and Wakefield.
8. J. Fisher et al., 'Constituency Campaigning in the 2010 British General Election', paper for presentation at the American Political Science Association, 2010. The research draws on responses from over 1,000 party agents during the 2010 election.

9. Fisher et al.'s study of campaign activity levels, as reported by agents, also reached the conclusion that Labour's grassroots activity was responsible for preventing the party suffering further losses.
10. Fisher et al., 'Constituency Campaigning'.
11. Of those contacted by the Conservatives, for example, 89% had had something through their letter box, compared to 18% by email, 9% who had been visited at home, or 5% who had been phoned. The leaflet/mail figures for Labour and the Lib Dems were 81% and 91% respectively.
12. In their February 2010 survey, for example, 60% of those contacted by a political party had been contacted by the Conservatives, compared to 43% for both Labour and the Liberal Democrats.
13. The figure rose with the age cohorts, from just 7% of 18–24 year olds, to some 28% of the those aged 65 or older.
14. C. Rallings et al., 'Much Ado about Not Very Much: The Electoral Consequences of Postal Voting at the 2005 British General Election', *British Journal of Politics and International Relations*, 12:2 (2010), 223–38.

12
Worms and Surges: The Polls

The 2010 election was dominated by opinion polls, both public and private. There were more of them than ever before, from more companies, and they drove many of the key decisions taken by the political parties. Despite his much ridiculed denials, opinion polls were the key factor behind Gordon Brown's decision not to call an election in 2007; the Conservatives' political and electoral strategies were both heavily driven by polling (although ironically, it would be the lack of polling on the key Big Society theme that would be one of the central criticisms of the Conservative campaign); and negative opinion polling was at least partly behind the Liberal Democrats' defenestration of Ming Campbell. Polls also had a major impact on the campaign itself, both in determining reporting of the Prime Ministerial debates and as a result in transforming coverage of Nick Clegg and the Liberal Democrats. Yet the accuracy of the final poll of the campaign – the exit poll, which for the second election running got the outcome of the election almost spot on – helped hide the fact that, more generally, the 2010 election was a mixed one for the polling industry.

Many of the more established polling outfits continued to poll for mainstream media clients: Populus polled for *The Times*, ICM for the *Guardian* and (sporadically) the *Telegraph* papers, Ipsos-MORI for Reuters, the *News of the World* and *London Evening Standard*, Harris for the *Daily Mail*, ComRes for the *Independent* (and *Independent on Sunday*), *Sunday Mirror*, and ITN. BPIX, based at the University of Essex, and fronted by a website that has been 'under construction' for five years, mostly polled for the *Mail on Sunday*. YouGov polled for a variety of outlets, including the *Telegraph*, from whom they broke in acrimonious circumstances, and ended up polling for the *Sunday Times* and *Sun*. Despite having got the 2005 result spot on, NOP soon afterwards parted company with the *Independent*, and virtually disappeared from the UK political polling scene. They were replaced by a variety of newcomers. The established Canadian company Angus Reid began polling for the politicalbetting.com website in 2009, and then for the *Sunday Express*. Opinium polled for the *Express* from 2009. They were also joined, intermittently, by TNS BRMB and OnePoll (for the *People*), and even one company from India, RNB India.

The methodology of polling has become increasingly varied and complex. For the first time in a UK election campaign, more pollsters conducted their fieldwork online than by telephone or (increasingly rare) face-to-face. In addition, the translation of raw data into the eventually published figures via an increasingly complicated mixture of filtering and weighting is conducted in different ways by the different companies, in attempts to counter the problems caused by differential turnout, selection bias and false reporting. The 'house effects' (or adjustments to raw data) of the polling companies could often be considerable, making comparison between data produced by different organisations largely meaningless (although that unfortunately did not stop plenty of people doing it).

The election campaign itself saw a record number of polls, more than 90, supplied by 11 different polling companies. This was nearly double the number of polls in 2005, and more than three times the number in 2001. The large increase in output can be attributed to three factors. The first was that the election looked like a close, and exciting, race. The second was the arrival on the UK polling scene of new pollsters attempting to break into a market which because of online polling now has relatively low costs of entry. And the third was the expansion in output from YouGov, which began to produce daily polls during the campaign – the company claimed they were the first genuinely daily polls using a fresh sample in an election campaign anywhere in the world – and YouGov's output alone was responsible for more than half of the polls produced during the election.

As in so many previous elections, minor shifts in the parties' standing could produce exaggerated claims about poll movements, with talk about the polls being 'all over the place'. In fact, to begin with they showed remarkable stability, once you took account of the natural variation resulting from sampling error. Every poll from the beginning of the campaign until the first TV debate on 15 April had the Conservatives on 38% (+/–3), with Labour on 30% (+/–3). With one exception, the Lib Dems were on 19% (+/–3). Random sampling error was sufficient to make the Conservative lead alter between 3 and 11 percentage points but the shares of the vote being received by the main parties were relatively constant, confirming the veteran pollster Bob Worcester's maxim that one should always look at the shares not the lead.

The impact of the polls was most felt with the leaders' debates, where they effectively determined the way the debates were reported. Each political party had a team ready to place its favoured interpretation on the outcome in the so-called 'spin room', a huge room of journalists and politicians all poised ready to provide post-debate opinion and comment for at least an hour after every debate. But for all their efforts, it was the post-debate polls which drove the story, and there was relatively little the politicians and their aides could do about it. When the Liberal Democrats began preparing for the debates, one of Nick Clegg's private worries had been that however well he did, it wouldn't matter – because the papers could write it up however they wanted. Yet within minutes of the first debate finishing, four polling companies showed Nick Clegg to be the clear winner (see Table 12.1), with both Brown and Cameron trailing far behind. It was difficult to spin that. One Conservative spinner put it bluntly: the polls 'wrote the story' and Peter Mandelson spoke of 'those bloody post-debate polls'. As one Conservative involved in their party's operation observed: 'They were all there – Charlie Whelan, Alastair Campbell, Peter Mandelson, like some ageing rock band, reunited for one last gig, and there was nothing they could do – their man had come bottom.'

Table 12.1 Debate winner polls

		Gordon Brown	*David Cameron*	*Nick Clegg*
First debate	Populus/*Times*	17	22	**61**
15 April	YouGov/*Sun*	19	29	**51**
	ComRes/ITN	20	26	**43**
	Angus Reid	18	20	**49**
	ICM/*Guardian*	19	20	**51**
Second debate	Angus Reid	23	32	**33**
22 April	ComRes/ITN	30	30	**33**
	YouGov/*Sun*	29	**36**	32
	Populus/*Times*	27	**37**	36
	ICM/*Guardian*	29	29	**33**
Third debate	Angus Reid	23	**36**	30
29 April	YouGov/*Sun*	25	**41**	32
	ComRes/ITN	26	**35**	33
	Populus/*Times*	25	**38**	**38**
	ICM/*Guardian*	29	**35**	27

Note: the 'winner' is in bold.

Viewers' reactions to the debates were also studied by a relatively new (in the UK, at least) dialling technique, sometimes called 'the worm'. Each member of a group has an electronic pad which he or she presses to register their instant reactions to what they hear and see. The research was carried out among undecided voters by ComRes for ITV and Ipsos-MORI for the BBC (as well as privately for the Conservatives). The overall outcomes of the worm exercises were largely the same as those for the polls – judging Clegg to be the clear winner of the first debate and Cameron and Clegg broadly equal in the second and third debates. But the worm allowed more detailed analysis of how voters viewed the candidates' performances. The ComRes exercise found that Cameron's remarks prompted the greatest variance among viewers. For example, in the first debate, he scored highly on his proposals for controlling immigration and the need for discipline in schools but poorly when he attacked Brown and when proposing to delay the retirement age. Brown was judged to be uncomfortable with the format and scored especially badly when he talked defensively about the Government's record on immigration. The format places a premium on the leaders appearing relaxed, answering the question, being positive and looking directly at the camera. But the ComRes analysis of their data noted one other interesting finding, which they summed up as 'Don't be too truthful.' As the report noted, 'the bad news and honesty that the institutes and think tanks are craving from our aspiring leaders doesn't go down well with the voters'. Every time there was a mention of a cut in a service, the worm dipped.[1]

The impact of the debates went way beyond those who actually watched them. Not only did the media replay clips from the debates, but they also widely reported the polls declaring Clegg the winner. The percentage who claimed to have watched the first debate (at 49%) was much higher than the percentage who actually did (overall, some 72% would claim to have watched at least one debate). The instant polls thus set the news agenda. Their results were so overwhelming that it was very difficult for anyone to argue anything other than that Nick Clegg had emerged victorious from the first debate. Without the polls, Clegg's performance would almost certainly not have been reported so positively, especially by the Conservative-supporting press. The polls influenced the media narrative, and in turn the media shaped public perceptions.

All but two of the instant polls used internet panels and without them the media reaction would have been different. ComRes and ICM were the exceptions, using telephone polling – in ComRes's case, utilising automated telephone polls, polling 9,000 viewers in less than 19 minutes of field time. The impact of internet-based surveys in the reporting of the leaders debates is almost certainly greater than the impact of all twitter accounts and blog sites combined. For those searching for the impact of the internet on the election, it could at least be found here.

Polls rely on interviewing a representative sample of the wider population. But with the televised debates, it is not obvious what that sample should be representative of. Should it be the general public as would be the case in any 'normal' opinion poll? Or should it be the viewing audience, those who are watching the debate? Those who watched the debates were more likely to be male, Conservative, and interested in politics. Weighting to their composition would therefore give an advantage to the Conservatives. But to weight to the population as a whole would mean skewing the results to those not involved (akin to weighting the results of a poll of UK voters according to the demographics of French voters). Pollsters differed in how they dealt with this, and whilst it would have made little difference in the first debate, given how overwhelming the outcome, it could matter in closer contests.

The first debate was also remarkable for a willingness of Conservative and Labour identifiers to say that they thought Nick Clegg had won. Populus found that more than half of those who said they were Conservatives thought Clegg won, along with 45% of those who were Labour voters. But by the second and third debates, reactions had become more partisan, being more obviously linked to voters' previously declared preferences; by the third debate Populus data showed 77% of Conservative voters thinking Cameron won; 69% of Labour voters believing Gordon Brown to be the victor. Such partisan responses clearly give an advantage to whichever party is already ahead in the polls, with the possibility that measures of 'victory' can be influenced by the extant standing of the parties, about as tautological an outcome as you can get.

Polls also measured other indications of how voters saw the debates – some of which were at least as interesting as crude measures of 'victory'. Populus polled across seven measures of a potential Prime Minister (see Table 12.2), both before the first debate, and then after each of the three. Their findings showed the huge improvement in Nick Clegg's rankings, so that following the third debate he was ahead on a majority of the characteristics. Yet Cameron also improved on some measures, and was seen by most voters as having the characteristics necessary to be Prime Minister. Those involved in Labour's debate preparation who had argued against the Prime Minister treating the debates as a likeability contest were spot on. Brown scored best on strength and the economy, dismally on likeability.

Table 12.2   Prime ministerial characteristics, before and after debates

	David Cameron		Gordon Brown		Nick Clegg	
	% after final debate	Change from before first debate	% after final debate	Change from before first debate	% after final debate	Change from before first debate
Strong	49	+7	40	+2	36	+22
Likeable	40	–13	13	–2	75	+21
Has what it takes to be Prime Minister	47	–3	38	+2	37	+18
Knows how to get our economy strong	36	+1	41	+8	25	+8
Has clear ideas to deal with the important problems facing Britain	45	+10	34	+1	48	+31
Will change this country for the better	37	–1	21	+1	44	+17
Is in touch with ordinary people	30	+1	21	–2	60	+22

Source: Populus.

The second impact of the debates on polling was that they legitimised the reporting of polls in a way that had become discouraged in recent elections. News broadcasts still rarely led with them (although they did twice, and in addition polls led the election part of the bulletins on five occasions), but the focus on the horse-race aspect of the election – who was ahead, who behind – was reinforced. Some 5% of front pages had a poll as a lead story, largely in the aftermath of the surge in Lib Dem support after the first TV debate. The polls also helped to translate the debates into a three stage horse race for the media. The contents of the debates were frequently overshadowed by the polls' reporting of what voters thought of the leaders.

The third impact of the polls following the debate was that they identified the remarkable transformation in the parties' standing – as a result of the Lib Dem 'surge' in the vote – which changed the nature of the rest of the campaign. Lib Dem support had been rising slightly before the first debate but the post-debate change was still astonishing. Almost overnight, the party increased its support by around 50% in comparable polls. There is no equivalent poll shift in a British general election since polling data began to be collected. From third, the party was suddenly in first place in some polls. Lib Dem support would begin to deflate somewhat over the next few weeks, but of the remaining 64 polls (conducted between 16 April and 5 May) they were first or second in 49, and only slipped back into third in 15.

For all the variation in the poll lead, the polls were pointing to a hung parliament for the entire campaign. The Conservatives had double-digit leads over Labour in just eight polls, and none of these was large enough to equate to an overall majority on the basis of uniform national swing. There were fewer constituency polls and fewer focus groups compared to 2005. But there was widespread interest in what was happening in the marginal seats and how much of a Conservative advantage that party's targeting of marginal seats was achieving. Several polls of marginal seats – by Populus for *The Times*, YouGov for Channel 4 – were conducted, consistently showing a better Conservative performance in the marginals, which helped to qualify any conclusions drawn from national samples.

The polls were often a useful corrective to much of what interested, even obsessed, the politicians and media in the Westminster village. Focus groups also showed that the media interest before the campaign about Lord Ashcroft's tax status and the allegations of Brown's bullying in Andrew Rawnsley's *The End of the Party* passed over most voters' heads, as did 'bigotgate' during the campaign. Throughout the campaign Cameron always led Brown as 'best Prime Minister', despite Clegg having the highest approval ratings on many other questions. The three most important issues for voters consistently were the economy, immigration and the NHS. Also telling was the reminder that voters' party loyalties could shape their evaluation of what the politicians say. A Populus/*Times* survey found that on some issues voters were still less likely to support a policy once it was identified with the Tory Party. For example, 12% said they would not support a policy of requiring foreign workers to speak English if it was a Conservative idea, but only 6% would do so if it was a Labour one.

The newspapers commission polls to generate newsworthy stories but at times also use them to advance a political agenda. The *Sun*, which had declared for Cameron the previous September, commissioned more polls than any other paper, given its daily tracker from YouGov. Yet it chose not to report a YouGov finding that if people thought the Lib Dems had a chance of winning, then 49% would vote for the party, compared to 26% Conservative and 19% Labour, just as it did not publish details of a poll showing that most people thought the Lib Dems were being the most honest party about future spending cuts. And, perhaps not surprising in view of its heavy coverage of the event, it did not report the finding that 83% said that Brown's 'bigot' remarks about Mrs Duffy in Rochdale would not affect their voting intention. But the information was quickly in the public domain because the findings were carried on YouGov's website, in accordance with the British Polling Council's transparency rules, and pored over on specialist sites such as politicalbetting.com or UK Polling Report. On the other side of the tabloid divide, the *Mirror* was also highly selective in its reporting of polls, seeking any opportunity to show Conservative support was falling and that Brown and Labour were gaining.

Nine opinion polls were published on the eve of the election, almost double the number in 2005. The final figures offered by the pollsters are listed in Table 12.3. Although the precise figures differed, the projected shares of the vote were relatively constant. The Conservatives were on 33–37% (although all but one company had them on 36+/–1); Labour on 24–29% (though all but one had them on 28+/–1) and the Lib Dem share ranged from 26 to 29% (although all but two were 28+/–1). The Lib Dem vote share had declined from its peak, following the first debate, but the party was still on course for its best-ever performance, and there was still the possibility that it would push Labour into third place.

Table 12.3   Eve of poll figures

Polling company	Field dates	Con %	Con Error	Lab %	Lab Error	LD %	LD Error	Average error
ICM/*Guardian*	3–4 May	36	–1	28	–2	26	+2	1.7
Populus/*Times*	4–5 May	37	0	28	–2	27	+3	1.7
MORI/*Standard*	5 May	36	–1	29	–1	27	+3	1.7
ComRes/ITN/*Independent*	4–5 May	37	0	28	–2	28	+4	2.0
Harris/*Daily Mail*	4–5 May	35	–2	29	–1	27	+3	2.0
Opinium/*Express*	4–5 May	35	–2	27	–3	26	+2	2.3
YouGov/*Sun*	4–5 May	35	–2	28	–2	28	+4	2.7
Angus Reid/ PoliticalBetting	4–5 May	36	–1	24	–6	29	+5	4.0
TNS BMRB	29 Apr–4 May	33	–4	27	–3	29	+5	4.0
Actual GB result		37		30		24		

Table 12.3 also sets out the eventual shares of the vote achieved by the parties – and the difference between those two figures. The overstating of the Lib Dem vote stands out. But the pollsters, apart from Angus Reid, were much better on the gap between Labour and Conservative, putting

the swing from the former to the latter at between 4.5 and 6%; in the event the final swing was just over 5%.

For the preceding two decades, eve-of-election polls in Britain had been beset by one continuing flaw, which was that they over-stated Labour's performance. That had been true in four of the five eve-of-election polls published in 2005. Indeed, in just one out of 21 polls over the last four elections, spread over almost 20 years, had a polling company's eve-of-election poll under-stated Labour's eventual performance. Yet, as is clear from the table, in 2010 no company over-stated Labour. Whilst the deviations from the actual result were not huge – with the obvious exception of Angus Reid's five points – they were consistently on one side of the divide, demonstrating a systemic error, rather than random fluctuations. The errors were even larger with the Liberal Democrats: every poll noticeably over-estimated the Lib Dem share of the vote, by between three and six points. The Lib Dem surge that had so dominated discussion of the election simply failed to materialise, and whilst the party did still poll better than its performance in 2005 – indeed, polling better than any third party since the Liberal–SDP Alliance in 1983 – the outcome was nothing like on the scale that the polls had been predicting. The polling industry appeared to have solved one longstanding problem, only for another to replace it.

Multiple explanations were put forward for this. Perhaps the Lib Dem 'surge' had never existed at all. The political parties' own canvassing – as monitored in their head offices – certainly never detected the same scale of surge as the polls were suggesting (see Chapter 11). The same applied to the ad hoc monitoring of the opening of postal votes that took place, which detected some rise in Lib Dem support but less than would have been predicted by the polls. This was as true of the Lib Dems as it was of the other two parties, and was one reason why some Lib Dem campaigners at Cowley Street were not quite so gung-ho as might have been expected, or as some of their supporters in the country were. One Labour strategist wondered if, after the first debate, people began to answer the polling questions differently, almost as a judgement on performance than on an intention to vote (what he called 'an X factor judgement'). It was, for example, noticeable that although declared support for the Lib Dems (largely) maintained after the first debate, support for them on other indicators, such as their policies, fell away more swiftly.

Alternatively, perhaps the problem lay in the type of people who were attracted to the party after the debate. All the evidence was that the new Lib Dem supporters were not previously committed supporters of the other parties, but were those who were previously unlikely to vote, including a disproportionate number of young voters. But the problem with attracting support from those who are normally less likely to vote is that they remain less likely to vote. Lib Dem supporters were less likely to say they were certain to vote, more likely to say that they might change their minds, and less likely to say that it mattered who won the election. This should have been taken into account – in that pollsters weight according to people's likelihood to vote – but it could be that the weightings were inadequate for the type of voter suddenly attracted to the Lib Dems.

Or perhaps, third, there was simply a late swing against the Lib Dems, as people suddenly baulked at voting for the party. A surge as sudden and dramatic as that following the first debate could presumably fade just as quickly (something that also worried many within the Lib Dem hierarchy). There was some evidence for this in Populus's eve-of-poll survey for *The Times*, which found a noticeable dropping away of support in the second day of the two-day polling. On the other hand, YouGov's last set of polling – again spread over two days – found exactly the opposite.

This was not a trivial question. The apparent surge in Lib Dem support had completely changed the way the election was conducted and discussed. If the surge had indeed just been a chimera produced by the polling industry, then dodgy polling had had serious consequences for the democratic process. On the other hand, if the Lib Dem surge had initially existed, only to fade and flop, then that was less worrying, being more of a comment on the voters – or on the appeal of Lib Dem policies – than on the pollsters.

A post-election exercise by ICM, involving calling back those they had previously interviewed, rejected many of these explanations: it found no evidence of differential turnout or that the Lib Dem vote was especially soft in practice, and suggested that the problem might be to do with shy Labour voters and/or the weighting that pollsters gave to recalled Lib Dem voting. Yet even that ICM exercise was based on an individual recalling how they voted – and if individuals were mis-reporting their vote at the time, they may well still have been doing so. Debate about exactly what happened to the Lib Dem 'surge' is likely to continue until pollsters again get a chance to measure Lib Dem support at the next election.

The blushes of the polling industry were spared somewhat by the accuracy of the exit poll (Table 12.4), which was conducted jointly by Ipsos-MORI and GfK-NOP and jointly commissioned by the BBC, ITN, and, for the first time, Sky.[2] The methods of analysis in 2010 were very similar to those utilised in 2005.[3] What differed were the sampling points, deliberately larger in order to capture more Labour–Lib Dem battlegrounds. It involved around 18,000 voters, interviewed at around 130 sites – of which 26 were new additions.

Table 12.4 The exit poll

	10pm	*10.45pm Revision*	*Eventual outcome*	*Difference*
Lab	255	255	258	–3
Con	307	305	307	0
LD	59	61	57	+2
Others	29	29	28	+1

Note: the figures include Thirsk & Malton as a Conservative seat.

The total average error, therefore, was just 1.5 seats, an astonishingly accurate prediction (although ironically, the original 10pm prediction was more accurate than its later revision). Just as in 2005, the poll had correctly predicted the majority (or, in this case, minority). The poll had noted that Labour was doing better in Scotland, in seats with incumbent Labour MPs, and where there was an above average ethnic minority population – all were true and explained its astonishing accuracy.

The Conservatives launched an ambitious private polling exercise early in Cameron's leadership, which continued throughout the lifetime of the parliament. It built on the work commissioned by Michael Ashcroft for the 2005 general election and published in *Smell the Coffee* (see p. 70). Labour, strapped for cash, did relatively little private polling, a contrast to 2005 when it outpolled the Conservatives and its relationship with the US pollsters it eventually appointed had effectively faded before the election campaign began. The Liberal Democrats, as ever, lacked the money to do much polling. All the parties also relied heavily on the ample public polling commissioned by the mass media. One Conservative insider said the party spent much of its time analysing the public data, adding 'We then work out exactly what we can't get from the public data and then poll on that.'

Deborah Mattinson, head of Chime Research, had polled for the Labour Party since 1986, and had effectively been Gordon Brown's private pollster since 1995, continuing in that role when Brown became party leader in 2007. The relationship was in part Brown's answer to Blair's close relationship with the political strategist Philip Gould and she became a key member of 'Team GB' (see above, p. 7). She quickly realised that Brown was not instinctively in touch with the public and lacked the antennae of Tony Blair or even David Cameron. For him polling was, according to a close adviser, 'an intellectual process, he did not get it instinctively'. But he was still an avid user of polls and focus groups – one of the reasons that his claims not to have been influenced by the polls in 2007 (see Chapter 1) were so ridiculed. Indeed, even the words he used on the doorstep of Number 10 the day he became Prime Minister had been checked in a focus group. Some critics complained that Mattinson dispensed only good news to Brown but in private she pointed to his shortcomings and regularly played clips from her focus groups to make him aware of what the public perceived as his strengths and weaknesses.[4]

It was always understood when Brown became leader that Mattinson would be complemented with a US pollster. In September 2007 Stan Greenberg was asked at short notice to poll in the marginal seats for a possible autumn general election. It was a pragmatic decision to recruit him; he already had done work on marginal seats in 2005. His findings, pointing to a narrow Labour majority, were such as to dissuade Brown from calling an election.

Mattinson's focus groups had already alerted the Prime Minister to the positive effect that George Osborne's inheritance tax proposals were having on floating voters (and indeed she had warned Brown of the salience of the issue well before Osborne's announcement).[5] In a case of shooting the messenger rather than the message Brown's relations with both pollsters and his chief of strategy Spencer Livermore soured after the election that never was. Mattinson continued to provide advice but had few interactions with Brown following the events of November 2007.

In January 2009 Douglas Alexander and David Muir, Brown's strategy adviser, talked to a number of Obama's operatives and decided to appoint the Benenson Strategy Group, as the party's private pollster. The idea was that the new team would initially report to Deborah Mattinson and, to save costs, the fieldwork would be done online by Peter Kellner of YouGov with Benenson providing the analysis. In the event, Mattinson's contacts with Brown faded away and the agency instead reported to Muir who forged a good relationship with Joel Benenson and Pete Brodnitz. The agency conducted three national polls, in March and September 2009 and February 2010, as well as work in April for the TV debates. The first poll, by telephone, was conducted by ICM, the others, online, by YouGov.

In one presentation in autumn 2009, Benenson pointed to the massive unpopularity of the Conservatives' inheritance tax proposals, which they called 'a tax cut for the rich' (but see p. 156). Building on the Obama success in overtaking Clinton to gain the Democrat nomination they urged Labour to adopt an 'insurgency' strategy. Muir conducted some focus groups himself and presented them and the Benenson work to political Cabinets. Some ministers felt that he could have been more open with the results of the research and may have held back some of the more negative findings about Brown and the Government. Others rejected that assessment and a defender in Number 10 said: 'I would understand it if he did. His job was also to boost morale, not least Gordon's.'

Some advisers were unhappy with Benenson's work. Labour's shortage of money meant that not only was there relatively little polling but also that Benenson and Brodnitz visited the UK less frequently than they wished, although they spoke to Brown regularly by phone. A decision was taken to divert the budget for a final election poll into one on the TV debates. Disagreement over the work of the US pollsters led to a confrontation in March between Muir, their main supporter, and Douglas Alexander. The latter felt that, as the campaign coordinator, he was not being fully kept abreast of the material. After the election he looked back and expressed regret that lack of finance meant the party was not able to benefit fully from Benenson's polling and strategic capability: 'the problem was that the pollsters provided a full service model and we could not afford it'.

On the eve of the election, the party then decided to give its campaign polling to YouGov's Peter Kellner, who conducted a large survey early in the campaign. A planned second survey was abandoned and the funds were instead diverted to add questions to YouGov's daily tracker polls for the *Sun* and *Sunday Times*, involving a fresh daily sample of 1,200–1,500 people. Philip Gould and Muir added four or five questions each day covering the Labour and Conservative parties' ratings on the economy and the NHS, and voters' expectations of life under a Tory or a Labour government. The negative expectations of a Labour victory concerned immigration and debt; for the Conservatives they concerned removing tax credits and prioritising the interests of the rich.

Labour's focus groups were conducted by Gould, Alice Cartner-Morley, Oliver Kempton and Greg Cook. Between the New Year and polling day they conducted some 75 groups, largely among 2005 Labour voters who were thinking of moving from the party. During the campaign a report of each evening's group was prepared for the key campaigners on the 'top table'. Cook conducted groups three evenings a week during the campaign outside London and found that the main issues of concern for voters were immigration, discipline in schools and Gordon Brown's leadership (all of which were damaging to Labour). Gould concentrated on London constituencies. Brown was often described as 'dull', 'a ditherer' and 'not a leader', although some also thought he had been a successful Chancellor and was a substantial politician. Greg Cook was so struck by the right-wing sentiments of lapsed Labour voters that he stated, 'with Michael Howard's 2005 platform and Cameron as leader the Tories would be unstoppable'. But the groups also found uncertainty about what the Conservative Party stood for and what a Cameron Britain would look like. The way to exploit this, according to Gould's report from his final focus group (on the Tuesday night before polling day), was to '"...*close on the economy and the economic choice*" [emphasis in original]. This should be a macro-choice about economic risk and a micro-choice about the direct financial costs of a Conservative government. Tax credits are central to this.'

As leader in the months following the 2005 election defeat, Michael Howard had appointed Michael Ashcroft as a deputy chairman of the party and a member of the party's board. The party accepted Ashcroft's offer to oversee the party's private polling, geared to target voters in the battleground seats (see p. 235). He invited Stephen Gilbert to commission regular surveys from Populus in the battleground seats, polling on the Liberal Democrats and other target voters from ICM, and focus groups from ORB. Between them Populus and ORB conducted over a hundred focus groups from the New Year to polling day. Cameron, Osborne and Hilton were the main regular recipients of the data and Gilbert's commentary on them, although by 2009 Hilton was taking little interest in the work. Ashcroft and Gilbert also made occasional presentations to the Shadow Cabinet. Populus pre-tested substantial parts of Osborne's 2007 conference speech and the work influenced his statement on inheritance tax (see p. 9) and his 2009 conference proposals for reducing part of the deficit.

In early 2010 the research concentrated not on the most marginal seats the party was attacking but a further 69 (all in England), the additional number needed to deliver a Parliamentary majority. The seats were selected on the basis of analysis by MOSAIC groups and other demographic and attitudinal factors.

Surveys during the Parliament showed that Cameron was regarded more positively than his party. During the second half of the Parliament, when the Conservatives were regularly gaining over 40% in the opinion polls and enjoyed double-digit leads over Labour, their private polling warned that nearly half said that the main or sometimes only reason people gave for voting Tory was to get rid of Labour, not because they liked the Conservatives. A similar proportion said they had not firmly decided how they would vote and might switch. Private and public polls showed that a large majority of voters were in favour of political change but only about half of those were prepared to vote Conservative. Because voters were still confused about the party's message and/or doubtful that the party had changed, one adviser urged it to sustain its message of modernisation. He added: 'But people are not sure what they are; they are a brand in transition.'

Populus developed 'mood boards' to study the Labour and Conservative images and reported each quarter. The most worrying finding for the Conservatives was the perception that they would, in a crunch, stick up for rich and privileged people. Cameron privately confessed late in 2008 that the persistence of this last image kept him awake at night. It was a factor in his Shadow Cabinet reshuffle in 2009 (see p. 87). That the perception declined only slightly by the time the election was called reflected the limits of Cameron's decontamination strategy. The party was also seen as opportunistic, 'jumping on bandwagons'. But Labour fared no better, being identified with single mums living on benefit and with 'fat lazy shirkers' rather than hard-working families. Compared with a similar survey of party brands in 1997 perceptions of Brown and Labour were as bad as they had been for John Major and the Conservatives in 1997.

During the campaign Populus polled in 69 seats in the eight clusters of target seats: East Midlands; Central Midlands; East Pennines; West Pennines; New Towns; Seaside Towns; Lib Dem rural, and Lib Dem urban. Two Labour clusters were added half way through the campaign, 'North' and 'Midlands & South' (see p. 235). The surveys covered party attributes, standings of the party leaders and 'momentum measures', the last referring to questions on awareness of campaign activity (especially direct mail), perceptions of who would win, locally as well as nationally, and the question: 'Overall would you say that you are moving towards or away from...' asked for each party. They found that Labour had solidified its vote in certain key clusters and, even more clearly, that the tide among the floating voters was moving away from the Conservatives in certain groups; in both the Pennine clusters and in the two Lib Dem clusters, the Conservatives were detecting a momentum problem even before the campaign began.

The Conservatives had originally planned that YouGov would conduct surveys of what people were saying about the parties during the campaign but decided to divert this budget into a weekly YouGov poll that would be the vehicle for the message polling that the American consultant Bill Knapp was seeking. Johnny Heald, of ORB, and Andrew Cooper and Rick Nye, of Populus, conducted focus groups in marginal seats with 2005 Labour voters who were thinking of switching, essentially the same groups

Labour was interviewing. The pollsters picked up the liking for Cameron and unpopularity of Brown, the sense that Labour was 'tired', had had its chance and it was time for a change. But many of the voters remained uncertain, a number commenting how difficult it was to imagine voting for the Conservatives ('my dad would be turning in his grave'). Heald also conducted private dial tests during the leaders' TV debates where 'soft' voters gave a second-by-second reaction to the debates.

The pollsters had no formal meetings with the party leaders and took no part in strategy discussions. Peter Kellner provided data for David Muir but was not a member of the Labour campaign team, although Gould and Greg Cook were. Kellner anyway wanted to preserve his distance because of his role as a media pundit, not least on election night television. For the Conservatives the material from Populus, ICM and ORB was sent directly to Stephen Gilbert. But Osborne, a keen student of the polls, had many informal discussions with Andrew Cooper, and in February 2010 the pollster was recruited to the campaign team, with a desk in party headquarters and liaised with the visiting American consultants (see p. 133).

Brought over from the US to help with message testing for the debate, Bill Knapp expressed surprise that the 'Big Society' language – the central spine of the Conservative manifesto – appeared not to have been tested beforehand. In a widely read post-election critique of the Conservative campaign, Tim Montgomerie, the editor of ConservativeHome, similarly attacked the failure to test the concept before it was launched. Steve Hilton, the brains behind the idea, thought it was ridiculous to test such a fundamental party belief. 'It is what the party is about, it is what you believe,' he told colleagues. For the past year at least he had become impatient that the polling had shown little progress on some of the key modernising themes he had promoted. Yet whilst it might be understandable that a party would not want to test its fundamental beliefs, they could have tested the language used to promote it. It was one of the paradoxes of the Conservative campaign that they tested so much, but not the Big Society.

The Liberal Democrats employed Hall & Partners, a commercial body which had done little political polling before and worked mainly on consumer branding. It was relatively cheap, and useful. During the election campaign, it polled samples of 1,500 voters each Saturday and concentrated questions on voting intention and the debates. The party also used open-ended questions with volunteer phone banks. It found that the party's 'fair taxes' policy tested the best, followed by education but the proposal for political reform was subsumed by the discussion about a hung parliament.

Beginning in late February the Conservatives did extensive online polling to test lines for the TV debates. Guided by Knapp, an expert in messaging, they tested alternative phrases to describe modern Conservatism, what Cameron stood for and how to characterise Brown and the Government. Labour's research was more modest. Before the debates began David Muir used snippets of the Brown rehearsals in focus groups. Benenson drew on their experience with Obama, mixing quantitative and qualitative research, using a tool called i-moderate. An innovation in British election campaigns, this spliced together clips of Brown and Cameron to do online testing and then talk to vote changers via an online chat mechanism. Before the final TV debate YouGov tested some lines about the Liberal Democrats. Brown had come to find Benenson's company reassuring and insisted he be with him before the final debate.

When the Conservatives' private polling re-interviewed 2,500 voters in the battleground seats after the election nearly a fifth said they had thought of voting Conservative but did not. When they were asked why not, the unprompted responses suggested a feeling that the party had not changed enough. For Labour, Philip Gould conducted a post-election focus group with people who, having voted for the party in 2005, had been thinking of switching to another party but returned to Labour in 2010. He found that apart from a feeling that the Conservatives had not changed enough Labour was perceived as the safest choice at a time of risk and there was a continuing sense of emotional attachment to Labour. In its post-election survey of 500 undecided voters who did not vote for the party the Lib Dems found that the two top reasons mentioned were that the party could not win and their policy on immigration.

Tim Montgomerie added to his criticisms of the Conservative campaign by arguing that the party in future should appoint a full-time professional pollster who would report directly to the party leader and market-test all policy initiatives. He suggested that a figure like Stephen Gilbert, who commissioned the research and reported the findings to politicians, should be dispensed with. The party leaders, he suggested, 'need their own Philip Gould'. The suggestion seems to be based on a misunderstanding of how Gould operated. Nobody concerned with the party's polling expressed any concerns about Gilbert's role and, although clearly a moderniser he presented the polling data to the party leadership, separate from his comments. Gould, by contrast, was and is a public and highly political figure, an ardent Labour moderniser, a forceful political strategist, and personally close to Tony Blair. Indeed this closeness made him suspect in the eyes of many Brownites and critics of New Labour, hardly the role model Montgomerie was recommending.

In 2010 the polls were followed as eagerly as ever, to see if Labour or the Lib Dems would finish second in the popular vote and if the Conservatives would cross the finishing line with a clear majority. The numerous public and private polls and focus groups consistently revealed that Labour's leader was unpopular and that voters felt its time was up, that the Lib Dems for all their popularity were not seen as a party of government, and that the Conservatives had still not changed enough for a majority of voters.

Notes

1. 'Learning from the Worm', London, ComRes, June 2010.
2. In addition, the exercise drew heavily on academic analysts, unseen and (largely) unsung, including the three authors of this volume's Appendix 2 – John Curtice (Strathclyde), Stephen Fisher (Oxford), and Robert Ford (Manchester), along with Jouni Kuha (LSE), Will Jennings (Manchester), and Clive Payne (Oxford).
3. See J. Curtice and D. Firth, 'Exit Polling in a Cold Climate: The BBC–ITV Experience in Britain in 2005', *Journal of the Royal Statistical Society A*, 171 (2008), 509–39.
4. See Deborah Mattinson, *Talking to a Brick Wall* (London: Biteback, 2010), esp. Chapters 10 and 11.
5. Ibid., p. 172.

13
The X-Factor Election: On the Air

Martin Harrison

The years since 2005 were far from easy for broadcasters. The commercial networks were hard hit by the recession and, for some, declining audiences and management changes. Channel Five's future was uncertain, ITN's 24-hour news channel closed, Channel 4 had severe funding difficulties and ITV pressed for a reduction in the burden of its regional news commitment. The scars from the clash between the Government and the BBC over the David Kelly affair and the subsequent Hutton report were still fresh. Under the Corporation's new charter its Board of Governors was replaced by the BBC Trust, with responsibility for strategy and budgets, and a new regulator, the Office of Communications (Ofcom). Relations between BBC management, the Trust and Ofcom had yet to bed down, and these new arrangements had still to find favour with politicians on either side of the House. Regardless of who won the election the Trust and Ofcom faced uncertain futures. Internally, there were bruising conflicts over newsroom redundancies, while reports on BBC coverage of the Middle East, the European Union and climate change had found it wanting. The Corporation was also held to have failed to adapt adequately to the devolved character of UK government. It had long had to contend with the unremitting hostility of sections of the press, but widely-publicised instances of financial laxity, and resentment at the expansion of its commercial activities now meant it could not count on the support of some of its traditional defenders. All the broadcasters had the challenge of bringing a general election to a public that was more than usually disaffected from politics and politicians in the wake of the parliamentary expenses scandal.

The broadcasters were helped by a timely innovation. Debates between party leaders had been proposed at every election for decades, but one side or another, usually the government of the day, had always found them inopportune. The possibility was raised afresh during the summer of 2009, but little progress had been made when, in early September, the head of Sky News, John Ryley, formally proposed a debate or debates and launched an online campaign. ITV and the BBC were irritated by what they saw as Sky grandstanding but Cameron and Clegg speedily assented; Brown agreed in principle but said the matter could be deferred until the election – when he must have known it would be too late to agree the necessary arrangements. Sky's political editor, Adam Boulton, raised the stakes by saying that if any party declined to participate Sky would go ahead with its chair empty.[1]

Divided, Labour vacillated. In an interview with Boulton Brown refused to be pinned down about his intentions and walked out. Later, he excised a commitment to participate from the advance text of his speech to the 2009 Labour conference. However, in early October he wrote to party activists signalling that he would go ahead.

Negotiations began shortly afterwards. Sue Inglish, BBC Head of Political Programming, recalled how hearts sank when the party representatives arrived at the first meeting bearing voluminous documentation about US experience. Indeed, with so much at stake everyone involved was initially extremely wary. Yet although the discussions were at times difficult and protracted more than one participant agreed they were 'remarkably positive'. They culminated in a 76-point agreement announced on 1 March.

There would be three 90-minute partly themed debates in prime time between the main national party leaders. (Brown initially favoured debates between ministers and their shadows, as well as leaders, as more appropriate to a system of cabinet government.) The debates would be held in north-west England, southern/south-west England and the Midlands and produced and moderated by ITV, BSkyB and the BBC, respectively. All parties would be treated equally – a customary Lib Dem demand that had always been resisted in the past. Cameron conceded this early on in the negotiations and was later criticised by senior colleagues as having thereby robbed the party of outright victory. Brown had preferred separate sessions with Cameron and Clegg, but this was not acceptable to the others. There would be additional debates in Scotland, Wales and Northern Ireland between representatives of qualifying parties in those countries.

The most sensitive issues turned on the composition and role of the studio audience and how the questions would be generated. Worried by, notably, recent experiences on BBC One's *Question Time*, the parties were determined at all costs to prevent discussion being interrupted, distracted or unbalanced by the audience. What eventually emerged from the haggling was that a 'representative' audience of about 200 would be recruited by the ICM polling organisation from people living within a 30-mile radius from the venue. It would be mute and passive, apart from applause at the beginning and end. There would be limited reaction shots. Questions would be filtered by a panel formed by the host broadcaster and had to be appropriate for answering by all three leaders – so avoiding questions tailored for or against any particular leader. The leaders would stand at podiums throughout. After brief initial statements they would answer questions in turn and then could challenge each other's replies. They would make short final statements. Some critics found the conditions stultifying; Dominic Lawson trenchantly declared that the entire affair would be 'characterised by a depressing combination of rigidity and superficiality'.[2]

In the event, the Prime Ministerial debates were preceded by something akin to a dry run – Channel 4's *Ask the Chancellors*, featuring Alistair Darling, George Osborne and Vince Cable, with Channel 4's economics editor, Krishnan Guru-Murthy as moderator. After brief initial statements the three answered questions on economic issues from a studio audience, which otherwise did not intervene, apart from one ripple of laughter and one spontaneous burst of applause. The chairman moved them along briskly, occasionally putting a supplementary question but never being intrusive. The politicians interrupted one another at times, but were unfailingly polite and serious, though with occasional flashes of humour and even agreement. This was a world away from the Commons bear pit. Was it just a shade too cosy? Even an hour was manifestly insufficient to exhaust the issues, yet that hour provided greater insight into the parties' perceptions and likely course of action than anything else in the campaign, particularly the agreement from all three men that the cuts to come would be even deeper than Margaret Thatcher's.

The agreed 76 'rules' did not have the stultifying effect some had feared. A greater constraint was that all three leaders were determined to avoid gaffes and on their best behaviour, so it was mildly surprising when Brown growled at Clegg to 'get real' over the Trident replacement and when Clegg called the Conservatives' associates in the European Parliament 'nutters'. The debate format had its limitations, chiefly arising from tackling eight or so substantial topics in under 90 minutes (see Table 13.1). Yet the answers could at least indicate the main lines of each party's approach and subject them to challenge. Thus the weaknesses of all three parties' proposals for immigration – on which there was a question in all three debates – became evident under scrutiny. What the debate format did not provide was the more sustained interrogation found in the best formal interviews. Andrew Gimson's verdict that the politicians 'descended to the level of some TV celebrity talent shows' was a classic example of what Lord Mandelson dismissed as 'hyperbole passing as journalism'.[3] But where else would voters have heard their political leaders explain themselves unmediated and at greater-than-soundbite length?

Table 13.1   Topics of questions asked in Prime Ministerial debates

First debate	Second debate	Third debate
Immigration	EU	Spending cuts
Crime	Climate change (personal contribution)	Taxes
Political reform	Pope's visit (stem cell research, contraception, gays, IVF, child abuse)	Bankers' bonuses/job losses
Education	Political reform	Help for manufacturing
Deficit	Pensions	Politicians/immigration
Military equipment/pay	All-party government	Housing
Health	Immigration	Benefits
Elderly care		Opportunities for children

Traditionalists fretted that the debates were making a parliamentary system increasingly presidential. Yet, unlike American campaigns, there were many substantial appearances elsewhere by ministers and their shadows, including not only the *Ask the Chancellors* session but nine short debates on specific issue areas carried by BBC Two's *Daily Politics Debates* and the separate series of debates in Scotland, Wales and Northern Ireland. In all, there was more direct engagement on air between politicians below leadership level in this election than in any previous campaign.

Broadcasters admitted being apprehensive that voters might tune in to the first debate from curiosity but drop out after a quarter of an hour, never to return. In the event, the first debate had an average audience of 9.4 million, opening at 8.8 million at 8.30pm and holding up to 9.3 million at 9.45pm. The second debate, which was not carried live by BBC One or ITV1, brought Sky News its largest ever audience, averaging 4.1 million. The final debate was seen by an average 8.1 million. Figures like these put the debates in the same ratings league as *Coronation Street* or a popular reality TV show. It would be wildly excessive to claim, as one broadcaster did, that the debates had saved democracy, but they certainly stimulated discussion well beyond the ranks of those who watched them, particularly among young voters, to the point that almost twice as many people subsequently claimed to have watched than actually did.

The prevailing view among broadcasters and politicians at a BAFTA review after polling day was that the debates had been a success and that they had come to stay, with only a little tweaking of the rules at the next election.[4] Not everyone shared that conclusion. The SNP and Plaid Cymru complained at being excluded. The SNP took its case to the BBC Trust and Ofcom. Rebuffed there it sought an interdict from the Court of Session in Edinburgh, again unsuccessfully; the court found its application 'far too late'. One awkwardness of the debates was that so many domestic matters are devolved to Scotland, Wales and Northern Ireland. Moderators had to remind viewers there that much of what was being said was not relevant to them. The separate debates in the devolved systems and compensatory exposure in regular output for the minor parties, including UKIP and the BNP did not entirely still all the complaints. In fact, smaller parties fared better in this election than in any previous campaign. Nevertheless, airtime is sure to be a bone of contention again at the next election.

Amid the predominantly favourable verdicts on the debates there was little disposition to reflect on the 'collateral damage' they engendered. The substantial preparation they required led to some interviews and press conferences being dropped (see p. 177). Both Brown and Cameron reportedly tried to duck out of interviews with Jeremy Paxman for *Newsnight*. Though these did take place they arguably lost some of their impact. The coverage bulletins and current affairs programmes gave to preparations for the debates, reactions to them, inquests on them and naming the winners also took time that would otherwise have been given to other matters. The most glaring examples were the futile interviews after each debate in which party spokesmen utterly predictably claimed that their man had won. There was also the potentially tedious deployment of The Worm, a program laboriously charting how panels of undecided voters pushing buttons reacted to words or phrases used by each leader.

News and Discussion

Enthusiasts had talked this up as the internet election, but radio and television remained the prime source of information for voters, albeit with a greatly increased interaction with social media. The scale of the

BBC's contribution was impressive. In addition to its regular national and regional news on radio and television there was news in Welsh for S4C and in Gaelic for Alba. Radio 1 had *Newsbeat* for young adults and CBBC's *Newsround* targeted an even younger age group. There were additional contributions from *Breakfast*, Radio 4's *Today, The World at One, PM, The World Tonight, Any Questions?, Question Time, Newsnight, The Daily Politics* (BBC One), *The Daily Politics Debates* (BBC Two) and, at weekends, *The Andrew Marr Show, The Politics Show*, Clive Anderson's mildly satirical *The Heckler* (Radio 4) and more comedy on Radio 1's *The Vote Now Show*. The Parliament Channel carried an eclectic mix of material from previous elections, current speeches and news conferences. This channel, the BBC News Channel, Sky News and Radio 5 Live were almost the only points outside the debates where politicians could be heard uninterrupted for more than 20 seconds.

There were also programmes for first-time voters on BBC Three, one on the implications of the election for the classical music industry (Radio 3) and another on Radio 6 on prospects for the popular music industry. ITV simply was not in the same league. Apart from its regular national and regional news output and the soft-focus *GMTV* its contribution was limited to profiles of the three party leaders and weekly editions of *Tonight*, with Jonathan Dimbleby, on the main issues in the election. In addition to news, Channel 4 had *Ask the Chancellors* and *Election Uncovered: What They Won't Tell Us*, an attempt to get behind the parties' unwillingness to discuss in detail how they would mend the economy. Shortly before the election Channel 4 had also run *Politicians for Hire*, in which retiring MPs were secretly filmed offering their services for lobbying.

Of the 305 BBC One, ITV1, Channel 4 and Radio 4 news programmes analysed for the period 17 April to 5 May every one made some reference to the election, albeit at times very briefly. However, unlike some earlier elections no bulletins were extended. Presentation was low-key; there were no dedicated election desks or presenters. The BBC flagged its election output with what looked like giant hatpins in the various party colours fanning out from an outline of the UK. ITN stayed with its regular presentation and Channel 4 displayed a simple Vote 2010 placard.

The election took between 50 and 55% of news time on the three main television networks – roughly in line with previous campaigns.[5] Radio 4 bulletins at 8am, 1pm and 10pm, that were immediately followed by analysis and discussion, gave the election 28% of their time, again much as usual. The half-hour free-standing bulletins at 6pm and midnight devoted, respectively, 31 and 25% of their time to the election. The flow slackened over weekends and Easter but whereas it had tended to fall back in the third week in previous elections it now held up well because the debates and the prospect of a hung parliament brought fresh material and excitement through to the final days.

During most elections some big non-political stories compete for airtime. This one had more than most: the crash of a Polish airliner near Smolensk cutting a deadly swathe through the country's political, military and cultural elite, headed bulletins on 10 and 11 April; volcanic ash from Iceland hugely disrupted air traffic, thwarting the travel plans of many thousands (15–22 April). So many people were directly or indirectly affected (and the shots of the volcano were so striking) that this received saturation coverage – though views of empty departure halls became as tedious as the Nth political photo opportunity. Other stories topping bulletins included social unrest in Greece (23 April and 1 May), a terrorist incident in New York (2 May), an international nuclear agreement (8 April), problems within the Roman Catholic church (22 April), a couple of murders (23–24 April) and the separation of conjoined twins (8 April).

Despite these other happenings, BBC One led on the election at both 6pm and 10pm on 18 of the 28 days between 8 April and the eve of poll, compared with ITV's 12 times in the early evening and 14 times at News at Ten – in keeping with ITV's generally less demanding approach. Channel 4's main news had 13 election leads. Radio 4's flagship 6pm bulletin, unburdened by the clutter of photo opportunities, spent less time on the campaign but led on it 19 times; the midnight news did so on 16 evenings. Usually when the election was not the lead story it came second, but on the occasional quiet day it sunk to eighth in the running order. The competition from other stories, the debates and the pressure to spend more time on the minor parties may explain why election news sometimes seemed even more compressed than usual.

The BBC and ITV both committed substantial resources to following the leaders. On most days, this gave rise to three packages on each leader, at roughly the same length, at roughly the same times and reporting roughly the same events to very similar agendas. Add the requirements of balance and their output had a sort of virtuous sameness. However, ITV seemed more receptive to items like Cameron being hit by an egg, which led its early evening election report on 21 April, or his encounter with an angry father whose child's special needs were not being met (1.30pm, 27 April). In general, nobody appeared to see elections as a time for awkward questions – in March the BBC had deferred transmission of a *Panorama* investigation of Lord Ashcroft after forceful representations by the Conservatives. His name was barely mentioned during the entire campaign. There was, however, one major difference between the BBC's and ITV's output. The BBC had a wide variety of programmes where issues were further explained and discussed; ITV did not.

Nowhere was more discussion more necessary than over the economy. In one or other of its manifold aspects it featured in no fewer than 227 of the 305 bulletins analysed. It was the main story through the first week and a recurring one for the rest of the campaign. The initial focus was on Conservative plans to tackle the problem immediately and halve a Labour increase in national insurance contributions – a 'tax on jobs' that it claimed would damage recovery. Labour would maintain the increase and defer cuts until recovery was further advanced. It accused the Conservatives of aggravating the deficit by forgoing £6 billion on national insurance. The conflicting approaches were outlined and explained many times in both the news and wider coverage, with the aid of the various channels' economics editors. Yet, despite all these efforts, it was subsequently reported that a sizeable fraction of the audience thought the Conservatives' proposed cut in insurance contributions was a Labour policy – an outcome providing food for thought to politicians and journalists alike (see p. 331).

The early clashes over national insurance and the timing of cuts were by no means unimportant but they sometimes seemed to serve as a diversion from the central questions about economic strategy. The snag was that none of the parties was prepared to come clean about its intentions, despite persistent attempts to get them to do so. The Institute for Fiscal Studies (IFS), an independent thinktank, produced a scathing report on the inadequacies of their policy statements. When Adam Boulton pressed Lord Mandelson for details about cuts he was curtly reminded that neither the IFS nor Boulton was standing in the election. 'Neither are you', came the irrepressible voice of Andrew Neil. A handful of details did emerge, such as the future of child trust funds, but on major issues like VAT nobody would be drawn. By the end, no sentient voter could have doubted that what lay ahead would be painful but he or she would have had little clear idea of where the blows would fall.

Nothing else was covered anywhere near as often as the economy. Other topics that featured relatively frequently were hung parliaments in 116 bulletins, the polls (95) and political reform (57). Education and the NHS (both 55), immigration (50), the EU (40) and crime (39) were also mentioned relatively often. 'Mentioned' is the operative word for several of those because highly compressed bulletins were prone to catch them up in a passing word or phrase. Most major areas were followed up in greater detail in other programmes, often on several occasions, but invariably to smaller audiences. Even so, little was heard about housing, the environment, transport or care of the elderly. Cameron's Big Society got coverage but, apart from his proposed tax concessions to married couples, which drew fire from other parties, much of it was too unfamiliar to attract wide discussion. Iraq had almost completely vanished from the agenda. The big parties touched on Afghanistan only when required to during the second debate. It was absent from non-election news because facilities visits for journalists were suspended during the campaign and because there were few deaths during the period to provide grim reminders of the war by the now-established ritual of announcing every death at least twice, followed by the people of Wootton Bassett paying their respects to the funeral cortège.

Towards the end of the campaign Labour tried unsuccessfully to persuade the other parties to join in representations to the broadcasters to focus more on policy analysis and less on personalities, Labour accepted that the manifestos had been fully, fairly and properly covered, but contended that, in the wake of the debates and the Lib Dem surge, 'the usual specialist examination of specific policy areas has not been done'.[6] Policy was in fact discussed right through to the closing stages, but to a lesser extent than in the first week or so. At times it seemed every bulletin and programme featured veteran commentators saying of the surge that something big was happening, they had never seen anything like it, though they could not say just what or why or where it would lead. In short, much time was spent on 'experts' saying they had nothing to say. The balance of attention shifted more towards the polls, tactical voting, a hung parliament and the leaders' increasingly frenetic travels, culminating with Cameron's final through-the-night sprint. These were all legitimate topics but it was a little too easy to lose track of what the election was actually about. Labour had a point.

According to a former campaign reporter one reason for trailing the leaders around the country from one boring event to the next was that something might happen that was not in the script. Every election throws up some such occasion. This time it was Brown's encounter with Gillian Duffy (see pp. 173–6). It led every bulletin for the rest of that day, refreshed by Brown hearing a play-back of the offending words for the first time on the Jeremy Vine show and his subsequent return to Duffy's home to seek absolution. The story ran at lengths reserved for Big Stories – 9'30" on BBC One's Ten O'Clock News, 12'53" on ITV1's News at Ten and 8'04" on Radio 4's midnight news, wiping out most other election coverage. Thereafter it was reprised from time to time until the campaign ended.

This was a compelling story for many reasons. Shots of Duffy's shock on learning of the Prime Minister's words and of Brown crumpling in that

Manchester studio on hearing the playback will linger in the memory as the most striking images of the 2010 campaign. But did the story really warrant quite so many repetitions – as much as six times in an hour – or the interviews with Duffy's niece and neighbours? Inevitably someone dredged up the lazy tag of 'bigotgate'. ITV reporters spoke of 'disaster', 'meltdown', 'self-destruct' and the 'defining moment of the campaign'.[7] BBC One's Ten O'Clock News declared that Labour's campaign was 'in chaos'. Two days later ITV even described Labour's campaign as 'accident prone' when a car hit a bus shelter during a Labour poster launch.[8] Somewhere in all of this a sense of proportion had been lost.

As always, news coverage concentrated on a relatively few people. While 249 different politicians were cited in the programmes analysed only 33 were reported six more times.[9] Labour, with its established ministerial team had 12, the Conservatives 6, the Lib Dems 4 and other parties 11. Only six survived from the 2005 tally (Brown, Jowell, Cable, Osborne, Salmon and Sturgeon). The major leaders were as dominant as ever – but no more so; Brown's 386 citations were 74% of those for Labour, Cameron's 375 citations were 71% of the Conservative tally, while Clegg's score was 328 – 72% of the Lib Dem total. (The next most cited person was Alex Salmond for the SNP with 56.) These are of course only the figures for news bulletins. If the full range of election programming were included in the tally, the results would look much less 'presidential' and the ranks of those making multiple appearances would be more substantial.

There was a flurry of comment after polling about the absence of women.[10] The number of female politicians cited six or more times actually rose by 20% compared with 2005 – from five to six. There were no Tories or Lib Dems, two were Labour (Yvette Cooper and Tessa Jowell) and four were from other parties – Caroline Lucas (Green), Margaret Richie (SDLP), Helena Sturgeon (SNP) and Helen Jones (Plaid). Women fared little better elsewhere. Andrew Neil pointedly remarked in *The Daily Politics* on the unwillingness of the parties to put up women to speak for them. Of the 31 panellists in the nine *Daily Politics Debates* only two were female. Out of 38 slots in the debates in the three devolved countries four were taken by women. Unlike 2005, one ethnic minority contender was cited over five times – ironically, this was Manish Sood, Labour's candidate in North-West Norfolk, who called Brown the worst prime minister in British history in the final days of the campaign. Members of ethnic minorities and women were much more common in vox pop collections or constituency items, for which reporters are briefed to achieve an equitable ethnic and gender mix. However, appearances there rarely exceeded 15 seconds. These constituency features also provided recurring reminders of popular disenchantment with politics and the impact of the expenses scandals, which did not otherwise feature prominently elsewhere in the news.

In some respects news coverage spanned an impressive range – but its limitations were never more apparent. It now had to take into account the debates, the greater number of parties qualifying for some form of recognition and the complicating realities of devolution. Always highly compressed it became more concentrated still; soundbites shrunk to minibites with several topics often touched on within a few seconds. It is questionable whether this served either the public or the parties. The wider output of course often provided correctives to overcompression in the news. But even there a greater diversity of perspectives would have been welcome. The IFS was well used but The King's Fund and the Constitution Unit less so. Business voices were heard loud and clear; the unions and the shop floor less so. Mainstream commentators abounded but more divergent thinkers or friendly assessments from abroad were scarce.

The Party Broadcasts

Only an older generation would remember when party election broadcasts running 20 minutes or so were the only way broadcasters acknowledged an election and only three parties benefitted from them. Those days are long gone. In 2010 the fragmentation of the old party system and the erosion of attention spans meant that 20 parties qualified for broadcasts of under five minutes to the whole UK or to Scotland, Wales or Northern Ireland. As many as 75 different versions were possible but, in the event, some carried the same content rebadged for the appropriate region.

Unloved and often derided, PEBs remained the one place where parties could present themselves to the voters in prime time, unconstrained by external agendas. Labour's first broadcast was estimated to have been seen by close on 9 million. Even if many were not actually attending to the screen the opportunity was well worth taking seriously, particularly by small parties – and larger ones as strapped for cash as Labour and the Lib Dems.[11]

The 2010 series reflected straitened times; not all the programmes would have been particularly cheap but none looked as if large chunks of cash had been thrown at it. In one, Clegg spoke from a nondescript corner of a nondescript office, Salmond spoke in a working-office setting; Cameron did one programme in his back garden, two of Labour's programmes featured minimalist sets, and Plaid Cymru's Ieuan Wyn Jones spoke against a completely blank background.

That was just one aspect of the challenge to every party: how to appeal to disenchanted voters. Cameron confronted the issue head-on, declaring in an obvious side-swipe at Clegg that any party claiming to have clean hands was lying; the politicians had been treating the public as mugs for 40 years. His 'big society' had the answer. Clegg's call for a change in how politics was run was even less well defined and inclined to over-rate the moralising potential of electoral reform and the recall. Alex Salmond roundly denounced the cosy club of Westminster politicians; UKIP, the BNP and the Socialists were even more forthright, while the English Democrats virtuously underlined that their candidates were paying their own way.

When politicians are in bad odour parties tend to resort to 'real people' (or actors passing as such). The technique served again in this campaign. One Lib Dem broadcast drew on people who had contacted the party via Facebook. The SNP had a suitably diverse group saying 'I'm a Nat' and explaining why. Labour featured people who had benefitted from its policies, while the Conservatives drew on a working mother, a charity worker and a small businessman for favourable assessments of the party's policies. In their differing ways the BNP, the Scottish Socialists and others took the same approach, hoping that people looking like those we meet every day would somehow be more believable than the politicians.

A key element of Labour's response was to use popular entertainers. Their first broadcast, and almost the only one to create substantial discussion in the press, was a mini-drama featuring actors Sean Pertwee (son of Jon, a former Dr Who) and David Tennant, another ex-Dr Who. A rumpled middle-aged man tramped through a desolate moorland landscape, ruminating about Gordon Brown's role in solving the international financial crisis and how the country was now turning the corner. Reaching a junction, he decided the right fork was too risky. Instead he walked forward towards a brightening sky and a 'future fair for all'. What was striking about this small-scale drama was its gently sidelong approach to a potentially unreceptive audience: Pertwee spoke his lines almost as a soliloquy that one happened to be overhearing. It was transmitted only in England; programmes for Scotland and Wales the same evening differed markedly in tone. Even these Labour heartlands were not given a glimpse of a politician as the film recalled the privations of the Thatcher years with funereal music and drab images of pit, factory and hospital closures, soaring interest rates, repossessions, unemployment and, in Scotland, the hated poll tax. Then, with lively music and brighter colours came the achievements of Labour's years. The Tories would take the two countries back to past hardships; only Labour could prevent that – the nationalists were not even mentioned, as irrelevant.

In the two succeeding programmes, stand-up comedian Eddie Izzard made 'two quick points then you can go and have a cup of tea'. He acknowledged in a disarming passing phrase that there had been 'problems along the way', but the Tories were Thatcher's children, who would take Britain backwards – in contrast to Labour's commitment to compassion and fairness. Rejecting Cameron's 'broken Britain' he celebrated a 'brilliant Britain'. Next Peter Davison (yet another former Dr Who) presented a sequence of cameos of people celebrating Labour achievements from greater numbers of doctors and nurses to the abolition of fox-hunting. He conceded that 'what we have done together is not enough; we must go further' – an imprecise pointer to a fourth Labour term if ever there was one.

In a fresh change of tactics Stephen Hopkins, whose credits included the horror film *Nightmare on Elm Street 5*, was brought in to raise the fear factor. His 'Nightmare on Your Street' depicted three typical Lambeth families in the wake of a Tory victory. They learned, respectively, that their child tax credit was terminated, that payments to baby bonds would cease and that an appointment with a cancer specialist was cancelled – an allegation that roused Conservative ire. Finally, Ross Kemp, best known as an actor in *EastEnders*, made a softly spoken attack, arguing that Labour cared for the many, not just a rich few; a Labour vote would save jobs and public services. At last acknowledging a threat from the Lib Dems he argued that a vote for them would put Cameron in Downing Street.

The Labour series prompts two reflections. Individual bits worked well but the series lacked coherence and consistency and meshed poorly with other aspects of the party's campaign. Second, while actors could chill viewers' blood about what the Conservatives might do, and so play a part in bringing people 'home to Labour', they could not speak with authority about what Labour would do with a fourth term. Only politicians could do that.

By contrast, since Cameron and Clegg were fighting their first election as leaders, their parties took the obvious course of putting them to the fore. The consistent Lib Dem message was that they were the uncontaminated agent of necessary change. Their first broadcast, which was the most ambitious, had Clegg talking to camera while walking through a variety of townscapes strewn with sheets of paper bearing promises like 'We will end boom and bust', broken by the 'old parties'. It was time for promises to be kept. The Lib Dems would bring 'change' and 'fairness' – repeatedly recurring expressions – to schools, the banks, housing, transport and employment. They would also clear 'the mess in the government's finances' – thus skating over the gravest problem in seven words. At Clegg's words all the crumpled papers vanished – they were, after all, not criminal litter, but computer-generated images that could be 'disappeared' at the touch of a button. In similar vein, in 'Don't Let Anyone Tell You It Can't be Different' Clegg presented the Lib Dems as the only party of true 'change'. As insistently optimistic about better politics, a fairer country and a better life, he gave no hint of awkward choices ahead. The series was good at mood music and projecting Clegg, much less so in conveying Lib Dem policies.

The Conservatives were equally insistent on the need for change and on showcasing their leader. They relied heavily on 'best of' compilations of clips from his speeches, skilfully edited to depict him as personable, energetic, decisive, even passionate. Every inch a prime-minister-in-waiting, he was heard respectfully by suitably diverse gatherings in equally diverse locations. He acknowledged public disenchantment with politicians – audacious stuff by party broadcast standards. His response was a Contract with the Voters, little mentioned elsewhere, emphasising that the people, not the politicians, were the masters. If the Conservatives failed to live up to their side of the bargain 'you should chuck us out' – a truism if ever there was one, but again rarely recognised so explicitly. 'The big society' was evoked at some length, allowing the party to show a positive side. The series was well thought through, with sufficient flexibility for a programme initially planned as an attack on Labour to be changed into a response to the Lib Dem surge and recorded in Cameron's garden.

One of the more unusual broadcasts from a smaller party came from the Greens. It featured party-coloured geometric shapes shifting around an otherwise blank screen to convey the message that they were not a single-issue party but had a wide range of attractive and distinctive policies on the NHS, pensions, transport, the minimum wage, job creation and the like. Similarly, UKIP projected itself (somewhat less convincingly) as offering more than hostility to the European Union. The SNP, through Alex Salmond – an able and experienced performer – opted for repetition of a few basic themes: that it was Scotland's only champion; if there were to be cuts Scotland would gladly offer the Scottish Office, the Trident replacement and the House of Lords. By a happy coincidence the party's first broadcast was scheduled immediately before the first Prime Ministerial debate, giving Salmond a golden opportunity for a spoiler, pointing out that the voice of Scotland would not be heard there (though his contention that most of the discussion would not apply to Scotland surely diminished his grievance). A leitmotif of the BNP broadcast was that, as a result of immigration, Britons were becoming second-class citizens in their own country. There was a heavy deployment of patriotic imagery: clips from the Second World War, a war memorial, Nick Griffin flanked by gallantry medals and a photograph of Churchill, with promises that the BNP would put Britain first, ending with 'Love Britain Vote BNP'.[12]

Election Night

For a while it seemed the traditional election night results programmes might fall victim to the preference of many councils for deferring the count until the day after polling. However, a spirited campaign by the ConservativeHome website with cross-party backing on Facebook produced a change of heart (see p. 198). So it was that a substantial proportion of the population camped before its televisions on 6 May, waiting for Big Ben to strike ten, marking the closing of the polls.

BBC One and ITV1 opened their heavily trailed coverage five minutes before that magic moment with countdowns setting out their stalls and with specially commissioned music. The BBC's stunning title sequence featured a computer-generated sweep across London, ending at the election studio, which was a wonder to behold. One of the largest sets the BBC had ever built, its two floors illuminated in blue and purple were crammed with people poised over computer screens. On the upper floor Jeremy Paxman was 'on the naughty step', as he put it, conducting interviews. This gaudy set was promptly dubbed Starship Enterprise, though older viewers may have been reminded of a mid-1950s palais de danse. Across the river, near the London Eye, was a barge containing Andrew Neil and assorted celebrities, which was no less promptly dubbed The Ship of Fools. One unresolved mystery was why the BBC, already under fire for extravagance, should spend so much, wasting Neil's talents in the process, soliciting the reactions of Joan Collins and Bruce Forsyth (among others) to the results. There were few regrets when the boat suffered power failure. In fairness, that was the only substantial criticism of the operation, which also included opt-outs for Scotland, Wales and Northern Ireland and in Gaelic and Welsh as well as on the BBC News Channel, and the Parliament Channel. Radios 4 and 5 Live had their own coverage and local radio stations carried results for their home areas.

ITV's offering was much more modest, as befitted an organisation only too well aware that, as usual on Great National Occasions, the BBC would pull much the larger audience. An unkind commentator described the scene as a 'windowless basement with five men in suits'. Where the BBC set out to impress by mustering vast resources ITV was more workaday – but it offered clean graphics, a team monitoring social network sites and a striking 'swingometer' designed to cope with the novel complexities of three-party politics. Guests were interviewed from a VIP reception in a plastic bubble on the terrace of County Hall. Sky's *Decision Time: The Result* was still more frugal, concentrating on a fast results service with a minimum of commentary. All three organisations offered high-definition transmission, though the HD audience was tiny. Channel 4 ran a four-hour *Alternative Election Night* of live comedy that attracted an average audience of 1,683,000 and appealed particularly to young adults. At times its audience exceeded ITV's.

On the first stroke of ten all networks flashed the results of their shared Ipsos-MORI exit poll: a hung parliament with the Conservatives 19 short of a majority. The only surprise was the Lib Dems gaining votes but losing seats. This triggered memories of the 1992 election when an inaccurate exit poll inspired analyses that were well wide of the mark. While the poll was as nearly right as anyone could reasonably expect, commentators were reluctant to commit themselves until they had a clutch of real results to hand. That took time. Meanwhile, a long hiatus was filled with speculative chat while a chain of athletic youngsters handed on ballot boxes in Sunderland's bid to beat its record time for a declaration. (They failed, just.) Once results started to flow it was soon obvious the exit polls had been near enough. By 1am the outcome was beyond doubt. With the results now a trickle and no 'Portillo moments' looming common sense suggested heading for bed and checking back at breakfast, even though the programmes still had many hours to go.

Across all television channels between 10pm and midnight the audience averaged 8.2 million, with BBC One beating ITV1 by over 4 million to 1.3 million. The ITV audience was little more than half its 2005 level. Yet, despite its greater resources the BBC did not invariably outshine its rivals; they may even have been an impediment at times. ITV was sometimes quicker on its feet, notably in covering reports of voters unable to vote at a number of polling stations. Sky concentrated on providing an efficient results service with good graphics and did that well, while radio was calm, clear, uncluttered and efficient.

Although the results were complete by Friday afternoon the election process was not. As one commentator remarked, a sprint now became a five-day marathon. As negotiations over the complexion of the new government dragged on weary reporting teams had to follow the story through; the rolling news channels were in their element, switching effortlessly from one development to the next up to Brown's dignified and emotional valedictory statement, also carried live on other networks. The combined BBC One and News Channel audience for the main evening news after the coalition agreement was announced reached 11.5 million. For the first time cameras followed a departing prime minister leaving Downing Street on foot with his wife and their two children who, one suddenly realised, one had never seen before. As on the opening day of the campaign the journey to the palace was tracked live by helicopter cameras. Shortly afterwards Cameron and his wife, made the same journey, again covered live, reaching Number 10 to announce the new coalition. Covering the politics of that coalition would raise new challenges for the broadcasters, not least how to adapt to a new style of politics and how best to cover elections under these novel arrangements.

Notes

1. *The Media Show*, 2 September 2009.
2. *Sunday Times*, 7 March 2010
3. *Daily Telegraph*, 22 April 2010; also Charles Moore, 'Politics is the loser', *Daily Telegraph*, 9 April 2010.
4. http://www.bafta.org/access-all-areas/videos/election-tv-debates/1098,BA. html
5. Calculations are net of opening and closing sequences, midway headlines and weather forecasts. BBC One bulletins collectively ran 20% more news and 25% more about the election than ITV1's.
6. *Guardian*, 26 April 2010.
7. *ITV News* 6.30pm, 28 April 2010; the language was more restrained at 10pm.
8. *ITV News* 1.30pm, 30 April 2010.
9. Citations across BBC One, ITV1, Channel 4 and Radio 4 news – Conservatives: Cameron 375, Osborne 30, Clarke and Hammond 23, Hague 11, Fox 10. Labour: Brown 386, Mandelson 32, Darling 25, Balls and Alexander 15, Hain and Johnson 12, E. Miliband 10, Sood 9, Cooper 8, Timms and Jowell 6. Lib Dem: Clegg 328, Cable 27, Davey 12, Huhne 6.
10. *Guardian*, 17 May 2010. This article discussed how few women were seen covering the election. Women were undeniably in the minority and the debates moderators and election night anchors were all male, but they were markedly more evident than in 2005. Broadcast coverage of the leaders' wives was much more low-key than in many national newspapers.
11. However, a survey for Cranfield University found that party broadcasts had only about a 4% share of the 'election experiences' of a panel of floating voters, compared with 6% mentioning radio news, 20% television news and 22% the debates.
12. A version of this broadcast appeared on the BNP website with a jar of Marmite on the top left of the screen. Unilever, owner of the Marmite brand, was unamused and obtained an injunction against the BNP. The incident recalled a spoof broadcast for the Hate Party that Marmite ran in the 2009 European election and is thought to have arisen from a BNP internal feud.

14
Labour No More: The Press

Margaret Scammell and Charlie Beckett[1]

It was to be expected that the novelty of Britain's first Prime Ministerial television debates would captivate the newspapers. However, it is doubtful that anyone guessed just how much. Commentators loved them and loathed them, but the debates defined the campaign in the press. They were largely responsible for what nearly all titles regarded as the most exciting contest in a generation, transforming what the press had expected to be a predictable two-horse race between a weary governing party and an opposition that had failed to convince. They created a three-way contest that kept a riveted press guessing from the first debate to the formation of the new government. Ultimately, what had seemed inconceivable to the entire national press for almost all the election came to pass with the Lib–Con coalition. Conservative papers that had denigrated Clegg mercilessly throughout the campaign now hailed the new special relationship: 'bring us sunshine', sang the *Sun*.

The Conservatives may have struggled for a majority with the electorate but they had their most benign press environment since 1992, and they won the support of six out of ten national dailies and five out of nine Sundays (see Tables 14.1 and 14.2). By contrast, this was a thoroughly wretched campaign for Labour. It lost the support of the *Guardian*, the *Financial Times* and Rupert Murdoch's stable of papers. It was left with the *Mirror* as its only ally, the worst press showing since the wilderness year of 1983. Moreover, the picture is bleaker still if the *Mirror*'s declining circulation is taken into consideration. Labour's share of the total circulation of national dailies was just 13% in 2010, lower than at any time since 1945, and an alarmingly steep descent from its 71% high during Tony Blair's pomp in 2001. In the press, even more than at the polls, this was well and truly the end of New Labour.

Table 14.1   Partisanship and circulation of national daily newspapers

Name of paper Ownership group (Chairman) Editor Preferred result	Circulation[a] (2005 in brackets) (000s)	Readership[b] (2005 in brackets) (000s)	% of readers in social grade (2005 in brackets)	
			ABC1	C2DE
Mirror Trinity Mirror (Sir Ian Gibson) Richard Wallace Labour victory[c]	1,240 (1,602)	3,425 (4,657)	39 (38)	61 (61)
Express Northern and Shell (Richard Desmond) Peter Hill Conservative victory	666 (884)	1,577 (2,132)	59 (60)	41 (40)
Sun News International (Rupert Murdoch) Dominic Mohan Conservative victory	2,956 (3,098)	7,761 (8,825)	38 (37)	62 (63)
Daily Mail Associated Newspapers (Viscount Rothermere) Paul Dacre Conservative victory	2,096 (2,278)	4,934 (5,740)	66 (66)	34 (34)
Daily Star Northern and Shell (Richard Desmond) Dawn Neesom No preference declared	823 (735)	1,577 (1,965)	31 (33)	69 (67)
Daily Telegraph Telegraph Group (Barclay brothers) Tony Gallagher Conservative victory	683 (868)	1,905 (2,181)	88 (87)	12 (13)
Guardian Scott Trust (Liz Forgan) Alan Rusbridger Liberal Democrat[c]	289 (327)	1,147 (1,068)	88 (89)	12 (11)
The Times News International (Rupert Murdoch) James Harding Conservative victory	507 (654)	1,773 (1,655)	86 (87)	14 (13)
Independent Independent Print Ltd (Evgeny Lebedev) Simon Kelner Liberal Democrat[c]	188 (226)	671 (643)	87 (87)	13 (13)
Financial Times Pearson plc (Glen Moreno) Lionel Barber Conservative victory	387 (132)	434 (453)	88 (92)	12 (8)

[a] Average net total circulation in the United Kingdom. Source: Audit Bureau of Circulation (April 2010).
[b] Source: National Readership Survey (January–December 2009).
[c] But vote tactically to keep Conservatives out.

Table 14.2   Partisanship and circulation of national Sunday newspapers

	Preferred winner 2010	(2005)	Circulation (000s)	Readership (000s)
News of the World	Con	(Lab)	2,906	7,642
Sunday Mirror	Lab (tactical vote for Lib Dem)	(Lab)	1,124	3,826
The People	Not Con	(Lab)	530	1,331
Mail on Sunday	Con	(Not Lab)	1,983	5,213
Sunday Express	Con	(Con)	574	1,622
Sunday Times	Con	(Con)	1,135	3,219
Observer	Lib Dem	(Lab)	332	1,212
Sunday Telegraph	Con	(Con)	510	1,677
Independent on Sunday	Lib Dem	(Lib Dem)	168	600

Note: Audit Bureau of Circulation (April 2010).

Source: ABC.

The Press since 2005

The newspapers' long-term decline in readership turned into a serious business crisis in the period after the 2005 election. The recession in 2008 and a steep reduction in advertising revenues meant that most titles were now losing money. At the same time they were all investing in websites that were attracting millions of online readers but earning relatively little income. The loss of readers happened across all sectors, but to varying degrees. The *Mirror* and the *Express* haemorrhaged heavily while the *Mail* and the *Sun* dropped relatively gently (Table 14.1). Among the broadsheets, the *Financial Times* managed to increase its readers, but generally, despite increasing pagination, the press could not halt the slide in sales.

Despite the gloom, there has been remarkable stability in the national daily market since 1997. No national title has disappeared and during 2005–10 only one changed ownership. In March 2010 Russian oligarch Alexander Lebedev bought the debt-ridden Independent Newspapers for £1 following his acquisition of the *London Evening Standard*.

The decline in revenue inevitably meant that newsrooms shrank, with major job losses at all titles. At the same time there was something of an existential crisis for newspapers, which became increasingly concerned at the growing challenge of the internet and the rapidly evolving blogosphere. The press increased its presence online but found itself in direct competition there with the broadcasters.

However, the *Telegraph*, in particular, proved that newspapers still had the power to set the news agenda and shake the political structures to their core. Its exposé of the scandalous nature of some MPs' expenses claims was by far the biggest story of 2009 (see Chapter 2). Perhaps surprisingly, however, the expenses scandal was not a leading issue during the campaign itself.

With the end of Tony Blair's premiership several newspapers reassessed their support for the Labour Government. The *Sun* was the first to jump ship. After 12 years of backing New Labour, the *Sun* announced its switch to the Conservatives in September 2009, on the same day as Gordon Brown's Labour Party conference speech. The decision was not a great surprise. In an echo of Blair's pre-1997 strategy, the new Conservative leader David Cameron had courted the Murdoch press. In August 2008 he flew to meet Rupert Murdoch in Santorini and it did not escape notice that the Conservative policy of downsizing the BBC and broadcast regulator Ofcom matched exactly the tenor of a speech given by Rupert's son James that same month at the Edinburgh TV festival. However, other newspapers, including Murdoch's *Times*, were slower to change their political endorsement and less enthusiastic in embracing Cameron himself.

For Prime Minister Brown, however, the honeymoon was short-lived. Rupert Murdoch and *Mail* editor Paul Dacre were known to admire him still. But Brown's reputation was battered, firstly by failing to call an election that he might well have won in the autumn of 2007 (see Chapter 1) and then by the economic crisis. Moreover, his pursuit of some of the more Blairite policies, such as Academy schools, and his divisive leadership style meant he also lost friends in the left-wing press, including the influential Polly Toynbee at the *Guardian*. With Labour looking decreasingly likely to win again it was no shock that the press turned against him.

How Individual Papers Covered the Campaign

'Labour's lost it', the *Sun* had declared when it announced its switch to the Conservatives in 2009. At the general election, no national paper worked harder to make that prediction come true. It invested significantly more coverage in this election compared with 2005 (see Table 14.3), and it devoted this to a dual-pronged personalised strategy. On the one hand, it sustained an uncompromising assault on Gordon Brown; on the other it took every opportunity to promote 'Cam the Man' as the people's champion. By its recent standards of half-hearted electioneering, it was a striking return to full-blooded partisanship. At times early on the *Sun* circled in its own singular orbit, unconnected to any reality reported by the rest of Fleet Street. It alone thought Cameron had won the first TV debate and it was highly selective in its use of opinion data to the point where it did not publish details from its own YouGov poll that indicated that voters were less afraid of a Clegg government than a Cameron one.

Table 14.3   Profile of press content

	Mean no. pages		Front-page election leads		Editorials on election (as % of all editorials)	
	2010	2005	2010	2005	2010	2005
Mirror	78	70	11	7	42	62
Express	76	76	10	11	48	50
Sun	72	58	15	7	74	57
Daily Mail	89	83	13	12	78	84
Daily Star	60	67	1	2	46	47
Daily Telegraph	64	50	19	16	39	42
Guardian	98	101	19	18	45	44
The Times	103	108	19	16	49	37
Independent	96	110	18	15	31	53
Financial Times	42	58	9	18	21	20

Note: Front-page leads and editorial analysis cover 22 issues between 12 April and 6 May (2005: 21 issues). Page count is for Monday–Friday only and excludes advertising sections.

The *Sun* stood apart from the rest of the right-wing press in terms of the quantity and stridency of the personal attacks on the Prime Minister. The man, who it had once admired as Labour's hero, had sunk to the 'nation's zero'. Brown was routinely derided as incompetent, a grotesque 'waster' of taxpayers' money, 'deceitful' and 'dithering'. He was the 'Prime Sinister', proclaimed the paper's editorial following the first TV debate (16 April). Amid the Liberal Democrat rise in the opinion polls, the *Sun* depicted Brown as both 'dead and buried' and willing to tell any lie to grab the potential lifeline of a Lib–Lab alliance. The paper adopted a hostile tone towards Nick 'Cleggomaniac', denouncing his arrogance for apparently seeking the premiership as the price for a deal with Labour, and repeatedly exposing his 'madcap schemes' to grant an amnesty to some illegal immigrants and to 'threaten our nuclear defences' (26 April). 'Why is Britain toying with [this] Brussels fanatic who would risk our economy for a collapsing currency,' its editorial (28 April) asked. Vote-Clegg-get-Brown it repeatedly warned its readers. At the same time, the *Sun* was easily Cameron's most unequivocal cheerleader in the national press. He was 'the change we need' following the manifesto launch, the 'Cam back kid' in the TV debates, 'Iron-man Cam' on the election trail and on polling day the *Sun* enlisted the iconic Barack Obama 'Hope' poster to depict the Tory leader in hues of red and blue. Under the headline 'Our Only Hope', the *Sun* declared that 'in Cameron we trust'. The election boiled down to a simple choice: 'five more years of exhausted Gordon Brown', or hope with Cameron's 'modern and positive Conservatives'.

Distinctively, the *Daily Mail* lamented a 'phoney campaign' that had never squarely confronted the key issues of immigration and especially the full scale of the deficit crisis. 'Dishonesty' was the motif of its election editorials; and the failure to come clean about public spending cuts was merely another act of deceit following 'years of lies and sleaze' in Westminster. The resulting public rage, it argued, largely explained the surge in Liberal Democrat support; it was effectively an anti-politics protest. The *Mail*, like much of the Conservative press, was taken off-guard by the strength of opinion poll spike for Nick Clegg. But it was at the forefront of the backlash. As the Tory papers fired at him from all directions, the *Mail* launched the most notorious attack: 'Clegg in Nazi Slur on Britain' was its front-page lead (22 April). The story, referring to a forgettable piece Clegg had written in 2002 about Britain's 'tenacious obsession' with World War II glories, was ridiculed on the internet.

Thereafter, the *Mail* maintained a lower-level but steady barrage against the Liberal Democrats. They were the 'real nasty party' according to star columnist Peter Oborne (22 April); Clegg was an elitist Westminster public schoolboy whose zealous Euro-fanaticism could threaten Britain's 'survival as a self-governing nation' (Tom Utley, 23 April). The paper kept up a continuous stream of stories questioning Clegg's squeaky-clean image on expenses, and expounding the 'disastrous' consequences of Lib Dem policies on defence and immigration. The underlying danger of a hung parliament was the *Mail*'s only true passion of this election. It retained some lingering respect for Brown, 'basically good' if misguided, and was not convinced by Cameron, who was too much an heir-to-Blair for the paper's taste. However, it was certain of the perils of a hung parliament and its political pages were filled with increasingly apocalyptic visions should Britain fail to elect a majority government. As riots against savage spending cuts erupted in the streets of Athens, the *Mail* warned that for Britain, as for Greece, public debt was 'the burning issue'. Britain needed strong government to immediately tackle the deficit; this 'alone can save us from Greece's fate', warned its polling day editorial. The *Mail* waited until late to formally endorse the Conservative Party (5 May); Cameron had grown in stature throughout the campaign, it argued, and was the best hope for avoiding economic chaos. However, above all, it urged its readers to vote decisively; the widespread belief that no clear winner would be a desirable outcome was dangerously wrong-headed. 'Whoever wins..., Britain will need bold decisive government if we are to avoid the nightmare into which Greece has been plunged.'

The *Daily Mirror* was the mirror image of the *Sun* in certain respects. It too was fiercely partisan; it too found most sport in attacking opponents and it too was highly selective in its use of opinion polls. However, unlike the *Sun*, the *Mirror* became increasingly isolated over the course of the campaign. The *Mirror* had enthused for Brown rather than Blair since the Iraq War and it continued to back its man gamely: Brown was the 'Man versus boys' in the first TV debate, he was substance rather than style and most importantly he was the architect of economic recovery following the banking crisis. The *Mirror* delighted at first in the Liberal Democrat poll surge, supporting Clegg against Tory press attacks and revelling in signs of cracks in the Conservative campaign. However, as Labour slipped to third position in several polls, the *Mirror* became less sure of itself. It had already begun to urge readers to vote tactically before Brown's 'bigot' gaffe destroyed any flickering hopes of a Labour triumph. It responded to that setback with an exclusive interview with Brown's wife Sarah: 'My Gord's so sorry'. But in its leader column that day (29 April) it told Labour to 'get off your knees and start fighting'.

However, the *Mirror*'s energy was directed mainly at attacking the Conservatives. It put Cameron's face in the second 'o' of the strap line 'Don't get Conned', which ran every day over its inside election coverage. It revived an old election trick of putting a man in a chicken suit and having him heckle Cameron at every opportunity. It devoted a good deal of space to accusing Cameron of campaigning incompetence: he was 'the man who blew one of the biggest poll leads in political history', said its leader (22 April). Most distinctively, though, it exhumed thoroughly retro class war. Through a succession of editorials and star columns it told readers that Eton-educated Cameron was not 'one of us'. As Tony Parsons put it on election day: Cameron 'just doesn't get us'. The *Mirror* capped its core vote strategy (6 May) by covering its front page with a Bullingdon Club picture of a young Cameron in evening suit: 'Our Prime Minister' ran the front-page headline. For your children's sake, it urged readers, 'vote Labour'.

The *Daily Express* continued in its role as the grumpy old man of Fleet Street and adopted a long-suffering tone. Even while it hailed the election as the most important for decades, it had no more appetite for this contest than in 2005 (Table 14.3). It reheated its old favourites: immigration and Euroscepticism and, in an echo of the Conservatives' 'broken Britain' slogan, it lamented the decay of the country's social fabric. Immigration was the top election issue on the front pages (see Table 14.4) and it was also the centre-piece of the paper's most spirited coverage, the pounding of the Liberal Democrats. The *Express* had welcomed the TV debates but then spent much of its time attacking their chief beneficiary. 'If Nick Clegg is the answer, what is the question,' asked columnist Leo McKinstry (19 April). According to subsequent editorials, 'Europe-loving' Clegg had a 'crazy' immigration policy, proposed an 'immoral' amnesty for illegal immigrants and was 'not in tune' with Middle England. The attacks gathered pace towards polling day, as the *Express* warned of the 'terrifying cost' of a Liberal Democrat vote. On 5 May it finally confirmed the obvious with a formal endorsement of the Conservatives: 'only Cameron can save Britain' proclaimed the editorial on the front page.

As usual, the *Daily Star* provided the slightest coverage, with just one front-page lead dedicated to the election (Table 14.3). Its celebrity-and-scandal diet had overhauled its stable-mate, the *Express*, in the circulation battle and it was one of only two papers to increase sales since 2005 (Table 14.1). The *Star* saw no reason to change a winning formula for the campaign, even if it was, as its leader column claimed (4 May), the most important election in a generation. Its issue agenda was conservative with a small 'c', primarily immigration. The paper made clear early on that it had had enough of Gordon Brown but it kept its distance from the Tory press Clegg-hunting party. If the Tories' only response was to clobber Clegg, it was no 'wonder why people see Clegg as a breath of fresh air', said its editorial (19 April). The *Star* was not hugely impressed with a campaign that had failed 'to make the earth move' and it declined to endorse any party, merely urging its readers to vote.

Among the upmarket press, the *Daily Telegraph* was the one to watch most closely. This was partly because of its standing as the market leader but also because its columnists included both Cameron's closest press allies and his most fierce right-wing critics. Ultimately, the *Telegraph* waged a strong pro-Conservative campaign but also maintained ideological diversity in its opinion pages. It made for entertaining reading; while Benedict Brogan praised 'booming' Cameron, Mary Riddell enthused over Clegg, and Simon Heffer denounced both of them as the latest charlatans to pique the interest of an uninterested public.

At the outset, the *Telegraph* labelled the election a contest between hope (Cameron) and fear (Brown) and this set the tone for its editorial line. For the first two weeks fear was the keyword; the Conservatives could pay heavily for allowing Nick Clegg to take part in the TV debates. In its news analysis and editorials the paper reflected the alarm in Conservative

Table 14.4 Front-page lead stories, 12 April–6 May

Date	Mirror	Express	Sun	Daily Mail	Daily Star	Daily Telegraph	Guardian	The Times	Independent	Financial Times
12 April	(Get him!)	Strangers in our own country	(Fizz Royal Highness)	Health chiefs' pay bonanza	(Kerry: is she fit to be a mum?)	Labour tries to win back Middle England	Brown: I will end 'take it or leave it' public services	Labour will force foreign workers to speak English	Brown's plan to win votes the Blair way	(Eurozone in €30bn loans deal for Greece)
13 April	(Jade's Jack raped me)	Expenses scandal MPs get legal aid	(Jade's Jack 'raped me')	(Mother of all defeats!)	(Jack Tweed 'raped' teen weeks after Jade's death)	VAT rise is a risk under Labour	Two visions of Britain	I'll put you in driving seat, says Cameron	Cameron champions 'people power' as voters back tax plan	Tory plan on foreign workers under fire
14 April	Have you been ad?	Civil servants' £1bn high life	(Paedo bikini)	(Civil servants' £1bn expenses)	(Jordan's holiday with 'other man')	Cameron: we need people power, not state power	Cameron's DIY revolution	Politicians' biggest fear is angry electorate	(The nuclear family)	'Hands off' vow to business
15 April	Gordon Brown is awesome!	(NHS sells off cancer drugs abroad)	(Paedo heaven on our High St)	(A tale of two payouts)	(Jordan holiday boobs horror)	Big lead for Tories in 100 key seats	Take me to your lectern: parties clash ahead of key TV debate	The screen test	Ninety minutes that could change Britain	Huge hole in party pledges
16 April	It's a man vs boys	(Britain is shut to the world)	Britain is paralysed by hot air	(Paralysed by the volcano)	(Britain is shut)	Clegg's star rises in great TV showdown	Clegg seizes his moment	Enter the outsider	Clegg comes of age	(Greece in key move towards bail-out)
17 April	(Vilecano)	(Volcano dust is deadly)	(Dead Enders)	(Million Britons stranded by ash)	(Jordan replaces Cowell as judge)	Cameron: it's a two-horse race	Knives out for Nick Clegg after dramatic poll boost	(Thousands stranded as dust cloud covers UK)	Mr Popularity [Clegg]	(Goldman charged with fraud)

Date										
19 April	('Suicide pills' in Bulger killer's cell)	(Volcanic cloud chaos: no end in sight)	(Spanish Airmada)	(Operation volcano!)	(Jordan: I want Alex out of my life)		('We need to get people home')	(Brown under pressure to get Britain flying)	Mandelson's Dunkirk	Investors fear effects of hung parliament
20 April	(They're toast!) [referring to Adrian Chiles leaving BBC]	(New volcano menace)	(T.G.I. Flyday)	(Volcano: a new blast of chaos)	(Jordan baby's bruised face and body)	(Met Office got it wrong over ban on flights)	Tory peerages for leaders of business attack on Labour	(Royal Navy is all at sea as airlines start to fly again)	(Sack Goldmans!)	(AIG eyes action on Goldman over CDOs)
21 April	Chicken hugget	(British skies open at last)	Clegg's secret election dossier found in cab	Abandoned to their fate	(Terror as plane hits ash cloud)	(Why was ban ever imposed?)	(Heathrow opens – and now recriminations start to fly)	The halo effect	I want to create an anti-Tory alliance [Brown]	(UK flights resume as airports reopened)
22 April	(Ash test dummies)	Clegg's crazy immigration policy	Clegg on his face	Clegg in Nazi slur on Britain	Brown: I quit	Nick Clegg, the Lib Dem donors and payments into his private account	Tories to send gay MP to curb EU extremists	Cameron: hung Parliament will risk economic disaster	Clegg raises the stakes	Ken Clarke unleashed to attack Lib Dems
23 April	One foot in the Dave	Cameron wins with passion	The Cam back kid	(Billions more for bankers)	(Jordan's lust for Pete's fab abs)	Cameron fights back	Clegg weathers the storm	Cameron nicks it	This time it's personal	(Goldman had two roles in Lloyds deal)
24 April	(Britain's bot talent)	(Thousands stranded for weeks)	Don't stop deceivin'	(The nine-bin nightmare)	(Jordan & Pete's sex factor)	Tories plan for a coalition	Tories target north-east and Northern Ireland for cuts	Brown rips up strategy to escape third place	(The universe... as seen by Hubble)	(Greece grasps €30bn lifeline)

continued

Table 14.4 continued

Date	Mirror	Express	Sun	Daily Mail	Daily Star	Daily Telegraph	Guardian	The Times	Independent	Financial Times
26 April	(My coke shame)	Fury over 1m illegal migrants	Minister of silly talks	Vatican fury at Britain's 'dark forces'	(Jordan & Alex baby party)	Cameron smash and grab raid on Labour	Clegg goes public on coalition – and looks to the Tories	Labour in turmoil as pressure on Brown grows	Splits emerge in Labour's election strategy	Brutal choices over deficit
27 April	(My story)	(Air fares go sky high)	Well hung... and shafted	Labour no longer trusted on NHS	(Gerro and Alex in love split hell)	Top heads back Tory pledge to free state schools	Clegg: I could work with Labour, just not with Brown	Tories switch target	Poll latest: Lib Dems now within one point of Tories	(Greek bond markets plunge)
28 April	Chicken coup	(BBC's 530 days of repeats in a year)	Pig deserts sinking ship	Secret tax bombshell	(Jade's Jack in wild booze hols orgy)	The story these men don't want you to read	Parties 'dishonest on cuts'	I want to be prime minister'	Tell us the truth	(IMF looks at offering more cash to Greece)
29 April	My Gord's so sorry	A hypocrite who shames Britain	Brown toast	Demonised: the granny who dared to utter the I-word	(Kerry's secret hols with Pete)	It was the day Gordon Brown met a real voter and, in his own words, it was a day of disaster	(Warning that Greek crisis could spread 'like ebola')	Trouble in Rochdale	Poll latest: Labour loses one voter	Brown: that was a disaster
30 April	New! Improved! Spin!	(Euro court hands our benefits to terrorists)	Scrambled Clegg and toast	(Teacher is cleared by a common sense jury)	(Jordan's new cancer scare)	Cameron on the money	Cameron wins third leg	The fight for a job	Brown last night came out fighting... is it too late?	(Greece agrees to €24bn of cutbacks)

Date										
1 May	(My brain just went ping)	(Fury over insult to war dead)	Only here for the Blears	This doctor gave her life to the NHS. Why won't the NHS now save her?	(Jordan ditches 'sex fiend' Alex)	I've paid a very high price	Nick Clegg: we have taken Labour's place in UK politics	Blair says a vote cast for Clegg is 'not serious'	(Black tide) [Louisiana oil spill]	Tories ramp up the pressure
3 May	(Sally: 'I didn't want to die')	(House prices set to soar)	Thy will be gone	Nurses cover for night GPs	(Jade's Jack in rape party shame)	Tories rule out Lib Dem alliance	We'll have six months to lay out cuts plan - Tories	Cameron outlines plans for first days in power	Cameron: 'I won't let Brown cling to power'	(Eurozone agrees Greek bail-out)
4 May	How to stop him	Scandal of 85m bill for pens and paper	Iron man Cam	Post vote fraud: the damning evidence	(Prem Ace's Hitler salute shame)	Cameron needs just 14 more seats	Battered PM finds his voice	Security chiefs condemn Lib Dem defence 'gamble'	Vote with your heads... not your hearts	Clegg open to Tory talks
5 May	Eton Rifles	Only Cameron can save Britain	Britain's got... to change	Vote decisively to stop Britain walking blindly into disaster	(Too moody to work)	Ulster pact could seal victory for Cameron	Labour split on poll strategy as Blair says don't vote tactically	Brown to voters: the best tactic is to back Labour	Britain has historic opportunity... It must not be missed	(Eurozone debt fears deepen)
6 May	Our Prime Minister? Really?	D-Day	Our only hope	Burning issue for Britain	(Gerro & Alex divorce agony)	Day of destiny	Cameron eyes the prize	The fate of the nation	The people's election	(Pru forced to abandon launch of rights issue)

ranks; the Clegg eruption had grounded the Tories, Brogan reported (20 April), and raised the prospect of a Lib–Lab alliance and electoral reform that could 'entrench centre-left politics and leave the Tories stuck on the sidelines for good'. However, as the campaign progressed the paper became increasingly optimistic of a slim Conservative victory and noticeably warmer towards Cameron, who had shown 'inner steel' and been 'commendably cool under fire' (5 May).

The *Telegraph* contributed in full measure to the Tory press broadside against Clegg with a raft of stories about his privileged background and the Liberal Democrats' 'half-baked' policies. Most distinctively, though, it returned its fire to the issue of financial propriety. It exclusively revealed that donors had paid money into Clegg's private account (22 April) and reported that as an MEP he had spent ten years on the European 'gravy train'. Thereafter, and in step with the other Conservative papers, the *Telegraph* reduced the stridency but not the quantity of critical commentary about the Liberal Democrats. The party suffered a 'multiple personality disorder', its leader said (3 May); it was irresponsible and the fortunate beneficiary of the anti-politics public mood (5 May). In an unpredictable contest, there was one certainty for the *Telegraph*: the 'end of New Labour'. The party had wasted an opportunity of historic proportions, it argued; it had gone on a spending binge but not delivered better public services than elsewhere in Europe. It was deplorable on immigration, had kept the country permanently at war and failed to reform the welfare system. On 5 May, the *Telegraph* delivered its formal verdict: 'We believe that only a Conservative government can restore the nation's fortunes.'

The *Guardian*, as usual, invested colossal resources in the campaign, running a six-page election section most days together with further attention in its comment pages and editorials. However, this time its diligence was rewarded with what it regarded as a hugely exciting contest; for once everyone was talking about electoral reform. The transformative potential was enormous, its editorial (5 May) argued, and could prove as significant for twenty-first-century British politics as the 1910 election had been for the twentieth century. The *Guardian* feasted on the TV debates lavishing multiple pages on the substance and the style; but even more, it revelled in their upshot, the rise of the Liberal Democrats. It could scarcely contain its enthusiasm for this potentially 'break-the-mould' moment, and its news analysis and opinion pieces gleefully picked over the possibilities of a hung parliament. Its editorial of 20 April proclaimed a 'new electoral reality', a genuine three-way contest, the serious prospect of electoral reform, 'and doesn't it actually feel rather good'.

On 1 May, the front-page lead story quoted Nick Clegg: 'we have taken Labour's place in British politics'. Certainly the Liberal Democrats took Labour's place in the *Guardian*. It was the first election since 1983 that it had not supported Labour as its first choice. Instead, the paper announced its 'enthusiastic' endorsement for the Liberal Democrats. At that point the decision came as no great surprise. The paper had been lukewarm to Labour from the outset; it had not been overly impressed with its manifesto, and well before the end its main interest in Labour was speculation about Brown's successor. The *Guardian* had urged Brown to stand down a year previously and had no desire for another five years of him. Ironically, the *Guardian* was the only national paper whose readers swung towards Labour in the period 2005–10 (see Table 14.5). However, it found more common ground with the Liberal Democrats on constitutional change, civil liberty, criminal justice, the EU, the environment and the Iraq War. 'A newspaper that is proudly rooted in the liberal as well as labour tradition … cannot ignore such a record. If not now, when? The answer is clear and proud. Now.'

Table 14.5   Party supported by daily newspaper readers

	2010 vote (%)			Con lead	Change since 2005 (%)			% Swing (Lab to Con)	Turn out %
	Con	Lab	LD		Con	Lab	LD		
All	37	30	24	7	+4	−6	+1	+5.0	65%
Readership (regular readers)									
Daily Express	53	19	18	35	+5	−9	0	+7.0	67%
Daily Mail	59	16	16	43	+2	−6	+2	+4.0	73%
Daily Mirror	16	59	17	−42	+5	−8	0	+6.5	68%
Daily Telegraph	70	7	18	63	+5	−6	+1	+5.5	81%
Guardian	9	46	37	−37	+2	+3	−4	−0.5	78%
Independent	14	32	44	−18	+1	−2	0	+1.5	79%
Daily Star	22	35	20	−13	+1	−19	+5	+10.0	43%
Sun	43	28	18	15	+10	−17	+6	+13.5	57%
The Times	49	22	24	27	+11	−5	−4	+8.0	80%
Daily Record*	12	65	6	−54	+5	+10	−10	−2.5	65%
None of these	32	31	26	2	+5	−6	−1	+5.5	61%

* *Daily Record* is Scotland's top seller. It is not a UK national paper.
Source: Ipsos MORI Final Election Aggregate Analysis. Base: 10,211 GB electors, March–May 2010.

No national daily enjoyed the campaign more than the *Independent*. Together with the *Guardian*, it was thrilled at the prospect of a hung parliament and the consequent likelihood of electoral reform. Like the *Guardian* it invested heavily in election coverage and it too was rewarded, not just with a nail-biting contest but also with a rare boost in its, admittedly meagre, net circulation for the month of April. Under new ownership, the *Indie* maintained its liberal editorial tone together with a lively range of political opinion. It offered some sharp commentary not least from Stephen Glover's beady-eyed review of other media, while Yasmin Alibhai-Brown spotted the irony that this supposedly mould-breaking election was still dominated by the 'old magic circle' of white, middle-class, Oxbridge-educated men. The feisty approach rattled rivals in the Murdoch press; in a widely reported incident, James Murdoch, accompanied by Rebekah Brooks (née Wade), chief executive of News International, angrily burst into the *Indie*'s offices to complain at an advertisement that stated: 'Rupert Murdoch won't decide this election – you will.'

The *Independent* rode the wave of 'Cleggmania'. The yellow surge was good for democracy, its editorial said (20 April), while on polling day it rejoiced in a campaign that had brought 'spectacular' and 'inspiring' engagement with voters. True, it admitted, there was something to the claim that the debates had brought about an 'X-Factor' election; but 'so what'? The debates had also generated a remarkable mood swing and presented a unique opportunity to transform the electoral system. The *Independent*'s Liberal Democrat leanings were never in doubt and it formally endorsed the party for the second successive election on 5 May. It urged a vote for the Lib Dems but also offered a guide to tactical voting to block the Tories.

By comparison with its main rivals, *The Times* had a relatively quiet election and maintained a clearer separation between factual reporting and opinionated commentary. It slightly increased its front-page election attention compared to 2005 (Table 14.3) and it carried extensive coverage inside and offered plenty of solid analysis and thoughtful opinion. Moreover, it was in no doubt that this was one of the most important and exciting elections for decades. It waited until 1 May to offer formal backing to the Conservatives, but its editorial inclination had long been clear. It had enthusiastically welcomed Cameron's 'Big Society' and was more consistent in its support for the idea than most of the Conservative-supporting press. It was *The Times*' first endorsement for the Tories in 18 years; the paper still had admiration for Tony Blair but it now liked Cameron's 'modern' Conservatives. They 'offer an optimistic vision for the renewal of Britain' and Cameron had shown 'the fortitude, judgement and character' to lead Britain to a stronger future. On polling day, its front-page editorial warned that 'a Greek tragedy' awaits us if Britain did not reduce its crippling public deficit; the 'fate of the nation' was in the balance.

Many papers claimed that government debt was *the* issue of the election. However, only the *Financial Times* consistently led on it. The paper's scrutiny of the manifestos revealed 'a huge' £37 billion hole in party pledges that, it said, would need to be filled by spending cuts or tax rises (15 April). Britain faced 'brutal choices' over the deficit, its front-page lead story warned (26 April), while inside it provided analysis of where those cuts might come. It linked its offline coverage to an online 'deficit buster' simulator, inviting readers to pick their own targets coupled with explanations of the often dire political and economic consequences. The stark choices facing Britain were set against the backdrop of the Greek deficit crisis, which consumed almost as much of the *FT*'s attention as the British election (Table 14.4).

The *FT* regretted a campaign that, it said, had focused too much on personality and not enough on substance. None of the parties had come clean on the key issue of how to tackle the £163 billion deficit and the paper was not hugely impressed with any of them. However, eventually it did come to a verdict and for the first time since 1987, the *Financial Times* backed the Conservatives (4 May). It had some praise for Gordon Brown as a 'crisis manager', but after 13 years Labour needed a spell in opposition to rejuvenate. The Conservatives were 'not perfect' and the paper harboured concerns about their hostility towards Europe. But, its editorial concluded: 'Britain needs stable and legitimate government to navigate the crisis and punch its weight abroad ... On balance, the Conservative party best fits the bill.'

In the press, as in the electorate, the campaign in Scotland was distinctive; the Conservatives struggled to gain a foothold and Gordon Brown was nowhere near the toxic presence he appeared to be in some of the London-based national dailies. With unemployment high in some parts of Scotland and immigration scarcely an issue outside Glasgow, the issue agenda was also distinctive. Scotland's top-selling newspaper, the *Daily Record*, traditionally supports Labour but this time its main concern was to 'stop David Cameron'. *Scotland on Sunday* came out for the Liberal Democrats, but neither the *Herald* nor the *Scotsman* summoned up enthusiasm for any of the major parties contesting north of the border. The *Herald* had given lukewarm support to Labour in 2005, but this time it chose 'not to presume to tell its readers how to vote'. The *Scotsman* admired Cameron's 'considerable effort' to reassure Scotland but still found itself unable 'to endorse any of the big four parties'.

The Campaign in Progress

Directly and indirectly, the TV debates dominated in the press. This was partly a matter of quantity. The debates topped the dailies' front-page agenda (Table 14.4). However, and more importantly, the debates defined the character of election reporting and, with two significant exceptions, dictated its flow.

By virtually unanimous consent they brought the election to life. The first few days of manifesto launches did not trouble the front-page headline writers of the popular tabloids (see Table 14.6), while the upmarket sector was dutiful rather than animated. The reaction to Labour's programme was distinctly lukewarm. The *Mirror* pronounced it 'radical yet realistic' and the *Guardian* thought Labour had done 'a decent enough job' but elsewhere praise was scant. The *Sun*'s headline, 'Out of ideazzz', captured the mood. The Conservatives' 'Big Society' impressed sufficiently to deserve a fair hearing, as the *Mail* put it, but only the *Telegraph* and the Murdoch papers raised enthusiasm. The Liberal Democrats' offer was mostly relegated to the inside pages as the papers prepared for the first

Table 14.6   Topics in front-page leads and editorials

	Front-page leads			Editorials		
	2010		2005	2010		2005
	Number	%	%	Number	%	%
TV debates	16	12	–	23	9	–
Party strategies/prospects	14	11	17	32	12	11
Brown	14	11	11*	18	7	7*
Deficit/public spending	12	9	6	12	5	6
Hung parliament	11	8	–	11	4	–
Cameron	10	8	–	20	8	–
Clegg	9	7	–	17	6	–
Exhortation to vote/advice on voting	7	5	3	18	7	7
Manifestos	7	5	–	19	7	8
Immigration	6	5	11	13	5	8
Opinion polls	6	5	5	3	1	–
Health/NHS	4	3	3	8	3	5
Economy	4	3	2	25	9	4
Defence	2	2	–	1	–	–
Law and order	–	–	3	3	1	7
Const. reform	–	–	–	4	2	–
Other	11	8	50	37	14	44
Total	*133*	*100*	*100*	*264*	*100*	*100*

* Blair in 2005.

TV debate. Both the *Independent* and the *Guardian* found it attractive, but others dismissed it as naïve, misguided or disappointing. The Liberal Democrats get five minutes of fame at election time, said the *Sun*. 'It's four more than they deserve.'

The first debate provided the spark. 'Ninety minutes that could change Britain', boomed the *Independent*, declaring a new era of politics. All the papers, especially the broadsheets, devoted an astonishing amount of space to every conceivable angle from pre-debate preparation to post-debate analysis of issues, performance, instant polls, voters' focus groups, viewers' 'wormlines', 'spin alley', body language and hairstyles. However, the full charge of shock and excitement only came a few days later as the papers began to realise the scale and consequences of the opinion poll boost for Nick Clegg and the Liberal Democrats. They split sharply along partisan lines: the liberal press was elated while the Conservative tabloids reacted with horror. One or two agreed with Boris Johnson in the *Telegraph* (19 April) that 'Cleggmania' would be short-lived: 'like the orange spores of an exploded puffball' the Liberal Democrats were everywhere today but would be 'gone with the wind' tomorrow. However, it was evident to most that the first debate had changed the game.

It led directly to two highly distinctive characteristics of this election. First, this was an extraordinarily leader-focused contest, even by recent standards of personalised campaigns. It was not just that the debates themselves intensified attention to the leaders and their performances; it was also that they cast a presidential framing over the entire contest. This can be seen in the prominence of leaders in the topic agenda (Table 14.6); this is a substantial increase over 2005 when only the then Prime Minister Tony Blair was a topic in his own right. It is also illustrated by the frequency of leaders in the headlines of the front-page lead stories (Table 14.4); the leaders featured in these twice as often as they had in 2005.[2] Table 14.7 also highlights the second, and arguably the most, distinctive characteristic: in the press, as in the opinion polls, this was a three-way contest. The big change is the prominence of Nick Clegg who attracted an unprecedented degree of attention for a Liberal Democrat leader. Table 14.5 demonstrates how significantly the Liberal Democrat party profile increased over 2005–10. The Lib Dems had not been the main subject of any front-page lead story in 2005, nor for that matter in 2001. One would need to return to the 1980s and the rise of the Social Democrat–Liberal Alliance to find anything like this much press interest in the third party.

Table 14.7   Election coverage of political parties in front-page lead stories and editorials (daily newspapers)

	2010 Number	%	2005 %
Front-page leads			
Conservative	39	29	19
Labour	45	34	73
Liberal Democrat	17	13	–
More than one party	32	24	8
Total	*133*	*100*	*100*
Editorials			
Conservative	57	22	14
Labour	65	25	56
Liberal Democrat	42	16	6
Other	8	3	1
More than one party	92	35	23
Total	*264*	*100*	*100*

Of course, much of the attention was hostile, as we have seen in the individual papers. The Tory press onslaught began in earnest on the day of the second TV debate (22 April) with the highly personal attack on Clegg, including the *Mail*'s infamous 'Nazi slur'. If the attack was no surprise, its ferocity was still a shock. It provoked much critical commentary in other sectors of the press. According to Johann Hari (*Independent*, 23 April) it was testament to the 'frenzied panic' in the right-wing press as they lost control of the parameters of permissible opinion. It also lent credence to an intriguing argument from David Yelland, former editor of the *Sun*. Writing in the *Guardian* (19 April) he revealed the high stakes for those papers that had systematically ignored the Liberal Democrats over many years. Should a 'Clegg miracle' happen, he said, the press would lose its normal two-party channels of influence and 'lock Murdoch and the media elite out of UK politics'.

Certainly, a sense of loss of control pervaded commentary among the more right-wing voices. They struggled to explain 'Cleggmania': was it an expression of protest from an angry public or evidence of the political immaturity of an X-Factor-fed audience, voting for a charming new face? It was inconceivable, apparently, that voters might reasonably prefer Clegg. In any event, television was culpable. Television had hijacked the election with 90 minutes of light entertainment called 'Britain's Got Politics', said Melanie Phillips in the *Mail* (19 April); the *Telegraph* editorialised that the debate marked a triumph for 'political escapism', while the *Sun* thought it had cast a 'spell of unreality over the election race'. The papers' problem, suggested Jon Snow in *The Times* (1 May), was that the debates had reduced their influence. Viewers had seen Clegg for themselves, and thus could discount the partisan bias of the press attacks.

Just two events punctured the debate-driven narrative. The first came on 28 April when papers seized on a report from the Institute for Fiscal Studies that accused all three major parties of failing to come clean about the colossal scale of cuts and tax rises that would be necessary to repair the public finances. The economy, the fragile recovery and the deficit crisis were underlying themes of this election. But, the *Financial Times* apart, this was the first time that they topped the press agenda. 'Tell us the truth,' demanded the *Independent*, summarising the tone of several front pages. 'The elephant in the room' could no longer be ignored in this phoney election, said the *Mail*'s leader column. But, however profound the crisis, it was drowned out the next day by the one major gaffe of the campaign: Gordon Brown's unguarded comments about his encounter in Rochdale with Labour-supporting pensioner Gillian Duffy, the details of which are described in Chapter 8.

'Bigotgate' was irresistibly ironic sport for the press. She 'popped out for a loaf' and came back with 'Brown Toast', exclaimed the *Sun*. 'Day of disaster' said the *Telegraph* and all the papers devoted pages of excruciating detail to the episode and Brown's subsequent grovelling apology. It exposed the hypocrisy of politicians and their arrogant disdain for ordinary voters, said the *Guardian* editorial in a widely echoed sentiment. For the *Mail*, Labour was the real bigot and Duffy was 'demonised' because she dared to utter the 'I-word'; and in the *Express*, Brown was 'a hypocrite who shames Britain'. Even the *Star* was moved to put politics on its front page: 'Bigots … That's what Brown thinks of you' it told its readers. The *Independent* offered a rare crumb of comfort for the Prime Minister: 'Poll latest: Labour loses one voter' was its verdict. The timing could scarcely have been worse for Brown. It came on the day of the final TV debate, on the topic of the economy, and was widely regarded as his last chance to contrast his substance to the young pretenders' style. In the event, he failed to make headway in the post-debate polls, and the *Financial Times* reported 'some in Mr Brown's party are already writing his obituary'. The *Guardian* compounded his miserable week by announcing its switch to the Liberal Democrats, leaving Brown utterly friendless in Fleet Street except for the lonely *Mirror*.

From the final debate until the end the Conservative broadsheets started to sound increasingly optimistic. The *Times* led on Cameron's plans for his first days in power, while the *Telegraph* reported mounting confidence that the Tories could govern alone. However, fears of an indecisive result were never far from the surface in any of the Tory-supporting papers, and the tabloids pressed home the point with a coalition disaster-fest in the final few days, epitomised by the *Sun*'s double-page editorial on the 'nightmare of a hung parliament'. Polling day dawned with the outcome still in considerable doubt, but the papers could unite at least on one thing: that this was a crucial election, and for many commentators, the most exciting in a generation.

The Sunday Newspapers

The Sundays followed their daily counterparts in the general shift away from Labour. The *Observer*, following its sister paper the *Guardian*, switched from Labour into the Liberal Democrat camp – the first time since 1983. Likewise, Britain's biggest selling newspaper, the *News of the World*, ensured that the entire Murdoch stable switched from New Labour to Cameron's Conservatives.

Like the dailies, the Sundays were discomforted by the resurgence of TV and their own struggling authority diminished both by falling sales and the 24/7 news cycle. Their campaign coverage was hugely disrupted by the inaugural TV debate and so the first Sunday in its wake set the tone for the following three weeks. It was actually the Icelandic volcano that dominated the front pages for the first weekend but in political news, Nick Clegg's name was now unexpectedly prominent, although opinions differed as to his merits and the implications of a close race. The *Independent on Sunday* was the main cheerleader for what it headlined as 'Cleggmania!' although their Labour-sympathetic main political commentators, John Rentoul and Alan Watkins, were both more cautious. The *Observer* was also positive about the Lib Dem surge with their main political columnist Andrew Rawnsley describing a hung parliament as 'jolly attractive'. Like the *Guardian* they maintained a steady critique of David Cameron while failing to drum up much enthusiasm for Gordon Brown.

For the Conservative-supporting Sundays there was a similarly mixed picture. The *Sunday Express* front page attempted to blame the British government for the volcano while inside a leader warned Cameron to 'get his act together'. All the right-wing Sundays recognised that there had been something of a seismic event in the campaign and they responded. The pro-Conservative *Mail on Sunday*'s front page declared that 'Clegg Nicks The Top Spot'. But turning inside there was a personal attack which attempted to suggest the Lib Dem leader was somehow foreign: 'Is There

Anything British About Lib Dem Leader?' asked one story. 'Vote Orange Get Brown' warned another.

The *Sunday Telegraph* reflected the rising Conservative panic on that first weekend. Its main political commentator Matthew d'Ancona attempted to distinguish between Clegg's personal and policy attraction to the voters while the news content attempted to raise 'Inconvenient Truths For Clegg'. The leader column tried to shift the agenda back onto 'the truth on the economy' that was stubbornly refusing to become an election issue. The *Sunday Times*, too, was strongly pro-Cameron but realistic enough to understand that the campaign had just changed radically. They announced 'Clegg Nearly As Popular As Churchill' and that it was now a three-way contest. Cameron, its editorial urged, needed to find 'a game-changer'. Throughout the campaign the *Sunday Times'* support for the Conservatives was often expressed by attacks on the idea of a hung parliament and by more general features showing Cameron and his wife in a positive light, or with negative stories on issues, such as immigration, that were seen as vote-winners for the Tories.

Labour's Sunday tabloid supporters entered the campaign with little gusto. Throughout, the election never led their front pages. The *Sunday Mirror* tried hard to characterise the Clegg surge as bad news for Cameron, but it made more of Sarah than Gordon Brown. As the Lib Dem surge opened up the prospect of a hung parliament all the Sunday papers ran stories warning or hailing that possibility; and their voting advice was framed in those terms rather than straightforward partisan advocacy. The tightness of the race encouraged a focus on polls and party strategy on the front pages, while the 25 election editorials were almost all devoted to campaign strategy or to advising readers on how to vote to secure or avoid a hung parliament. Thus, the *Sunday Times* warned that 'Dangers Lurk Behind Lib Dem Charm', while the *Sunday Telegraph* claimed that 'We Won't Get Brave Decisions From A Coalition'. Conversely, the *Observer* was happy to announce that 'Cameron Leaves Door Open To Coalition'.

By the final weekend, the most passionately loyal Conservative papers were hopeful of a return to the narrative of a 'normal' majority victory. Extensive and highly partisan coverage made the most of the Gillian Duffy 'Bigotgate' affair. However, only the *Mail on Sunday* led on a directly anti-Brown story, with Duffy telling them that, unsurprisingly: 'Gordon Won't Be Getting My Vote'. The other Tory Sundays continued a twin-track approach of warning against Nick Clegg and the prospect of a coalition while enthusiastically promoting David Cameron. The *News of the World* asserted that its final opinion poll meant we were heading for 'Cameron By 4 Seats'. Intriguingly, it did not follow its sister paper, the *Sun*, in personal attacks on Gordon Brown, but instead concentrated on boosting his Conservative rival. It featured a personal article by Cameron saying he would 'Change The Face Of Britain In A Year' while the pro-Cameron leader article said it was 'Time For A Leader of Vision'. Likewise, the *Sunday Telegraph* carried a huge feature describing Cameron as 'The Man Born To Be Prime Minister'. The *Sunday Times* also fore-grounded Cameron's personality in its endorsement, stating that the Conservatives' 'Deserve A Chance' while stressing that voters 'Love Clegg But Hate His Policies'.

By this point Labour was left with only the *Sunday Mirror* to give it unambiguous, if tired and predictable, support. It presented David Cameron in Downing Street as a horror movie in the making, while Brown was given ample space to insist 'We Can Still Win It!' But its stablemate, the *People*, had abandoned its traditional Labour position and urged its readers to vote for a 'balanced parliament'. The *Independent on Sunday*, meanwhile, joined the *Observer* in declaring that 'Clegg Is The Candidate For Change'.

The Weeklies

The *Spectator* had the clearest line of the three main weekly political magazines. Its editor Fraser Nelson, who was also the main political columnist for the *News of the World*, took the magazine's editorial line to the right of Cameron but it was solidly behind the Conservatives. It was praying for a majority in its final leader where it said that 'Cameron must avoid doing deals with the Liberal Democrats' and instead stick to a minority government guided by undiluted Conservative principles. *The Economist* also supported the Conservatives from a vantage point that was both more free-market and liberal-libertarian than Cameron. Thus its final leader offered grudging support: 'They plainly have faults ... We dislike their Europhobic fringe and their exaggerations about Britain's broken society ... But Mr Cameron is much closer to answering the main question facing Britain than either of his rivals is.'

The *New Statesman* retained its historic loyalty to Labour but felt that it had run out of ideological steam: 'somewhere along the way, the revolution was postponed. The ideals of New Labour were inevitably compromised by the pragmatism of power.' It was certain that the Prime Minister was now a liability: 'Mr Brown has struggled as Prime Minister, unable to command the unity of his cabinet and incapable of connecting or communicating successfully with the wider electorate.

He has equivocated and dithered.' During the campaign it consistently hailed the possibility of a hung parliament as a 'progressive moment' and in the end it argued for tactical voting to engineer a coalition between Labour and the Liberal Democrats.

Newspapers and Magazines Online

Many of these titles now have a significant readership on the internet. The *Mail* online is the most popular with 2.3 million daily browsers, according to the Audit Bureau of Circulation, with the *Guardian* in second place with 1.8 million and the *Telegraph* on 1.6 million. Even the *Independent* regularly has more than 500,000 daily online visits. Of course, many of these visitors might be international and most internet users spend less time looking at a newspaper's website than they would reading a hard copy. It is also true that some papers, such as the *Mail*, emphasise lighter material online to attract the expanding global internet audience. Nonetheless, the 'quality' newspapers, especially, exploited the potential for interactive data on their websites, offering more sophisticated fare than their printed graphics and features. Some of this would have been helpful for voters intent on voting tactically in marginal seats. Generally, it meant that no reader was more than a few clicks away from detailed information on candidates and policies. The newspapers and the weekly magazines also created forums where the public could engage interactively by commenting on opinion columns and news articles. Additionally, the internet gave newspapers the opportunity to match the broadcasters' 24-hour continuity of coverage.

The *Spectator* had already established a vibrant community of political blogs, while in the year before the election, the *Statesman* transformed its social media offering by giving its columnists regular blogs and a lively presence on Twitter. All this allowed newspapers and weekly magazines to provide their internet audiences with more diverse and dynamic coverage through the week. The *Guardian* and *The Times* created live blogs written by their political staff at key moments, including during the TV debates. These provided multi-dimensional coverage that provided links to social media, such as blogs, Twitter and Facebook, as well as to other media and party political online information and reportage. Typically, discussions of media influence on politics separate the internet from newspapers and television; this election showed that now the press, and even the weeklies, are intimately networked into the continuous stream of news in the digital age.

Advertising

This election was remarkable for the absence of party political advertising. The Liberal Democrats, alone among the parties, invested in press advertising with a one-page insertion in *The Times* (5 May) with Nick Clegg offering a personal guarantee. All told, across the campaign there were only five pages of election-related political advocacy, from pressure groups concerned to keep the ban on fox-hunting, or warning against a hung parliament or urging a vote to stop the British National Party. This was by some distance the slightest show of political advertising in modern campaigns. It compares to 35 pages of party advertising in 2005.

Conclusion

The press often seemed marginalised during this campaign. This was more emphatically than ever a television election. It was defined by the TV debates and 24-hour broadcasting generally provided the key moments. Sky News broke the 'Bigotgate' story and, together with BBC News, it offered blanket coverage of the campaign trail and the gripping aftermath as the coalition deal was hammered out. Newspaper deadlines have become decreasingly relevant. As a result, the parties provided less press-targeted material. Additionally, there was a striking decline in political advertising as parties shifted their publicity to online, squeezing the life out of what was once a valuable revenue stream. The gradual drift to the internet for daily news, reduced staffing and declining readerships further undermined newspapers' confidence.

At times there was a palpable sense of loss. It was manifested partly in complaints about the TV debates from commentators across the ideological spectrum; the debates had sucked the oxygen out of all other campaign events, and focused too much on the trivialities of personality. But mostly it was evident in the Tory papers' collective baring of teeth at Nick Clegg. They quickly choked back the hyperbolic excesses of the first assault, as they drew less fear, more ridicule and disgust from other sectors of the media and the blogosphere. The snarling did not stop, as we have seen, but changed direction and tone, to focus on Liberal Democrat policy and the twin 'nightmares' of a hung parliament and the possibility that Clegg would prop up Brown.

It is tempting to see this campaign as confirmation of dwindling newspaper power. The papers generally followed, rather than set, the agenda. More significantly still, even though the Conservative-supporting press commanded 74% of total national daily circulation, it failed to deliver what it desperately wanted: a clear majority for David Cameron. However, Ipsos-MORI's poll of voter behaviour by newspaper readership offers some mixed signals. Table 14.5 shows that the national readership swing from Labour to Conservative was 5%, the same as for the electorate as a whole. Only the Scottish *Daily Record*, reflecting the different situation north of the border, and the *Guardian*, went against the tide. To that extent, the press was simply in tune with the national mood.

However, the stand-out figure in Table 14.5 is the suggestively high 13.5% swing to the Conservatives among *Sun* readers. It may be accounted for partly by the paper's high proportion of readers from the social grades C2 and DE; at 7% these groups switched to the Conservatives by a larger than national average swing. The *Star*, with a similar readership profile, also saw a large swing, despite offering little political content and no party endorsement. Moreover, the polls say nothing about the direction of the causal arrow, and doubtless there was an interaction effect as readers influenced papers and vice versa. However, with its huge daily readership and willingness to flex its political muscles, it would be foolish to dismiss the significance of the *Sun*. The *Sun* did not win or lose it; but Cameron, like Blair before him, has cause to be grateful to Rupert Murdoch's support.

Notes

1. Many thanks to research assistants Max Hanska-Ahy, Irene Lee, Jessica Siegel and Alex Telka; to Martin Harrop for his continuing guidance; and to Bob Worcester and Roger Mortimore of Ipsos-MORI.
2. M. Scammell and M. Harrop, 'The Press: Still for Labour Despite Blair', in D. Kavanagh and D. Butler, *The British General Election of 2005* (Basingstoke: Palgrave Macmillan, 2005), pp. 119–45.

15
More Diverse, Yet More Uniform: MPs and Candidates

Byron Criddle

The 2010 election set a series of records. It was contested by more candidates than ever before, and came after a higher number of retirements than in any post-war election. It also saw larger numbers of women and ethnic minority MPs elected, as a result of vigorous attempts by the parties to increase the diversity of their candidates. Less obviously, however, the changes to the nature of the intake – including a noticeable rise in the professional politician, and the almost complete elimination of the manual worker MP – has resulted in the parliamentary parties becoming more similar to each other in their composition.

A total of 4,133 candidates contested the election, and the average number of candidates per constituency was 6.3, compared to 5.5 in 2005.[1] The Conservative, Labour and Liberal Democrat parties contested 631 mainland seats, avoiding only Speaker Bercow's seat at Buckingham. The SNP fought all 59 Scottish seats and Plaid all 40 Welsh seats. Four minor parties fielded more than a hundred candidates: UKIP 558 (496 in 2005), BNP 338 (119), the Green Party 335 (183) and the English Democrats 104. The greater number of these and other minor party candidates and of independents accounted for the highest total of candidates on record in a general election, 578 more than in 2005.[2]

Of the 650 MPs elected, 232 were new to the House, more than a third (36%) of its membership. Five were MPs who had sat in previous parliaments: John Cryer, Geraint Davies, Chris Leslie and Stephen Twigg, all Labour victims at the 2005 election, and the Conservative, Jonathan Evans, who was returning after having lost his seat in 1997.[3] For those who had anticipated a clear Conservative victory, the size of the new intake was smaller than had been expected. It was smaller than that in 1997, when 260 MPs, or 40%, were new to the Commons, 183 of whom were Labour compared with 148 new Conservatives in 2010. The rest of the new intake consisted of 67 Labour, ten Liberal Democrats, and seven others (one each for SNP, Plaid, Green, SDLP and Alliance, and two DUP). The Conservative new intake comprised a slightly larger proportion of the party's parliamentary strength (48%) than Labour's 1997 intake (44%).

If the scale of replacement of MPs was slightly less dramatic than expected, the scale of retirements was considerably greater than in any post-war parliament, including 1945 when, despite a ten-year gap since the previous election, the total of retiring MPs was 129. In 2010 149 MPs left the House, 23% of its membership. The average at all elections since 1979, excluding 1997, was 12%. In 1997 the figure had been 117, or 18%. In one way, the circumstances of 2010 were not dissimilar to those of 1997: the anticipated end of an electoral cycle, with the expectation of a change of government, prompting low morale among the ranks of the governing party. Some 102 Labour Members dominated the list of 149 retiring MPs in 2010, just as 72 Conservatives dominated the list of 117 in 1997.

Retirement of MPs is usually attributable to age, infirmity, personal scandal or political discordance, and each of these were at work in 2010. Most of the 102 departing Labour MPs were aged over sixty, 35 of them over sixty-five. Of the 37 retiring Conservatives, all but seven were over 60. The most conspicuously age-related retirement was that of the former DUP leader, Revd Ian Paisley (b. 1926) who at 84 had been the oldest MP since the death in 2007 of Labour's Piara Khabra (b. 1924). Paisley had thought of continuing into the next parliament, but left as Lord Bannside, with his constituency dynastically transferred to the care of his son. Labour's departing MPs included two who were in their eightieth year: Alan Williams (b. 1930), the outgoing Father of the House, and the last MP to have been elected in 1964; and Bob Wareing (b. 1930), whose departure followed his deselection as a Liverpool MP. The former Deputy Prime Minister, John Prescott (b. 1938), headed a long list of departing Labour ex-ministers, many of whom were at an age when retirement is not unexpected. MPs who departed and were colourful in different ways, included the celebrated Commons rebel Bob Marshall-Andrews, the herald of New Labour power-dressing in the late 1990s, Barbara Follett, and Labour's last Old Etonian MP, Mark Fisher.

With the welcome prospect of a change of government most Conservative retirements were easily explicable in terms of age or infirmity.

Eight were septuagenarians or on the cusp of 70. They included Sir Patrick Cormack, who had been first elected in 1970 when he unexpectedly defeated Aneurin Bevan's widow Jennie Lee at Cannock. A devoted parliamentarian, he had polled a mere nine votes when running for the Speakership in 2009, coming ninth in a field of ten. Another of the 1970 vintage was John Gummer, probably best remembered for feeding his daughter a beef burger as Agriculture Minister during a scare about mad cow disease. Also from the 1970 intake, though then elected for Labour, was John Horam who eventually sat in the House under three different party labels. He had defected to the SDP in 1981, was defeated in 1983, eventually to re-emerge in 1992 as a Conservative MP. He was the last MP from the 30-strong Gadarene rush to the SDP out of the Labour Party, having managed dexterously to have sustained a Commons career, if at the price of being likened by Dennis Skinner to the Vicar of Bray.

Of five other septuagenarian retiring Members – Michael Mates (b. 1934), Sir Michael Lord (b. 1938), Sir Peter Viggers (b. 1938), Sir Nicholas Winterton (b. 1938) and Anthony Steen (b. 1939), age alone did not account for the retreat of the last three, as will be considered below. Still in their sixties were three other Conservatives worthy of note: Michael Howard, who as Leader had begun the climb towards regaining power by eroding Labour's large majority in 2005; Ann Widdecombe, who had stood out in her party as an almost lone opponent of hunting and whose labelling in 1997 of Michael Howard ('something of the night') stuck; and Sir Michael Spicer, departing Chairman of the 1922 Committee, who had established an effective line in pithy didactic interventions at Prime Minister's Questions. The former Conservative Chief Whip, David Maclean, was also leaving, having suffered multiple sclerosis.

Scandal of a sort involving personal, invariably sexual, behaviour accounted for two exits in 2010. The Liberal Democrat, Mark Oaten, suffered tabloid exposure early in 2006 for an encounter of a sexual nature, as did the Labour MP Nigel Griffiths, and both left parliament in 2010, Griffiths ostensibly for a challenging new job. The marital life of the Conservative MP, James Gray, also attracted much attention. He overcame attempts locally to deselect him and successfully contested the election.

A further source of retirement in 2010 was the impact of the Boundary Commission's review, which had the effect of reducing the number of Labour-held seats and served to dislodge a number of Labour MPs. Only two Conservative MPs were similarly affected. James Brokenshire (Hornchurch), who had lost out to his parliamentary neighbour Angela Watkinson (Upminster) in the new combined seat of Hornchurch &

Upminster, was eventually safely relocated to the vacated seat of Old Bexley & Sidcup. John Greenway, however, MP for the abolished seat of Ryedale, lost to Anne McIntosh, whose Vale of York seat had been merged with his to form a new (in fact revived) seat of Thirsk & Malton, and retired. Rather more Labour MPs had to accept the same fate. On Merseyside Eddie O'Hara (Knowsley South) lost to George Howarth (Knowsley North) in a contest for the redrawn Knowsley seat, and Claire Curtis-Thomas (Crosby) decided not to contest the new seat of Sefton Central. Both retired. In Birmingham any problems from the reduction of Labour-held seats by one was resolved by the exit of Lynne Jones (Selly Oak), though not before she suggested as she left that she might not vote for Roger Godsiff, a beneficiary of her leaving, in the redrawn Hall Green seat. In South Yorkshire, Mick Clapham (Barnsley West & Penistone) retired rather than contest the new Penistone & Stocksbridge seat against its other claimant Angela Smith, a Sheffield MP. In Greater Manchester, Ian Stewart (Eccles), alleged his rivals had received favourable treatment as he was squeezed by competition from Hazel Blears and Barbara Keeley for the new Salford & Eccles and Worsley & Eccles South seats, and was obliged to retire. Perhaps most conspicuous of all the boundary review problems was in west Yorkshire, where the Normanton seat of Ed Balls had merged into his wife's adjacent seat of Pontefract & Castleford, leaving him with a slight claim on the new seat of Morley & Outwood, which was duly made available for him by the other claimant, Colin Challen (Morley & Rothwell) deciding to retire.

To these sources of retirement in 2010 must be added the deselection of MPs by their local constituency organisations. Three such cases involved Labour MPs. As already noted, the serially rebellious Campaign Group left-winger Bob Wareing was deselected in Liverpool West Derby in September 2007 in a contest with the Blairite ex-Minister Stephen Twigg, who had lost his London seat in 2005. Denouncing his deselection as the work of a 'New Labour mafia', Wareing announced his intention of fighting the seat as an independent and resigned the Labour whip. In the event he did not stand at the general election. In Stockton North another elderly left-winger Frank Cook (b. 1935) was replaced by a local councillor, Alex Cunningham, who claimed the local activists wanted someone who had lived in the area all his life, and wanted change. Cook went on to fight the seat against the new Labour candidate in 2010, polling a slight 1,577 (4%). The fate of both these MPs was perhaps poetic justice, for each had been beneficiaries in the early 1980s of the deselection or defection of the two right-wing Labour MPs, Eric Ogden in Liverpool West Derby, and Bill Rodgers in Stockton, each of whom went on to create the SDP. Their replacements, Wareing and Cook, in their turn nearly 30 years later had been deselected.

A third Labour deselection casualty was Anne Moffat (who stood as Anne Picking in 2005) in East Lothian, ousted after a long dispute over her alleged shortcomings as a constituency MP and as early as 2007 had received bad publicity for apparently high travel expense claims. Having suffered a brain haemorrhage in 2009, she alleged intimidation and pressure from leading party figures and the Whips' Office to make her retire. She was ousted in a deselection vote in March 2010. To these Labour departures should be added the self-deselection of the disaffected former cabinet minister, Clare Short, who had resigned belatedly from the Blair cabinet over the Iraq War in 2003, and who resigned the Labour whip in September 2006, declaring herself 'profoundly ashamed' of the Government's 'craven support' for American foreign policy, opposing the replacement of Trident, proposing proportional representation, and hoping for a hung parliament. She left the Commons in 2010.

Three Conservative MPs lost the whip in the course of the Parliament and each left the Commons in 2010, though two of them fought the election against their Conservative replacement candidate. One who went quietly was Derek Conway (Old Bexley & Sidcup), whose problems prefigured by over a year the revelations about MPs' expenses that began in May 2009. As early as January 2008 it was revealed that he had employed his son as a parliamentary aide despite him being away at university in Newcastle. An investigation by the Standards and Privileges Committee found against Mr Conway, who lost the whip. He apologised to the Commons in 2009 and left at the dissolution in 2010. Another Conservative in difficulties was Andrew Pelling who had won the marginal Croydon Central seat in 2005. Following arrest for alleged assault on his wife, for which he was subsequently not charged, he lost the whip and was replaced as candidate for the next election. Amid confusion as to whether he had been given an option of resuming his candidacy and claims that he had neglected his duties and suffered from depression, he fought the seat as an independent in 2010, and garnered 3,239 votes (6.5%). More idiosyncratic was the case of Bob Spink, MP for Castle Point, and a populist right-winger on crime, immigration, and specifically Europe. In March 2008 there was some dispute as to whether he had resigned the whip over lack of support for his efforts to repel local attempts at his deselection or whether he had had the whip removed. Expressing his disillusion with Conservative policy on Europe, there were claims he had defected to UKIP in the following month, becoming its first MP (see p. 117), but he later left and fought the 2010 election as a

'Green Belt' candidate. He polled a remarkable 12,174 (27%), the largest vote of any candidate standing independently of the Westminster parties.

Age, infirmity, personal scandal, boundary revision and deselection accounted for many retirements in 2010. But extraneous factors such as the collapsed morale in the Parliamentary Labour Party as it faced inevitable defeat, and disillusion across all parties following the expenses revelations, were also important. The 2005 election had produced through the vagaries of the electoral system a lucky victory for Labour on a low vote share and with many MPs sitting on knife-edged majorities. The change of Prime Minister had not made any difference. It was clear that defeat beckoned, prompting MPs with indefensible majorities, such as those in the string of six North Kent marginals stretching from Dartford to Thanet South, to quit (as three of them did), and also prompting the exit of many ex-cabinet ministers who featured among the 'under-age' retirements, notably Des Browne (b. 1952), Stephen Byers (b. 1953), Patricia Hewitt (b. 1950), Geoff Hoon (b. 1953), John Hutton (b. 1955), Alan Milburn (b. 1958), and, more conspicuously given their youth, Ruth Kelly (b. 1968), James Purnell (b. 1970) and, though not a former cabinet minister, Kitty Ussher (b. 1971). Most of the above had been strong Blairites. Some 40 of Labour's retiring MPs were former ministers, many of whom had much left of their working lives. It was evident that career politicians were quitting for new careers in anticipation of Labour's defeat.

The expenses revelations, and their orchestration by the *Daily Telegraph*, reinforced the sense of malaise across the Commons and persuaded MPs to retire regardless of their own expenses records. For many Members the sense of public opprobrium was too much to bear. The Labour MP Dick Caborn spoke of wives seeing their husbands lose public esteem and urging them to leave; Labour's Harry Cohen, who had encountered criticism of his housing arrangements, spoke of his wife's worsening health; and the Conservative MP, Nadine Dorries mentioned the possibility of a suicide. More practically, there was concern about the effect of a serious tightening up of the allowances available to MPs in the wake of the revelations, with, for example, the withdrawal of the resettlement grant for defeated or departing MPs, which, available in 2010, might not be at a future election. MPs also expressed concern over attempts to restrict their outside earnings. The GP Howard Stoate (retiring from highly vulnerable Dartford) had continued to work part-time as a locum, claiming his effectiveness as a health specialist in the Commons depended on his employment, and citing that, rather than the certainty of his defeat, as the reason for his decision to retire. The retiring Conservative MP, Paul Goodman, who was returning to journalism, feared that a ban on outside work would lead to yet more professional politicians. Another fear, closer to home, was of a ban on MPs employing their spouses as secretaries, a point cited by the retiring Labour ex-minister, Jane Kennedy. Thus it was that all MPs were affected by the revelations regardless of whether their retirements were more obviously prompted by them. About two-thirds of the announced retirements post-dated the expenses revelations in May 2009.

On the Conservative side some MPs quit very soon after the first *Daily Telegraph* disclosures in May 2009. The MP whose expenses record came to symbolise the entire saga was Anthony Steen (Totnes), partly because of his defiant defence of arboricultural work in the grounds of his large house. He claimed the public were simply jealous and had no right to interfere in his private life. Apologising for this initial outburst, he promptly announced he would quit. Douglas Hogg (Sleaford & North Hykeham), though denying he had specifically claimed for 'moat cleaning' on his Lincolnshire estate, also swiftly announced he would retire. Sir Peter Viggers (Gosport), who had (unsuccessfully) claimed for provision of a 'duck house' on his pond, announced his intention to retire, allegedly after a conversation with David Cameron. The party leadership was not sorry to see these departures of 'bed-blocking' older MPs to release their seats for a new generation. In the same category were Sir Nicholas and Ann Winterton, MPs for Macclesfield and Congleton, who had been investigated in 2008, well before the revelations of May 2009, by the Standards and Privileges Committee for allegedly improper claims relating to a London property. At the time Sir Nicholas blamed an 'ageist' campaign against him and affirmed his intention to seek re-election. But when the matter resurfaced in 2009 the Wintertons swiftly announced they would retire. Of a younger generation was the married couple Andrew Mackay (Bracknell) and Julie Kirkbride (Bromsgrove) who both announced their retirements following criticism of their second housing allowance claims, he having already swiftly quit as David Cameron's PPS. Later in 2009 David Wilshire, MP for Spelthorne, faced with allegations of improperly processed office allowances, announced his retreat, blaming a 'witch hunt' against MPs, and with some hyperbole noted that branding a whole group of people as undesirables had led to Hitler's gas chambers. These were the more obvious Conservative casualties.

At least five Labour MPs lost their careers as a direct consequence of the revelations, because all were suspended from the PLP and barred by the National Executive Committee from standing again for election. Elliot Morley (Scunthorpe) allegedly claimed for payments relating to a mortgage that had been paid off, David Chaytor (Bury North) had allegedly made irregular claims for rent, and Jim Devine (Livingstone) had allegedly made improper claims for office equipment and repairs. Margaret Moran (Luton South) had most conspicuously claimed for repairs to a property in Southampton, neither near London nor Luton. Ian Gibson (Norwich North) was criticised for allegedly improper claims made on a property, and he reacted to his loss of the whip and ban from standing again by immediately resigning his seat and prompting a by-election which Labour lost. Extraneous factors therefore contributed to a larger scale of retirement from the House of Commons than in any other post-war parliament.

Candidate selection had been dominated during the previous 20 years by the question of diversifying the composition of the House of Commons, with the objective being a more demographically representative parliament. Primarily this had meant augmenting the number of women MPs. In all three main parties a key problem had been the paucity of supply, the low proportion, under 30%, of women on the parties' approved list of candidates – the shallowness of the pool of eligibles. The first party to do anything about this was Labour, initially by compulsorily short-listing women, and eventually introducing a policy of all-women shortlists (AWS), which by 2010 involved excluding men from selection in about half of the seats where replacements were needed for retiring MPs. This mechanical means of increasing the supply of women candidates had not been adopted by the Conservatives or the Liberal Democrats, who traditionally relied on exhortation both to get more women onto the approved list and to persuade local parties to shortlist and select them. Nevertheless it was the sight of about 100 women on Labour's benches continuously after 1997 that finally led the Conservatives to adopt measures which, whilst short of AWS, did lead in 2010 to a trebling of the number of Conservative women MPs.

After the 2005 election the Conservatives set the pace for innovative selection procedures, through a 'priority' list of candidates and open primaries. The idea of a priority list, or 'A-list' as it became known, had been trailed by Andrew Lansley MP, a former head of the Conservative Research Department, and by a former Party Chairman Theresa May MP. Both had envisaged a list of the 100 'best' candidates, composed equally of men and women, with Theresa May observing that 'if we cannot find fifty grade-A top-class women who want to offer themselves as Conservative candidates we should probably give up now'.[4] Before the 2005 election the party had already reformed its candidate screening process under the advice of an occupational psychologist in order to improve the supply of candidates with appropriate aptitudes and competences. The problem still remained the low proportion of women on the approved list (27%) and the disparity between that modest figure and the proportion of Tory MPs in 2005 who were women (17 out of 198, or 9%). The A-list, dating from June 2006, was intended to increase the supply of women candidates by creating a gender balance of 50%-50% on a reduced pool of eligibles, in place of the 73%-27% imbalance on the approved candidates list, and then to advertise seat vacancies in the target seats only to names on that list and to require local Conservative Associations to select from that list.

According to a leaked report the first version of the list (periodically topped-up) contained 101 names of whom 54 were female and seven ethnic minority aspirants. This skewing of the supply pool of candidates was intended to increase the chances of women being chosen, and yet still permitted a reduced pool of male candidates capable of standing and winning selection. Supporters of the system met charges of tokenism by arguing that any selected woman would have to prove herself against male opposition, because the short-listing at local level in target seats would be guided by CCHQ, and by the requirement for shortlists to be gender-balanced.

Predictably, these steps to redress the shortage of women in the parliamentary party met with resistance from local male aspirants waiting to step into the shoes of retiring male MPs. Tim Montgomerie, of the ConservativeHome website, also opposed the centralising impulse of the A-list procedure and the limiting of the autonomy of local Conservative associations. He accepted the need for more women MPs but suggested that diversity was about more than just gender and questioned why so many Conservative MPs were from the City, the law, the private sector, the South and private schools. He noted that many of the 68 candidates on the first version of the A-list who had fought previous elections had achieved below-average swings, causing him to wonder at the objectivity of the process of selection for the list.[5] For the MP Edward Leigh, the A-list was blighting careers, discouraging activists and was contrary to natural justice. John Maples MP, Deputy Chairman for Candidates, dismissed such complaints bluntly in March 2007: 'I would like to be able to run this like a dictator. I would achieve what I want. I could get the right candidates in the right seats, the right percentages of women and ethnic minority candidates, but the party's not going to wear that, and each association has autonomy.'

These bullish remarks concealed a recognition of the unease which had met the imposition of the A-list, for in January 2009 he announced changes to selection rules which reduced the salience of the list by restoring safe and target seat selections from the approved list but requiring all selections to be exactly gender balanced. Constituency associations agreeing to this would be allowed to select from the traditional approved list. The reversion to selection from the approved list was in order to placate thwarted favourite son aspirants, though it was seen in CCHQ as a reflection that the A-list had succeeded in its aim of achieving more diverse selections.

Another innovation in Conservative selection processes was the open primary, allowing registered electors who were not party members to attend the final selection meeting. The intention was to open out the party to the wider public, recruit more members for the party and achieve greater press coverage. In safe seats it could give the wider electorate the impression of taking part in the choice of the MP, though only 15 of the 116 seats where open primaries were held were Conservative-held. Nor did the increased choice of candidate emerging from the primary process give a greater advantage to aspiring women MPs; just 22 were selected by such means, although 48 of the seats holding primaries were gained by the party at the election. It was estimated that the possibilities of 'entryism' – the swamping of the meeting by outsiders – was slight, with the non-party members usually comprising no more than a minority of those attending the open primaries. The outsiders selected from a predetermined shortlist and the primary's verdict required endorsement by a subsequent general meeting of the membership.

Another innovation, employed in two constituencies, was the all-postal primary, where the entire electorate was offered a postal vote in the selection of the Conservative candidate. These were used in the Conservative-held seats of Totnes and Gosport. In both cases the shortlists, over which the wider electorate had no say, appeared carefully balanced. At Totnes it consisted of one man and two women, the man being a local mayor, one of the women a local council leader, and the other a near-local GP who had been in the party only two years. The latter, Sarah Wollaston, the least political of the three, won. At Gosport, a shortlist of four was gender balanced and ethnically diverse, with one of the men from the BME (black and minority ethnic) community. A well known, more political figure who had fought a nearby seat before, Caroline Dinenage, won. Few conclusions may be drawn from such a small sample but the turnout, 25% in Totnes and 18% in Gosport, hardly justified the CCHQ-provided sum of £38,000 for the Totnes primary. Nor was the relatively non-political victor at Totnes typical of the party's standard-bearers in 2010.

In a further move to open the party out to the wider public and create in the words of a CCHQ official 'a parliamentary party that would look like the country it is governing', David Cameron in the wake of the expenses revelations opened the candidates list to anyone who, though never politically involved, had a desire to 'clean up' politics. Some 4,000 people responded, of whom about 400 were put through the candidate screening process; 200 passed and eventually four were selected for Conservative-held seats which they retained at the election. These four: Bob Stewart, a soldier, Daniel Poulter, a doctor, Jo Johnson, a financial journalist, and Rory Stewart a former diplomat and soldier and traveller in the Muslim world with echoes of T.E. Lawrence, may have been new to party politics, but in social and professional background and gender, they cut a very traditional dash.

Nevertheless, the quest for diversity saw the number of women candidates in winnable seats increased to the extent that had the party secured a Commons majority at the election it would have had 62 women elected in place of the 17 elected in 2005. As it was, the total rose to 49. It also produced a significant rise in the number of MPs from ethnic minorities. But two disputes in late 2009 and early 2010 symbolised the concern at the grass roots over the centralising measures required to achieve these results. At Norfolk South West the candidate, Elizabeth Truss, faced an ultimately unsuccessful deselection attempt over her past private life, and in Surrey East, where the BME candidate Sam Gyimah had been selected, his business affairs were questioned. But the underlying concerns in both cases were about the prioritising of women over local men, of gender-balanced shortlists, and of shortlists of the sort imposed by CCHQ at Surrey East, where the five people short-listed did not include a single heterosexual white man. It was also evident that the women in the new intake were less likely than men to have local connections with the constituencies they had won, such had been their peripatetic quest to land a seat. Even more was that true of the BME victors. Yet in late 2009 David Cameron had threatened the imposition of all-women shortlists, and drawn from Iain Dale, an aspiring candidate and internet commentator on Conservative politics, the comment, 'I can just about stomach a final shortlist having to consist of three men and three women, but for me it is this far and no further.'

The centre had always been ill at ease with the periphery in Conservative politics, but this time the leadership was able to use the leverage it had on a party anxious to win power. Yet the gains were still modest: an increase of 32 women MPs on the 17 elected in 2005. CCHQ had skewed the pool of eligibles in the direction of equality, so increasing the supply of women candidates, but it had not, as Labour was doing, guaranteed their selection by way of all-women shortlists.

Labour's candidate selection process after 2005 followed established lines. With little expectation of gaining seats, if it was to stay ahead of the Conservatives in the provision of women and ethnic minority MPs it would have to use seats where MPs were retiring. In 2006 it reaffirmed a 'requirement' by the NEC of achieving at least 40% of the PLP being women after the election. This was an ambitious target given that the 98 seats then occupied by women comprised only 28% of the PLP. To reach 40% would require, in a then 355-member PLP, an additional 50 seats, an impossible target at a time when the party was looking at probable defeat at the next election. Reaching the 40% target would require a ruthless policy of applying AWS in seats from which Labour MPs were retiring. To this end the NEC set down guidelines for determining the allocation of all-women shortlists, seeking agreement with constituency parties, but insisting that final decisions rested at the centre regardless of the preferences of local party members. The NEC sought to allocate AWS in vacated Labour-held seats by taking into account the gender of neighbouring MPs and the representation of women in each region as a whole. In some regions the party had proportionately far fewer women MPs than others, with levels in the North (19%), Scotland (20%), the West Midlands (23%) and Wales (24%), lower than the figure of 30% exceeded in some other regions. By the time shortlist allocation was completed a virtual balance between open and all-women lists had been achieved in vacated Labour-held seats. Ultimately, all-women lists were applied in 63 seats, 46 of them seats from which MPs were retiring, with the majority of seats allocated to women being seen as statistically safe on the basis of the last election. The other 17 seats allocated all-women shortlists were target seats which the party had lost in 2005. Of the 46 Labour-held seats, 18 were duly lost at the election, but the targeting had secured 28 more women MPs, with four more who had been selected by way of open shortlists. It had made a notable difference in the North East where, in the kingdom of Andy Capp, the previous total of four women MPs was augmented to ten.

Inevitably, the AWS strategy met with resistance from ambitious local sons. In Burnley the resistance secured an open list instead of an all-women list, although a woman was still selected. The NEC used delays to the selection process caused by Burnley's resistance, to justify introducing complete central control of short-listing after 1 January 2010, creating a Special Selections Panel with power to determine shortlist composition regardless of local opinion. A number of the selections made thereafter met with local criticism, less over the selection of women, than over the claim that the NEC was parachuting favoured metropolitan figures or others without local claims into vacated safe seats. Throughout the entire selection period traditional complaints were aired. At Erith & Thamesmead, it was claimed local candidates were being thwarted by influential national party insiders organising support for the 22-year-old daughter of the former party pollster Lord Gould, with allegations of postal voting irregularities. A local candidate, Teresa Pearce, prevailed and was subsequently elected. At Barrow & Furness it was claimed that the Downing Street aide John Woodcock received favourable access to the CLP membership list and orchestrated local press coverage. At Airdrie & Shotts selection was delayed for two years, allegedly to frustrate a local favourite son, and ultimately, when the NEC had full powers, from an all-women selection emerged Pamela Nash, the former political aide, as it happened, to the outgoing MP, John Reid. At Liverpool Wavertree, local hackles rose against the successful quest for selection of Luciana Berger, a London-based lobbyist with supposedly important connections at national level, and the support of the departing MP, Jane Kennedy. At Stoke Central there was resentment at the selection with backing from Lord Mandelson of the television celebrity historian Tristram Hunt. There was comment too at the 'parachuting' of the union leader Jack Dromey into Birmingham Erdington on the eve of the election. In fact these well-publicised complaints about top-down interference were less justified by analysis of the list of the new Labour intake which showed the great majority had credible local links, many in local government. And a number of the parliamentary aides who were elected had been working for the MP they were replacing.

The Liberal Democrats, after the 2005 election had made some changes in the way they dealt with candidate screening and selection. They employed an occupational psychologist who had earlier advised the Conservatives on a more professional system of candidate screening for access to their candidates list, testing for skills in leadership, communication, judgement, and application of the party's values. Assessors at the sessions had also received 'diversity training' to ensure open access for all applicants. By these means some 200 new candidates reached the approved list of some 1,000 people, but this came too late to affect most candidate selections for 2010. The party's reliance on recycling more than 40% of its candidates from previous elections was much higher than in the case of the two larger parties.

The party was traditionally apprehensive over gender balancing having rejected a call for AWS in 2001. But its selection rules did now require balancing of shortlists, with the inclusion of one or two people of either gender, depending on the size of the shortlist. For some years the party also had had a Campaign for Gender Balance, which sought to mentor aspiring women in a way similar to Labour Women's Network and Conservative2Win.

But the obstacle to innovation was, as ever, not the shallow pool of eligibles from which it chose its candidates – about a quarter on the list were women – but the shallow pool of winnable seats. In a traditionally male-dominated political world, and with no more than three score of seats the party had any experience of winning, there was little room for discriminating in favour of women as the two other parties were doing through A-listing or AWS. The shortage of winnable seats supply and lack of many women MPs as role models worked against change.[6] As it was, in 2010 with seven male MPs retiring and one of the seats divided into two, of the candidates selected for the eight seats, four of the candidates were women. But all lost whilst three of the four men selected to fight the other seats were elected, so confirming the party's heavy reliance on incumbency in creating and holding 'safe' seats. For the Liberal Democrats, it was seats, not women, that were in short supply.

Table 15.1   Women candidates 2005–10

	Conservative	Labour	Lib Dem
2010	153 (24%)	191 (30%)	134 (20%)
2005	122 (19%)	166 (26%)	145 (23%)

Table 15.2   Women MPs 2005–10

	2005	By-elections 2005–10	Deaths 2002–10	Retiring 2010	Defeated 2010	New MPs 2010	Total
Conservative	17	+1	–	–5	–	36	49
Labour	98	–	–2	–24	–23	32	81
Lib Dem	10	–	–1	–	–3	1	7
SNP	0	–	–	–	–	1	1
SDLP	0	–	–	–	–	1	1
DUP	1	–	–	1	–	–	0
Alliance	0	–	–	–	–	1	1
Sinn Fein	1	–	–	–	–	–	1
UUP/Independent	1	–	–	–	–	–	1
Green	0	–	–	–	–	1	1
Total	*128*	*+1*	*–3*	*–30*	*–36*	*+73*	*143*

The three parties fielded 478 women, 153 Conservatives, 191 Labour and 134 Liberal Democrats. The total had not increased much, and in the case of the Liberal Democrats had actually fallen. The key development, in the Conservative Party had been the targeting of women in winnable seats, a policy replicating Labour's over the past five elections.

The total of women MPs at 143 (21% compared with 20% in 2005) was a record. With Labour on an ebb tide it had been expected that its numbers of women MPs would fall, but its success in placing women candidates in its safer seats compensated for its electoral retreat. Its 31% of the PLP was a slight rise on 2005 (28%). But the Conservatives' increase (16% of their Commons strength compared to 9% in 2005) was crucial in sustaining and increasing the overall total. Despite the modest nature of its net gain of 32 seats, the result was remarkable when set against the party's historic inability to rise above the total of the 20 seats acquired when it last took office in 1992, and served to challenge Labour's established dominance of the diversity agenda.

The virtual doubling of the number of MPs from ethnic minorities came with virtually no increase in the number of BME candidates. Classification of candidates of mixed ethnic origin is problematic and no totals are ever definitive, but the approximate figures (2005 figures in brackets) were: Conservative 43 (41), Labour 46 (36), Liberal Democrat 46 (42). With effective targeting in 2010 the total number of non-white MPs rose from 15 (13 Labour, 2 Conservative) in 2005, to 27: 16 Labour, 11 Conservative. In 2005, by electing two BME candidates in Windsor and Cambridgeshire North West, constituencies with only slight BME populations (8.5% and 3.3% respectively on 2001 Census figures) the Conservatives had challenged the assumption that overwhelmingly white constituencies were electorally risky locations for non-white candidates, and in the run-up to 2010 a group of favoured BME candidates was recommended to safe seats until they each struck lucky. One, Sam Gyimah, who was eventually selected in Surrey East, was even given a run in one of the only two all-ballot primaries, in Gosport. CCHQ presided over the selection of six BME candidates in constituencies where the BME population was minimal (in the highest case, at Spelthorne, 5.7%). The six beneficiaries were Priti Patel (Witham) a public relations executive and the first Conservative female Asian MP; Helen Grant (Maidstone & The Weald), a solicitor; Sam Gyimah (Surrey East), a businessman; Sajid Javid (Bromsgrove), a banker; Kwasi Kwarteng (Spelthorne), another banker; and Nadhim Zahawi (Stratford-on-Avon), a businessman. Barring electoral meltdown, these MPs, and the two elected in 2005, by occupying safe seats in the suburbs, green belts and rolling shires, had every prospect of enjoying uninterrupted careers, a prediction less tenable in the case of the three other non-white Conservative MPs elected in 2010 in seats gained from Labour: Rehman Chishti (Gillingham & Rainham), a barrister who was a former Labour candidate at Horsham in 2005, and whose inclusion on the A-list caused some comment; Alok Sharma (Reading West), an accountant; and Paul Uppal (Wolverhampton South West), a businessman.

Conscious of the risks of losing its dominance as the parliamentary face of ethnic diversity, Labour provided the first three female Muslim MPs: Rushanara Ali (Bethnal Green & Bow), a political staffer and researcher; Yasmin Qureshi (Bolton South East), a barrister; and Shabana Mahmood (Birmingham Ladywood), also a barrister. In addition to these three new MPs, four others of Labour's eight new BME MPs were also elected for safe seats: Chi Onwurah (Newcastle Central), an electrical engineer; Lisa Nandy (Wigan), a political aide; Anas Sarwar (Glasgow Central), a dentist; and Chuka Umunna (Streatham), a solicitor. Of the newcomers only Valerie Vaz (Walsall South), a solicitor, occupied a marginal seat. Labour had taken care not to apply all-women shortlists in the more densely BME seats where a woman-only list might meet with some Asian resistance to women candidates; indeed two of their three Muslim women MPs came through on open shortlists, as did two other of their new female BME MPs. Thus Labour, having lost five of its 13 BME MPs from the previous parliament (one from retirement, one from death, and three from defeat), more than held its own, even if the remarkable Conservative leap from two to 11 BME MPs, eight of whom in safe seats, served to rival Labour's ownership of the ethnic part of the diversity agenda.

The age profile of the Commons is set out in Table 15.3, with little change in the median age of MPs by party, other than some ageing of Liberal Democrat MPs. The ebbing Labour tide was reflected in the ageing of the PLP, 60% of whom were now over 50, the reverse of the position among Conservative MPs, 60% of whom were under 50. The oldest MP was Sir Peter Tapsell (b. February 1930).[7] Two other Conservatives were over 70: Bill Cash (b. 1937) and Sir Alan Haselhurst (b. 1937). Labour's septuagenarians comprised a larger phalanx of 12.

They were led by Sir Gerald Kaufman (b. 1930), Dennis Skinner (b. 1932), David Winnick (b. 1933), Joe Benton (b. 1933), Austin Mitchell (b. 1934), Paul Flynn (b. 1935), Glenda Jackson (b. 1936), Ann Clwyd (b. 1937), Alan Keen (b. 1937), Sir Stuart Bell (b. 1938), Geoffrey Robinson (b. 1938), and Michael Meacher (b. 1939). That 15 MPs were in their twenties was due less to the influx of new young Conservatives, than to

Labour's selection of very young candidates in safe seats usually reserved for more experienced campaigners. While the youngest Conservative MP was James Wharton (b. February 1984), the youngest overall was Labour's Pamela Nash (b. June 1984).

Table 15.3   Age of candidates

	Conservative		Labour		Liberal Democrat	
	Elected	*Unelected*	*Elected*	*Unelected*	*Elected*	*Unelected*
Age (at 1 Jan 2010)						
Under 20	–	2	–	1	–	2
20–29	4	51	10	64	1	61
30–39	71	113	31	78	12	114
40–49	107	102	63	83	13	138
50–59	94	49	95	111	18	155
60–69	27	8	47	36	13	75
70–79	3	–	12	–	–	3
Unknown	–	–	–	–	–	26
Total	*306*	*325*	*258*	*373*	*57*	*574*
Median age						
2010	47	39	52	45	50	47
2005	48	38	53	40	46	45

For the third Parliament in succession the Member with the longest service was Sir Peter Tapsell, first elected in Harold Macmillan's 'Never Had It So Good' election of 1959, and who with unbroken service from 1966 finally became Father of the House in 2010. The last Labour survivor from the 1960s was David Winnick who sat for Croydon South from 1966 to 1970, and was then returned at Walsall North in 1979. Eight Conservatives from the 1970s were led by the two survivors of Edward Heath's 1970 intake, when Kenneth Clarke and Sir Alan Haselhurst both won marginal seats from Labour. Following them were three MPs elected in 1974: Sir Malcolm Rifkind, Sir John Stanley and Sir George Young, the 1975 by-election entrant Peter Bottomley, and the 1979 survivors Stephen Dorrell and Richard Shepherd. The attitudes of most of this small group had been formed in the pre-Thatcherite One Nation tradition. On the Labour side lingered ten Members from the Wilson–Callaghan years of the 1970s, three from the 1970 election: Kaufman, Skinner, one of Labour's six surviving coal miners, and Michael Meacher, a perennial non-Cabinet minister under Tony Blair. Margaret Beckett, the Commons' longest surviving woman, was first elected in October 1974, Geoffrey Robinson, and Austin Mitchell at by-elections in 1976 and 1977 respectively, and

Frank Dobson, Frank Field, Barry Sheerman and Jack Straw in 1979. The lone Liberal Democrat survivor from this era was Sir Alan Beith, elected in 1973. With under 50 Conservative MPs remaining from the 1980s – the years of the Thatcherite high tide – and with twice as many dating from the less politicised years of the Labour hegemony, it was unclear how the great weight of the inexperienced 2010 new intake would be felt. Nor was it apparent how the majority of Liberal Democrat MPs dating from the period of tacit Lib–Lab electoral pacts with which they secured their seats between 1992 and 2005, would ultimately judge the Coalition government formed in 2010. Of Labour's 183-strong 1997 intake, only 52 (28%) remained, but the bulk of those elected in subsequent elections bore the stamp of the de-ideologised party of government ushered in by Tony Blair in 1997, and comprised half the PLP.

Table 15.4 Parliamentary experience of MPs

First elected	Conservative	Labour	Liberal Democrat
1959–69	1	1	–
1970–79	8	10	1
1980–92	48	53	7
1993–97	25	59	13
1998–2005	73	68	26
2006–10	151	67	10
Total	306	258	57

The family connections of MPs remained modest, but continued to reflect a tradition of political families, sustained mainly by the Conservatives. Of 18 MPs who were the sons, or in two cases the daughter of a former MP, 12 were Conservative, five Labour, and one, a Democratic Unionist. Seven of these were in the new intake: the Conservatives' Ben Gummer (Ipswich), Mark Pawsey (Rugby), Laura Sandys (Thanet South) and Robin Walker (Worcester); the Labour MPs John Cryer (Leyton & Wanstead) and Anas Sarwar (Glasgow Central); and Ian Paisley Jnr (Antrim North), son of the Revd Ian Paisley. Mr Sarwar and Mr Paisley were seamlessly following their fathers into the same seat, in a manner now rare.[8] Mr Sarwar's father had represented his Glasgow seat from 1997 to 2010, whereas Mr Paisley had his father's 40-year occupancy of Antrim North to build on. Mark Pawsey and Robin Walker were taking on their fathers' former seats after a break: Mr Pawsey's father, James, had represented Rugby from 1983 to 1997, and Peter Walker, a Cabinet minister in the Heath and Thatcher years, had sat for Worcester from

1961 to 1992. Of the sons of MPs, the returning John Cryer had the rare distinction of having followed both parents into the Commons; he and his mother, Ann Cryer (Keighley) were both elected in 1997, he being defeated in 2005 and she retiring in 2010. Ben Gummer was arriving just as his father John Gummer was departing, after 31 years as a Suffolk MP, though originally elected in Lewisham in 1970.

Nine MPs were the grandchildren of former MPs, and in three of these cases, the great grandchildren as well. Labour's Hilary Benn, and the Conservative Nicholas Soames had an unbroken thread of parliamentary forebears stretching back to the 1890s in Mr Benn's case, but in Mr Soames' case into the mists of time with his maternal descent from the Spencer-Churchills. Nick Hurd was the fourth consecutive member of the Hurd family to sit in the Commons dating, almost unbroken since his great grandfather, Sir Percy Hurd was first elected in 1918. Echoes of that sort of lineage featured in the family background of the new Conservative MP for Richmond Park, Zac Goldsmith, both of whose grandfathers had been MPs, Frank Goldsmith who had sat from 1924 to 1929, and his maternal grandfather Viscount Castlereagh (1931–45), who became the 8th Marquess of Londonderry. With these links Mr Goldsmith numbered amongst his MP forebears successive generations of the Londonderry (Vane-Tempest-Stewart) dynasty, including the early-nineteenth-century statesman Viscount Castlereagh, and the prominent cabinet minister of the Baldwin years, the 7th Marquess, husband of the leading 1930s socialite, Lady Londonderry.

Laura Sandys, newly elected for Thanet South, was the child of the second marriage of Duncan Sandys (a cabinet minister in the Macmillan years), whose first wife was a daughter of Winston Churchill. She was via her half-sisters, both of whom married Conservative MPs, linked to the Spencer-Churchill dynasty. Two Conservatives had dynastic associations with the Royal Family. The re-elected Ian Liddell-Grainger (Bridgwater & West Somerset) was the great, great, great grandson of Queen Victoria, whilst his leader, David Cameron, apart from descent from three MPs on his mother's side stretching back from his great grandfather, enjoyed a direct line of descent from one of William IV's children by his mistress Dora Jordan.

The family connections of Labour MPs, Hilary Benn apart, were rather less prestigious. The dissolution and election depleted the number of married couples in the House, with the re-elected Ed Balls and Yvette Cooper joined by the re-elected Harriet Harman and her newly arrived husband, Jack Dromey (Birmingham Erdington). The sibling count rose with, in addition to David and Ed Miliband, and Angela and Maria Eagle, the election of Valerie Vaz (Walsall South) who with her re-elected brother Keith Vaz, formed the first brother and sister pair since Gwilym and Megan Lloyd George in the 1945–50 House, and, before that, Victor and Thelma Cazalet in the parliaments elected in 1931 and 1935.

The educational background, specifically the schooling, of MPs implies more about their social origins than data on university education, given that only a relatively small minority of MPs had not become graduates of some sort.

In Table 15.5 the word 'private' has been substituted for 'public' (as used in previous books in this series) in order to make the distinction clearer between state and non-state schooling. In 2010 the increase in the number of Conservative MPs from 198 in 2005 to 306, predictably increased the number who had been to private fee-paying schools, from 118 to 166. However, as a proportion of all Conservative MPs the percentage of the privately educated dropped from 60% to 54%. At the four most recent elections won by the party the percentage of MPs elected at private schools was: 1979 73%, 1983 70%, 1987 68%, 1992 62%. With the drop to 54% in 2010, this perceptible downward trend quickened, with a move toward a party with a balanced composition of state and non-state schooled MPs. Indeed, amongst the new intake of 2010 there was a 50–50 split between state and non-state educated MPs.

Furthermore, within the private school category, the presence of the famous elite schools has waned. The prospect of the first 'Eton and Oxford' Prime Minister since 1963 prompted speculation before the election about 'the return of the Etonians', and yet with 19 Conservative Etonian MPs, compared with 16 elected in 2005, the proportion dropped from 8% to 6% – the lowest on record. Again, the trend had been downwards for some decades: in 1951 the proportion was 24%; in 1959 20%; in 1992 10%. Of the 19 elected in 2010, five were in the new intake: Jacob Rees-Mogg, Jesse Norman, Jo Johnson, Rory Stewart and Kwasi Kwarteng.[9] The Liberal Democrats retained one Etonian MP, John Thurso, actually Viscount Thurso, grandson of the war-time Liberal leader, Sir Archibald Sinclair, for whose constituency, Caithness & Sutherland, he sits. With the retirement of Mark Fisher the Labour Party lost the last of its Etonian MPs, making the 2010 House the first since 1923 in which the ranks of the PLP did not contain an Etonian.[10]

The decline of Eton was partly offset by the new Conservative intake containing three Harrovians, where previously there had been none since the election of 1992. But the broader trend had been away from the great schools in particular and from all private schools in general. A further indicator of greater social diversity was reflected in the proportion of Oxbridge graduates. In comparable years, when the party had won elections with about 330 MPs, the proportion of Oxbridge graduates was 50% in 1979, 45% in 1992, and 34% in 2010, a trend further confirmed by the proportion of the new intake of 2010 who were graduates of either university: 27%.

Table 15.5 Education of candidates

	Conservative		Labour		Liberal Democrat	
	Elected	*Unelected*	*Elected*	*Unelected*	*Elected*	*Unelected*
Secondary school	15	34	27	41	2	47
Secondary + poly/coll	25	26	42	59	4	106
Secondary + univ	100	172	153	209	29	316
Private school	5	1	–	1	1	4
Private sch + poly/coll	16	6	2	2	4	5
Private sch + univ	145	86	34	49	17	81
Unknown	–	–	–	12	–	15
Total	*306*	*325*	*258*	*373*	*57*	*574*
Oxford	72	28	30	21	10	35
Cambridge	32	18	15	17	6	36
Other universities	141	212	142	220	30	326
All universities[a]	*245*	*258*	*187*	*258*	*46*	*397*
	(80%)	*(80%)*	*(73%)*	*(70%)*	*(80%)*	*(70%)*
Eton	19	5	–	–	1	3
Harrow	3	1	–	–	–	–
Winchester	2	2	–	–	–	–
Other private schools	142	85	36	52	21	87
All private schools	*166*	*93*	*36*	*52*	*22*	*90*
	(54%)	*(29%)*	*(14%)*	*(14%)*	*(40%)*	*(16%)*

a Of graduates, the following had attended post-1992 universities: MPs: Conservative 4, Labour 6, Liberal Democrat 0; Unelected candidates: Conservative 26, Labour 24, Liberal Democrat 44.

Labour had never been marked by any significant reliance on private schools or elite universities. In 2010 the 14% of its MPs from private schools was around its usual mark, and its Oxbridge graduates comprising 18%, compared with 16% in 2005, and also 16% in 1992, the last time it had lost an election and had a similar number of seats. The Liberal Democrat MPs' educational profile was closer to the Conservatives', with 40% privately educated and 30% Oxbridge graduates, unchanged from the previous election.

Table 15.6   Occupation of candidates

	Conservative		Labour		Liberal Democrat	
	Elected	Unelected	Elected	Unelected	Elected	Unelected
Professions						
Barrister	27	20	9	10	2	14
Solicitor	29	19	17	44	2	20
Doctor/Dentist/Optician	6	6	2	6	1	12
Architect/Surveyor	6	1	–	1	1	4
Civil/chartered engineer	2	3	4	6	–	16
Accountant	13	17	2	7	2	18
Civil service/local govt	2	9	13	35	3	38
Armed services	15	3	1	1	–	7
Teachers: university	–	4	9	7	4	23
Poly/college	–	1	12	9	–	13
School	4	18	14	29	6	65
Other consultant	3	5	3	6	1	15
Science/research	–	1	3	7	–	4
Total	*107*	*107*	*89*	*168*	*22*	*249*
	(35%)	*(33%)*	*(35%)*	*(45%)*	*(39%)*	*(43%)*
Business						
Company director	50	30	4	5	3	20
Company executive	50	38	4	18	4	37
Commerce/insurance	10	15	1	6	3	35
Managerial/clerical	2	9	5	13	–	18
General business	8	21	6	6	–	33
Management consultant	5	11	–	2	1	4
Total	*125*	*124*	*20*	*50*	*11*	*147*
	(40%)	*(38%)*	*(8%)*	*(13%)*	*(20%)*	*(26%)*
Miscellaneous						
Miscellaneous white collar	2	19	15	22	4	50
Politician/political organiser	31	22	52	44	7	31
Union official	–	–	29	20	–	–
Journalist/publisher	18	21	15	19	5	26
Public relations	11	11	3	9	2	14
Charity/voluntary sector	2	7	13	22	3	21
Farmer	8	4	–	–	2	3
Housewife	–	–	–	–	–	5
Student	–	4	–	–	–	10
Total	*72*	*88*	*127*	*136*	*23*	*160*
	(24%)	*(27%)*	*(49%)*	*(37%)*	*(40%)*	*(28%)*
Manual worker	*2*	*6*	*22*	*16*	*1*	*11*
	(1%)	*(2%)*	*(9%)*	*(4%)*	*(2%)*	*(2%)*
Unknown	–	–	–	3	–	7
Grand total	*306*	*325*	*258*	*373*	*57*	*574*

The occupational composition of the Commons remained much as before, with, in the Conservative case, the broad occupational groupings – professional, business, and the miscellaneous category (which in Table 15.6 is broken down more fully into constituent occupations) – were broadly similar to when the party last formed a government in 1992. Nor was the new intake significantly different occupationally from the rest of the party, apart from a slight drift away from the professions and toward business and finance. In Labour's case the main change was the enlarged proportion of the PLP in the miscellaneous category (up from 43% in 2005), attributable to the large number, at least a fifth of Labour MPs and some two-fifths of the new intake, who came from previous employment as ministerial or Members aides. The rise was largely at the expense of the teaching profession which was barely represented in the new intake.

The growth of the professional politician was apparent in the other parties as well, and coupled with the achievement of diversity in representation of gender and race, and to a comparatively much more limited extent in education, and with the virtual eradication of the manual worker MP, the differences between the public faces of the parties could be said to be eroding.[11] Yet there remained Labour's conspicuously weak presence as reflected in the PLP in the business sector, and the public sector background of most of its MPs. As the 2010 Parliament ran its course, what remained of Labour's distinctive parliamentary face would doubtless be put to the test.

Notes

1. Of the 4,133 candidates, 3,272 were men and 861 (21%) women.
2. House of Commons Library Research Paper 10/36.
3. Apart from the five returning MPs, seven other former Members contested the election: Peter Duncan, for the Conservatives; Andy King, Ivan Henderson and Philip Sawford for Labour, and Parmjit Gill and David Rendel for the Liberal Democrats, all in their former or redrawn constituencies. All lost, as did Dave Nellist, the former expelled left-wing Labour MP who had sat for Coventry South from 1983 to 1992, but had contested a Coventry seat at every election since, this time polling 1,592 votes (3.7%) in Coventry North East.
4. Quoted in Robert McIlveen, 'Ladies of the Right: An Interim Analysis of the A List', *Journal of Elections, Public Opinion and Parties*, 19:2 (May 2009), 147–59.
5. Tim Montgomerie, ConservativeHome website, 8 February 2009.
6. Elizabeth Evans, 'Supply or Demand? Women Candidates and the Liberal Democrats', *British Journal of Politics and International Relations*, 10 (2008), 590–606.
7. His age is represented in Table 15.3 as at January 2010.

8. Only the retiring Labour MP Hilary Armstrong in Durham North West had enjoyed a similar transmission of her seat from her father in 1987, and, further back, Labour's Greville Janner, who inherited his seat in Leicester from his father in 1970, and established a continuous occupation of the seat spanning 52 years between 1945 and 1997.

9. Of the 16 Etonians elected in 2005 Douglas Hogg retired and David Heathcoat-Amory was defeated.

10. The ten Etonian Labour MPs were: William Pethwick-Lawrence 1923–31 and 1935–45, Hugh Dalton 1924–31 and 1935–59, John Oldfield 1929–31, Oliver Baldwin 1929–31 and 1945–47, John Strachey 1929–31 and 1945–63, Dick Mitchison 1945–64, Reginald Paget 1945–74, Tam Dalyell 1962–2005, Ben Whittaker 1966–70 and Mark Fisher 1983–2010. Five of them sat contemporaneously in the 1945 Parliament.

11. Of the 25 former manual workers, seven were coal miners, including the Conservative Chief Whip Patrick McLoughlin.

16
A Landmark Election: The Campaign in Retrospect

The election outcome ensured that 2010 would have a significant place in the history books. A remarkable election confirming the importance of multi-party politics, it paved the way for the formation of the first peace-time coalition government for more than 70 years and the first formed afresh after a general election since the mid-nineteenth century – when Disraeli famously warned that 'England does not love coalitions'. The campaign itself was also notable, not just for the introduction of the televised leaders' debates, but also for the context. The nation's financial deficit and the scandals associated with the abuses of expenses in the outgoing parliament provided a gloomy backdrop. Whichever party won the election would have to introduce unpopular measures – so unpopular that the Governor of the Bank of England was quoted as saying that the winner would subsequently be out of office for a generation.

The parties acknowledged at the outset of the campaign that the TV debates would dominate, although few anticipated how far-reaching, even disruptive, the changes would be or the extent to which the success of Nick Clegg and the presidentialising effect would lead to genuine three-party politics in the reporting. Traditional campaign routines like the well-planned campaign grid, early morning press conferences to launch initiatives and issue challenges to the other parties, lengthy set-piece broadcast interviews and the party election broadcasts were all marginalised. The 24/7 media and the focus on the party leaders and the debates made it exhausting for the leaders and their entourages. Running throughout the campaign was speculation about the possible effects of the much-bruited anti-politics popular mood, the widespread sense of time for change from Labour, lingering distrust of the Conservatives and, towards the end, growing interest about how the parties would react to a likely hung parliament. Uncertainty about which party would win, high sales of party manifestos, and the public interest in the TV debates led many to expect a high turnout on polling day. The final ComRes poll reported that 'a whopping 71% are absolutely certain to vote'. In the event the figure was 65.1%, a modest rise of 4% on 2005.[1] The public were said to have found it an interesting election – or at least not a boring one – but they hardly flocked back to the polls.

The TV debates dominated coverage of the campaign, as reported in Chapters 13 and 14. They transformed the nature of the campaign and also elevated Nick Clegg (and his party) to such an extent that he had become a credible figure as Deputy Prime Minister when the coalition government was formed. An aide who accompanied Clegg throughout the campaign was reminded of the movies: 'We were like that mousy girl who goes to the proms in films, takes off her glasses, and shakes her hair, and suddenly everyone realises how beautiful she is.'

One merit of the debates was that they brought the leaders face-to-face in front of the public. They hammered away with their favoured lines, usually blunt warnings of what lay ahead if the other side was elected – 'Labour's tax on jobs', 'let's get real', 'the need for tough choices', 'be honest', 'the two old parties', 'the Tory tax cut for the richest 3,000 estates', 'fairness', 'change', and don't risk a Conservative government which 'would set back the economic recovery' or 'another five years of Gordon Brown'. But how far did they help to clarify policy choices? Researchers in the parties had prepared detailed policy guides and briefings for press conferences but because so few were held they were not used. A Labour press conference on the economy, attended by many senior economic commentators, elicited only 'what if' questions about hung parliaments.

Still, complaining about the downside of the debates may well be pointless – they appear to be here to stay – and it is hardly as if what they replaced was a feast of democratic intellectual engagement. At the end of the first week of the campaign, before the first debate had been held, a Populus poll for *The Times* revealed that voters were decidedly foggy about what divided the parties. Voters attributed four out of eight key policy pledges to the wrong party. Even National Insurance, the subject of a week of intense claim and counter-claim, was wrongly classified: a majority of voters thought that cutting National Insurance was a Labour policy. It was a salutary reminder that most campaigning goes over voters' heads.

In an implied admission that the media attention on the debates – preparations, build-up and post-debate analysis – squeezed the amount of discussion of policies a senior Conservative admitted: 'We were quite happy with the coverage, thank you very much. Without the coverage of the debates and the process we'd have had days of Labour exploiting the voters' fears of us.' George Osborne thought the media interest on process protected his party 'from weeks of heavy Labour pounding over issues like tax credits'. Labour strategists, aware of this, were frustrated. Osborne had been stung by the success of Labour tactics in the 2001 and 2005 elections when they had exploited voters' fears of Conservative 'cuts'. This time, 'we killed off Brown's tax and spend line', he said.

All parties struggled to come to terms with the unfamiliar campaign terrain represented by the debates, the need to treat the Liberal Democrats as a major party, the economic crisis and the curtailment of expenditure 'offers' to attract support. Labour was fighting the election at a particular disadvantage: trying for a fourth successive term of office, burdened by a 13-year accumulation of voters' complaints and resentments; the worst economic recession since the 1930s which had ruined the party's reputation for economic competence; an unpopular Prime Minister; support only from the *Daily Mirror* among the ten main daily papers and only the *Sunday Mirror* of nine Sunday papers. There was also a massive imbalance in campaign resources, with the Conservatives spending roughly four times as much as Labour during the campaign and perhaps even more in the months before. Labour's staffing levels at the campaign centre were down by two-thirds from 2005; it did very little polling, cut back on its direct mail before the campaign and ran only one poster during it. And yet thanks to the efforts of some established MPs and their activists and the voters' loyalty to the party, Labour still managed to hold 258 seats. Appendix 2 reports in detail on the high degree of variance in performances across seats, particularly for Labour. It also reports how incumbency helped all the three national parties, particularly where the candidate had been first elected in 2005. An effect of 2010 may be to incentivise incumbents in marginal seats to go it alone, further weakening party HQ.

Once again the general election could hardly be called an internet one and Britain still lagged well behind the United States in the use of the new technology. Expectations had been raised because of the success of the Obama internet campaign in fund-raising in 2008. But this dampener needs to be qualified. Large numbers 'meshed', watching television while online, and there were many online reactions to the debates and election broadcasts. Most candidates now have a web presence. William Hague's online appeal raised over £100,000. The use of blogging, social networking sites, tweets and independent campaigns such as Rage Against the Election have made it difficult for parties and the traditional print media to exercise the control over political messages they once did, and are sure to become more important in future elections. By contrast, press advertising was markedly reduced and party election broadcasts continued to decline in significance.

The campaign mattered. If Labour's share of the vote hardly differed between the beginning and the end of the campaign, the Lib Dems ended 3–4% higher and the Conservatives 2–3% lower. The slight drop in Conservative support was probably the margin between being the largest party in a hung parliament and having a (slim) majority of its own. That there was no winner may have been the voters' choice, even if they could not vote for such an outcome; polls suggested that many did not mind the prospect and, later, the outcome.

All parties advocated change in general and political reform in particular. For the first time in nearly a century the political system was an issue although there was broad agreement about many reforms. Direct election of members of the House of Lords, reform of the electoral system, fixed-term parliaments, recall of errant MPs, and a reduction in the number of MPs were all up for consideration. Some of the interest was a reaction to the anti-politics mood triggered by the recent expenses scandal, some a consequence of the likelihood of a hung parliament and some an anticipation of the Liberal Democrats gaining perhaps nearly a third of the vote but few seats. Party strategists and the commentators considered the lessons which might be learnt from the coalitions in the Scottish and Welsh legislatures, local government and some European countries, while the Conservatives warned of the potential shortcomings of a hung parliament. But focus groups reported that media discussion about different electoral systems, hung parliaments and coalitions passed over the heads of voters. More cynical observers noted that electoral reform at Westminster had been promised in Labour manifestos in 1997, 2001 and 2005, and not followed up.

Because the party leaders dominated the media, as a consequence of the debates and decline of press conferences, only a handful of significant frontbenchers received attention. Labour had talked of presenting 'the team' but it was hardly evident. George Osborne, concentrating on his campaign-coordinating duties, was far from prominent and Michael Gove and William Hague took up some of the slack. Some research suggested that when Osborne and Cameron were seen together it increased voters' fears about the youth, inexperience and poshness of the top Tory leadership. Vince Cable was a casualty of the increased media interest in his leader; before the first TV debate Clegg had rarely been seen on television without Cable at his side.

Women were notable by their absence from the front line of the campaign. Harriet Harman complained to Peter Mandelson about Labour's male-dominated campaign, although Labour strategists reflected that the party lacked high-profile women, and that Harman's complaints were not entirely altruistic. 'More time for women means more time for Harriet,' reflected one cynical witness of the exchange. But the wives of the leaders attracted extensive media attention and a number of newspapers analysed their clothing. The coverage prompted some commentators to wonder whether the political leader's spouse is now a campaign fixture.

Labour's campaign was based on the fear of 'Tory cuts' and an appeal to some strong Labour values. The Conservatives called for a change of direction and for the removal of Gordon Brown. The Lib Dems dismissed the other two parties as 'failed' and asked people to vote for real change. Yet all parties were left with if onlys. Could Labour under a different leader have overcome the prevailing mood of time for change and held the extra seats required to form a majority coalition with the Lib Dems? What more could the Conservatives have done to remove the voters' lingering distrust of their past and gain the extra seats to give them a majority? And how could the Liberal Democrats have better capitalised on the rise in support generated by the leaders' debates?

Clegg's rise prompted hitherto-muted Conservative criticisms of David Cameron for having allowed him equal billing in the debates in the first place. Cameron's claim to be the candidate of 'change' had abruptly been appropriated by a new figure, as Clegg rode the anti-politics mood. 'The Conservatives have spent £10 million on a branding exercise and it has gone up in smoke in less than an hour,' commented a Labour strategist. Observers of Cameron's debate preparation had been so impressed by Jeremy Hunt acting the part of Clegg that one said 'We should have realised the danger at once.' Yet in the wake of the expenses scandal this complaint fails to take account of the need for greater political transparency and accountability and voter engagement. Cameron and most of his aides were unapologetic about the arrangement, believing the innovation a good thing in itself. They also calculated that the focus on Cameron would help them answer voters' doubts about the party.

The Conservatives had seen their handsome poll lead whittled away since the turn of the year. Cautious members of the Cameron team had long warned of the mountain the party had to climb and the need for so many factors to work in its favour: a 6.9% swing, the party's biggest since 1945, and the Lib Dems to underperform in the Con–Lib Dem marginals. After polling day the party could point to some campaign successes. The attacks on Labour's 'jobs tax' in the first week mobilised heavyweight business support and gave it the initiative. The TV debates limited Labour's opportunities to focus on potential tax increases and spending cuts under a Cameron government. The party successfully integrated its polling in the battleground seats with its direct mail to answer Labour charges it planned cuts to services affecting key groups of voters. It achieved a swing against Labour of 5.1%, the third highest since 1945, gained 97 seats, its largest number since 1931, and ended its longest period in opposition since the eighteenth century.

But few considered it a good campaign, considering the resources at the party's disposal and its many advantages over Labour. Tim Montgomerie, founder of the ConservativeHome website, spoke for many when he complained of 'an inadequate campaign', 'a woeful campaign', one that had missed the open goal presented by Labour's huge election handicaps. Nearly two-thirds of Montgomerie's sample of party members judged the campaign 'poor'. The party had enjoyed double-digit leads over Labour during 2009; faced a tired government led by an unpopular Prime Minister; the recession had left voters feeling unhappy and Labour had shed its reputation for economic competence. Why then did the Conservatives fail to achieve a clear majority? Four major factors held back the party, of which not all were under the party's control once the campaign began.

The first was the residual public distrust of the Conservative brand. The effectiveness of Labour leaflets warning that the Conservatives would take away tax credits and other benefits may have reflected the incomplete progress Cameron had made over the previous four years in rebranding his party. Crucially, the point was made in a party post-election survey of voters in battleground seats who had thought of voting Conservative. The most mentioned reasons such voters gave for not turning to the party covered fears that it was still for the rich and not for ordinary people as well as concerns about spending cuts or removing benefits such as tax credits or free bus passes for the elderly, fears summarised in the phrase 'the same old Tories'. Public surveys showed that voters were still less willing to support policies once they knew they were Conservative policies, and whilst some three-quarters of voters agreed it was time for a change from Labour less than 40% agreed it was time for a change to the Conservatives. Focus groups for both Labour and the Conservatives found a general uncertainty or lack of optimism about what a future Conservative government would be like. Cameron's campaign team spent much time debating what to do about this problem and never resolved whether they should talk more about themselves or more about Labour.

In analysing the results Conservative strategists noted that they had made few inroads in Labour seats which contained a large ethnic minority vote and/or a large public-sector workforce or many on welfare benefits (what some Cameroons called 'Labour's client state'). Scotland continued to be a no go country for Conservatives where it was fourth in share of the vote and had only one seat. Twenty years after the downfall of Mrs Thatcher it remained unScottish to vote Conservative. These weaknesses go back for a generation at least. Cameron had tried to make up ground by promising to reduce the number of public service targets and to trust the professional judgement of people working in the public service, as well as by selecting from a more diverse range of candidates, including more from ethnic minorities. He had limited success.

Second, there was a lack of a consistent political message, apart from linking Gordon Brown's name to the themes of waste, the financial deficit, poor public services, and over-centralisation, climaxing with the threat of 'five more years' of Gordon Brown. But elsewhere there was switching between tackling the deficit and promoting the Big Society. Cameron's six-point message for the spring conference bore little resemblance to his final days' 'Contract' message to voters which suddenly referred to immigration, crime and reforming the welfare state, not mentioned in the spring message. The idea of the Big Society was a particular bugbear for some activists and candidates who found the theme and the concept difficult to communicate on the doorstep. Steve Hilton, the brains behind the idea, was reported as thinking that the idea of testing the concept 'preposterous' because it was never designed to be a doorstep message. He regarded it as the heart of modern Conservatism: 'It was not a campaign strategy, not a leaflet, not a slogan,' he told friends.

A different claim is that the party was fighting the wrong campaign. Some activists, along with some Conservative-supporting newspapers, wanted more emphasis on immigration, Europe and tax cuts, the agenda on which the party had lost so decisively in 2001 and 2005 and which would have subverted Cameron's modernising project. Table 16.1 suggests that this agenda was unlikely to have been a vote-winner. It shows that when voters were asked about the most important issues facing the country the economy was top by a wide margin followed by immigration/ asylum and crime. But it also shows that when asked about the issues most important for them and their family the top four issues all related to the economy with crime and immigration/asylum well down the list. Cameron discussed his plans for curbing immigration in all three debates;

in target seats three pieces of direct mail were addressed to households where voters had raised concerns about immigration; and the party's final campaign newsletter covered it as one of the three key issues of the campaign, along with the NHS and the economy. Given the large lead the Conservatives already enjoyed on the issue of immigration one wonders what further benefit would have been gained by talking about it more, and it may merely have weakened the party's standing among the liberal-minded people Cameron had been trying to court.

Table 16.1   Most important issues facing...

The Country	
The economy/credit crunch/jobs/unemployment	70%
Immigration/asylum	49%
Crime/law and order/police	42%
Health/NHS/hospitals	36%
You and Your Family	
Prices/inflation/cost of living	60%
The economy/credit crunch/jobs/unemployment	58%
Pensions/social security/poverty in Britain	35%
Immigration/asylum	20%

Source: YouGov.

A YouGov poll conducted after the election found that only 12% of Conservative supporters felt that Cameron's drive for modernisation had abandoned traditional Tory policies on taxation, immigration and crime whereas 68% thought he had struck the right balance between modernising and sticking to traditional Conservatism. Reflecting on the campaign, one of Cameron's closest supporters noted that when he looked at where the party had failed to make headway – in Scotland, with ethnic minority voters, and with public sector workers – he struggled to see how the way to achieve greater success with these groups was to shift to the right.

And looking ahead, such a campaign would not have helped Cameron in his efforts to court Liberal Democrats after polling day or Clegg to persuade his party to join forces with the Conservatives. That the Conservatives were able to agree the terms of a coalition with the Liberal Democrats was a mark of Cameron's progress in changing his party, at elite level at least, even if it had not delivered a majority of seats on polling day.

Third, the party had hoped for more success in its battleground seats. If some results were spectacular, other well-funded local campaigns failed to deliver and there was particular disappointment in the Pennines seats. The party captured the 154th most marginal seat but failed in the 39th most marginal. It won 25 seats on an above 5% swing but failed to win nine with a less than 5% swing. Some of the battleground gains are down to the extra resources poured into the seats and they strengthened Cameron's hand in the days after polling day. Had there been a uniform national swing, the Conservatives would have fallen to 291 seats, Labour increased to 264 and the Lib Dems would have had 64. Cameron would have missed even a second best 300+ seat target and Labour would have had sufficient seats to form a majority in coalition with the Lib Dems. But it is still striking how such a huge investment in the key seats produced a relatively modest return. Lord Ashcroft who had invested heavily – in both time and money – in the programme felt that his 'ground war' had been subverted by the 'air war', because of the media focus on the leaders' debates and the boost it provided to the Lib Dems.

Finally, political geography still works against the Conservatives or, alternatively, helps Labour. Labour's 35.2% share of the vote and 2.8% lead in votes over the Conservatives gave it a handsome majority of seats in 2005. But in 2010 the Conservatives' 37% vote share and 7% lead over Labour left it well short of a majority. To gain a 20-seat majority Labour now needs only a 4% lead in votes over the Conservatives but the latter need a 13% lead over Labour to achieve the same majority. The bias is partly an effect of the continuing over-representation of Scotland and Wales (de facto in the former, de jure in the latter), partly because Conservatives 'waste' votes in safe seats, and partly because of out-of-date Boundary Commission recommendations (see Appendix 2).

Some of the other criticisms of the campaign mentioned by Montgomerie and the Tory activists were more accurate. The management problems identified in the near term campaign were not corrected. Some at the centre continued to talk of three silos, represented by the separate interests of Osborne (the economy), Hilton (the big picture) and Coulson (the news cycle), and complained of the lack of clear campaign direction, as used to be exercised by strong party chairmen or by Lynton Crosby in 2005. 'We do have a flat management structure, I suppose,' said one key actor wryly. As noted on page 132, such was Cameron's preference, but it did not lead to a well-focused campaign.

But activists' criticism of the campaign focus on Cameron was hardly fair. Party leaders have become increasingly dominant as the carrier of their party's election message which was even truer once Britain introduced the TV debates. An Ipsos-MORI poll found that for the first time voters mentioned leaders as frequently as policies as having the most influence on their vote. Several surveys showed that Cameron was more popular than his party and his senior colleagues. ICM surveys reported that voters rated Brown and Clegg ahead of Cameron for honesty and 'substance not spin' but on the key questions of being the most competent Prime Minister and moving Britain in the right direction he was a clear leader (see Table 16.2).

Table 16.2   Leaders' ratings (%)

	14 March 2010	6 May 2010
Who is likely to prove the most competent PM?		
Cameron	42	38
Brown	28	26
Clegg	8	19
Who is likely to move Britain in the right direction?		
Cameron	39	35
Brown	28	25
Clegg	10	24

Source: ICM.

Labour campaigners had mixed views about the campaign. Paradoxically, there was less ill-will in defeat towards the leadership than there had been after the Blair victory in 2005. Despite having suffered a net loss of 90 seats and nearly a million votes from 2005 there was some immediate relief and satisfaction that the party had ended up with 258 seats. At one point, particularly after Brown's encounter with Mrs Duffy, some campaign staff feared a meltdown to 220 or even 200 seats and being overtaken in vote share by the Lib Dems. That would have been an inglorious conclusion to the careers of Brown, Mandelson, Campbell, Gould et al., all associated with so many past election victories. Instead, the party was still negotiating for a continued spell in power four days after polling day. Douglas Alexander took pride in the success of the party's ground war which produced 'a 1983 vote share but a 1992 seat share'. The party's essentially (although undeclared) defensive strategy of concentrating the limited resources on Labour's less vulnerable seats – to deny the Conservatives a clear majority – was vindicated.

Philip Gould agreed: 'In many ways, of all the campaigns, this one gave me the most satisfaction, because it was the hardest and despite our lack of resources, advertising, funds or much polling, and fighting at a massive strategic disadvantage we stopped our opponents getting an overall majority and stopped our share of votes and seats falling to irretrievable levels.' And some Labour values, particularly the belief in active government, still resonated with voters. A post-election Greenberg poll found that 71% agreed it was 'time for government to be more involved' versus 22% agreeing it was 'time to depend more on the market'. By a 2 to 1 majority voters favoured government investment in new industries and sectors rather than a system of less regulation and more free enterprise.

The view of many Labour figures was: 'It could have been worse.' But it was a sign of just how bad it could have been that the eventual result in 2010 was in any way considered a success. The election returns made grim reading for Labour. Its 29.7% share of the vote was the lowest since the 1983 disaster and its second worst since 1918 when it first fought elections as a national party. For the first time in its history the party had lost vote share in three successive general elections. It might be consoled that some of its core vote remained loyal, particularly in inner-London, the north of England and Scotland. But an Ipsos-MORI post-election survey (Table 16.3) shows a substantial Lab to Con swing among the C2DE voters. Appendix 2 shows that Labour support fell disproportionately in working class seats which had suffered above average rises in unemployment (with Merseyside and Scotland being the exceptions). Labour also lost ground heavily among men in the 25–34 age group and in much of so-called middle England. In the new parliament over a quarter of Labour MPs were drawn from Scotland and Wales. Many of the seats, particularly in the South East, that New Labour had gained in 1997 and held in 2001 and 2005, had been lost.

A YouGov survey showed a disconnection between Labour members' analysis of the party's campaign and that of the public. Members thought the main reasons for the party's defeat was its subservience to the United States on foreign policy, that it was out of touch with ordinary voters and that it did not do enough for its working class supporters. But the public lived on a different planet. They mentioned immigration, the recession and Gordon Brown.

Some Labour campaigners were dismayed by the repeated messages from focus groups that many former supporters no longer saw the party as being on the side of ordinary people who said they felt threatened by immigration (for them often not a question of race but of fairness) and resented shirkers receiving welfare benefits, rather than the hard-working families who played by the rules. Many of the complaints echoed those in Giles Radice's influential 1992 pamphlet *Southern Discomfort*, a text that inspired New Labour's attempt to recapture the support of the aspirational working class. Table 16.4 shows that many voters regarded

Table 16.3   How Britain voted in 2010

	Con %	Lab %	LD %	Oth %	Con lead over Lab ±%	Turnout %	Con ±%	Lab ±%	LD ±%	Turnout ±%	Lab–Con swing %
	Voting						*Change since 2005*				
All	37	30	24	10	7	65%	+4	–6	+1	+4	5.0
Gender:											
Male	38	28	22	12	10	66%	+4	–6	0	+4	5.0
Female	36	31	26	8	4	64%	+4	–7	+3	+3	5.5
Age:											
18–24	30	31	30	9	–2	44%	+2	–7	+4	+7	4.5
25–34	35	30	29	7	4	55%	+10	–8	+2	+6	9.0
35–44	34	31	26	9	4	66%	+7	–10	+3	+5	8.5
45–54	34	28	26	12	6	69%	+3	–7	+1	+4	5.0
55–64	38	28	23	12	10	73%	–1	–3	+1	+2	1.0
65+	44	31	16	9	13	76%	+3	–4	–2	+1	3.5
Social class:											
AB	39	26	29	7	13	76%	+2	–2	0	+5	2.0
C1	39	28	24	9	11	66%	+2	–4	+1	+4	3.0
C2	37	29	22	12	8	58%	+4	–11	+3	0	7.5
DE	31	40	17	12	–10	57%	+6	–8	–1	+3	7.0
Housing tenure:											
Owned	45	24	21	11	21	74%	+1	–5	+1	+3	3.0
Mortgage	36	29	26	9	7	66%	+5	–7	+1	+6	6.0
Social renter	24	47	19	11	–23	55%	+8	–8	0	+4	8.0
Private renter	35	29	27	9	6	55%	+8	–7	–1	+4	7.5

Source: Ipsos-MORI.

Labour as being on the side of immigrants and non-white Britons rather than 'ordinary working people', a perception that was driving Labour voters away from the party. And where 59% of the public thought that much of the extra money Labour spent on public services was wasted, only 12% of Labour members agreed. In *The Scotsman* (8 May), Tony Blair's former political secretary John McTernan referred to 'the dark heart of this election, the issue that everyone was talking about – except the politicians – immigration'. It was a theme that came through repeatedly in Labour focus groups.

Immediately after the election some former ministers, now leadership candidates, complained of how they had worried that the party in government had failed to 'connect' with the much-lauded 'hard-working families', was seen as soft on immigration and ordinary voters felt betrayed by an out-of-touch liberal elite. Brown privately regretted that the government had not been more robust in curbing immigration but those around him would caustically note that the ministers in question had never once raised the subject.

Table 16.4   Perceptions of the parties

Which two or three of these groups do you think Labour most wants to help? (Tick up to three) (%)	
Immigrants and non-white Britons	44
Single parent families	35
Ordinary working people	24
The rich	21
The poor	21
Traditional families (married couples with children)	20
Which two or three of these groups do you think the Conservatives most want to help? (Tick up to three) (%)	
Traditional families (married couples with children)	54
The rich	45
Ordinary working people	29
Immigrants and non-white Britons	8

Source: YouGov.

Labour's campaign, even allowing for the lack of resources, itself left many dissatisfied. The internal divisions between the campaigners were never resolved. 'We had no compelling message or narrative apart from warning about the same old Tories,' said one, 'We've got a slogan, but not a message, apart from "Don't Trust the Tories",' said another. One of its authors complained about the neglect of the manifesto and how it was not integrated into the rest of the campaign. Peter Mandelson had long been uneasy about the credibility of the party's message on the economy (see pp. 64–5) and after the election reflected, 'Our line on spending cuts was simply not convincing to people. It made it more not less difficult to attack the Tory position.' Brown rarely led the news bulletins, except for his embarrassing exchange with Mrs Duffy. Conservatives, struck by how negative Labour's campaign was, acknowledged the effectiveness of claims that 'Tory cuts' would threaten pensioners' winter fuel allowance and pension credit, tax credits and the right to see a cancer specialist promptly, all disseminated in Labour's final election broadcast and in direct mail. Brown and those around him remained convinced that they needed a standard of living argument, and that ruling out a VAT increase would have made a difference. It would not, however, have helped with the credibility issue.

At times Labour's campaign seemed improvised, with Brown's activities arranged late in the day and the campaign grid followed only fitfully. In part this was a legacy of the lack of clarity about roles and arrangement until late in the day. Brown and the team touring with him grew increasingly frustrated with the last-minute decisions. An experienced campaigner in Victoria Street said, 'This was the least organised, least resourced campaign I have been in' and a key figure in the party's communications strategy reflected 'We never had a clear narrative, we were too reactive.' One of the party's most experienced and senior strategists commented: 'The 1997 campaign was a Rolls Royce operation; 1987 was a Ford Cortina; 2010 was somewhere between a Vauxhall Astra and a Robin Reliant – modest, cheap to run but when driven carefully, holds the road.' Mandelson's considered view was, 'if you lack a shared vision of what you are fighting on, then your message will be weak and the campaign will have less impact'.

Gordon Brown's defenders – and indeed, even some of his critics – will argue that history will judge him more positively than the electorate did in 2010. It will forget the peripheral and trivial, and focus on the fact that – when it came to high-stakes and vital decisions – he showed leadership, vision, and judgement. The decisions to save the banks, they claim, will be remembered when Mrs Duffy has been long forgotten.

But as a campaigner he was wooden, 'the cork in the bottle' one adviser sighed and 'a drag on our ratings' said another. Steve Richards in the *Independent* on 22 April compared him to 'King Lear wandering from place to place with his entourage', and the accompanying media were pretty dismissive of his early forays into the constituencies. Ironically, Brown and his team shared the media dissatisfaction with his 'safe' encounters with party supporters in the first part of the campaign and wanted to break out of it. Brown suffered in comparison with his two younger and more change-oriented rivals. Private polls revealed that when his name was attached to propositions support fell compared with those that referred to just 'Labour'. Candidates made little use of his name on the doorstep or in local literature but he showed great resilience after his embarrassment in Rochdale when his mood, according to aides, was 'dark'. In the last few days he found his voice at the CitizensUK, Bradford, and Manchester events, hammering home his strongest message – the protection of front-line services and warning about Conservative threats to tax credits.

In Victoria Street Brown's closest aides had appealed for him to display more energy, drive and passion. The feedback from the surveys and the voters had been disheartening, saying how tired, downbeat and old he looked. Philip Gould, impressed by voters' uncertainty and the likelihood of a hung parliament, thought that Labour could still become the biggest party if it finished strongly. Having successfully called in the last week for the slogan 'A Future Fair For All' to be rebranded as 'Fighting For Your Future', his final focus report concluded that recovery required Brown to overcome his 'core weakness, his lack of energy and tiredness. What he must be doing at all times is linking passion, fight and substance.' It echoed advice given to Brown by one adviser before the campaign started, that his best chance of victory was, paradoxically, to assume defeat. He had to relax 'and face the prospect of life after government with equanimity. Then he is more likely to come across to the public as Doctor Gordon – the authentic, decent, fallible but determined standard-bearer of progressive values.' The advice was prophetic.

Leadership was clearly a problem for Labour. But the bigger problems – being in office for 13 years, the economic recession, and the lack of a credible message for the future – went beyond the Prime Minister.

The Liberal Democrats entered the campaign expecting a rise in support, largely because they would receive more generous broadcasting coverage, doubly so because of the television debates. Of the three party leaders Clegg put most effort into preparing for those debates. The party won the support of three quality national newspapers, although this did not compensate for the attacks from the centre-right newspapers. Even party optimists never expected to reach 30% of the polls – the veteran chair of the campaign committee, John Sharkey, confessed to being 'shocked'. But once the surge began, the other parties and a hostile press subjected the party's policies to intense scrutiny, particularly the proposed amnesty for illegal immigrants and policies on Europe.

The Lib Dems struggled to withstand the pressure that followed being treated as a serious contender for power. As one member of their campaign team remarked, there are two tests of a manifesto. 'Does it fall apart under pressure, is it properly costed? And it passed that test. The second test is: is it popular? Nick put forward a well-thought-through case for an alternative approach to immigration. But it wasn't popular, as we learnt to our cost.' Or as another key member of the Lib Dem team remarked, more bluntly: 'This is a party that spends five years writing 35 policy papers, and nine months writing a manifesto, and it manages to come up with just one policy which wins votes, two policies which lose votes, and 7,000 policies that no one gives a flying fuck about.'

In the last days of the campaign the Lib Dems were squeezed as the other parties warned that a vote for it would produce not a Lib Dem government but either a Gordon Brown or a Conservative government. Clegg may also have suffered by talking late in the campaign about process issues, about what he would do if he held the balance of power and the conditions that he would seek. Opinion polls warned that Lib Dem support was soft and the increased support occurred largely among young and undecided voters, traditionally the groups least likely to turn out and vote. An indicator of potential fragility was that YouGov detected a rise in approval for Lib Dem policies after the first debate, then a decline, before a slight fall in voting support. Despite the evidence that the party was being squeezed, the exit poll and results on polling day still came as a surprise.

Compared with 2005 the party had lost five seats and increased its vote share by only 1%. Its 'Northern Strategy' failed almost entirely. Yet a post-election poll by Stan Greenberg found that 30% of voters had 'very seriously' or 'somewhat seriously' thought of voting Lib Dem but did not, compared with 21% who considered voting Conservative but did not and 19% who considered Labour but did not. Despite falling short of their expectations the party now figured as a serious force in government for the first time in nearly a century, and it would fight the next election as a party of government.

The election also confirmed the long-term decline in support for the two large parties and the increasing importance of the other parties (see Appendix 2). But the success of the 'other' parties in the European elections and the devolved parliaments was again not replicated in the general election. Whilst the first Green MP was elected, there was no seat for UKIP or BNP, Respect lost its single MP, and the two independents were ousted. Both UKIP and the BNP boosted their votes, partly because they ran many more candidates than in 2005. The BNP total vote was double that of the Green Party's, more than the SNP's and the combined total of the two parties was nearly 1.5 million, or 2% of the total. In Appendix 2, John Curtice, Stephen Fisher and Robert Ford show that the interventions of UKIP, the BNP and the Greens reduced support for the Conservatives, Labour and the Lib Dems, respectively. Among the 'other' parties the BNP was helped by the recession, the decline of Respect helped Labour to recover support among Muslims, and a modest rise in SNP support enabled it to regain second place in vote share in Scotland from the Lib Dems.

For all the words written and spoken, several topics received little attention, including localism (despite the Big Society), further devolution for Scotland and Wales, Britain's relations with the European Union and its military presence in Afghanistan and Iraq. Indeed an outsider might have been struck by the parochialism of Britain in 2010. Above all, to what extent had the campaign prepared the voters for the substantial cuts in spending or tax rises which were sure to follow? On 6 May a *Times* editorial stated that the election was the most important for a generation, and added 'as an exercise in democracy this election has already risen to the occasion'. Yet two days earlier in the same paper Rachel Silvester had complained of 'a lack of honesty about the scale of public spending cuts that will be required whoever wins power'. Did the parties rise to the challenge of the economic crisis?

Surveys showed that many voters thought the cuts could largely be magicked away by efficiency savings without any harm to front-line services. Analysis from the Institute for Fiscal Studies mid-way through the campaign reported that the Lib Dem plans for tax increases and spending cuts had identified only a quarter of the savings necessary over the next five years, the Conservatives only a fifth and Labour only an eighth. The parties were specific about their spending increases but shared a 'striking reticence', according to the IFS, about specific cuts in spending programmes or tax increases. Brown resisted references to

" ...WE WOULD SAIL UP THE AVENUE, BUT WE HAVEN'T GOT A YACHT
WE WOULD DRIVE UP THE AVENUE, BUT THE HORSE WE HAD WAS SHOT
WE WOULD RIDE IN A TROLLEY CAR, BUT WE HAVEN'T GOT THE FARE
SO WE'LL WALK UP THE AVENUE ..."

("WE'RE A COUPLE OF SWELLS"–EASTER PARADE)

'...We would sail up the avenue'

Garland, *Daily Telegraph*, 6 January 2010
(© Telegraph Media Group Ltd 2010)

spending or programme cuts in the manifesto, and the Conservatives were diffident about announcing planned cuts. The TV debates failed to shed light, and (as reported on p. 248) any leader mentioning cuts during the debate saw their ratings drop. Politicians could hardly be blamed for not rushing forward with detail about spending cuts. A Cameroon later admitted, 'I guess there was a sort of mutual pact between the parties about not being too upfront about future pain; everyone wanted to avoid debate about what was to come.'

As Appendix 2 makes clear, the hung parliament did not occur by chance. Whilst the individual aspects of the 2010 election are important, it also needs to be seen in the broader context of political change in Britain, especially the fragmenting of the party system, decade-on-decade. A hung parliament was increasingly likely as a result of changes to the electoral geography and the increasing inability of the two main parties to maintain voters' affections and loyalty. To focus on the detail of the Lib Dems' performance – and the fact that they failed (yet again) to break through – is to ignore the fact that (yet again) they formed a sizeable bloc in the Commons, on a par with that seen in the 1920s.

The election results and formation of the coalition brings Westminster into line with what is happening in other parts of the UK. There are five parties in the Northern Ireland Executive, Plaid and Labour are in coalition in Wales; the SNP has formed a minority government in Scotland, and the Conservatives and Liberal Democrats are in coalition at Westminster. As of late 2010, therefore, ten parties exercised national-level power and none of the four arrangements has one party majority government, for so long seen as an essential feature of the British model of party government.

The 2010 election has left many established features of British politics in a state of flux. For much the post-war period the prospect of an accommodation between Labour and the Lib Dems (or its predecessors) has been a fixture in political debate. A realignment of the centre-left goes back to before 1914 and was an original objective (along with electoral reform) of Blair's New Labour project, only dashed by the scale of Labour's landslide in 1997. But a number of key figures in both parties, particularly an older generation of Lib Dem leaders, still hankered after moving to a 'progressive' alliance that would keep the Conservatives out of office. Yet it was David Cameron, having attacked the prospect of backstairs deals between parties in a hung parliament, who negotiated a coalition with the Lib Dems, opening the possibility of a centre-right realignment. The new Prime Minister now spoke of the merits of 'partnership' and defended it as the form of government needed to protect 'the national interest', as in 1916, 1931 and 1940.

It poses, however, an interesting question: whether the Conservatives – or at least David Cameron's type of Conservative – were better off having failed to achieve an overall majority. Even if they had they scraped past the 323 seat line, the Conservatives would have struggled to have secured more than a tiny majority, which would have made it politically difficult to implement the many difficult decisions on public spending which all the parties accepted were imminent. The new coalition, however, produced a majority of 80 (a majority which, if secured by one party we would almost describe as a landslide), and the possibility of power for four to five years, with the government's activities given running cover by the Liberal Democrats. The process of detoxification may have been necessary in order to make the coalition work; but the coalition may well continue and exaggerate the process of detoxification. Cameron may claim – as he does – to have preferred a Conservative majority. But then he also claimed not to be preparing for any post-election deals.

As the election approached, Nick Clegg was careful never to say he would be the kingmaker in the event of a hung parliament. The voters, he claimed, were the kingmakers. Yet that was not what happened. The public gave an ambiguous answer, one which could have produced (at least) two kings. The final paradox of the election is that it was the Liberal Democrats – the weakest of the three parties – who decided who should form the government – and on the basis of a policy of immediate expenditure cuts which was diametrically opposed to the one on which they had fought the election. The general election did not determine who would be Prime Minister; the Liberal Democrats did. Moreover, the crucial policy agreement that cemented the Con–Lib Dem coalition was a referendum on the Alternative Vote, a policy that in the election both the Conservatives and Lib Dems had opposed, and which had been supported only by Labour (and to which, after the election, Labour promptly declared themselves opposed).

A referendum on AV is likely to be held at some point in 2011. Whether that referendum is successful or not (but especially if it is), we may need to get used to such outcomes. Such developments in turn raise questions about the continued importance of party manifestos or the idea of the mandate. What is the point of manifestos if large parts of them can be jettisoned in post-election negotiations? And how much legitimacy do policies cobbled together in (smoke free) rooms enjoy? Immediately after the election, the government tried to argue that its coalition agreement enjoyed the same status as a manifesto, and that therefore the Salisbury

Convention – that opposition parties in the Lords do not vote against the manifesto – would apply. Labour peers (sensibly) did not accept the argument. The process of 'coalitionising' British politics – to use a phrase of the Cabinet Secretary's – is one that we may need to get used to over the coming years.

Within days of the election, it was possible to read a wide variety of predictions about the future of British politics: how the coalition would all be over in months; how it would last the full five years; how it was a disastrous outcome for Labour; or the Conservatives; or the Liberal Democrats. There were predictions that it would all end in tears. There were predictions that this was a Brave New World. The truth was that no one knew. Everyone was making it up. But for good or ill, the future looked – for those interested in politics – as intriguing as the election that had preceded it.

Note

1. This is the figure for turnout in the UK as a whole; turnout in Great Britain (as discussed in Appendix 2) was 65.3%.

Appendix 1: The Voting Statistics

Table A1.1   Votes and seats, 1945–2010

	Electorate	Votes	Conservative[a]	Labour	Liberal (Democrats)[b]	Scottish and Welsh Nationalists	Communists	Other
1945[c]	73.3% 32,836,419	100%–640 24,082,612	39.8%–213 9,577,667	48.3%–393 11,632,191	9.1%–12 2,197,191	0.2% 46,612	0.4%–2 102,760	2.1%–20 525,491
1950	84.0% 34,269,770	100%–625 28,772,671	43.5%–299 12,502,567	46.1%–315 13,266,592	9.1%–9 2,621,548	0.1% 27,288	0.3% 91,746	0.9%–2 262,930
1951	82.5% 34,645,573	100%–625 28,595,668	48.%–321 13,717,538	48.8%–295 13,948,605	2.5%–6 730,556	0.1% 18,219	0.1% 21,640	0.5%–3 159,110
1955	76.8% 34,858,263	100%–630 26,760,493	49.7%–345 13,311,936	46.4%–277 12,404,970	2.7%–6 722,405	0.2% 57,231	0.1% 33,144	0.8%–2 230,807
1959	78.7% 35,397,080	100%–630 27,859,241	49.4%–365 13,749,830	43.8%–258 12,215,538	5.9%–6 1,638,571	0.4% 99,309	0.1%–1 30,897	0.5%–1 145,090
1964	77.1% 35,892,572	100%–630 27,655,374	43.4%–304 12,001,396	44.1%–317 12,205,814	11.2%–9 3,092,878	0.5% 133,551	0.2% 45,932	0.6% 169,431
1966	75.8% 35,964,684	100%–630 27,263,606	41.9%–253 11,418,433	47.9%–363 13,064,951	8.5%–12 2,327,533	0.7% 189,545	0.2% 62,112	0.7%–2 201,032
1970	72.0% 39,342,013	100%–630 28,344,798	46.4%–330 13,145,123	43.%–288 12,178,295	7.5%–6 2,117,033	1.3%–1 381,819	0.1% 37,970	1.7%–5 486,557
Feb. '74	78.1% 39,770,724	100%–635 31,340,162	37.8%–297 11,872,180	37.1%–301 11,646,391	19.3%–14 6,058,744	2.6%–9 804,554	0.1% 32,743	3.1%–14 958,293
Oct. '74	72.8% 40,072,971	100%–635 29,189,178	35.8%–277 10,464,817	39.2%–319 11,457,079	18.3%–13 5,346,754	3.5%–14 1,005,938	0.1% 17,426	3.1%–12 897,164

1979	76.0%	100%-635	43.9%-339	37.%-269	13.8%-11	2.%-4	0.1%	3.2%-12
	41,093,264	31,221,361	13,697,923	11,532,218	4,313,804	636,890	38,116	1,001,447
1983	72.7%	100%-650	42.4%-397	27.6%-209	25.4%-23	1.5%-4	0.2%	2.9%-17
	42,197,344	30,671,136	13,012,315	8,456,934	7,780,949	457,676	53,848	90,875
1987	75.3%	100%-650	42.3%-376	30.8%-229	22.6%-22	1.7%-6	0.3%	2.3%-17
	43,181,321	32,536,137	13,763,066	10,029,778	7,341,290	543,559	89,753	762,615
1992	77.7%	100%-651	41.9%-336	34.4%-271	17.8%-20	2.3%-7	0.5%	3.%-17
	43,249,721	33,612,693	14,092,891	11,559,735	5,999,384	783,991	171,927	1,004,765
1997	71.5%	100%-659	30.7%-165	43.2%-418	16.8%-46	2.5%-10	0.2%	6.6%-20
	43,757,478	31,286,597	9,602,857	13,516,632	5,242,894	782,570	63,991	2,077,653
2001	59.4%	100%-659	31.7%-166	40.7%-412	18.3%-52	2.5%-9	0.6%	6.2%-20
	44,403,238	26,368,798	8,357,622	10,724,895	4,812,833	660,197	166,487	1,646,764
2005	61.2%	100%-646	32.4%-198	35.2%-356	22.0%-62	2.2%-9	–	8.2%-21
	44,261,545	27,123,652	8,772,473	9,547,944	5,981,874	567,105	–	2,234,267
2010	65.1%	100%-650	36.1%-307	29.0%-258	23.0%-57	2.2%-9	–	9.6%-19
	45,610,369	29,687,409	10,726,555	8,606,518	6,836,188	656,780	–	2,861,368

a Includes Ulster Unionists 1945–70.
b Liberals 1945–79; Liberal–SDP Alliance 1983–87; Liberal Democrats 1992–.
c The 1945 figures exclude University seats and are adjusted for double counting in the 15 two-member seats.

Northern Ireland party votes

Party	Votes	% share (change)	Seats (change)	Candidates	Lost deposits
Alliance	42,762	6.3 (+2.4)	1 (+1)	18	10
DUP	168,216	25.0 (–8.7)	8 (–1)	16	0
SDLP	110,970	16.5 (–1.0)	3 (0)	18	2
Sinn Fein	171,942	25.5 (+1.2)	5 (0)	17	4
TUV	26,300	3.9 (–)	0 (–)	10	2
UCU	102,361	15.2 (–2.9)	0 (–1)	17	2
Others	51,320	7.6 (+5.2)	1 (+1)	12	9

Note: UCU calculation for 2005 includes UUP plus Conservative vote, where Conservatives stood.

Minor party votes (GB only)

Party	Votes	% Share	Average % share	Candidates	Lost deposits
BNP	564,321	1.9	3.8	338	266
Christian Party	18,623	0.1	0.6	71	71
English Democrats	64,826	0.2	1.3	107	106
Greens	285,616	1.0	1.8	335	328
Respect	33,251	0.1	6.4	11	8
Scottish Socialist	3,157	0.0	0.8	10	10
UKIP	919,486	3.1	3.5	558	459

Table A1.2 National and regional results

United Kingdom

	Seats won in 2010 (change since 2005)					Turnout	Share of votes cast 2010 (% change since 2005)				
	Con	Lab	Lib Dem	Nat & Other			Con	Lab	Lib Dem	Nat	Other
England	298 (+92)	191 (−87)	43 (−4)	1 (−1)	England	65.5 (+4.5)	39.6 (+3.9)	28.1 (−7.4)	24.2 (+1.3)	0 (0)	8.1 (+2.2)
North	43 (+23)	104 (−24)	11 (+1)	0 (0)	North	62.3 (+4.6)	30.7 (+3.5)	38.4 (−7.6)	22.4 (+1.0)	0 (0)	8.5 (+3.1)
Midlands	64 (+27)	39 (−25)	2 (−1)	0 (−1)	Midlands	65.7 (+4.4)	40.3 (+4.3)	30.2 (−8.6)	20.6 (+2.1)	0 (0)	8.9 (+2.2)
South	191 (+42)	48 (−38)	30 (−4)	1 (0)	South	67.1 (+4.5)	43.9 (+3.8)	22.0 (−6.8)	26.5 (+1.2)	0 (0)	7.7 (+1.8)
Wales	8 (+5)	26 (−4)	3 (−1)	3 (0)	Wales	64.8 (+2.0)	26.1 (+4.7)	36.2 (−6.5)	20.1 (+1.7)	11.3 (−1.3)	6.3 (+1.3)
Scotland	1 (0)	41 (0)	11 (0)	6 (0)	Scotland	63.8 (+3.0)	16.7 (+0.9)	42.0 (+2.5)	18.9 (−3.7)	19.9 (+2.3)	2.5 (−1.9)
Great Britain	307 (+97)	258 (−91)	57 (−5)	10 (−1)	Great Britain	65.3 (+4.3)	37.0 (+3.7)	29.7 (−6.5)	23.6 (+0.9)	2.3 (0)	7.5 (+1.8)
Northern Ireland	0 (0)	0 (0)	0 (0)	18 (0)	Northern Ireland	57.6 (−7.8)	0 (−0.4)	0 (0)	0 (0)	0 (0)	100 (+0.4)
United Kingdom	307 (+97)	258 (−91)	57 (−5)	28 (−1)	United Kingdom	65.1 (+4.0)	36.1 (+3.8)	29.0 (−6.2)	23.0 (+1.0)	2.2(0)	9.6 (+1.4)

Regions

	Seats won in 2010 (change since 2005)					Turnout	Share of votes cast 2010 (% change since 2005)				
	Con	Lab	Lib Dem	Nat & Other			Con	Lab	Lib Dem	Nat	Other
South East	135 (+27)	44 (−25)	12 (−2)	1 (0)	South East	66.6 (+5.0)	44.1 (+3.8)	24.3 (−6.2)	24.0 (+0.8)	0 (0)	7.6 (+1.7)
Greater London*	28 (+7)	38 (−6)	7 (0)	0 (−1)	Greater London*	64.3 (+6.9)	34.5 (+2.6)	36.6 (−2.3)	22.1 (+0.2)	0 (0)	6.7 (−0.5)
Inner London	5 (+1)	21 (0)	2 (0)	0 (−1)	Inner London	61.6 (+8.7)	26.1 (+2.9)	44.0 (+0.5)	23.7 (+0.8)	0 (0)	6.3 (−4.3)
Outer London	23 (+)	17 (−6)	5 (0)	0 (0)	Outer London	65.9 (+5.8)	39.6 (+2.8)	32.2 (−4.2)	21.2 (−0.2)	0 (0)	7.0 (+1.6)
Rest of South East	107 (+20)	6 (−19)	5 (−2)	1 (+1)	Rest of South East	67.9 (+3.9)	49.6 (+4.7)	17.4 (−8.7)	25.0 (+1.1)	0 (0)	8.1 (+2.9)
Outer Met. Area	59 (+10)	3 (−10)	0 (0)	0 (0)	Outer Met. Area	68.3 (+4.6)	51.1 (+4.9)	17.4 (−9.4)	23.7 (+1.6)	0 (0)	7.8 (+2.9)
Other South East	48 (+10)	3 (−9)	5 (−2)	1 (+1)	Other South East	67.5 (+3.3)	47.9 (+4.5)	17.3 (−8.0)	26.4 (+0.7)	0 (0)	8.3 (+2.8)
South West*	36 (+11)	4 (−8)	15 (−3)	0 (0)	South West*	68.9 (+2.7)	42.8 (+4.2)	15.4 (−7.4)	34.7 (+2.2)	0 (0)	7.1 (+1.0)
Devon & Cornwall	11 (+5)	2 (−1)	5 (−4)	0 (0)	Devon & Cornwall	68.2 (+2.4)	42.6 (+6.5)	12.4 (−6.5)	36.1 (−0.4)	0 (0)	8.9 (+0.4)
Rest of S.W.	25 (+6)	2 (−7)	10 (+1)	0 (0)	Rest of S.W.	69.2 (+2.9)	42.9 (+3.2)	16.8 (−7.9)	34.1 (+3.4)	0 (0)	6.2 (+1.3)
East Anglia	20 (+4)	0 (−5)	3 (+1)	0 (0)	East Anglia	67.8 (+4.0)	44.7 (+3.3)	18.8 (−10.4)	27.0 (+2.6)	0 (0)	9.5 (+4.5)
East Midlands*	31 (+12)	15 (−11)	0 (−1)	0 (0)	East Midlands*	67.1 (+4.8)	41.2 (+4.1)	29.8 (−9.2)	20.8 (+2.4)	0 (0)	8.2 (+2.8)
West Midlands*	33 (+15)	24 (−14)	2 (0)	0 (−1)	West Midlands*	64.6 (+4.2)	39.5 (+4.5)	30.6 (−8.1)	20.5 (+1.9)	0 (0)	9.4 (+1.7)

Table A1.2 continued

Regions

	Seats won in 2010 (change since 2005)				Share of votes cast 2010 (% change since 2005)					
	Con	Lab	Lib Dem	Nat & Other	Turnout	Con	Lab	Lib Dem	Nat	Other
W. Mids. Met. Co.	7 (+3)	19 (−4)	2 (+1)	0 (0)	61.3 (+3.7)	33.5 (+4.0)	37.6 (−6.8)	19.3 (+1.3)	0 (0)	9.6 (+1.5)
Rest of W. Mids.	26 (+12)	5 (−10)	0 (−1)	0 (−1)	67.4 (+4.5)	44.4 (+4.8)	25.0 (−9.1)	21.3 (+2.4)	0 (0)	9.3 (−1.8)
Yorks & Humber*	19 (+10)	32 (−9)	3 (−1)	0 (0)	62.9 (+4.0)	32.8 (+3.7)	34.4 (−9.2)	22.9 (+2.3)	0 (0)	9.9 (+3.2)
S. Yorks Met. Co.	0 (0)	13 (0)	1 (0)	0 (0)	60.8 (+5.9)	20.6 (+2.6)	42.0 (−10.7)	23.7 (+2.4)	0 (0)	13.7 (+5.7)
W. Yorks Met. Co.	7 (+6)	13 (−7)	2 (+1)	0 (0)	64.2 (+4.5)	32.9 (+5.1)	37.4 (−8.5)	20.7 (+2.1)	0 (0)	9.0 (+1.3)
Rest of Yorks & Humb	12 (+4)	6 (−2)	0 (−2)	0 (0)	62.9 (+2.2)	41.7 (+3.5)	25.0 (−9.5)	25.1 (+2.4)	0 (0)	8.2 (+3.7)
North West	20 (+11)	44 (−12)	5 (+1)	0 (0)	61.9 (+5.3)	31.1 (+3.2)	40.2 (−5.8)	21.4 (+0.2)	0 (0)	7.4 (+2.4)
Gtr. Mancs. Met. Co.	2 (+1)	22 (−1)	3 (0)	0 (0)	59.3 (+4.8)	27.3 (+3.6)	40.3 (−6.9)	23.8 (+0.5)	0 (0)	8.6 (+2.8)
Merseyside Met. Co.	1 (0)	13 (0)	1 (0)	0 (0)	60.7 (+6.8)	21.1 (+1.7)	52.3 (−1.5)	20.8 (−2.0)	0 (0)	5.8 (+1.9)
Rest of N.W.	17 (+10)	9 (−11)	1 (+1)	0 (0)	65.2 (+5.1)	39.6 (+3.7)	34.0 (−7.0)	19.4 (+1.0)	0 (0)	7.0 (+2.4)
North	4 (+2)	28 (−3)	3 (+1)	0 (0)	62.3 (+4.1)	26.6 (+3.8)	41.2 (−8.4)	23.7 (+0.3)	0 (0)	8.5 (+4.3)
Tyne and Wear Met. Co.	0 (0)	12 (0)	0 (0)	0 (0)	59.9 (+4.3)	21.4 (+4.0)	48.7 (−7.1)	21.7 (−1.5)	0 (0)	8.3 (+4.7)
Rest of North	4 (+2)	16 (−3)	3 (+1)	0 (0)	63.5 (+3.9)	29.2 (+3.7)	37.4 (−9.1)	24.8 (+1.3)	0 (0)	8.6 (+4.1)
Wales*	8 (+5)	26 (−4)	3 (−1)	3 (0)	64.8 (+2.0)	26.1 (+4.7)	36.2 (−6.5)	20.1 (+1.7)	11.3 (−1.3)	6.3 (+1.3)
Industrial S. Wales	3 (+2)	20 (−1)	1 (0)	0 (−1)	63.3 (+2.0)	22.9 (+3.6)	41.7 (−7.1)	19.6 (+2.3)	8.5 (−0.6)	7.3 (+1.8)
Rural Wales	5 (+3)	6 (−3)	2 (−1)	3 (+1)	67.2 (+2.1)	31.2 (+6.5)	27.5 (−5.5)	20.9 (+0.9)	15.7 (−2.4)	4.7 (+0.5)
Scotland*	1 (0)	41 (0)	11 (0)	6 (0)	63.8 (+3.0)	16.7 (+0.9)	42.0 (+2.5)	18.9 (−3.7)	19.9 (−2.3)	2.5 (−1.9)
Ayrshire & Borders	1 (0)	5 (0)	1 (0)	0 (0)	65.3 (+1.0)	25.8 (+0.5)	39.8 (+1.0)	16.2 (−2.0)	17.2 (+2.9)	1.0 (−2.4)
Clydeside	0 (0)	19 (0)	1 (0)	0 (0)	61.5 (+3.6)	11.4 (+0.8)	55.4 (+4.8)	12.8 (−4.6)	17.8 (+2.3)	2.7 (−3.3)
Rest of Central Belt	0 (0)	10 (0)	1 (0)	0 (0)	66.8 (+3.4)	16.8 (+0.5)	42.2 (+2.4)	20.2 (−4.8)	18.2 (+3.4)	2.6 (−1.5)
NE & Fife	0 (0)	7 (0)	3 (0)	5 (0)	63.4 (+3.1)	19.3 (+1.5)	32.7 (+1.8)	20.4 (−3.2)	25.5 (+0.4)	2.2 (−0.6)
Highlands & Islands	0 (0)	0 (0)	5 (0)	1 (0)	64.7 (+2.3)	14.6 (+1.4)	21.0 (−2.0)	40.4 (−2.5)	19.4 (+4.1)	4.5 (−0.9)
N Ireland	0 (0)	0 (0)	0 (0)	18 (0)	57.6 (−7.8)	0 (−0.4)	0 (0)	0 (0)	0 (0)	100 (+0.4)

Notes:

The English Regions are the eight *Standard Regions*, now obsolete but used by the OPCS until the 1990s.

The *Outer Metropolitan Area* comprises those seats wholly or mostly in the Outer Metropolitan Area as defined by the OPCS. It includes: the whole of Surrey and Hertfordshire; the whole of Berkshire except Newbury; and the constituencies of Bedfordshire South West; Luton North; Luton South (Bedfordshire; Beaconsfield; Chesham & Amersham; Wycombe (Buckinghamshire); Basildon South & Billericay; Basildon South & East Thurrock; Brentwood & Ongar; Castle Point; Chelmsford; Epping Forest; Harlow; Rayleigh & Wickford; Rochford & Southend East; Southend West; Thurrock (Essex); Aldershot; Hampshire North East (Hampshire); Chatham & Aylesford; Dartford; Faversham & Kent Mid; Gillingham & Rainham; Gravesham; Maidstone & The Weald; Rochester & Strood; Sevenoaks; Tonbridge & Malling; Tunbridge Wells (Kent); Arundel & South Downs; Crawley; Horsham; Sussex Mid (West Sussex).

Industrial Wales (a description no longer entirely accurate but used for continuity with previous volumes) includes Gwent, the whole of Glamorgan, and the Llanelli constituency in Dyfed.

Ayrshire & Borders comprises: Ayr, Carrick & Cumnock; Ayrshire Central; Ayrshire North & Arran; Berwickshire, Roxburgh & Selkirk; Dumfries & Galloway; Dumfriesshire, Clydesdale & Tweeddale; and Kilmarnock & Loudoun.

Clydeside includes all Glasgow seats, both Dunbartonshire seats, both Paisley & Renfrewshire seats, plus Airdrie & Shotts; Coatbridge, Chryston & Bellshill; Cumbernauld, Kilsyth & Kirkintilloch East; East Kilbride, Strathaven & Lesmahagow; Inverclyde; Lanark & Hamilton East; Motherwell & Wishaw; Renfrewshire East; and Rutherglen & Hamilton West.

Rest of Central Belt includes all Edinburgh seats, plus East Lothian; Falkirk; Linlithgow & East Falkirk; Livingston; Midlothian; and Stirling.

NE & Fife includes both Aberdeen seats, both Dundee seats, plus Aberdeenshire West & Kincardine; Angus; Banff & Buchan; Dunfermline & West Fife; Fife North East; Glenrothes; Gordon; Kirkcaldy & Cowdenbeath; Moray; Ochil & South Perthshire; and Perth & North Perthshire.

Highlands & Islands includes Argyll & Bute; Caithness, Sutherland & Easter Ross; Inverness, Nairn, Badenoch & Strathspey; Na H-Eileanan An Iar; Orkney & Shetland; Ross, Skye & Lochaber.

Where boundary changes (as explained on p. 387) have taken place, the calculations for seat changes are based on notional figures for what would have happened if the new boundaries had been in force in 2005, drawn from Colin Rallings and Michael Thrasher (ed), *Media Guide to the New Parliamentary Constituencies* (Plymouth: Local Government Chronicle Elections Centre, 2007).

In all but four cases the European constituencies are covered in the table above. These constituencies are indicated with an asterisk (*). The results for the four other European constituencies are:

	Seats won in 2010 (change since 2005)					Share of votes cast 2010 (% change since 2005)			
	Con	Lab	Lib Dem	Nat & Other	Turnout	Con	Lab	Lib Dem	Other
North East	2 (+1)	25 (−2)	2 (+1)	0 (0)	61.1 (+3.9)	23.7 (+4.2)	43.6 (−9.3)	23.6 (+0.2)	9.1 (+4.9)
North West	22 (+12)	47 (−13)	6 (+1)	0 (0)	62.4 (+5.3)	31.7 (+3.0)	39.4 (−5.7)	21.6 (+0.3)	7.2 (+2.4)
Eastern	52 (+10)	2 (−11)	4 (+1)	0 (0)	67.6 (+4.1)	47.1 (+3.8)	19.6 (−10.2)	24.1 (+2.2)	9.2 (+4.2)
South East	75 (+14)	4 (−13)	4 (−2)	1 (+1)	68.1 (+3.9)	49.9 (+4.9)	16.2 (−8.1)	26.2 (+0.8)	7.7 (+2.5)

Table A1.3 Constituency results

These tables list the votes in each constituency in percentage terms.
With the exception of Scotland, the constituencies are listed alphabetically within counties, as defined in 1974. In Greater London the constituencies are listed alphabetically within each borough (and allocated to a single borough in cases where they cross borough boundaries). The Scottish results are not arranged within counties as too many of the constituencies cross boundaries.
The figure in the 'Other' column is the total percentage received by all other candidates than the parties listed in the table.
As above, where boundary changes have taken place, the calculations are based on notional figures for what would have happened if the new boundaries had been in force in 2005 (as explained on p. 387).

* denotes a seat won by different parties in 2005 and 2010
† denotes a seat that changed hands in a by-election between 2005 and 2010
‡ denotes a seat held by the Speaker in 2005 or 2010.

Swing is given in the conventional (total vote or 'Butler') form – the average of the Conservative % gain (or loss) and the Labour % loss (or gain) (measured as % of the total poll). It is only reported for seats where those parties occupied the top two places in 2005 and 2010. This is the practice followed by previous books in this series since 1955.

ENGLAND	Turnout %	Turnout +/-	Con %	Con +/-	Lab %	Lab +/-	LD %	LD +/-	Grn %	UKIP %	BNP %	Other No. & %	Swing
Avon, Bath	70.6	+1.5	31.4	-0.5	6.9	-7.5	56.6	+11.2	2.4	1.9	–	(4) 0.9	–
Bristol East	64.8	+1.8	28.3	+0.2	36.6	-8.9	24.4	+4.7	1.8	3.4	4.4	(2) 1.2	+4.5
North West*	68.5	-0.3	38.0	+5.5	25.9	-12.2	31.5	+6.6	1.0	2.3	–	(1) 1.3	+8.9
South	61.6	+2.6	22.9	+3.3	38.4	-10.1	28.7	+4.9	2.5	2.6	3.6	(2) 1.3	–
West	66.9	+3.3	18.4	+2.0	27.5	-9.0	48.0	+9.0	3.8	1.2	–	(2) 1.1	–
Filton & Bradley Stoke	70.0	+7.5	40.8	+5.3	26.4	-7.4	25.3	-3.1	0.9	3.1	2.7	(2) 0.8	+6.4
Kingswood*	72.2	+3.0	40.4	+8.3	35.3	-10.6	16.8	-1.2	0.8	3.2	2.7	(1) 0.7	+9.4
Somerset North	75.0	+3.2	49.3	+7.5	11.1	-10.6	35.7	+5.5	–	3.9	–	–	–

Somerset North East	75.4	+3.9	41.3	+2.2	31.7	−7.0	22.3	+2.7	1.3	3.4	−	−	+4.6
Thornbury & Yate	75.2	+1.6	37.2	+6.3	7.0	−3.8	51.9	−2.4	−	3.5	−	(2) 0.4	−
Weston-Super-Mare	67.2	+1.5	44.3	+4.0	10.9	−7.7	39.2	+3.1	−	2.7	2.1	(2) 0.8	−
Bedfordshire, Bedford*	66.7	+4.7	38.9	+5.4	35.9	−5.7	19.9	−2.0	0.9	2.5	1.7	(1) 0.3	+5.5
Bedfordshire Mid	72.2	+3.5	52.5	+5.9	14.8	−7.7	24.9	+1.4	1.4	5.1	−	(1) 1.3	−
North East	71.2	+2.8	55.8	+5.9	16.1	−9.1	21.7	+0.8	−	4.1	2.3	−	+7.5
South West	66.3	+3.5	52.8	+4.5	19.6	−10.6	20.0	+3.2	−	4.2	3.4	−	+7.6
Luton North	65.5	+8.6	31.8	−0.4	49.3	+0.7	11.1	−4.5	1.1	3.6	3.1	−	−0.5
South	64.7	+10.9	29.4	+1.3	34.9	−7.9	22.7	+0.1	0.9	2.3	3.1	(6) 6.8	+4.6
Berkshire, Bracknell	67.8	+5.1	52.4	+2.5	16.8	−11.1	22.3	+4.5	1.6	4.4	2.4	(1) 0.1	+6.8
Maidenhead	73.7	+3.4	59.5	+7.6	7.1	−2.1	28.2	−8.0	0.9	2.3	1.5	(1) 0.5	−
Newbury	74.0	+1.4	56.4	+7.4	4.3	−1.7	35.5	−7.1	0.8	2.5	−	(2) 0.4	−
Reading East	66.7	+8.2	42.6	+6.9	25.5	−8.5	27.3	+3.0	2.1	2.2	−	(2) 0.3	+7.7
West*	65.9	+6.0	43.2	+9.6	30.5	−14.5	20.1	+4.3	1.2	3.2	−	(1) 1.8	+12.1
Slough	58.0	+4.1	34.3	+7.9	45.8	−0.4	14.5	−2.2	1.1	3.2	−	(1) 1.0	+4.1
Windsor	71.3	+7.2	60.8	+11.4	9.9	−8.0	22.4	−4.7	1.3	3.3	1.9	(1) 0.4	−
Wokingham	71.5	+3.7	52.7	+4.6	10.1	−4.9	28.0	−4.7	1.0	3.1	−	(3) 5.1	−
Buckinghamshire, Aylesbury	68.3	+5.9	52.2	+3.8	12.6	−5.7	28.4	−0.4	−	6.8	−	−	−
Beaconsfield	70.0	+6.8	61.1	+7.0	11.7	−7.8	19.6	−2.4	1.5	4.9	−	(2) 1.3	−
Buckingham‡	64.5	−3.8	47.3	−10.9	−	−	−	−	−	17.4	2.0	(8) 33.3	−
Chesham & Amersham	74.6	+7.8	60.4	+6.8	5.6	−8.0	28.5	+2.3	1.5	4.1	−	−	−
Milton Keynes North*	65.4	+2.0	43.5	+7.3	26.8	−11.1	22.1	+1.4	1.4	3.3	2.1	(3) 0.8	+9.2
South*	63.9	+2.5	41.6	+3.9	32.2	−8.6	17.7	+2.5	1.4	3.7	2.7	(2) 0.6	+6.2
Wycombe	65.6	+4.1	48.6	+1.2	17.3	−12.8	28.8	+10.9	−	4.4	−	(2) 0.9	+7.0
Cambridgeshire, Cambridge	65.3	+6.3	25.6	+8.3	24.3	−8.2	39.1	−5.6	7.6	2.4	−	(2) 1.0	−
Cambridgeshire North East	71.1	+12.0	51.6	+4.7	17.8	−12.8	20.0	+3.0	−	5.4	3.4	(2) 1.8	+8.7
North West	65.6	+2.3	50.5	+4.3	16.9	−8.7	21.9	−1.0	−	8.3	−	(1) 2.4	+6.5
South	74.8	+6.6	47.4	+0.9	10.2	−9.5	34.1	+5.8	1.8	3.2	−	(1) 3.3	−
South East	69.3	+5.1	48.0	+0.8	7.6	−13.8	37.6	+6.2	1.3	3.7	−	(2) 1.7	−
Huntingdon	64.9	+2.3	48.9	−1.9	11.0	−7.4	28.9	+2.3	1.2	6.0	−	(3) 4.0	−
Peterborough	63.9	+4.9	40.4	−2.9	29.5	−4.8	19.6	+2.9	1.2	6.7	−	(2) 2.6	+0.9

ENGLAND	Turnout %	Turnout +/-	Con %	Con +/-	Lab %	Lab +/-	LD %	LD +/-	Grn %	UKIP %	BNP %	Other No. & %	Swing %
Cheshire, Chester, City Of*	68.3	+3.9	40.6	+3.8	35.1	-3.9	19.1	-2.7	1.1	2.6	-	(2) 1.5	+3.9
Congleton	68.9	+4.8	45.8	+0.4	17.2	-10.5	31.9	+5.0	-	4.2	-	(3) 0.9	+5.4
Crewe & Nantwich*†	65.9	+6.0	45.8	+12.9	34.0	-14.4	15.0	-3.7	-	2.8	2.0	(1) 0.3	+13.7
Eddisbury	67.7	+2.6	51.7	+4.8	21.6	-10.5	22.5	-4.5	-	4.3	-	-	+7.6
Ellesmere Port & Neston	67.4	+6.1	34.9	+2.1	44.6	-4.1	15.1	-0.7	-	3.7	-	(1) 1.8	+3.1
Halton	60.0	+6.4	20.2	+0.3	57.7	-5.4	13.8	-3.2	1.6	3.0	3.8	-	+2.9
Macclesfield	68.2	+5.7	47.0	-2.7	20.3	-8.7	23.1	+3.5	1.7	2.8	-	(1) 5.2	+3.0
Tatton	68.9	+4.9	54.6	+3.1	17.3	-6.5	22.6	+0.8	-	-	-	(2) 5.6	+4.8
Warrington North	62.7	+7.4	30.2	+5.9	45.5	-7.3	20.8	+2.1	-	-	-	(1) 3.4	+6.6
South*	69.3	+7.8	35.8	+3.7	33.0	-8.3	27.5	+3.5	0.8	3.0	-	-	+6.0
Weaver Vale*	65.4	+9.8	38.5	+6.9	36.3	-9.4	18.6	-1.1	0.8	2.3	2.4	(3) 1.0	+8.1
Cleveland, Hartlepool	55.5	+4.2	28.1	+16.7	42.5	-9.0	17.1	-13.3	-	7.0	5.2	-	-
Middlesbrough	51.4	+2.7	18.8	+2.3	45.9	-11.7	19.9	+1.2	-	3.7	5.8	(1) 5.9	-
South & Cleveland East	63.6	+2.7	35.6	+3.8	39.2	-11.1	15.9	+2.1	-	4.1	3.4	(1) 1.8	+7.4
Redcar*	62.5	+4.5	13.8	-4.1	32.7	-18.6	45.2	+25.0	-	4.5	3.5	(1) 0.3	-
Stockton North	59.2	+1.1	25.9	+4.7	42.8	-12.0	16.1	-2.6	-	3.9	4.4	(2) 6.9	+8.3
South*	68.1	+5.6	38.9	+4.7	38.3	-9.4	15.1	-1.0	-	2.9	3.1	(2) 1.7	+7.0
Cornwall, Camborne & Redruth*	66.4	+3.2	37.6	+12.0	16.3	-12.4	37.4	+1.6	1.4	5.1	-	(2) 2.2	-
Cornwall North	68.2	+3.7	41.7	+6.3	4.2	-8.3	48.1	+5.7	-	4.9	-	(1) 1.1	-
South East*	68.7	+1.0	45.1	+10.1	7.1	-3.4	38.6	-8.1	1.7	6.2	-	(1) 1.3	-
St. Austell & Newquay	62.7	-2.2	40.0	+5.1	7.2	-6.6	42.7	-4.5	-	3.7	2.2	(1) 4.2	-
St. Ives	68.6	+0.8	39.0	+11.7	8.2	-4.4	42.7	-9.1	2.8	5.6	-	(2) 1.7	-
Truro & Falmouth*	69.1	+4.0	41.7	+10.0	9.6	-9.4	40.8	-0.1	1.8	3.9	-	(1) 2.1	-
Cumbria, Barrow & Furness	64.0	+5.1	36.3	+3.7	48.1	+2.9	10.0	-7.8	1.2	1.9	1.9	(1) 0.6	+0.4
Carlisle*	64.7	+6.1	39.3	+5.9	37.3	-9.6	15.6	-1.0	1.5	2.3	2.6	(2) 1.5	+7.7
Copeland	67.6	+5.4	37.1	+3.6	46.0	-0.7	10.2	-3.7	0.9	2.3	3.4	-	+2.1
Penrith & The Border	69.9	+3.2	53.4	+2.0	12.9	-6.1	28.5	2.6	-	2.8	2.4	-	-

Westmorland & Lonsdale	76.9	+6.1	36.2	-8.1	2.2	-5.6	60.0	+14.1	–	1.6	–	–	–
Workington	65.9	+3.4	33.9	+4.8	45.5	-6.5	13.5	-0.9	–	2.2	3.8	(1) 1.1	+5.7
Derbyshire, Amber Valley*	65.5	+1.5	38.6	+4.7	37.4	-9.0	14.4	+2.1	–	2.0	7.0	(1) 0.6	+6.9
Bolsover	60.6	+4.4	24.6	+7.3	50.0	-15.2	15.5	-2.0	1.3	3.9	6.0	–	–
Chesterfield*	63.8	+3.8	15.7	+7.5	39.0	-1.6	37.8	-9.1	–	3.1	–	(2) 3.0	–
Derby North	63.1	+0.6	31.7	+5.8	33.0	-9.0	28.0	+0.5	–	1.8	4.4	(2) 1.0	–
South	58.0	-6.7	28.5	+8.7	43.3	-9.8	20.5	-3.7	–	4.4	–	(1) 3.3	–
Derbyshire Dales	73.8	+6.3	52.1	+5.6	19.4	-6.3	22.5	-1.9	1.7	3.8	3.6	(2) 0.6	+6.0
Mid	71.7	+5.1	48.3	+1.1	24.5	-10.2	20.5	+4.5	–	2.6	–	(1) 0.5	+5.7
North East	65.9	+4.7	33.0	+7.0	38.2	-10.1	23.3	+1.8	–	5.6	–	–	+8.6
South*	71.4	+4.5	45.5	+8.1	31.4	-11.5	15.9	+3.0	1.1	2.4	4.3	(1) 0.5	+9.8
Erewash*	68.4	+5.8	39.5	+10.4	34.2	-10.5	17.5	+4.0	1.8	1.8	4.9	(1) 1.0	+10.5
High Peak*	70.4	+4.3	40.9	+3.6	31.6	-9.5	21.8	+2.4	1.9	3.4	–	(2) 0.5	+6.5
Devon, Devon Central	75.7	+5.8	51.5	+7.7	6.9	-4.7	34.4	-4.4	1.5	5.3	–	–	–
East	72.6	+4.6	48.3	+1.1	10.8	-7.5	31.2	+3.1	1.4	8.2	–	–	–
North	68.9	+0.6	36.0	+0.3	5.2	-3.7	47.4	+0.9	1.3	7.2	1.2	(3) 1.6	–
South West	70.4	+2.2	56.0	+11.6	12.4	-11.8	24.1	+0.3	1.9	6.2	1.4	–	+11.7
West & Torridge	71.4	+0.2	45.7	+3.4	5.3	-5.3	40.3	+3.4	1.5	5.5	1.3	–	–
Exeter	67.7	+3.4	33.0	+8.1	38.2	-4.0	20.3	-0.7	1.5	3.7	–	(1) 2.1	+6.0
Newton Abbot*	69.7	+0.7	43.0	+8.0	7.0	-4.4	41.9	-3.6	1.0	6.4	–	(1) 0.2	–
Plymouth Moor View	61.0	+2.7	33.3	+8.3	37.2	-7.2	16.9	-2.1	2.1	7.7	3.5	(1) 0.5	+7.8
Sutton & Devonport*	60.2	+4.7	34.3	+4.7	31.7	-9.0	24.7	+2.1	1.5	6.5	–	(2) 0.8	+6.9
Tiverton & Honiton	71.5	+1.0	50.3	+3.6	8.9	-4.4	33.3	+4.2	1.0	6.0	–	–	–
Torbay	64.6	+4.4	38.7	+2.9	6.6	-7.9	47.0	+5.2	2.5	5.3	1.4	(2) 1.4	–
Totnes	70.4	+0.7	45.9	+3.0	7.4	-4.7	35.6	-1.5	–	6.0	1.3	(1) 0.6	–
Dorset, Bournemouth East	61.9	+2.9	48.4	+3.1	13.3	-5.3	30.9	-0.4	–	6.9	–	(1) 1.1	–
West	58.1	+4.2	45.1	+5.6	14.8	-8.1	31.7	-0.2	–	7.2	–	–	–
Christchurch	71.8	+1.4	56.4	+1.1	9.8	-5.8	25.3	1.2	–	8.5	–	–	–
Dorset Mid & Poole North	72.4	+0.3	44.5	+7.7	5.9	-4.2	45.1	-4.9	–	4.5	–	–	–
North	73.4	+4.1	51.1	+4.6	5.4	-4.2	37.0	-0.9	1.0	5.2	–	(1) 0.4	–
South*	68.1	-1.3	45.1	+7.1	30.3	-11.4	19.0	+3.3	1.2	4.0	–	(1) 0.5	+9.3

ENGLAND	Turnout %	Turnout +/-	Con %	Con +/-	Lab %	Lab +/-	LD %	LD +/-	Grn %	UKIP %	BNP %	Other No. & %	Swing
West	74.6	-1.8	47.6	+1.1	6.7	-1.1	40.7	-1.2	1.2	3.8	-	-	-
Poole	65.3	+1.3	47.5	+4.1	12.7	-10.0	31.6	+2.5	-	5.3	2.5	(1) 0.4	-
Durham, Bishop Auckland	60.2	+4.0	26.3	+3.4	39.0	-11.1	22.3	-1.3	-	2.7	4.9	(1) 4.8	-
Darlington	62.9	+3.5	31.5	+5.4	39.4	-12.9	23.4	+5.0	-	2.8	2.9	-	+9.1
Durham, City Of	67.2	+3.7	13.3	+3.9	44.3	-2.9	37.7	-2.1	-	1.9	2.5	(1) 0.4	-
North	60.7	+5.3	21.0	+4.3	50.5	-13.6	21.0	+1.9	-	3.3	4.1	-	-
North West	62.3	+4.4	20.0	+3.6	42.3	-11.6	24.9	+5.0	-	2.9	4.2	(1) 5.6	-
Easington	54.7	+2.8	13.7	+3.0	58.9	-12.4	16.0	+3.1	-	4.7	6.6	-	-
Sedgefield	62.1	-0.2	23.5	+9.3	45.1	-13.9	20.0	+8.2	-	3.7	5.2	(1) 2.6	+11.6
East Sussex, Bexhill & Battle	67.4	+0.5	51.6	-2.6	12.0	-5.9	28.0	+5.3	-	-	3.6	(1) 4.9	-
Brighton Kemptown*	64.7	+5.9	38.0	+3.8	34.9	-4.1	18.0	+1.1	5.5	3.2	-	(1) 0.5	+4.0
Pavilion*	70.0	+7.7	23.7	+0.4	28.9	-7.5	13.8	-2.2	31.3	1.8	-	(3) 0.4	+3.9
Eastbourne*	67.0	+3.8	40.7	-2.3	4.8	-6.0	47.3	+5.6	-	2.5	1.8	(3) 2.9	-
Hastings & Rye*	64.3	+5.3	41.1	+3.0	37.1	-3.5	15.7	-0.1	-	2.8	2.6	(1) 0.7	+3.3
Hove*	69.5	+6.7	36.7	+0.3	33.0	-4.5	22.6	+4.6	5.2	2.4	-	(1) 0.2	+2.4
Lewes	72.9	+3.1	36.7	+2.1	5.0	-4.3	52.0	+0.5	1.5	3.4	1.2	(1) 0.2	-
Wealden	71.8	+5.5	56.6	+6.1	9.6	-7.1	25.3	+0.6	2.5	6.0	-	-	-
Essex, Basildon & Billericay	63.4	+1.2	52.7	+6.7	23.1	-11.7	15.7	+2.5	-	3.8	4.7	-	+9.2
Basildon South & East Thurrock*	62.2	+3.0	43.9	+5.3	31.0	-9.7	13.4	+2.8	-	5.9	5.6	(1) 0.3	+7.5
Braintree	69.1	+4.9	52.6	+2.7	19.9	-10.8	18.8	+5.2	-	5.0	2.2	-	+6.7
Brentwood & Ongar	73.0	+5.1	56.9	+2.9	9.9	-4.9	23.5	-3.4	1.5	4.0	2.9	(3) 1.7	-
Castle Point	66.9	+0.3	44.0	-4.3	14.7	-15.7	9.4	-0.9	-	-	4.9	(1) 27.0	+5.7
Chelmsford	70.4	+9.3	46.2	+6.7	11.0	-16.0	36.8	+6.6	0.9	2.8	1.6	(2) 0.7	-
Clacton	64.2	+1.6	53.0	+8.6	25.0	-10.9	12.9	-0.6	1.2	-	4.6	(2) 3.2	+9.7
Colchester	62.3	+5.8	32.9	+0.8	12.3	-7.9	48.0	+0.3	1.5	2.9	1.5	(3) 0.8	-
Epping Forest	64.5	+2.9	54.0	+1.2	14.3	-7.2	21.5	+3.4	1.4	4.0	4.3	(1) 0.6	+4.2
Harlow*	64.9	+2.6	44.9	+4.1	33.7	-7.7	13.7	+0.7	-	3.6	4.0	(1) 0.2	+5.9

Harwich & North Essex	69.3	+2.3	46.9	+4.3	19.9	-10.9	23.6	+4.3	1.9	5.2	2.2	(1) 0.3 +7.6
Maldon	67.9	+5.0	59.8	+3.5	12.7	-11.5	19.3	+4.3	-	5.1	3.1	+7.5
Rayleigh & Wickford	69.2	+5.2	57.8	+3.9	14.5	-12.0	15.1	-0.3	-	4.2	4.1	(1) 4.2 +8.0
Rochford & Southend East	58.3	+2.8	46.9	+1.5	20.3	-11.3	19.4	+4.7	1.7	5.8	4.5	(1) 1.5 +6.4
Saffron Walden	71.5	+2.7	55.5	+4.6	9.7	-4.5	27.4	-2.2	1.4	4.1	1.9	-
Southend West	65.2	+4.0	46.1	-0.1	13.4	-9.2	29.4	+5.4	1.5	3.9	3.1	(2) 2.7 -
Thurrock*	58.9	+4.4	36.8	+3.6	36.6	-9.6	10.7	-0.4	-	7.4	7.9	(1) 0.6 +6.6
Witham	69.9	+6.4	52.2	+2.5	18.5	-13.9	19.8	+4.6	3.0	6.5	-	+8.2
Gloucestershire, Cheltenham	66.8	+4.4	41.2	+2.4	5.1	-6.7	50.5	+11.1	-	2.3	-	(1) 0.9 -
Cotswolds, The	71.5	+4.2	53.0	+3.7	10.7	-7.9	29.6	+1.5	1.7	4.2	-	(1) 0.8 -
Forest Of Dean	71.3	+0.4	46.9	+6.0	24.2	-12.4	21.9	+4.7	1.9	5.2	-	+9.2
Gloucester*	64.0	+1.5	39.9	+5.3	35.2	-12.4	19.2	+5.6	1.0	3.6	-	(1) 1.1 +8.9
Stroud*	74.0	+3.9	40.8	+2.5	38.6	-1.5	15.4	+1.5	2.7	2.2	-	(1) 0.2 +2.0
Tewkesbury	70.4	+8.2	47.2	-1.0	11.6	-8.7	35.5	+7.1	1.0	4.1	-	(1) 0.6 -
Greater London												
Barking and Dagenham, Barking	61.4	+13.2	17.8	+1.2	54.3	+4.7	8.2	-2.6	0.7	2.9	14.6	(4) 1.5 -1.7
Dagenham & Rainham	63.4	+6.6	34.3	+0.9	40.3	-8.9	8.6	-0.4	0.7	3.5	11.2	(2) 1.4 +4.9
Barnet, Chipping Barnet	67.4	+4.7	48.8	+2.9	25.2	-8.6	20.2	+4.9	2.0	2.8	-	(1) 0.9 +5.8
Finchley & Golders Green	66.7	+3.9	46.0	+6.2	33.7	-5.4	17.0	-0.1	1.6	1.7	-	+5.8
Hendon*	63.6	+4.7	42.3	+5.2	42.1	-3.0	12.4	-1.7	1.1	2.1	-	+4.1
Bexley, Bexleyheath & Crayford	66.4	+1.8	50.5	+3.9	26.5	-7.7	12.7	-0.4	0.9	3.6	4.7	(1) 1.1 +5.8
Erith & Thamesmead	60.8	+7.1	31.5	+5.0	44.9	-7.7	12.0	-0.8	0.8	2.7	5.1	(3) 3.0 +6.3
Old Bexley & Sidcup	69.2	+4.0	54.1	+4.1	19.3	-8.7	15.4	+1.5	0.8	3.4	4.7	(3) 2.3 +6.4
Brent, Brent Central*	61.2	+5.7	11.2	-1.9	41.2	-8.9	44.2	+13.1	1.5	-	-	(3) 1.9 -
North	62.3	+3.9	31.5	+2.2	46.9	-2.5	17.0	-2.5	1.4	0.7	-	(3) 2.5 +2.3
Bromley, Beckenham	72.0	+6.7	57.9	-1.8	14.5	-4.9	20.6	+4.5	1.3	3.3	2.1	(1) 0.5 +1.5
Bromley & Chislehurst	67.3	+4.6	53.5	+8.5	16.6	-7.9	22.0	-1.8	1.4	3.3	2.4	(1) 0.9 +8.2
Orpington	72.2	-0.2	59.7	+8.5	9.0	+3.0	24.5	-15.9	1.0	2.8	2.5	(1) 0.4 -
Camden, Hampstead & Kilburn	65.7	+9.9	32.7	+9.8	32.8	-3.5	31.2	-4.0	1.4	0.8	0.6	(2) 0.4 -
Holborn & St. Pancras	62.9	+9.7	20.4	-0.5	46.1	+1.0	27.9	+1.8	2.7	1.1	1.4	(3) 0.4 -
Croydon, Croydon Central*	65.2	+5.1	39.5	-0.9	33.5	-7.6	13.2	+0.4	1.2	2.0	2.9	(4) 7.7 +3.3

ENGLAND	Turnout %	Turnout +/-	Con %	Con +/-	Lab %	Lab +/-	LD %	LD +/-	Grn %	UKIP %	BNP %	Other No. & %	Swing
North	60.6	+8.0	24.1	+1.9	56.0	+2.4	14.0	-3.2	2.0	1.7	-	(4) 2.2	-0.3
South	69.3	+5.8	50.9	-1.1	20.0	-4.0	22.8	+2.4	1.7	4.4	-	-	+1.5
Ealing, Ealing Central & Acton*	67.2	+11.2	38.0	+6.8	30.1	-3.2	27.6	-3.0	1.6	1.6	-	(2) 1.0	+5.0
North	65.2	+5.1	30.9	+2.6	50.4	+3.5	13.2	-6.0	1.1	1.4	2.2	(1) 0.9	-0.4
Southall	63.8	+8.9	29.8	+10.8	51.5	-5.8	14.9	-3.3	1.6	-	-	(2) 2.1	+8.3
Enfield, Edmonton	63.2	+5.7	29.8	+2.3	53.7	-2.3	10.5	-1.5	1.3	2.6	-	(2) 2.1	+2.3
Enfield North	67.1	+6.8	42.3	-0.8	38.5	-2.3	12.2	+0.7	1.1	2.1	2.8	(3) 2.1	+0.7
Southgate	69.1	+5.7	49.4	+5.7	32.2	-8.8	13.8	+2.7	1.4	1.1	-	(4) 1.1	+7.2
Greenwich, Eltham	67.0	+8.6	37.5	+2.9	41.5	-0.7	12.6	-4.7	1.0	2.4	4.2	(5) 1.9	+1.8
Greenwich & Woolwich	62.9	+9.6	24.5	+7.0	49.2	-3.3	18.2	-1.5	2.6		2.8	(2) 0.8	-
Hackney, Hackney North & Stoke Newington	62.8	+13.4	14.5	+0.0	55.0	+6.0	23.9	+0.8	4.6			(4) 2.7	-
South & Shoreditch	58.8	+7.4	13.5	-0.2	55.7	+3.0	22.4	+1.1	3.5	1.5		(6) 2.0	-
Hammersmith	65.6	+7.0	36.4	+2.4	43.9	+1.5	15.9	-3.0	1.5	1.2	0.9	(7) 3.3	-
Haringey, Hornsey & Wood Green	68.9	+7.1	16.7	+4.0	34.0	-4.3	46.5	+3.2	1.5			(1) 0.3	+0.5
Tottenham	58.2	+10.4	14.9	+1.4	59.3	+1.4	17.7	+0.9	2.3	1.1		(2) 0.5	-
Harrow, Harrow East*	67.1	+5.8	44.7	+6.1	37.6	-7.9	14.3	+0.1	2.4	1.9		(5) 4.6	+7.0
West	67.3	+2.9	36.8	+6.4	43.6	-5.0	16.2	-2.5	1.7	2.1		-	+5.7
Havering, Hornchurch & Upminster	68.0	+4.7	51.4	+3.9	20.8	-10.3	13.9	+5.4	1.4	5.3	6.4	(2) 1.1	+7.1
Romford	65.2	+3.2	56.0	-1.7	19.5	-9.5	12.0	+3.6	1.0	4.4	5.2	(3) 1.9	+3.9
Hillingdon, Hayes & Harlington	57.5	+2.2	29.4	+1.7	54.8	-1.6	8.7	-1.1	0.8	-	3.6	(3) 2.6	+1.6
Ruislip, Northwood & Pinner	70.8	+8.5	57.5	+2.8	19.5	-4.5	16.6	+0.3	1.5	2.7	-	(2) 2.2	+3.6
Uxbridge & South Ruislip	61.0	+2.4	48.3	+3.8	23.4	-3.0	20.0	-2.7	1.1	2.7	3.1	(2) 1.5	+3.4
Hounslow, Brentford & Isleworth*	64.4	+11.5	37.2	+6.5	33.6	-5.4	23.7	+0.7	1.5	1.6	1.3	(4) 1.1	+6.0
Feltham & Heston	59.9	+12.0	34.0	+5.2	43.6	-4.5	13.7	-2.9	1.1	2.0	3.5	(4) 1.9	+4.8
Islington, Islington North	65.4	+11.5	14.2	+2.4	54.5	+3.3	26.7	-3.2	3.0	1.6	-	-	-
South & Finsbury	64.4	+10.8	19.4	+4.6	42.3	+2.4	34.1	-4.2	1.6	1.6	-	(2) 1.0	-

Kensington and Chelsea, Kensington	53.1	+1.2	50.1	+6.2	25.5	-4.1	19.6	-0.6	2.1	2.1	–	(1) 0.6	+5.2
Chelsea & Fulham	60.2	+7.6	60.5	+5.2	18.5	-6.9	16.2	+2.2	1.7	1.2	1.0	(3) 1.0	+6.1
Kingston & Surbiton	70.4	+2.7	36.5	+3.5	9.3	-3.8	49.8	-1.3	1.0	2.5	–	(2) 0.8	–
Lambeth, Streatham	62.8	+11.0	18.3	+2.0	42.8	-4.2	35.8	+6.3	1.8	–	–	(3) 1.2	–
Vauxhall	57.7	+9.3	21.5	+7.0	49.8	-2.0	25.1	-2.1	1.6	–	–	(5) 1.9	–
Lewisham, Lewisham Deptford	61.5	+10.6	13.5	+0.8	53.7	-1.7	23.4	+5.4	6.7	–	–	(2) 2.7	–
East	63.3	+8.5	23.6	-0.7	43.1	-4.6	28.2	+8.3	1.5	1.8	–	(2) 1.8	+1.9
West & Penge	63.1	+5.7	25.5	+3.9	41.1	-5.2	28.1	+1.0	2.1	2.5	–	(1) 0.7	–
Merton, Mitcham & Morden	66.4	+5.6	25.2	+0.6	56.4	-0.3	11.9	-2.1	0.9	2.0	3.2	(2) 0.4	+0.4
Wimbledon	72.1	+4.3	49.1	+7.7	22.3	-13.4	25.0	+6.8	1.2	1.9	–	(1) 0.5	+10.6
Newham, East Ham	55.6	+8.0	15.2	+1.4	70.4	+16.8	11.6	+0.8	1.2	–	–	(1) 1.6	–
West Ham	55.0	+10.2	14.7	+2.6	62.7	+10.9	11.5	+1.3	1.4	1.6	3.3	(4) 8.2	+3.7
Redbridge, Ilford North	62.9	+1.7	45.7	+2.0	34.2	-5.4	12.7	-1.1	1.2	1.9	–	(1) 1.0	-0.2
Ilford South	58.3	+4.7	27.4	+0.1	49.4	+0.6	17.0	-3.6	2.6	2.2	–	(1) 1.5	–
Richmond, Richmond Park*	76.2	+3.0	49.7	+10.1	5.0	-4.2	42.8	-3.8	1.0	1.1	–	(2) 0.4	–
Twickenham	74.1	+1.8	34.1	+1.7	7.7	-3.7	54.4	+2.7	1.1	1.5	1.1	(2) 0.2	–
Southwark, Camberwell & Peckham	59.3	+7.3	13.0	+3.1	59.2	-4.1	22.4	+1.9	2.9	–	–	(7) 2.5	–
Bermondsey & Old Southwark	57.5	+8.8	17.1	+4.1	29.2	-2.4	48.4	+0.7	1.6	–	3.1	(2) 0.6	–
Dulwich & West Norwood	66.2	+9.3	22.2	-2.3	46.6	+2.3	27.2	+4.0	2.6	1.5	–	–	-2.3
Sutton, Carshalton & Wallington	69.0	+4.8	36.8	-0.6	8.7	-8.6	48.3	+7.9	0.8	2.9	2.4	–	–
Sutton & Cheam	72.8	+5.5	42.4	+1.7	7.0	-4.9	45.7	-1.2	0.5	2.0	2.1	(4) 0.4	–
Tower Hamlets, Bethnal Green & Bow*	62.4	+10.9	13.9	+2.0	42.9	+8.5	20.1	+7.8	1.7	–	2.8	(6) 18.5	–
Poplar & Limehouse	62.3	+12.2	27.1	+2.6	40.0	+4.7	11.2	-2.8	1.0	1.2	–	(5) 19.6	-1.0
Waltham Forest, Chingford & Woodford G.	66.5	+3.5	52.8	-0.4	22.7	-3.0	16.8	-0.9	1.5	2.6	3.0	(2) 0.6	+1.3
Leyton & Wanstead	63.2	+9.3	22.2	-0.5	43.6	-2.2	27.6	+2.9	1.4	2.7	1.4	(2) 1.1	–
Walthamstow	63.4	+8.8	14.0	-4.2	51.8	+1.5	28.7	+1.6	1.9	2.0	–	(3) 1.6	–
Wandsworth, Battersea*	65.7	+6.5	47.3	+7.5	35.1	-5.6	14.7	+0.3	1.1	1.0	–	(2) 0.7	+6.5
Putney	64.4	+4.6	52.0	+9.7	27.4	-10.2	16.9	+0.6	1.4	1.1	1.1	–	+9.9
Tooting	68.9	+9.5	38.5	+8.0	43.5	+0.8	14.8	-4.8	1.2	1.2	–	(2) 0.7	+3.6
Westminster, Cities Of London & W.	55.3	+4.1	52.2	+3.9	22.2	-3.1	20.5	+2.0	2.1	1.8	–	(4) 1.3	+3.5
Westminster North	59.3	+8.5	38.5	+5.2	43.9	+4.0	13.9	-5.7	1.2	0.8	0.8	(4) 0.8	+0.6

ENGLAND	Turnout %	Turnout +/-	Con %	Con +/-	Lab %	Lab +/-	LD %	LD +/-	Grn %	UKIP %	BNP %	Other No. & %	Swing
Greater Manchester, Altrincham & Sale W.	68.4	+0.6	48.9	+1.9	22.4	-7.0	25.5	+3.6	-	3.2	-	-	+4.5
Ashton Under Lyne	56.9	+5.4	24.7	+4.6	48.4	-10.1	14.8	+3.2	-	4.4	7.6	-	+7.3
Blackley & Broughton	49.2	+3.4	18.3	+5.3	54.3	-8.2	14.2	-4.9	-	2.6	7.2	(2) 3.4	-
Bolton North East	64.7	+10.2	36.5	+2.2	45.9	-0.4	13.0	-3.1	-	4.2	-	(1) 0.4	+1.3
South East	57.0	+5.7	25.6	+2.9	47.4	-8.3	15.9	-2.2	-	3.9	5.1	(1) 0.5	+5.6
West	66.7	+5.5	38.3	+4.9	38.5	-6.8	17.2	-1.8	-	4.0	-	(2) 0.8	+5.9
Bury North*	67.3	+5.7	40.2	+3.4	35.2	-6.6	17.0	+1.9	-	2.9	4.1	(2) 0.7	+5.0
South	65.6	+7.1	33.6	+5.5	40.4	-10.5	18.2	+1.1	-	2.1	3.6	(1) 1.0	+8.0
Cheadle	73.3	+4.6	40.8	+0.5	9.4	-0.5	47.1	-0.7	-	2.7	-	-	-
Denton & Reddish	58.1	+5.6	24.9	+5.8	51.0	-6.7	17.9	+1.6	-	5.5	-	(1) 0.8	+6.2
Hazel Grove	67.4	+6.1	33.6	+3.3	12.5	-3.6	48.8	-1.5	-	5.1	-	-	-
Heywood & Middleton	57.5	+3.7	27.2	+5.4	40.1	-8.2	22.7	+2.5	-	2.6	7.0	(1) 0.4	+6.8
Leigh	58.4	+7.1	20.9	+4.5	48.0	-9.8	18.2	-0.9	-	3.5	6.1	(3) 3.3	-
Makerfield	59.4	+9.8	18.8	+5.2	47.3	-14.8	16.2	+4.8	-	-	7.4	(2) 10.4	+10.0
Manchester Central	44.3	+2.5	11.8	+1.3	52.7	-6.6	26.6	+5.6	2.3	1.5	4.1	(4) 1.0	-
Gorton	50.5	+4.7	11.0	+1.2	50.1	-3.0	32.6	-0.9	2.7	-	-	(4) 3.5	-
Withington	60.5	+5.2	11.1	+0.8	40.5	-0.4	44.7	+2.4	1.8	1.6	-	(2) 0.5	-
Oldham East & Saddleworth	60.7	+3.9	26.4	+8.7	31.9	-10.7	31.6	-0.5	-	3.9	5.7	(1) 0.5	-
West & Royton	58.6	+4.6	23.7	+2.6	45.5	-2.9	19.1	-2.1	-	3.2	7.1	(1) 1.5	-
Rochdale	58.1	+0.9	18.1	+7.6	36.4	-4.5	34.4	-6.1	-	4.4	-	(3) 6.7	-
Salford & Eccles	55.0	+9.5	20.5	+3.6	40.1	-15.3	26.3	+3.5	-	2.6	6.3	(3) 4.2	-
Stalybridge & Hyde	58.7	+4.9	32.9	+6.8	39.6	-10.1	17.0	+1.4	1.7	3.3	5.5	-	+8.5
Stockport	62.2	+8.2	25.3	+1.8	42.7	-9.6	25.0	+3.6	1.7	2.2	3.1	-	+5.7
Stretford & Urmston	63.3	-0.6	28.7	-1.4	48.6	-2.8	16.9	+3.0	2.0	3.4	-	(1) 0.4	+0.7
Wigan	58.4	+6.3	24.7	+5.8	48.5	-9.6	15.4	-1.5	-	5.7	5.7	-	+7.7
Worsley & Eccles South	57.5	+3.2	32.5	+4.8	42.9	-10.4	16.5	+3.6	-	4.9	-	(1) 3.2	+7.6
Wythenshawe & Sale East	51.0	-0.2	25.6	+3.3	44.1	-8.0	22.3	+0.9	-	3.4	3.9	(1) 0.7	+5.7

Hampshire, Aldershot	63.5	−0.1	46.7	+2.7	12.1	−9.6	34.4	+5.5	−	4.5	−	(2) 2.3	−
Basingstoke	67.2	+6.3	50.5	+11.7	20.4	−12.2	24.5	+2.6	−	4.1	−	(1) 0.5	+11.9
Eastleigh	69.3	+4.9	39.3	+2.1	9.6	−11.5	46.5	+8.2	−	3.6	−	(3) 0.9	−
Fareham	71.6	+4.7	55.3	+5.6	14.2	−11.4	23.8	+2.1	1.5	4.1	−	(1) 1.1	+8.5
Gosport	64.5	+3.2	51.8	+7.0	16.9	−14.5	21.1	+4.5	1.2	3.2	2.1	(4) 3.7	+10.8
Hampshire East	71.0	+6.3	56.8	+9.7	7.9	−8.6	30.5	−3.5	−	2.9	−	(2) 2.0	−
North East	73.3	+10.7	60.6	+7.5	9.8	−6.8	25.5	−1.6	−	4.2	−	−	−
North West	70.4	+4.3	58.3	+7.8	13.1	−7.7	23.4	−1.5	−	5.2	−	−	−
Havant	63.0	+2.5	51.1	+6.8	17.7	−11.0	23.4	+3.2	−	5.9	−	(1) 1.8	+8.9
Meon Valley	72.7	+1.5	56.2	+10.4	6.4	−4.2	32.6	−8.4	−	2.9	−	(3) 1.9	−
New Forest East	68.7	+2.6	52.8	+3.4	9.8	−2.4	30.3	−3.0	2.0	5.0	−	−	−
West	69.6	+3.5	58.8	+2.9	9.8	−6.7	23.3	+4.1	2.2	5.9	−	−	−
Portsmouth North*	62.7	+2.6	44.3	+6.5	27.8	−10.8	20.1	−0.2	1.0	4.1	−	(2) 2.7	+8.6
South	57.1	−0.3	33.3	−0.4	13.7	−8.7	45.9	+4.2	1.7	2.1	2.1	(2) 1.3	−
Romsey & Southampton North*	71.7	+5.3	49.7	+6.6	6.4	−4.6	41.3	−2.4	−	2.6	−	−	−
Southampton Itchen	59.6	+4.8	36.3	+9.0	36.8	−11.5	20.8	+0.1	1.4	4.3	−	(1) 0.4	+10.3
Test	61.4	+5.4	33.0	+8.0	38.5	−5.7	22.3	−1.8	2.0	3.9	−	(1) 0.3	+6.9
Winchester*	75.8	+3.9	48.5	+11.2	5.5	−3.9	43.1	−7.0	−	2.0	−	(1) 0.9	−
Hereford and Worcester, Bromsgrove	70.7	+3.1	43.7	−7.3	21.8	−8.1	19.6	+4.6	−	5.7	3.7	(3) 5.5	+0.4
Hereford & South Herefordshire*	67.2	+1.1	46.2	+5.2	7.2	−3.0	41.1	−2.3	−	3.4	2.0	−	−
Herefordshire North	71.1	+1.8	51.8	−0.7	7.1	−8.4	31.0	+6.9	3.2	5.7	−	(1) 1.2	−
Redditch*	64.2	+0.6	43.5	+5.0	30.3	−13.4	17.6	+3.2	0.9	3.4	3.2	(4) 1.2	+9.2
Worcester*	67.2	+2.8	39.5	+4.4	33.4	−8.4	19.4	+3.2	1.5	2.8	2.5	(3) 0.8	+6.4
Worcestershire Mid	70.6	+4.0	54.5	+3.2	14.9	−9.1	23.4	+3.1	1.2	6.0	−	−	+6.1
West	74.2	+4.2	50.4	+5.4	6.8	−3.7	37.8	−1.2	1.2	3.9	−	−	−
Wyre Forest*	66.3	+2.4	36.9	+7.8	14.3	−8.2	11.9	−	−	2.9	2.2	(1) 31.7	−
Hertfordshire, Broxbourne	64.0	+4.7	58.8	+4.9	17.6	−7.9	13.4	+1.1	−	4.1	4.7	(1) 1.4	+6.4
Hemel Hempstead	68.0	+3.7	50.0	+9.9	20.8	−18.9	22.9	+6.0	−	2.5	3.3	(1) 0.5	+14.4
Hertford & Stortford	70.6	+4.1	53.8	+3.6	13.8	−10.5	26.0	+7.5	−	3.1	2.3	(2) 1.0	+7.1
Hertfordshire North East	69.8	+3.2	53.5	+5.5	16.4	−11.9	23.4	+3.1	1.7	4.1	−	(3) 0.8	+8.7
South West	72.5	+3.8	54.2	+7.2	11.5	−9.3	27.9	−2.1	−	2.6	2.3	(1) 1.5	−

ENGLAND	Turnout %	Turnout +/-	Con %	Con +/-	Lab %	Lab +/-	LD %	LD +/-	Grn %	UKIP %	BNP %	Other No. & %	Swing
Hertsmere	64.7	+1.7	56.0	+2.8	18.8	-8.4	17.4	-1.0	1.3	3.6	3.0	-	+5.6
Hitchin & Harpenden	74.1	+5.4	54.6	+5.2	13.6	-8.4	26.7	+0.2	1.5	3.0	-	(4) 0.7	-
St. Albans	75.4	+6.9	40.8	+3.5	17.6	-16.7	36.4	+11.0	1.4	3.8	-	-	+10.1
Stevenage*	64.8	+2.1	41.4	+6.4	33.4	-9.7	16.6	-1.7	-	4.5	2.3	(4) 1.8	+8.0
Watford*	68.6	+3.6	34.9	+5.3	26.7	-6.8	32.4	+1.1	1.6	2.2	2.2	-	-
Welwyn Hatfield	68.0	-0.2	57.0	+7.4	21.4	-14.9	16.4	+2.2	1.6	3.4	-	(1) 0.3	+11.1
Humberside, Beverley & Holderness	67.1	+2.9	47.1	+6.2	21.1	-13.6	22.7	+3.0	1.3	3.5	3.9	(1) 0.4	+9.9
Brigg & Goole*	65.1	+2.4	44.9	+6.9	33.1	-12.7	14.6	+1.4	-	4.0	3.4	-	+9.8
Cleethorpes*	64.0	+2.4	42.1	+4.8	32.6	-10.8	18.2	+3.5	-	7.1	-	-	+7.8
Great Grimsby	53.8	+2.1	30.5	+6.7	32.7	-14.4	22.4	+3.1	-	6.2	4.6	(2) 3.5	+10.5
Haltemprice & Howden	69.4	-1.1	50.2	+3.2	15.7	+2.2	26.4	-10.0	1.4	-	3.2	(1) 3.0	-
Hull East	50.6	+3.0	16.6	+3.6	47.9	-8.1	22.8	+2.6	-	8.0	-	(2) 4.7	-
North	52.0	+5.9	13.1	-0.2	39.2	-13.1	37.3	+11.3	1.4	4.1	4.3	(1) 0.6	-
West & Hessle	55.0	+10.3	20.2	-0.5	42.5	-12.6	24.2	+3.2	-	5.4	4.5	(2) 3.3	-
Scunthorpe	58.7	+4.3	32.6	+5.8	39.5	-12.5	18.3	+1.2	1.1	4.6	3.9	-	+9.2
Yorkshire East	64.0	+2.8	47.5	+2.1	20.3	-11.8	21.2	+2.2	1.5	4.2	3.6	(1) 1.8	+6.9
Isle of Wight, Isle Of Wight	63.9	+1.9	46.7	-2.3	11.6	-5.6	31.7	+2.2	1.3	3.5	2.1	(4) 3.1	-
Kent, Ashford	67.9	+2.5	54.1	+2.7	16.7	-9.7	22.8	+7.2	1.8	4.5	-	-	+6.2
Canterbury	66.4	+0.0	44.8	+0.3	16.1	-12.0	32.5	+11.1	2.3	3.9	-	(1) 0.4	+6.1
Chatham & Aylesford*	64.5	+3.8	46.2	+9.4	32.3	-12.7	13.3	-0.2	0.9	3.0	3.1	(2) 1.2	+11.1
Dartford*	65.7	+2.4	48.8	+7.6	27.6	-15.5	14.7	+4.6	-	3.7	-	(3) 5.3	+11.6
Dover*	70.1	+2.8	44.0	+9.1	33.5	-11.8	15.8	+0.0	-	3.5	2.2	(3) 1.0	+10.4
Faversham & Kent Mid	70.3	+5.0	56.2	+6.1	16.6	-12.5	19.6	+2.9	1.9	3.7	-	(2) 2.0	+9.3
Folkestone & Hythe	67.7	-1.0	49.4	-4.5	10.8	-1.8	30.3	+0.7	1.2	4.6	3.1	(1) 0.5	-
Gillingham & Rainham*	66.1	+2.1	46.2	+5.5	27.7	-13.1	18.1	+2.8	0.8	3.2	2.5	(3) 1.5	+9.3
Gravesham	67.4	+1.6	48.5	+4.8	28.8	-13.4	13.3	+2.6	1.4	4.8	-	(2) 3.1	+9.1
Maidstone & The Weald	68.9	+3.7	48.0	-3.8	9.7	-12.6	36.0	+13.2	1.3	3.3	-	(2) 1.6	-

Rochester & Strood	65.0	+2.6	49.2	+6.6	28.5	-13.1	16.3	+3.9	1.5	–	–	(1) 4.5	+9.8
Sevenoaks	71.0	+5.0	56.8	+5.5	13.2	-8.0	21.4	-0.8	–	3.6	2.8	(2) 2.2	–
Sittingbourne & Sheppey	64.0	-1.2	50.0	+8.3	24.6	-17.1	16.4	+3.6	–	5.4	2.7	(2) 1.0	+12.7
Thanet North	63.2	+4.0	52.7	+4.7	21.5	-11.1	19.4	+3.8	–	6.5	–	–	+7.9
South	65.6	+0.5	48.0	+6.8	31.4	-8.1	15.1	+2.9	–	5.5	–	–	+7.4
Tonbridge & Malling	71.5	+3.1	57.9	+5.1	12.6	-11.2	22.5	+3.0	1.5	3.7	–	(2) 1.7	+8.2
Tunbridge Wells	68.1	+2.2	56.2	+5.5	10.8	-9.6	25.3	+0.0	1.8	4.1	1.4	(1) 0.3	–
Lancashire, Blackburn	62.9	+5.2	26.1	+3.5	47.8	+5.7	15.2	-5.4	–	2.1	4.7	(3) 4.0	-1.1
Blackpool North & Cleveleys*	61.5	+3.9	41.8	+4.5	36.5	-9.2	13.3	-0.4	–	4.1	3.8	(1) 0.5	+6.9
South	55.8	+3.5	35.8	+4.9	41.1	-7.5	14.4	-0.7	–	3.8	4.2	(1) 0.7	+6.2
Burnley*	62.8	+3.3	16.6	+5.8	31.3	-7.1	35.7	+12.0	–	2.2	9.0	(2) 5.2	–
Chorley	69.2	+7.0	38.0	+3.6	43.2	-7.6	14.0	-0.7	–	4.1	–	(1) 0.7	+5.6
Fylde	66.3	+7.0	52.2	-2.1	19.7	-5.9	22.1	+6.2	1.5	4.5	–	–	+1.9
Hyndburn	63.5	+4.7	33.8	+1.9	41.1	-4.6	11.8	-2.6	1.1	3.5	5.0	(3) 3.7	+3.3
Lancashire West	65.7	+7.6	36.2	+2.2	45.1	-2.9	13.6	-0.5	1.0	3.7	–	(1) 0.4	+2.6
Lancaster & Fleetwood*	63.4	+3.9	36.1	+2.5	35.3	-7.1	19.1	+3.5	4.4	2.4	2.2	(1) 0.5	+4.8
Morecambe & Lunesdale*	62.4	+0.9	41.5	+4.2	39.5	-9.5	13.3	-0.3	1.4	4.2	–	–	+6.9
Pendle*	67.8	+4.1	38.9	+7.1	30.9	-6.2	20.2	-3.0	–	3.3	6.4	(1) 0.3	+6.6
Preston	51.5	-2.7	21.7	+0.7	48.2	-0.5	24.4	+4.5	–	4.5	–	(2) 1.2	+0.6
Ribble Valley	67.2	+5.7	50.3	+5.4	22.0	-7.8	20.5	-2.1	–	6.7	–	(1) 0.4	+6.6
Rossendale & Darwen*	64.4	+2.8	41.8	+7.1	32.2	-10.7	18.1	+3.2	–	3.4	2.0	(4) 4.4	+8.9
South Ribble*	67.9	+4.4	45.5	+6.6	34.7	-9.6	14.1	-0.6	–	3.7	–	–	+8.1
Wyre & Preston North	71.1	+7.8	52.4	-2.3	21.3	-5.9	21.5	+5.4	–	4.8	–	–	+1.8
Leicestershire, Bosworth	70.0	+4.3	42.8	+0.2	16.0	-15.9	33.5	+11.9	–	2.0	4.5	(2) 1.1	+8.0
Charnwood	75.6	+11.7	49.6	+1.3	19.7	-9.9	21.5	+2.5	–	3.4	5.8	–	+5.6
Harborough	70.5	+4.1	48.9	+7.5	12.7	-5.9	31.1	-2.3	–	2.7	3.1	(2) 1.4	–
Leicester East	65.8	+3.9	24.4	+4.6	53.8	-5.0	14.2	-2.3	1.5	1.5	3.5	(1) 1.0	+4.8
South	61.1	+3.4	21.4	+3.6	45.6	+6.2	26.9	-3.7	1.6	1.5	3.0	–	+7.6
West	55.2	+2.6	27.2	+2.8	38.4	-12.4	22.6	+4.4	1.8	2.5	6.0	(4) 1.6	+7.6
North West*	72.9	+6.1	44.6	+8.6	30.1	-15.4	16.6	+4.6	–	2.2	6.5	–	+12.0
South	71.2	+6.0	49.5	+4.1	20.9	-8.8	21.0	+2.0	–	3.6	5.0	–	+6.4

ENGLAND	Turnout %	Turnout +/-	Con %	Con +/-	Lab %	Lab +/-	LD %	LD +/-	Grn %	UKIP %	BNP %	Other No. & %	Swing %
Loughborough*	74.4	+11.4	41.6	+4.3	34.5	-6.7	18.3	+0.4	–	1.8	3.9	–	+5.5
Rutland & Melton	71.5	+6.2	51.1	-0.1	14.3	-10.6	25.8	+7.2	–	4.6	3.2	(1) 1.1	+5.3
Lincolnshire, Boston & Skegness	64.2	+5.3	49.4	+3.1	20.6	-10.9	14.8	+5.4	–	9.5	5.3	(1) 0.4	+7.0
Gainsborough	67.5	+2.8	49.3	+5.4	15.6	-10.5	27.8	+1.8	–	4.2	3.1	–	+8.0
Grantham & Stamford	67.7	+4.7	50.3	+3.4	18.0	-13.2	22.2	+5.7	–	3.0	4.7	(1) 1.8	+8.3
Lincoln*	70.2	+12.9	37.5	+3.3	35.2	-8.5	20.2	+1.9	–	2.2	3.0	(2) 1.8	+5.9
Louth & Horncastle	65.1	+2.8	49.6	+3.2	17.3	-8.0	22.2	+1.6	–	4.3	4.4	(2) 2.2	+5.6
Sleaford & North Hykeham	70.1	+3.3	51.6	+1.0	16.9	-9.5	18.2	+0.1	–	3.6	3.3	(1) 6.4	+5.3
South Holland & The Deepings	65.8	+4.3	59.1	+2.1	14.0	-10.5	15.5	+2.6	1.4	6.5	3.6	–	+6.3
Merseyside, Birkenhead	56.3	+6.3	18.9	+2.4	62.5	-2.3	18.6	-0.1	–	–	–	–	–
Bootle	57.8	+7.0	8.9	+1.5	66.4	-4.6	15.1	-1.4	–	6.1	2.3	(1) 1.1	–
Garston & Halewood	60.1	+6.8	16.1	+6.3	59.5	+1.6	20.1	-9.9	–	3.6	–	(1) 0.6	–
Knowsley	56.3	+2.6	9.0	-2.3	70.9	-0.9	13.4	-0.4	–	2.6	4.2	–	–
Liverpool Riverside	52.1	+9.4	10.9	+1.9	59.3	+0.0	22.7	-0.6	3.5	1.7	1.8	–	–
Walton	54.8	+8.1	6.5	+0.1	72.0	+0.2	14.2	-2.7	–	2.6	3.2	(2) 1.4	–
Wavertree	60.6	+12.8	7.5	+1.0	53.1	+3.6	34.2	-6.4	1.6	2.3	0.4	(2) 0.9	–
West Derby	56.7	+11.0	9.3	+1.0	64.1	+3.6	12.5	-2.7	–	3.1	–	(2) 11.0	–
St. Helens North	59.4	+3.7	22.3	+3.5	51.7	-5.6	20.2	-0.7	–	4.7	–	(1) 1.1	–
South	59.1	+5.9	17.8	+5.7	52.9	-2.7	22.2	-6.6	–	2.7	4.4	–	–
Sefton Central	71.8	+11.0	33.9	+0.4	41.9	-3.7	19.9	+0.7	–	4.2	–	–	+2.0
Southport	65.1	+4.1	35.8	-1.2	9.4	-3.4	49.6	+3.3	–	5.1	–	–	–
Wallasey	63.2	+5.4	31.4	+0.9	51.8	-2.7	13.7	+0.9	–	2.9	–	(1) 0.3	+1.8
Wirral South	71.2	+3.5	39.5	+6.3	40.8	-1.7	16.6	-5.0	–	3.2	–	–	+4.0
West	71.5	+3.4	42.5	+0.7	36.3	-4.0	16.8	+0.5	–	2.3	–	(2) 2.1	+2.3
Norfolk, Broadland	72.7	+8.3	46.2	+2.8	13.8	-9.8	32.4	+2.9	1.4	4.5	1.7	–	–
Great Yarmouth*	61.2	+1.2	43.1	+5.0	33.2	-12.4	14.4	+3.3	1.0	4.8	3.3	(1) 0.2	+8.7
Norfolk Mid	68.4	+2.8	49.5	+2.9	17.4	-12.8	22.2	+3.0	2.9	5.5	2.5	–	+7.9

North	73.2	+0.5	32.1	-3.9	5.8	-3.1	55.5	+2.3	1.0	5.4	–	(1) 0.2	–
North West	65.3	+3.7	54.2	+4.3	13.3	-18.3	23.2	+8.5	1.6	3.9	3.8	–	+11.3
South	72.2	+3.1	49.3	+5.2	13.2	-9.0	29.4	-1.3	1.8	4.2	2.0	–	–
South West	66.2	+4.1	48.3	+3.4	18.6	-11.4	21.6	+2.4	1.7	6.2	3.6	(2) 0.6	+7.4
Norwich North*	65.7	+3.8	40.6	+10.1	31.4	-15.7	18.3	+2.2	2.9	4.4	1.8	(1) 0.2	+12.9
South*	64.6	+5.6	22.9	+1.1	28.7	-8.7	29.4	-0.6	14.9	2.4	1.5	–	–
North Yorkshire, Harrogate & Knaresb.*	71.1	+4.4	45.7	+9.9	6.4	-2.7	43.8	-8.3	–	2.0	2.1	–	+4.4
Richmond (Yorks)	66.3	+1.7	62.8	+3.5	15.3	-5.3	19.1	+2.2	2.8	–	–	(2) 0.9	+6.9
Scarborough & Whitby	65.3	+1.7	42.8	+1.8	26.3	-12.0	22.5	+6.5	1.5	3.0	2.9	(1) 1.3	+9.7
Selby & Ainsty	71.1	+2.1	49.4	+2.3	25.7	-17.1	17.7	+7.7	–	3.2	2.7	(3) 0.9	–
Skipton & Ripon	70.9	+4.7	50.6	+0.6	10.0	-8.2	32.4	+5.8	–	3.5	2.6	(1) 3.7	+5.4
Thirsk & Malton	49.6	-16.2	52.9	+1.0	13.6	-9.8	23.3	+4.5	–	6.6	–	(1) 0.3	+6.0
York Central	60.8	+0.2	26.1	+3.2	40.0	-8.9	25.2	+5.0	3.6	2.4	2.5	–	–
Outer*	70.2	+5.8	43.0	+6.7	17.1	-9.9	36.1	-0.7	–	2.1	1.8	–	+3.3
Northamptonshire, Corby*	69.5	+3.9	42.2	+2.2	38.7	-4.4	14.4	+1.7	–	–	4.7	(1) 2.3	+7.8
Daventry	72.5	+4.6	56.5	+3.5	15.8	-12.1	19.4	+4.9	1.5	4.5	–	(2) 2.2	+9.4
Kettering	68.8	-0.4	49.1	+6.2	29.9	-12.7	15.8	+3.6	–	–	2.9	(3) 1.2	+6.9
Northampton North*	65.1	+7.9	34.1	+4.4	29.3	-9.4	27.9	+1.0	1.1	3.1	3.3	(5) 8.5	+9.6
South	61.8	+2.9	40.8	+3.0	25.4	-16.1	19.4	+5.9	0.9	4.9	–	(1) 1.2	+7.5
Northamptonshire South	73.0	+5.4	55.2	+3.7	17.3	-11.4	21.0	+3.9	1.1	4.0	–	(4) 2.0	+10.8
Wellingborough	67.2	+1.4	48.2	+5.5	25.4	-16.0	17.1	+5.6	0.9	3.2	3.1	–	–
Northumberland, Berwick Upon Tweed	67.9	+4.6	36.7	+7.7	13.2	-5.2	43.7	-8.9	–	3.2	3.2	(2) 3.0	+6.1
Blyth Valley	61.3	+5.1	16.6	+2.7	44.5	-10.5	27.2	-3.9	–	4.3	4.4	(2) 5.1	–
Hexham	72.0	+3.4	43.2	+0.8	19.0	-11.4	29.9	+4.2	–	–	2.8	(2) 1.3	–
Wansbeck	61.9	+3.5	17.5	+2.6	45.8	-9.3	27.5	+1.0	1.6	2.5	3.7	(2) 3.1	+6.4
Nottinghamshire, Ashfield	62.3	+5.2	22.2	-2.2	33.7	-15.0	33.3	+19.5	–	1.9	5.8	(1) 0.8	+0.7
Bassetlaw	64.8	+4.0	33.9	-1.2	50.5	-2.5	11.2	-0.7	0.8	3.6	–	–	+2.6
Broxtowe*	73.9	+4.9	39.0	+1.8	38.3	-3.4	16.9	+0.8	–	2.3	2.7	–	+2.9
Gedling	68.0	+4.1	37.3	+0.3	41.1	-5.5	15.3	+1.5	–	3.0	3.3	–	+9.5
Mansfield	60.4	+3.5	26.3	+7.6	38.7	-11.4	15.4	+1.4	–	6.2	4.4	(1) 9.0	+4.7
Newark	71.4	+8.1	53.9	+3.4	22.3	-6.0	20.0	+1.6	–	3.8	–	–	–

ENGLAND	Turnout %	Turnout +/-	Con %	Con +/-	Lab %	Lab +/-	LD %	LD +/-	Grn %	UKIP %	BNP %	Other No. & %	Swing
Nottingham East	56.4	+7.5	23.7	+1.2	45.4	-1.3	24.3	+2.5	2.8	3.4	–	(1) 0.4	+1.3
North	54.2	+5.8	24.8	+6.7	48.6	-10.6	17.1	-0.3	–	3.9	5.7	–	+8.7
South	60.5	+9.1	32.9	+6.2	37.3	-8.6	23.1	-0.4	1.5	2.4	2.8	–	+7.4
Rushcliffe	73.6	+3.6	51.2	+3.1	20.7	-6.7	21.7	+4.4	2.3	4.1	–	–	+4.9
Sherwood*	68.5	+6.7	39.2	+5.8	38.8	-10.6	14.9	+1.4	–	3.0	3.6	(1) 0.4	+8.2
Oxfordshire, Banbury	66.7	+2.2	52.8	+5.9	19.2	-8.9	20.4	+2.9	1.7	5.0	–	(1) 0.9	+7.4
Henley	73.2	+5.4	56.2	+3.0	10.9	-4.1	25.2	-0.9	2.5	3.4	1.9	–	–
Oxford East	63.1	+5.6	18.8	+1.5	42.5	+6.5	33.6	-1.6	2.4	2.3	–	(2) 0.4	–
West & Abingdon*	65.3	-1.7	42.3	+9.6	10.6	-5.2	42.0	-4.1	2.1	2.7	–	(1) 0.3	–
Wantage	70.0	+1.9	52.0	+8.9	13.9	-10.0	27.9	+0.3	1.9	4.3	–	–	–
Witney	73.3	+4.3	58.8	+9.4	13.0	-9.4	19.4	-3.1	4.1	3.5	–	(5) 1.2	–
Shropshire, Ludlow	73.1	+1.1	52.8	+7.7	6.7	-4.0	32.8	-7.9	0.9	4.4	2.1	(1) 0.4	–
Shrewsbury & Atcham	70.3	+1.0	43.9	+6.3	20.6	-13.5	29.0	+6.1	1.1	3.1	2.2	(1) 0.2	+9.9
Shropshire North	65.7	+2.4	51.5	+1.9	18.1	-7.8	20.9	+1.2	1.6	4.7	3.2	–	+4.8
Telford	63.5	+4.8	36.3	+3.2	38.7	-9.5	15.5	+1.4	–	5.9	3.7	–	+6.3
Wrekin, The	70.1	+4.2	47.7	+5.6	27.1	-12.1	17.4	+2.4	–	4.5	3.3	–	+8.9
Somerset, Bridgwater & West Somerset	66.3	+2.3	45.3	-0.1	17.1	-8.5	28.3	+5.7	1.6	4.8	2.4	(1) 0.6	+4.2
Somerton & Frome	74.3	+5.1	44.5	+1.9	4.4	-6.4	47.5	+3.8	–	3.2	–	(1) 0.4	–
Taunton Deane	70.5	+1.2	42.2	+1.1	5.1	-7.0	49.1	+4.7	–	3.6	–	–	–
Wells*	66.9	-0.8	42.5	-1.0	7.5	-8.1	44.0	+6.1	1.1	3.1	1.8	–	–
Yeovil	69.4	+5.6	32.9	-1.2	5.2	-5.3	55.7	+4.2	–	4.1	2.0	–	–
South Yorkshire, Barnsley Central	56.5	+8.8	17.3	+2.5	47.3	-10.4	17.3	-2.0	–	4.7	8.9	(3) 4.6	–
East	56.1	+7.3	16.5	+3.8	47.0	-23.9	18.2	+4.1	–	4.5	8.6	(3) 5.2	–
Don Valley	59.8	+6.5	29.7	+2.7	37.9	-18.6	17.1	+0.6	–	4.4	4.9	(2) 6.1	+10.6
Doncaster Central	57.2	+5.2	24.8	+6.1	39.7	-11.3	21.1	-2.6	–	3.4	4.2	(3) 6.8	–
North	57.9	+5.2	21.0	+1.8	47.3	-3.8	14.9	-0.8	–	4.3	6.8	(2) 5.6	+2.8
Penistone & Stocksbridge	67.9	+5.8	31.2	+7.5	37.8	-7.4	21.1	-3.7	–	4.2	4.7	(1) 1.1	–

Rother Valley	64.2	+6.5	28.4	+5.3	40.9	−10.6	17.3	+1.2	–	5.6	7.7	–	+8.0
Rotherham	59.0	+4.9	16.7	+3.4	44.6	−13.1	16.0	−0.4	–	5.9	10.4	(1) 6.3	–
Sheffield Brightside & Hillsborough	57.1	+7.1	11.5	+1.7	55.0	−14.6	20.0	+6.9	–	4.1	7.8	(1) 1.7	–
Central	59.6	+4.6	10.1	+1.0	41.3	−5.2	40.9	+9.5	3.8	1.6	2.2	(1) 0.1	–
Hallam	73.7	+5.8	23.5	−6.6	16.1	−1.7	53.4	+7.1	1.8	2.3	–	(4) 2.8	–
Heeley	62.0	+4.3	17.3	+3.0	42.6	−11.5	28.4	+7.0	2.4	3.7	5.5	–	–
South East	61.5	+6.8	17.4	+3.0	48.7	−11.6	23.3	+6.4	–	4.6	5.7	(1) 0.3	–
Wentworth & Dearne	58.0	+3.6	17.6	+3.8	50.6	−11.2	16.1	−0.1	–	8.1	7.6	–	–
Staffordshire, Burton*	66.5	+6.1	44.5	+7.2	31.9	−10.2	15.8	+3.4	–	2.9	4.8	–	+8.7
Cannock Chase*	61.1	+3.7	40.1	+10.1	33.1	−17.9	17.0	+3.0	–	3.5	4.8	(3) 1.6	+14.0
Lichfield	71.0	+4.3	54.4	+5.7	19.8	−12.4	20.1	+4.2	–	5.7	–	–	+9.0
Newcastle Under Lyme	62.2	+4.0	34.4	+9.4	38.0	−7.4	19.6	+0.7	1.1	8.1	–	–	+8.4
Stafford*	71.1	+4.1	43.9	+4.7	33.0	−10.2	16.3	2.0	–	3.4	2.2	–	+7.4
Staffordshire Moorlands	70.5	+2.7	45.2	+5.4	29.9	−6.0	16.7	−0.8	–	8.2	–	–	+5.7
South	68.3	+30.7	53.2	+2.5	20.3	+0.3	16.7	+3.3	–	5.5	3.8	(1) 0.5	+1.1
Stoke On Trent Central	53.2	+4.5	21.0	+3.7	38.8	−13.6	21.7	+3.1	–	4.3	7.7	(5) 6.4	–
North	55.8	+4.9	23.8	+6.0	44.3	−11.5	17.7	+4.2	–	6.2	8.0	–	+8.8
South	58.6	+4.4	28.4	+4.2	38.8	−8.1	15.9	+0.8	1.0	3.4	9.4	(2) 4.1	+6.2
Stone	70.4	+3.4	50.6	+2.2	20.7	−9.0	22.4	+3.8	–	5.3	–	–	+5.6
Tamworth*	64.5	+3.4	45.8	+8.7	32.7	−10.3	16.2	+2.1	4.3	4.9	–	(1) 0.5	+9.5
Suffolk, Bury St. Edmunds	69.3	+2.5	47.5	+1.2	16.6	−10.7	26.4	+6.7	1.7	5.1	–	–	+5.9
Ipswich*	62.0	+1.9	39.1	+8.0	34.7	−8.2	18.2	−2.9	2.7	2.9	2.7	(3) 0.7	+8.1
Suffolk Central & Ipswich North	70.5	+3.4	50.8	+6.2	16.2	−12.3	25.0	+4.7	2.0	4.4	–	(2) 0.9	+9.3
Coastal	71.2	+4.0	46.4	+1.8	16.1	−10.1	29.8	+7.7	–	5.7	–	–	+6.0
South	70.9	+2.1	47.7	+5.7	14.3	−10.1	30.8	+2.4	–	7.1	3.0	–	–
West	64.7	+3.9	50.6	+1.7	14.7	−14.2	23.4	+6.2	–	6.4	–	(2) 1.9	+7.9
Waveney*	65.1	+1.5	40.2	+6.9	38.7	−6.6	13.3	−1.8	–	5.2	–	(1) 0.2	+6.8
Surrey, Epsom & Ewell	68.8	+2.6	56.2	+1.2	11.9	−8.1	26.8	+5.3	2.3	4.6	–	(1) 0.5	–
Esher & Walton	72.4	+10.1	58.9	+13.2	10.7	−8.8	24.8	−4.7	–	3.3	–	(4) 2.3	–
Guildford	72.1	+5.0	53.3	+9.9	5.1	−4.8	39.3	−4.0	–	1.8	–	(1) 0.5	–
Mole Valley	74.5	+3.1	57.5	+2.8	7.0	−3.7	28.7	−1.7	1.6	5.1	–	–	–

ENGLAND	Turnout %	Turnout +/-	Con %	Con +/-	Lab %	Lab +/-	LD %	LD +/-	Grn %	UKIP %	BNP %	Other No. & %	Swing
Reigate	69.8	+4.6	53.4	+4.8	11.3	-10.2	26.2	+3.1	2.2	4.2	2.7	-	-
Runnymede & Weybridge	66.4	+8.0	55.9	+4.5	13.4	-9.6	21.6	+3.8	1.4	6.5	-	(1) 1.1	+7.1
Spelthorne	67.1	+4.4	47.1	-3.4	16.5	-10.8	25.9	+8.8	-	8.5	-	(5) 2.1	+3.7
Surrey East	71.1	+5.2	56.7	+0.6	9.0	-5.8	25.9	+2.0	-	6.9	-	(2) 1.5	-
Heath	69.6	+5.2	57.6	+6.2	10.2	-6.5	25.8	-3.0	-	6.3	-	-	-
South West	74.8	+4.9	58.7	+8.1	6.0	-1.9	30.2	-9.2	1.2	2.6	1.1	(2) 0.2	-
Woking	71.5	+8.1	50.3	+2.9	8.0	-8.3	37.4	+4.3	-	3.8	-	(2) 0.5	-
Tyne and Wear, Blaydon	66.2	+4.0	15.9	+7.9	49.6	-2.0	29.3	-8.5	-	-	5.1	-	-
Gateshead	57.5	+3.8	14.9	+4.8	54.1	-7.3	21.3	+0.6	1.0	2.9	4.7	(2) 1.0	-
Houghton & Sunderland South	55.3	+2.1	21.4	+5.2	50.3	-11.7	13.9	-0.6	-	2.7	5.2	(1) 6.5	+8.4
Jarrow	60.3	+5.5	20.6	+7.8	53.9	-4.9	18.5	-4.0	-	-	7.0	-	-
Newcastle Upon Tyne Central	56.5	-0.1	19.4	+2.8	45.9	-4.6	24.1	-3.4	1.7	2.2	6.7	-	-
East	58.7	+3.4	16.0	+3.0	45.0	-7.7	33.3	+1.5	1.6	-	3.5	(1) 0.5	-
North	65.5	+3.8	18.1	+3.4	40.8	-9.0	33.1	+0.1	0.7	2.9	4.3	-	-
South Shields	57.7	+7.0	21.6	+4.0	52.0	-8.8	14.2	-5.0	2.1	-	6.5	(4) 3.6	-
Sunderland Central	57.0	+6.3	30.1	+5.6	45.9	-4.1	16.9	+0.1	-	2.6	4.5	-	+4.8
Tynemouth	69.6	+3.6	34.4	-2.2	45.3	-3.0	14.9	-0.2	1.0	1.7	2.7	-	+0.4
Tyneside North	59.7	+4.3	18.3	-0.3	50.7	-8.7	22.9	+0.9	-	2.8	4.0	(1) 1.3	-
Washington & Sunderland West	54.2	+6.8	21.8	+6.9	52.5	-16.2	17.1	+0.9	-	3.4	5.1	-	-
Warwickshire, Kenilworth & Southam	75.2	+5.0	53.6	+3.2	14.3	-11.2	27.7	+5.6	1.2	2.5	-	(1) 0.7	+7.2
Nuneaton*	65.8	+6.9	41.5	+4.6	36.9	-9.8	15.3	+2.8	-	-	6.3	-	+7.2
Rugby*	68.9	+1.5	44.0	+5.7	31.4	-12.1	19.9	+4.9	1.0	0.9	2.9	-	+8.9
Stratford On Avon	72.7	+3.5	51.5	+0.3	9.5	-6.0	29.1	+1.7	1.0	3.7	2.2	(2) 3.0	-
Warwick & Leamington*	72.3	+6.6	42.6	+8.2	35.4	-9.3	18.3	+2.4	1.4	1.9	-	(1) 0.4	+8.8
Warwickshire North*	67.4	+4.5	40.2	+8.1	40.1	-7.3	11.6	-1.9	-	2.8	4.5	(1) 0.9	+7.7
West Midlands, Aldridge-Brownhills	65.5	+2.0	59.3	+11.1	19.8	-12.9	17.7	+5.8	2.2	-	-	(1) 1.0	+12.0
Birmingham Edgbaston	60.6	+3.3	37.6	-1.5	40.6	-2.5	15.4	+2.6	1.1	1.8	2.9	(2) 0.7	+0.5

Erdington	53.5	+5.1	32.6	+9.7	41.8	-11.1	16.2	+0.3	-	2.4	5.1	(3) 1.9 +10.4
Hall Green	63.6	+7.7	15.0	+0.1	32.9	-9.4	24.6	-1.8	-	1.9	-	(2) 25.5 -
Hodge Hill	56.6	+0.9	11.6	+1.0	52.0	+5.1	27.7	-2.1	-	1.7	5.5	(1) 1.5 -
Ladywood	48.7	+3.5	11.9	+3.5	55.7	+3.0	27.5	-1.9	2.4	2.5	-	-
Northfield	58.6	+3.4	33.6	+3.2	40.3	-10.1	15.7	+3.3	1.0	3.3	5.5	(1) 0.7 +6.6
Perry Barr	59.0	+5.1	21.3	+4.0	50.3	+4.0	22.0	-4.1	-	4.0	-	(2) 2.5 -
Selly Oak	62.2	+1.9	31.1	+1.4	38.5	-8.3	22.3	+4.9	1.4	2.4	3.9	(1) 0.3 +4.8
Yardley	56.5	+2.0	19.2	+8.6	32.2	-2.5	39.6	-2.5	-	2.9	5.3	(1) 0.9 -
Coventry North East	59.4	+6.0	22.1	+3.3	49.3	-7.6	16.6	+0.1	-	3.0	4.3	(2) 4.7 +5.5
North West	63.9	+3.8	29.3	+2.7	42.8	-5.2	17.9	-0.5	1.1	2.8	3.6	(3) 2.5 +3.9
South	62.4	+3.0	33.4	+2.8	41.8	-4.0	18.0	+0.4	1.4	3.8	-	(1) 1.5 +3.4
Dudley North	63.5	+2.2	37.0	+5.6	38.7	-3.9	10.5	+0.0	-	8.5	4.9	(1) 0.4 +4.7
South	63.0	+2.8	43.1	+8.1	33.0	-11.0	15.7	+3.0	-	8.2	-	- +9.5
Halesowen & Rowley Regis	65.7	+2.6	41.2	+4.6	36.6	-9.7	14.8	+2.3	-	6.4	-	(1) 1.0 +7.1
Meriden	63.4	+3.3	51.7	+4.0	20.5	-11.7	17.8	+1.0	1.3	2.6	4.8	(1) 1.3 +7.9
Solihull*	72.3	+4.9	42.6	+2.9	8.9	-6.7	42.9	+3.5	-	2.2	2.9	(1) 0.6 -
Stourbridge*	67.8	+3.9	42.7	+3.4	31.7	-10.4	16.4	+0.4	0.8	4.5	3.6	(1) 0.4 +6.9
Sutton Coldfield	67.9	+5.2	54.0	+1.4	20.4	-5.5	18.0	+1.4	1.1	3.1	3.5	- +3.4
Walsall North	55.9	+3.8	34.3	+6.8	37.0	-11.2	13.1	+0.8	-	4.8	8.1	(2) 2.7 +9.0
Walsall South	63.0	+3.1	35.4	+6.9	39.7	-9.5	14.4	+4.6	-	8.4	-	(2) 2.2 +8.2
Warley	61.0	+3.8	24.8	+1.9	52.9	-2.0	15.5	+2.3	-	6.8	-	- +1.9
West Bromwich East	60.6	+2.4	28.9	+6.1	46.5	-9.2	13.2	+0.8	-	2.6	5.8	(1) 3.0 +7.7
West	55.8	+4.1	29.3	+6.6	45.0	-8.7	12.0	+1.8	-	4.3	9.4	- +7.6
Wolverhampton North East	59.2	+4.2	34.3	+4.7	41.4	-13.3	13.5	+1.9	-	3.3	6.6	(1) 1.0 +9.0
South East	58.0	+5.7	28.6	+5.6	47.6	-12.0	15.2	+2.9	-	7.7	-	(1) 1.0 +8.8
South West*	68.2	+5.2	40.7	+2.6	39.0	-4.5	16.0	+2.5	-	3.7	-	(1) 0.6 +3.5
West Sussex, Arundel & South Downs	72.9	+2.1	57.8	+7.4	8.6	-8.7	27.9	+1.4	-	5.7	-	-
Bognor Regis & Littlehampton	66.2	+3.0	51.4	+6.3	14.0	-11.0	23.5	+1.6	-	6.5	4.0	(1) 0.5 +8.6
Chichester	69.6	+4.4	55.3	+7.4	10.5	-8.1	27.4	-0.3	-	6.8	-	-
Crawley*	65.3	+6.9	44.8	+5.8	32.3	-6.8	14.4	-1.1	1.3	2.9	3.5	(2) 0.9 +6.3
Horsham	72.0	+4.9	52.7	+3.4	7.5	-9.2	32.2	+4.5	1.0	5.1	-	(3) 1.4 -

ENGLAND	Turnout %	Turnout +/-	Con %	Con +/-	Lab %	Lab +/-	LD %	LD +/-	Grn %	UKIP %	BNP %	Other No. & %	Swing
Sussex Mid	72.4	+3.5	50.7	+2.5	6.6	-6.2	37.5	+1.8	1.2	2.5	1.0	(1) 0.5	-
Worthing East & Shoreham	65.4	+3.6	48.5	+4.6	16.7	-8.8	25.5	+1.2	2.3	6.2	-	(1) 0.8	+6.7
West	64.7	+2.7	51.7	+4.1	11.8	-7.4	27.9	+1.1	2.0	6.0	-	(1) 0.6	-
West Yorkshire, Batley & Spen	66.6	+5.8	33.6	+1.9	42.2	-3.1	15.8	+0.4	1.2	-	7.2	-	+2.5
Bradford East*	62.1	+8.0	26.8	+9.4	32.8	-11.3	33.7	+3.9	-	-	4.6	(3) 2.1	-
South	59.8	+6.3	29.1	+4.8	41.3	-7.0	18.3	+3.8	-	3.5	7.0	(1) 0.8	+5.9
West	64.9	+8.9	31.1	-0.2	45.3	+5.6	11.7	-7.4	2.3	2.0	3.4	(2) 4.1	-2.9
Calder Valley*	67.3	+1.3	39.4	+3.6	27.0	-11.5	25.2	+6.3	1.7	2.3	3.5	(3) 1.0	+7.6
Colne Valley*	69.1	+3.8	37.0	+4.1	26.4	-9.0	28.2	+3.7	1.6	2.1	3.4	(1) 1.3	+6.5
Dewsbury*	68.4	+9.2	35.0	+3.3	32.2	-8.4	16.9	+3.2	1.6	-	6.0	(2) 8.3	+5.9
Elmet & Rothwell*	71.8	+2.0	42.6	+8.1	34.5	-11.4	16.3	-1.0	-	2.9	3.2	(1) 0.4	+9.8
Halifax	61.9	+0.9	34.0	+0.9	37.4	-4.5	19.1	+1.2	-	1.5	6.3	(1) 1.7	+2.7
Hemsworth	60.4	+6.1	24.3	+2.2	46.8	-11.9	12.9	-2.8	-	-	7.0	(1) 9.0	+7.0
Huddersfield	61.1	+4.5	27.8	+6.7	38.8	-7.6	24.7	+0.6	4.0	-	3.9	(1) 0.8	-
Keighley*	72.4	+3.2	41.9	+7.7	35.8	-9.0	14.8	+3.0	-	3.1	4.1	(1) 0.3	+8.3
Leeds Central	46.0	+1.7	20.2	+1.6	49.3	-10.2	20.8	-0.7	-	-	8.2	(2) 1.5	-
Leeds East	58.4	+2.3	23.2	+2.9	50.4	-9.4	17.5	+0.3	-	-	7.8	(1) 1.1	+5.5
North East	70.0	+5.4	33.1	+2.9	42.7	-3.0	19.6	-2.1	-	1.8	1.6	(1) 1.3	+3.0
North West	66.5	+3.7	26.6	-0.3	21.0	-10.9	47.5	+10.6	1.2	1.4	1.8	(2) 0.6	-
West	57.5	+4.7	19.7	+5.6	42.3	-13.9	24.2	+6.8	4.7	2.9	6.1	-	-
Morley & Outwood	65.8	+7.4	35.3	+10.3	37.6	-8.4	16.8	+6.7	-	3.1	7.2	-	+9.3
Normanton, Pontefract & Castleford	56.2	+2.9	24.5	+7.9	48.2	-17.1	16.4	+5.3	-	-	8.4	(1) 2.6	+12.5
Pudsey*	70.9	+4.9	38.5	+4.8	35.1	-10.3	20.8	+2.7	-	2.5	3.2	-	+7.6
Shipley	73.0	+4.9	48.6	+9.7	28.4	-9.4	20.0	+4.8	3.0	-	-	-	+9.6
Wakefield	62.7	+1.3	35.6	+9.1	39.3	-4.8	16.3	-2.5	2.0	-	5.8	(1) 1.0	+6.9
Wiltshire, Chippenham	72.6	+5.8	41.0	+3.3	6.9	-9.9	45.8	+3.3	0.9	3.4	1.2	(2) 0.8	-
Devizes	68.8	+3.5	55.1	+4.0	10.2	-12.2	27.0	+4.7	1.8	4.5	-	(2) 1.5	+8.1

	Turnout %	Turnout +/-	Con %	Con +/-	Lab %	Lab +/-	LD %	LD +/-	Plaid %	Plaid +/-	Grn %	UKIP %	BNP %	Others No & %	Swing
Salisbury	71.9	+3.4	49.2	+2.8	7.6	-11.0	36.9	+10.0			1.0	2.9	1.6	(2) 0.8	+7.6
Swindon North*	64.2	+3.4	44.6	+5.7	30.5	-14.6	17.2	+4.4			1.0	3.7	3.1	–	+10.1
South*	64.9	+5.9	41.8	+4.9	34.3	-6.2	17.6	+0.6			1.3	4.3	–	(2) 0.7	+5.5
Wiltshire North	73.4	+3.9	51.6	+1.9	6.7	-5.3	36.2	+1.8			1.2	3.9	–	(1) 0.4	–
South West	68.4	+3.8	51.7	+2.5	11.5	-5.7	30.5	+0.3			–	5.5	–	(1) 0.9	–
WALES															
Clwyd, Aberconwy*	67.2	+5.2	35.8	+6.8	24.5	-8.5	19.3	+0.2	17.8	+3.8	–	2.1	–	(1) 0.5	+7.6
Alyn & Deeside	65.5	+5.8	32.3	+7.1	39.6	-9.2	18.3	+0.9	3.9	+0.2	–	2.5	3.4	–	+8.1
Clwyd South	64.5	+3.3	30.2	+4.8	38.4	-6.8	17.2	+1.7	8.7	-0.8	–	2.4	3.2	–	+5.8
West	65.8	+0.7	41.5	+5.4	24.7	-11.3	15.2	+1.9	15.4	+4.5	–	2.3	–	(2) 0.9	+8.4
Delyn	69.2	+5.5	34.6	+8.5	40.8	-4.9	15.5	-2.4	5.0	-2.4	–	1.8	2.3	–	+6.7
Vale Of Clwyd	63.7	-2.1	35.2	+3.5	42.3	-3.6	12.6	+0.7	5.8	-1.4	–	1.4	2.3	(1) 0.4	+3.6
Wrexham	64.8	+1.5	25.4	+5.4	36.9	-9.2	25.8	+2.2	6.2	+0.4	–	2.3	3.4	–	–
Dyfed, Carmarthen East & Dinefwr	72.6	+1.8	22.4	+8.7	26.5	-1.8	12.1	+2.4	35.6	-10.2	–	3.4	–	–	–
West & Pembrokeshire South*	69.7	+2.5	41.1	+9.8	32.7	-4.0	12.1	-2.1	10.4	-5.1	–	2.8	–	(1) 0.9	+6.9
Ceredigion	65.4	-2.6	11.6	-0.8	5.8	-6.3	50.0	+13.5	28.3	-7.6	1.8	2.6	–	–	–
Llanelli	67.3	+3.4	14.4	+0.7	42.5	-4.5	10.4	-2.5	29.9	+3.5	–	2.8	–	–	+5.0
Preseli Pembrokeshire	69.0	-1.0	42.8	+6.4	31.2	-3.7	14.5	+1.5	9.2	-3.3	–	2.3	–	–	–
Gwent, Blaenau Gwent*	61.8	-4.4	7.0	+4.7	52.4	20.1	10.1	+5.9	4.1	+1.7	–	1.5	3.7	(2) 21.1	–
Islwyn	63.2	+3.0	14.0	+3.0	49.2	-15.1	10.4	-1.8	13.0	+0.6	1.3	2.7	3.8	(2) 6.9	–
Monmouth	72.1	-1.3	48.3	+1.4	25.9	-11.1	19.4	+6.6	2.7	+0.6	–	2.4	–	–	+6.2
Newport East	63.3	+5.4	23.0	-0.5	37.0	-8.2	32.2	+8.5	2.1	-1.7	–	2.0	3.4	(1) 0.4	–
West	64.0	+4.7	32.3	+2.8	41.3	-3.6	16.6	-1.3	2.8	-0.8	1.1	2.9	3.0	–	+3.2
Torfaen	61.5	+2.2	20.0	+4.2	44.8	-12.1	16.6	+0.9	5.3	-0.9	1.2	2.3	4.4	(2) 5.4	+8.2
Gwynedd, Arfon*	63.3	+5.1	16.9	+0.5	30.4	-3.5	14.1	-1.7	36.0	+3.9	–	2.6	–	–	–
Dwyfor Meirionnydd	63.7	+2.3	22.3	+8.1	13.9	-7.8	12.2	+1.3	44.3	-6.4	–	2.7	–	(1) 4.5	–
Ynys Mon	68.8	+1.3	22.5	+11.4	33.4	-1.3	7.5	+0.7	26.2	-4.9	–	3.5	–	(2) 6.9	–

WALES	Turnout %	Turnout +/-	Con %	Con +/-	Lab %	Lab +/-	LD %	LD +/-	Plaid %	Plaid +/-	Grn %	UKIP %	BNP %	Others No & %	Swing
Mid-Glamorgan, Bridgend	64.4	+4.7	30.4	+5.4	36.3	-6.6	22.6	+0.5	5.9	-1.0	–	2.1	2.7	–	+6.0
Caerphilly	62.3	+5.8	17.1	+2.4	44.9	-10.5	14.7	+4.7	16.7	-1.4	–	2.4	4.2	–	–
Cynon Valley	59.0	-1.3	10.1	+1.5	52.5	-10.5	13.8	+1.6	20.3	+6.8	–	3.4		–	–
Merthyr Tydfil	58.6	+3.2	7.5	-1.4	43.7	-16.8	31.0	+17.0	5.1	-4.9	–	2.7	3.7	(2) 6.4	–
Ogmore	61.8	+2.3	15.6	+1.4	53.8	-7.1	15.2	+0.5	9.6	-0.6	–	2.3	3.6	–	–
Pontypridd	63.0	-0.2	16.2	+4.6	38.8	-15.4	31.2	+11.2	7.3	-3.7	1.0	3.4		(2) 2.2	–
Rhondda	60.3	-1.5	6.4	+0.9	55.3	-12.8	10.6	+0.2	18.1	+2.2	–	1.2		(1) 8.4	–
Powys, Brecon & Radnorshire	72.5	+3.0	36.5	+1.9	10.5	-4.5	46.2	+1.3	2.5	-1.1	0.9	2.3		(2) 1.1	–
Montgomeryshire*	69.4	+3.1	41.3	+13.8	7.1	-5.2	37.8	-12.5	8.3	+1.3	–	3.3		(2) 2.1	–
South Glamorgan, Cardiff Central	59.1	+0.0	21.6	+12.3	28.8	-5.5	41.4	-8.4	3.4	-0.1	1.6	2.1		(3) 1.1	–
North	72.7	+2.2	37.5	+1.0	37.1	-1.9	18.3	-0.4	3.3	-0.9	0.8	2.4		(1) 0.6	+1.5
South & Penarth	60.2	+2.0	28.3	+4.4	38.9	-7.7	22.3	+2.4	4.2	-1.1	1.2	2.6		(3) 2.5	+6.0
West	65.2	+7.0	29.6	+7.0	41.2	-3.6	17.5	+0.5	7.0	-5.9	1.8	2.7		–	+5.3
Vale Of Glamorgan*	69.3	+0.8	41.8	+4.4	32.9	-7.8	15.2	+2.0	5.5	+0.3	0.9	3.1		(1) 0.5	+6.1
West Glamorgan, Aberavon	60.9	+1.5	14.2	+4.1	51.9	-8.1	16.3	+2.5	7.1	-4.7	–	1.6	4.1	(2) 4.8	–
Gower	67.5	+2.1	32.0	+6.5	38.4	-4.0	19.1	+0.6	6.6	-1.2	–	1.6	2.3	–	+5.3
Neath	64.8	+2.3	13.1	+1.5	46.3	-6.3	14.9	+0.6	19.9	+2.8	–	2.2	3.6	–	–
Swansea East	54.6	+1.0	14.8	+4.7	51.5	-5.1	18.3	-1.8	6.7	-0.2	1.0	2.6	5.2	–	–
West	58.0	+1.3	20.8	+4.8	34.7	-7.2	33.2	+4.3	4.0	-2.5	1.1	2.0	2.6	(2) 1.6	–

SCOTLAND	Turnout %	Turnout +/-	Con %	Con +/-	Lab %	Lab +/-	LD %	LD +/-	SNP %	SNP +/-	Grn %	UKIP +/-	BNP	Others No & %	Swing
Aberdeen North	58.2	+2.4	12.4	+2.9	44.4	+2.0	18.6	-5.3	22.2	-0.1	–	–	1.7	(1) 0.7	–
South	67.2	+5.1	20.7	+3.6	36.5	-0.2	28.4	-5.1	11.9	+2.0	1.0	–	1.2	(1) 0.3	–
Aberdeenshire West & Kincardine	68.4	+4.8	30.3	+1.9	13.6	+0.5	38.4	-7.9	15.7	+4.4	–	0.9	1.1	–	–
Airdrie & Shotts	57.5	+2.8	8.7	-1.1	58.2	-0.9	8.1	-3.4	23.5	+7.0	–	1.5	–	(1) 1.5	–
Angus	60.4	-0.1	30.9	+1.5	17.2	-0.7	10.8	-6.7	39.6	+5.9	1.7	–	–	–	–
Argyll & Bute	67.3	+3.0	24.0	+0.5	22.7	+0.3	31.6	-4.9	18.9	+3.4	–	–	–	(2) 0.9	+0.3
Ayr, Carrick & Cumnock	62.6	+0.7	25.5	+2.4	47.1	+1.8	9.3	-4.8	18.0	+4.9	–	–	–	–	–
Ayrshire Central	64.2	+1.1	20.4	-1.8	47.7	+1.3	11.9	-4.1	19.0	+7.5	–	–	–	(1) 1.0	-1.5
North & Arran	62.1	+1.6	15.6	-2.7	47.4	+3.5	10.0	-6.4	25.9	+8.0	–	–	–	(1) 1.0	-3.1
Banff & Buchan	59.8	+3.2	30.8	+11.4	14.0	+2.0	11.3	-2.0	41.3	-9.9	–	–	2.6	–	–
Berwickshire, Roxburgh & Selkirk	66.4	+2.3	33.8	+4.9	10.2	-5.7	45.4	+3.5	9.2	+0.6	–	1.2	–	(1) 0.3	–
Caithness, Sutherland & Easter Ross	60.9	+1.5	13.0	+2.8	24.6	+3.7	41.4	-9.1	19.2	+5.8	–	–	–	(1) 1.8	–
Coatbridge, Chryston & Bellshill	59.4	+2.0	8.1	+0.9	66.6	+2.1	8.5	-3.6	16.8	+3.3	–	–	–	–	–
Cumbernauld, Kilsyth & Kirkintilloch E.	64.3	+3.4	8.3	+1.3	57.2	+5.4	9.5	-5.3	23.8	+1.6	–	1.3	–	(1) 1.2	-4.3
Dumfries & Galloway	70.0	+0.4	31.6	-3.7	45.9	+4.8	8.8	+0.5	12.3	+0.2	–	1.4	–	–	+2.6
Dumfriesshire, Clydesdale & T.	68.9	+0.3	38.0	+1.9	28.9	-3.4	19.8	-0.5	10.8	+1.6	1.1	–	–	–	–
Dunbartonshire East	75.2	+2.1	15.5	-1.0	34.1	+1.0	38.7	-3.1	10.5	+4.7	–	1.1	–	–	–
West	64.0	+2.7	7.7	+1.2	61.3	+9.4	8.1	-6.3	20.1	-1.6	1.3	1.6	–	(1) 1.2	–
Dundee East	62.0	-0.5	15.2	+2.4	33.3	-2.9	10.6	-0.8	37.8	+0.6	–	1.1	–	(1) 0.6	–
West	58.9	+2.8	9.3	+1.0	48.5	+3.9	11.4	-3.0	28.9	-1.2	–	–	–	(2) 1.9	–
Dunfermline & West Fife†	66.5	+6.6	6.8	-3.6	46.3	-1.2	35.1	+14.9	10.6	-8.3	–	1.3	–	–	–
East Kilbride, Strathaven & L.	66.6	+3.1	13.0	+3.0	51.5	+2.8	9.9	-6.6	23.0	+5.1	2.0	1.1	–	(1) 0.6	–
East Lothian	67.0	+2.3	19.7	+3.7	44.6	+3.1	16.9	-8.0	16.0	+2.9	1.8	–	–	–	–
Edinburgh East	65.4	+4.5	10.9	+0.6	43.4	+3.4	19.4	-5.0	20.4	+3.4	5.1	–	–	(1) 0.7	–
North & Leith	68.4	+6.0	14.9	-3.7	37.5	+3.2	33.8	+4.6	9.6	-0.5	2.2	–	–	(4) 1.9	–
South	73.8	+4.4	21.6	-2.5	34.7	+1.5	34.0	+1.7	7.7	+1.5	2.0	–	–	–	–
South West	68.5	+3.5	24.3	+1.0	42.8	+3.0	18.0	-3.0	12.2	+1.6	1.9	–	–	–	–
West	71.3	+3.0	23.2	+3.7	27.7	+9.1	35.9	-13.6	13.2	+4.1	–	–	–	(2) 0.8	-1.0
Falkirk	62.0	+2.4	11.2	+1.3	45.7	-5.1	10.3	-5.7	30.3	+8.9	–	2.5	–	–	–

SCOTLAND	Turnout %	Turnout +/-	Con %	Con +/-	Lab %	Lab +/-	LD %	LD +/-	SNP %	SNP +/-	Grn %	UKIP +/-	BNP	Others No & %	Swing
Fife North East	63.8	+1.7	21.8	+2.3	17.1	+4.4	44.3	-7.8	14.2	+3.8	–	2.6	–	–	–
Glasgow Central	50.9	+7.0	7.1	+0.8	52.0	+3.8	16.4	-1.4	17.5	+2.7	2.6	0.8	2.0	(2) 1.6	–
East†	52.0	+3.8	4.5	-2.4	61.6	+0.9	5.0	-6.8	24.7	+7.7	–	0.6	2.1	(1) 1.4	–
North	57.5	+7.1	7.1	-1.7	44.5	+5.1	31.3	+3.9	11.9	-1.0	3.2	–	1.0	(1) 1.0	–
North East‡(†)	49.1	+3.4	5.3	–	68.3	+15.0	7.7	–	14.1	-3.5	–	–	2.7	(3) 1.8	–
North West	58.3	+3.1	9.9	+0.4	54.1	+4.9	15.8	-3.7	15.3	+1.5	2.5	–	2.0	(1) 0.5	–
South	61.6	+5.6	11.5	-1.1	51.7	+4.5	11.8	-7.2	20.1	+7.5	2.4	–	1.6	(1) 0.9	–
South West	54.6	+4.5	6.6	+0.8	62.5	+2.3	9.0	-2.6	16.3	+1.0	–	–	2.6	(1) 2.9	–
Glenrothes	59.8	+3.6	7.2	+0.1	62.3	+10.4	7.7	-5.0	21.7	-1.6	–	1.0	–	–	–
Gordon	66.4	+4.6	18.7	+1.0	20.1	-0.1	36.0	-9.0	22.2	+6.2	1.5	–	1.4	–	–
Inverclyde	63.4	+2.5	12.0	+1.8	56.0	+5.2	13.4	-3.6	17.5	-2.0	–	1.2	–	–	–
Inverness, Nairn, Badenoch & S.	64.9	+1.1	13.3	+3.0	22.1	-8.8	40.7	+0.4	18.7	+5.2	1.7	1.2	–	(3) 2.3	–
Kilmarnock & Loudoun	62.8	+0.6	14.2	+2.8	52.5	+5.3	7.3	-3.8	26.0	-1.7	–	–	–	–	–
Kirkcaldy & Cowdenbeath	62.3	+3.9	9.3	-1.0	64.5	+6.4	9.3	-3.7	14.3	-0.2	–	1.7	–	(3) 0.9	–
Lanark & Hamilton East	62.3	+3.2	15.0	+2.2	50.0	+3.9	11.3	-7.4	21.0	+3.2	–	1.3	–	(1) 1.4	–
Linlithgow & East Falkirk	63.6	+3.1	11.9	+0.1	49.8	+2.1	12.8	-2.5	25.4	+1.9	–	–	–	–	–
Livingston	63.1	+4.6	10.8	+0.6	48.5	-2.6	11.1	-4.3	25.9	+4.4	–	0.9	2.0	(2) 0.8	–
Midlothian	63.9	+1.3	11.9	+2.5	47.0	+1.5	17.1	-9.1	20.6	+3.7	1.5	0.9	–	(2) 0.9	–
Moray	62.2	+3.0	26.1	+4.1	17.1	-3.3	14.5	-4.7	39.7	+3.1	–	2.6	–	–	–
Motherwell & Wishaw	58.5	+1.8	9.4	+0.1	61.1	+3.6	9.8	-2.2	18.2	+1.7	–	–	–	(1) 1.6	–
Na H-Eileanan An Iar	67.6	+2.2	4.4	+0.0	32.9	-1.6	7.5	-0.5	45.7	+0.8	–	–	–	(1) 9.6	–
Ochil & South Perthshire	67.2	+1.2	20.5	-1.0	37.9	+6.5	11.4	-1.9	27.6	-2.3	–	1.4	–	–	–
Orkney & Shetland	58.5	+4.1	10.5	-2.8	10.7	-3.5	62.0	+10.5	10.6	+0.2	1.2	6.3	–	–	–
Paisley & Renfrewshire North	68.6	+3.8	14.6	+1.0	54.0	+8.3	10.5	-7.7	19.1	+0.2	–	–	–	(2) 1.8	–
South	65.4	+2.4	9.9	+1.5	59.6	+7.0	9.5	-8.1	18.1	+0.5	–	–	–	(3) 2.8	–
Perth & North Perthshire	66.9	+3.0	30.5	+0.2	16.4	-2.3	12.3	-3.8	39.6	+5.9	–	–	–	(1) 1.1	–
Renfrewshire East	77.3	+5.1	30.4	+0.5	50.8	+6.9	9.2	-9.0	8.9	+2.0	–	0.7	–	–	-3.2
Ross, Skye & Lochaber	67.2	+2.6	12.2	+2.2	15.1	+0.2	52.6	-6.1	15.1	+5.5	2.2	1.9	–	(1) 0.8	–
Rutherglen & Hamilton West	59.2	+0.8	9.7	+1.3	60.8	+5.2	12.0	-6.4	16.1	+2.2	–	1.4	–	–	–
Stirling	70.8	+2.6	23.9	-1.1	41.8	+5.8	14.5	-6.2	17.3	+4.7	1.6	0.8	–	–	-3.5

N. IRELAND	Turnout %	Turnout +/-	UCU %	UCU +/-	DUP %	DUP +/-	APNI %	APNI +/-	SF %	SF +/-	SDLP %	SDLP +/-	Other %
Antrim East	50.7	-6.6	23.7	-1.4	45.9	-1.0	11.1	-3.6	6.8	+1.4	6.6	-0.8	6.0
North	57.8	-7.8	10.9	-4.1	46.4	-10.4	3.2	+0.1	12.4	-1.8	8.8	-2.2	18.2
South	53.9	-8.2	30.4	+0.9	33.9	-6.4	7.7	-0.6	13.9	+3.2	8.7	-2.5	5.4
Belfast East*	58.4	-0.3	21.2	-10.5	32.8	-19.6	37.2	+26.1	2.4	+0.0	1.1	-1.0	5.4
North	56.5	-1.1	7.7	-1.8	40.0	-3.0	4.9	+2.0	34.0	+7.0	12.3	-4.4	1.1
South	57.4	-5.1	17.3	-4.9	23.7	-5.9	15.0	+7.8	–	–	41.0	+10.8	3.0
West	54	-13.5	3.1	+0.6	7.6	-3.2	1.9	+1.8	71.1	+2.5	16.4	+0.4	0.0
Down North*	55.2	-0.9	20.4	-32.7	–	–	5.6	-2.0	0.7	+0.1	2.0	-1.1	71.3
South	60.2	-8.5	7.3	-1.5	8.6	-7.5	1.3	+0.0	28.7	+1.7	48.5	+1.6	5.7
Fermanagh & South Tyrone	68.9	-6.9	–	–	–	–	0.9	–	45.5	+7.3	7.6	-7.2	45.9
Foyle	57.5	-12.5	3.2	+0.9	11.8	-2.3	0.6	–	31.9	-1.4	44.7	-1.7	7.7
Lagan Valley	56	-6.6	21.1	-1.8	49.8	-8.5	11.4	+0.5	4.0	-0.3	5.0	+1.5	8.6
Londonderry East	55.3	-8.4	17.8	-1.9	34.6	-6.4	5.5	+3.1	19.3	1.9	15.4	-3.9	7.4
Newry & Armagh	60.4	-13.3	19.1	+5.2	12.8	-5.6	1.2	–	42.0	+0.6	23.4	-1.8	1.5
Strangford	53.7	-3.4	27.8	+2.9	45.9	-8.9	8.7	+0.5	3.6	-0.1	6.7	-1.7	7.3
Tyrone West	61	-14.2	14.2	+7.3	19.8	2.0	2.3	–	48.4	+9.5	14.0	+4.9	1.4
Ulster Mid	63.2	-12.3	11.0	+0.4	14.4	-9.1	1.0	–	52.0	+4.4	14.3	-3.1	7.3
Upper Bann	55.4	-9.2	25.7	+0.1	33.8	-3.8	3.0	+0.8	24.7	+3.7	12.7	-0.2	0.0

Notes:
UCU: Ulster Conservatives and Unionists – New Force. Comparison with 2005 is with the UUP vote, plus the Conservative vote in seats where Conservatives stood in 2005.
DUP: Democratic Unionist Party
APNI: Alliance Party of Northern Ireland
SF: Sinn Fein
SDLP: Social Democratic and Labour Party

Table A1.4   Seats changing hands

Con Gains from Labour
Aberconwy
Amber Valley
Basildon South & East Thurrock
Battersea
Bedford
Blackpool North & Cleveleys
Brentford & Isleworth
Brigg & Goole
Brighton Kemptown
Bristol North West
Broxtowe
Burton
Bury North
Calder Valley
Cannock Chase
Cardiff North
Carlisle
Carmarthen West & Pembrokeshire South
Chatham & Aylesford
Chester, City Of
Cleethorpes
Colne Valley
Corby
Crawley
Crewe & Nantwich
Croydon Central
Dartford
Derbyshire South
Dewsbury
Dorset South
Dover
Dudley South
Ealing Central & Acton
Elmet & Rothwell
Erewash
Gillingham & Rainham
Gloucester
Great Yarmouth
Halesowen & Rowley Regis
Harlow
Harrow East
Hastings & Rye
Hendon
High Peak
Hove
Ipswich
Keighley
Kingswood
Lancaster & Fleetwood
Leicestershire North West

Lincoln
Loughborough
Milton Keynes North
Milton Keynes South
Morecambe & Lunesdale
Northampton North
Northampton South
Norwich North
Nuneaton
Pendle
Plymouth Sutton & Devonport
Portsmouth North
Pudsey
Reading West
Redditch
Rossendale & Darwen
Rugby
Sherwood
South Ribble
Stafford
Stevenage
Stockton South
Stourbridge
Stroud
Swindon North
Swindon South
Tamworth
Thurrock
Vale Of Glamorgan
Warrington South
Warwick & Leamington
Warwickshire North
Watford
Waveney
Weaver Vale
Wolverhampton South West
Worcester

Con Gains from Lib Dems
Camborne & Redruth
Cornwall South East
Harrogate & Knaresborough
Hereford & South Herefordshire
Montgomeryshire
Newton Abbot
Oxford West & Abingdon
Richmond Park
Romsey & Southampton North
Truro & Falmouth
Winchester
York Outer

Con Gains from Others
Wyre Forest

Lib Dem Gains from Labour
Bradford East
Brent Central
Burnley
Norwich South
Redcar

Lib Dem Gains from Con
Eastbourne
Solihull
Wells

Labour Gains from Lib Dem
Chesterfield

Labour Gains from Others
Bethnal Green & Bow
Blaenau Gwent

Other Gains
Arfon Plaid from Lab
Brighton Pavilion Green from Lab
Belfast East Alliance from DUP
Down North Independent from UCU
    (with MP remaining same)

Table A1.5 Exceptional results

Ten highest turnouts (GB) (%)
77.3 Renfrewshire East
76.9 Westmorland & Lonsdale
76.2 Richmond Park
75.8 Winchester
75.7 Devon Central
75.6 Charnwood
75.4 Somerset North East
75.4 St. Albans
75.2 Kenilworth & Southam
75.2 Thornbury & Yate

Five highest turnouts (NI) (%)
68.9 Fermanagh & South Tyrone
63.2 Ulster Mid
61.0 Tyrone West
60.4 Newry & Armagh
60.2 Down South

Ten lowest turnouts (%)
44.3 Manchester Central
46.0 Leeds Central
48.7 Birmingham Ladywood
49.1 Glasgow North East
49.2 Blackley & Broughton
(49.6 Thirsk & Malton)
50.5 Manchester Gorton
50.6 Hull East
50.9 Glasgow Central
51.0 Wythenshawe & Sale East

Ten smallest majorities		*Votes*	%
Fermanagh & South			
Tyrone	SF	4	0.0
Hampstead & Kilburn	Lab	42	0.1
Warwickshire North	Con	54	0.1
Camborne & Redruth	Con	66	0.2
Thurrock	Con	92	0.2
Bolton West	Lab	92	0.2
Oldham East &			
Saddleworth	Lab	103	0.2
Hendon	Con	106	0.2
Sheffield Central	Lab	165	0.4
Solihull	LD	175	0.3

Ten best Con results (% change)
+16.7 Hartlepool
+13.8 Montgomeryshire
+13.2 Esher & Walton
+12.9 Crewe & Nantwich
+12.3 Cardiff Central
+12.0 Camborne & Redruth
+11.7 Basingstoke
+11.7 St. Ives
+11.6 Devon South West
+11.4 Ynys Mon

Ten best Lab results (% change)
+20.1 Blaenau Gwent
+16.8 East Ham
+10.9 West Ham
+10.4 Glenrothes

Table A1.5   continued

+9.4 Dunbartonshire West
+9.1 Edinburgh West
+8.5 Bethnal Green & Bow
+8.3 Paisley & Renfrewshire North
+7.0 Paisley & Renfrewshire South
+6.9 Renfrewshire East

Ten best Lib Dem results (% change)
+25.0 Redcar
+19.5 Ashfield
+17.0 Merthyr Tydfil
+14.9 Dunfermline & West Fife
+14.1 Westmorland & Lonsdale
+13.5 Ceredigion
+13.2 Maidstone & The Weald
+13.1 Brent Central
+12.0 Burnley
+11.7 Bosworth

Ten largest SNP votes (%)
45.7 Na H-Eileanan An Iar
41.3 Banff & Buchan
39.7 Moray
39.6 Perth & North Perthshire
39.6 Angus
37.8 Dundee East
30.3 Falkirk
28.9 Dundee West
27.6 Ochil & South Perthshire
26.0 Kilmarnock & Loudoun

Ten largest Plaid votes (%)
44.3 Dwyfor Meirionnydd
36.0 Arfon
35.6 Carmarthen East & Dinefwr
29.9 Llanelli
28.3 Ceredigion
26.2 Ynys Mon
20.3 Cynon Valley
19.9 Neath
18.1 Rhondda
17.8 Aberconwy

Ten largest UKIP votes (%)
17.4 Buckingham
9.5 Boston & Skegness
8.5 Christchurch

8.5 Spelthorne
8.5 Dudley North
8.4 Walsall South
8.3 Cambridgeshire North West
8.2 Dudley South
8.2 Devon East
8.2 Staffordshire Moorlands

Ten largest Green votes (%)
31.3 Brighton Pavilion
14.9 Norwich South
7.6 Cambridge
6.7 Lewisham Deptford
5.5 Brighton Kemptown
5.2 Hove
5.1 Edinburgh East
4.7 Leeds West
4.6 Hackney North & Stoke
     Newington
4.4 Lancaster & Fleetwood

Ten largest BNP votes (%)
14.6 Barking
11.2 Dagenham & Rainham
10.4 Rotherham
9.4 Stoke On Trent South
9.4 West Bromwich West
9.0 Burnley
8.9 Barnsley Central
8.6 Barnsley East
8.4 Normanton, Pontefract &
     Castleford
8.2 Leeds Central

Largest deposit saving other votes (GB) (%)
31.7 Wyre Forest (IKHHC)
27.0 Castle Point (Ind)
25.1 Birmingham Hall Green
     (Respect)
21.4 Buckingham (Ind)
19.9 Blaenau Gwent (Ind)
17.5 Poplar & Limehouse (Respect)
16.8 Bethnal Green & Bow (Respect)
9.6 Na H-Eileanan An Iar (Ind)
9.3 Liverpool West Derby (Liberal)
9.0 Hemsworth (Ind)
9.0 Mansfield (Ind)

8.4 Rhondda (Ind)
7.8 Makerfield (Ind)
7.1 Dewsbury (Ind)
6.5 Croydon Central (Ind)
6.5 Houghton & Sunderland South
  (Ind)
6.5 Ynys Mon (Ind)
6.4 Sleaford & North Hykeham (Ind)
6.3 Rotherham (Ind)
5.9 Middlesbrough (Ind)
5.8 Merthyr Tydfil (Ind)
5.8 Northampton South (Ind)
5.6 Durham North West (Ind)

5.2 Doncaster North (English
  Democrat)
5.2 Macclesfield (Ind)
5.0 Buckingham (Ind)

Major parties lost deposits (%)
4.8 Eastbourne (Lab)
4.5 Glasgow East (Con)
4.4 Somerton & Frome (Lab)
4.4 Na H-Eileanan An Iar (Con)
4.3 Newbury (Lab)
4.2 Cornwall North (Lab)
2.2 Westmorland & Lonsdale (Lab)

Table A1.6   By-election results, 2005–10

	Date	Con %	Lab %	Lib Dem %	Best Other %	Rest % (no.)	Turnout %
Cheadle	2005	40.4	8.8	48.9	1.0 (UKIP)	0.9 (1)	69.6
	15.7.05	42.4	4.6	52.2	0.6 (Veritas)	0.2 (1)	55.2
	2010	40.8	9.4	47.1	2.7 (UKIP)		72.5
Livingston	2005	10.1	51.1	15.4	21.6 (SNP)	1.8 (1)	58.5
	29.9.05	6.8	41.8	14.8	32.7 (SNP)	3.9 (6)	38.6
	2010	10.8	48.5	11.1	25.9 (SNP)	3.7 (4)	63.1
Dunfermline & West Fife	2005	10.5	48.1	20.4	19.2 (SNP)	3.1 (2)	59.9
Lib Dem gain	9.2.06	7.8	30.6	35.8	21.0 (SNP)	4.7 (5)	48.7
Lab regain	2010	6.8	46.3	35.1	10.6 (SNP)	1.3 (1)	66.4
Blaenau Gwent	2005	2.3	32.3	4.3	58.2 (Ind)	2.9 (2)	66.1
	29.6.06	3.7	37.0	5.4	46.2 (Ind)	7.7 (2)	51.7
Labour gain	2010	7.0	52.4	10.1	19.9 (Ind)	10.5 (4)	61.8
Bromley & Chislehurst	2005	51.1	22.2	20.3	3.2 (UKIP)	3.2 (1)	64.9
	29.6.06	40.0	6.6	37.8	8.1 (UKIP)	7.5 (7)	40.5
	2010	53.5	16.6	22.0	3.3 (UKIP)	4.7 (3)	67.3
Ealing Southall	2005	21.6	48.8	24.4	4.6 (Grn)	0.6 (1)	56.4
	19.7.07	22.5	41.5	27.6	3.1 (Grn)	5.0 (8)	42.9
	2010	29.8	51.5	14.9	1.7 (Grn)	2.2 (2)	70.8
Sedgefield	2005	14.4	58.9	11.9	10.2 (Ind)	4.6 (11)	61.8
	19.7.07	14.6	44.8	19.9	8.9 (BNP)	11.7 (8)	41.5
	2010	23.5	45.1	20.0	5.2 (BNP)	6.3 (2)	62.1
Crewe & Nantwich	2005	32.6	48.8	18.6			60.3
Con gain	28.5.07	49.5	30.6	14.6	2.2 (UKIP)	3.2 (6)	57.7
	2010	45.9	34.0	15.0	2.8 (UKIP)	2.4 (2)	66.0

Table A1.6   continued

	Date	Con %	Lab %	Lib Dem %	Best Other %	Rest % (no.)	Turnout %
Henley	2005	53.5	14.7	26.0	3.3 (Grn)	2.5 (1)	68.8
	26.6.08	56.9	3.1	27.8	3.8 (Grn)	8.4 (8)	50.3
	2010	56.2	10.9	25.2	3.4 (UKIP)	4.4 (2)	71.4
Haltemprice & Howden	2005	47.5	12.7	36.8	1.7 (BNP)	1.4 (1)	69.7
	10.7.08	71.6			7.4 (Grn)	21.1 (11)	34.1
	2010	50.2	15.7	26.4	3.3 (BNP)	4.5 (2)	69.2
Glasgow East *SNP gain* *Lab regain*	2005	6.9	60.7	11.8	17.0 (SNP)	3.5 (1)	48.4
	24.7.08	6.3	41.7	3.5	43.1 (SNP)	5.5 (5)	42.2
	2010	4.5	61.6	5.0	24.7 (SNP)	4.2 (3)	52.3
Glenrothes	2005	7.1	51.9	12.7	23.4 (SNP)	5.0 (3)	55.7
	6.11.08	3.8	55.1	2.6	36.5 (SNP)	2.1 (4)	52.3
	2010	7.2	62.3	7.7	21.7 (SNP)	1.0 (1)	59.7
Norwich North *Con gain*	2005	33.2	44.9	16.2	2.7 (Grn)	3.0 (2)	60.6
	23.7.09	39.5	18.2	14.0	11.8 (UKIP)	16.5 (8)	45.8
	2010	40.6	31.4	18.3	4.4 (UKIP)	5.3 (4)	65.2
Glasgow North East *Lab 'gain' from Speaker*	2005				53.3 (Speaker)	17.7 (SNP)	45.8
	12.11.09	5.2	59.4	2.3	20 (SNP)	13.1 (9)	33.0
	2010	5.3	68.4	7.7	14.1 (SNP)	4.4 (4)	49.1

Appendix 2: An Analysis of the Results

John Curtice, Stephen Fisher and Robert Ford

In the immediate post-war period Britain came to be regarded as having a classic two-party system: few voters backed anyone other than a Conservative or Labour candidate; even fewer MPs belonged to anything other than the Conservative or Labour parties; and one party almost always managed to secure an overall majority.

This characterisation has, though, looked increasingly dubious. It looks even less accurate in the wake of the outcome of the 2010 election. To begin with, just two-thirds (66.6%) of the votes in Great Britain were cast for either the Conservatives or Labour.[1] That represented a drop of nearly three points on the equivalent figure five years before and was the lowest proportion since and including the 1922 election, the first to be held after the partition of Ireland and the first at which Labour overtook the Liberals in the popular vote. As well as almost one in four votes (23.6%) going to the Liberal Democrats – the second highest vote share to be secured by the party or its predecessors since 1923 – nearly one in ten voters in Great Britain (9.7%) voted for someone other than the three main parties, up nearly two points on the last election and higher than at any previous election in the country's history.[2]

Meanwhile, as many as 85 MPs (including 18 from Northern Ireland) were elected under a banner other than Conservative or Labour. A slight fall, of seven seats, compared with the position in 2005, this still constituted confirmation of a continued step change in the level of third party representation that first became apparent in 1997 (see Appendix 1, Table A1.1). More importantly, it was sufficient to help ensure that for only the second time in the post-war period no single party was able to secure an overall majority.

Given this backdrop it is perhaps hardly surprising that the performance of the major party that 'lost' the election was by historical standards little short of dire. Labour's share of the total vote, 29.7%, was its second lowest share since 1918; only the party's performance in the calamitous defeat in 1983 was worse. The 6.5 point drop in its share of the vote almost matches the worst ever reverse between two elections suffered by an incumbent Labour government, that is the 6.7 point drop suffered by the party following the collapse of Ramsay MacDonald's government in 1931. The party's performance constituted no less than a 14.6 point fall in its support since it first secured power in 1997, a fall that outstrips the previous biggest loss of support suffered by any post-war government, the 13.4 point drop in Conservative support between 1979 and 1997.

Even the achievement of the plurality winner, the Conservatives, was no more than modest. At 37.0%, the party's share of the vote represented its fifth lowest tally amongst the 24 elections held since and including 1922. Never before has the party managed to secure office (albeit on this occasion as part of a coalition) on as low a share of the vote. Despite starting from a relatively low base, at 3.8 points the increase in the Conservatives' share of the vote was lower than the equivalent figure on the three previous occasions when the party succeeded in ejecting an incumbent Labour government from power.

Even so, it was still enough to give the Conservatives a lead of 7.3 points over Labour. That exceeds the 7.1 point lead that Margaret Thatcher obtained when she first won power in 1979, and is much larger than the 2.3 point lead obtained by Edward Heath in 1970 or anything that the party achieved during the heyday of two-party politics in the 1950s. On each of those occasions such a lead was sufficient to ensure the electoral system delivered a Conservative overall majority. This time it was not, and instead of a single party majority government Britain found itself being governed by a Conservative/Liberal Democrat coalition. Evidently this time around the electoral system did not perform in the manner that it once did.

Still, there was one apparent bright spot for all politicians. Despite fears that the MPs' expenses scandal of the previous year would engender widespread cynicism amongst the electorate – and thus a reluctance to vote at all – turnout increased by four points to 65.3%. Even so, this hardly represented renewed enthusiasm for the political process. Between 1922 and 1997 turnout had never been lower than 70%, before falling precipitately to just 59% in 2001 and 61% in 2005. While the anticipated closeness of the election outcome might have helped bring some voters to the polls, it would appear that the British electorate can no longer be relied upon to vote simply out of duty or habit.[3]

This overview of the outcome of the 2010 election clearly raises a number of important questions. Why did Labour suffer such a large reversal of votes? Why was the Conservative advance so modest? How do we account for the increase in votes for parties other than Conservatives and Labour? And perhaps above all, why did the electoral system fail to deliver an overall majority for any one party, even though the representation of third parties did not increase in line with their support?

In this appendix we aim to cast some light on the answers to each of these questions by analysing the constituency election results, concentrating in particular on the rises and falls in party support since the previous election in 2005. Although such an approach cannot provide a full answer to our questions, many of which also need to be addressed through evidence collected via sample surveys, it is particularly useful in helping us understand the link between votes cast and seats won, and thus in understanding why Britain now has a coalition rather than a single party majority government.

We do, though, face one methodological difficulty in undertaking such an exercise. Apart from Scotland, the 2010 election was fought on new electoral boundaries, following a review conducted by the Boundary Commissions.[4] Only 73 of the constituencies in England and Wales were left wholly unchanged. Thus in order to be able to analyse the change in party support since the last election, we have to rely on estimates of what the outcome of the 2005 election would have been if that election had been contested on the new constituency boundaries. We use estimates that were compiled for the three main broadcasting organisations together with the Press Association and which were widely used in reporting of the election.[5] Inevitably, however, this means that a degree of potential measurement error surrounds the changes in vote share we quote for any individual constituency, although the impact of such error can be expected to even itself out when looking at the outcome in groups of constituencies.

Table A2.1 provides some key statistics on the changes in party performance since 2005. We show for each of the three largest parties not only the change in their overall share of the vote, but also the average or mean change across all the individual constituencies, together with the median. All of the analysis of change in this appendix is based on mean change, which proved to be much the same as the overall change.[6] In Labour's case, however, the median (or middle) value of all the individual constituency level changes represents a much bigger decline than either the overall or mean change. This suggests that the party performed atypically (relatively) well in a minority of constituencies, and that in much of the country its vote fell rather more heavily than suggested by the overall change in its support. This is a point to which we will return.

The table also shows for each of the three largest parties the standard deviation of the change in their share of the vote across all constituencies. This is a measure of the degree to which party performance varied from one constituency to another. Again Labour's performance stands out, as varying far more than that of both the Liberal Democrats and (especially) the Conservatives. However, some care needs to be exercised in interpreting this statistic, as it will be inflated by any errors in the estimates of what the outcome of the 2005 election would have been on the new constituency boundaries. Even so, comparison with the equivalent statistics for other recent elections indicates that the variation in Labour's vote was particularly high (even when compared with previous elections where a boundary review had just taken place), even if the same cannot be said of either the Conservatives or the Liberal Democrats.[7]

Table A2.1　Measures of change since 2005

	Overall	*Mean*	*Median*	*Standard Deviation*
Change in Con vote	+3.8	+3.8	+3.6	3.4
Change in Lab vote	−6.5	−6.5	−7.6	5.6
Change in Lib Dem vote	+1.0	+0.8	+0.9	4.5
Total vote swing	+5.1	+5.2	+5.8	3.7
Two-party swing	+7.6	+7.9	+8.5	5.1
Change in turnout	+4.0	+4.2	+3.9	3.6

The following constituencies are excluded from the calculation of the mean, median and standard deviation of all statistics apart from turnout: Buckingham (no Labour or Liberal Democrat candidate in 2010); Glasgow North East (no Conservative or Liberal Democrat candidate in 2005); Wyre Forest (no Liberal Democrat candidate in 2005). These three seats are excluded from all analysis of party performance in this appendix. The delayed election in Thirsk & Malton is included.

'Total vote swing' is the average of the change in the Conservative share of the vote and the Labour share of the vote. 'Two-party swing' is the change in the Conservative share of the votes cast for Conservative and Labour only (that is, the two-party vote). In both cases a plus sign indicates a swing to the Conservatives, a minus sign a swing to Labour.

The table also shows the equivalent statistics for two measures of 'swing'. Both measures summarise the change in the relative strength of the Conservative and Labour parties, and have been much used in the analysis of previous British elections. In both cases they reflect what we have already learnt from the equivalent figures for Conservative and Labour separately – the median swing from Labour to the Conservatives was bigger than either the overall or the mean swing, reflecting an apparent asymmetry in Labour's performance. But the value of looking at swing is more limited in an era when the Conservatives and Labour Party no longer dominate votes cast or even seats won. Thus for the most part we focus our analysis on the change in the share of the vote won by individual parties rather than any measure of swing.

We begin by examining what happened to the vote of the defeated government. This, after all, was the vote that changed most overall and for which the degree of change varied most from one constituency to another. We then examine the relatively limited advance made by the Conservatives, before turning to the Liberal Democrats. Thereafter we look in some depth at the record vote cast for parties other than these three. Finally, following a brief look at turnout, we examine the link between votes and seats, and aim to explain why on this occasion single member plurality failed to deliver a government with an overall majority.

Labour

Governments that preside over an ailing economy are often thought to be punished by voters at the ballot box.[8] Given the economic backdrop against which the election was fought, one reason why Labour might have lost so heavily in 2010 is that voters were disenchanted by its handling of the economy.[9] If so, then the party should have lost ground most heavily in constituencies that had suffered most from the recession.[10] At the same time, however, perhaps those working in the public sector were particularly concerned that the advent of a Conservative government committed to making deeper public expenditure cuts would threaten the security of their jobs. We might therefore expect to find that Labour's vote fell rather less in those constituencies that contain relatively large numbers of public sector workers.

The recession does indeed seem to have cost Labour dear. Where unemployment (as measured by the claimant count) as a proportion of the electorate had increased by less than 1.25 percentage points since 2005, Labour's vote fell on average by just 4.4 points. In contrast, the party's vote fell by almost twice that amount, 8.2 points, in constituencies where unemployment had increased by more than 2.5 points. Those parts of the country that had suffered most from the recession were indeed the most likely to have lost faith in Labour's ability to govern.

One important feature of those constituencies where unemployment had increased most since 2005 is that they are often ones where a relatively large proportion of those in employment are engaged in occupations that are classified by government statisticians as routine or semi-routine, and more widely as 'working class'.[11] They are thus constituencies that contain high proportions of voters who would traditionally have been expected to vote Labour. However, the link between individual membership of a social class and voting Labour has weakened since the 1990s.[12] Equally, between 1997 and 2001 Labour lost support particularly heavily in constituencies with a relatively large proportion of working class voters,[13] a pattern that was not reversed in 2005. Given where unemployment had risen most since 2005 and the apparent impact that rise had had on Labour support, perhaps the impact of the recession helped now to weaken those links yet further.

Indeed, at 7.9 points the mean fall in Labour's share of the vote in those constituencies in which more than 25% of the economically active population aged 16–74 are in a working class occupation was as much as three points higher than the equivalent statistic (4.9 points) for those constituencies where less than 18% are in such occupations. Labour particularly lost ground in seats where there were both many working class voters and there had been a large increase in unemployment; in these circumstances the drop in Labour's vote was as much as 9.4 points. In other words, a large increase in unemployment proved especially toxic for Labour where it occurred in what might have once been regarded as a 'traditional' Labour constituency.

However, there is one potential pitfall in our analysis so far. There were over 100 constituencies where Labour won less than 20% of the vote in 2005, and indeed more than a dozen where it won less than 10%. In such circumstances there is a limit to the degree to which Labour's vote could fall. As most of these are relatively middle class constituencies where it is the Liberal Democrats rather than Labour who are the principal challengers to the Conservatives, there is a danger that the above average Labour performance in more middle class constituencies (that had experienced lower increases in unemployment) is simply an arithmetic artefact.

Labour's support did indeed fall less where there were relatively few Labour voters last time. On average its vote fell by just 4.9 points in seats where the party won less than 20% of the vote in 2005, and by just 2.7 points where it had won less than 10%. However, this does not account for the patterns noted above. If we exclude from our analysis all seats where Labour won less than 20% of the vote in 2005, there is still no less than a five point difference between the fall in the party's share of the vote in seats with the highest increase in unemployment and in those with the lowest. Equally, there is little over a four point gap in respect of seats with the highest and lowest proportions of working class voters.

But did voters' fears of public expenditure cuts matter too? It seems that they did. Constituencies containing a relatively large number of people working in the public sector proved to be relatively loyal to Labour. In constituencies where over 28% of those aged 16–74 who are economically active are employed in public administration, education or health, Labour's vote fell on average by 4.7 points.[14] In contrast, where that proportion was less than 22%, the party's vote fell by no less than 8.6 points. As we might have anticipated, constituencies in which unemployment had increased most are typically those in which a relatively small proportion work in the public sector, but even if we take that into account, it is still clear that Labour's vote fell less where the public sector plays a larger role in the local economy.[15] As a result of this pattern a new political gap seems to have opened up in Britain's electoral geography. In 2005 Labour's vote was on average almost as high (37.2%) in seats with relatively low proportions of public sector workers as it was in seats with a relatively large proportion (37.5%). There is now a four point difference in the level of support Labour secures in the two kinds of constituency.

While Labour may have lost ground particularly heavily in working class constituencies, not all areas of traditional Labour strength rejected the party. As is evident from Table A1.2 in Appendix 1, the party's overall vote share actually increased by 2.5 points in Scotland, even though it had suffered two catastrophic by-election defeats during the course of the last parliament (both of which were reversed) and had lost power to the SNP in the 2007 Scottish Parliament election. Labour also performed relatively well on Merseyside and in particular in the five constituencies located wholly or mostly in the city of Liverpool where on average the party's vote increased by 1.8 points. Perhaps in these areas, which had suffered relatively badly from the impact of the policies pursued by the previous Conservative administration in the 1980s, voters were still inclined to look to Labour to defend their interests despite the experience of the more recent recession.

Labour also appears to have recovered some ground in constituencies where some of the decisions it had made between 2001 and 2005 had caused it difficulties in 2005. Perhaps the most controversial decision it had made in that earlier period was to join the invasion of Iraq in 2003, a decision that proved to be particularly unpopular in constituencies with large numbers of Muslim voters.[16] That damage appears to have been repaired. As Table A2.2 shows, Labour's vote held up far better in those seats that contain a relatively large proportion of Muslim voters.

The main beneficiaries of Labour's difficulties in constituencies with many Muslim voters in 2005 had been, first, the Liberal Democrats, who uniquely amongst the major parties had opposed the war, together with Respect, a far left grouping that had strongly campaigned against the war. Table A2.2 shows that the Liberal Democrat vote only fell back slightly in the wake of Labour's recovery in such seats. However, Respect, which had suffered a split in 2007, fielded less than half as many candidates in 2010 (11) as it had done in 2005 (26). In only three instances did the party stand where it had fought the nearest equivalent seat in 2005. Labour clearly benefitted from the consequent reversal in Respect's fortunes. On average Labour's vote increased by 3.0 points in those seats where Respect had won over 4% of the vote in 2005, and two of the three largest increases in Labour's vote, in East Ham (+16.8) and West Ham (+10.9), occurred in seats where Respect had performed strongly in 2005 but did not contest the seat in 2010.

Table A2.2   Change in share of vote by proportion Muslim

	Mean change in share of vote won by			
% Muslim	Con	Lab	Lib Dem	
Up to 1%	+3.9	−7.3	+0.9	(378)
1–5%	+3.9	−7.1	+1.4	(149)
5–10%	+3.9	−4.4	+0.2	(63)
More than 10%	+2.6	−0.8	−0.3	(39)

'% Muslim' is the proportion of the population identifying themselves as Muslim in response to the 2001 Census.

However, Labour's relative success in Muslim seats may not have been occasioned only by fading passions about Iraq. For the party generally performed well in more or less any constituency with a large ethnic minority population, whether predominantly Muslim or not. Labour's vote fell on average by only 0.7 points in seats where, according to the 2001 Census, more than a quarter regard themselves as something other than white. It may be that the emphasis the Labour government gave to reducing discrimination against black and Asian people helped retain the loyalty of voters in these constituencies. In any event, Labour's performance in seats with relatively large numbers of Muslim and/ or ethnic minority voters helps to account for its relative success in Inner London where, as Appendix 1 Table A1.2 shows, its overall vote increased slightly.

Another decision that caused Labour difficulties in 2005 was the introduction of university 'top-up' fees. The party's vote fell more heavily in 2005 in seats that it was defending where there were relatively large numbers of students (defined as seats where more than 8% of the adult population aged under 75 was classified by the 2001 census as a student). This distinctive loss too seems to have been reversed this time around. In those seats that Labour won in 2001 with a relatively large student population Labour's vote fell by just 3.2 points, far less than the 7.3 point drop elsewhere.

Two implications flow from these findings. First, they demonstrate that groups of voters for whom a government decision is particularly controversial are willing to hold the government to account by changing their voting behaviour accordingly. Second, however, such behaviour is not necessarily long-lasting in its consequences; disaffected voters may be willing to return to the fold once the particular cause of their discontent has faded. This suggests that the reasons for the heavy loss of votes that Labour suffered between 2005 and 2010 lie primarily in voters' reactions to the events of the previous five years rather than their feelings about the government's record over the whole of its term of office since 1997.

One of the features of recent British elections has been a tendency for MPs – and especially those in marginal seats – to develop a 'personal vote'.[17] MPs are seemingly able to attract a degree of support for themselves as individuals rather than because of the party they represent by being highly visible and active within their constituency. Thanks in part to the MPs' expenses scandal – though also perhaps because of a realisation that the party was likely to lose the election – an unusually large number of Labour MPs opted not to stand again. Only 248 of the 348 seats that Labour was defending at this election (according to the estimates of the outcome of the 2005 election on the new boundaries) were fought by the person who had been the incumbent MP for all or most of the new constituency during the previous five years.

Labour might well have had reason to fear that the loss of personal votes would cost it vital support in some marginal seats. On the other hand at this election having a high voluntary turnover of existing MPs might prove to be advantageous. Perhaps voters' anger about the MPs' expenses scandal meant that they were inclined to vote against any incumbent MP who was standing again, especially if the MP had been embroiled in the scandal.[18]

In practice it appears that the turnover amongst its MPs did cost Labour votes. At 7.4 points, the decline in the party's vote in those of its seats that were not defended by the incumbent MP was more than two points higher than the equivalent statistic in seats where the incumbent stood again (–5.2).[19] However, incumbent Labour MPs who had been seriously implicated in the MPs' expenses scandal do also appear to have been punished.[20] In 39 such instances Labour's vote dropped on average by 6.5 points, 1.5 points higher than the equivalent figure for all other incumbents. Even so, incumbents who had been caught up in the expenses scandal still performed better than non-incumbent candidates who were attempting to defend a Labour held seat.

Of the ethnic minority candidates that stood under Labour's banner, 11 were incumbent MPs defending their seat. This group proved relatively successful. At 2.1 points, the fall in their share of the vote was well below even the average for incumbent Labour MPs. However, the difference can be accounted for by the fact that most were fighting constituencies with large Muslim and/or ethnic minority populations, constituencies where Labour generally performed relatively well in any event. Indeed, even ethnic minority candidates who were contesting a seat that Labour did not win in 2005 but which also had a substantial ethnic minority population (that is constituencies where more than 10% of the population regard themselves as something other than white) only saw their vote fall on average by 3.4 points.[21] However, ethnic minority Labour candidates fighting constituencies that were not won by Labour in 2005 and which did not have large ethnic minority populations seem to have suffered some electoral disadvantage; their vote fell on average by no less than 10.7 points.[22] Whereas selecting an ethnic minority candidate may be somewhat advantageous for Labour in an area with a relatively large ethnic minority population, it seems that the opposite may be the case where a white population predominates.

On the other hand, there is no consistent evidence that female Labour candidates performed any better or any worse than their male counterparts. In seats that Labour had not won in 2005, the fall in Labour's vote was almost exactly the same in seats fought by female candidates (–7.4 points) as it was in those fought by men (–7.3 points). True, the vote of incumbent female Labour MPs fell on average by rather more (5.8 points) than that of male incumbents (–5.0) but the difference is not statistically significant. Meanwhile the fall in Labour's vote was no less where a female candidate replaced a male incumbent Labour MP (–7.4) than where a male incumbent was replaced by another man (–7.5 points).[23]

We noted above that Labour's performance varied more than that of the other parties and to a greater extent than it had done at previous elections. Now we can begin to see why. Labour's performance was affected by voters' different reactions to the recession that had already occurred and the public expenditure cuts that were anticipated. At the same time distinctive losses that the party suffered in 2005 were reversed, most notably amongst the Muslim community. Meanwhile one part of the UK, Scotland, simply behaved entirely differently from the rest of the country, while the loss of the personal votes of retiring Labour MPs added a further twist to the party's fortunes. Labour's performance varied so much because voters in different parts of the country reacted systematically differently to the record they were asked to judge.

We can also now see why the median fall in Labour's vote was greater than the mean. In a relatively small set of constituencies, in particular those with a large Muslim/ethnic minority population and in Scotland, the party performed particularly well, in some instances enjoying an increase in its share of the vote. This had a marked impact on the party's overall performance, but such results were atypical. In most of the country the picture was of a heavy drop in support, and one that was usually closer to the median drop of 7.6 points than the mean of 6.5. In truth, in much of the country the scale of the reverse suffered by Labour was rather greater than immediately hits the eye.

Conservatives

A successful opposition profits from the misfortune of the incumbent government. We have seen that Labour lost support particularly heavily in seats that had experienced a large increase in unemployment together with seats with a relatively large working class. If the Conservatives were taking full advantage of the electorate's discontent with the incumbent government, we might expect them to have advanced particularly strongly in such seats.

The evidence for such a pattern is either weak or non-existent. At 3.9 points the average increase in the Conservatives' share of the vote in those seats where unemployment as a percentage of the electorate had increased by 2.5 points or more was no higher than where unemployment had increased by 1.25 points or less. The party did advance somewhat more strongly in seats with a relatively large working class (as defined above) than in those with a relatively small one. But at 0.9 points the difference in the party's performance between the two kinds of seats was but a pale reflection of the three point difference we observed earlier in Labour's performance.[24] It seems as though one reason at least why the Conservatives did not make a stronger advance in the election is that even when voters had particularly strong doubts about the performance of the incumbent government, this did not necessarily translate into a willingness to switch to the Conservatives.

At the same time, voters living in constituencies with a relatively large public sector were relatively reluctant to switch to the Conservatives. On average the party's vote increased by as much as 5.1 points in those seats where less than 22% of the workforce are in public administration, health or education, but by only 3.1 points in places where over 28% are in those occupations. So not only did the party apparently fail to profit from the unemployment that had already occurred, but it also appears to have suffered from concern about the scale of the party's policy of sharp public spending cuts.[25]

Meanwhile, the party had particular difficulties in Scotland, where its overall share of the vote advanced by just 0.9 points, even less of an advance than we have seen Labour managed north of the border. The party's share of the Scottish vote was not only as much as nine points below what it had been when the party had last won a general election, in 1992, but was also still 0.8 points lower than it had been in 1997 when it had suffered a wipeout. Scottish Conservatives have, it seems, still been unable to shake off the impression of being an 'English' party, a legacy from both the economic difficulties Scotland suffered in the 1980s and the party's opposition to devolution in the 1990s. Certainly the party's failure to add to its existing tally of one seat in Scotland was central to its inability to secure an overall majority, for the 306 Tory MPs elected from England and Wales would have been sufficient to secure an overall majority in a House of Commons that did not include any representatives from Scotland. Meanwhile, the party's poor performance in Scotland stood in sharp contrast to its achievements in the more rural half of the other part of Great Britain to enjoy devolved government, Wales, where, as Appendix 1 Table A1.2 shows, the party was particularly successful, adding 6.5 points to its overall share of the vote.

Prior to the election, the party's hopes of securing an overall majority appeared to rest quite heavily on being able to perform better than average in marginal seats being defended by Labour or the Liberal Democrats against a Conservative challenger. In order to help achieve such an outcome, during the course of the last parliament the party engaged in an exercise supervised and partly funded by the party's Deputy Chairman, Lord Ashcroft, to target resources on marginal seats that appeared to be winnable (for more details see pp. 234–6). If the party could perform better than average in such seats, then it would increase its chances of winning an overall majority for any particular share of the overall national vote. Fearful of this prospect, Labour MPs frequently criticised the Conservatives' reliance on Lord Ashcroft's money in the months and years leading up to the election.

Table A2.3 would appear to suggest that this strategy had a degree of success. On average the increase in the Conservative share of the vote was greatest in those seats that Labour was defending against a second placed Conservative challenger. However, the added advantage that the party enjoyed in these seats was only a small one of 0.7 of a point; in keeping with the low standard deviation in the change in the party's share of the vote since 2005. Indeed, what is most remarkable about the Conservative column in Table A2.3 is the relative uniformity of the party's performance in seats with very different tactical situations. Meanwhile, there is certainly no evidence that the party was particularly successful in its second battleground, those seats where it was the principal challenger in a Liberal Democrat held seat.

Table A2.3   Party performance by tactical situation

| Winning/Second party 2005 | Mean change in share of vote won by | | | |
	Con	*Lab*	*Lib Dem*	
Lab/Con	+4.5	−7.0	+0.6	(213)
Con/Lib Dem	+4.1	−6.8	+0.5	(81)
Lib Dem/Lab	+4.0	−4.0	−0.9	(16)
Lib Dem/Con	+3.7	−4.7	−0.4	(45)
Con/Lab	+3.6	−9.9	+3.3	(128)
Lab/Lib Dem	+3.0	−5.2	+0.4	(107)
All seats	+3.8	−6.5	+0.8	(629)

Seats where a party other than Conservative, Labour or Liberal Democrat won first or second place not shown. Such seats are, however, included in the calculation for 'All seats'.

If we look further at those seats where the Conservatives were challenging Labour, there appears to be something of a paradox. As we have noted, if Lord Ashcroft's efforts were to reap a dividend the Conservatives' advance needed to be particularly strong in more marginal Labour held seats, and especially so in those constituencies where the swing required for a Conservative victory was close to the 6.9% mark that, on the assumption of a uniform swing, would bring the Conservatives an overall majority.[26] Yet there is no evidence that in general the Conservative advance was strongest of all in these seats. Where the Conservatives started off between 10 and 15 points behind Labour (that is seats where they required a swing of between 5% and 7.5%) the party's vote increased on average by 4.4 points. Meanwhile where Labour's initial lead was just somewhat higher, that is between 15 and 20 points, the equivalent figure is, at 4.8 points, only a little higher. Neither figure is markedly different from the 4.6 point increase the Conservatives achieved in seats where Labour started off less than ten points ahead (most of which the Conservatives might have anticipated winning without any special effort) or the 4.3 point increase where Labour's 2005 majority was greater than 20 points (that is seats that for the most part would be regarded as safe). It would seem that even on a generous reading of the evidence the exercise headed by Lord Ashcroft had limited success at most in ensuring that the Conservatives generally performed particularly well in key Labour held marginal seats – and certainly not success on the scale that Labour had feared.

Given that the Conservatives were anticipating making an advance in the election, they perhaps had less reason to worry about decisions by their incumbent MPs to retire. Even so, as many as 57 of the 209 seats the party was defending were not fought by incumbents.[27] As in Labour's case, that turnover appears to have cost the Conservatives votes. The party's vote only rose on average by 2.9 points in Conservative held seats that were not being defended by an incumbent, compared with 4.1 points where the incumbent MP was still in place. In contrast, incumbent Conservative MPs who first won their seats in 2005 – and who thus will have had the opportunity over the previous five years to acquire a personal vote for the first time – saw their vote increase on average by 5.6 points, while those who had been in the Commons longer only enjoyed an average increase of 3.8 points. The above average performance of Conservative MPs newly elected in 2005 helps to explain why the Conservatives performed relatively well in marginal seats they were defending[28] (the average increase in the party's vote in all such seats was no less than 5.1 points), though in truth it seems that Conservative candidates of all descriptions tended to perform relatively well in such seats.

Still, it seems that Mr Cameron may have been wise to try to limit the fallout from the expenses scandal, for as in Labour's case, Conservative MPs who had become seriously embroiled in the MPs' expenses scandal appear to have cost their party votes. On average their vote increased by just 2.8 points, whereas that of incumbents who had not been involved at all in the scandal enjoyed an increase of 4.4 points. However, it seems that persuading an MP who had been caught up in the scandal to step down did not necessarily insulate the party from loss. On average the Conservative vote only increased by 2.1 points where the incumbent MP had stood down in the wake of the expenses scandal, whereas it increased by 3.6 points in seats that were being defended by a non-incumbent candidate and where the previous MP had not been particularly involved in the scandal. Here though the pattern was far from consistent – for example, the Conservative vote increased by seven points in Gosport, where, in one of the most celebrated incidents in the scandal, the previous MP, Sir Peter Viggers, had been required to stand down (see p. 27).

Prior to the expenses scandal, Mr Cameron had, as a part of a strategy to 'modernise' the image of his party, encouraged it to select more female and ethnic minority candidates. There is no evidence that female Conservative candidates consistently did better or worse than their male counterparts. The same, however, is not true of ethnic minority candidates. Where an ethnic minority Conservative contested a seat that had been fought by a white candidate in 2005, the Conservative vote increased on average by just 2.3 points, a full one and a half points below the equivalent statistic for seats that were fought by a white candidate on both occasions. Indeed, in five instances where an ethnic minority candidate defended a Conservative seat that had previously been represented by a white MP, the party's share of the vote fell back on average, by 2.3 points. As in Labour's case, the degree to which potential Conservative voters were reluctant to back an ethnic minority candidate varied according to the racial composition of the electorate. In seats where more than 10% of the population regards itself as something other than white, the Conservative vote increased on average by 3.5 points where an ethnic minority Conservative candidate stood; elsewhere the party's vote only increased on average by 1.3 points.[29] One difficulty this pattern creates for the party is that nominating an ethnic minority candidate is more likely to cost the party votes in those seats that it has some chance of winning. The apparent reluctance of Conservative members to nominate ethnic minority candidates in such seats evidently reflects an outlook that still exists amongst a section of the party's potential electorate.[30]

One particular mechanism David Cameron used to try to broaden the social background of Conservative candidates was the creation of an 'A' list of supposedly particularly able applicants to whom constituencies were encouraged to give priority when selecting their candidate (for further details see pp. 313–15). There is no consistent evidence that this move either helped, or – as some critics within the party feared – hindered the party's quest for votes. True, the average increase in their party's vote secured by A list candidates was, at 2.5 points, a little lower than the increase enjoyed by non-incumbent non-A list candidates who were defending a Conservative seat (+3.0 points). On the other hand, in those seats not won by the Conservatives in 2005, the average increase in the party's support obtained by A list candidates was, at 5.0 points, rather higher than that enjoyed by non-A list candidates (3.6 points). The record of A-list female candidates proved to be equally mixed.[31]

We now have some important clues as to why the Conservatives' advance was relatively modest in 2010. Although voters in those parts of the country where the recession had hit particularly hard had lost confidence in Labour, they were not especially persuaded that a Conservative government would be preferable. At the same time the party's message on how to handle the deficit was not attractive to those living where public sector employment is particularly prevalent. Meanwhile, the party's efforts to enhance its prospects by focusing organisational resources on Labour held marginal seats brought an uncertain dividend, while the promotion of a more diverse set of candidates did not have any apparent beneficial impact on the party's fortunes. Mr Cameron may have tried hard to change his party and its image during the previous five years, but it seems that it still left many voters less than impressed.

Liberal Democrats

One of the most important sources of variation in Liberal Democrat performance at past elections has been tactical voting.[32] A voter is said to vote tactically if they decide to vote for a party other than the one they most prefer because that party appears better placed to secure the defeat of a party that they particularly dislike. Voters have particularly been inclined to vote for whichever of Labour or Liberal Democrat seemed best placed to defeat the Conservatives locally. This has meant that the Liberal Democrats have often found it relatively difficult to win votes in seats where they were third behind both Labour and the Conservatives, but have prospered in seats where Labour were third.

Such tactical voting was particularly in evidence between 1997 and 2005, when the Conservatives were particularly unpopular. In 1997 voters appeared to switch from the Liberal Democrats to Labour in more or less any seat that the Conservatives were defending against a Labour challenge, while in seats where the Liberal Democrats seemed to have a credible prospect of winning voters seemed even more willing than before to switch from Labour to the Liberal Democrats.[33] Neither pattern was reversed in 2001 or 2005.[34] However, now that the Conservatives were no longer so unpopular (or indeed Labour so popular), perhaps fewer voters would feel the impetus to vote against the Conservatives and would revert to voting for the party they most preferred.

A glance back at Table A2.3 gives reason to believe that perhaps this may indeed have happened. The Liberal Democrat vote went up most strongly in seats that the Conservatives were defending against a second placed Labour challenge. At the same time Labour performed worse in these seats than in any other category of seats in the table.[35] It would seem that voters were particularly likely to switch from Labour to the

Liberal Democrats in these seats – perhaps because they decided they no longer wished to vote tactically.

However, if this pattern is a consequence of a general 'tactical unwind', we would also expect to find that the Liberal Democrats performed relatively well – again at Labour's expense – in the more marginal seats that Labour was defending against a Conservative challenge. After all, many of these will also have been amongst the seats that the Conservatives were defending in 1997 when tactical voting against a Conservative incumbent was so commonplace. However, of this there is no sign. In seats where Labour started off with a lead of less than ten points over a second placed Conservative, the average increase in the Liberal Democrat vote was only 1.2 points, little different from the overall national average.[36] If some Liberal Democrat supporters did indeed return to the fold in 2010 because they no longer wished to vote tactically for Labour, they only did so in seats that were already in Conservative hands – perhaps because, given that the Conservatives were advancing in the polls, they reckoned that continuing to vote tactically against the Conservatives was likely to prove ineffective.

Meanwhile if those who had previously voted tactically for the Liberal Democrats rather than backing Labour had now decided to do so no longer, we would expect the Liberal Democrats to have performed particularly badly – and Labour relatively well – in seats where the Conservatives and the Liberal Democrats shared first and second place. Table A2.3 indicates that on average the Liberal Democrats did indeed fall back a little where they were defending a seat against a second placed Conservative, while Labour tended to lose less ground in such circumstances. However the Liberal Democrats also performed relatively poorly where they were defending a seat against a Labour rather than a Conservative challenge. This suggests that while the Liberal Democrats may have had their difficulties in seats they were defending, it is unlikely that the explanation simply lies in the unwinding of past tactical support by erstwhile Labour supporters.

One possibility might be the loss of MPs' personal votes. Such votes have previously been particularly important for the party. The relative weakness of the party's national appeal has meant that the ability of Liberal Democrat MPs to secure votes on the basis of their personal popularity and local activity has often been crucial to their election and re-election. So the fact that of the 62 seats that the party was defending, as many as ten (including one new seat that was not currently represented by a Liberal Democrat MP) were being fought by non-incumbents always seemed likely to cause the party difficulties.

On average the party's vote fell by no less than 4.7 points in seats that were being defended by a non-incumbent, whereas incumbent MPs on average saw their vote increase by 0.6 of a point, little different from the party's performance nationwide. However, as we would anticipate, it was those incumbents who had first captured their seat in 2005 who typically performed best of all; their vote rose on average by 3.1 points. Other incumbent Liberal Democrat MPs, in contrast, performed relatively poorly, suffering a slight drop of 0.3 of a point in their support.

However, there is yet a further distinction to be drawn amongst incumbent Liberal Democrat MPs. Those who had been personally implicated in the MPs' expenses scandal saw their vote fall on average by 4.6 points.[37] Amongst other incumbent MPs who had first won their seat before 2005, the Liberal Democrats' share of the vote increased on average by 1.8 points. In short once we take into account both the impact of (lost) personal votes and the MPs' expenses scandal, there is no clear evidence that the Liberal Democrats suffered any particular loss of support in seats that they were defending, whether as a result of a reversal of tactical switching or for any other reason.

Still, it should also be noted that the party performed relatively poorly too in seats where they started off in second place to the Conservatives, but were only ten points or less behind. In these seats the party's vote fell back on average by 0.6 of a point, while at 5.7 points the fall in Labour's vote in these seats was also somewhat lower than average. Perhaps here there is evidence of tactical unwinding? But again, it seems unlikely. First, all but two of these marginal Conservative/Liberal Democrat contests were seats where Labour won less than 20% of the vote last time, and where, as we have already seen, Labour's vote fell less, irrespective of the nature of the local tactical situation. Second, the seats where the Liberal Democrat vote fell back most were typically either seats that the Conservatives had captured from the Liberal Democrats in 2005[38] or else were ones where, as a result of boundary changes, much of the seat had previously had a Liberal Democrat MP who was no longer standing.[39] In these circumstances the personal vote that had previously been accumulated locally seems this time around to have been lost.[40]

We should note too that the Liberal Democrats also performed relatively poorly in seats where the party locally was challenging Labour. In seats where the Labour majority over the Liberal Democrats in 2005 had been less than ten points, the Liberal Democrat vote fell back on average by as much as 2.2 points, while Labour's vote hardly dropped at all (–0.3). These are certainly not seats where some voters had previously made a tactical switch from Labour to the Liberal Democrats.[41] In part, the reasons for this outcome are similar to those (as outlined in the previous paragraph) that pertain in seats where the Liberal Democrats had been challenging the Conservatives.[42] But it is also a consequence of two other sources of variation in the Liberal Democrat performance.

First, three of the most marginal Labour/Liberal Democrat contests were in Scotland where, as we have already seen, Labour's vote actually increased, and where the Liberal Democrats performed poorly in the wake of this Labour advance. The party's overall share of the Scottish vote fell by no less than 3.7 points. (Indeed, a similar pattern applied in another area where we have seen Labour also performed unusually well, Merseyside. In the five seats wholly or mostly in the city of Liverpool, the Liberal Democrat vote fell by 4.5 points.[43]) Second, as many as five of the Labour/Liberal Democrat marginals were seats where over 5% of the population are Muslim and thus were seats where, as we discussed earlier, the Liberal Democrats typically lost some of the particularly strong advance that they had made in 2005 in the wake of the Iraq War.[44]

Something of a consistent picture is emerging from this analysis. It seems that, for a variety of reasons, the Liberal Democrats often found it rather more difficult to make headway in the kinds of seats where Labour were relatively strong.[45] Indeed, in seats where Labour won between 20% and 40% of the vote in 2005, the Liberal Democrat vote increased on average by 2.2 points. In contrast, in seats where Labour won more than 40% in 2005, the increase in the Liberal Democrat vote averaged just 0.4 of a point. This pattern is the reverse of what happened in 2005, when the Liberal Democrats advanced most strongly in areas of Labour strength, thereby enabling the party to mount a stronger assault on Labour held seats than ever before. It seems that some of that distinctive progress in what had hitherto been relatively barren territory for the party was lost.

As in the case of both Labour and the Conservatives, there is no discernible difference between the performances of Liberal Democrat male and female candidates. However, at first glance, the party's ethnic minority candidates do seem to have fared rather worse than their white colleagues. In 29 seats where an ethnic minority Liberal Democrat candidate stood this time, but a white candidate was nominated in 2005, the party's share of the vote fell, on average by 1.5 points. However, much of this poor performance can be accounted for by the distinctive character of the constituencies that were contested by ethnic minority Liberal Democrats. Nearly two-thirds of those who stood where a white candidate had done in 2005 did so in constituencies where over 5% of the population are Muslim – that is seats where the party generally performed relatively poorly, although ethnic minority Liberal Democrats who fought a Muslim seat for the first time do seem to have had particular difficulty in maintaining their party's share of the vote.[46] In any event, it seems that ethnic minority Liberal Democrats who fought predominantly white constituencies were not under the same disadvantage as many Conservative and even some Labour candidates in such circumstances.

The Liberal Democrat 'surge' in the opinion polls dominated much of the national campaign. Yet, in practice, it seems that local factors once again played a central role in its actual performance. Personal, local popularity – either won or lost – apparently still mattered heavily in accounting for which Liberal Democrats managed to win and who lost out. At the same time, many Liberal Democrat MPs apparently continued to profit from switching undertaken in response to the local tactical situation. However, in contrast to 2005, it is not apparent that discontent with particular decisions made by the incumbent Labour government reaped the party any identifiable systematic benefit.[47] It was perhaps the performance of a party that captured the support of those who wanted 'none of the above' – so long as the candidate and party locally were able to capture and galvanise that mood.

Minor parties

As we noted earlier, more people than ever before voted for a party other than Conservative, Labour or Liberal Democrat. By far the biggest challenge was mounted by the Eurosceptic United Kingdom Independence Party (UKIP), which fought no less than 558 of the 632 seats in Great Britain. This represented the largest minor party challenge ever to be mounted, and generated the largest share of the vote ever won by a minor party, some 3.2% of the overall vote in Great Britain, clearly outpacing the previous best performance by any minor party, the 2.7% won by the Referendum Party in 1997. UKIP's average vote in the seats it actually contested was 3.5%, compared with 2.8% in the 496 seats it had fought in 2005. The party continued to perform best in more middle class constituencies that contain relatively large numbers of older voters, and in particular such constituencies on or near the southern and eastern coasts of England. However, the 0.8 point average increase in its vote in seats it had also fought in 2005 largely occurred across the board – but with one notable exception. The party's vote often fell back a little where it had performed particularly well in 2005. On average in seats where it had managed to win more than 5% of the vote last time around, its tally this time fell back on average by 0.2 of a point. It seems that the party still has to learn how to build on local success from one election to another.

The British National Party (BNP) also made an advance, albeit more partial. Fielding 338 candidates, substantially more than the 119 it stood in 2005, the party won 1.9% of the overall votes cast in Great Britain, easily the highest vote ever cast for a far right party in a UK general election. However, its average share of the vote in those seats it actually fought was, at 3.8%, in fact slightly down on the 4.3% the party achieved in 2005. For the most part this reflects the fact that in increasing the number of constituencies it fought, the party fought more seats where its appeal was less strong; in those seats where the party did not fight any of the component constituencies in 2005, the party's average vote was just 2.9%. However, it is notable that the party's vote also appears to have fallen back somewhat in those places where it had performed best in 2005.[48] This included the Barking seat contested by the party's leader, Nick Griffin, whose hopes of becoming the party's first elected MP in the constituency were dashed.

As in 2005 the BNP was most successful in relatively deprived urban constituencies with relatively large Asian or Muslim populations – and less well educated working class ones too – and in particular such constituencies located along the Pennines, in the West Midlands and in the east end of London together with adjoining constituencies in Essex. But these familiar patterns were not the only ones of note; the BNP also performed well in places that had experienced a relatively large increase in unemployment since 2005. This is illustrated in Table A2.4, which shows that even in those seats where the BNP had not fought any of the component old constituencies in 2005 – which were disproportionately and mostly seats without a large ethnic minority population – the party's average vote was relatively high in seats that had experienced a relatively large increase in unemployment irrespective of their class composition. The BNP's success was apparently not simply fuelled by concern about immigration but also by fears engendered by the recent recession.

In contrast to her counterpart in the BNP, the leader of the Greens, Caroline Lucas, did succeed in making it to the House of Commons. But her success in Brighton Pavilion, thanks to a 9.4 point increase in her party's vote there, was an isolated one. Even though the party contested more constituencies than ever before, 335 (compared with 202 in 2005), at 1.0%, its overall share of the vote was slightly lower (by 0.1 of a point) than five years previously. At 1.8%, the party's average share of the vote in the constituencies that it fought was well down on the record 3.4% it achieved in 2005. Its vote was also down on average by 1.4 points in those seats that it had previously contested in 2005. Apart from Brighton Pavilion, the only other seat in which the party made significant progress was Norwich South (+7.5 points). The Greens had opted to target their efforts on these two seats, in both of which they had already established a significant local government presence. Such targeting appears capable of bringing the party dividends.

Table A2.4   Level of BNP support by class composition and change in unemployment

% Working class	Change in unemployment 2005–10			All seats
	Low	Medium	High	
Low	2.0	2.3	3.1	2.2
	(29)	(48)	(3)	(78)
High	2.0	3.2	3.8	3.3
	(10)	(77)	(42)	(129)
All seats	2.0	2.9	3.7	2.9
	(39)	(125)	(45)	(209)

% Working class: Low: % economically active adults aged 16–74 in routine and semi-routine occupations according to the 2001 Census less than 21%; High: % adults in such occupations greater than 21%.
Change in unemployment: Low: unemployment claimant count as a proportion of the electorate increased by less than 1.25 points between May 2005 and March 2010; Medium: unemployment increased by between 1.25 and 2.5 points; High: unemployment increased by more than 2.5 points.
   Table confined to seats fought by the BNP in 2010 but where the party did not fight any portion of the seat in 2005. Buckingham is excluded.

Despite having performed poorly in 2005 and having come first in the 2007 Scottish Parliament election, the Scottish National Party (SNP) only made a modest advance. Its vote increased on average by just 2.3 points, though in the event this proved enough for the party to reclaim the second place in votes across the whole of Scotland that it had lost in 2005 to the Liberal Democrats. Still, the SNP's fortunes compared favourably with those of the nationalist party in Wales, Plaid Cymru, whose vote on average actually fell back, by 1.1 points. At 11.3% the party's share of the vote was no higher than it had been in 1970, the first occasion on which it fought all the seats in Wales. The party's heaviest losses were typically in its Welsh speaking heartlands in Dyfed and Gwynedd, while the party's vote held steady or even increased in many seats close to the border with England in Clwyd, Gwent and Powys. Plaid Cymru has attempted in recent years to increase its appeal to more anglicised Wales and perhaps this has begun to have an impact. Or equally, maybe the party's more traditional supporters have been particularly unhappy with the party's decision in 2007 to enter a coalition with Labour in the Welsh Assembly.

Between them UKIP, the BNP, the Greens and the two nationalist parties account for nearly 87% of the vote cast for minor party candidates and independents. Their collective success, and especially that of the three British-wide parties, is of interest not only in itself but also for the impact it may have had on the fortunes of the larger parties. Did an advance by these parties come at the expense of one of the large parties in particular?

The Conservative Party has long been fearful of the success of Eurosceptic parties.[49] UKIP's performance at this election will not have assuaged that concern. True, there is little sign in those seats that UKIP fought in both 2010 and in 2005 that the variation in Conservative performance was consistently related to the variation in UKIP's performance. However, it is notable that, at just 2.6 points, the increase in the Conservative share of the vote in seats that UKIP contested this time around but had not fought in 2005, was noticeably lower than the national average increase in the Conservative vote. In contrast the performance of both Labour and the Liberal Democrats appears to have been little affected by the entry of a UKIP candidate into the fray. It appears that while changes in UKIP's popularity may not particularly affect the Conservatives' vote, the party's 'baseline' vote does come disproportionately from those who would otherwise vote Conservative.

Labour, meanwhile, appeared particularly concerned before polling day about the rise of the BNP. The far right party has tended to perform best in constituencies where typically Labour is relatively strong, appealing to less well educated working class voters who would often be regarded as part of Labour's 'core' vote.[50] Labour's concern appears to have been justified too. We have already noted that the BNP performed particularly well in constituencies that had experienced a relatively large increase in unemployment – that is precisely the kind of constituency in which we also noted earlier that Labour performed particularly badly. The two phenomena do indeed appear to be linked. At 7.4 points the decline in Labour's vote in seats that the BNP fought in 2010 but did not fight in 2005 was far higher than the 4.8 point drop the party suffered in those seats that the BNP did not fight at either election.

Moreover, this link between the decline in Labour's vote and BNP performance was a consequence of what happened in seats that had experienced a relatively large increase in unemployment in particular. In seats where the increase in unemployment since 2005 represented less than 1.25% of the electorate, Labour's vote actually fell less where the

BNP fought the seat in 2010 after having not done so in 2005 (down 3.7 points) than it did where the BNP did not fight in 2005 or 2010 (down 4.7 points). But in seats where the increase in unemployment represented more than 2.5% of the electorate, the picture was very different. The drop in Labour's vote in a constituency that the BNP contested in 2010 but not in 2005 was no less than 8.2 points, compared with just 3.1 points in seats that the BNP continued not to contest. It seems that it was in those places that had lost out most from the recession where Labour's fears of losing votes to the BNP proved all too prescient.

So far as the Liberal Democrats are concerned, the Greens have previously appeared to be the minor party that potentially posed the greatest threat to their prospects. The Greens' environmental message tended to appeal to much the same kind of relatively well-educated middle class voter amongst whom the Liberal Democrats tend to do relatively well. At first glance, that apparent threat does not appear to have been realised in 2010. The Liberal Democrat vote rose on average by 0.6 of a point in seats that were fought by the Greens in 2010 but not in 2005, little different from the 0.7 of a point increase the party enjoyed in seats that the Greens did not fight at either election. However, seats that the Greens fought in 2010 after not having done so in 2005 were more likely than those that the party did not fight on either occasion to be seats where the Conservatives started off ahead of Labour – and a glance back at Table A2.3 reminds us that these were generally seats where the Liberal Democrats performed particularly well. Once we take that into account, it becomes evident that a decision by the Greens to fight a seat anew did cost the Liberal Democrats support. For example, in seats where the Conservatives were first and Labour second in 2005, the average increase in the Liberal Democrat vote was 2.8 points where the Greens fought anew compared with 3.4 points where they did not fight at all. Equally, in Labour/Conservative contests the equivalent figures are 1.0 and 0.2 respectively. In contrast no such systematic difference arose in respect of the Conservative or Labour performance.

Overall, then, one key reason for the record level of support acquired collectively for minor parties was the ability of each of UKIP, the BNP and the Greens to fight more constituencies than ever before. More voters simply had the opportunity to vote for these parties and thus did so. But at the same time UKIP, and to a lesser extent the BNP, also managed to strengthen their appeal; the latter in particular seems to have been able to profit from fear of unemployment in a manner that the Conservatives could not. Yet it was the Greens that demonstrated an ability to build upon past local success and thereby make a breakthrough into the House of Commons. It remains to be seen which proves to be the more important achievement in the longer term, but it is clear that in 2010 at least none of the larger parties could afford to ignore the potential challenge from the more ideological 'fringe' of British politics. That is certainly a very different world from one in which competition for votes is dominated by just two heavyweight parties.

Turnout

One obvious potential explanation for the four point increase in turnout is that voters felt that the outcome of the election was uncertain. Most opinion polls published during the campaign were reported as pointing to a hung parliament, while they also suggested that the Liberal Democrats might overtake Labour as the second largest party in votes (see Chapter 12). Previous experience has suggested that turnout tends to be higher when opinion polls suggest that the result will be close.

But if that was the reason for the increase in turnout, it is somewhat curious that it was not particularly marked in seats where the contest was apparently close locally. In seats where the lead of the largest party over the second party in 2005 was less than ten points, turnout increased on average by 3.9 points, slightly below the overall average of 4.2 points. In contrast turnout rose by no less than 4.9 points in seats where the largest party enjoyed a lead of 30 points or more.

However, in many seats where the outcome locally appeared close, this would also have been the case in 2005 and perhaps even earlier, and so the incentive to vote provided by a close contest locally might have been no greater than before. Indeed, in seats where the lead of the largest party had also been less than ten points in 2001, turnout increased by just 2.5 points. In contrast, in seats that had not been so marginal on that occasion, the average increase was as much as 4.8 points. Indeed, more generally, in seats where the majority in 2005 had been less than that four years before, turnout increased by 4.5 points, compared with 2.8 points where the 2005 result had been less close. In short, some voters do appear to have been encouraged to vote when their local constituency had newly become marginal.[51]

Nevertheless, this is far from being the most striking pattern in the change in turnout. Above all, turnout simply increased most where it had previously been relatively low. In seats where participation had been more than four points below the national average in 2005, that is 57% or less, turnout increased on average this time by no less than 6.1 points. In contrast where the turnout last time had been between 57% and 65%, the average increase was 4.1 points, and where it had been over 65% in 2005, only 2.7 points. In short, it was those parts of Britain that had previously appeared least engaged with the political process – and places that in many cases had also been those where turnout had fallen most in 2001 and 2005 – where voters were apparently most likely to return to the ballot box, though whether this was because they were particularly influenced by the apparent closeness of the election or for some other reason we cannot be sure.[52]

However, not all the variation in turnout resulted in higher increases in turnout in places where it had previously been relatively low. Other things being equal, turnout increased rather less in constituencies with relatively high levels of social deprivation.[53] It increased rather more in places with a relatively large number of graduates.[54] But it seems that, despite some of the fears that were expressed before the election, there certainly is not any systematic evidence that those sections of the population that were already relatively disconnected from the electoral process became even less inclined to vote in the wake of the expenses scandal.[55]

The electoral system

There are two issues to consider in assessing how the electoral system converted votes into seats. The first is whether the variation in the change in party support affected the outcome in seats. How does the result compare with what would have happened if the changes in party support had been exactly the same across the whole country? Then second, how do we account for the failure of the electoral system to deliver an overall majority? Was it a one-off accident unlikely ever to be repeated? Or was it the result of longer-term developments that raise questions about whether single member plurality can be expected to produce overall majorities in future?

If support for the three main parties had risen or fallen in line with the overall change in their share of the vote across the country as a whole, the outcome would have been Conservative 291 seats, Labour 264, and the Liberal Democrats 64, while 31 seats (including 18 in Northern Ireland) would have been won by other parties.[56] The result would have still been a hung parliament, but one in which a majority government could have been formed by Labour and the Liberal Democrats combined as well as by the Conservatives and the Liberal Democrats together. The variation in party performance around the overall national result thus had an important impact on the bargaining power of the various parties in the subsequent negotiations to form a new government.

The principal reason for this Conservative advantage lay in the fact that the party made a net gain of 87 seats from Labour rather than the tally of 73 seats they would have obtained if the change in party support had been the same in every constituency. In particular the Conservatives captured 23 seats from Labour where the total vote swing required for them to win locally was greater than the 5.1% total vote swing from Labour to Conservative that occurred across the country as a whole, only partly counterbalanced by the fact that Labour managed to defend successfully nine seats where the Conservatives required less than a 5.1% swing to win.

This divergence from what would have happened in the event of a uniform national swing owed more to the pattern of Labour success and failure than it did to particularly good or bad Conservative performances. At 7.3 points, the average change in the Conservative share of the vote in the 23 'additional' seats the party captured from Labour was 3.5 points above the party's overall national performance, while at 10.7 points, the average fall in Labour's vote in these seats was as much as 4.2 points greater than it was nationally. The equivalent statistics in the nine seats that Labour retained against the national trend were 1.4 points for the Conservatives, 2.4 points below their national performance, and an increase of 0.1 of a point for Labour, no less than 6.6 points better than the party's national performance.

Comparison of the characteristics of these two sets of constituencies indicates that they differed in respect of a number of characteristics that we have seen systematically affected Labour's performance, but not always that of the Conservatives. None of the nine seats that Labour managed to hold against the national trend had experienced an increase in unemployment of more than 2.5 points, while only one of the 23 additional seats the Conservatives captured had seen unemployment increase by less than 1.25 points. Five of the nine seats are ones with a relatively small working class population (less than 18%), while no less than 11 of the 23 contain relatively large such populations (of more than 25%) and none have relatively small populations. In five of the nine seats Muslims comprise 5% or more of the population, while in six more than 10% of the population belong to an ethnic minority. Only one of the 23 seats contains an ethnic minority or Muslim population of any size at all. At the same time, not only were two of the seats that Labour saved against the tide located in Scotland or on Merseyside, but all bar one was defended by an incumbent MP. In contrast, nearly half (11) of the seats that Labour failed to retain were not defended by an incumbent Labour MP.[57]

Although variation in performance cost Labour a net total of 14 seats to the Conservatives some of that loss was compensated for by the fact that the party both successfully defended eight seats that, on the national result, the party would have lost to the Liberal Democrats, and also actually captured one seat from the Liberal Democrats. In contrast the Liberal Democrats only gained four seats from Labour that they would not have captured if the result locally had been in line with the national trend. It was this pattern that primarily accounted for the Liberal Democrats' failure to make an advance in seats despite securing a modest increase in their overall vote.[58] Seven of the nine seats that elected Labour rather than Liberal Democrat MPs despite the national trend were being defended by an incumbent Labour MP, six had experienced increases in unemployment of less than 1.25 points, and five had relatively small working class populations (and none had a large one), while four had ethnic minority populations of more than 10%, three had Muslim populations of more than 5%, and three were in Scotland. In short it was the Liberal Democrats' misfortune that many of the seats in which they potentially posed a serious challenge to Labour were in the event ones where typically Labour's vote held up relatively well.[59]

Still, although the outcome in seats departed somewhat from what would have happened if the movement of votes since 2005 had been the same everywhere, this was not the reason why the electoral system failed to deliver an overall majority for only the second time since 1945. Given the outcome in votes, Britain was heading for a hung parliament anyway. That in itself suggests that the failure to deliver an overall majority may not have been a one-off accident, but rather was the consequence of longer-term trends in Britain's electoral geography.

There are, in fact, three developments that between them help us to understand why the electoral system delivered a hung parliament. First, the system is no longer as effective as it once was at denying representation to the Liberal Democrats together with other smaller parties. Second, fewer seats are marginal between Labour and the Conservatives. Third, nowadays the electoral system treats Labour more favourably than it does the Conservatives.[60]

As we noted at the beginning of this appendix, the 23.6% of the vote in Great Britain won by the Liberal Democrats in 2010 was not the largest share of the vote to be won by Britain's third largest party in the post-war period. That accolade still belongs to the 26% of the vote won by the former Liberal/SDP Alliance in 1983. However, whereas then the Alliance won just 23 seats, this time around the Liberal Democrats won 57. Indeed, this was the third election in a row in which the party won over 50 seats, whereas between the whole of the period between 1945 and 1992 it had never reached as much as the two dozen mark.

So evidently the electoral system has come to treat the Liberal Democrats more kindly than it once did. The explanation for this is relatively simple. The main reason why the Alliance profited so little from its success in 1983 is that its vote was geographically very evenly spread.[61] The standard deviation of its share of the vote across all constituencies in 1983 was just 7.3, far less than the equivalent figure at that election for the Conservatives of 13.2, and for Labour of 15.7. As a result the party came second in many constituencies, but first in relatively few. At more recent elections, in contrast, the Liberal Democrat vote has varied rather more from one constituency to another. In 2010 the standard deviation of the Liberal Democrat vote was 10.4.[62] Thus although the Liberal Democrats are still disadvantaged by the electoral system compared with Labour and the Conservatives, that disadvantage has lessened at recent elections.

Meanwhile, apart from the 57 seats won by the Liberal Democrats, 28 were captured by Scottish and Welsh nationalists, a Green, and 18 MPs from Northern Ireland in 2010. Such additional third party representation has become commonplace at recent elections, not least because since the 1970s the party system in Northern Ireland has largely been divorced from that in the rest of the UK. If there is a relatively large phalanx of some 80–90 MPs who belong to neither the Conservatives nor Labour, then inevitably the chances of a hung parliament occurring are greater than if, as was the case in the 1950s and 1960s, no more than a dozen or so such MPs are elected.

However, those chances have been increased by a further long-standing development, a decline in the number of seats that are marginal between Labour and the Conservatives.[63] If the single member electoral system is to deliver an overall majority for one party, even if that party has won less than half the vote and has only secured a relatively small lead over its principal competitor, there needs to be a relatively large number of seats where the lead of the current incumbent is sufficiently small that it is likely to be overturned if the country as a whole swung modestly in the opposite direction. If there are fewer such seats, then a small lead for either the Conservatives or Labour may no longer be sufficient to ensure that the plurality winner enjoys an overall majority.

For this purpose, we can define as a marginal seat one where the Conservative share of those votes cast for either Labour or the Conservatives (the 'two-party vote') would lie between 45% and 55% in the event that, as a result of a uniform swing between them across the country as a whole, those two parties were to have exactly the same tally of votes. Until 1974 there were always 150 or more seats that fell into that category, almost enough to ensure that for any 1% two-party swing between those two parties as many as 3% of the seats would change hands. However in February 1974, the first occasion in the post-war period when the electoral system failed to deliver an overall majority, the number of such seats fell to 119, a fall that has never since been reversed. Indeed by 1983 the number of such seats had fallen to just 80. And while by 2001, at 114 the tally had almost returned to the level that obtained in 1974, it has since fallen away once again. After dropping once more to 104 in 2005, it has fallen yet further to just 85. At this level only around 1.5% of the seats are likely to change hands for any 1% swing in votes.

A full explanation of the long-term trend in the number of marginal seats is beyond the scope of this appendix.[64] But at its simplest, the fall has occurred because parts of Britain where Labour were already relatively strong moved yet further (as compared with the country as a whole) in Labour's direction, whereas the opposite happened in the case of areas where the Conservatives were already relatively strong. When that happens, some constituencies become increasingly (relatively) Labour while others become more Conservative, thereby leaving fewer marginal seats where both parties are competitive. Such a pattern was again in evidence in 2010. On average the two-party swing in seats that the Conservatives already held was as much as 10.2 points; in contrast the swing in seats that Labour was defending was only 6.4 points.[65] In general, those parts of Britain that had already embraced the Conservatives switched more readily to the party than did those where Labour had hitherto been the strongest party – thereby serving to reduce the number of marginal seats once more.

Despite the decline in the number of marginal seats, in 2005 Labour was still able to win a comfortable overall majority, despite winning only 36% of the total vote and enjoying only a three point lead over the Conservatives. In contrast the seven point lead secured by the Conservatives in 2010 proved insufficient to secure the party an overall majority. Whatever may have happened to the number of third party MPs or the number of marginal seats it would appear that a third vital ingredient in the failure of the electoral system to deliver an overall majority in 2010 was that it treated the Conservatives less generously than Labour.[66]

There are two main reasons why single member plurality may favour one of the two largest parties over the other.[67] The first is that the seats won by one of those parties contain fewer voters than those won by its principal opponent. This possibility was very much in evidence in 2010, even though in England and Wales the election was fought on new constituency boundaries designed to ensure the geographical distribution of constituencies matched more closely the current distribution of the electorate. The average electorate in those seats won by the Conservatives in 2010 was, at 72,375, no less than 3,811 higher than the equivalent figure of 68,564 in those seats that were won by Labour.

This discrepancy arose because of two different patterns. First Wales continues to be deliberately over-represented in the House of Commons, while although the provisions of the Scotland Act 1998 had resulted in 2005 in a reduction in the number of Scottish constituencies, those provisions still failed to achieve their apparent intention of equalising the size of Scottish and English constituencies.[68] Thus in 2010 constituencies in Wales contained on average only 56,626 electors and those in Scotland 65,526. Seats in England, in contrast, contained on average no less than 71,876. Second, the supposedly new constituencies in England and Wales had in fact been created using electorates for 2000 (England) or 2002 (Wales). They were thus already considerably out of date, while the population in Britain had continued to shift out of (Labour-voting) urban areas to more suburban and rural (and more Conservative) ones, and from the (Labour-voting) north to the (more Conservative inclined) south. Even in the five years since 2005, on average the electorate in those seats won by the Conservatives in 2010 had increased by nearly 800 more than it had done in those seats that were won by Labour.

However, differences in the size of the electorate are not the only reason why Conservative seats contained more voters. The turnout in such seats was also higher. Although on average turnout increased more in those seats won in 2010 by Labour (+4.8 points) than in those won by the Conservatives (+3.9 points), this still meant that the average turnout in Labour seats (61.1%) was some seven points below that in Conservative ones (68.3%). The effect of this turnout gap was that the average difference of 3,811 in the number of electors in Conservative and Labour seats turned into one of no less than 7,594 when it came to the number of votes actually cast.[69]

The second main reason why single member plurality may favour one of the two largest parties over the other is that its vote is more efficiently distributed. A party's vote is efficiently distributed if it wins a relatively large number of seats with a relatively small lead over its principal national rival. Such a distribution means that a party is 'wasting' relatively few votes in either losing or piling up large majorities. At recent elections, Labour's vote has tended to be more efficiently distributed than that of the Conservatives and that tendency was still in evidence in 2010.[70] Meanwhile, the Conservatives also lose out because they waste considerably more votes than Labour losing in seats that are won by one of the third parties.[71]

The combined effect of these three developments on the relationship between seats and votes can be seen in Table A2.5. Throughout this table we assume that the Liberal Democrats and minor parties win the same share of the vote in every constituency as they did in 2010, while the turnout and electorate are the same too. What we do vary is the Conservative and Labour share of the vote, doing so by applying various hypothetical total-vote swings that are deemed to occur in each and every constituency. Thus, for example, our estimate of what would happen if the Conservatives were to have a 4.1 point lead over Labour, rather than the 7.3 point lead that they actually secured, is obtained by assuming there was a 1.6 point total vote swing from Conservative to Labour in every constituency. In that way we acquire a picture of how the electoral system operates given the electoral geography of party support and degree of third party success that pertained in 2010.

Table A2.5   Relationship between votes and seats

| | Votes (GB %) | | | Seats (UK) | | |
Con	Lab	Con lead	Con	Lab	LD	Others
31.4	35.4	−4.0	226	336	62	26
32.0	34.7	−2.7	239	326	59	26
33.2	33.2	0.0	255	306	61	28
35.4	31.3	4.1	282	281	59	28
37.0	29.7	7.3	307	258	57	28
39.0	27.8	11.2	327	233	62	28
39.7	27.0	12.7	336	225	62	28

The continuing bias against the Conservatives is very clear. If the Conservatives and Labour were to secure the same overall share of the vote, Labour would have as many as 51 more seats than the Conservatives. The Conservatives need to be four points ahead of Labour in votes before they emerge ahead in seats. And whereas Labour would win an overall majority (for which the requirement is 326 seats) with a lead of a little under three points, the Conservatives would require one of over 11 points.

Just as important is the wide range that lies between the lead that produces a Conservative majority and that which produces a Labour one.

Indeed, reflecting the further fall in marginal seats and the continuing relatively high level of third-party representation, comparison of this table with equivalent tables compiled after previous elections indicates that that range has never been wider.[72] In short, it seems that under the conditions that now prevail in Britain most narrow outcomes in votes are likely to produce a hung parliament. Indeed, the prospects of any party emerging with what might be regarded as a safe overall majority able to withstand by-election defeats and the occasional backbench rebellion, now look rather poor. To acquire a majority of 20 Labour require a lead of four points, and the Conservatives one of nearly 13 points.

The Conservative/Liberal Democratic coalition is committed to making changes to the electoral system. One of its aims is to reduce the bias against the Conservatives by ensuring that constituencies in Wales and Scotland are not systematically smaller than those in England and by reducing the length of time it takes to implement new boundaries. While this change can be expected to reduce the bias against the Conservatives, it cannot be expected to eliminate it, not least because, as we have already seen, differences in electorate size are only one of the sources of that bias.[73] But in any event any reduction in the lead that the Conservatives require to achieve a majority can be expected to be matched by a corresponding increase in the lead that Labour requires to obtain one. The chances of another hung parliament occurring in future will remain relatively high.[74]

The prospects of a hung parliament are likely to be increased yet further if a further proposal put forward by the coalition – the introduction of the alternative vote – secures the approval of the electorate in a referendum. Under the alternative vote, voters do not simply place an 'X' on their ballot paper, but rather rank the candidates standing in their constituency in order of preference. If no candidate secures 50% of the first preference votes the votes of those candidates at the bottom of the poll are successively redistributed until eventually that threshold is reached. Because many voters express a second preference for the Liberal Democrats, the party can be expected to win more seats that it does under single member plurality. On the basis of data on the second preferences of voters collected shortly before polling day, we estimate that the party might have won some 79 seats if the alternative vote had been in place in 2010, while the Conservatives would have won 281, Labour 262, and others 28.[75] That would have meant a hung parliament in which the Liberal Democrats would have been able to form a majority coalition with either Labour or the Conservatives.

Conclusion

Our analysis has helped uncover why the 2010 election proved to be a contest that Labour lost, but the Conservatives could not win. Labour was punished for the onset of the worst recession since the 1930s; the sharper its edge locally the more that voters defected. Once unusually good performances in certain constituencies, most notably in Scotland and in areas with substantial Muslim populations, are left aside, the scale of Labour's defeat was even more dramatic. However, the Conservatives struggled to capitalise on this legacy. They did not perform particularly well in areas where unemployment increased most; rather that was a feat achieved by the BNP. Voters living in constituencies that contain a relatively large number of public sector employees were hesitant about voting for a party that promised deeper public expenditure cuts. And although the party managed to win more seats than it would have done if the change in party support across the country as a whole had been even, its attempts to do particularly well in Labour held marginal seats did not produce sufficient dividend to overcome the anti-Conservative bias in the electoral system together with the long-term decline in marginal seats.

Britain thus ended up with its first hung parliament in over 30 years and its first peace-time coalition since the 1930s. This certainly represented a major interruption to Britain's post-war two party system of alternating single party majority governments. Whether it will prove temporary or permanent remains to be seen, but unless the nation's electoral geography or support for the Liberal Democrats and smaller parties is very different at the next election from what it was in 2010, there certainly is no guarantee that normal service will be resumed – even if, despite the Liberal Democrats' hopes, that election is still fought with first past the post still firmly in place.

Notes

1. Unless otherwise stated, all figures in this appendix refer to Great Britain, excluding Northern Ireland. For discussion of the results in Northern Ireland see pp. 193–4.
2. The previous record high was in 1918, when the party system was particularly fluid. On that occasion 8.8% of the vote was cast for someone other than a Conservative, Labour or Liberal candidate.
3. S. Butt and J. Curtice, 'Duty in Decline? Trends in Attitudes to Voting', in A. Park, J. Curtice, K. Thomson, M. Phillips, E. Clery and S. Butt (eds), *British Social Attitudes: The 26th Report* (London: Sage, 2010).
4. Boundary Commission for England, *Fifth Periodical Report*, Cm 7032 (London: The Stationery Office, 2007); Boundary Commission for Wales, *Fifth Periodical*

Report on Parliamentary Constituencies and First Report on National Assembly for Wales Electoral Regions, HC 743 (London: The Stationery Office, 2005).

5. C. Rallings and M. Thrasher, *Media Guide to the New Parliamentary Constituencies* (Plymouth: Local Government Chronicle Elections Centre, 2007). On occasion we also make reference to what happened in a constituency in 2001. These are based on estimates we have constructed by taking Rallings and Thrasher's estimates of the outcome in each constituency in 2005 and applying to them the weighted average of the change in party vote shares between 2001 and 2005 in the component old constituencies, the weights representing the proportion of the new seat that came from each component old seat.

6. For the most part we illustrate our findings by reporting differences in mean change in different groups of constituencies. However, our analysis is informed by extensive multivariate modelling of each party's performance, modelling that enables us both to take account of the possibility that an apparent relationship is spurious (that is a knock-on consequence of other, more important patterns) and to determine whether the patterns we report are statistically significant, given the number of seats involved and the degree of variation around the mean change in question.

7. J. Curtice and M. Steed, 'Appendix 2: An Analysis of the Voting', in D. Butler and D. Kavanagh, *The British General Election of 1983* (London: Macmillan, 1984), pp. 334–5; J. Curtice and M. Steed, 'Appendix 2: Analysis', in D. Butler and D. Kavanagh, *The British General Election of 1987* (London: Macmillan, 1988), p. 319; J. Curtice and M. Steed, 'Appendix 2: The Results Analysed', in D. Butler and D. Kavanagh, *The British General Election of 1997* (London: Macmillan, 1997), p. 298; J. Curtice and M. Steed, 'Appendix 2: The Results Analysed', in D. Butler and D. Kavanagh, *The British General Election of 2001* (Basingstoke: Palgrave Macmillan, 2001), p. 306; J. Curtice, S. Fisher and M. Steed, 'Appendix 2: The Results Analysed', in D. Kavanagh and D. Butler, *The British General Election of 2005* (Basingstoke: Palgrave Macmillan, 2005), p. 237.

8. There is a voluminous literature on this subject. See for example, R. Duch and R. Stevenson, *The Economic Vote: How Political and Economics Institutions Condition Election Results* (New York: Cambridge University Press, 2007).

9. For survey evidence on the impact of economic evaluations on the decline in Labour support between 2005 and 2010 see J. Curtice, 'How Labour Lost: Wrong Policies or Poor Delivery?', *Public Policy Research*, 17 (2010), 3–9.

10. R. Johnston and C. Pattie, 'It's the Economy Stupid – But Which Economy? Retrospective Economic Evaluations and Voting at the 1997 British General Election', *Regional Studies*, 35 (2001), 309–19.

11. Office for National Statistics, *Standard Occupational Classification 2000* (Basingstoke: Palgrave Macmillan, 2000).

12. See for example A. Heath, R. Jowell and J. Curtice, *The Rise of New Labour: Party Policies and Voter Choices* (Oxford: Oxford University Press, 2001).

13. Curtice and Steed, 'Appendix 2', in Butler and Kavanagh, *British General Election of 2001*, pp. 310–3.

14. Data on the proportion of people in each constituency who are employed in the public sector are not available. But those who work in the industrial sectors, 'public administration and defence', 'education' and 'health and social

care' for which data are available from the 2001 Census are mostly employed in the public sector and constitute the majority of public sector workers.

15. For example, amongst constituencies where unemployment as a proportion of the electorate had increased by more than 2.5 points between 2005 and 2010, Labour's vote fell on average by 9.2 points where less than 22% work in public sector jobs, but by only 3.6 points where more than 28% work in that sector.

16. Curtice et al., 'Appendix 2', in Kavanagh and Butler, *British General Election of 2005*, pp. 239–40.

17. See 'Appendix 2', in Kavanagh and Butler, *British General Election of 2005*, pp. 247–8, and previous volumes back to 1992.

18. Of course some personal votes might also have been lost at this election as a result of the boundary changes. An MP fighting a redrawn seat might well find that some of those who were willing to support him or her personally no longer lived in the constituency. Unless otherwise stated, in our analysis an 'incumbent MP' is one defending a new seat the largest proportion of which consists of the MP's former seat and which would have been won by his or her party on the estimated results of the 2005 election on the new boundaries.

19. It is possible that MPs who stood down did so because they were aware of their personal unpopularity, and that it was this unpopularity that cost Labour votes at the election. However, this implies a high degree of self-awareness on the part of incumbent MPs. We also note that there is no evidence that Labour's vote generally fell particularly heavily where a Labour MP who had been implicated in the expenses scandal (and who might have been personally unpopular as a result) stood down.

20. These are MPs for whom one or more items of expenditure totalling more than £10,000 were judged to have been impermissible or unreasonable and/ or had claimed more than £5,000 for gardening and/or had been allegedly involved in any of the following: 'flipping' their nominated second home for apparent financial advantage; charging full costs for a home where adult children or friends were living or where the mortgage was in joint names; making a claim for a property where they had lived rent free or for which there was no longer a mortgage; not paying capital gains tax on their nominated second home after sale; claiming for a second home that was located close to regular home or one not located in either London or in/ near the MP's constituency; claiming for a second home but not regularly attending the Commons; making any other claim that appeared a serious breach of the rules.

   We also identified separately those who had been 'moderately' implicated in the scandal. These were MPs who were judged to have made claims of between £5,000 and £10,000 that were unreasonable or impermissible and/ or making such a claim for more than £10,000 but the money had already been returned and/or making a claim that was inadequately documented and/or had making a claim for expensive hotels/hotels located near the MP's home and/or claiming for expenditure of less than £5,000 on PR materials that were judged to be political. In Labour's case this group of allegedly more moderate offenders does not appear to have suffered any electoral penalty.

21. We note, further, that in only one case had the seat in question been contested by an ethnic minority candidate in 2005. However, that seat, Bethnal Green

& Bow, was one where there was a large drop in the vote for Respect, and a consequent large increase (of 8.5 points) in Labour's share of the vote. Even so, the average fall in Labour's vote in the remaining seats in this group was still only 5.8 points.

22. Only two of these seats had been contested by an ethnic minority candidate in 2005. Meanwhile, we note that non-incumbent ethnic minority candidates defending seats that were won by Labour in 2005 only suffered an average drop in their share of the vote of 4.5 points where there was a substantial ethnic minority population, but one of 11.9 points where there was not. (This analysis excludes Glasgow Central where a non-incumbent ethnic minority candidate replaced an incumbent ethnic minority MP.)

23. In particular it might be noted that despite the controversy that the use of the procedure sometimes invoked, there is no evidence that those women who were selected via an all-women shortlist performed any worse than those women elected via an open contest. If anything the opposite was the case; on average Labour's vote fell on average by only 5.0 points where a female Labour candidate had been selected via an all-women shortlist.

24. The Conservative vote increased by 4.2 points in constituencies with a relatively large working-class population compared with 3.3 points in those with a relatively small one.

25. Though we note that the two point difference in the Conservative performance in the two kinds of constituency is only half the equivalent difference in the Labour performance.

26. Rallings and Thrasher, *Media Guide to the New Parliamentary Constituencies.*

27. In part this figure was inflated by the fact that the Conservatives were deemed by the estimates of the outcome of the 2005 election on the new boundaries to be defending some seats that in practice had not had a Conservative MP between 2005 and 2010.

28. Defined as seats where in 2005 the Conservative lead over whoever was second was less than ten points.

29. We note too that where a white Conservative candidate fought a constituency that had been contested by an ethnic minority Conservative candidate in 2005, at 4.9 points, the average increase in the party's share of the vote was just over a point higher than in seats fought by a white candidate on both occasions. Moreover the increase was particularly high, 5.8 points, in those seats with a relatively small ethnic minority population.

30. For evidence of such reluctance at previous elections, see, for example, Curtice et al., 'Appendix 2', in Kavanagh and Butler, *British General Election of 2005*, p. 249. We note too that the party's promotion of ethnic minority candidates does not seem to have enabled the party to enhance its appeal in constituencies with a relatively large ethnic minority population. We have already seen in Table A2.2 above that the Conservative vote increased rather less on average in constituencies where more than 10% of the population is Muslim. In addition, at 3.0 points, the average increase in the Conservative vote in all seats where more than 25% of the population regard themselves as something other than white, was also somewhat below the national average.

31. At 2.9 points, the average increase in the party's vote obtained by female A-list candidates defending a Conservative held seat was, on the one hand, rather better than that of female non-A list candidates (+1.6 points), but, on the

other hand, no better than that of male non-A list candidates (+3.2 points). Similarly, although at 4.7 points, the average increase in the Conservative vote in seats fought by A-list female candidates standing in a seat not won by the Conservatives in 2005 was rather higher than that obtained by non-A list female candidates in such seats (+3.0 points), it was still less than that obtained by male A-list candidates (+5.6 points).

Meanwhile, just six A-list ethnic minority candidates stood in the election, three in seats that were won by the Conservatives in 2005, and three in seats that were not, too few to come to any firm conclusion about the performance of such candidates. A-list ethnic minority candidates certainly suffered the disadvantage that most ethnic minority Conservative candidates did, but it is not clear that they consistently did so to any greater or lesser degree than did non-A list ethnic minority candidates.

32. Also known as 'strategic voting' in much of the academic literature outside the UK.

33. Curtice and Steed, 'Appendix 2', in Butler and Kavanagh, *British General Election of 1997*, pp. 309–11; G. Evans, J. Curtice and P. Norris, 'New Labour, New Tactical Voting?', in D. Denver, J. Fisher, P. Cowley, and C. Pattie (eds), *British Elections and Parties Review Volume 8* (London: Frank Cass, 1998), pp. 65–79.

34. Curtice and Steed, 'Appendix 2', in Butler and Kavanagh, *British General Election of 2001*, pp. 316–23; J. Curtice and S. Fisher, 'Tactical Unwind? Changes in Party Preference Structure and Tactical Voting from 2001 to 2005', *Journal of Elections, Public Opinion and Parties*, 16 (2006), 55–76.

35. More generally, our suspicion that there might be a particularly strong link between Liberal Democrat and Labour performance is further heightened by the fact that, at –0.53, the correlation between the change in the Labour vote and that in the Liberal Democrat vote is far higher than the correlation between Liberal Democrat and Conservative performance (–0.28) or indeed that between Labour and Conservative performance (–0.29).

36. And, indeed, no different at all from what happened in seats where Labour started off with a majority of more than 20 points, and where typically there had previously been little tactical switching.

37. Either seriously or moderately. See note 20 above.

38. Guildford, where the Liberal Democrat vote fell by 4.0 points, Ludlow (–7.9) and Newbury (–7.1).

39. Devon Central (4.4 point drop in Liberal Democrat vote), of which 36% was previously part of Teignbridge (Liberal Democrat held in 2005) and 21% from Devon West & Torridge (Liberal Democrat held between 2001 and 2005), and Meon Valley (–8.4), 42% of which was previously in Winchester (Liberal Democrat held before 2010).

40. We also note that in the one instance, Solihull, where boundary changes had turned what was previously a Liberal Democrat seat into one that the Conservatives would have won marginally in 2005 and where the incumbent Liberal Democrat MP did stand again, the Liberal Democrat vote rose by 3.5 points.

41. There had been some evidence of tactical switching from Conservative (rather than Labour) to Liberal Democrat in these seats (see Curtice et al., 'Appendix 2', in Kavanagh and Butler, *British General Election of 2005*, p. 245), but the

relatively poor performance of the Conservatives in Labour/Liberal Democrat contests (see Table A2.3) does not suggest that this particular form of switching systematically unwound either.

42. A third of the Hampstead & Kilburn constituency, where the Liberal Democrat vote fell by 4.0 points, was previously in Brent East (Liberal Democrat held). Just under 10% of Oxford East (–1.6) had previously been in Oxford West & Abingdon (Liberal Democrat held until 2010). Meanwhile Leicester South (–3.7) had been lost by the Liberal Democrats in 2005 after winning it in a by-election the previous year.

43. This followed a decline at recent elections in the party's hitherto strong local government vote in the city, as a result of which the party lost control of the council to Labour in the contemporaneous local elections in the city in 2010.

44. We note, however, that the recovery in Labour's vote in seats with relatively large student populations (see above) seemingly did not particularly hurt the Liberal Democrats who had performed relatively well in such seats in 2005. Amongst those seats that Labour won in 2001 and had a relatively large student population (that is more than 8%), the Liberal Democrat vote rose on average by 0.5 of a point, only a little below the equivalent figure of 0.9 of a point in former Labour seats that contained fewer students.

45. The one exception to this pattern comprises seats where Labour won less than 20% of the vote in 2005 and where, as we have already seen, Labour's vote fell rather less. In these seats the Liberal Democrat vote fell on average by 0.3 of a point.

46. In seats where over 5% of the population are Muslim, an ethnic minority Liberal Democrat candidate stood in 2010, but a white candidate stood in 2005, the Liberal Democrat vote fell on average by 1.8 points. In similar seats fought by a white candidate on both occasions the Liberal Democrat vote rose by 0.5 of a point. In seats where less than 1% of the population is Muslim the equivalent figures are 1.5 points and 1.6 points respectively. In making this calculation we exclude three seats in Scotland newly fought by an ethnic minority candidate on the grounds that the party generally performed poorly north of the border – though all three candidates in question performed particularly poorly even in comparison with the party's performance in general in Scotland.

47. In particular, although there are some signs that the party's vote increased most where unemployment increased most, this relationship disappears once we take account of some of the patterns we have already described. Much the same can be said for an apparent tendency for the party to advance rather less in seats that contain a relatively large proportion of public sector workers.

48. Our ability to analyse the change in the BNP vote between 2005 and 2010 is limited by the fact that the estimates we use of the outcome of the 2005 election on the new constituency boundaries do not include any separate figures for the BNP. Our comment here is based on an informal examination of how well the BNP did in 2010 and 2005 in those constituencies where the party performed best in 2005 and where extensive boundary changes did not take place. It is on account of the lack of such estimates that much of our analysis of the variation in the BNP's performance is based on what happened in those constituencies where the BNP did not have a presence in any of their component parts in 2005.

49. Curtice and Steed, 'Appendix 2', in Butler and Kavanagh, *British General Election of 1997*, pp. 305–8; Curtice and Steed, 'Appendix 2', in Butler and Kavanagh, *British General Election of 2001*, pp. 326–7; Curtice et al., 'Appendix 2', in Kavanagh and Butler, *British General Election of 2005*, pp. 246–7.

50. R. Ford and M. Goodwin, 'Angry White Men: Individual and Contextual Predictors of Support for the British National Party', *Political Studies*, 58 (2010), 1–25.

51. For a similar finding at previous elections see also Curtice and Steed, 'Appendix 2', in Butler and Kavanagh, *British General Election of 2001*, p. 308; Curtice et al., 'Appendix 2', in Kavanagh and Butler, *British General Election of 2005*, p. 249 as well as earlier appendices in this series. It is also quite clear that voters are discouraged from voting if the final outcome of the election nationally is already known. The biggest increase in turnout (+30.7 points) occurred in Staffordshire South where the poll had been delayed in 2005 by the death of a candidate. The largest drop (–16.2 points) was in Thirsk & Malton where the poll this time was not held until 27 May for the same reason.

52. We should though note that in general the electorate increased least between 2005 and 2010 in those seats that had the lowest turnout in 2005. It is thus possible that some of the increase in turnout may be occasioned either by returning officers in such areas, which are typically urban areas with more mobile populations, being more rigorous in admitting names onto the register or less effective at persuading those people with little interest in politics to apply to be on the register. However, although there is some evidence that turnout did indeed increase most where the size of the electorate increased least, this pattern does not by any means fully account for the link between the level of turnout in 2005 and the change in turnout between 2005 and 2010.

53. For example, amongst those constituencies where turnout had been less than 57% in 2005, turnout increased on average by 7.4 points in those seats where over 65% of adults reported in the 2001 Census that they were in good health, but by only 4.4 points in those seats where less than 65% said they were in good health. This pattern may, however, also reflect an apparent tendency for voting to go up more in seats with relatively large numbers of young people, a group amongst whom turnout fell particularly heavily in 2001 and 2005. See C. Bromley and J. Curtice, 'Where Have All the Voters Gone?', in A. Park, J. Curtice, K. Thomson, L. Jarvis and C. Bromley (eds), *British Social Attitudes: The 19th Report* (London: Sage, 2002).

54. The combination of the fact that turnout increased more in seats where turnout had previously been low and in those with more graduates helps in part to explain why turnout increased particularly heavily in Inner London (see Appendix 1, Table A1.2). It may be further accounted for some, albeit inconsistent evidence, that turnout increased more in seats where there are more young people and in those with relatively large ethnic minority populations.

55. We also note that we have not been able to find any link between the change in turnout and whether or not the local MP had been particularly implicated in the MPs' expenses scandal.

56. In making this calculation we have assumed that support for SNP and PC candidates increased by 0.1 of a point (that is the change in the overall level

of support across Great Britain or the two parties combined), while that of the best placed minor candidate increased by 1.9 points (that is the change in the overall level of support won by all such parties across Britain as a whole).

57. Though only two of the 12 incumbents were implicated in the expenses scandal, which seems not to have had a significant effect on the turnover of seats in relation to votes.

58. Movements above and below the national tide only resulted in a net total of two more seats being won by the Conservatives instead of the Liberal Democrats. The Conservatives gained nine seats from the Liberal Democrats that would not have changed hands on the national trend, but the Liberal Democrats both retained four seats despite the national tide and at the same time also captured three seats from the Conservatives. We note that the four seats the Liberal Democrats unexpectedly retained, together with one of the seats it nominally gained (Solihull), were all fought by the incumbent Liberal Democrat MP. In contrast, four of the nine seats the Liberal Democrats lost because of movements larger than that which occurred nationally were not fought by incumbents, while four of the five incumbents who lost had endured unfavourable publicity in the wake of the expenses scandal. The personal votes and popularity of Liberal Democrat MPs evidently played an important role in determining their individual fates.

59. Labour's vote in the nine seats that they managed to defend against the tide rose on average by 0.1 of a point, thereby outpacing the party's national performance by 6.6 points. The Liberal Democrat vote dropped on average in these same seats by 2.9 points, a smaller deficit of 3.9 points. Meanwhile, of the four seats that the Liberal Democrats captured on movements greater than the national trend, three were seats that had experienced increased in unemployment of more than 2.5 points, while the fourth seat (Brent Central) was contested by an existing Liberal Democrat MP (Sarah Teather) who had previously represented nearly half of the seat in the previous parliament. Intriguingly, however, three of the four seats were ones where more than 5% of the population are Muslim.

60. A. Blau, 'A Quadruple Whammy for First-Past-The-Post', *Electoral Studies*, 23 (2004), 431–53.

61. G. Gudgin and P. Taylor, *Seats, Votes and the Spatial Organisation of Elections* (London: Pion, 1979).

62. However, we should note that the standard deviation of both the Conservative and the Labour shares of the vote was also somewhat higher in 2010. The Conservative figure increased from 14.0 in 2005 to 14.6 in 2010, and that for Labour from 15.1 to 15.9.

63. See for example J. Curtice, 'Neither Representative nor Accountable: First-Past-The-Post in Britain', in B. Grofman, A. Blais and S. Bowler (eds), *Duverger's Law of Plurality Voting* (New York: Springer, 2009).

64. See J. Curtice and M. Steed, 'Electoral Choice and the Production of Government: The Changing Operation of the Electoral System in the United Kingdom since 1955', *British Journal of Political Science*, 12 (1982), 249–98.

65. Readers may, perhaps, initially be somewhat surprised at this result given that, as Table A2.3 shows, the Conservative vote increased rather more heavily in seats the party was challenging Labour than it did in seats where the party was previously ahead. However, this is outweighed by the fact that Labour's

vote fell most heavily in seats where it had previously been second to the Conservatives.

66. This development was also not new in 2010. See for example R. Johnston, D. Rossiter and C. Pattie, *From Votes to Seats: The Operation of the UK Electoral System since 1945* (Manchester: Manchester University Press, 2001); Curtice et al., 'Appendix 2', in Kavanagh and Butler, *British General Election of 2005*, p. 252; Curtice, 'Neither Representative nor Accountable'.

67. R. Johnston, *Political, Electoral and Spatial Systems* (Oxford: Clarendon Press, 1979).

68. J. Curtice, 'Reinventing the Yo-Yo? A Comment on the Electoral Provisions of the Scotland Bill', *Scottish Affairs*, 23 (1998), 41–53.

69. However, it should be borne in mind that because the Liberal Democrats typically perform better in seats where the Conservatives are stronger, the difference between Conservative and Labour held seats in the average number of votes cast for those two parties alone is a more modest 4,970.

70. This can be illustrated by the following calculation. The mean Conservative share of the two-party vote in seats won by either Conservative or Labour and contested by both parties was 53.1%. We reduce the Conservative share of the two-party vote in every constituency by 3.1 points in order to simulate what the outcome would be in those seats if Conservative and Labour had the same share of the overall vote in those constituencies and if those constituencies had the same electorate size and turnout. Labour would win 288 seats, in 32% of which the party's share of the two-party vote would be less than 60%. The Conservatives would win 276, of which just 27% would be ones where the party's share of the two-party vote would be less than 60%.

71. On average the Conservatives won 28.4% of the vote in seats won by third parties, but Labour only 16.6%.

72. See, for example, Curtice and Steed, 'Appendix 2', in Butler and Kavanagh, *British General Election of 1987*, p. 357; Curtice and Steed, 'Appendix 2', in Butler and Kavanagh, *British General Election of 1992*, p. 351; Curtice and Steed, 'Appendix 2', in Butler and Kavanagh, *British General Election of 1997*, p. 316; Curtice and Steed, 'Appendix 2', in Butler and Kavanagh, *British General Election of 2001*, p. 331; Curtice et al., 'Appendix 2', in Kavanagh and Butler, *British General Election of 2005*, p. 251.

73. Even under the provisions of the proposed new legislation, the electorates upon which constituencies are based would still be nearly five years out of date by the time an election was held, and thus in practice, given the current pattern of population movement, there could well still be some difference between the average electorate of Conservative and Labour constituencies.

74. A proposed reduction in the size of the House of Commons from 650 to 600 may result in a small reduction in the range of results that produces a hung parliament, but it is unlikely to be large.

75. Opinion poll conducted by ComRes for the *Independent* newspaper and published on 27 April 2010.

Select Bibliography

Books

Ashcroft, M., *Smell the Coffee: A Wake-up Call for the Conservative Party* (Michael Ashcroft, 2005).

Astle, J., Laws, D. and Marshall, D. (eds), *Britain After Blair: A Liberal Agenda* (Profile Books, 2006).

Bale, T., *The Conservative Party from Cameron to Thatcher* (Polity Press, 2010).

Brack, D., Grayson, R. and Howarth, D. (eds), *Reinventing the State: Social Liberalism for the 21st Century* (Politico's, 2007).

Brazier, A. and Kalitowski, S. (eds), *No Overall Control? The Impact of a 'Hung Parliament' on British Politics* (Hansard Society, 2008).

Cable, V., *Free Radical* (Atlantic, 2009).

Cable, V., *The Storm: The World Economic Crisis and What it Means* (Atlantic, 2009).

Callus, G. and Dale, I., *Total Politics Guide to the 2010 General Election* (Biteback, 2010).

Cameron, D., *Social Responsibility: The Big Idea for Britain's Future* (Conservative Party, 2007).

Campbell, M., *My Autobiography* (Hodder & Stoughton, 2008).

Casey, T. (ed.), *The Blair Legacy: Politics, Policy, Governance and Foreign Affairs* (Palgrave Macmillan, 2009).

Cowley, P., *The Rebels: How Blair Mislaid His Majority* (Politico's, 2005).

Copsey, N., *Contemporary British Fascism: The British National Party and the Quest for Legitimacy* (Palgrave Macmillan, 2nd edition, 2008).

Duch, R. and Stevenson, R., *The Economic Vote: How Political and Economics Institutions Condition Election Results* (Cambridge University Press, 2007).

Eatwell, R. and Goodwin, M. (eds), *The New Extremism in 21st Century Britain* (Routledge, 2010).

Edwards, G. and Isaby, J., *Boris v. Ken: How Boris Johnson Won London* (Politico's, 2008).

Elliott, F. and Hanning, J., *Cameron: The Rise of the New Conservative* (Fourth Estate, 2007).

Felp, C. (ed.), *Conservative Revival* (Politico's, 2006).

Griffiths, S. and Hickson, K. (eds), *British Party Politics and Ideology After New Labour* (Palgrave Macmillan, 2010).

Gyimah, S. (ed.), *From the Ashes... The Future of the Conservative Party* (Bow Group, 2005).

Hazell, R. and Paun, A. (eds), *Making Minority Government Work: Hung Parliaments and the Challenges for Westminster and Whitehall* (Constitution Unit and Institute for Government, 2009).

Hennessy, P., *Having it So Good: Britain in the Fifties* (Allen Lane, 2006).

Heppell, T., *Choosing the Labour Leader: Labour Leadership Elections from Wilson to Brown* (International Library of Political Studies, 2010).

Heppell, T., *Choosing the Tory Leader: Conservative Party Leadership Elections from Heath to Cameron* (Tauris, 2008).

Hurst, G., *Charles Kennedy: A Tragic Flaw* (Politico's, 2006).

Hurst, G. (ed.), *The Times Guide to the House of Commons* (Times Books, 2010).

Jones, D., *Cameron on Cameron: Conversations with Dylan Jones* (Fourth Estate, 2008).

Jones, N., *Campaign 2010* (Biteback, 2010).

Lee, S., *Best For Britain? The Politics and Legacy of Gordon Brown* (Oneworld, 2007).

Lee, S. and Beech, M. (eds), *The Conservatives under David Cameron: Built to Last?* (Palgrave Macmillan, 2009).

Lee, S. and Beech, M. (eds), *Ten Years of New Labour* (Palgrave Macmillan, 2008).

Mandelson, P., *The Third Man* (HarperPress, 2010).

Mattinson, D., *Talking to a Brick Wall* (Biteback, 2010).

O'Hara, K., *After Blair: David Cameron and the Conservative Tradition* (Ica Books, 2007).

Park, A. et al., *British Social Attitudes: The 25th Report* (Sage, 2009).

Park, A. et al., *British Social Attitudes: The 26th Report* (Sage, 2010).

Price, L., *Where Power Lies: Prime Ministers v The Media* (Simon & Schuster, 2010).

Rallings, C. and Thrasher, M., *British Electoral Facts* (Total Politics, 2009).

Rallings, C. and Thrasher, M., *Media Guide to the New Parliamentary Constituencies* (Plymouth: Local Government Chronicle Elections Centre, 2007).

Rawnsley, A., *The End of the Party: The Rise and Fall of New Labour* (Viking, 2010).

Riddell, R. and Haddon, C., *Transitions: Preparing for Changes of Government* (Institute for Government, 2009).

Rosenblatt, G., *A Year in the Life: From Member of Public to Member of Parliament* (Hansard Society, 2006).

Russell, A. and Fieldhouse, E., *Neither Left nor Right? The Liberal Democrats and the Electorate* (Manchester University Press, 2005).

Seldon, A. (ed.), *Blair's Britain, 1997–2007* (Cambridge University Press, 2007).

Seldon, A., with Snowden, P. and Collings, D., *Blair Unbound* (Simon & Schuster, 2007).

Snowdon, P., *Back from the Brink: The Inside Story of the Tory Insurrection* (HarperPress, 2010).

van der Eijk, C. and Franklin, M., *Elections and Voters* (Palgrave Macmillan, 2009).

Watt, P., *Inside Out* (Biteback, 2010).

Whiteley, P., Seyd, P. and Billinghurst, A., *Third Force Politics: Liberal Democrats at the Grassroots* (Oxford University Press, 2006).

Winnett, R. and Rayner, G., *No Expenses Spared* (Bantam Press, 2009).

Zetter, L., *Blue Print: The Policies, Principles and Personalities of the New Conservative Government* (Total Politics, 2009).

Journals

Abedi, A. and Lundberg, T.C., 'Doomed to Failure? UKIP and the Organisational Challenges Facing Right-Wing Populist Anti-Disestablishment Parties', *Parliamentary Affairs*, 62:1 (2009), 72–87.

Bale, T., 'Between a Soft and a Hard Place? The Conservative Party, Valence Politics and the Need for a New "Eurorealism"', *Parliamentary Affairs*, 59:3 (2006), 385–400.

Bale, T., '"A bit less bunny-hugging and a bit more bunny-boiling"? Qualifying Conservative Change under David Cameron', *British Politics*, 3:3 (2008), 270–99.

Bale, T., 'Cometh the Hour, Cometh the Dave: How Far is the Conservative Party's Revival All Down to David Cameron', *The Political Quarterly*, 80:2 (2009), 222–32.

Birch, S., 'Real Progress: Prospects for Green Party Support in Britain', *Parliamentary Affairs*, 62:1 (2009), 53–71.

Birch, S. and Allen, N., 'How Honest do Politicians Need to Be?', *The Political Quarterly*, 81:1 (2010), 49–56.

Borisyuk, G., Rallings, C., Thrasher, M. and Johnston, R., 'Parliamentary Constituency Boundary Reviews and Electoral Bias: How Important are Variations in Constituency Size?', *Parliamentary Affairs*, 63:1 (2010), 4–21.

Brack, D., 'Liberal Democrat Leadership: The Cases of Ashdown and Kennedy', *The Political Quarterly*, 78:1 (2007), 78–88.

Carter, N., 'The Green Party: Emerging from the Political Wilderness?', *British Politics*, 3:2 (2008), 223–40.

Carter, N., '"Sharing the Proceeds of Growth": Conservative Economic Policy under David Cameron', *The Political Quarterly*, 80:2 (2009), 259–69.

Childs, S., Webb, P. and Marthaler, S., 'The Feminization of the Conservative Parliamentary Party: Party Members' Attitudes', *The Political Quarterly*, 80:2 (2009), 204–13.

Cole, M., 'Growing Without Pains? Exploring Liberal Democrat MPs' Behaviour', *British Journal of Politics and International Relations*, 2:2 (2009), 259–79.

Cowley, P., 'The Parliamentary Party', *The Political Quarterly*, 80:2 (2009), 214–21.

Cowley, P. and Stuart, M., 'There was a Doctor, a Journalist and Two Welshmen: The Voting Behaviour of Independent MPs in the United Kingdom House of Commons, 1997–2007', *Parliamentary Affairs*, 62:1 (2010), 19–31.

Cowley, P. and Stuart, M., 'Where Has All the Trouble Gone? British Intra-Party Parliamentary Divisions during the Lisbon Ratification', *British Politics*, 5:2 (2010), 133–48.

Curtice, J., 'Back in Contention? The Conservatives' Electoral Prospects', *The Political Quarterly*, 80:2 (2009), 172–83.

Curtice, J., 'How Labour Lost: Wrong Policies or Poor Delivery?', *Public Policy Research*, 17:1 (2010), 3–9.

Curtice, J. and Firth, D., 'Exit Polling in a Cold Climate: The BBC–ITV Experience in Britain in 2005', *Journal of the Royal Statistical Society A*, 171 (2008), 509–39.

Curtice, J. and Fisher, S., 'Tactical Unwind? Changes in Party Preference Structure and Tactical Voting from 2001 to 2005', *Journal of Elections, Public Opinion and Parties*, 16:1 (2006), 55–76.

Denham, A., 'Far From Home: Conservative Leadership Selection from Heath to Cameron', *The Political Quarterly*, 80:4 (2009), 479–94.

Denham, A., 'From Grey Suits to Grass Roots: Choosing Conservative Leaders', *British Politics*, 4:2 (2009), 217–35.

Denham, A. and Dorey, P., 'The Caretaker Leader Cleans Up: The Liberal Democrat Leadership Contest of 2006', *Parliamentary Affairs*, 60:1 (2007), 26–45.

Denham, A. and Dorey, P., 'Just the Ticket? The Labour Party's Deputy Leadership Election of 2007', *The Political Quarterly*, 78:4 (2007), 527–35.

Denham, A. and Dorey, P., '"Meeting the Challenge"? The Liberal Democrats' Policy Review of 2005–2006', *The Political Quarterly*, 78:1 (2007), 68–77.

Denham, A. and Dorey, P., 'A Tale of Two Speeches: The Conservative Party Leadership Election', *The Political Quarterly*, 77:1 (2006), 35–41.

Denham, A. and O'Hara, K., 'Cameron's Mandate: Democracy, Legitimacy and Conservative Leadership', *Parliamentary Affairs*, 60:3 (2007), 409–23.

Denham, A. and O'Hara, K., 'The "Three Mantras": Modernisation and the Conservative Party', *British Politics*, 2:2 (2007), 167–90.

Denver, D., '"A Historic Moment?" The Results of the Scottish Parliament Elections 2007', *Scottish Affairs*, 60 (2007), 61–79.

Denver, D. and Fisher, J., 'Evaluating the Effects of Traditional and Modern Modes of Constituency Campaigning in Britain 1992–2005', *Parliamentary Affairs*, 62:2 (2009), 196–210.

Dorey, P., 'Election Reports: The Welsh Assembly Election 2007', *Representation*, 43:4 (2007), 315–21.

Dorey, P., 'A New Direction or Another False Dawn? David Cameron and the Crisis of British Conservatism', *British Politics*, 2:2 (2007), 137–66.

Dorey, P., '"Sharing the Proceeds of Growth": Conservative Economic Policy under David Cameron', *The Political Quarterly*, 80:2 (2009), 259–69.

Dunleavy, P., 'Facing up to Multi-Party Politics: How Partisan Dealignment and PR Voting Have Fundamentally Changed Britain's Party Systems', *Parliamentary Affairs*, 58:3 (2005), 505–32.

Evans, E., 'Supply or Demand? Women Candidates and the Liberal Democrats', *British Journal of Politics and International Relations*, 10:4 (2008), 590–606.

Evans, S., 'Consigning its Past to History? David Cameron and the Conservative Party', *Parliamentary Affairs*, 61:2 (2008), 291–314.

Fieldhouse, E. and Cutts, D., 'The Effectiveness of Local Party Campaigns in 2005: Combining Evidence from Campaign Spending and Agent Survey Data', *British Journal of Political Science*, 39:2 (2009), 367–88.

Fielding, S., 'Cameron's Conservatives', *The Political Quarterly*, 80:2 (2009), 168–71.

Finlayson, A., 'Making Sense of David Cameron', *Public Policy Research* (Mar–May 2007), 3–10.

Fisher, J., 'Hayden Phillips and Jack Straw: The Continuation of British Exceptionalism in Party Finance?', *Parliamentary Affairs*, 62:2 (2009), 298–317.

Fisher, J., Denver, D. and Hands, G., 'Unsung Heroes: Constituency Election Agents in British General Elections', *British Journal of Politics and International Relations*, 8:4 (2006), 569–86.

Flinders, M., 'Bagehot Smiling: Gordon Brown's "New Constitution" and the Revolution That Did Not Happen', *The Political Quarterly*, 81:1 (2010), 49–56.

Foley, M., 'Gordon Brown and the Role of Compounded Crisis in the Pathology of Leadership Decline', *British Politics*, 4:4 (2009), 498–513.

Ford, R. and Goodwin, M., 'Angry White Men: Individual and Contextual Predictors of Support for the British National Party', *Political Studies*, 58:1 (2010), 1–25.

Francis, M., 'The Bland Leading the Bland: Electing the Liberal Democrat Leader 1988–2007', *Representation*, 46:1 (2010), 91–100.

Gallagher, T., 'Labour and the Scottish National Party: The Triumph of Continuity in a Changing Scotland', *The Political Quarterly*, 80:4 (2009), 533–44.

Gamble, A., 'British Politics and the Financial Crisis', *British Politics*, 4:4 (2009), 450–62.

Goodwin, M., 'Activism in Contemporary Extreme Right Parties: The Case of the British National Party (BNP)', *Journal of Elections, Public Opinion and Parties*, 20:1 (2010), 31–54.

Green, J., 'When Voters and Parties Agree: Valence Issues and Party Competition', *Political Studies*, 55:3 (2007), 629–55.

Heppell, T. and Hill, M., 'Transcending Thatcherism? Ideology and the Conservative Party Leadership Mandate of David Cameron', *The Political Quarterly*, 80:3 (2009), 388–99.

Hayton, R., 'Towards the Mainstream? UKIP and the 2009 Elections to the European Parliament', *Politics*, 30:1 (2010), 26–35.

Holmes, A., 'Devolution, Coalitions and the Liberal Democrats: Necessary Evil or Progressive Politics?', *Parliamentary Affairs*, 60:4 (2007), 527–47.

John, P. and Margetts, H., 'The Latent Support for the Extreme Right in British Politics', *West European Politics*, 32:3 (2009), 496–513.

Johns, R., Mitchell, J., Denver, D. and Pattie, C., 'Valence Politics in Scotland: Towards an Explanation of the 2007 Election', *Political Studies*, 57:1 (2009), 207–33.

Johnston, R., Maclean, I., Pattie, C. and Rossiter, D., 'Can the Boundary Commissions Help the Conservative Party? Constituency Size and Electoral Bias in the United Kingdom', *The Political Quarterly*, 80:4 (2009), 479–94.

Johnston, R. and Pattie, C., 'Funding Political Parties in England and Wales: Donations and Constituency Campaigns', *The British Journal of Politics and International Relations*, 9:3 (2007), 365–95.

Johnston, R., Rossiter, D. and Pattie, C., 'Disproportionality and Bias in the Results of the 2010 General Election: Evaluating the Electoral System's Impact', *Journal of Elections, Public Opinion and Parties*, 16:3 (2006), 37–54.

Johnston, R., Rossiter, D. and Pattie, C., 'Far Too Elaborate About So Little: New Parliamentary Constituencies for England', *Parliamentary Affairs*, 61:1 (2008), 4–30.

Jones, P., 'The Smooth Wooing: The SNP's Victory in the 2007 Scottish Parliamentary Elections', *Scottish Affairs*, 60 (2007), 6–23.

Kalitowski, S., 'Hung Up over Nothing? The Impact of a Hung Parliament on British Politics', *Parliamentary Affairs*, 61:2 (2008), 396–407.

Kellner, P., 'Britain's Oddest Election?', *The Political Quarterly*, 80:4 (2009), 469–78.

Kelso, A., 'Parliament on its Knees: MPs' Expenses and the Crisis of Transparency at Westminster', *The Political Quarterly*, 80:3 (2009), 329–38.

Kerr, P., 'Cameron's Chameleon and the Current State of Britain's "Consensus"', *Parliamentary Affairs*, 60:1 (2007), 46–65.

Kettell, S. and Kerr, P., 'One Year On: The Decline and Fall of Gordon Brown', *British Politics*, 3:4 (2008), 490–510.

Kirby, J., 'From Broken Families to Broken Society', *The Political Quarterly*, 80:2 (2009), 243–7.

Konstantinidis, I., 'Actors or Subjects: How Far Do the Liberal Democrats Control Their Own Fate?', *Representation*, 42:2 (2006), 139–47.

Lebo, M.J. and Norpoth, H., 'The PM and the Pendulum: Dynamic Forecasting of British Elections', *British Journal of Political Science*, 37:1 (2007), 71–87.

Lebo, M.J. and Young, E., 'The Comparative Dynamics of Party Support in Great Britain: Conservatives, Labour and the Liberal Democrats', *Journal of Elections, Public Opinion and Parties*, 19:1 (2009), 73–103.

Leith, M.S. and Steven, M., 'Party over Policy? Scottish Nationalism and the Politics of Independence', *The Political Quarterly*, 81:2 (2010), 263–9.

Lynch, P. and Whitaker, R., 'A Loveless Marriage: The Conservatives and the European People's Party', *Parliamentary Affairs*, 61:1 (2008), 31–51.

McAllister, L. and Cole, M., 'Pioneering New Politics or Re-arranging the Deckchairs? The 2007 National Assembly for Wales Elections and Results', *The Political Quarterly*, 78:4 (2007), 536–46.

McIlveen, R., 'Ladies of the Right: An Interim Analysis of the A List', *Journal of Elections, Public Opinion and Parties*, 19:2 (2009), 147–59.

Nagel, J.H. and Wlezien, C., 'Centre Party Strength and Major-Party Divergence in Britain, 1945–2005', *British Journal of Political Science*, 40:2 (2010), 279–304.

Norton, P., 'The Future of Conservatism', *The Political Quarterly*, 79:3 (2008), 324–32.

O'Hara, K., 'The Iron Man: Is Cameron True Blue?', *Public Policy Research* (Sept–Nov 2007), 181–5.

Quinn, T., 'The Conservative Party and the "Centre Ground" of British Politics', *Journal of Elections, Public Opinion, and Parties*, 18:2 (2008), 179–99.

Quinn, T., 'Leasehold or Freehold? Leader-Eviction Rules in the British Conservative and Labour Parties', *Political Studies*, 53:4 (2005), 793–815.

Rallings, C., Thrasher, M. and Borisyuk, G. (2010), 'Much Ado about Not Very Much: The Electoral Consequences of Postal Voting at the 2005 British General Election', *British Journal of Politics and International Relations*, 12:2 (2010), 223–38.

Randall, N., 'No Friends in the North? The Conservative Party in Northern England', *The Political Quarterly*, 80:2 (2009), 184–92.

Rhodes, J., 'The Political Breakthrough of the BNP: The Case of Burnley', *British Politics*, 4:1 (2009), 22–46.

Tilley, J., Evans, G. and Mitchell, C., 'Consociationalism and the Evolution of Political Cleavages in Northern Ireland, 1989–2004', *British Journal of Political Science*, 38:4 (2008), 699–717.

Tonge, J. and Evans, J., 'Northern Ireland: Unionism Loses More Leaders', *Parliamentary Affairs*, 63:4 (2010), 158–75

Usherwood, S., 'The Dilemmas of a Single-Issue Party: The UK Independence Party', *Representation*, 44:3 (2008), 255–64.

Weale, M. and Riley, R., 'Immigration and Its Effects', *National Institute Economic Review*, 198 (2006), 4–9.

Webb, P., 'The Continuing Advance of the Minor Parties', *Parliamentary Affairs*, 58:4 (2005), 757–75.

Whiteley, P., 'Where Have All the Members Gone?' The Dynamics of Party Membership in Britain', *Parliamentary Affairs*, 62:2 (2009), 242–57.

Wilks-Hegg, S., 'The Canary in a Coalmine? Explaining the Emergence of the British National Party in English Local Politics', *Parliamentary Affairs*, 62:3 (2009), 277–398.

Wills, D. and Reeves, S., 'Facebook as a Political Weapon: Information in Social Networks', *British Politics*, 4:2 (2009), 265–81.

Index

Compiled by Sue Carlton